W9-BIQ-340

Algebra Two

Third Edition

Joseph N. Payne

Arthur F. Coxford

Francis G. Lankford, Jr.

Floyd F. Zamboni

with Trigonometry

Harcourt Brace Jovanovich

New York   Chicago   San Francisco   Atlanta   Dallas   *and*   London

ISBN 0-15-353935-6

We do not include a *Teacher's Edition* automatically with each shipment of a classroom set of textbooks. We prefer to send a *Teacher's Edition* only when it is requested by the teacher or administrator concerned or by one of our representatives. A *Teacher's Edition* can easily be mislaid when it arrives as part of a shipment delivered to a school stockroom and, since it contains answer materials, we want to be sure that it is sent directly to the person who will use it or to someone concerned with the use or selection of textbooks.

If your class assignment changes and you no longer are using or examining the *Teacher's Edition*, you may want to pass it on to a teacher who has use for it.

Contents

Mathematical Content

Mathematical Models

Selecting the appropriate <u>mathematical model</u> is frequently the most difficult step in problem solving. In *Algebra One* and *Algebra Two with Trigonometry,* mathematical models are used to help make the meaning of the mathematics clearer to the student. The application of this concept to the biological, physical, and social sciences connects the abstract art of mathematics with real problems in the physical world. Emphasizing these applications provides motivation to the students not only in their study of mathematics but also in helping students with their selection of possible career areas.

With respect to mathematics and careers, you will find a number of pages devoted to a wide range of careers in which varying levels of mathematical competency is necessary. Too often, students feel that the study of mathematics is primarily aimed at careers in the physical sciences and engineering. In these pages, students will find information regarding educational requirements, as well as the nature of the work that is involved.

Mathematical models are also used because of their importance in mathematics itself. In the third editions of *Algebra One, Geometry,* and *Algebra Two with Trigonometry,* the connection between geometric ideas and ideas of number is stressed. Number ideas are used as a mathematical model of geometric ideas and vice versa. The important one-to-one correspondence between the set of real numbers and the set of points on a line is but one example. Others include the correspondence between ordered pairs of real numbers and points in the plane, between ordered triples of real numbers and points in space, and between complex numbers and points in the plane.

Graphing is perhaps the most useful illustration of the connection of numbers to geometry. It is begun early in *Algebra One,* used repeatedly, and extended in each of the other two books. Algebra and geometry are consistently and continually related, which is absolutely essential in later mathematics, particularly the calculus.

Systems of Numbers

The structure of the real and the complex number systems emerges from a sound intuitive base that is built on many specific examples. It is important that this structure — that of the field — have a solid intuitive base if the students are to be able to make conjectures and to apply what they have learned. Real numbers are dealt with extensively in the opening chapters of *Algebra One* and complex numbers are introduced in the very first chapter of *Algebra Two with Trigonometry.* The structure of the real number system is also reviewed in the algebra review sections of *Geometry.* To provide contrasting examples of systems, finite number fields, other finite systems (see Chapter 11 of *Algebra One*), and matrices are all utilized.

Functions and Relations

Functions and relations provide a main theme for the study of algebra, and a clear understanding of these concepts is a primary goal. The ordered-pair definition provides the main framework from which students view the topic of relations and functions. Ample attention is given within this framework to the rule (or correspondence) that determines a function or a relation. In this context, the concept of a <u>mapping</u> enables the students to see the significance of the rule for a function or relation clearly.

Specific functions, such as the linear, quadratic, polynomial, trigonometric, exponential, and logarithmic functions, as well as the general idea of what a relation or a function is, are vital to further progress in mathematics or a science.

Proof

Increased sophistication in the handling of deductive proofs should be a very long-range goal of mathematics students. Some leading mathematicians have said that the role of proof is "to convince." However, the authors have taken as a goal to help students gain increased understanding of, and sophistication with, deductive proof. However, the level of sophistication is geared to the maturity of the learners at each level. A program in high school algebra must be designed to be effective with students of all abilities, including those who do not benefit from a rigorous approach.

In *Algebra One,* for example, difficult proofs that students must accomplish on their own are optional and are placed in the C exercises, clearly designating them for the students of higher ability. Direct and indirect proof and some formal logic are treated in Chapter 11 of *Algebra One,* an optional chapter.

Increased use of proof is evident in *Algebra Two with Trigonometry* and, of course, in *Geometry.* Even here, however, the development of topics is such that teachers who wish to omit the formal arguments may easily do so.

Mathematical Skills

Skill development is carefully planned within the broader framework of developing mathematical ideas. Just as skill in computation is one of the basic aims of the elementary and junior high school curriculums, skill in algebraic manipulation is a major goal of the secondary school mathematics program. This skill requires careful analysis of the way that each student's facility can be effectively developed. To meet the needs of those students in first-year algebra who are not proficient in basic computational skills, the authors have included a *Review of Basic Skills* section in *Algebra One.* Similarly, a *Review of Algebra One* section is part of *Algebra Two with Trigonometry.*

Reasonable competence in computation, algebraic methods, and proof is often necessary to the further development of important concepts. At the time a new idea is being developed, it is essential that students have the skills needed to handle it. Thus, a brief set of exercises entitled *Remember* is included at appropriate places throughout both algebra texts as an aid in maintaining prior learned skills that will be used in the lesson or lessons that follow.

Mathematics and Science

In most secondary schools, students are expected to take at least one course in science for which some algebra is required. Similarly, students who take more than one course in secondary school mathematics are frequently the same students who take more than one course in secondary science. Thus, the content has been carefully adjusted to reflect the anticipated needs that these students will have. Ratio, proportion, and variation—concepts utilized in all science courses—are developed thoroughly and carefully. Exponents are introduced early in *Algebra One,* since this topic is important to study in biology. The quadratic function is introduced in Chapter 8 of *Algebra One,* because of the essential need for it in physical science or earth science courses that may be taught in the ninth grade, as well as in later courses in mathematics and science. Students in chemistry and physics will need the mathematics that is presented in *Geometry* and *Algebra Two with Trigonometry,* Third Edition.

Using the Texts

Here is a list of the main features of the Third Edition.

Format

Expositions are short and to the point. Main ideas are displayed prominently and illustrated through the use of carefully worked-out examples and tables.

With few exceptions, each section is restricted to the development of one major concept and can be covered in a one- or two-day lesson. Emphasis is placed on thoroughly worked out examples and tabular-type material. This has, in turn, reduced much of the need for elaborate explanations.

Review of Skills

To meet the needs of students who have deficiencies in the area of arithmetic skills, *Algebra One* contains a section in the back portion of the student edition entitled *Review of Basic Skills*. The authors do not recommend that a first course in algebra begin with extensive review and teaching of basic skills. They believe that the study of algebra begins with algebra and that basic skills are reviewed as students progress through the course.

Students entering the second year of algebra may have certain shortcomings in first-year algebra, particularly where a year of geometry occurs between first- and second-year algebra. To accommodate this, *Algebra Two with Trigonometry* contains a section immediately preceding Chapter 1 entitled *Review of Algebra One*.

Try These Exercises

These are included in almost every section (lesson), just before the *Exercises*. The *Try These* concentrate on the most fundamental aspects of the lesson. They can be used orally or in written form to measure how well each student understood the lesson before assigning homework from the *Exercises*. You can also let the students do the *Try These* as a self-check since answers are provided in the student edition.

Remember Exercises

This group of exercises is designed as a maintenance device that provides a brief review of a prior-taught skill. Usually, the skill is one that is needed as background for the following section(s). For this reason, the *Remember* exercises appear as the last portion of an exercise set. Since the *Remember* exercises are self-checking, answers are provided in the student's book at the end of each chapter.

Chapter Objectives and Review

The objective(s) for each section are listed at the end of each chapter. Each objective is stated in simple language for the student and is cross-referenced to a given section. Following the statement of each objective are exercises that pertain directly to the stated objective.

The chapter objectives are intended to help the teacher focus with greater clarity on what is to be done next and on what results to expect. Because these results can be measured, the teacher can evaluate the lesson and know with some precision what follow-up activities are necessary.

Chapter Test

A short test is provided at the end of each chapter. Students can use this as a practice test or for review purposes. Answers are provided in the back of the book so that the student can determine area(s) of weakness before taking a formal chapter test.

Cumulative Review

A Cumulative Review appears after Chapters 4, 7, and 10 in *Algebra One* and after Chapters 4, 7, 11, and 14 in *Algebra Two with Trigonometry*. Each cumulative review is presented in a multiple-choice format. This not only permits students to go through many questions rapidly, but familiarizes them with the format of a standardized test.

Provision for Different Abilities

The textbooks can easily be adapted to many levels of interest and ability. This is reflected especially in the exercise sets, which include exercises that are coded A, B, and C. Students who are successful with the A Exercises—the minimal level—will be able to follow subsequent topics and achieve success with them. More able students will be challenged by the B Exercises, which deal with the topic of the given section in more depth than the A Exercises. The C Exercises are designed to challenge the most able students.

Of particular importance in attending to the varying ability of students is the suggested timetable that is structured for three ability levels. It can be found on page M-9 of this Teacher's Edition. A special feature of the table is the provision for a one-and-a-half year sequence in each of the three books of the series. This schedule is intended for students who need more time to cover the usual year's work. This schedule, for example, permits a student to complete a first-year algebra-geometry sequence in three years.

Following the suggested timetable you will find a suggested assignment guide for each section of a given chapter. This is also structured for three ability levels.

Puzzles

Most chapters contain at least two mathematical puzzles. Some puzzles will challenge the most able students; others can be solved by students of less ability.

Careers

Attention is paid to the need of students with regard to potential career selection. Information about certain careers—training required, the need for the study of mathematics, and some mention of the nature of the work of people in these careers—is provided in an attractive photographic format.

Computer Programming

The last chapter of each algebra textbook is on computer mathematics using the language of BASIC. Each section of the computer chapter is related directly to particular mathematical topics covered in the textbook. No prior knowledge of BASIC or programming is required to pursue these optional chapters. Further, the chapters may be studied without access to a computer. However, computer access is strongly recommended.

Special Topics

Both algebra textbooks contain material on certain topics that can be treated as optional. The format of these topics is distinguishable from the rest of the content, as they are either one- or two-page "lessons," depending on the material. For example, Chapter 1 of *Algebra One* contains a full page on linear units of measure in the metric system and a two-page treatment in Chapter 2 on other units of measure in the metric system. Some of the other topics treated in *Algebra One* are: equivalence relations, linear programming, and continued fractions.

In *Algebra Two with Trigonometry*, the first special topic is on synthetic division in Chapter 2.

The use of these special topics is, of course, dependent on the teacher. Clearly, most of these special topics can be used as an extension of the basic text by more able students. However, some topics can be used effectively with the class as a whole.

Individualized Instruction

The theme of this Teacher's Manual is the concern of the authors to build a program of instruction that meets the needs of a wide range of abilities. This is also the intent of those schools that make provision for individualized instruction. To properly implement any mode of individualized instruction, the key element with respect to materials is a textbook that makes provision for a wide range of abilities, such as containing material for remediation (*Review of Basic Skills in Algebra One*, *Review of Algebra One* in *Algebra Two with Trigonometry*), maintenance (*Remember* exercises), daily monitoring (*Try These* exercises), graded exercises, and extension (*Special Topics* and optional sections).

Further, the Teacher's Edition must contain the kind of assistance to the teacher that will help in the implementation of a program of individualized instruction, such as the two-page overviews that contain suggested assignments for each section of a given chapter on a day-to-day basis. (See pages M-10 through M-39.)

It is important that <u>both</u> the teacher and student know what the objectives are for each section of a given chapter, such as those stated in the *Chapter Objectives and Review*.

A testing program based on the objectives is an essential ingredient for individualization. Two separate test booklets, (see next column) are available for each of the algebra and geometry textbooks. The *Form A* test booklet can be used as a posttest and *Form B* as a second posttest for those students whose performance on *Form A* required them to go back over certain sections of the chapter.

Since *Form A* and *Form B* are equivalent, either form can be used as a pretest and the other form as a posttest for a given chapter.

Teacher's Edition

This *Teacher's Edition* consists of the following.

A general overview.

A specific overview of the textbook.

Individual overviews for each chapter, including a suggested section-by-section timetable of assignments for three levels of instruction.

The student's pages with annotated answers to all exercises and puzzles.

An Answer Key for those answers too lengthy for annotation in the text.

Answers to the tests in the *Testing Program*.

Testing Program

A testing program is available for each of the three books in the series. Separate tests—two forms, A and B—are available for *Algebra One*, *Geometry*, and *Algebra Two with Trigonometry*. The testing program can be used both for diagnosing difficulties that students are having and for assessing progress. Thus, valuable teacher time is saved in preparation of tests. Each form contains a test for each chapter and five cumulative tests.

Alternate Answers Editions

Also available are *Alternate Answers Editions* of *Algebra One* and *Algebra Two with Trigonometry*. These editions contain the answers to the odd-numbered exercises.

Solution Key

Complete *Solution Keys* are available as separate publications for the third editions of *Algebra One* and *Algebra Two with Trigonometry*.

Algebra 500 and Geometry 500

Also available for use with these books are two slide programs—*Algebra 500* and *Geometry 500*. Each is a unique visual resource that provides instantaneous access to full color representations of algebraic and geometric figures. Through the use of Daylight Blackboard Projection slides, figures that are most needed in teaching algebra and geometry can be put on the blackboard in seconds, in detail, and with great accuracy. This visual resource provides a way of saving time in and before class, and is extremely beneficial in the motivation it provides.

Overview

The approach to mathematical content differentiates one algebra textbook from another. The topics emphasized, the methods developed, and the details of each topic are the vital parts of the course. The arrangement of the content is also important. Seven major content areas in *Algebra Two with Trigonometry* are emphasized, as well as the two important areas of review. A good understanding of these areas will prepare students for further courses in mathematics or science. Also, the seven content areas provide the understanding and the various skills that will be needed in later life by those students taking *Algebra Two with Trigonometry, Third Edition,* as their final course in high school mathematics.

Content

The Structure of the Complex Number System

Understanding of the structure of the complex number system is a primary goal of second-year algebra. To achieve this goal, the real number system is reviewed in a review section preceding Chapter 1, entitled *Review of Algebra One*. This review is maintained and extended in Chapter 1, with particular emphasis on irrational numbers appearing in radical form. The review of the real number system builds on the substantial background that pupils bring to second-year algebra from their previous study.

Next, the complex numbers are introduced and operations on them defined. The authors feel that some new content is needed at the beginning of the second course in algebra that would be interesting to the student. A detailed and extensive review of the real number system has proved uninteresting to both students and teachers. The early introduction of complex numbers motivates a review of computational skills and ideas developed in first-year algebra. Similarly, this allows one to interweave the needed review of previously developed ideas and skills with the real numbers. Also, early introduction of complex numbers permits the complete treatment of polynomials, factoring, and graphing when the topics are first introduced. This enables a more thorough teaching job on complex numbers than has been previously possible.

For example, complex numbers are used in Chapter 2 when factoring polynomials and when performing operations on polynomials. Having complex numbers permits complete factorization of any polynomial with real coefficients. Particular emphasis is placed on factoring quadratic polynomials with real coefficients, a skill needed in dealing with quadratic equations in Chapter 6. Similarly, in Chapter 2, operations with rational expressions include the polynomials with complex coefficients. In Chapter 4, graphing is done on the complex plane, and complex numbers are related to vectors. After the study of trigonometry, complex numbers are expressed in polar form in Chapter 14.

The early introduction and integration of complex numbers leaves time for other topics. At the same time, it enables the student to expand his or her understanding of algebraic structure earlier and more thoroughly.

Coordinate Geometry

Because geometry as a high school course now includes both two-dimensional and three-dimensional geometry, it is essential to extend the concepts of coordinate geometry from two to three dimensions in *Algebra Two with Trigonometry*. The main ideas are the connection between ordered pairs of real numbers and points in the plane and between ordered triples of real numbers and points in space. Equations for the conic sections, the circle, ellipse, parabola, and hyperbola are derived and each is graphed.

Graphs aid the study of properties of linear, quadratic, exponential, logarithmic, and trigonometric functions.

The emphasis on graphing is used frequently as motivation for other concepts. For example, graphs of the exponential function provide the motivation for defining negative integral exponents, rational exponents, and irrational exponents.

Problem Solving

A primary goal of algebra is the use of mathematical ideas in solving problems—problems ranging from everyday applications to applications in the physical and biological sciences.

The unique tool used in *Algebra Two with Trigonometry* to help students solve problems is the identification of the conditions within the verbal statement of the problem, and the use of these conditions in developing a mathematical model that describes the problem. Frequently, the conditions are expressed in a mathematical model that is an equation or an inequality. Section 3–7 discusses the concept of a mathematical model.

Mathematical Models

Mathematical models are utilized in the discussion of coordinate geometry and in dealing with number systems as well as in problem solving. Section 4–8 provides an extensive discussion of the use of mathematical models in coordinate geometry. Vectors are used as a mathematical model of the real number system (one-dimensional vectors) and of the complex number system (two-dimensional vectors). This discussion begins with Section 4–10 and continues through the remainder of Chapter 4.

Relations and Functions

Linear and quadratic functions are reviewed and extended in *Algebra Two with Trigonometry*. In addition, a thorough treatment of exponential and logarithmic functions as inverse functions is given. Sufficient computation with exponents and logarithms is provided to maintain ideas and skills needed for practical uses. Also, sufficient concept development is provided to insure a firm base for uses of logarithms and exponents in further mathematics work.

Proof

Deductive proof is stressed more in *Algebra Two with Trigonometry* than in *Algebra One*. In *Algebra Two with Trigonometry*, the goal is to use deductive proof as an natural way to derive formulas and to establish the important theorems of algebra. The difficulty level of the proofs is compatible with the content studied and the background of the student. Difficult proofs are placed in C exercises so that a teacher can reserve them for more able students.

Probability

Many students find probability to be the most interesting topic of second-year algebra. The content of Chapter 12 will have particular importance for students who plan to make careers in the social sciences. Unfortunately, lack of time may force teachers to use this chapter as independent work for more able students. However, the content of this chapter is appropriate for most students.

Trigonometry

For schools that include trigonometry with second-year algebra, trigonometric functions are treated in two chapters, Chapters 13 and 14. These chapters contain a treatment of high school trigonometry which is adequate for the beginning study of analysis and calculus. Particular stress is placed upon the important ideas of periodicity and amplitude. If trigonometry is included, Chapters 13 and 14 should be studied; if not, the content in Chapters 1–11 will suffice for a course in second-year algebra.

Review of Algebra One

This *Review of Algebra One* checks students' understanding of the major ideas in first-year algebra. This review unit consists of four parts. Each part contains a diagnostic test, a review unit, and a mastery test. The diagnostic tests provide a quick way to assess the students' deficiencies. Each item in the diagnostic tests is keyed to one or more items in the review unit that follows. The purpose of each review unit is to serve as a vehicle for reteaching. Each mastery test provides a final check on comprehension.

It is recommended that this material be used as the need arises. For example, you may want to use one day of each of the first four weeks of the school year to study the four parts that constitute the *Review of Algebra One*. Another way the material can be handled is to refer students to it on an individual basis. In any case, it is not recommended that you spend the first week or two of the school year exclusively on this material. However the material is used, make sure students know the nature of the material and urge them to use it for personal review.

Other Important Topics

Many new and interesting topics have been included in *Algebra Two with Trigonometry*. These include work with <u>matrices</u> (Sections 7–9 and 7–10), <u>vectors</u> (Sections 4–11 and 4–12), and <u>computer programming</u> (Chapter 15). Of particular import is the inclusion of special topics, such as mathematical induction, natural logarithms, proof by contradiction, and others, that can be used for enrichment purposes. The new content has been included as it fits naturally into a well-planned sequential development of second-year algebra and trigonometry. It can, however, be omitted by teachers who are pressed for time to complete the basic course.

Psychology and Pedagogy

Careful Sequencing of Topics

Algebra Two with Trigonometry reflects the authors' extensive experience in teaching by emphasizing the careful sequencing of topics. It has been demonstrated that careful sequencing is a primary factor for retention of ideas and the development of skills.

Skill Development

In this book the authors have aimed to develop the really essential skills that a student needs for success in algebra, as well as in later mathematics courses. Experience in the classroom demonstrates that this textbook is effective in building manipulative skills, including operations on complex numbers, solving systems of equations, simplifying algebraic expressions, factoring polynomials, operating with rational expressions, exponents, and logarithms. At no time, however, is the skill work handled so that the student feels he or she is learning skills for their own sake.

Motivation

For day-to-day teaching it is doubtful that any source of motivation is as powerful as the individual success of the student in learning. A learner who is successful seems to develop a great intrinsic interest and seems to be much more of a "self-starter." The authors have had this success motive clearly in mind as each chapter was written and as each set of exercises was prepared. Not only is the language of the textbook simple and direct and addressed to the student, but also the many aids that are discussed in the general overview are used. These include the self-checking exercises: the *Remember* for maintenance and review, the *Try These* for determining how well the student understands a given section (lesson) before the Exercises are assigned, and the *Chapter Test*, for determining how well the student understands a given chapter before taking the formal chapter test. Since these three types of exercises are self-checking, answers are provided in the student textbook.

The optional sections indicated in the suggested timetable, the special topics, the B and C Exercises, the *Puzzles*, the *More Challenging Problems*, and the optional chapters illustrate the authors' concern for making provision for more able students.

Suggested Timetable

There are two main ways to provide for different abilities in a class, by depth and by the pace of presentation. The suggested timetable below provides for differences in the pace for a class, depending on the overall ability of the students. It is, at best, a rough approximation of the time the authors would allot to the various chapters. Three ability levels are provided for. Level One is the minimal course, Level Two the standard course, and Level Three the course for students of above average ability. The sections suggested as optional for average and below average students are indicated by (0). These sections may be omitted without loss of continuity. The pace and depth should ultimately be determined by the teacher.

Chapter	Level One		Level Two		Level Three	
	Sections	Days	Sections	Days	Sections	Days
1	All	16	All	14	All	11
2	(0) 15	27	All	22	All	19
3	(0) 8	14	(0) 8	12	All	10
4	All	18	All	14	All	12
5	(0) 6, 7	11	All	10	All	9
6	(0) 6, 12	18	(0) 12	17	All	15
7	(0) 7, 8, 9, 10	10	(0) 9, 10	13	All	12
8	(0) 7, 8	12	All	13	All	10
9	(0) 9, 10	14	All	15	All	12
10	(0) 8, 9, 10	15	(0) 9, 10	12	All	12
11	(0) 6	9	All	10	All	8
12	OMIT CHAPTER	0			All	8
13	OMIT CHAPTER	0	Selected topics	13	All	13
14	OMIT CHAPTER	0			All	11
15	OMIT CHAPTER	0			Selected topics	4
Semester Reviews		6		5		4
Total		170		170		170

Chapter Overviews

On the pages that follow are *Overviews* for each of the chapters. Each *Overview* consists of a brief discussion of the *Plan of the Chapter*, suggestions for *Teaching the Chapter* that include comments on the sections that comprise the chapter, and a suggested table of assignments. This table gives suggested assignments for three ability levels on a day-to-day basis for each section.

Overview for Chapter 1

The objectives for this chapter are on pages 34–35.

The real and the complex number systems provide the core of the content for this first chapter. After an introduction to various kinds of numbers, postulates are stated for operations on real numbers. There is a review of radicals and methods of combining them as a transition into operations on complex numbers.

Plan of the Chapter

The opening section recalls the various subsets of the real numbers and the properties of these numbers under the operations of addition and multiplication.

Radicals are reviewed in Section 1–2 because of the need for them in the study of complex numbers, but only square roots are included. Much of the study of radicals provides deeper insight into rational and irrational numbers as well as the skill needed with complex numbers. This review of radicals should provide a smooth transition to imaginary numbers.

Motivation for imaginary numbers arises from the fact that no real number is the square root of a negative number. After expressing pure imaginary numbers in i-form—as the product of i and a real number—complex numbers are introduced. Definitions of equality and operations on complex numbers complete the chapter.

Teaching the Chapter

The authors realize that students must begin the year's work with a good understanding of the real numbers. Review may therefore be necessary, particularly where a year of geometry occurs between first and second year algebra. The *Review of Algebra One* contains Diagnostic Tests, which the teacher may use to determine how much review a particular class needs. The Review may serve as a chapter to be studied page-by-page by the entire class, or it may be used on an individual basis. It is recommended that the class begin the year with Chapter 1 and only refer to the *Review of Algebra One* as the need arises.

1–1 In this opening section on various kinds of real numbers, you can refer frequently to the chart on page 3.

In the discussion of a rational number $\frac{a}{b}$ as a terminating or nonterminating decimal, you can show that upon division of a by b, there can be no more than $b - 1$ repeating digits.

The postulates for addition and multiplication on page 4 will be familiar to most students.

1–2 through **1–4** These three sections on radicals occur early in this book as necessary background for the introduction to complex numbers in Section 1–5.

The definition of absolute value on page 7 is an especially good point at which to encourage students to refer to $-x$ as "the opposite of x" in order to emphasize that $-x$ is not necessarily negative. You can also relate absolute value to the idea of distance from the origin to a point on the number line.

The set of *Remember* exercises on page 8 is the first of several that run throughout the book. They usually provide preparation for the following section(s).

1–5 Complex numbers are introduced early in the book for several reasons. First, their introduction provides interest in a new system of numbers and thereby is a great help in motivating students. Also, the plan allows fuller discussion of several topics: complete solution sets of quadratic equations, an extension of factoring, and operations with polynomial expressions. The early introduction of the complex number system enables the teacher to go directly to the heart of second-year algebra. This allows the class to cover more interesting material during the course of the school year than could otherwise be done.

1–6 An important structural difference between the set of complex numbers and the set of real numbers is that the latter can be <u>ordered</u> and the former cannot. Thus, statements such as "$2 - 3i < 5$" are meaningless. Another difference is the definition of equality on page 21. This definition has no useful analogue for real numbers.

1–7 through **1–9** Operations with complex numbers have an interesting resemblance to operations with real numbers. On this level, the work of these sections provides an opportunity to review skills in an interesting new context.

You will want to point out that the set of complex numbers satisfies the list of postulates (the field postulates) for real numbers found on page 560.

Suggested Timetable of Assignments

Section	Level One	Level Two	Level Three
1	A: 1–31 Odds *Second day* A: 33–42 All	A: 1–41 Odds	A:1–41 Odds B: 43–46 All
2	A: 1–13 Odds 14–17 All 19–25 Odds	A: 1–13 Odds 14–17 All 19–25 Odds	A: 1–25 Odds B: 26–29 All
3	A: 2–20 Evens *Second day* A: 21–40 All	A: 2–28 Evens *Second day* A: 30–40 Evens B: 42–56 Evens, 57	A: 3, 6, 9, · · ·, 39 B: 42–56 Evens 57
4	A: 1–13 All *Second day* A: 14–24 All	A: 2–20 Evens *Second day* A:21–24 All B: 27, 30, 33, 36	A: 3, 6, 9, · · ·, 24 B: 27, 30, 33, 36
5	A: 1–12 All 13–21 Odds *Second day* A: 22–36 All	A: 1–27 Odds *Second day* A: 28–36 All B: 37–45 All	A: 3, 6, 9, · · ·, 36 B: 37–45 All
6	A: 1–18 All *Second day* A: 19–30 All	A: 1–15 Odds 17–30 All B: 31	A: 1–15 Odds 17–30 All B: 31, 33
7	A: 2–34 Evens	A: 2–34 Evens 35	A: 3, 6, 9, · · ·, 33 35 B: 36–39 All
8	A: 1–21 Odds	A: 3, 6, 9, · · ·, 21 B: 22, 23, 25, 26	A: 3, 6, 9, · · ·, 21 B: 22, 23, 25, 27 C: 28, 29
9	A: 1–9 All 10–16 Evens	A: 2–16 Evens B: 20–26 Evens	A: 3, 6, 9, 10–16 Evens B: 18–26 Evens C: 28
Total* Days	16	14	11

*NOTE: The total number of days includes two extra days: One for review and one for testing.

Overview for Chapter 2

The objectives for this chapter are on pages 96–99.

Plan of the Chapter

The chapter opens with the definition of a polynomial and is followed by several sections on operations with polynomials, including factoring. These culminate in a section (2–8) on the <u>Remainder Theorem</u> and <u>Factor Theorem</u>. A section on solving polynomial equations by factoring is followed by several sections on operations with rational expressions. A section on the <u>Binomial Theorem</u> completes the chapter.

Teaching the Chapter

An effective technique in teaching polynomials is to make two lists on the chalkboard, one denoting polynomials, the other denoting expressions that are not polynomials. Ask students to tell what part of the definition of a polynomial the non-polynomial expressions fail to satisfy.

In factoring a complicated expression, it may help to have students replace common binomial expressions by a single variable first. Then factor and substitute back. You may need to give special attention to the Factor and Remainder Theorems. The Factor Theorem offers an effective technique for introducing the factoring patterns for the sum and difference of cubes.

2–1 For the classification of polynomials by the nature of the coefficients, emphasize that you see the smallest set of numbers containing all of the coefficients. Otherwise, all polynomials would be polynomials over the complex numbers.

2–2 and **2–3** When operating with polynomials, students can use either the "vertical" arrangement or the "horizontal" one depending on whether ease of manipulation or structure is being stressed.

2–4 through **2–6** In all factoring, stress the fact

that expressions are factorable over some sets of numbers but perhaps not over some others. Thus, in Example 5 of Section 2–4 the expression $a^2 + b^2$ is not factorable over the integers. However, it is factorable over the complex numbers in Section 2–6.

2–7 For the Exponent Properties for Division, you should illustrate the rationale for the subtraction of exponents by using the definition of integral exponents. You will want to take time to illustrate $x^0 = 1$ fully, since many students will think that $x^0 = 0$.

2–8 Division of polynomials leads naturally to the Remainder Theorem. Its proof closely resembles the illustration on page 64. Suppose that $Q(x)$ is the quotient when a polynomial $P(x)$ is divided by $x - a$. If r is the remainder, then

$$(x - a)\, Q(x) + r = P(x)$$

For $x = a$, $\qquad 0 \cdot Q(a) + r = P(a)$

or, $\qquad\qquad\qquad r = P(a).$

For the Factor Theorem you may want to study the special topic on *If and Only If* on page 129.

2–9 In Example 2, students can use the Factor Theorem for the first factor and then use their skill in factoring quadratics for the other two factors.

2–10 through **2–14** In teaching the rules of operations for rational expressions, it is a good idea to begin with the special case in which the expression is a rational number.

2–15 This section is considered optional for Level One students.

The special topic for this chapter is *Synthetic Division*. This method of finding the quotient and remainder when a polynomial is divided by $x - a$ can be learned by all students. You may want to use this special topic when you are dealing with division by $x - a$ or immediately after.

Suggested Timetable of Assignments

Section	Level One	Level Two	Level Three
1	A: 1–24 All	A: 2–24 Evens B: 34–36 All	A:' 2–24 Evens B: 26–36 Evens
2	A: 1–29 Odds	A: 3, 6, 9, · · ·, 30 B: 31–37 Odds	A: 4, 8, 12, · · ·, 28 B: 31–37 Odds C: 39–43 All
3	A: 2–20 Evens *Second day* A: 22–30 Evens 31, 32, 34, 35, 36, 38	A: 3, 6, 9, · · ·, 36 B: 39, 41	A: 4, 8, 12, · · ·, 36 B: 39–42 All C: 43
4	A: 2–22 Evens *Second day* A: 23–47 Odds	A: 3, 6, 9, · · ·, 48	A: 4, 8, 12, · · ·, 48 B: 52, 56; C: 60, 64

5	A: 1–10 All
	   11–19 Odds
	Second day A: 20–32 All
		A: 1–25 Odds
		Second day A: 27–32 All
		      B: 33, 39
			A: 4, 8, 12, · · ·, 32
			B: 33, 36, 39
			C: 42, 45

6	A: 1–15 All *Second day* A: 16–27 All	A: 1–21 Odds *Second day* A: 22–27 All B: 28–30 All	A: 3, 6, 9, · · ·, 27 B: 30, 33, 36
7	A: 1–5 All; 6, 8, 10 *Second day* A: 12–22 Evens	A: 3, 6, 9, · · ·, 21	A: 4, 8, 12, 16, 20 B: 24, 27 C: 30, 33

8	A: 1–15 Odds
	Second day A: 16–24 Evens
	         25, 27
		A: 2–16 Evens
		Second day A: 18–32 Evens
		      B: 39, 40
			A: 3, 6, 9, · · ·, 30
			Second day B: 34, 36, 38
			         39–44 All

9	A: 1–11 All *Second day* A: 12–19 All	A: 1–21 Odds	A: 1–21 Odds B: 22, 23
10	A: 1–11 All *Second day* A: 12–30 Evens	A: 8–30 Evens	A: 8, 12, 16, · · ·, 28 B: 31–36 All
11	A: 1–15 Odds *Second day* A: 16–24 Evens	A: 2–24 Evens	A: 4, 8, 12, · · ·, 24 B: 27–33 All
12	A: 1–12 All *Second day* A: 14–22 Evens	A: 2–20 Evens *Second day* A: 22, 24, 26 B: 28–32 All	A: 4, 8, 12, · · ·, 24 B: 30, 33, 36
13	A: 1–21 Odds	A: 5–27 Odds	A: 5–27 Odds
14	A: 1–15 Odds *Second day* A: 16–26 Evens	A: 2–20 Evens *Second day* A: 22–26 Evens B: 27, 28, 30, 33, 35	A: 7–25 Odds *Second day* B: 27–43 Odds C: 45
15	OMIT SECTION	A: 1–11 Odds 13, 16 B: 26	A: 8, 9, 12, 16 B: 17, 18, 20, 25, 28 C: 29
Total Days	27	22	19

Overview for Chapter 3

The objectives for this chapter are on pages 130–131.

The main purpose of Chapter 3 is mastery of solving equations involving rational expressions. The work is motivated throughout by appeal to applications and mathematical models.

Plan of the Chapter

The chapter opens with three sections on the solving of equations. In the first of these sections, the idea of equivalent sentences is developed. The second section stresses techniques previously developed and applies them to the solution of equations for a variable.

In the next section absolute value equations are discussed. In this important section, a single equation involving an absolute value is shown to be equivalent to a compound or sentence.

The next section introduces solutions to linear inequalities with much emphasis on graphic representation. There follow two sections on the solving of verbal problems. The chapter closes with an optional section on inequalities involving absolute value.

Teaching the Chapter

The equation-solving techniques that are developed in the first three sections are the basis for other major topics in this chapter: inequalities, equations with absolute value, and problem solving.

3-1 In discussing equivalent equations, mention that multiplication by 0 does not lead to an equivalent equation. Rather, it leads to an equation $0x = 0$ which is true for all replacements.

In doing the exercises of this section, you may wish also to let students subtract or divide rather than add the opposite and multiply by the reciprocal. You should show that the two approaches are equivalent.
Remember: The exercises here review the LCM skill. It is used in the next section.

3-2 Apparent solutions are often called extraneous roots. When students check a possible

solution, they should do so in the original equation.

The point in Example 2 is that multiplying both sides of an equation by an expression containing a variable may result in an expression that is not equivalent to the original. You may want to add some detail to the steps given in the example, especially in multiplying by the LCD.

3-3 You may want to ask what the opening two equations represent. These and similar equations in the exercises are useful in a wide variety of occupations. This section is especially important for students taking science courses.

3-4 The key notion in working with absolute value equations is to rewrite them as equivalent compound sentences. Then you proceed with each clause as before. You probably will need to review the idea of a compound sentence. Stress that the or means that the solutions to both clauses are in the solution set.

3-5 For the table at the top of page 116, show that multiplication by −1 reflects the numbers multiplied through zero, so that the positions are reversed. Thus, the inequality sign is reversed. You can also demonstrate that the sign changes by defining "$a < b$" as follows: "$a < b$ if and only if there is a positive number c such that $a + c = b$." Multiplying by −1 gives, $-a - c = -b$ or $-a = -b + c$. By this alternate definition, this last equation means that $-a > -b$.

3-6 Ask students to identify common situations that might be represented by the rates given at the top of page 119.

This example and the following one lead to Example 3, in which the most familiar case (the case in which $a = 1$) is demonstrated. Most of the exercises are of the type represented by Example 3.

3-7 You will want to remind students always to check solutions in the original problem to see whether they make sense. They should not check an answer in an equation derived from the problem because an error may have been made in writing the equation.

3-8 (This section is considered optional for Level One and Level Two students.) For $|x| < 2$, it is worth taking some time to show why the solution set comes out to be the intersection of two sets. You can compare the result with the solution set of the sentence $|x| > 2$. In this case, the resulting solution set is the union of two sets.

An alternate method of solving absolute value inequalities is to solve the related absolute value equality first. This usually gives you two points.

You check the points in the three disjoint sets formed by these two points in the original inequality. The sets that work form the solution set of the original inequality.

The special topic for this chapter, *If and Only If*, considers conditional and biconditional statements as they relate to definitions and theorems. Answers to the *Can You Solve These?* are on page M-72.

Suggested Timetable of Assignments

Section	Level One	Level Two	Level Three
1	A: 2–16 Evens *Second day* A: 18–30 Evens	A: 3, 6, 9, · · ·, 30 *Second day* B: 31–39 Odds	A: 17, 23, 24, 26, 29 B: 33, 36, 39 C: 42
2	A: 1–11 Odds *Second day* A: 13–25 Odds	A: 3, 6, 9, · · ·, 24	A: 8, 12, 16, 20, 24 B: 27, 30, 33, 36 C: 39
3	A: 1–13 Odds *Second day* A: 15–27 Odds	A: 1–17 Odds *Second day* A: 19–27 Odds B: 30, 38	A: 6, 12, 18, 24 B: 30, 33, 36, 39, 42
4	A: 1–13 Odds	A: 3, 6, 9, · · ·, 21	A: 6, 12, 16, 18 B: 25, 27 C: 29
5	A: 1–9, 11, 13 *Second day* 12–26 Evens	A: 7–25 Odds	A: 6, 12, 18, 24 B: 27–31 All C: 32
6	A: 1, 2, 4, 6	A: 2–8 Evens B: 11	A: 2–8 Evens B: 9, 12
7	A: 1, 3, 5, 7, 8 *Second day* A: 9–12 All	A: 1–11 Odds *Second day* A: 12, 13 B: 14–17 All	A: 3, 5, 8, 10, 13 B: 16, 19
8	OMIT SECTION	OMIT SECTION	A: 8, 10 B: 12–24 Evens
Total Days	14	12	10

Overview for Chapter 4

The objectives for this chapter are on pages 174–175.

In Chapter 4, the Cartesian coordinate plane is discussed. The study of vectors is taken up and graphical methods for the solution of problems involving vector quantities are presented and applied.

Plan of the Chapter

Students learn (or review) how (1) to plot points in the coordinate plane, (2) to determine the distance between two points, (3) to find the midpoint of a segment, and (4) to find the slopes of parallel and perpendicular lines. The section on writing equations of straight lines includes the point-slope form, slope-intercept form, and standard form.

The study of complex numbers is continued in this chapter. Complex numbers are associated with ordered pairs of real numbers, and the four operations are expressed in terms of ordered pairs. These operations provide an interesting parallel to the earlier definitions for the operations given in Chapter 1. Also, the ordered pair definition of complex numbers makes graphing easier and leads naturally to a discussion of the vectors associated with complex numbers. Following this discussion is a section on vector addition.

Teaching the Chapter

4–1 Point out that the scales on the x and y axes may be changed to accomodate plotting points with large coordinates. However, point out that when different scales are used, distortion in the graph occurs unless the scales on the two axes are the same.

4–2 The definition of distance between two points can be used to find the distance between points on the x axis, y axis, and on lines parallel to either axis. Sometimes the definition is stated as two formulas: $|x_1 - x_2|$ or $|x_2 - x_1|$ for points on the x axis or lines parallel to it; $|y_1 - y_2|$ or $|y_2 - y_1|$ for points on the y axis or lines parallel to it.

4–3 After Example 2 is discussed you may wish to give the students a couple of new examples before going over Example 3.

4–4 In the definition of slope stress that the order in which you subtract the coordinates is unimportant as long as the differences between x and y are taken in the same order.

4–5 If you prove Theorem 4–3 in class, you can model the proof after Exercise 18 on page 152.

4–6 The point-slope form of the equation of a line is the basic one used in this development. The remaining forms are derived from this form and should be clearly related to it. Emphasize that the point-slope form does not exist for vertical lines, because these lines do not have slope.

4–7 This section tries to help the student become more familiar with the interplay between the geometric and algebraic representations of a mathematical idea. In the exercises, it might be worthwhile to ask students to name the geometric model they draw for Exercises 1–20, or to describe the geometric model verbally.

4–8 This section illustrates the fact that the symbol (a, b) can serve as a model for a variety of ideas, such as a point, a vector, or a complex number.

You may want to mention that the plane for graphing the complex numbers is sometimes called the Argand Plane.

All students should try to do some of Exercises 21–28.

4–9 Vectors are models for a variety of physical concepts such as force, displacement, and velocity. These ideas can be used to help students understand that the vector has both direction and magnitude or length.

You may want to mention that vectors that begin at the origin and end at a point in the plane are called position vectors. When other vectors are used, they must be translated to the standard position to determine the complex number for which they stand.

4-10 Point out that addition can also be done by using the parallelogram law—drawing each addend vector from the origin as the sum or resultant vector. This could be illustrated using forces or velocities.

Subtraction of a vector can, of course, be done by adding the opposite vector.

The special topic for this chapter is *Coordinate Geometry in Three-Space*. It is a natural extension of the chapter, as it is concerned with plotting points in three-space and finding the distance between points in three-space.

Answers to the *Can You Solve These?* are on page M-72.

Suggested Timetable of Assignments

Section	Level One	Level Two	Level Three
1	A: 1–27 All 29	A: 2–24 Evens 25–35 All	A: 6, 12, 18, 24 25–35 All B: 36–38 All
2	A: 1–12 All *Second day* A: 13–22 All	A: 3, 6, 9, 12 13–21 Odds B: 23	A: 10, 12, 13–21 Odds B: 23, 24, 26 C: 27
3	A: 1–9 All 11, 13	A: 2–8 Evens 9–14 All B: 16	A: 2–14 Evens B: 15–18 All
4	A: 1–13 All *Second day* A: 14–21 All	A: 2–8 Evens, 9–13 All *Second day* A: 14–21 All B: 22, 24, 28	A: 2–8 Evens, 9–13 All, 14, 16, 18, 20, 21 B: 22, 24, 28
5	A: 1–7 All *Second day* A: 8–12 All	A: 2–12 Evens B: 15	A: 3, 6, 9, 12 B: 13–15 All C: 16, 17
6	A: 1–9 Odds, 10–15 All *Second day* A: 16–24 Evens 25–32 All	A: 2–24 Evens *Second day* A: 25–32 All B: 33–37 All	A: 4, 8, 12, · · ·, 24 26–32 Evens B: 34, 35, 36, 37, 40, 42, 43
7	A: 1–15 Odds *Second day* A: 17–28 All	A: 3, 6, 9, · · ·, 18 21–28 All	A: 3, 6, 9, · · ·, 27 B: 29, 30, 31, 33
8	A: 2–40 Evens	A: 2–40 Evens	A: 2–40 Evens B: 41, 42
9	A: 1–7 All *Second day* 8–16 All	A: 1–13 Odds 14–16 All	A: 1–13 Odds 14–16 All B: 17–20 All
10	A: 1–10 All	A: 1–19 Odds B: 21	A: 3, 6, 9, · · ·, 18 B: 21, 22
Total Days	18	14	12

Overview for Chapter 5

The objectives for this chapter are on pages 208–209.

Chapter 5 takes up the study of two important concepts in mathematics, relations and functions. Special functions and the more general idea of mappings are discussed.

Plan of the Chapter

Following intuitive and formal work on relations, the concept of a function is introduced. In using functional notation, care is taken to emphasize that $f(x)$ is another way to denote y, the second member of a function.

A discussion of mapping follows the discussion of functions. The concept of a mapping provides an approach to relations that emphasizes action. The authors feel that this approach will strengthen students' understanding of function and relation. Note that in this course the word mapping refers to relations in general and not just to functions.

The discussion of mapping is followed by a consideration of these special functions: the *constant function, identity function, linear function, direct variation function, absolute value function,* and the *greatest integer function.* Direct variation is treated as a special case of the linear function. It is also represented by means of proportions.

The zeros of a function are considered next. Students learn how to determine the zeros of a given function graphically and algebraically. The formal definition of a composite function which follows is illustrated by an example showing how two functions f and g can define a new function $g(f)$, the composite of g and f. A further example illustrates that the composition of functions is not necessarily commutative.

In the last section on inverse relations, the inverse, M^{-1}, of the relation M is defined as the set of ordered pairs (y, x), where (x, y) is an element of M.

Teaching the Chapter

5-1 In Example 2 you should make the distinction between the relation defined by the equation $y = 2x + 4$ and the equation itself. Then you may explain that the phrase "defined by the equation" is often omitted when discussing relations. Emphasize also that when the domain of a relation is not specified, it is understood to be the set of real numbers.

5-2 Function notation often causes trouble. You will want to make sure that students understand that $f(x)$ does not equal f times x. Insisting that students read $f(x)$ as "f at x" will help avoid the problem. In graphing functions given in the function notation, identify the $f(a)$ with the value of y when $x = a$. That is, encourage the students to think of "$f(x)$" as "y". Here you should continue to give examples of functions defined in ways other than by a single equation. The students will see enough of this sort of definition later.

5-3 A mapping emphasizes the basic components of a function, domain, range, and rule, and provides a graphic way of associating the elements of the two sets.

5-4 The first three of the special functions illustrated in Example 1 are seen often in later work in mathematics. The greatest integer function is useful in number theory.

You may want to mention that direct variation can also be defined by a proportion $\frac{y_1}{x_1} = \frac{y_2}{x_2}$. The advantage of the proportion is the fact that the constant of variation need not be found.

5-5 The zeros of a function are used in sketching graphs. To stress the fact that zeros are the values of x corresponding to the places where the graph crosses the x axis, you can say that "x is a zero" implies that "y *is* zero."

5-6 (This section is considered optional for Level One students.) A good way to help students understand composite functions is to illustrate the process using mapping diagrams. In so doing, the learner can see that dual role of the middle set—the range of the first function and the domain of the second.

5-7 (This section is considered optional for

Level One students.) You may want to explain that some inverses are of great importance. Examples are the inverse of the exponential function (the logarithmic function) and the inverse of several trigonometric functions.

Care should be taken to see that the students do not confuse M^{-1} with M raised to the -1 exponent. Note that the inverse of a nonconstant linear function is always a function. Point out also that other functions may not have functions for their inverses.

The special topic for this chapter is *Inverse and Contrapositive*. This topic can be used in conjunction with the special topic in Chapter 3, *If and Only If*. Answers to the *Can You Solve These?* are on page M-72.

Suggested Timetable of Assignments

Section	Level One	Level Two	Level Three
1	A: 1–19 All	A: 1, 2, 3 5–19 Odds B: 28, 32, 34	A: 1–19 Odds B: 32–39 Odds
2	A: 1–15 All *Second day* A: 16–25 All	A: 2–20 Evens 22–25 All	A: 2–20 Evens 22–25 All C: 26–30 Evens
3	A: 1–10 All *Second day* A: 11, 12	A: 1–14 All	A: 1–14 All B: 15, 17
4	A: 1–9 All *Second day* A: 10–20 All	A: 1–9 All 10–16 Evens 17–20 All	A: 2–20 Evens C: 39, 40
5	A: 1–12 All *Second day* A: 13–21 All	A: 1–8 All, 9–19 Odds 20, 21 B: 22	A: 1–8 All 9–21 Odds B: 22, 23, 24
6	OMIT SECTION	A: 1–19 Odds	A: 1–19 Odds B: 20, 21
7	OMIT SECTION	A: 2–20 Evens *Second day* A: 21–24 All B: 25–37 All	A: 2–24 Evens B: 26–36 Evens C: 38, 39, 40
Total Days	11	10	9

Overview for Chapter 6

The objectives for this chapter are on pages 252–253.

The aim is to investigate the properties of quadratic functions and quadratic equations.

Plan of the Chapter

A major application of quadratic functions, variation as the square, opens the chapter. Then the definition of a quadratic function is stated and represented graphically. The effect of the parameters a, b, and c on graphs of $y = ax^2 + bx + c$ is studied. Symmetry is defined algebraically, and the equation of the axis of symmetry of the quadratic function is derived. Problems on maximum and minimum values are solved.

Quadratic equations are first solved graphically by reading off the zeros of the function. The method of completing the square is employed to derive the quadratic formula. The discriminant, $b^2 - 4ac$, is used to determine the nature of the roots of a quadratic equation.

Teaching the Chapter

6-1 You could contrast variation as the square with inverse variation (see Section 10-6). An example of the latter would be the amount of light and the distance from the light source.

6-2 Here you can begin by summarizing the characteristics of a linear function. Then develop the major distinguishing characteristic: that the quadratic must have a second degree term.

6-3 through **6-5** These sections ought to be thought of as a unit in which the properties of the parabola are examined in relation to the coefficients on the terms defining the function. For the function $y = ax^2 + bx + c$, the a controls the width of the graph and determines whether it opens upward or downward. The c slides the curve along the y axis, and the b moves the curve both up or down and left or right.

6-6 (This section is considered optional for Level One students.) Stress the key idea of trying to find a product of two expressions, both involving the variable, and then to find the axis of symmetry of the resulting quadratic function.

6-7 Remind students that the zeros of a function give the solution set of the corresponding equation. Using the graph, show that a quadratic equation can have two, one, or no real roots.

6-8 The skill developed in this section is vital to the next few sections and should be mastered before going on. In Example 1 some students will need to be reminded of the difference between the ordered pair $(3, -3)$ and the solution set $\{3, -3\}$. Note also in Example 4 that the equation given is not an "incomplete" quadratic, yet it has the form of $x^2 = k$. Thus, the previous methods should also apply. This points out the relative unimportance of the term "incomplete" quadratic.

6-9 The main goal of the section is to develop the skill needed to derive the quadratic formula in the next section. Before doing Example 1, you may need to review an example of a perfect square trinomial.

6-10 In deriving the quadratic formula, it is a good idea to begin with a numerical example and mark the key steps. Then do the same thing again with literal coefficients.

6-11 Once the students have become familiar with the quadratic formula, the material of this section should be easy. Students should memorize the various results for the discriminant being negative, zero, or positive, and be able to use the discriminant to determine the nature of the solutions of quadratic equations.

6-12 This section is considered optional for Level One and Level Two students.

Suggested Timetable of Assignments

Section	Level One	Level Two	Level Three
1	A; 1–14 All	A: 1–13 Odds B: 15, 16	A: 3, 6, 9, 12 B: 15, 16 C: 17–20 All
2	A: 1–7 All *Second day* A: 8–13 All	A: 1–5 All 7–12 All	A: 1–13 Odds B: 14, 15 C: 17
3	A: 1–10 All *Second day* A: 11–16 All	A: 1–14 All	A: 1–14 All B: 17, 20
4	A: 1–13 All *Second day* A: 14–19 All	A: 1–13 All *Second day* A: 14, 16, 18, 19 B: 20–22 All	A: 1, 2, 3–17 Odds, 18, 19 B: 20, 21, 22
5	A: 1–11 Odds	A: 1–11 Odds *Second day* B: 13, 15, 17, 19, 20, 21	A: 3, 6, 9, 12 B: 16–21 All C: 24
6	OMIT SECTION	A: 1–7 All *Second day* A: 8, 9, 10 B: 11, 12	A: 1–10 All *Second day* B: 11, 12 C: 14, 15, 17
7	A: 2–8 Evens	A: 3, 6, 9, 12 B: 13, 14	A: 4, 8 B: 13 C: 17, 19, 21
8	A: 1–23 Odds *Second day* A: 24–31 All	A: 3, 6, 9, · · ·, 36	A: 6, 12, 18, · · ·, 36 B: 38–46 Evens C: 48
9	A: 1–9 All *Second day* A: 10–24 Evens	A: 2–8 Evens 12, 15, 18, 21, 24	A: 6, 12, 18, 24 B: 27, 30, 33, 36, 39
10	A: 3, 6, 9, 12, 15 *Second day* A: 16–24 Evens	A: 3, 6, 9, · · ·, 18 *Second day* A: 19–22 All 25, 26	A: 18–24 Evens B: 28–34 Evens 35, 38
11	A: 1–15 Odds	A: 1–15 Odds 16, 17 B: 18–20 All	A: 3, 6, 9, 12, 15, 16, 17 B: 18–24 Evens C: 26
12	OMIT SECTION	OMIT SECTION	A: 2–22 Evens
Total Days	18	17	15

Overview for Chapter 7

The objectives for this chapter are on pages 288–289.

Plan of the Chapter
Students begin by finding the solution set of a system of equations by graphing and then by the more accurate algebraic methods of addition and substitution. Word problems appear throughout the chapter to emphasize the practical applications of these algebraic methods. Inconsistent systems are defined, their graphs drawn, and the algebraic methods associated with them discussed. Consistent, independent, and dependent systems are similarly treated.

Pairs of linear equations are used to solve problems. Then systems of linear inequalities are solved. These techniques are applied to solving systems of three inequalities in two variables.

The final three sections introduce systems with three variables. Matrix methods for solving systems are explored in the next-to-last section. In the final section, dependent and inconsistent systems are considered. Here students use matrix methods to study systems of equations that have either infinitely many solutions or the empty set for their solution.

Teaching the Chapter
The addition method is sometimes called the "addition and subtraction" method. When given a choice, most students prefer the addition method over the substitution method. They should, however, know how to use both methods, for the substitution method is often simpler. The graphical method for solving a system of linear equations, while not exact, presents a picture that helps students understand why they take the steps they do. Have students attempt the solution of some inconsistent and dependent systems using the methods of addition and substitution. Then have them graph such systems to help them discover the reason for the "failure" of algebraic methods.

Only graphical methods can be used to state the solution sets in problems dealing with systems of inequalities.

7–1 through **7–3** The key idea to stress in these sections is that a system of linear equations has a unique, finite solution when the lines intersect in a unique point.

One way to prove Theorem 7–1 is to write the equations in the standard linear form. Multiply each equation by a constant and add the two equations. You will get $k(ax + by + c) + h(dx + ey + f) = 0$. Suppose that (r, s) satisfies each original equation. Then it is obvious that the same coordinates satisfy the equation written above. Thus, the theorem is proved.

7–4 Consistent systems are the only ones that have solutions. Thus, consistent systems are the only ones that are dependent or independent. The best way to illustrate the difference is to show a set of graphs representing the various situations.

7–5 In Example 1, contrast the solution presented with one you could do using only one variable.

In Exercises 3 and 4, you may first need to review the ideas of complementary and supplementary angles.

7–6 It may be a good idea to begin by reviewing the word and and its relationship to intersection of sets. This can be stressed as the students choose the test points for locating the solution set.

7–7 (This section is considered optional for Level One students.) The idea of polygonal convex set is the basis for the topic of linear programming.

7–8 (This section is considered optional for Level One students.) The ability quickly to sketch a plane will be helpful in the last three sections of this chapter. Finding the traces of the plane in each of the three coordinate reference planes is a good way to start.

7–9 and **7–10** (These sections are considered optional for Level One and Level Two students.) In showing how to solve equations using matrices, it is a good idea to compare the matrix method with the addition method by doing one example twice, once by each method. The corresponding steps of the two methods can be placed side-by-side on the chalkboard.

The special topic for this chapter is *Proof by* *Contradiction.* It is important that students in second-year algebra be given the opportunity to study various methods of proof. Using the indirect method to prove that $\sqrt{2}$ is irrational is most appropriate.

Suggested Timetable of Assignments

Section	Level One	Level Two	Level Three
1	A: 1–9 Odds *Second day* A: 8, 10–16 All	A: 1–15 Odds	A: 3, 6, 9, 12, 15 B: 17, 18
2	A: 1–15 Odds	A: 1–15 Odds	A: 3, 6, 9, 12, 15 B: 16, 17, 18 C: 27, 29
3	A: 1–3, 5, 7, 9	A: 1–9 Odds B: 10, 14	A: 3, 6, 9 B: 12, 15, 18 C: 20
4	A: 1–9 Odds	A: 1–9 Odds *Second day* B: 11–21 Odds	A: 3, 6, 9 B: 12, 15, 18, 21
5	A: 1–5 All *Second day* A: 6–10 All	A: 1–5 All *Second day* A: 6–14 Evens	A: 2–14 Evens B: 16
6	A: 1–9 Odds	A: 1–9 Odds B: 10	A: 3, 6, 9 B: 10, 11, 12
7	OMIT SECTION	A: 1–9 Odds	A: 3, 6, 9 B: 10, 11, 12
8	OMIT SECTION	A: 2, 4, 6 *Second day* A: 8 B: 13, 14	A: 2, 6 B: 10, 13, 14 C: 15
9	OMIT SECTION	OMIT SECTION	A: 6, 8, 10 B: 11, 12
10	OMIT SECTION	OMIT SECTION	A: 4, 8 B: 9, 13, 15, 16 C: 19, 20
Total Days	10	13	12

Overview for Chapter 8

The objectives for this chapter are on pages 318–319.

Plan of the Chapter

In Section 8–1, the equation $y = 2^x$ is graphed, using only positive integral values of x. The properties of exponents which are positive integers are stated and then extended to include zero and negative exponents. Scientific notation is presented, giving students an immediate use for negative integral exponents. Scientific notation will also be used in the chapter on logarithms.

Section 8–3 on simplifying expressions with negative exponents illustrates the writing of a fraction with negative exponents, as a fraction with positive exponents, and also the inverse of this operation.

The desire to "fill in more points" on the graph of $y = 2^x$ leads to the inclusion of rational numbers as exponents. Thus, in Section 8–4, the definition of rational exponents is given and rational exponents are related to radicals.

Changing the index of a radical is discussed, the purpose being to be able to combine radicals. Radical equations and radical equations reducible to quadratics, covered in Sections 8–6 and 8–7 respectively, are used in Chapter 10 in deriving the equations of the conic sections.

In the last section, skills learned in the preceding sections are used to solve exponential equations. This section also prepares for the next chapter on exponents and logarithms.

Teaching the Chapter

Show the need for zero and negative exponents by drawing the graph of an exponential equation, such as that given on page 294. Leave it on the board for several days, filling in points as the definition of exponents is extended.

When you have covered Section 8–4 on rational number exponents, fill in additional points on the graph of the exponential equation. Motivate the extension of the definition of exponents to the real numbers by discussing with the class which numbers still remain to be included on the graph.

Give your students ample practice in changing the index of a radical and in solving radical equations. Before dealing with radical equations reducible to quadratics, you will find it helpful to review the methods of solving quadratic equations: factoring, completing the square, and using the quadratic formula.

8–1 Stress that the purpose of the section is to extend the concept of exponent to include the negative integers.

8–2 This section is exceptionally useful to science students. The key idea is that every real number can be expressed as a product of the number between 1 and 10 and a power of 10.

8–3 In this section, students apply what they have learned about negative exponents.

8–4 This section extends the work of Section 8–1. In the exercises, it may be a good idea to do some of Exercises 53–63 orally with the class, since they illustrate all the various ways of representing fractional exponents.

8–5 You may want to use the term "like radicals" for radicals having the same index and radicand. In working with like radicals, you can compare the procedures with those developed for like terms in algebraic expressions.

In Example 5, the introduction of the decimal form is done so that students will feel comfortable with the logarithm work done in the next chapter. You may want to explain this to the students.

Before assigning Exercises 28–30, it may be well to discuss the example that precedes them.

8–6 This work on radical equations is important background for calculating distances in the coordinate plane and for proving theorems using coordinate methods. You may want to illustrate a few geometric theorems, such as "The medians of an equilateral triangle are congruent," that can be proved using coordinates and that involve distances.

The work with apparent solutions emphasizes the need to check answers in the original equation.

8-7 (This section is considered optional for Level One students.) The type of radical equation illustrated in Examples 1 and 2 is exactly the type used in the work on conic sections in Chapter 10. The key to the procedure is to square twice.

8-8 (This section is considered optional for Level One students.) It may be a good idea to illustrate with numerical examples the property that appears at the top of page 314. In doing Examples 1 and 2, stress that the goal is to get the bases to be the same. Exponential equations that are solvable with the aid of logarithms are studied in Chapter 10.

Suggested Timetable of Assignments

Section	Level One	Level Two	Level Three
1	A: 2–28 Evens, 29–36 All *Second day* A: 37–44 All 45–53 Odds	A: 1–27 Odds 29–44 All 45–53 Odds	A: 1–27 Odds, 29–44 All 45–53 Odds B: 54
2	A: 1–13 All	A: 1–13 All	A: 1–13 All
3	A: 1–16 All *Second day* A: 17–28 All	A: 1–24 All *Second day* A: 25–28 All B: 29–33 All	A: 1–27 Odds B: 29–33 All
4	A: 2–40 Evens *Second day* A: 41–48 All 53–59 All	A: 2–52 Evens *Second day* A: 53–63 Odds B: 64–75 All	A: 4, 8, 12, · · ·, 60 B: 65–79 Odds
5	A: 1–16 All *Second day* A: 17–27 All	A: 1–16 All *Second day* A: 17–30 All	A: 2–30 Evens B: 32, 34, 36
6	A: 1–14 All	A: 2–30 Evens	A: 3, 6, 9, · · ·, 30 B: 33, 36, 39
7	OMIT SECTION	A: 1–10 All	A: 2–10 Evens B: 12–20 Evens
8	OMIT SECTION	A: 1–10 All	A: 1–21 Odds
Total Days	12	13	10

Overview for Chapter 9

The objectives of this chapter are on pages 354–356.

Plan of the Chapter

The exponential function is defined and illustrated by means of an example. Intuitive understanding of this function is then developed through exercises. Section 9–2 prepares the way for the introduction of the logarithmic function.

Computations using logarithms to base 2 lead to common logarithms, or base 10 logarithms. The student learns how to use tables of logarithms and how to find antilogarithms. The known relations of exponents lead to the proof of the three important properties of logarithms.

Scientific notation is used to introduce the terms characteristic and mantissa, following which students apply logarithms to computation.

The principle of interpolation is illustrated graphically by using similar triangles to analyze the method of interpolation. Following a number of exercises requiring a knowledge of interpolation, logarithms are used to solve practical problems.

Section 9–10 is devoted to exponential equations and Examples show how to solve such equations by inspection and by means of logarithms.

Teaching the Chapter

The restriction $a \neq 1$ in the definition of an exponential function is necessary, since $a = 1$ would result in a constant function. Negative values for b are also avoided since these would produce a discontinuous function with points above and below the x axis.

9–1 Point out that the graph of $y = a^x$ rises or falls from left to right, depending on whether $a > 1$ or $a < 1$. Note also that all exponential functions contain the point (0, 1) whether the base a is greater than or less than 1.

9–2 and **9–3** Most the work of the first of these sections is readiness work for the introduction to logarithms in Section 9–3. To help alleviate the problem of the unfamiliar terminology and symbolism of logarithms, sufficient time should be spent on Section 9–2 where the idea of a logarithm is presented without the symbolism.

When introducing the logarithm as the inverse of $y = 10^x$, mention that the inverse could be expressed as $x = 10^y$ or $y = \log_{10} x$. This may help students to identify logarithm with exponent. In reviewing inverse, you can have students recall that a function and its inverse are symmetric with respect to the line $y = x$.

9–4 One good way to begin this section is to have some rapid oral practice on changing from logarithmic to exponential form and vice-versa.

Point out that although many other bases could be used to express the logarithm of a number, base 10 is used because it vastly reduces the number of table entries needed.

9–5 Exercises 25–40 are very good for class discussions.

9–6 One way to introduce the log of a number larger than ten is to give the number, ask the class to write it in scientific notation and then ask for the logarithm of the product. Once this is done, you can name the integral part as characteristic and the log of the number between 1 and 10 as the mantissa.

In discussing the form of the answer to Example 3 ($8.5340 - 10$), point out that this is the most useful form, but that other forms, such as $18.5340 - 20$ and $21.5340 - 23$ are also mathematically correct.

9–7 and **9–8** In the work on interpolation, stress that the logarithmic curve is nearly linear over small intervals. Thus, any error is not too great.

9–9 (This section is considered optional for Level One students.) If calculators are available, you can have students use them to check the results of Example 1.

9–10 (This section is considered optional for Level One students.) In Example 2, alert the students to the fact that they must not subtract when they are dividing logarithms.

The special topic for this chapter is *Natural Logarithms*. This topic is a natural extension of the content of this chapter.

Answers to the *Can You Solve These?* are on page M-72.

Suggested Timetable of Assignments

Section	Level One	Level Two	Level Three
1	A: 1–6 All	A: 1–13 All	A: 1–13 All B: 14–17 All
2	A: 2–16 Evens	A: 2–24 Evens	A: 2–24 Evens C: 29, 30
3	A: 1–12 All *Second day* A: 19–33 All	A: 1–35 Odds	A: 3, 6, 9, · · ·, 36 B: 37, 42, 43, 45 C: 46
4	A: 1–27 Odds	A: 1–27 Odds	A: 1–27 Odds
5	A: 1–4 All 12–15 All 25–34 All	A: 1–4 All, 12–15 All, 25–39 Odds B: 41, 42	A: 1–4 All, 12–15 All 25–39 Odds B: 41–45 Odds; C: 47
6	A: 1–8 All 9, 12, 15, · · ·, 27 *Second day* A: 30–46 Evens	A: 1–8 All 9, 12, 15, · · ·, 27 *Second day* A: 30–46 Evens	A: 3, 6, 9, · · ·, 45
7	A: 1–11 Odds *Second day* A: 4, 15, 16 17, 18	A: 1–13 Odds *Second day* A: 15, 17 B: 19, 20	A: 1, 7, 9, 15, 17 B: 20 C: 21
8	A: 1–23 Odds *Second day* A: 25, 27, 33, 37	A:1–23 Odds *Second day* A: 25, 28, 37, 42 B: 46	A: 3, 6, 9, · · ·, 21 27, 36, 42 B: 46, 49
9	OMIT SECTION	A: 4, 5, 7, 9	A: 4, 5, 7 B: 15 C: 18
10	OMIT SECTION	A: 1, 3, 6, 9 13–21 Odds	A: 3, 6, 9, 12, 13, 17 19, 21 C: 22a, 23
Total Days	14	15	12

Overview for Chapter 10

The objectives for this chapter are on pages 387–390.

Plan of the Chapter

The equations of the circle, ellipse, and hyperbola centered at the origin are derived and illustrated. The more general case of each conic with center at an arbitrary point (h, k) is also considered.

A section on applications includes *inverse variation, inverse variation as the square,* and *joint variation.*

The last part of the chapter discusses the solution sets of systems of equations where one or both members of a system are second degree equations. A section on graphing precedes the discussion.

With the intuitive background developed, attention is turned to solving the systems algebraically. First considered is a system in which one of the equations is of the first-degree. In Section 10–9, systems of two second-degree equations are presented. In the final section of the chapter, students are shown how to graph second-degree inequalities.

Teaching the Chapter

After this chapter is completed, all students should be able to graph the conics and to name a conic from its equation. However, for some students it is advisable that you omit the derivations of the equations except, perhaps, for the circle. This is especially true if you have omitted Section 8–7 as recommended in the suggested timetable for Level One students.

10–1 The circle is the most familiar of the conics. It illustrates the use of the distance formula in the derivation of the equation. It would be a good idea to do some of the *Remember* exercises on page 361 before deriving the formula for the ellipse in the next section.

10–2 A nice way to draw an ellipse is to tack a piece of string at two fixed points and draw the figure by keeping the string taut with the drawing

instrument. You can illustrate how this procedure fits the definition.

10–3 Emphasize that the parabola is one of the most useful curves. For example, many reflectors for telescopes and automobile headlights are parabolic in their cross sections. The light arrives (or originates) at the focus.

10–4 For the hyperbola as for the ellipse, a always represents the length of the semimajor axis (also called the transverse axis) and b represents the semiminor axis (also called the conjugate axis). Show that the minor axis, unlike the minor axis of the ellipse, does not have its endpoints on the graph.

10–5 For students who are interested, you may want to develop the coordinates of the vertices of $xy = k$. If so, they are $(\sqrt{k}, \sqrt{k})$ and $(-\sqrt{k}, -\sqrt{k})$ for $k > 0$ and $(-\sqrt{k}, \sqrt{k})$ and $(\sqrt{k}, -\sqrt{k})$ for $k < 0$.

10–6 Some students may prefer another method for solving problems involving inverse variation; namely, to solve for the constant of variation and then use this for finding the unknown variable. For example, in Example 2, $y = 9$ when $x = 5$; thus $k = 45$. If $x = 25$, then $25y = 45$ and $y = 1\frac{4}{5}$.

10–7 Graphical analysis of the various possible intersections of conics and conics, or conics and lines, helps students to gain understanding of the nature of the real solutions of such systems. This insight will be very useful when they are asked to solve similar systems algebraically because they will have the intuition to help them understand the various outcomes of the algebraic manipulations.

10–8 (This section is considered optional for Level One students.) The maximum number of solutions to these systems is two, but one and no real solutions also occur. Stress that a sketch of the graphs of the two equations will help determine the number of real solutions you can expect.

10–9 (This section is considered optional for Level One and Level Two students.) As is usually the case, graphs help determine the solutions. So students should sketch at least some of the graphs.

10–10 (This section is considered optional for Level One and Level Two students.) The key here is to graph, determine the boundary (or boundaries), and then try points in the various regions determined by the graphs.

Suggested Timetable of Assignments

Section	Level One	Level Two	Level Three
1	A: 1–10 All *Second day* A: 11–16 All	A: 1–15 Odds B: 17–23 Odds	A: 3, 6, 9, 12, 15 B: 17–25 All
2	A: 1–7 All *Second day* A: 8–14 All	A: 1–9 Odds 10–14 All B: 15, 16	A: 3, 6, 9, 11–14 B: 15–23 All
3	A: 1–6 All *Second day* A: 7–15 All	A: 2–8 Evens 9–16 All B: 17, 18	A: 2–16 Evens B: 17, 18 C: 19, 20
4	A: 1–7 All *Second day* A: 8–13 All	A: 1–7 All, 9 *Second day* A: 8, 10–15 All	A: 2–8 Evens 10–15 All B: 16, 17

5	A: 1–15 Odds
	   17, 18
		A: 1–15 Odds
		   18, 19
			A: 1–15 Odds
			   18, 19
			B: 21

6	A: 1–9 All *Second day* A: 13–19 All	A: 1–9 All *Second day* A: 13–19 All B: 20, 22	A: 1–19 Odds B: 20–22 All

7	A: 1–9 All
	Second day A: 10–13 All
		A: 1–9 Odds
		   10–14 All
			A: 1–9 Odds
			   10–14 All

8	OMIT SECTION	A: 1, 8, 13, 14, 20	A: 1, 13, 20 B: 26, 27
9	OMIT SECTION	OMIT SECTION	A: 1, 3, 5 B: 7
10	OMIT SECTION	OMIT SECTION	A: 2–12 Evens B: 13
Total Days	15	12	12

Overview for Chapter 11

The objectives for this chapter are on pages 412–413.

Chapter 11 introduces arithmetic and geometric sequences and series, the formulas associated with them, and the method used to find the sums of infinite geometric series.

Plan of the Chapter

The definition of <u>sequence</u> is given in terms of a function whose demain is the set of positive integers and whose range is the set of terms of the sequence. <u>Arithmetic</u> and <u>geometric sequences</u> are defined and the formulas for the nth terms are given. Then arithmetic and geometric series are defined as the indicated sum of an arithmetic or geometric sequence. Formulas for the sum of each series are motivated by examples. A number of problems are included in the exercises where the formulas developed are applied to the solution of practical problems.

The sum of an <u>infinite series</u> is defined as the <u>limit</u> of the sequence of partial sums associated with the series. In the last section, the limit of an infinite geometric series is discussed. The formula for the sum of a finite geometric series is used to determine terms in the sequence of partial sums of an infinite geometric series.

Teaching the Chapter

Stress that a sequence is a function and that the terms of the sequence are numbers in the range of the function. The idea of function clarifies the later ideas.

Introduce arithmetic and geometric sequences by examples. Students should discover that each term after the first can be found by adding a constant to the preceding term or multiplying by a constant. Using this idea, students should be able to derive the general term of a sequence.

In the section on arithmetic series, the distinction between a sequence and a series is illustrated.

To motivate the theorem for finding the sum of an arithmetic series, write a specific example on the board. Add the first term to the last term, the second term to the next to last term, and so forth. Then make the theorem for finding the sum of an arithmetic series plausible by doing the same thing to a general series.

An effective way to present a geometric series is to relate it to an arithmetic series. Note that the general term of a geometric series is the same as the general term of the corresponding geometric sequence. Again, motivate the theorem for finding the sum of a geometric series by working a specific example. Then make the theorem plausible by use of a general series.

11–1 For each of the sequences at the top of page 392, you could have the students seek a general expression that will give each term for the appropriate value of n. In doing this, set up a correspondence, such as in the example, and look for a way of operating on the integers to get the terms of the sequence.

11–2 You can introduce arithmetic sequences by referring to some of the results obtained in Exercise 20 on page 393. Ask the students to characterize the sequence before presenting the general definition. The point to emphasize is that there is a fixed or common difference between a term and the subsequent term and that this difference is the same for all adjacent terms.

Give several examples of arithmetic means and how to calculate them. In the *Try These* exercises, mastery is needed for working the exercises that follow.

11–3 The geometric sequence is one in which working from the recursive definition to the general term is very successful.

The geometric mean between two numbers x and y is $\pm\sqrt{xy}$. This fact can be discussed in the work on the geometric mean.

11–4 Stress the difference between a sequence and a series. Notice also that the series is not the <u>sum</u> (if such sum exists) of the series.

There are two forms for the sum of an arithmetic series. The first given in Theorem 11–1 can be shown equivalent to the one following it by noting that the term a_n equals $a_1 + (n-1)d$. Thus,

$2a_1 + (n - 1)d$ reduces to $a_1 + a_n$. If one formula can be committed to memory, then the other can always be derived as needed.

Exercises 26–31 could be used effectively for oral class work.

11–5   The procedures in this section are similar to those in the previous section.

11–6   (This section is considered optional for Level One classes.) A nice introduction to the idea of limit is suggested in this section. You may want to expand on that introduction with other examples of the thinking involved in finding a limit. The key concept to stress is that for large values of n, r^n is very small when $|r|$ is less than one.

The calculator could be very effectively used to illustrate this. Simply punch in 0.5 and raise it to the 20th power. The result is 0.0000009.

The special topic that in included in this chapter is *Finite Fields*. For many students, this chapter may represent the end of the course. Therefore, it is felt that the inclusion of some study of a field would be most appropriate to culminate the year's work, since a basic understanding of a field will be helpful in later mathematics courses.

Answers to the *Can You Solve These?* are on page M-72.

Suggested Timetable of Assignments

Section	Level One	Level Two	Level Three

1	A: 1–3 All
	   5–15 Odds
		A: 1–3 All
		   5–15 Odds
		B: 17–21 Odds
			A: 5–15 Odds
			B: 16–21 All

2	A: 1–10 All *Second day* A: 11–20 All	A: 1–14 All *Second day* A: 15–20 All B: 21–25 All	A: 7–19 Odds B: 21–33 Odds
3	A: 1–9, 14–17, 22, 24	A: 1–25 Odds	A: 3, 6, 9, · · ·, 24 B: 27–35 All C: 36
4	A: 1–10 All *Second day* A: 12–22 All	A: 2–24 Evens	A: 3, 6, 9, · · ·, 24 B: 26–32 Evens C: 34
5	A: 1–10 All	A: 1–10 All *Second day* B: 13–18 All	A: 4–10 Evens B: 11–18 All
6	OMIT SECTION	A: 1–15 Odds B: 16	A: 5–15 Odds B: 16, 18, 19
Total Days	9	10	8

Overview for Chapter 12

The objectives for this chapter are on pages 436–437.

This chapter introduces and develops the principal ideas of permutations, combinations, and probability. Sample spaces are used to present and illustrate some important theorems in probability.

Plan of the Chapter

In Section 12–1, permutation formulas are developed for a permutation of n things taken r at a time and of n things taken n at a time.

Students next examine the problem of finding permutations of elements that are not all different. Through discussion and examples they are led to the formula on the total number of permutations of n things of which p are alike of one kind, q are alike of another kind, r are alike of another kind, and so on. Following this, combinations and the problem of determining arrangements without regard to order are studied. The definition of a combination is presented. The formula for determining the number of combinations of n different things taken r at a time is given.

The remainder of the chapter develops basic ideas of probability. The approach adopted in Section 12–5 is intuitive. Included in this section are three postulates on probability. The chapter closes with a section on mutually exclusive events.

This chapter is considered optional for Level One students. Selected topics can be used with Level Two students.

Teaching the Chapter

12–1 In introducing permutations, you can begin with two elements, a and b. There are two different ordered arrangements of a and b: ab and ba. These are the two permutations. Next, you can move to three elements. Have the students organize their search for the permutations in a systematic manner. Show that the permutations beginning with a are two in number. The same is true for those beginning with b and with c. Thus, there are 3×2 permutations in all. Now you can look at the 4×6 array of permutations of four items. Note that for each of the new fourth letters,

each of the six permutations of the previous three letters gives a permutation. Thus, there are $4 \times 3 \times 2 \times 1$ permutations of the four objects. Generalize this to n objects to get the formula given at the bottom of page 418.

To introduce the idea of $_nP_r$, consider the first position in a row of r objects. Ask how many ways you can fill that spot if you have n books. Clearly, there are n ways. For each of these ways, how many ways can you fill the second spot? Since you have already used one book, you only have $n-1$ books with which to fill it. Thus, you can fill the first two spots in $n(n-1)$ ways. The same procedure is continued until you have filled all of the r spots. Then you can show the short way to note this as is done at the bottom of page 419.

The definition of 0! is always troublesome to students. Point out that we are free to define it in any way we wish, but we want a definition that will disturb the least of what we already know about factorials.

12–2 One way to begin this section is to consider a white die and two red dice. Here there are six permutations if you can tell one red die from the other. Show these on the board. Now erase the means of distinguishing the red dice. Notice that there are $\frac{6}{2}$ or three distinguishable permutations. Now examine the illustration given in the book. Draw the generalization that the number of distinguishable permutations of n objects of which p are alike is $\frac{_nP_n}{p!}$. Point out that you always begin with the permutation of n things taken n at a time and divide by each of the numbers of permutations of the indistinguishable objects. The formula is given on the bottom of page 422.

Note in the exercises involving circular permutations in a plane that clockwise and counterclockwise arrangements are counted as different arrangements. However, in space, two such arrangements are not counted as different arangements.

12–3 In combinations, stress that order is *not* important.

In connection with the Example, illustrate that $_{30}C_3 = {}_{30}C_{27}$ or, in general, $_nC_r = {}_nC_{n-r}$.

12–4 Begin the section by reviewing the Binomial Theorem. Review again the property illustrated immediately above and provided in Exercise 7 on page 426. Show how this property is useful in the Binomial Theorem.

12–5 Some students may raise the terminology of the "odds" for or against an event's occurring. "Odds of m to n" translates into a probability of

$$\frac{m}{m+n} \text{ or } \frac{n}{m+n}.$$

12–6 Contrast the events given in Examples 2 and 3. In the second instance, the events are not mutually exclusive and the sets overlap. When events are mutually exclusive, the probability of one or the other happening is the sum of the probabilities of the individual events. However, when they are not mutually exclusive, a correction must be made in the probability to take care of the overlapping of the two events. This is summarized in Theorem 12–1.

The special topic included in this chapter is *Mathematical Induction*. For those students who are able to study this topic, you can assign some of the theorems in Chapter 11. Answers to the *Can You Solve These?* are on page M-72.

Suggested Timetable of Assignments

Section	Level One	Level Two	Level Three
1	OMIT CHAPTER	SELECTED TOPICS	A: 1–15 Odds B: 17, 18, 21
2			A: 1–8 All B: 10, 11, 13
3			A: 1–13 Odds B: 14, 15
4			A: 3–10 All
5			A: 2–14 Evens
6			A: 1–8 All 9, 11, 13
Total Days	0	The total number of days will depend upon the topics selected.	8

Overview for Chapter 13

The objectives for this chapter are on pages 472–475.

The purpose of Chapter 13 is to introduce the six trigonometric functions and to give students a working knowledge of some of the fundamental methods of trigonometry.

This chapter is considered optional for Level One students. Selected topics can be assigned to Level Two students.

Plan of the Chapter

In the first section, general angle (positive and negative) is discussed. This is followed by the definitions of the sine, cosine, and tangent functions. Functions of special angles are discussed and the measures of the sides of 30-60-90 and 45-45-90 right triangles are found. The right triangle definitions for the sine, cosine, and tangent are presented and applied in solving right triangles. Angles of elevation and depression are discussed and problems using these ideas are solved.

Interpolation is explained, followed by a section on computation with logarithms of trigonometric functions. Angles with negative measures are introduced and functional values found. Theorems expressing the sine, cosine, and tangent of angles of the form $180 - \theta$, $180 + \theta$, $360 - \theta$, $90 - \theta$, and $90 + \theta$ in terms of functions of an acute angle are also presented.

Finally, the *Law of Sines* and the *Law of Cosines* are presented, proofs given, and applications shown. The reciprocal trigonometric functions are introduced and the secant, cosecant, and cotangent are found for given angular measures.

Teaching the Chapter

13–1 The definition of angle given in this section associates the angle more naturally with its measure than the "union of rays" definition often found in geometry.

13–2 One way to illustrate Theorem 13–1, at least for the first two quadrants, is to attach a string of about 50 cm at about the 50 cm mark of a meter stick. Then attach a 20 cm string at the 20 cm mark of the same stick. Attach two small weights one to each string at its free end. Now rotate the stick about the 0 cm mark to a variety of positions.

13–3 and **13–4** These two sections will be geometry-review material for many students.

13–5 It may be necessary to review the general idea of interpolation as done earlier with logarithms before beginning interpolation with trigonometric functions.

13–6 One way to introduce the work here is by first finding the sine of 17°20′ in the table. Emphasize that this is a number. Now look up the logarithm of the number in the logarithm table. Then turn to the tables of logarithms of sines, and look up log sin 17°20′ directly. They should be nearly the same.

13–7 The stick-string-weight model referred to earlier will work for illustrating the functions of negative angles also.

13–8 You may want to mention that although the reduction formulas of Theorem 13–3 through 13–7 are most easily understood using positive values of θ less than 90°, they really are true for all real values of θ.

13–9 Emphasize that the reciprocals of the defining ratios are also functions of the angles.

13–10 You can begin this section with a question: "Is there a proportional relationship between the sides of a triangle and its angles?" The conjecture $\frac{a}{A} = \frac{b}{B} = \frac{c}{C}$ suggests itself and is easily shown false. It is then natural to test the conjecture "The sides of a triangle are proportional to the sines of the opposite angles" (not to the angles themselves).

13–11 Point out that the Pythagorean Theorem is a special case of the Law of Cosines.

Suggested Timetable of Assignments

Section	Level One	Level Two	Level Three
1	OMIT CHAPTER	SELECTED TOPICS	A: 2–24 Evens B: 25–31 All 32
2			A: 1–15 Odds 17–21 All B: 22–31 All
3			A: 3, 4, 5, 7 B: 13–21 Odds 22
4			A: 1–11 All B: 12–16 All
5			A: 3, 6, 9, 12 15–18 All B: 20
6			A: 1–21 Odds B: 23
7			A: 4, 8, 12, 16 B: 17–20 All
8			A: 2–20 Evens 22–27 All
9			A: 1–15 Odds B: 17–20 All
10			A: 2–10 Evens
11			A: 1–5 Odds B: 7, 9 C: 10
Total Days	0	The total number of days will depend upon the topics selected.	13

Overview for Chapter 14

The objectives for this chapter are on pages 506–507.

In Chapter 14, the ideas in Chapter 13 are extended and developed. <u>Radian measure</u> is defined, the graphs of the trigonometric functions are discussed, <u>trigonometric identities</u> are introduced, and the inverses of sin x, cos x, and tan x are also discussed.

Plan of the Chapter

A radian is defined, and relationships are given for converting degrees to radians and radians to degrees. Numerous exercises develop the ideas presented. Finding trigonometric functions of angles expressed in radian measure are then treated. The graphs of the sine and cosine functions are presented and discussed. The characteristics of these graphs are analyzed through questions concerning their domain, range, period, and amplitude. The graph of the tangent function is then introduced.

Graphing is followed by sections on the <u>fundamental identities</u>, <u>sum and difference identities</u>, and <u>trigonometric identities</u>. The identities given include reciprocal identities, ratio identities, and Pythagorean identities. Additional identities, such as those for the sine and cosine of the sum and difference of angles, double angle, and half-angle, are discussed.

Inverse trigonometric functions are then presented. Definitions are given for $y = $ arc sin x, $y = $ arc cos x, and $y = $ arc tan x, and for the principal values of each of these inverse functions.

The last section is on trigonometric equations.

This chapter is considered optional for Level One students. Selected topics can be used with Level Two students.

14–1 Example 2 can be considered for the case when the radius of the circle is 1. Then it easily follows that 2π is the measure both of the circumference of the circle and its central angle. Thus, 2π radians are 360 degrees and π radians are 180 degrees.

14–2 You may wish to point out that in spite of the apparent strangeness of functions such as sin 0.8727, in more advanced work this method of representing trigonometric functions turns out to be superior to trigonometric functions that use degrees.

14–3 Period and amplitude are among the most useful and important ideas associated with the trigonometric functions. Examine several functions with different amplitudes to illustrate the effect of varying the coefficient. Note that if $A = -1$, the curve is reflected in the x axis.

14–4 This is a good place to review the meaning of *asymptote,* showing how it is illustrated in the tangent function. You will want to emphasize that, unlike the sine and cosine functions, the period of the tangent function is π.

14–5 The study of trigonometric identities is perhaps best begun by reviewing some algebraic identities. Consideration of a few conditional algebraic equations and even a trigonometric conditional equation (although this anticipates Section 14–9) might also be a good idea in order to show that trigonometric equations, like algebraic ones, may be true for <u>all</u>, <u>some</u>, or <u>no</u> allowable replacements of the variable.

14–6 The sum and difference identities for sine and cosine are particularly fundamental. Some students are able to remember the two formulas of Theorem 14–6 by memorizing, sing-song fashion, the phrase, "sine sine, cosine sine, cosine cosine, sine sine."

14–7 No specific method can be given to prove an identity. The best advice is to manipulate the given functions as well as one can. If nothing else seems to work, change everything to sines and cosines.

14–8 Review the manner in which you can graph the inverse of a function by reflecting over the line $y = x$. Do this for the sine function. Discuss the graph and note that the inverse is not a function. It is a good idea to keep stressing that the arc function values are angle measures in the same way that you earlier stressed that the logarithmic function values are exponents.

14–9 This section contains applications of the arc functions discussed in the previous section.

The special topic for this chapter is *Complex Numbers in Polar Form*. This topic is a natural extension of trigonometry, since it exhibits a relationship between complex numbers and the sine and cosine.

Answers to the *Can You Solve These?* are on page M-72.

Suggested Timetable of Assignments

Section	Level One	Level Two	Level Three
1	OMIT CHAPTER	SELECTED TOPICS	A: 3, 6, 9, · · ·, 30 B: 31–33 C: 34, 35
2			A: 2–18 Evens B: 20–28 Evens
3			A: 7–17 All B: 18–22 Evens
4			A: 1–3 All B: 4–12 All
5			A: 3, 6, 9, · · ·, 18 B: 21, 24, 27
6			A: 1–11 Odds 13–16 All B: 17, 19, 21
7			A: 6, 12 B: 17, 18, 19, 23
8			A: 3, 6, 9, · · ·, 21 23 B: 24
9			A: 3, 6, 9, 12, 15 17, 20
Total Days	0	The total number of days will depend upon the topics selected.	11

Overview for Chapter 15

This chapter on computer programming in the BASIC language may be studied without access to a computer. However, the programming lessons may be hard to motivate if students cannot actually run their programs. Therefore, computer access, while not absolutely necessary, is strongly recommended. No previous programming experience is assumed.

Plan of the Chapter

There are two ways in which to use this chapter with a class:

1. by itself covering all or most of the eight sections over a period of several days, or
2. as a supplement to earlier algebra topics taking up each computer section only when it is needed.

Some lessons may be omitted without loss of continuity in the programming units. Sections 15–1 and 15–2 are essential to the units that follow. Section 15–4, which introduces the FOR—NEXT loop, should be studied if either Section 15–6 or 15–8 is studied.

Space limitation in the student's book did not permit discussion of variations in the BASIC language from one system to another. You will need to point out to students any program statements that must be revised for your particular computer system. Students should also be referred to the system's programming manual for other ways of writing the programs. Only those features of BASIC needed for the programs shown are covered. For other aspects of the language, students can be referred to the many texts on BASIC (see *Computer Programming in the BASIC Language*, © 1975, by Neal Golden and published by Harcourt Brace Jovanovich, Inc., New York).

Teaching the Chapter

15–1 BASIC stands for "Beginners' All-purpose Symbolic Instruction Code." It was invented in the mid-1960's at Dartmouth College especially for time-sharing computer systems.

Only one type of BASIC variable is used in this chapter, namely, one letter (A, B, C, ..., Z). (There are several other types.) A programmer is free to choose any letter for a variable.

It is helpful to trace the logical flow of a program by pretending to be the computer, taking the DATA values as they are listed, and working through the program. This technique will be useful in the next lesson.

15–2 In Program 2, you can show students the necessity of the two GO TO 3∅ statements by removing, say, line 6∅, and tracing the program to show the error that results.

In the instructions for the exercises, students are told to "be sure that the DATA chosen produces each possible outcome at least once." You may have to amplify this instruction. For instance, in Exercise 4, the DATA should include at least one set of numbers that can be the lengths of the sides of a right triangle and at least one set that cannot.

15–3 Program 4 shows that DATA may continue for more than one line as long as each line is numbered and begins with the word DATA.

15–4 Program 5 simply prints a table of values that students could then use to draw their own graph of a function. However, most computer systems offer a "library" program that draws graphs on the terminal.

15–5 Each BASIC system has other MAT commands in addition to those listed on page 523. Consult the manual of your system.

Exercise 1 can be done by solving the general form of the system to obtain formulas for *x* and *y*, by thinking in terms of determinants, or by using matrices. You could assign a different group of students to program each approach. The program can also be extended to handle larger systems of equations, for which the matrix approach becomes most advantageous.

15–6 In Program 8, the variable I is the index of the FOR—NEXT loop, 2 is the initial value of the index and N is its final value. The understood STEP of one is the increment. Lines 4∅ and 5∅ constitute the body of the loop.

The index may or may not enter the calculations in the body of a loop. For example, in Program 5, the index X was used to generate values of Y. On the other hand, in Program 8, I merely counts the number of times the loop is executed.

15-7 In Program 10, students may ask about 2Ø LET F = 1. If so, remove it and have them trace the resulting program, remembering that in BASIC all variables begin with a default value of Ø. The students will notice that line 4Ø keeps producing Ø as the value of F.

The RANDOMIZE command used in Program 11 may not be available on your system. If it is not, then the program shown may not produce a different number of heads and tails each run.

15-8 The table on page 528 lists four trigonometric functions available in BASIC. The SQR function was introduced earlier in the chapter. Additional functions available on most systems (although the three-letter abbreviations may vary) are: CLG (for common logarithm), LOG (for natural logarithm), EXP (for powers of e), INT (greatest integer function), and ABS (absolute value function).

Suggested Timetable of Assignments

Section	Level One	Level Two	Level Three
1	OMIT CHAPTER	SELECTED TOPICS	A: 4–8 Evens 10, 15, 16, 17
2			A: 3–5 B: 6
3			A: 1, 3 B: 5, 8, 11
4			A: 1, 5, 7, 9
5		·	*Optional Section* A: 2–5
6			*Optional Section* A: 1, 2, 3, 7 B: 9
7			*Optional Section* A: 1 B: 2–4
8			*Optional Section* A: 1, 2, 3 B: 6
Total Days	0	The total number of days will depend upon the topics selected.	4

Answer Key

Chapter 1

Page 19

50.

Addition	Subtraction	Division
46. Neither	Neither	Pure imaginary
47. Pure imaginary	Real	Real
48. Real	Pure imaginary	Real
49. Pure imaginary or zero	Pure imaginary or zero	Real

Page 28

28. $(0 + 0 \cdot i)(a + bi) = 0(a + bi) + 0i(a + bi) = (0 \cdot a + 0 \cdot bi) + (0 \cdot ai - 0 \cdot b)$
$= (0 \cdot a - 0 \cdot b) + (0 \cdot b + 0 \cdot a)i = 0 + 0 \cdot i = 0$

29.

Statements	Reasons
1. $(a + bi)(c + di)$ $= a(c + di) + bi(c + di)$	**1.** Definition of Mult. of complex numbers.
2. $= (ac + adi) + [bci + (bi)(di)]$	**2.** Dist. Prop.
3. $= (ac + bci) + [adi + (bi)(di)]$	**3.** Comm. Prop. of Add.
4. $= c(a + bi) + di(a + bi)$	**4.** Dist. Prop.
5. $= (c + di)(a + bi)$	**5.** Dist. Prop.

30.

Statements	Reasons
1. $[(a + bi)(c + di)](e + fi)$ $= [a(c + di) + bi(c + di)](e + fi)$	**1.** Definition of Mult. of complex numbers.
2. $= [a(c + di)e + bi(c + di)e]$ $+ [a(c + di)fi + bi(c + di)fi]$	**2.** Same as **1.**
3. $= [a(c + di)e + a(c + di)fi]$ $+ [bi(c + di)e + bi(c + di)fi]$	**3.** Comm. Prop. and Assoc. Prop. of Add.
4. $= [a(c + di)(e + fi)]$ $+ [bi(c + di)(e + fi)]$	**4.** Dist. Post.
5. $= (a + bi)[(c + di)(e + fi)]$	**5.** Dist. Post.

31.

Statements	Reasons
1. $(a + bi)[(c + di) + (e + fi)]$ $= (a + bi)[(c + e) + (d + f)i]$	**1.** Definition of Add. of complex numbers.
2. $= a[(c + e) + (d + f)i]$ $+ bi[(c + e) + (d + f)i]$	**2.** Def. of Mult. of complex numbers.
3. $= a(c + e) + a(d + f)i$ $+ bi(c + e) + bi^2(d + f)$	**3.** Dist. Prop.
4. $= ac + ae + adi + afi$ $+ bci + bei - bd - bf$	**4.** Dist. Prop.
5. $= (ac - bd) + (bc + ad)i$ $+ (ae - bf) + (be + af)i$	**5.** Comm. and Assoc. Prop.
6. $= (a + bi)(c + di) + (a + bi)(e + fi)$	**6.** Mult. of complex numbers.

Here is one way to do the problem: For ease in explanation, the coins are numbered 1 through 12.

I. Place 1, 2, 3, 4 on one side of the scale and 5, 6, 7, 8 on the other side. There are 2 possibilities: **a.** the coins balance or **b.** the coins do not balance. This is weighing 1.

II. **a.** The coins balance: This means the counterfeit coin is one of 9, 10, 11, or 12. Weighing 2: The test for 3 coins: Place 9 and 10 on the left side and 11 and any good coin on the right. This leads to 3 possibilities: a) they balance, b) the left side is heavier, or c) the right side is heavier.

a) If they balance, then 12 is counterfeit. For weighing 3, test 12 against a good coin to see if it is lighter or heavier.

b) If the left side is heavier, either 9 or 10 is heavier or 11 is lighter. For weighing 3, test 9 against 10. If 9 and 10 balance, the counterfeit coin is 11, and it is lighter. If 9 and 10 do not balance, the heavier coin is counterfeit.

c) If the right side is heavier, either 9 or 10 is lighter or 11 is heavier. For weighing 3, test 9 against 10. If they balance, 11 is counterfeit, and it is heavier. If 9 and 10 do not balance, the lighter of 9 and 10 is the counterfeit.

II. **b.** The coins do not balance: Mark the 4 coins that weigh more as "heavier"—here denoted by a square around a numeral; mark the other 4 coins as "lighter"—denoted by a circle around a numeral. Suppose $\boxed{1}$, $\boxed{2}$, $\boxed{3}$, $\boxed{4}$ are "heavier" and $\circled{5}$ $\circled{6}$ $\circled{7}$ $\circled{8}$ are "lighter." Test $\boxed{1}$, $\boxed{2}$, $\circled{5}$, against $\boxed{3}$, $\circled{6}$, G (denoting a good coin). If they balance, use the test for 3 coins (shown above) with $\boxed{4}$, $\circled{7}$, $\circled{8}$. (First test $\circled{7}$ against $\circled{8}$.) If they do not balance, and the left side is heavier, use the test for 3 coins with $\boxed{1}$, $\boxed{2}$, $\circled{6}$. (First test $\boxed{1}$ against $\boxed{2}$). If the right side is heavier, then either $\circled{5}$ is lighter or $\boxed{3}$ is heavier. Test either of these coins against G.

Chapter 2

37.

Statements	Reasons
1. $\dfrac{P}{Q} \div \dfrac{R}{S} = \dfrac{\frac{P}{Q}}{\frac{R}{S}}$	1. Meaning of division.
2. $= \dfrac{\frac{P}{Q} \cdot \frac{S}{R}}{\frac{R}{S} \cdot \frac{S}{R}}$	2. $\dfrac{\frac{S}{R}}{\frac{S}{R}} = 1$; the mult. ident.
3. $= \dfrac{\frac{P}{Q} \cdot \frac{S}{R}}{1}$	3. $\dfrac{R}{S}$ and $\dfrac{S}{R}$ are mult. inverses.
4. $= \dfrac{P}{Q} \cdot \dfrac{S}{R}$	4. 1 is the mult. identity.
5. $= \dfrac{PS}{QR}$	5. Multiplication of rational expressions.

47.

Statements	Reasons
1. $\dfrac{P}{Q} + \dfrac{R}{S} = \left(\dfrac{P}{Q}\right)\left(\dfrac{S}{S}\right) + \left(\dfrac{R}{S}\right)\left(\dfrac{Q}{Q}\right)$	1. If the numerator and denominator of a rational expression are multiplied by the same nonzero polynomial, an equal rational expression is obtained.
2. $\phantom{\dfrac{P}{Q}} = \dfrac{PS}{QS} + \dfrac{RQ}{SQ}$	2. Definition of multiplication of rational expressions.
3. $\phantom{\dfrac{P}{Q}} = \dfrac{PS}{QS} + \dfrac{QR}{QS}$	3. Commutative Postulate.
4. $\phantom{\dfrac{P}{Q}} = \dfrac{PS + QR}{QS}$	4. Definition of addition of rational expressions with like denominators.

Page 93

1. $x^4 + 4x^3y + 6x^2y^2 + 4xy^3 + y^4$ 2. $r^7 + 7r^6s + 21r^5s^2 + 35r^4s^3 + 35r^3s^4 + 21r^2s^5 + 7rs^6 + s^7$
3. $c^3 - 3c^2d + 3cd^2 - d^3$ 4. $m^6 - 6m^5n + 15m^4n^2 - 20m^3n^3 + 15m^2n^4 - 6mn^5 + n^6$
5. $x^5 + 15x^4 + 90x^3 + 270x^2 + 405x + 243$ 6. $16r^4 + 32r^3 + 24r^2 + 8r + 1$ 7. $w^3 - 12w^2$
$+ 48w - 64$ 8. $243m^5 + 810m^4 + 1080m^3 + 720m^2 + 240m + 32$ 9. $16x^4 - 96x^3$
$+ 216x^2 - 216x + 81$ 10. $81x^4 + 216x^3y + 216x^2y^2 + 96xy^3 + 16y^4$ 11. $32a^5 - 240a^4b$
$+ 720a^3b^2 - 1080a^2b^3 + 810ab^4 - 243b^5$ 12. $x^3 + 0.6x^2 + 0.12x + 0.008$ 20. $1024x^{10}$
$- 3840x^8y^2 + 5760x^6y^4 - 4320x^4y^6 + 1620x^2y^8 - 243y^{10}$ 31. $3^n + \dfrac{n}{1} \cdot 3^{n-1}(n) + \dfrac{n(n-1)}{1 \cdot 2}$
$\cdot 3^{n-2}(n)^2 + \dfrac{n(n-1)(n-2)}{1 \cdot 2 \cdot 3} \cdot 3^{n-3}(n)^3$, or $3^n + 3^{n-1}n^2 + \dfrac{3^{n-2}}{2}n^3(n-1) + \dfrac{3^{n-3}}{6}$
$n^4(n-1)(n-2)$ 32. $2^n + \dfrac{n}{1} \cdot 2^{n-1}(-n) + \dfrac{n(n-1)}{1 \cdot 2} \cdot 2^{n-2}(-n)^2 + \dfrac{n(n-1)(n-2)}{1 \cdot 2 \cdot 3}$
$\cdot 2^{n-3}(-n)^3$ or $2^n - 2^{n-1}n^2 + \dfrac{2^{n-2}}{2}n^3(n-1) - \dfrac{2^{n-3}}{6}n^4(n-1)(n-2)$

Page 93
Puzzle

$10^2 - 6^2 = 64 = 4^3$; $15^2 - 10^2 = 125 = 5^3$; $21^2 - 15^2 = 216 = 6^3$; $28^2 - 21^2 = 343 = 7^3$;
$36^2 - 28^2 = 512 = 8^3$
Yes, the squares of successive terms do always differ by a cube.
$\left(\dfrac{n(n+1)}{2}\right)^2 - \left(\dfrac{(n-1)(n)}{2}\right)^2 = n^3$, or $\left(\dfrac{(n+1)(n+2)}{2}\right)^2 - \left(\dfrac{n(n+1)}{2}\right)^2 = (n+1)^3$

Chapter 4

Page 152

16. $P\left(\dfrac{b}{2}, \dfrac{c}{2}\right)$ is the midpoint of the segment joining $(0, 0)$ and (b, c). $Q\left(\dfrac{a+b}{2}, \dfrac{c}{2}\right)$ is
the midpoint of the segment joining $(a, 0)$ and (b, c). The slope of the line joining P
and Q is 0. Therefore, $\overline{PQ}$ is parallel to the x axis. Since the third side of the triangle
lies on the x axis, $\overline{PQ}$ is parallel to the third side of the triangle. $PQ = \left|\dfrac{b}{2} - \dfrac{a+b}{2}\right| = $
$\left|-\dfrac{a}{2}\right|$ The length of the segment joining $(0, 0)$ and $(a, 0)$ is $|a|$. Thus $\overline{PQ}$ is one-half
as long as the segment joining $(0, 0)$ and $(a, 0)$.

17. Use $(0, 0)$, $(a, 0)$, (b, c), and (d, e) as the coordinates of the quadrilateral. $P\left(\frac{a}{2}, 0\right)$ is the midpoint of the segment joining $(0, 0)$ and $(a, 0)$; $Q\left(\frac{a+d}{2}, \frac{e}{2}\right)$ is the midpoint of the segment joining $(a, 0)$ and (d, e); $R\left(\frac{b+d}{2}, \frac{c+e}{2}\right)$ is the midpoint of the segment joining (b, c) and (d, e); $S\left(\frac{b}{2}, \frac{c}{2}\right)$ is the midpoint of the segment joining $(0, 0)$ and (b, c). The slope of the line joining P and Q and the line joining S and R is $\frac{e}{d}$. The slope of the line joining S and P and the line joining R and Q is $\frac{c}{b-a}$. Therefore the quadrilateral has both pairs of opposite sides parallel and, by definition, is a parallelogram.

18. Reason: **1.** Given. **2.** Construction. In a plane, there is one and only one line perpendicular to a given line at a given point on the line. **3.** If two parallel lines are cut by a transversal, corresponding angles are congruent. **4.** Perpendicular lines form right angles, and definition of right triangle. **5.** Two right triangles are similar if an acute angle of one is congruent to an acute angle of the other. **6.** Corresponding sides of similar triangles are proportional. **7.** Distance formula and definition of slope.

Page 161 **1.** All points on the line 2 units right of the y axis. **2.** All points on the line 3 units above the x axis. **3.** All points on and to the right of the line 2 units left of the y axis. **4.** All points on and below the line 4 units below the x axis. **5.** All points on the line through $(0, 0)$ and $(1, 1)$. **6.** All points on the line through $(0, 0)$ and $(-1, 1)$. **7.** All points on and above the x axis. **8.** All points on and left of the y axis. **9.** All points on the line passing through $(0, -2)$ and $(1, 1)$. **10.** All points on the line passing through $(0, 5)$ and $(1, 3)$. **11.** All points on the line passing through $(0, 2)$ and $(4, 0)$. **12.** All points on the line passing through $(0, 6)$ and $(3, 0)$. **13.** All points below the line passing through $(0, 2)$ and $(6, 0)$. **14.** All points above the line passing through $(0, 8)$ and $(-4, 0)$. **15.** All points on and above the line passing through $(0, -3)$ and $(1, -1)$. **16.** All points on and below the line passing through $(0, 7)$ and $(1, 3)$. **17.** All points 3 units or more to the right of the y axis and 2 units or more below the x axis. **18.** All points more than 1 unit left of the y axis and 4 or more units above the x axis. **19.** All points on or below the line passing through the points $(0, 2)$ and $(6, 0)$ and on or above the line passing through $(0, 4)$ and $(2, 0)$. **20.** All points on or above the line passing through $(0, -8)$ and $(4, 0)$ and on or below the line passing through $(0, 1)$ and $(-2, 0)$.

Page 171 **22.** Graph $P(2, 3)$ and draw $\overrightarrow{OP}$. Start at P. Move 1 unit left and 5 units down to $Q(1, -2)$. Draw $\overrightarrow{PQ}$ which represents $(-1, -5)$. Start at Q. Move 2 units right and 1 unit down to $R(3, -3)$. Draw $\overrightarrow{QR}$ which represents $(2, -1)$. Draw $\overrightarrow{OR}$. $\overrightarrow{OR}$ represents $\overrightarrow{OP} + \overrightarrow{PQ} + \overrightarrow{QR}$. Thus $(2, 3) + (-1, -5) + (2, -1) = (3, -3)$.

Chapter 5

24. The parabola with vertex at (0, 0) also passing through (−2, 4) and (2, 4).
25. All points below the line $y = x$.   **26.** All points on or above the line $y = x + 5$.
27. All points on or below the line $y = 2x − 3$.

18. The graph consists of two half-lines, one from (0, −3) directed to the left, parallel to the x axis, and one from (0, 3) directed to the right, parallel to the x axis. (The endpoints (0, −3) and (0, 3) are represented by small circles, since they are not included.)   **19.** The graph consists of the point (0, 0) and two half-lines, one from (0, −2) directed to the left, parallel to the x axis, and one from (0, 2) directed to the right, parallel to the x axis. (The endpoints (0, −2) and (0, 2) are represented by small circles, since they are not included.)   **20.** The graph consists of the ray from (0, 0) through (2, 2) and the half-line from (0, −4) directed to the left, parallel to the x axis. (The point (0, −4) is not included.)   **21.** The graph consists of the point (0, 6) and two half-lines, one from (0, 0) through (2, 2), and the other from (0, 0) through (−2, 2). (The endpoint of the half-lines, (0, 0), is not included.)

21. A straight line passing through (0, 0) and (1, 1).   **22.** A straight line passing through (0, 0) and (−1, 1).   **23.** A straight line 3 units above and parallel to the x axis.   **24.** A straight line 3 units below and parallel to the x axis.   **25.** The graph of $y = |x|$ is shown in Ex. **32.**   **26.** The graph of $y = −|x|$ is shown in Ex. **34.**
27. The graph consists of an infinite number of line segments (in each case with the right endpoint deleted). For example, from (−3, −3) to (−2, −3), from (−2, −2) to (−1, −2), from (−1, −1) to (0, −1), from (0, 0) to (1, 0), from (1, 1) to (2, 1), from (2, 2) to (3, 2), etc.   **28.** The graph consists of an infinite number of line segments (in each case with the right endpoint deleted). For example, from (−3, 3) to (−2, 3), from (−2, 2) to (−1, 2), from (−1, 1) to (0, 1), from (0, 0) to (1, 0), from (1, −1) to (2, −1), etc.   **29.** A line passing through (0, 0) and (2, 1).

20. A line through (0, 10) and (−2, 0). Zero is −2.   **21.** A line through (0, −3) and ($\frac{3}{2}$, 0). Zero is $\frac{3}{2}$.   **22.** A parabola with vertex at (0, −1) passing through (−1, 3) and (1, 3). Zeros are $-\frac{1}{2}$ and $\frac{1}{2}$.   **23.** A parabola with vertex at (3, −9) passing through (1, −5) and (5, −5). Zeros are 0 and 6.   **24.** If $a^x = 0$ then $a \cdot a \cdot \cdots \cdot a = 0$, and $a = 0$. But $a > 0$ was given. Thus, $a^x \neq 0$ and the function has no zeros.

25. $f\left(\dfrac{-b + \sqrt{b^2 - 4ac}}{2a}\right) \overset{?}{=} 0$; $a\left(\dfrac{-b + \sqrt{b^2 - 4ac}}{2a}\right)^2 + b\left(\dfrac{-b + \sqrt{b^2 - 4ac}}{2a}\right) + c \overset{?}{=} 0$;

$a\left(\dfrac{b^2}{4a^2} - \dfrac{2b\sqrt{b^2 - 4ac}}{4a^2} + \dfrac{b^2}{4a^2} - \dfrac{4ac}{4a^2}\right) + b\left(\dfrac{-b}{2a} + \dfrac{\sqrt{b^2 - 4ac}}{2a}\right) + c \overset{?}{=} 0$; $\dfrac{b^2}{4a} - \dfrac{b\sqrt{b^2 - 4ac}}{2a}$

$+ \dfrac{b^2}{4a} - c - \dfrac{b^2}{2a} + \dfrac{b\sqrt{b^2 - 4ac}}{2a} + c \overset{?}{=} 0$; $0 = 0$. In a similar way, it can be shown that

$f\left(\dfrac{-b - \sqrt{b^2 - 4ac}}{2a}\right) = 0$.

21. Graph of f: The points $(2, 1)$, $(1, 3)$, $(5, -2)$, $(3, -4)$. Graph of f^{-1}: The points $(1, 2)$, $(3, 1)$, $(-2, 5)$, $(-4, 3)$. **22.** Graph of f: The line through $(0, 0)$ and $(2, -2)$. Graph of f^{-1}: The same line. **23.** Graph of f is a line through $(0, -3)$, $(3, 3)$, and $(1, -1)$. Graph of f^{-1} is a line through $(-3, 0)$, $(3, 3)$, and $(-1, 1)$. **24.** Graph of f is a line through $(0, 5)$ and $(1, 2)$. Graph of f^{-1} is a line through $(5, 0)$ and $(2, 1)$.
25. Graph of f is a parabola with vertex at $(0, 0)$ passing through $(2, 4)$ and $(-2, 4)$. Graph of f^{-1} is a parabola with vertex at $(0, 0)$ passing through $(4, 2)$ and $(4, -2)$.
26. Graph of f is a line through $(0, 0)$ and $(2, 2)$. Graph of f^{-1} is the same line.
27. Graph of $f(x) = |x|$: See Ex. **32**, on page 193. Graph of $f^{-1}(x)$, or $x = |y|$: See Ex. **33**, on page 193. **28.** Graph of f is a parabola which passes through $(4, 2)$ and $(4, -2)$. The vertex is at $(0, 0)$. Graph of f^{-1} is a parabola which passes through $(2, 4)$ and $(-2, 4)$. The vertex is $(0, 0)$. **29.** If the inverse of the relation is a function, then no horizontal line intersects the graph of the relation in more than one point. The test described in Ex. **29** can be used to answer Ex. **30–37**.

41. The graph of Ex. **40** represent the functions $f(x) = -2x - 2$ and $f^{-1}(x) = -\frac{1}{2}x - 1$; $f[f^{-1}(x)] = -2(-\frac{1}{2}x - 1) - 2 = x + 2 - 2 = x$; $f^{-1}[f(x)] = -\frac{1}{2}(-2x - 2) - 1 = x + 1 - 1 = x$
42. Label the points $A(a, b)$ and $B(b, a)$. The slope of $y = x$ is 1. The slope of the line passing through A and B is $\dfrac{b - a}{a - b} = \dfrac{-(a - b)}{a - b} = -1$. The slopes are negative reciprocals, so the graph of $y = x$ is perpendicular to $\overline{AB}$. Let $P(x, y)$ be any point on the line $y = x$. By the distance formula, $AP = \sqrt{(a - x)^2 + (b - y)^2}$ and $BP = \sqrt{(b - x)^2 + (a - y)^2} = \sqrt{(a - y)^2 + (b - x)^2}$. Since $y = x$, replace y by x in these equations. Then $AP = BP = \sqrt{(a - x)^2 + (b - x)^2}$.

Chapter 6

12. The three parabolas have the same size and shape, but have different positions with respect to the x and y axes. The graphs of $y = x^2 - 4$ and $y = x^2$ both have the y axis as axis of symmetry, but the vertex of $y = x^2 - 4$ is at $(0, -4)$, while the vertex of $y = x^2$ is at $(0, 0)$. The axis of symmetry for $y = x^2 - 8x + 12$ is the line $x = 4$ and its vertex is at $(4, -4)$. All graphs open upward.

x	-3	-2	-1	0	1	2	3
$y = x^2$	9	4	1	0	1	4	9
$y = x^2 - 4$	5	0	-3	-4	-3	0	5

x	1	2	3	4	5	6	7
$y = x^2 - 8x + 12$	5	0	-3	-4	-3	0	5

13. These three graphs have the same size and shape, but have different positions with respect to the x and y axes.

function	axis of symmetry	vertex
$y = 2x^2$	y axis	(0, 0)
$y = 2x^2 - 8x + 8$	$x = 2$	(2, 0)
$y = 2x^2 - 8x + 10$	$x = 2$	(2, 2)

x	−3	−2	−1	0	1	2	3	4	5
$y = 2x^2$	18	8	2	0	2	8	18		
$y = 2x^2 - 8x + 8$			18	8	2	0	2	8	18
$y = 2x^2 - 8x + 10$			20	10	4	2	4	10	20

14. Both parabolas have the same axis of symmetry, have the same size and shape and open in the same direction. Their positions with respect to the x axis are different if $c_1 \neq c_2$.   **15.** Graphs of parabolas have the same vertex (0, c) and the axis of symmetry is the y axis in each case. The greater the absolute value of a, the steeper the curve. If a_1 or a_2 is positive, the curve opens upward; if negative, the curve opens downward.   **17.** When the rocket hits the ground s = 0. Therefore, $80t - 4.9t^2 = 0$; $t(80 - 4.9t) = 0$; $t = 0$ or $80 - 4.9t = 0$; $t = 0$ or $t = 16.3$. The object will hit the ground in 16.3 seconds. The highest altitude is 326.5 meters which is reached after 8.2 seconds.

13. (a) $x = -\frac{1}{2}$ (b) $(-\frac{1}{2}, -\frac{25}{4})$ (c) (−3, 0) and (2, 0) (d) (0, −6) and (−1, −6) **14.** (a) $x = 2$ (b) $V(2, -4)$ (c) (0, 0), (4, 0) (d) (3, −3) and (1, −3) **15.** (a) $x = \frac{7}{2}$ (b) $V(\frac{7}{2}, -\frac{25}{4})$ (c) (1, 0), (6, 0) (d) (5, −4) and (2, −4) **16.** (a) $x = \frac{1}{2}$ (b) $(\frac{1}{2}, -\frac{25}{2})$ (c) (3, 0) and (−2, 0) (d) (2, −8) and (−1, −8) **17.** (a) $x = \frac{3}{4}$ (b) $(\frac{3}{4}, -\frac{75}{8})$ (c) $(-\frac{1}{2}, 0)$ and (2, 0) (d) (0, −6) and $(\frac{3}{2}, -6)$ **18.** (a) $x = \frac{1}{2}$ (b) $(\frac{1}{2}, -4)$ (c) $(\frac{3}{2}, 0)$ and $(-\frac{1}{2}, 0)$ (d) (0, −3) and (1, −3).   **19.** They are congruent since $|a| = |1| = |-1|$ and have the same axis of symmetry, $x = 2$. They also have the same zeros. The graphs are also symmetric with respect to the x axis. The graphs have different vertices. The vertex of $y = x^2 - 4x + 1$ is $V(2, -3)$ and the vertex of $y = 4x - x^2 - 1$ is $V(2, 3)$. Also, the graph of $y = x^2 - 4x + 1$ opens upward and the graph of $y = 4x - x^2 - 1$ opens downward.   **24.** $y = a(x - h)^2 + k$, or $y = ax^2 - 2ahx + ah^2 + k$. The abscissa of the vertex of $y = ax^2 + bx + c$ is $\frac{b}{2a}$.

By comparison, the abcissa of the vertex of $y = ax^2 + (-2ah)x + (ah^2 + k)$ is $-\frac{(-2ah)}{2a} = h$. The ordinate of the vertex of $y = ax^2 + bx + c$ is $-\frac{b^2}{4a} + c$. By comparison, the vertex of $y = ax^2 + (-2ah)x + (ah^2 + k)$ is $-\frac{(-2ah)^2}{4a} + ah^2 + k = -ah^2 + ah^2 + k = k$.

Therefore the vertex is at (h, k).

25.

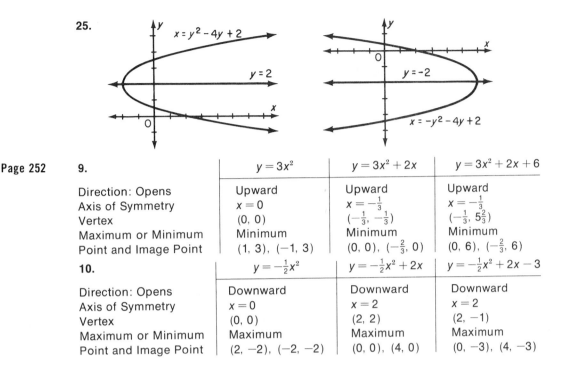

9.

	$y = 3x^2$	$y = 3x^2 + 2x$	$y = 3x^2 + 2x + 6$
Direction: Opens	Upward	Upward	Upward
Axis of Symmetry	$x = 0$	$x = -\frac{1}{3}$	$x = -\frac{1}{3}$
Vertex	$(0, 0)$	$(-\frac{1}{3}, -\frac{1}{3})$	$(-\frac{1}{3}, 5\frac{2}{3})$
Maximum or Minimum	Minimum	Minimum	Minimum
Point and Image Point	$(1, 3), (-1, 3)$	$(0, 0), (-\frac{2}{3}, 0)$	$(0, 6), (-\frac{2}{3}, 6)$

10.

	$y = -\frac{1}{2}x^2$	$y = -\frac{1}{2}x^2 + 2x$	$y = -\frac{1}{2}x^2 + 2x - 3$
Direction: Opens	Downward	Downward	Downward
Axis of Symmetry	$x = 0$	$x = 2$	$x = 2$
Vertex	$(0, 0)$	$(2, 2)$	$(2, -1)$
Maximum or Minimum	Maximum	Maximum	Maximum
Point and Image Point	$(2, -2), (-2, -2)$	$(0, 0), (4, 0)$	$(0, -3), (4, -3)$

Chapter 7

A passer-by hears the children debating how to divide the horses and offers to help. He first gets off his own horse and leads it to the other horses so that the number of horses becomes 18. The first child then gets nine horses, the second six, and the third two. The passer-by then retrieves the remaining horse (his own) and rides off.

23. and 24.

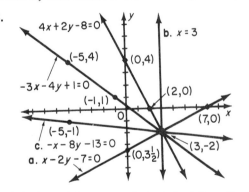

26. If (x_1, y_1) is the point common to both $4x + 2y - 8 = 0$ and $-3x - 4y + 1 = 0$, then it is true that $(4x_1 + 2y_1 - 8) + (-3x_1 - 4y_1 + 1) = 0 + 0 = 0$. For any m, $m(4x_1 + 2y_1 - 8) = 0$, since $m \cdot 0 = 0$. For any n, $n(-3x_1 - 4y_1 + 1) = 0$, since $n \cdot 0 = 0$. Therefore, $m(4x_1 + 2y_1 - 8) + n(-3x_1 - 4y_1 + 1) = 0 + 0 = 0$, and (x_1, y_1) satisfies the equation $m(4x + 2y - 8) + n(-3x - 4y + 1) = 0$ also.

Page 274

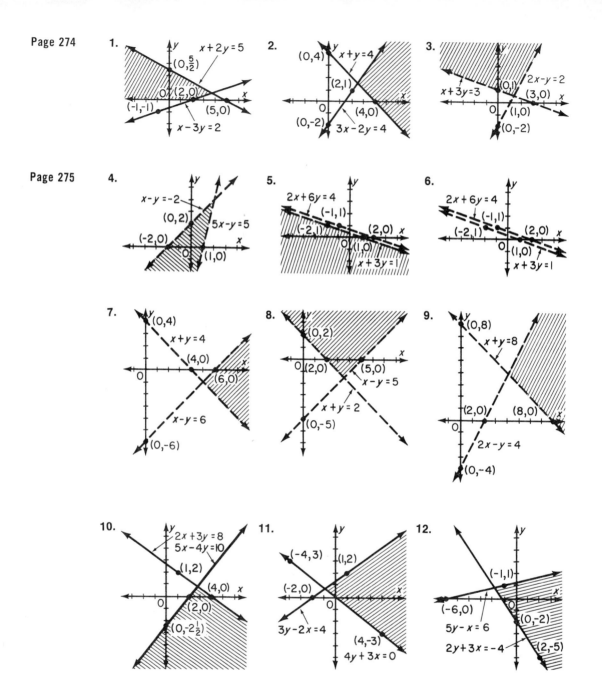

Page 275

1. $x \geq 1$, $y \geq 1$, $x + y \leq 5$. The solution set is the polygonal convex set bounded by the triangle whose vertices are $(1, 1)$, $(4, 1)$ and $(1, 4)$. **2.** The triangle with vertices $(1, 1)$, $(1, -6)$, and $(8, 1)$. **3.** The triangle with vertices $(-1, 1)$, $(-1, \frac{5}{2})$, and $(-4, 1)$. **4.** The triangle with vertices $(0, 0)$, $(-6, 0)$, and $(0, -3)$. **5.** The triangle with vertices $(0, 0)$, $(0, 4)$, and $(-3, 2)$. **6.** The triangle with vertices $(5, 5)$, $(6, 1)$, and $(1, 3)$. **7.** The triangle with vertices $(2, 2)$, $(3, -3)$, and $(-3, 1)$. **8.** $\emptyset$. The sets of points do not intersect. **9.** The triangle with vertices $(0, 4)$, $(\frac{5}{2}, \frac{3}{2})$, and $(\frac{10}{3}, \frac{7}{3})$.

10.

11. The solution set is the convex polygonal set bounded by the quadrilateral whose vertices are $(0, 0)$, $(0, 6)$, $(4, 0)$, and $(3, 3)$.

12. The quadrilateral with vertices $(0, 0)$, $(0, 4)$, $(4, 6)$, and $(8, 3)$.

16.   **17.**   **18.**

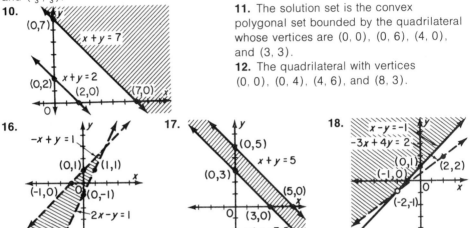

Chapter 8

46. $7 \cdot 10^3 + 6 \cdot 10^2 + 5 \cdot 10^1 + 4 \cdot 10^0$ **47.** $8 \cdot 10^3 + 3 \cdot 10^2 + 2 \cdot 10^1 + 5 \cdot 10^0 + 7 \cdot 10^{-1}$ **48.** $5 \cdot 10^2 + 3 \cdot 10^{-2}$ **49.** $1 \cdot 10^3 + 2 \cdot 10^2 + 3 \cdot 10^1 + 4 \cdot 10^0 + 5 \cdot 10^{-1} + 6 \cdot 10^{-2} + 7 \cdot 10^{-3}$ **50.** $9 \cdot 10^{-5}$ **51.** $2 \cdot 10^4 + 3 \cdot 10^3 + 7 \cdot 10^{-2}$ **52.** $7 \cdot 10^4 + 5 \cdot 10^3$ **53.** $7 \cdot 10^1 + 5 \cdot 10^0 + 4 \cdot 10^{-3}$

54. The graph of $y = 2^x$, for the replacement set given, consists of the ordered pairs in the table below.

x	-5	-4	-3	-2	-1	0	1	2	3	4	5
2^x	$\frac{1}{32}$	$\frac{1}{16}$	$\frac{1}{8}$	$\frac{1}{4}$	$\frac{1}{2}$	1	2	4	8	16	32

55. The graph of $y = (-2)^x$, for the replacement set given, consists of the ordered pairs in the table below. This graph is different from the graph of $y = 2^x$. Points lie both above and below the x axis (above when x is even and below when x is odd)

x	-5	-4	-3	-2	-1	0	1	2	3	4	5
$(-2)^x$	$-\frac{1}{32}$	$\frac{1}{16}$	$-\frac{1}{8}$	$\frac{1}{4}$	$-\frac{1}{2}$	1	-2	4	-8	16	-32

32. $(x^{-1}+y^{-1})^{-1} = \dfrac{1}{x^{-1}+y^{-1}} = \dfrac{1}{\dfrac{1}{x}+\dfrac{1}{y}} = \dfrac{xy}{y+x}$. Since $\dfrac{xy}{y+x} \neq x+y$, for all values of x

and y, $(x^{-1}+y^{-1})^{-1} = x+y$ is usually a false statement. **33.** $(x+y)^{-1} = \dfrac{1}{x+y}$ and

$x^{-1}+y^{-1} = \dfrac{1}{x}+\dfrac{1}{y} = \dfrac{y+x}{xy}$. Since $\dfrac{1}{x+y} \neq \dfrac{y+x}{xy}$, for all values of x and y, $(x+y)^{-1} =$

$x^{-1}+y^{-1}$ is usually a false statement.

37. Since $(\sqrt[n]{a} \cdot \sqrt[n]{b})^n = ab;\ [(\sqrt[n]{a} \cdot \sqrt[n]{b})^n]^{\frac{1}{n}} = (ab)^{\frac{1}{n}};\ \sqrt[n]{a} \cdot \sqrt[n]{b} = (ab)^{\frac{1}{n}}$ or
$\sqrt[n]{a} \cdot \sqrt[n]{b} = \sqrt[n]{ab}$

Chapter 9

13. The graph of $y = 2^x$ is a smooth curve which passes through the points:

x	-5	-4	-3	-2	-1	0	1	2	3	4	5
y	$\frac{1}{32}$	$\frac{1}{16}$	$\frac{1}{8}$	$\frac{1}{4}$	$\frac{1}{2}$	1	2	4	8	16	32

The graph of $y = (\frac{1}{2})^x$ is a smooth curve which passes through the points:

x	-5	-4	-3	-2	-1	0	1	2	3	4	5
y	32	16	8	4	2	1	$\frac{1}{2}$	$\frac{1}{4}$	$\frac{1}{8}$	$\frac{1}{16}$	$\frac{1}{32}$

The graphs are symmetric with respect to the y axis. The graphs of $y = 3^x$ and $y = (\frac{1}{3})^x$ are also symmetric with respect to the y axis. For these pairs of graphs, the y axis is the perpendicular bisector of the line segments joining any two corresponding points on the two graphs. (See Ex. **2** and **5** for a description of the graphs of $y = 3^x$ and $y = (\frac{1}{3})^x$.)

18. The graph of $y = 2^x$ passes through the points:

x	-5	-4	-3	-2	-1	0	1	2	3	4	5
y	$\frac{1}{32}$	$\frac{1}{16}$	$\frac{1}{8}$	$\frac{1}{4}$	$\frac{1}{2}$	1	2	4	8	16	32

The graph of $x = 2^y$ passes through the points:

x	$\frac{1}{32}$	$\frac{1}{16}$	$\frac{1}{8}$	$\frac{1}{4}$	$\frac{1}{2}$	1	2	4	8	16	32
y	-5	-4	-3	-2	-1	0	1	2	3	4	5

The graphs are symmetric with respect to the line $y = x$. The graph of $y = 2^x$ is asymptotic to the negative half of the x axis. The graph of $x = 2^y$ is asymptotic to the negative half of the y axis. **19.** When $x = m$ and $x = -m$, corresponding points on

the two graphs are: $A(m,\ a^m)$ on $y = a^x$, and $B\left(-m,\ \left(\dfrac{1}{a}\right)^{-m}\right)$ on $y = \left(\dfrac{1}{a}\right)^x$. Since

$\left(\dfrac{1}{a}\right)^{-m} = a^m$, these two points are seen to be $A(m,\ a^m)$ and $B(-m,\ a^m)$, so both lie on a line

parallel to the x axis. Thus, the y axis is perpendicular to the line containing $\overline{AB}$. Since

the midpoint of $\overline{AB}$ is $\left(\dfrac{m+(-m)}{2},\ \dfrac{a^m+a^m}{2}\right)$ or $(0,\ a^m)$, it is clear that the y axis is the

perpendicular bisector of $\overline{AB}$.

46. Since $t = \log_{10}M$ and $r = \log_{10}N$, $M = 10^t$ and $N = 10^r$ and $M \times N = 10^t \cdot 10^r = 10^{t+r}$. Then, $\log_{10}(M \times N) = t + r$. Substituting: $\log_{10}(M \times N) = \log_{10}M + \log_{10}N$. **47.** As in Exercise **46**, $M = 10^t$ and $N = 10^r$. $\dfrac{M}{N} = \dfrac{10^t}{10^r} = 10^{t-r}$. Then, $\log_{10}\left(\dfrac{M}{N}\right) = t - r$. Substituting: $\log_{10}\left(\dfrac{M}{N}\right) = \log_{10}M - \log_{10}N$. **48.** Since $\log_{10}M = t$, $10^t = M$ and $M^s = (10^t)^s = 10^{st}$, $s \in R$. Then, $\log_{10}M^s = st$. Substituting: $\log_{10}M^s = s\log_{10}M$.

22. a.

$$\text{Let } x = \log_a N$$
$$a^x = N$$
$$\log_b(a^x) = \log_b N$$
$$x \log_b a = \log_b N$$
$$\log_a N \log_b a = \log_b N$$
$$\log_a N = \frac{\log_b N}{\log_b a}$$

b.

$$\text{Let } x = \log_a b$$
$$a^x = b$$
$$x \log_b a = \log_b b$$
$$\log_a b \log_b a = 1$$
$$\log_a b = \frac{1}{\log_b a}$$

Chapter 10

26. Let $A = C$, and $B = 0$. Then $Ax^2 + Ay^2 + Dx + Ey + F = 0$. $x^2 + y^2 + \dfrac{D}{A}x + \dfrac{E}{A}y$

$+ \dfrac{F}{A} = 0$ or $\left(x^2 + \dfrac{D}{A}x\right) + \left(y^2 + \dfrac{E}{A}y\right) = \dfrac{-F}{A}; \left[x^2 + \dfrac{D}{A}x + \left(\dfrac{D}{2A}\right)^2\right] + \left[y^2 + \dfrac{E}{A}y + \left(\dfrac{E}{2A}\right)^2\right]$

$= \dfrac{-F}{A} + \left(\dfrac{D}{2A}\right)^2 + \left(\dfrac{E}{2A}\right)^2; \left(x + \dfrac{D}{2A}\right)^2 + \left(y + \dfrac{E}{2A}\right)^2 = \dfrac{-4AF + D^2 + E^2}{4A^2};$ Let $R = \dfrac{-4AF + D^2 + E^2}{4A^2}$

If $R > 0$, $\left(x + \dfrac{D}{2A}\right)^2 + \left(y + \dfrac{E}{2A}\right)^2 = R$ is the equation of a circle with center at

$\left(-\dfrac{D}{2A}, -\dfrac{E}{2A}\right)$ and radius $= \sqrt{R}$. If $R = 0$, the radius $= 0$ and $\left(x + \dfrac{D}{2A}\right)^2 + \left(y + \dfrac{E}{2A}\right)^2 = 0$

is the point $\left(\dfrac{-D}{2A}, \dfrac{-E}{2A}\right)$. If $R < 0$, the graph of $\left(x + \dfrac{D}{2A}\right)^2 + \left(y + \dfrac{E}{2A}\right)^2 = R$ does not exist

in the real number plane since radius $= \sqrt{R}$ which is an imaginary number.

24. $BF' + BF = \sqrt{b^2 + c^2} + \sqrt{b^2 + c^2} = 2\sqrt{b^2 + c^2}$; $AF' + AF = (2c + a - c) + (a - c)$ $= 2a$. From the definition of an ellipse, the sum of the distances from the foci of the ellipse to any point on the ellipse is a constant. Therefore, $BF' + BF = AF' + AF$; $2\sqrt{b^2 + c^2} = 2a$, $\sqrt{b^2 + c^2} = a$, $b^2 + c^2 = a^2$, or $c^2 = a^2 - b^2$.

19. $y + 2 = -\frac{1}{4}(x - 2)^2$. The graph opens downward; vertex $(2, -2)$; focus $(2, -3)$; directrix $y = -1$; y intercept $(0, -3)$. **20.** $x + 1 = \frac{1}{2}(y + 2)^2$. The graph is a parabola that opens to the right; vertex $(-1, -2)$; focus $(-\frac{1}{2}, -2)$; directrix $x = -\frac{3}{2}$; x intercept $(1, 0)$. **21.** $y - 12 = -2(x + 2)^2$. The graph is a parabola that opens downward; vertex $(-2, 12)$; focus $(-2, 11\frac{7}{8})$; directrix $y = 12\frac{1}{8}$; y intercept $(0, 4)$

22. $x - 4 = -\frac{3}{2}(y + 1)^2$. The graph opens to the left; vertex $(4, -1)$; focus $(3\frac{5}{6}, -1)$; directrix $x = 4\frac{1}{6}$; x intercept $(2\frac{1}{2}, 0)$.

1. Vertices: $(4, 0)$ and $(-4, 0)$; opens horizontally; asymptotes: $y = \frac{1}{2}x$ and $y = -\frac{1}{2}x$

2. Vertices: $(5, 0)$ and $(-5, 0)$; opens horizontally; asymptotes: $y = \frac{3}{5}x$ and $y = -\frac{3}{5}x$

3. Vertices: $(0, 7)$ and $(0, -7)$; opens vertically; asymptotes: $y = \frac{7}{6}x$ and $y = -\frac{7}{6}x$

4. Vertices: $(0, 8)$ and $(0, -8)$; opens vertically; asymptotes: $y = \frac{8}{5}x$ and $y = -\frac{8}{5}x$

5. Vertices: $(0, 3)$ and $(0, -3)$; opens vertically; asymptotes: $y = \frac{1}{3}x$ and $y = -\frac{1}{3}x$

6. Vertices: $(6, 0)$ and $(-6, 0)$; opens horizontally; asymptotes: $y = \frac{1}{2}x$ and $y = -\frac{1}{2}x$

7. Vertices: $(2, 0)$ and $(-2, 0)$; opens horizontally; asymptotes: $y = \frac{5}{2}x$ and $y = -\frac{5}{2}x$

8. Vertices: $(0, 3)$ and $(0, -3)$; opens vertically; asymptotes: $y = \frac{3}{2}x$ and $y = -\frac{3}{2}x$

9. Vertices: $(3, 0)$ and $(-3, 0)$; opens horizontally; asymptotes: $y = x$ and $y = -x$

15. 4. $(0, \sqrt{89})$ and $(0, -\sqrt{89})$; **5.** $(0, \sqrt{90})$ and $(0, -\sqrt{90})$ or $(0, 3\sqrt{10})$ and $(0, -3\sqrt{10})$; **6.** $(3\sqrt{5}, 0)$ and $(-3\sqrt{5}, 0)$; **7.** $(\sqrt{29}, 0)$ and $(-\sqrt{29}, 0)$; **8.** $(0, \sqrt{13})$ and $(0, -\sqrt{13})$; **9.** $(3\sqrt{2}, 0)$ and $(-3\sqrt{2}, 0)$ **16.** Center $(3, 2)$; vertices $(7, 2)$ and $(-1, 2)$; opens horizontally; asymptotes are the line that passes through the points $(7, 5)$ and $(-1, -1)$, and the line that passes through the points $(-1, 5)$ and $(7, -1)$. **17.** Center $(0, 3)$; vertices $(0, 10)$ and $(0, -4)$; opens vertically; the asymptotes are the line passing through the points $(-5, 10)$ and $(5, -4)$, and the line passing through the points $(-5, -4)$ and $(5, 10)$. **18.** Center $(1, 0)$; vertices $(-2, 0)$ and $(4, 0)$; opens horizontally; asymptotes are the line that passes through the point $(-2, -2)$ and $(4, 2)$, and the line that passes through the points $(-2, 2)$ and $(4, -2)$.

17. This is a rectangular hyperbola in quadrants I and III. A possible table of values is:

x	1	2	3	6	9	18	-1	-2	-3	-6	-9	-18
y	18	9	6	3	2	1	-18	-9	-6	-3	-2	-1

18. $xy = -18$ is a rectangular hyperbola in quadrants II and IV. A possible table of values is:

x	1	2	3	6	9	18	-1	-2	-3	-6	-9	-18
y	-18	-9	-6	-3	-2	-1	18	9	6	3	2	1

19. This is a rectangular hyperbola in quadrants I and III. A possible table of values is:

x	1	3	9	-1	-3	-9
y	9	3	1	-9	-3	-1

20. This is a rectangular hyperbola in quadrants II and IV. A possible table of values is:

x	1	3	9	-1	-3	-9
y	-9	-3	-1	9	3	1

1. The graph is the set of points outside the circle with center at $(0, 0)$ and radius 6.
2. The graph is the set of points inside the circle with center at $(0, 0)$ and radius $\sqrt{10}$.
3. The graph is the set of points inside the parabola with vertex at $(0, 0)$, opening upward.   **4.** The graph is the set of points outside the ellipse with center at $(0, 0)$ and intercepts $(4, 0)$, $(-4, 0)$, $(0, 3)$ and $(0, -3)$.   **5.** The graph is the set of points inside the ellipse with center $(0, 0)$ and intercepts $(5, 0)$, $(-5, 0)$, $(0, 4)$ and $(0, -4)$.
6. The graph is the set of points inside both branches of the hyperbola with center at $(0, 0)$ and vertices $(2, 0)$ and $(-2, 0)$.   **7.** The graph is the set of points outside the parabola with vertex at $(0, 0)$, opening to the right.   **8.** The graph is the set of points inside and on the parabola with vertex at $(\frac{3}{2}, -\frac{9}{4})$, opening upward, with x intercepts $(0, 0)$ and $(3, 0)$.   **9.** The graph is the set of points between the two branches of the rectangular hyperbola $xy = 16$, with vertices at $(4, 4)$ and $(-4, 4)$.   **10.** The graph is the set of points on and outside the parabola with vertex at $(0, 0)$, opening to the left.   **11.** The graph is the set of points on and between the two branches of the rectangular hyperbola with vertices at $(\sqrt{15}, -\sqrt{15})$ and $(-\sqrt{15}, \sqrt{15})$.   **12.** The graph is the set of points inside the ellipse with center at $(0, 0)$ and intercepts $(\sqrt{3}, 0)$, $(-\sqrt{3}, 0)$, $(0, \frac{1}{2}\sqrt{6})$ and $(0, -\frac{1}{2}\sqrt{6})$.   **13.** The solution set is the set of points within and on the circle with center at $(0, 0)$ and radius 5 *and* within and on the parabola with vertex at $(0, 0)$, opening upward.   **14.** The solution set is the set of points outside and on the circle with center at $(0, 0)$ and radius 5 *and* within and on the circle with center at $(0, 0)$ and radius 6.   **15.** The solution set is the set of all points within and on the circle with center $(0, 0)$ and radius 7 *and* outside and on the parabola opening downward with vertex at $(0, 0)$.

2. Since $b \neq 3a$, $b - 3a \neq 0$ and $(b - 3a)^2 > 0$. Squaring we find that $b^2 - 6ab + 9a^2 > 0$. Adding $6ab$ to both sides, $b^2 + 9a^2 > 6ab$. Dividing both sides by $3ab$, which is positive since $a > 0$ and $b > 0$,

$$\frac{b^2 + 9a^2}{3ab} > \frac{6ab}{3ab} \text{ or } \frac{b^2}{3ab} + \frac{9a^2}{3ab} > 2, \text{ or } \frac{b}{3a} + \frac{3a}{b} > 2.$$

3. $(a^2 - 4)^2 \geq 0$ is always true. Squaring, $a^4 - 8a^2 + 16 \geq 0$. Adding $8a^2$ to both sides, $a^4 + 16 \geq 8a^2$. Dividing through by a^2, which is positive since $a \neq 0$, $a^2 + \dfrac{16}{a^2} \geq 8$.

7. x intercepts: $(3, 0)$, and $(-3, 0)$; y intercepts: $(0, 6)$ and $(0, -6)$; foci: $(0, 3\sqrt{3})$ and $(0, -3\sqrt{3})$ **8.** x intercepts: $(2, 0)$ and $(-2, 0)$; y intercepts: $(0, 8)$ and $(0, -8)$; foci: $(0, 2\sqrt{15})$ and $(0, -2\sqrt{15})$ **9.** x intercepts: $(4, 0)$ and $(-4, 0)$; y intercepts: $(0, 5)$ and $(0, -5)$; foci: $(0, 3)$ and $(0, -3)$

12. Horizontal axis of symmetry; opens to the right; vertex: $(0, 0)$; focus: $(9, 0)$; directrix: $x = -9$ **13.** Vertical axis of symmetry; opens down; vertex: $(0, 0)$; focus: $(0, -16)$; directrix: $y = 16$

14. Horizontal axis of symmetry; opens to the left; vertex: $(0, 0)$; focus: $(-1, 0)$; directrix: $x = 1$ **17.** Vertices: $(6, 0)$ and $(-6, 0)$; opens horizontally; asymptotes: $y = \frac{1}{3}x$ and $y = -\frac{1}{3}x$ **18.** Vertices: $(0, 8)$ and $(0, -8)$; opens vertically; asymptotes: $y = 2x$ and $y = -2x$ **19.** Vertices: $(3, 0)$ and $(-3, 0)$; opens horizontally; asymptotes: $y = \frac{5}{3}x$ and $y = -\frac{5}{3}x$

Chapter 11

Page 397

35. Let x be the first term in an arithmetic sequence a_n and y, the third term in the sequence. Therefore, a_2 will be the arithmetic mean between x and y. $y = a_3 = a_1 + (3 - 1)d$; $a_3 = y = x + 2d$ and $d = \frac{y - x}{2}$. The arithmetic mean $a_2 = a_1 + d = x + \frac{y - x}{2} = \frac{x + y}{2}$. This is the same as the average of the numbers x and y.   **36.** Let a and b be arithmetic sequences: $a = a_1, a_2, a_3, \cdots, a_n, \cdots$; $a_n - a_{n-1} = d$; $b = b_1, b_2, b_3, \cdots, b_n, \cdots$; $b_n - b_{n-1} = c$. If $s = a + b$ then $s_n - s_{n-1} = (a_n + b_n) - (a_{n-1} + b_{n-1}) = (a_n - a_{n-1}) + (b_n - b_{n-1}) = d + c$. Since the difference between any two consecutive terms of the sequence, s, is the constant, $d + c$, s is an arithmetic sequence.   **37.** Let $a = 2, 4, 6, 8, \cdots$, and $b = 4, 7, 10, 13, \cdots$. Therefore, $p = a \cdot b = 8, 28, 60, 104, \cdots$. The difference between the first and second terms is 20; between the second and third terms is 32; between the third and fourth is 44; etc. Since there is not a common difference between consecutive terms, the sequence, p, is not an arithmetic sequence.   **38.** Let $a = a_1, a_2, a_3, \cdots, a_n, \cdots$; $a_n - a_{n-1} = d$. Consider this sequence multiplied by a constant c: $ca = ca_1, ca_2, ca_3, \cdots, ca_n, \cdots$; $ca_n - ca_{n-1} = c(a_n - a_{n-1}) = cd$. Since cd is a constant, the sequence, ca, is an arithmetic sequence.

Page 401

37. If a_1, a_2, a_3 forms a geometric sequence, the ratio between consecutive terms is a constant r. $\frac{a_2}{a_1} = r$ and $\frac{a_3}{a_2} = r$. Therefore, $\frac{a_3^2}{a_2^2} = \frac{a_3 \cdot a_3}{a_2 \cdot a_2} = \frac{a_3}{a_2} \cdot \frac{a_3}{a_2} = r \cdot r = r^2$, $\frac{a_2^2}{a_1^2} = \frac{a_2 \cdot a_2}{a_1 \cdot a_1} = \frac{a_2}{a_1} \cdot \frac{a_2}{a_1} = r \cdot r = r^2$. Since there is a constant ratio of r^2 between consecutive terms, the sequence is a geometric sequence.

Page 405

35. Since $a_1 + a_2 + a_3 + a_4 + a_5 + \cdots$ is an arithmetic series, $a_n - a_{n-1} = d$ for consecutive terms of the sequence $a_1, a_2, a_3, a_4, a_5, \cdots$. The difference between consecutive terms of the sequence $a_1, a_3, a_5, \cdots$ can be written: $a_n - a_{n-2} = (a_n - a_{n-1}) + (a_{n-1} - a_{n-2}) = d + d = 2d$. Since the difference between any two terms of this sequence is a constant, the sequence is an arithmetic sequence. Thus the series $a_1 + a_3 + a_5 + \cdots$ is an arithmetic series.

Chapter 12

Page 421

23. $_nP_r = \dfrac{n!}{(n-r)!} = \dfrac{n(n-1)(n-2)\cdots(n-r+1)(n-r)!}{(n-r)!}$

$= \dfrac{n(n-1)(n-2)\cdots(n-r+1)(n-r)(n-r-1)\cdots(3)(2)(1)}{(n-r)!}$

$n(_{n-1}P_{r-1}) = n\left[\dfrac{(n-1)!}{(n-1-(r-1))!}\right] = n\left[\dfrac{(n-1)!}{(n-r)!}\right]$

$= n\left[\dfrac{(n-1)(n-2)\cdots(n-r+1)(n-r)!}{(n-r)!}\right]$

$= n\left[\dfrac{(n-1)(n-2)\cdots(n-r+1)(n-r)(n-r-1)\cdots(3)(2)(1)}{(n-r)!}\right]$

$= \dfrac{n(n-1)(n-2)\cdots(n-r+1)(n-r)(n-r-1)\cdots(3)(2)(1)}{(n-r)!}$

Since both expressions are equal, $_nP_r = n(_{n-1}P_{r-1})$.

Page 426

6. By Theorem 12–3 when $r = n$; $_nC_n = \dfrac{n!}{n!(n-n)!} = \dfrac{n!}{n!0!} = \dfrac{n!}{n!} = 1$

When $r = 1$, $_nC_1 = \dfrac{n!}{1!(n-1)!} = \dfrac{n(n-1)(n-2)\cdots3\cdot2\cdot1}{1\cdot(n-1)(n-2)\cdots3\cdot2\cdot1} = \dfrac{n}{1} = n$

7. $_nC_{n-r} = \dfrac{n!}{(n-r)![n-(n-r)]!} = \dfrac{n!}{(n-r)!r!} = \dfrac{n!}{r!(n-r)!} = {}_nC_r$

Page 427

5. $16x^4 + 96x^3y + 216x^2y^2 + 216xy^3 + 81y^4$　　**6.** $32a^5 - 40a^4b + 20a^3b^2 - 5a^2b^3$

$+ \dfrac{5}{8}ab^4 - \dfrac{1}{32}b^5$　　**7.** $a^5 + 5a^4b + 10a^3b^2 + 10a^2b^3 + 5ab^4 + b^5$　　**8.** $a^3 + 6a^2b + 12ab^2 + 8b^3$

Page 433

7. 1. $E_1 = \{S_2, S_3, S_4, S_5, S_6, S_7, S_8, S_9, S_{10}, S_J, S_Q, S_K, S_A\}$;
$E_2 = \{D_2, D_3, D_4, D_5, D_6, D_7, D_8, D_9, D_{10}, D_J, D_Q, D_K, D_A\}$
2. $E_1 = \{S_Q, D_Q, H_Q, C_Q\}$; $E_2 = \{H_2, H_3, H_4, H_5, H_6, H_7, H_8, H_9, H_{10}, H_J, H_Q, H_K, H_A\}$
3. $E_1 = \{S_J, S_Q, S_K, D_J, D_Q, D_K, H_J, H_Q, H_K, C_J, C_Q, C_K\}$;
$E_2 = \{S_2, S_3, S_4, S_5, S_6, S_7, S_8, S_9, S_{10}, D_2, D_3, D_4, D_5, D_6, D_7, D_8, D_9, D_{10}, H_2, H_3, H_4,$
$H_5, H_6, H_7, H_8, H_9, H_{10}, C_2, C_3, C_4, C_5, C_6, C_7, C_8, C_9, C_{10}\}$　　**4.** $E_1 = \{B_3, B_6, B_8, B_{10}\}$;
$E_2 = \{R_2, R_3, R_4, R_5, R_8, R_9\}$　　**5.** $E_1 = \{R_2, R_3, R_4, R_5, R_8, R_9\}$; $E_2 = \{R_8, B_8, B_{10}\}$
6. $E_1 = \{B_3, B_6, B_8, B_{10}\}$; $E_2 = \{R_2, R_3, R_5, B_3\}$

Page 437

10. $_nC_r = \dfrac{n!}{r!(n-r)!} = \dfrac{n!}{(n-r)!r!} = \dfrac{n!}{[(n-r)!(n-(n-r))!]} = {}_nC_{n-r}$
11. $_4C_0x^4 - {}_4C_1x^3y + {}_4C_2x^2y^2 - {}_4C_3xy^3 + {}_4C_4y^4$
12. $_7C_0x^7 + {}_7C_1x^6y + {}_7C_2x^5y^2 + {}_7C_3x^4y^3 + {}_7C_4x^3y^4 + {}_7C_5x^2y^5 + {}_7C_6xy^6 + {}_7C_7y^7$
13. $_5C_0(2a)^5 - {}_5C_1(2a)^4(3b) + {}_5C_2(2a)^3(3b)^2 - {}_5C_3(2a)^2(3b)^3 + {}_5C_4(2a)(3b)^4 - {}_5C_5(3b)^5$

Chapter 13

Page 441

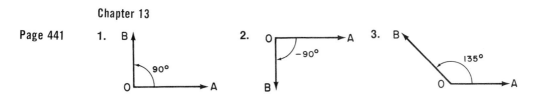

1. B, 90°　　**2.** −90°　　**3.** B, 135°

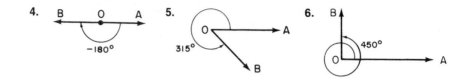

4. B O A −180°

5. 315° O A, B

6. B 450° O A

Page 450 **20.** Let $\alpha = 3\theta$; then $\sin^2 3\theta + \cos^2 3\theta = (\sin \alpha)^2 + (\cos \alpha)^2$. $\sin \alpha = \dfrac{y}{r}$, hence

$(\sin \alpha)^2 = \dfrac{y^2}{r^2}$. $\cos \alpha = \dfrac{x}{r}$, hence $(\cos \alpha)^2 = \dfrac{x^2}{r^2}$. By the Pythagorean Theorem,

$x^2 + y^2 = r^2$, multiply by $\dfrac{1}{r^2}$; $\dfrac{x^2}{r^2} + \dfrac{y^2}{r^2} = 1$, substituting, $(\cos \alpha)^2 + (\sin \alpha)^2 = 1$, hence

$\cos^2 3\theta + \sin^2 3\theta = 1$. **21.** $\tan 60° = \dfrac{\sqrt{3}}{1}$, $\sin 60° = \dfrac{\sqrt{3}}{2}$, $\cos 60° = \dfrac{1}{2}$, hence $\dfrac{\sin 60°}{\cos 60°} =$

$\dfrac{\frac{\sqrt{3}}{2}}{\frac{1}{2}}$, or $\dfrac{\sqrt{3}}{2} \cdot \dfrac{2}{1}$ or $\dfrac{\sqrt{3}}{1}$ or $\tan 60°$; $\therefore \dfrac{\sin 60°}{\cos 60°} = \tan 60°$ **22.** $\sin^2 \theta + \cos^2 \theta =$

$\left(\dfrac{y}{r}\right)^2 + \left(\dfrac{x}{r}\right)^2 = \dfrac{y^2 + x^2}{r^2} = \dfrac{r^2}{r^2} = 1$; $\tan \theta = \dfrac{y}{x} = \dfrac{\frac{y}{r}}{\frac{x}{r}} = \dfrac{\sin \theta}{\cos \theta}$

Page 453 **5.** $\angle$ D: $\dfrac{d}{e}, \dfrac{f}{e}, \dfrac{d}{f}$; $\angle$ F: $\dfrac{f}{e}, \dfrac{d}{e}, \dfrac{f}{d}$ **6.** $\angle$ K: $\dfrac{k}{h}, \dfrac{g}{h}, \dfrac{k}{g}$; $\angle$ G: $\dfrac{g}{h}, \dfrac{k}{h}, \dfrac{g}{k}$ **7.** $\angle$ X: $\dfrac{x}{y}, \dfrac{z}{y}, \dfrac{x}{z}$;

$\angle$ Z: $\dfrac{z}{y}, \dfrac{x}{y}, \dfrac{z}{x}$ **8.** Represent CD by x, AD by c_1, DB by c_2. Then the sine, cosine, and

tangent of the acute angles are as follows. $\angle$ A: $\dfrac{x}{b}, \dfrac{c_1}{b}, \dfrac{x}{c_1}$; $\angle$ 1: $\dfrac{c_1}{b}, \dfrac{x}{b}, \dfrac{c_1}{x}$;

$\angle$ B: $\dfrac{x}{a}, \dfrac{c_2}{a}, \dfrac{x}{c_2}$; $\angle$ 2: $\dfrac{c_2}{a}, \dfrac{x}{a}, \dfrac{c_2}{x}$;

Page 460 **20.** If $\theta < 180°$, reference triangles are similar in quadrants I and II; if $\theta > 180°$, (but $\theta < 360°$) reference triangles are similar in quadrants III and IV.

Page 465 **1.** $\sin \theta = \dfrac{7}{25}$, $\cos \theta = -\dfrac{24}{25}$, $\tan \theta = -\dfrac{7}{24}$, $\csc \theta = \dfrac{25}{7}$, $\sec \theta = -\dfrac{25}{24}$, $\cot \theta = -\dfrac{24}{7}$

2. $\sin \theta = -\dfrac{5\sqrt{41}}{41}$, $\cos \theta = \dfrac{4\sqrt{41}}{41}$, $\tan \theta = -\dfrac{5}{4}$, $\csc \theta = -\dfrac{\sqrt{41}}{5}$, $\sec \theta = \dfrac{\sqrt{41}}{4}$, $\cot \theta = -\dfrac{4}{5}$

3. $\sin \theta = -\dfrac{12}{13}$, $\cos \theta = -\dfrac{5}{13}$, $\tan \theta = \dfrac{12}{5}$, $\csc \theta = -\dfrac{13}{12}$, $\sec \theta = -\dfrac{13}{5}$, $\cot \theta = \dfrac{5}{12}$

4. $\sin \theta = 0$, $\cos \theta = 1$, $\tan \theta = 0$, $\csc \theta$ is undefined, $\sec \theta = 1$, $\cot \theta$ is undefined.

M-56 Answer Key

10. Let d = horizontal distance from the top of the lighthouse to the point directly above the buoy. Let y = height of the tide. Then $\tan A = \dfrac{x}{d}$ and $d = \dfrac{x}{\tan A}$, $\tan B = \dfrac{x+y}{d}$ and $d = \dfrac{x+y}{\tan B}$. Thus, $\dfrac{x}{\tan A} = \dfrac{x+y}{\tan B}$. Solving for y: $y = \dfrac{x \tan B}{\tan A} - x$ and $y = x(\cot A \tan B - 1)$. **11.** Let x = height of tower above $\overline{AB}$. Let y = horizontal distance from B to base of tower. Then $\tan\theta = \dfrac{x}{c+y}$ and $y = \dfrac{x - c\tan\theta}{\tan\theta}$, $\tan\phi = \dfrac{x}{y}$ and $y = \dfrac{x}{\tan\phi}$. Thus, $\dfrac{x}{\tan\phi} = \dfrac{x - c\tan\theta}{\tan\theta}$, $x(\tan\theta - \tan\phi) = -c\tan\theta\tan\phi$, $x = \dfrac{c\tan\theta\tan\phi}{\tan\phi - \tan\theta}$.

Chapter 14

θ in radians	$\sin\theta$	$\cos\theta$	$\tan\theta$	$\cot\theta$	$\sec\theta$	$\csc\theta$
13. 0.7156	0.6561	0.7547	0.8693	1.1504	1.325	1.524
14. 1.3963	0.9848	0.1736	5.6713	0.1763	5.759	1.015
15. 1.4923	0.9969	0.0785	12.706	0.0787	12.75	1.003
16. 0.3054	0.3007	0.9537	0.3153	3.1716	1.049	3.326
17. 0.8116	0.7254	0.6884	1.0538	0.9490	1.453	1.379
18. 0.1949	0.1937	0.9811	0.1974	5.0658	1.019	5.164

12.

x	0	$\dfrac{\pi}{6}$	$\dfrac{\pi}{4}$	$\dfrac{\pi}{3}$	$\dfrac{\pi}{2}$	$\dfrac{2\pi}{3}$	$\dfrac{3\pi}{4}$	$\dfrac{5\pi}{6}$	π
y	0	.8660	1	.8660	0	$-.8660$	-1	$-.8660$	0

x	$\dfrac{7\pi}{6}$	$\dfrac{5\pi}{4}$	$\dfrac{4\pi}{3}$	$\dfrac{3\pi}{2}$	$\dfrac{5\pi}{3}$	$\dfrac{7\pi}{4}$	$\dfrac{11\pi}{6}$	2π
y	.8660	1	.8660	0	$-.8660$	-1	$-.8660$	0

The graph of $y = \sin 2x$ has the same general shape as a sine curve, but it repeats itself more often. It makes 2 cycles, while $y = \sin x$ makes one between $x = 0$ to $x = 2\pi$.

15.

x	0	$\dfrac{\pi}{6}$	$\dfrac{\pi}{4}$	$\dfrac{\pi}{3}$	$\dfrac{\pi}{2}$	$\dfrac{2\pi}{3}$	$\dfrac{3\pi}{4}$	$\dfrac{5\pi}{6}$	π
y	1	.5	0	$-.5$	-1	$-.5$	0	.5	1

x	$\dfrac{7\pi}{6}$	$\dfrac{5\pi}{4}$	$\dfrac{4\pi}{3}$	$\dfrac{3\pi}{2}$	$\dfrac{5\pi}{3}$	$\dfrac{7\pi}{4}$	$\dfrac{11\pi}{6}$	2π
y	.5	0	$-.5$	-1	$-.5$	0	.5	1

The graph of $y = \cos 2x$ has the same general shape as a cosine curve, but it repeats itself more often. It makes two cycles, while $y = \cos x$ makes one between $x = 0$ and $x = 2\pi$.

1. The graph of $y = \tan x$ over the interval $-\dfrac{\pi}{2} \le x \le \dfrac{5\pi}{2}$ consists of 3 identical curves.

Asymptotes are $x = -\dfrac{\pi}{2}$, $x = \dfrac{\pi}{2}$, $x = \dfrac{3\pi}{2}$, and $x = \dfrac{5\pi}{2}$. The zeros are at 0, π, and 2π.

(See page 486.)

4. The graph has the general shape of $y = \tan x$, but the period is 4π.

x	-2π	$-\dfrac{4\pi}{3}$	$-\pi$	$-\dfrac{2\pi}{3}$	0	$\dfrac{2\pi}{3}$	π	$\dfrac{4\pi}{3}$	2π
y	Undefined	-1.732	-1	$-.5774$	0	.5774	1	1.732	Und.

8. The graph has the general shape of $y = \tan x$, but it has a period of $\dfrac{\pi}{3}$. Therefore, the graph repeats itself 6 times in the interval $x = -\pi$ to $x = \pi$. The zeros of the graph are located at $x = -\pi$, $-\dfrac{2\pi}{3}$, $-\dfrac{\pi}{3}$, 0, $\dfrac{\pi}{3}$, $\dfrac{2\pi}{3}$, and π. The asymptotes are located at

$x = -\dfrac{5\pi}{6}$, $-\dfrac{\pi}{2}$, $-\dfrac{\pi}{6}$, $\dfrac{\pi}{6}$, $\dfrac{\pi}{2}$, and $\dfrac{5\pi}{6}$.   **9.** The graph has the general shape of $y = \tan x$,

but it has a period of 3π. A continuous portion of the curve lies between $x = -\dfrac{3\pi}{2}$ and

$x = \dfrac{3\pi}{2}$, which are the asymptotes in the interval from $x = -2\pi$ to $x = 2\pi$. A zero of the

function occurs at $x = 0$.   **10.** The graph has the general shape of $y = \tan x$, but it

has a period of $\dfrac{\pi}{3}$. Also, the ordinate of every point on the curve is $\frac{1}{2}$ the ordinate of the

corresponding point on the curve of $y = \tan 3x$, given in Exercise **8**. The curve repeats

itself 3 times in the interval $x = -\dfrac{\pi}{2}$ to $x = \dfrac{\pi}{2}$. The zeros of the function are located at

$x = -\dfrac{\pi}{3}$, 0, and $\dfrac{\pi}{3}$. The asymptotes are at $x = -\dfrac{\pi}{2}$, $-\dfrac{\pi}{6}$, $\dfrac{\pi}{6}$, and $\dfrac{\pi}{2}$.   **11.** The graph has

the general shape of $y = \tan x$, but it has a period of 3π. Also, the ordinate of every
point on this curve is two times the ordinate of the corresponding point on the curve of

$y = \tan \dfrac{1}{3}x$, given in Exercise **9**. One complete continuous portion of the curve lies on

the given interval. The endpoints of the interval are the asymptotes of the curve. A zero
of the function occurs at $x = 0$.

19. $\csc \theta = \dfrac{r}{y} = \dfrac{1}{\dfrac{y}{r}} = \dfrac{1}{\sin \theta}$, since $\dfrac{y}{r} = \sin \theta$; $\sin \theta \ne 0$; r, y real numbers; r, $y \ne 0$

20. $\cos \theta \cdot \sec \theta = \dfrac{x}{r} \cdot \dfrac{r}{x} = 1$; $\cos \theta \ne 0$; x, r real numbers; x, $r \ne 0$ **21.** $\tan \theta$

$\cdot \cot \theta = \dfrac{y}{x} \cdot \dfrac{x}{y} = 1$; $\tan \theta$, $\cot \theta \ne 0$; x and y are real numbers; x, $y \ne 0$ **22.** $\tan \theta = \dfrac{y}{x}$

$= \dfrac{\dfrac{y}{r}}{\dfrac{x}{r}} = \dfrac{\sin \theta}{\cos \theta}$; $\cos \theta \ne 0$; x, y, r are real numbers; x, $r \ne 0$

23. $\cot \theta = \dfrac{x}{y} = \dfrac{\frac{x}{r}}{\frac{y}{r}} = \dfrac{\cos \theta}{\sin \theta}$; $\sin \theta \neq 0$; x, y, r are real numbers; r, $y \neq 0$

24. $\tan \theta = \dfrac{y}{x} = \dfrac{\frac{y}{xy}}{\frac{x}{xy}} = \dfrac{\frac{1}{x}}{\frac{1}{y}} = \dfrac{\frac{r}{x}}{\frac{r}{y}} = \dfrac{\sec \theta}{\csc \theta}$; $\cos \theta$, $\sin \theta \neq 0$; x, y, r are real numbers; x, y, $r \neq 0$

25. $\cot \theta = \dfrac{x}{y} = \dfrac{\frac{x}{r}}{\frac{y}{r}} = \dfrac{x}{r} \cdot \dfrac{r}{y} = \cos \theta \cdot \csc \theta$; $\sin \theta \neq 0$; x, y, r are real numbers; y, $r \neq 0$

26. $\cos^2 \theta = \left(\dfrac{x}{r}\right)^2 = \dfrac{x^2}{r^2} = \dfrac{x^2}{x^2 + y^2} = \dfrac{x^2 + y^2 - y^2}{x^2 + y^2} = \dfrac{x^2 + y^2}{x^2 + y^2} - \dfrac{y^2}{x^2 + y^2} = 1 - \dfrac{y^2}{r^2} = 1 - \sin^2 \theta$;

x, y, r are real numbers; $r \neq 0$ **27.** $\tan^2 \theta + 1 = \dfrac{y^2}{x^2} + 1 = \dfrac{y^2 + x^2}{x^2} = \dfrac{r^2}{x^2} = \sec^2 \theta$;

$\cos \theta \neq 0$; x, y, r are real numbers; $x \neq 0$

Page 494   **13.** $\sin(45° + \theta) = \dfrac{\sqrt{2}}{2}(\cos \theta + \sin \theta)$; $\cos(45° + \theta) = \dfrac{\sqrt{2}}{2}(\cos \theta - \sin \theta)$

14. $\sin(45° - \theta) = \dfrac{\sqrt{2}}{2}(\cos \theta - \sin \theta)$; $\cos(45° - \theta) = \dfrac{\sqrt{2}}{2}(\cos \theta + \sin \theta)$ **15.** $\sin$

$(270° + \theta) = -\cos \theta$; $\cos(270° + \theta) = \sin \theta$ **16.** $\sin(270° - \theta) = -\cos \theta$;
$\cos(270° - \theta) = -\sin \theta$

Page 496   **1.** $(1 - \tan \theta)^2 = 1 - 2\tan \theta + \tan^2 \theta = (1 + \tan^2 \theta) - 2\tan \theta = \sec^2 \theta - 2\tan \theta$

2. $(1 - \sin^2 \theta)(1 + \tan^2 \theta) = \cos^2 \theta \cdot \sec^2 \theta = \cos^2 \theta \cdot \dfrac{1}{\cos^2 \theta} = 1$

3. $\dfrac{\cos^2 \theta}{\sin \theta} + \sin \theta = \dfrac{\cos^2 \theta + \sin^2 \theta}{\sin \theta} = \dfrac{1}{\sin \theta} = \csc \theta$

4. $\tan \theta + \cot \theta = \dfrac{\sin \theta}{\cos \theta} + \dfrac{\cos \theta}{\sin \theta} = \dfrac{\sin^2 \theta + \cos^2 \theta}{\cos \theta \sin \theta} = \dfrac{1}{\cos \theta \sin \theta} = \dfrac{1}{\cos \theta} \cdot \dfrac{1}{\sin \theta} = \sec \theta \cdot \csc \theta$

5. $\dfrac{\tan \theta}{1 - \cos^2 \theta} = \dfrac{\tan \theta}{\sin^2 \theta} = \dfrac{\sin \theta}{\cos \theta \sin^2 \theta} = \dfrac{1}{\cos \theta \sin \theta} = \dfrac{1}{\cos \theta} \cdot \dfrac{1}{\sin \theta} = \sec \theta \cdot \dfrac{1}{\sin \theta} = \dfrac{\sec \theta}{\sin \theta}$

6. $\dfrac{\cot \theta}{\cos \theta} + \dfrac{\sec \theta}{\cot \theta} = \dfrac{\frac{\cos \theta}{\sin \theta}}{\cos \theta} + \dfrac{\frac{1}{\cos \theta}}{\frac{\cos \theta}{\sin \theta}} = \dfrac{\cos \theta}{\sin \theta \cos \theta} + \dfrac{\sin \theta}{\cos^2 \theta} = \dfrac{\cos^2 \theta + \sin^2 \theta}{\sin \theta \cos^2 \theta} = \dfrac{1}{\sin \theta \cos^2 \theta}$

$= \dfrac{1}{\sin \theta} \cdot \dfrac{1}{\cos^2 \theta} = \csc \theta \cdot \sec^2 \theta$

7. $\dfrac{\cos x - \sin x}{\cos x} = \dfrac{\cos x}{\cos x} - \dfrac{\sin x}{\cos x}$

$= 1 - \tan x$

8. $\dfrac{\cot \theta + 1}{\cot \theta} = \dfrac{\cot \theta}{\cot \theta} + \dfrac{1}{\cot \theta}$

$= 1 + \tan \theta$

9. $\tan x \, (\tan x + \cot x)$
$= \tan^2 x + \tan x \cot x$
$= \tan^2 x + 1$
$= \sec^2 x$

10. $(\sec \theta - \tan \theta)(\sec \theta + \tan \theta)$
$= \sec^2 \theta - \tan^2 \theta$
$= (\tan^2 \theta + 1) - \tan^2 \theta$
$= (\tan^2 \theta - \tan^2 \theta) + 1$
$= 1$

11. $\sec^4 x - \tan^4 x$
$= (\sec^2 x + \tan^2 x)(\sec^2 x - \tan^2 x)$
$= (\sec^2 x + \tan^2 x)(\tan^2 x + 1 - \tan^2 x)$
$= (\sec^2 x + \tan^2 x)(1)$
$= \sec^2 x + \tan^2 x$

12. $\sin^4 x + 2 \sin^2 x \cos^2 x + \cos^4 x$
$= (\sin^2 x + \cos^2 x)^2$
$= (1)^2$
$= 1$

13. $\dfrac{\sin^4 \theta - \cos^4 \theta}{1 - \cot^4 \theta} = \dfrac{\sin^4 \theta - \cos^4 \theta}{1 - \dfrac{\cos^4 \theta}{\sin^4 \theta}}$

$= \dfrac{\sin^4 \theta - \cos^4 \theta}{\dfrac{\sin^4 \theta - \cos^4 \theta}{\sin^4 \theta}}$

$= \sin^4 \theta$

14. $\dfrac{1 - 2 \sin x - 3 \sin^2 x}{\cos^2 x}$

$= \dfrac{(1 - 3 \sin x)(1 + \sin x)}{1 - \sin^2 x}$

$= \dfrac{(1 - 3 \sin x)(1 + \sin x)}{(1 - \sin x)(1 + \sin x)}$

$= \dfrac{1 - 3 \sin x}{1 - \sin x}$

15. $\csc \theta + \dfrac{\tan \theta}{\sin \theta} - \sec \theta = \csc \theta + \dfrac{\dfrac{\sin \theta}{\cos \theta}}{\sin \theta} - \dfrac{1}{\cos \theta} = \csc \theta + \dfrac{1}{\cos \theta} - \dfrac{1}{\cos \theta}$

$= \csc \theta = \dfrac{1}{\sin \theta} = \dfrac{1}{\sin \theta} \cdot \dfrac{\cos \theta}{\cos \theta} = \dfrac{\cos \theta}{\sin \theta \cos \theta} = \dfrac{\cos \theta}{\sin \theta} \cdot \dfrac{1}{\cos \theta} = \dfrac{\cot \theta}{\cos \theta}$

16. $\dfrac{\sec x - \sin x}{\tan x - 1} = \dfrac{\left(\dfrac{1}{\cos x} - \sin x\right)}{\left(\dfrac{\sin x}{\cos x} - 1\right)} \cdot \dfrac{\left(\dfrac{\sin x}{\cos x} + 1\right)}{\left(\dfrac{\sin x}{\cos x} + 1\right)} = \dfrac{\dfrac{\sin x}{\cos^2 x} - \dfrac{\sin^2 x}{\cos x} + \dfrac{1}{\cos x} - \sin x}{\dfrac{\sin^2 x}{\cos^2 x} - 1}$

$= \dfrac{\cos^2 x \left(\dfrac{\sin x}{\cos^2 x} - \dfrac{\sin^2 x}{\cos x} + \dfrac{1}{\cos x} - \sin x\right)}{\sin^2 x - \cos^2 x} = \dfrac{\sin x - \cos x \sin^2 x + \cos x - \sin x \cos^2 x}{(1 - \cos^2 x) - \cos^2 x}$

$= \dfrac{\sin x - \cos x (1 - \cos^2 x) + \cos x - \sin x (1 - \sin^2 x)}{1 - 2 \cos^2 x} = \dfrac{\sin^3 x + \cos^3 x}{1 - 2 \cos^2 x}$

Page 497

17. $\tan (\alpha + \beta) = \dfrac{\sin (\alpha + \beta)}{\cos (\alpha + \beta)} = \dfrac{\sin \alpha \cos \beta + \cos \alpha \sin \beta}{\cos \alpha \cos \beta - \sin \alpha \sin \beta}$

$= \dfrac{\dfrac{\sin \alpha \cos \beta}{\cos \alpha \cos \beta} + \dfrac{\cos \alpha \sin \beta}{\cos \alpha \cos \beta}}{\dfrac{\cos \alpha \cos \beta}{\cos \alpha \cos \beta} - \dfrac{\sin \alpha \sin \beta}{\cos \alpha \cos \beta}} = \dfrac{\tan \alpha + \tan \beta}{1 - \tan \alpha \tan \beta}$

18. $\tan (\alpha - \beta) = [\tan \alpha + (-\beta)] = \dfrac{\tan \alpha + \tan (-\beta)}{1 - \tan \alpha \tan (-\beta)} = \dfrac{\tan \alpha - \tan \beta}{1 + \tan \alpha \tan \beta}$

19. $\cos 2x = \cos (x + x)$
$= \cos x \cos x - \sin x \sin x$
$= \cos^2 x - \sin^2 x$

20. $\cos 2x = \cos^2 x - \sin^2 x$
$= \cos^2 x - (1 - \cos^2 x)$
$= \cos^2 x - 1 + \cos^2 x$
$= 2 \cos^2 x - 1$

21. $\cos 2x = 2\cos^2 x - 1$
$= 2(1 - \sin^2 x) - 1$
$= 1 - 2\sin^2 x$

22. $\tan 2x = \tan(x + x)$
$= \dfrac{\tan x + \tan x}{1 - \tan x \tan x}$
$= \dfrac{2\tan x}{1 - \tan^2 x}$

23. $\cos\left(\dfrac{\theta}{2} + \dfrac{\theta}{2}\right) = 2\cos^2\left(\dfrac{\theta}{2}\right) - 1$

$\cos\theta = 2\cos^2\left(\dfrac{\theta}{2}\right) - 1$

$2\cos^2\left(\dfrac{\theta}{2}\right) = 1 + \cos\theta$

$\cos^2\left(\dfrac{\theta}{2}\right) = \dfrac{1 + \cos\theta}{2}$

$\cos\left(\dfrac{\theta}{2}\right) = \pm\sqrt{\dfrac{1 + \cos\theta}{2}}$

24. $\tan\dfrac{\theta}{2} = \dfrac{\sin\left(\dfrac{\theta}{2}\right)}{\cos\left(\dfrac{\theta}{2}\right)}$

$= \pm\dfrac{\sqrt{\dfrac{1 - \cos\theta}{2}}}{\sqrt{\dfrac{1 + \cos\theta}{2}}}$

$= \pm\sqrt{\dfrac{1 - \cos\theta}{1 + \cos\theta}}$

25. $\tan\dfrac{\theta}{2} = \pm\sqrt{\dfrac{1 - \cos\theta}{1 + \cos\theta}}$

$= \pm\sqrt{\dfrac{(1 - \cos\theta)}{(1 + \cos\theta)} \cdot \dfrac{(1 + \cos\theta)}{(1 + \cos\theta)}}$

$= \pm\sqrt{\dfrac{1 - \cos^2\theta}{(1 + \cos\theta)^2}}$

$= \pm\sqrt{\dfrac{\sin^2\theta}{(1 + \cos\theta)^2}}$

$= \pm\dfrac{\sin\theta}{1 + \cos\theta}$

Page 503

13. $\left\{2k\pi + \dfrac{\pi}{2},\ 2k\pi + \dfrac{7\pi}{6},\ 2k\pi + \dfrac{11\pi}{6}\right\}$, where k is any integer.

14. $\left\{2k\pi + \dfrac{2\pi}{3},\ 2k\pi + \dfrac{4\pi}{3},\ 2k\pi\right\}$, where k is any integer.

Page 503

More Challenging Problems **1.** Both graphs are of the general shape of the sine curve with amplitude 1 and period π. The y intercept for $y = \sin 2x$ is $(0, 0)$ and for $y = \sin\left(2x + \dfrac{\pi}{2}\right)$ is $(0, 1)$. The graph of $y = \sin\left(2x + \dfrac{\pi}{2}\right)$ leads the graph of $y = \sin 2x$ by $\dfrac{\pi}{4}$.
2. Both graphs are of the general shape of the sine curve with amplitude 1 and period $\dfrac{2\pi}{3}$. The y intercept for $y = \sin 3x$ is $(0, 0)$, and for $y = \sin\left(3x + \dfrac{\pi}{2}\right)$ is $(0, 1)$. The graph of $y = \sin\left(3x + \dfrac{\pi}{2}\right)$ leads the graph of $y = \sin 3x$ by $\dfrac{\pi}{6}$. **3.** $\tan\theta \cdot \cos\theta \cdot \csc\theta = 1$;
$\tan\theta \cdot \cos\theta \cdot \dfrac{1}{\sin\theta}$; $\tan\theta \cdot \dfrac{\cos\theta}{\sin\theta}$; $\tan\theta \cdot \cot\theta$; $\tan\theta \cdot \dfrac{1}{\tan\theta}$; $1 = 1$ **4.** $\cos^2\theta \cdot \sec\theta$
$= \sin\theta \cdot \cot\theta$; $\cos^2\theta \cdot \dfrac{1}{\cos\theta} = \sin\theta \cdot \dfrac{\cos\theta}{\sin\theta}$; $\cos\theta = \cos\theta$ **5.** $\cos 3\theta = \cos(\theta + 2\theta)$
$= \cos\theta\cos 2\theta - \sin\theta\sin 2\theta = \cos\theta\,(2\cos^2\theta - 1) - \sin\theta \cdot 2\sin\theta\cos\theta = 2\cos^3\theta - \cos\theta - 2(1 - \cos^2\theta)\cos\theta = 2\cos^3\theta - \cos\theta - 2\cos\theta + 2\cos^3\theta = 4\cos^3\theta - 3\cos\theta$ **6.** $\sin^2\theta + \cos^2\theta = 1$; $\dfrac{\sin^2\theta}{\cos^2\theta} + \dfrac{\cos^2\theta}{\cos^2\theta} = \dfrac{1}{\cos^2\theta}$, $\cos^2\theta \neq 0$; $\tan^2\theta + 1 = \sec^2\theta$ or $1 + \tan^2\theta = \sec^2\theta$

7. $1 + 2\cot^2\theta + \cot^4\theta = (1 + \cot^2\theta)^2 = (\csc^2\theta)^2 = \csc^4\theta$ **8.** $\sin\alpha\cos\beta = \frac{1}{2}$
$[\sin(\alpha+\beta) + \sin(\alpha-\beta)] = \frac{1}{2}(\sin\alpha\cos\beta + \cos\alpha\sin\beta + \sin\alpha\cos\beta - \cos\alpha\sin\beta)$
$= \frac{1}{2}(2\sin\alpha\cos\beta)$; $\sin\alpha\cos\beta = \sin\alpha\cos\beta$ **9.** $\cos\alpha\sin\beta = \frac{1}{2}[\sin(\alpha+\beta) - \sin(\alpha-\beta)] = \frac{1}{2}(\sin\alpha\cos\beta + \cos\alpha\sin\beta - \sin\alpha\cos\beta + \cos\alpha\sin\beta) = \frac{1}{2}(2\cos\alpha\sin\beta)$;
$\cos\alpha\sin\beta = \cos\alpha\sin\beta$ **10.** $\cos\alpha\cos\beta = \frac{1}{2}[\cos(\alpha+\beta) + \cos(\alpha-\beta)] = \frac{1}{2}(\cos\alpha\cos\beta - \sin\alpha\sin\beta + \cos\alpha\cos\beta + \sin\alpha\sin\beta) = \frac{1}{2}(2\cos\alpha\cos\beta)$; $\cos\alpha\cos\beta = \cos\alpha\cos\beta$ **11.** $\sin\alpha\sin\beta = \frac{1}{2}[\cos(\alpha-\beta) - \cos(\alpha+\beta)] = \frac{1}{2}(\cos\alpha\cos\beta + \sin\alpha\sin\beta - \cos\alpha\cos\beta + \sin\alpha\sin\beta) = \frac{1}{2}(2\sin\alpha\sin\beta)$; $\sin\alpha\sin\beta = \sin\alpha\sin\beta$ **14.** Show that $\tan(\text{Arc}\cos\frac{3}{5} + \text{Arc}\sin\frac{5}{13}) = \frac{63}{16}$.

$\tan(\text{Arc}\cos\frac{3}{5} + \text{Arc}\sin\frac{5}{13}) = \dfrac{\tan(\text{Arc}\cos\frac{3}{5}) + \tan(\text{Arc}\sin\frac{5}{13})}{1 - \tan(\text{Arc}\cos\frac{3}{5})\tan(\text{Arc}\sin\frac{5}{13})} = \dfrac{\frac{4}{3} + \frac{5}{12}}{1 - \frac{4}{3}\cdot\frac{5}{12}} = \dfrac{63}{16}$.

We must also check that $\text{Arc}\cos\dfrac{3}{5} + \text{Arc}\sin\dfrac{5}{13} < \dfrac{\pi}{2}$, since $\tan\dfrac{\pi}{2}$ is undefined. This

follows, as $\text{Arc}\cos\dfrac{3}{5} < \dfrac{\pi}{3}$, and $\text{Arc}\sin\dfrac{5}{13} < \dfrac{\pi}{6}$. Therefore, $\text{Arc}\cos\dfrac{3}{5} + \text{Arc}\sin\dfrac{5}{13} =$

$\text{Arc}\tan\dfrac{63}{16}$.   **15.** Show that $\text{Arc}\tan x + \text{Arc}\cot x = \dfrac{\pi}{2} = \text{Arc}\sin 1$, or that $\sin(\text{Arc}\tan$

$x + \text{Arc}\cot x) = 1$. But $\sin(\text{Arc}\tan x + \text{Arc}\cot x) = \sin(\text{Arc}\tan x)\cos(\text{Arc}\cot x)$

$+ \cos(\text{Arc}\tan x)\sin(\text{Arc}\cot x) = \dfrac{x}{\sqrt{x^2+1}}\cdot\dfrac{x}{\sqrt{x^2+1}} + \dfrac{1}{\sqrt{x^2+1}}\cdot\dfrac{1}{\sqrt{x^2+1}} = \dfrac{x^2}{x^2+1}$

$+ \dfrac{1}{x^2+1} = \dfrac{x^2+1}{x^2+1} = 1$ **16.** $K = \frac{1}{2}bc\sin A = \frac{1}{2}bc\left(2\sin\dfrac{A}{2}\cos\dfrac{A}{2}\right) = bc\left(\sin\dfrac{A}{2}\cos\dfrac{A}{2}\right)$

$= bc\sqrt{\dfrac{1-\cos A}{2}}\sqrt{\dfrac{1+\cos A}{2}}^* = bc\sqrt{\dfrac{(s-b)(s-c)}{bc}}\sqrt{\dfrac{s(s-a)}{bc}}$;
$K = \sqrt{s(s-a)(s-b)(s-c)}$

* Using the Law of Cosines (see below).

$\dfrac{1-\cos A}{2} = \dfrac{1 - \left(\dfrac{b^2+c^2-a^2}{2bc}\right)}{2} = \dfrac{2bc - b^2 - c^2 + a^2}{4bc}$

$= \dfrac{a^2 - c^2 + 2bc - b^2}{4bc} = \dfrac{a^2 - (c-b)^2}{4bc} = \dfrac{[a+(c-b)][a-(c-b)]}{4bc}$

$= \dfrac{(a+c-b)(a+b-c)}{4bc} = \dfrac{1}{bc}\left(\dfrac{a+c-b}{2}\right)\left(\dfrac{a+b-c}{2}\right) = \dfrac{(s-b)(s-c)}{bc}$

Also, $\dfrac{1+\cos A}{2} = \dfrac{1 + \left(\dfrac{b^2+c^2-a^2}{2bc}\right)}{2} = \dfrac{2bc + b^2 + c^2 - a^2}{4bc}$

$= \dfrac{(b+c)^2 - a^2}{4bc} = \dfrac{(b+c+a)(b+c-a)}{4bc}$

$= \dfrac{1}{bc}\left(\dfrac{b+c+a}{2}\right)\left(\dfrac{b+c-a}{2}\right) = \dfrac{s(s-a)}{bc}$

14. General shape of sine curve; domain: $-2\pi \le x \le 2\pi$; range: $-2 \le y \le 2$; amplitude $= 2$; period $\dfrac{2\pi}{3}$.   **15.** General shape of cosine curve; domain: $-2\pi \le x \le 2\pi$; range: $-\dfrac{1}{4} \le y \le \dfrac{1}{4}$; amplitude $= \dfrac{1}{4}$; period 4π.   **16.** General shape of tangent curve; domain: $-2\pi \le x \le 2\pi$; range: $-\infty \le y \le \infty$; no amplitude; period $\dfrac{\pi}{2}$.

17. $(1 - \sin^2 x)(1 + \tan^2 x) = (\cos^2 x)(\sec^2 x) = (\cos^2 x)\left(\dfrac{1}{\cos^2 x}\right) = 1$ **18.** $\sec x$

$\csc x - \dfrac{\sin x}{\cos x} = \dfrac{1}{\cos x} \cdot \dfrac{1}{\sin x} - \dfrac{\sin x}{\cos x} = \dfrac{1 - \sin^2 x}{\sin x \cos x} = \dfrac{\cos^2 x}{\sin x \cos x} = \dfrac{\cos x}{\sin x} = \cot x$

19. $\sin^4 x - 2\sin^2 x + 1 = (\sin^2 x)^2 - 2(\sin^2 x) + 1 = (1 - \cos^2 x)^2 - 2(1 - \cos^2 x)$
$+ 1 = 1 - 2\cos^2 x + \cos^4 x - 2 + 2\cos^2 x + 1 = \cos^4 x$ **20.** $\dfrac{1 + \sin x}{\cot^2 x} = \dfrac{1 + \sin x}{\csc^2 x - 1}$

$= \dfrac{1 + \sin x}{(\csc x - 1)(\csc x + 1)} = \dfrac{\sin x\left(\dfrac{1}{\sin x} + 1\right)}{(\csc x - 1)(\csc x + 1)}$

$= \dfrac{\sin x(\csc x + 1)}{(\csc x - 1)(\csc x + 1)} = \dfrac{\sin x}{\csc x - 1}$

Chapter 15

There is never just one way to write a program. For simple programs different variables could be used. For more complicated programs, in addition to different choices of variables, decisions could be worded differently or in a different order. Consequently the "answers" provided below are just a guide and show one valid way of writing each program.

Also the DATA chosen for each run can vary. The DATA listed in each program is chosen primarily to cause each possibility to occur at least once; that is, to test the logic of the program to make sure it handles all cases. To save space, some lines that would not be broken in an actual program are shown broken here.

```
9. 1Ø READ L,W
   2Ø LET A = L*W
   3Ø PRINT "AREA =";A
   4Ø GO TO 1Ø
   5Ø DATA 6,5,11.3,9.1,186,32
   6Ø END
```

```
10. 1Ø READ W,L
    2Ø LET P = W/(W+L)*1ØØ
    3Ø PRINT "PCT. =";P
    4Ø GO TO 1Ø
    5Ø DATA 1,1Ø,9,Ø,31,15
    6Ø END
```

```
11. 1Ø READ S
    2Ø LET P = 4*S
    3Ø PRINT "PERIMETER =";P
    4Ø GO TO 1Ø
    5Ø DATA 5,11,31.2
    6Ø END
```

12. Replace statements 2Ø and 3Ø in Exercise 11 by:

```
    2Ø LET A = S*S
    3Ø PRINT "AREA =";A
```

13.
```
1Ø READ X,Y
2Ø LET A = (X+Y)/2
3Ø PRINT "AVERAGE =";A
4Ø GO TO 1Ø
5Ø DATA 8,6,-13,21,37.6,81.2
6Ø END
```

14.
```
1Ø READ X,Y,Z
2Ø LET A = (X+Y+Z)/3
3Ø PRINT "AVERAGE =";A
4Ø GO TO 1Ø
5Ø DATA 8,9,1Ø,-17,-5,31,
          61.8,73.2,68.7
6Ø END
```

15.
```
1Ø READ B,H
2Ø LET A = .5*B*H
3Ø PRINT "AREA =";A
4Ø GO TO 1Ø
5Ø DATA 1Ø,7,6.5,3.2,11,17
6Ø END
```

16.
```
1Ø READ R,O,H,T
2Ø LET G = R*H + O*T
3Ø PRINT "GROSS PAY =";G
4Ø GO TO 1Ø
5Ø DATA 2.25,4.5,4Ø,Ø,2.25,
          4.5,4Ø,3.5
6Ø END
```

17.
```
1Ø READ R
2Ø LET C = 3.14159*2*R
3Ø PRINT "CIRCUMFERENCE =";C
4Ø GO TO 1Ø
5Ø DATA 5,7.5,11.8
6Ø END
```

18. Replace statements 2Ø and 3Ø in Exercise 17 by:
```
2Ø LET A = 3.14159*R*R
3Ø PRINT "AREA =";A
```

1.
```
1Ø READ S
2Ø LET D = S*SQR(2)
3Ø PRINT "DIAGONAL =";D
4Ø GO TO 1Ø
5Ø DATA 5,11,31.2
6Ø END
```

2.
```
1Ø READ S
2Ø LET A = S*S*SQR(3)/4
3Ø PRINT "AREA =";A
4Ø GO TO 1Ø
5Ø DATA 5,1Ø,24.6
6Ø END
```

3.
```
1Ø READ X,Y
2Ø IF X = Y THEN 6Ø
3Ø IF X > Y THEN 8Ø
4Ø PRINT X;" < ";Y
5Ø GO TO 1Ø
6Ø PRINT X;" = ";Y
7Ø GO TO 1Ø
8Ø PRINT X;" > ";Y
9Ø GO TO 1Ø
1ØØ DATA 3,4,9,9,1Ø,7
11Ø END
```

4.
```
1Ø READ A,B,C
2Ø A↑2 + B↑2 = C↑2 THEN 7Ø
3Ø IF A↑2 + C↑2 = B↑2 THEN 7Ø
4Ø IF B↑2 + C↑2 = A↑2 THEN 7Ø
5Ø PRINT A;B;C; "DO NOT FORM A
                RIGHT TRIANGLE"
6Ø GO TO 1Ø
7Ø PRINT A;B;C; "DO FORM A
                RIGHT TRIANGLE"
8Ø GO TO 1Ø
9Ø DATA 6,6,6,3,4,5,2,3,5
1ØØ END
```

5.
```
1Ø READ X
2Ø IF X < Ø THEN 5Ø
3Ø PRINT X,X
4Ø GO TO 1Ø
5Ø LET Y = -X
6Ø PRINT X,Y
7Ø GO TO 1Ø
8Ø DATA 7,Ø,-3
9Ø END
```

6.
```
1Ø READ A,B,C,D
2Ø READ N
3Ø IF A*N+B=C*N+D THEN 6Ø
4Ø PRINT N;"IS NOT A SOLUTION"
5Ø GO TO 2Ø
6Ø PRINT N;"IS A SOLUTION"
7Ø GO TO 2Ø
8Ø DATA 6,-5,3,4,3,-1,Ø
9Ø END
```

7.
```
1Ø READ A,B,C,D
2Ø READ N
3Ø IF A*N+B < C*N+D THEN 6Ø
4Ø PRINT N; "IS NOT A SOLUTION"
5Ø GO TO 2Ø
6Ø PRINT N;"IS A SOLUTION"
7Ø GO TO 2Ø
8Ø DATA 6,-5,3,4,3,-1,1Ø
9Ø END
```

1.
```
10 READ X1,Y1,X2,Y2
15 PRINT "SLOPE OF THE LINE THROUGH
   (";X1;",";Y1;") AND
   (";X2;",";Y2;") IS ";
20 IF X2-X1=0 THEN 50
30 PRINT (Y2-Y1)/(X2-X1)
40 GO TO 10
50 PRINT "UNDEFINED"
60 GO TO 10
70 DATA 6,-2,8,10,4,0,4,-2,-6,7,-3,7
80 END
```

2. Add these statements to Program 4:
```
11 IF B < 0 THEN 14
12 PRINT A;"+";B;"I+";
13 GO TO 15
14 PRINT A;B;"I+";
15 IF D < 0 THEN 18
16 PRINT C;"+";D;"I=";
17 GO TO 20
18 PRINT C;D;"I=";
```

3.
```
10 READ X1,Y1,X2,Y2
20 LET D=SQR((X2-X1)↑2+
   (Y2-Y1)↑2)
30 PRINT "DISTANCE =" D
40 GO TO 10
50 DATA 0,0,3,4,-2,1,5,
   -7,-6,-6,6,6
60 END
```

4.
```
10 READ X1,Y1,X2,Y2
20 PRINT "MIDPOINT=(";(X1+X2)/2;
   ",";(Y1+Y2)/2;")"
30 GO TO 10
40 DATA 0,0,3,4,-2,1,5,-7,-6,
   -6,6,6
50 END
```

5.
```
10 READ X1,Y1,X2,Y2,X3,Y3,X4,Y4
20 LET D1=SQR((X2-X1)↑2+(Y2-Y1)↑2)
30 LET D3=SQR((X4-X3)↑2+(Y4-Y3)↑2)
40 IF D1<>D3 THEN 100
50 LET D2=SQR((X3-X2)↑2+(Y3-Y2)↑2)
60 LET D4=SQR((X1-X4)↑2+(Y1-Y4)↑2)
70 IF D2<>D4 THEN 100
80 PRINT "PARALLELOGRAM"
90 GO TO 10
100 PRINT "NOT A PARALLELOGRAM"
110 GO TO 10
120 DATA 0,0,3,0,3,3,0,3,-3,-2,-2,4,
    3,8,10,-5,4,2,4,2,14,2,17,6
130 END
```

6.
```
10 READ X1,Y1,M
20 IF M=0 THEN 50
30 PRINT M;"X - Y =";
   M*X1-Y1
40 GO TO 10
50 PRINT "Y = ";Y1
60 GO TO 10
70 DATA 6,4,1,-3,7,-2,
   -10,6,0
80 END
```

7.
```
10 READ M,B
20 IF M = 0 THEN 50
30 PRINT -M;"X + Y =";B
40 GO TO 10
50 PRINT "Y = ";B
60 GO TO 10
70 DATA 6,-2,10,-1,0,3
80 END
```

8.
```
10 READ X1,Y1,X2,Y2
20 IF X2-X1=0 THEN 70
30 IF Y2-Y1=0 THEN 90
40 LET M = (Y2-Y1)/(X2-X1)
50 PRINT M;"X - Y =";M*X1-Y1
60 GO TO 10
70 PRINT "X = ";X1
80 GO TO 10
90 PRINT "Y = ";Y1
100 GO TO 10
110 DATA 6,-1,6,8,-3,4,5,4,-1,-1,
    2,2
120 END
```

9.
```
10 READ A,B
20 PRINT "ABSOLUTE VALUE =";
   SQR(A↑2+B↑2)
30 GO TO 10
40 DATA 6,0,0,-3,3,4
50 END
```

10.
```
10 READ A,B
20 IF B<=0 THEN 50
30 PRINT A;" - ";B;"I"
40 GO TO 10
50 PRINT A;" + ";-B;"I"
60 GO TO 10
70 DATA 6,-1,-3,5,8,0,0,-7
80 END
```

```
11. 10 READ A,B                          80 GO TO 10
    20 IF A<>0 THEN 40                   90 PRINT A1;B1;"I"
    30 IF B = 0 THEN 110                 100 GO TO 10
    40 LET A1 = A/(A↑2+B↑2)              110 PRINT "NO RECIPROCAL"
    50 LET B1 = -B/(A↑2+B↑2)             120 GO TO 10
    60 IF B1<0 THEN 90                   130 DATA 3,4,1,-1,0,0
    70 PRINT A1; " + ";B1;"I"            140 END

12. 10 READ X,Y                          120 GO TO 10
    15 PRINT "(";X;",";Y;") ";           130 IF Y > 0 THEN 160
    20 IF X = 0 THEN 80                  140 PRINT "IV"
    30 IF Y = 0 THEN 110                 150 GO TO 10
    40 IF X > 0 THEN 130                 160 PRINT "I"
    50 IF Y > 0 THEN 200                 170 GO TO 10
    60 PRINT "III"                       180 PRINT "BOTH AXES"
    70 GO TO 10                          190 GO TO 10
    80 IF Y = 0 THEN 180                 200 PRINT "II"
    90 PRINT "Y-AXIS"                    210 GO TO 10
    100 GO TO 10                         220 DATA 1,3,0,0,-1,6,-2,-5,6,
    110 PRINT "X-AXIS"                         -1,0,7,-6,0
                                         230 END
```

Page 521

```
1. 10 READ A,B,C                    2. Replace statement 20 in
   20 PRINT "VERTEX = (";              Exercise 1 by:
      -B/(2*A);",";
      C-B↑2/(4*A);")"                   20 PRINT "AXIS OF SYMMETRY:
   30 GO TO 10                              X=";-B/(2*A)
   40 DATA 2,-3,7,-1,0,5,0,0
   50 END
```

```
3. 10 READ A,B,C                    4. 10 READ A,B,C
   20 IF A < 0 THEN 50                 20 PRINT "DISCRIMINANT =";
   30 PRINT "VERTEX IS A                  B↑2-4*A*C
      MINIMUM"                         30 GO TO 10
   40 GO TO 10                         40 DATA 2,-3,7,1,-4,4,2,7,1
   50 PRINT "VERTEX IS A               50 END
      MAXIMUM"
   60 GO TO 10
   70 DATA 2,-3,7,-1,0,5,1,0,0
   80 END
```

```
5. 10 READ A,B,C                    6. 10 READ A,B,C
   20 LET D = B↑2 - 4*A*C              20 PRINT "SUM OF ROOTS = ";
   30 IF D < 0 THEN 70                    -B/A
   40 IF D = 0 THEN 90                 30 PRINT "PRODUCT OF ROOTS = ";
   50 PRINT "TWO REAL ROOTS"             C/A
   60 GO TO 10                         40 GO TO 10
   70 PRINT "NO REAL ROOTS"            50 DATA 2,-3,7,1,-4,4,2,7,1
   80 GO TO 10                         60 END
   90 PRINT "ONE REAL ROOT"
   100 GO TO 10
   110 DATA 2,-3,7,1,-4,4,2,7,1
   120 END
```

7.
```
1Ø READ A,B,C
2Ø READ D,E
3Ø IF A*D↑2-A*E↑2+B*D+C<>Ø THEN 7Ø
4Ø IF 2*A*D*E+B*E<>Ø THEN 7Ø
5Ø PRINT "IS A ROOT"
6Ø GO TO 2Ø
7Ø PRINT "NOT A ROOT"
8Ø GO TO 2Ø
9Ø DATA 1,-6,25,3,4,3,-4,
   Ø,6,1,Ø
1ØØ END
```

8.
```
1Ø READ A,B,C
2Ø READ X1,Y1
3Ø IF A*X1↑2+B*X1+C<Ø THEN 6Ø
4Ø PRINT "(";X1;",";Y1;")
   IS NOT IN THE SOLUTION SET"
5Ø GO TO 2Ø
6Ø PRINT "(";X1;",";Y1;")
   IS IN THE SOLUTION SET"
7Ø GO TO 2Ø
8Ø DATA 1,-6,25,3,5,Ø,Ø,
      -1,7,3,4

9Ø END
```

9.
```
1Ø READ X1,X2
2Ø LET B = -X1-X2
3Ø LET C = X1*X2
4Ø IF B<Ø THEN 8Ø
5Ø IF C<Ø THEN 13Ø
6Ø PRINT "X↑2 +";B;
   "X +";C;" = Ø"
7Ø GO TO 1Ø
8Ø IF C<Ø THEN 11Ø
9Ø PRINT "X↑2 -";-B;
   "X +";C;" = Ø"
1ØØ GO TO 1Ø
11Ø PRINT "X↑2 -";-B;
    "X -";-C;" = Ø"
12Ø GO TO 1Ø
13Ø PRINT "X↑2 +";B;
    "X -";-C;" = Ø"
14Ø GO TO 1Ø
15Ø DATA 7,-3,.75,2,1Ø,5,
        3,-11,6,6
16Ø END
```

Page 524

1.
```
1Ø READ A,B,C,D,E,F
2Ø IF A*E-B*D<>Ø THEN 6Ø
3Ø IF A*F-C*D=Ø THEN 6Ø
4Ø PRINT "INCONSISTENT"
5Ø GO TO 1Ø
6Ø PRINT "CONSISTENT"
7Ø GO TO 1Ø
8Ø DATA 1,-2,6,2,1,17,
        1,1,4,2,2,8,3,
        -1,1Ø,9,-3,12
9Ø END
```

2.
```
1Ø READ A,B,C,D,E,F
2Ø IF A*E-B*D=Ø THEN 5Ø
3Ø PRINT "INDEPENDENT"
4Ø GO TO 1Ø
5Ø IF A*F-C*D<>Ø THEN 3Ø
6Ø PRINT "DEPENDENT"
7Ø GO TO 1Ø
8Ø DATA 1,-2,6,2,1,17,1,1,4,2,2,
        8,3,-1,1Ø,9,-3,12
9Ø END
```

3.
```
1Ø READ A,B,C,D,E,F
2Ø LET T = A*E - B*D
3Ø IF T = Ø THEN 8Ø
4Ø LET X = (C*E-B*F)/T
5Ø LET Y = (A*F-C*D)/T
6Ø PRINT "SOLUTION IS
   (";X;",";Y;")"
7Ø GO TO 1Ø
8Ø PRINT "NO UNIQUE
   SOLUTION"
9Ø GO TO 1Ø
1ØØ DATA 1,-2,6,2,1,17,
        1,1,4,2,2,8,3,
        -1,1Ø,9,-3,12
11Ø END
```

4.
```
1Ø READ A,B,C,D,E,F
2Ø READ X1,Y1
3Ø IF A*X1+B*Y1>=C THEN 7Ø
4Ø IF D*X1+E*Y1>=F THEN 7Ø
5Ø PRINT "(";X1;",";Y1;") IS IN
   THE COMMON SOLUTION SET"
6Ø GO TO 2Ø
7Ø PRINT "(";X1;",";Y1;") IS NOT
   IN THE COMMON SOLUTION SET"
8Ø GO TO 2Ø
9Ø DATA 1,-1,6,2,1,17,Ø,Ø,8,1,
        15,2,-1,6
1ØØ END
```

5.
```
10 DIM M(3,3)
20 MAT READ M
30 LET D1 = M(1,1)*(M(2,2)*M(3,3)-M(2,3)*M(3,2))
40 LET D2 = M(2,1)*(M(1,2)*M(3,3)-M(1,3)*M(3,2))
50 LET D3 = M(3,1)*(M(1,2)*M(2,3)-M(1,3)*M(2,2))
60 PRINT"DETERMINANT =";  D1-D2+D3
70 GO TO 20
80 DATA 1,3,2,2,1,3,3,1,2,3,5,1,6,-2,2,8,-1,4,-2,1,-1,2,5,
       -1,5,2,1
90 END
```

1. Delete 20 PRINT A; and 50 PRINT A; change 70 PRINT to 70 PRINT A.

2.
```
10 READ A,D,N
20 LET S = N*(2*A+(N-1)*D)/2
30 PRINT "SUM =";S
40 GO TO 10
50 DATA 5,3,10,6,-.5,8,
        -12,3.5,15
60 END
```

3.
```
10 READ A,D,N
20 LET S = A
25 PRINT S;
30 FOR I = 2 TO N
40 LET A = A + D
50 LET S = S + A
60 PRINT S;
70 NEXT I
80 PRINT
90 GO TO 10
100 DATA 5,3,10,6,-.5,8,-12,
         3.5,15
110 END
```

4.
```
10 READ A,R,N
20 PRINT A;
30 FOR I = 2 TO N
40 LET A = A*R
50 PRINT A;
60 NEXT I
70 PRINT
80 GO TO 10
90 DATA 3,3,5,8,.25,
        10,1,-4,4
100 END
```

6.
```
10 READ A,R,N
20 LET S = A
30 PRINT S;
40 FOR I = 2 TO N
50 LET A = A * R
60 LET S = S + A
70 PRINT S;
80 NEXT I
90 PRINT
100 GO TO 10
110 DATA 3,3,5,8,.25,10,1,-4,4
120 END
```

5. In Exercises **4**, delete 20 and 50 and change 70 to 70 PRINT A .

7. From Exercise **6**, delete 30 and 70 and change 90 to 90 PRINT S .
```
50 PRINT "NO INFINITE SUM"
60 GO TO 10
70 DATA .5,.5,1,2,-32,-.5
80 END
```

8.
```
10 READ A,R
20 IF ABS(R)>= 1 THEN 50
30 PRINT "INFINITE SUM =";
   A/(1-R)
40 GO TO 10
```

9.
```
10 READ A,B,N
20 LET D = (B-A)/(N+1)
30 FOR I = 1 TO N
40 LET A = A + D
50 PRINT A;
60 NEXT I
70 PRINT
80 GO TO 10
90 DATA 4,16,5,14,17,1,6,
        11,3
100 END
```

10.
```
10 READ A,B,N
20 LET R = (B/A)↑(1/(N+1))
30 FOR I = 1 TO N
40 LET A = A * R
50 PRINT A;
60 NEXT I
70 PRINT
80 GO TO 10
90 DATA 4,32,2,2,8,1,3,.1875,3
100 END
```

1.
```
10 PRINT "N","N FACTORIAL"
20 PRINT
30 LET N = 0
40 LET F = 1
50 PRINT N,F
60 FOR N = 1 TO 10
70 LET F = F * N
80 PRINT N,F
90 NEXT I
100 END
```

2.
```
10 READ N,R
20 LET F = 1
30 FOR I = N-R+1 TO N
40 LET F = F*I
50 NEXT I
60 PRINT " NUMBER OF PERMU-
        TATIONS =";F
70 GO TO 10
80 DATA 10,6,7,7,6,2
90 END
```

3.
```
10 READ N,R,P
20 LET F = 1
30 FOR I = N-R+1 TO N
40 LET F = F*I
50 NEXT I
60 LET P1 = 1
70 FOR J = 1 TO P
80 LET P1 = P1*J
90 NEXT J
100 PRINT "NUMBER OF
        PERMUTATIONS ="; F/P1
110 GO TO 10
120 DATA 10,3,5,2,8,1
130 END
```

4.
```
10 READ N,R
20 LET F = 1
30 IF R<N/2 THEN 40
35 LET R = N-R
40 FOR I = N-R+1 TO N
50 LET F = F*I
60 NEXT I
70 LET G = 1
80 FOR I = 2 TO R
90 LET G = G*I
100 NEXT I
110 PRINT "NUMBER OF
        COMBINATIONS =";F/G
120 GO TO 10
130 DATA 100,2,5,3,30,5
140 END
```

1.
```
10 READ X,Y
20 LET R = SQR(X↑2+Y↑2)
25 IF R = 0 THEN 160
30 PRINT "SIN(P) =";Y/R
40 PRINT "COS(P) =";X/R
50 IF X = 0 THEN 120
60 PRINT "TAN(P) =";Y/X
70 PRINT "SEC(P) =";R/X
80 IF Y = 0 THEN 140
90 PRINT "COT(P) =";X/Y
100 PRINT "CSC(P) =";R/Y
110 GO TO 10
120 PRINT "TAN AND SEC
        UNDEFINED"
130 GO TO 80
140 PRINT "COT AND CSC
        UNDEFINED"
150 GO TO 10
160 PRINT "ALL FUNCTIONS
        UNDEFINED"
170 GO TO 10
180 DATA 3,4,0,0,0,7,-3,0,-1,1
190 END
```

2. For all parts of Exercise **2,** use the figure on the right for notation for sides and angles.

a) HA case

```
10 READ C,A1
20 PRINT "ANGLES ARE:";
   A1;90-A1
30 LET A1 = A1*3.14159/180
40 LET A = C*SIN(A1)
50 LET B = C*COS(A1)
60 PRINT "SIDES ARE:";A;B;C
70 PRINT
80 GO TO 10
90 DATA 10,40,12,30,400,27
100 END
```

b) LA case

```
10 READ A,A1
20 PRINT "ANGLES ARE:";A1;90-A1
30 LET A1 = A1*3.14159/180
40 LET B = A/TAN(A1)
50 LET C = A/SIN(A1)
60 PRINT "SIDES ARE:";A;B;C
70 PRINT
80 GO TO 10
90 DATA 10,30,532,42,250,45
100 END
```

c) HL case

```
10 READ C,A
20 LET B = SQR(C↑2 - A↑2)
30 PRINT "SIDES ARE:";A;B;C
40 LET A1 =ATN(A/B)
50 LET A1 = A1*180/3.14159
60 PRINT "ANGLES ARE:";A1;
   90-A1
70 PRINT
80 GO TO 10
90 DATA 10,5,18,15,210,143
100 END
```

d) LL case

```
10 READ A,B
20 LET C = SQR(A↑2 + B↑2)
30 PRINT "SIDES ARE:";A;B;C
40 LET A1 = ATN(A/B)
50 LET A1 = A1*180/3.14159
60 PRINT "ANGLES ARE:";A1;
   90-A1
70 PRINT
80 GO TO 10
90 DATA 25.3,60,15,15,10,20
100 END
```

3.
```
10 READ A,S1,B,S2,C
20 LET D = (C-A)*(S2-S1)/(B-A)
30 PRINT "SIN(";C;") =";S1+D
40 GO TO 10
```

```
50 DATA 29,.4848,30,.5,29.5,
   55
51 DATA .8192,56,.8290,55.3
60 END
```

4.
```
10 READ X
20 IF X<-270 THEN 180
30 IF X = -270 THEN 200
40 IF X<-180 THEN 220
50 IF X = -180 THEN 240
60 IF X<-90 THEN 260
70 IF X = -90 THEN 280
80 IF X<0 THEN 160
90 IF X = 0 THEN 300
100 IF X<90 THEN 180
110 IF X = 90 THEN 200
120 IF X<180 THEN 220
130 IF X = 180 THEN 240
140 IF X<270 THEN 260
150 IF X = 270 THEN 280
160 PRINT "QUADRANT IV"
170 GO TO 10
```

```
180 PRINT "QUADRANT I"
190 GO TO 10
200 PRINT "POSITIVE Y-AXIS"
210 GO TO 10
220 PRINT "QUADRANT II"
230 GO TO 10
240 PRINT "NEGATIVE X-AXIS"
250 GO TO 10
260 PRINT "QUADRANT III"
270 GO TO 10
280 PRINT "NEGATIVE Y-AXIS"
290 GO TO 10
300 PRINT "POSITIVE X-AXIS"
310 GO TO 10
320 DATA 0,33,90,110,180,210,270,
    300,-15,-90,-100,-180,
    -195,-270,-295
330 END
```

5. For all parts of Exercise 5, use the figure on
   the right for notation for sides and angles.

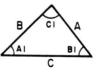

a) SSS case

```
1Ø READ A,B,C
2Ø LET T = (B↑2+C↑2-A↑2)/(2*B*C)
3Ø LET A1 = ATN(SQR(1-T↑2)/T)
4Ø LET S = B*SIN(A1)/A
5Ø LET B1 = ATN(S/SQR(1-S↑2))
6Ø LET A1 = A1*18Ø/3.14159
7Ø LET B1 = B1*18Ø/3.14159
8Ø PRINT "ANGLES ARE:";A1;B1;
   18Ø-A1-B1
9Ø PRINT
1ØØ GO TO 1Ø
11Ø DATA 4,5,7,25,4Ø,58,8,9,13
12Ø END
```

b) ASA case

```
1Ø READ A1,C,B1
2Ø LET C1 = 18Ø-A1-B1
3Ø PRINT "ANGLES ARE:"A1;
   B1;C1
4Ø LET C1 = C1*3.14159/18Ø
5Ø LET A1 = A1*3.14159/18Ø
6Ø LET B1 = B1*3.14159/18Ø
7Ø LET A = C*SIN(A1)/SIN(C1)
8Ø LET B = C*SIN(B1)/SIN(C1)
9Ø PRINT "SIDES ARE:";A;B;C
1ØØ PRINT
11Ø GO TO 1Ø
12Ø DATA 32,1.5,54,41,36,
        15,54,24Ø,74
13Ø END
```

c) SAA case

```
1Ø READ A,A1,B1
2Ø LET C1 = 18Ø-A1-B1
3Ø PRINT "ANGLES ARE:";
   A1;B1;C1
4Ø LET A1 = A1*3.14159/18Ø
5Ø LET B1 = B1*3.14159/18Ø
6Ø LET C1 = C1*3.14159/18Ø
7Ø LET B = A*SIN(B1)/SIN(A1)
8Ø LET C = A*SIN(C1)/SIN(A1)
9Ø PRINT "SIDES ARE:";A;B;C
1ØØ GO TO 1Ø
11Ø DATA 16.5,38,54,224,84,
        21.1,75.36,18,32
12Ø END
```

6.

```
1Ø READ A,B,C
2Ø LET S = (A+B+C)/2
3Ø PRINT "AREA =";
   SQR(S*(S-A)*(S-B)*(S-C))
4Ø GO TO 1Ø
5Ø DATA 3,4,5,6,6,6,17,12,21
6Ø END
```

Answers to Can You Solve These?

Page 71   **7.** Yes   **8.** Yes   **9.** No   **10.** Yes   **11.** No   **12.** No

Page 129   **1.** Conditional: If a number is an integer, then the number is a real number; Converse: If a number is a real number, then it is an integer; Biconditional: A number is an integer if and only if it is a real number.   **2.** Conditional: If a number is divisible by 4, then it is an even number; Converse: If a number is an even number, then it is divisible by 4; Biconditional: A number is divisible by 4 if and ony if it is a real number.
3. For Exercise 1: True, False, False; For Exercise 2: True, False, False

Page 173   **1.** Move 3 units from 0 along the positive x axis, then 4 units to the right, then 5 units up.
2. Move 2 units from 0 along the negative x axis, 4 units to the right, and 3 units down.
3. Move 1 unit from 0 along the negative x axis, 6 units to the left, and 6 units up.
4. $AB = \sqrt{(-3-4)^2 + (-4-5)^2 + (2-6)^2} = \sqrt{146} \approx 12.1$ **5.** The z coordinate
6. $P_1P_3 = \sqrt{(x_2-x_1)^2 + (y_2-y_1)^2}$; $P_2P_3 = \sqrt{(y_2-y_2)^2 + (z_2-z_1)^2}$; $(P_1P_2)^2 = (P_1P_3)^2 + (P_2P_3)^2$, or $P_1P_2 = \sqrt{(x_2-x_1)^2 + (y_2-y_1)^2 + (z_2-z_1)^2}$

Page 207   **1.** Inverse: If a number is not divisible by 9, then it is not a multiple of 3; Contrapositive: If a number is not a multiple of 3, then it is not divisible by 9.   **2.** Inverse: If a number is not an integer, then it is not a rational number; Contrapositive: If a number is not a rational number, then it is not an integer.   **3.** For Exercise 1: False, True; For Exercise 2: False, True

Page 353 $7.86

Page 411   **1.** 0;1   **2.** E;0   **3.** k   **4.** Commutative postulate for multiplication, multiplicative inverse postulate

Page 435   **1.** i. Let $n = 1$, $1 = 1^2$; ii. Assume the statement is true for $n = k$: $1 + 3 + 5 + \cdots + (2k - 1) = k^2$; iii. Let $n = k + 1$; $1 + 3 + 5 + \cdots + (2k - 1) + (2(k + 1) - 1) = k^2 + (2(k + 1) - 1) = k^2 + 2k + 1 = (k + 1)^2$. Therefore, by the Mathematical Induction Theorem, $1 + 3 + 5 + \cdots + (2n - 1) = n^2$ for any natural number, n.   **2.** i. Let $n = 1$, $n^2 + n = 1^2 + 1 = 2$ which is divisible by 2. ii. Assume the statement is true for $n = k$: $k^2 + k$ is divisible by 2. iii. Let $n = k + 1$; $(k + 1)^2 + (k + 1) = k^2 + 3k + 2 = (k^2 + k) + (2k + 2)$. $(k^2 + k)$ is divisible by 2 (from ii). $(2k + 2) = 2(k + 1)$ which is divisible by 2. Thus, by the Mathematical Induction Theorem, $n^2 + n$ is divisible by 2 for any natural number, n.

Page 505   **1.** $r = 6$, $\theta = 110°$ **2.** $r = 7$, $\theta = 270°$ **3.** $r = 3$, $\theta = 210°$ **4.** $r = 4$, $\theta = 70°$
5. $r = 5$, $\theta = -210°$, or $150°$ **6.** $r = 6$, $\theta = -40°$, or $320°$

Answers to Testing Program

The following are the answers to the test items of the Testing Program for *Algebra Two with Trigonometry*, Third Edition. There are two booklets, *Form A* and *Form B*. Each form contains a test for each chapter, except for the chapter on computer programming. Five cumulative tests are also found in each form.

FORM A

Chapter 1　**1.** 0.785, $-3\frac{2}{5}$, $-0.\overline{43}$　**2.** Associative Postulate for Addition　**3.** -7　**4.** $8, 9$
5. $5x\sqrt{3}$　**6.** $60\sqrt{3}$　**7.** $\dfrac{\sqrt{15}}{3}$　**8.** $-2\sqrt{x}$　**9.** $-31\sqrt{3}$　**10.** $9i$　**11.** $-2\sqrt{6}$

12. $\dfrac{\sqrt{5}}{2}$　**13.** $6 - 6i$; 6; -6　**14.** $\sqrt{7} + 0i$　**15.** $-22 + 0i$　**16.** $-\sqrt{5} + 10i$

17. $34 + 0i$　**18.** $56 - 2\sqrt{6}i$　**19.** $-4 + 2\sqrt{5}i$　**20.** $-\dfrac{14}{29} - \dfrac{23}{29}i$

Chapter 2　**1.** a, b　**2.** 4; 3(trinomial), real　**3.** $9x^3 + 13x^2 + 2x - 14$　**4.** $6n^3 - 3n^2 + 4n + 4$
5. $-6a^5b^5$　**6.** $4x^2 - 12x + 9$　**7.** $2y^3 + 3y^2 - 5y + 12$　**8.** $(3a + 5b)(3a - 5b)$
9. $6a^2b(a + 2a^2b^2 - 3b)$　**10.** $(a - 5b)^2$　**11.** $(x + 6)(x - 3)$　**12.** $(2y + 3)(3y - 4)$
13. $(\sqrt{6}x + \sqrt{5}y)(\sqrt{6}x - \sqrt{5}y)$　**14.** $-6x + 8xy + 12y$　**15.** 4　**16.** No, it is not a
factor.　**17.** $\{8, -3\}$　**18.** $\dfrac{a}{b}$　**19.** $a(a - 1)$　**20.** $\dfrac{a - 1}{a + 4}$　**21.** $\dfrac{-x + 2}{3}$　**22.** $\dfrac{7a - 17}{6}$

23. $\dfrac{2x - 1}{x(x - 1)}$　**24.** $x^3 - 9x^2 + 27x - 27$　**25.** $120a^7b^3$

Chapter 3　**1.** $\{4\}$　**2.** $\{-1\}$　**3.** $\{.3\}$　**4.** $\{21\}$　**5.** $\{6\}$　**6.** $\{3, -2\}$　**7.** $\{2\}$　**8.** $\dfrac{5F - 160}{9}$

9. $\dfrac{L - a + d}{d}$　**10.** $\{x: x > -2\}$　**11.** $\{y: y \le 4\}$　**12.** $4\frac{4}{9}$ hours　**13.** $\frac{3}{7}$
14. 8 meters　**15.** $\{y: 2 \le y \le 10\}$; The graph is a line segment between 2 and 10. The circles at 2 and 10 are filled.　**16.** $\{w: w > 4\} \cup \{w: w < -16\}$; The graph consists of two arrows, one starting at 4 and going to the right, the other starting at -16 and going to the left. The circles at 4 and -16 are empty.

Chapter 4   1. $(-2, -3)$ 2. The point 3 spaces right and 4 spaces down from the origin.
3. $2\sqrt{5}$ 4. 24   5. $(1, -6)$ 6. $(10, 10)$ 7. $\frac{1}{2}$ 8. A line going through $(0, 7)$
and $(-4, 1)$.   9. $-\frac{3}{2}$ 10. -2 11. $5x - 4y - 8 = 0$ 12. $3x - 4y - 32 = 0$
13. A line going through $(0, -5)$ and $(2, -1)$.   14. $-5 + 11i$ 15. A segment with
an arrow head from $(0, 0)$ to $(3, -4)$; Length $= 5$ 16. The sum vector goes from
$(0, 0)$ to $(7, 2)$; Length $= \sqrt{53}$

Chapter 5   1. $\{-1, 0, 1, 2\}$; $\{2, 1, 5\}$ 2. Real numbers   3. $\{6, 3, 2\}$ 4. Yes   5. F   6. $\frac{9}{16}$
7. $\{(0, 5), (2, 5), (-3, -2), (1, -2)\}$ 8. The x value -2 maps onto the y value 4, 0
maps onto 2, 2 maps onto -1, and 4 maps onto 6.   9. $\{4.5, \sqrt{9}, \frac{3}{2}, 0, 17\}$ 10. 12
11. -2 and 5   12. -4 and 1   13. $\{(1, -2), (2, -3), (3, -4)\}$; $\{1, 2, 3\}$;
$\{-2, -3, -4\}$ 14. $9x^2 - 12x$; $3x^2 - 14$ 15. No.   16. One line through $(-1, -3)$
and $(1, 3)$ and another line through $(3, 1)$ and $(-3, -1)$; Yes.

Cumulative Test (Chapters 1–5)   1. $.\overline{23}, -3\frac{2}{3}, \sqrt{16}$ 2. $60\sqrt{6}$ 3. $\frac{\sqrt{42}}{3}$ 4. $7\sqrt{2} - 8i$
5. $-3y^3 + 4y^2 + 10y + 6$ 6. $12c^2 + 7cd - 10d^2$ 7. $(6a + 5b)(6a - 5b)$ 8. $\{-7, 3\}$
9. $\frac{x - y}{3}$ 10. $\frac{4y + 4}{y}$ 11. $\{-5\}$ 12. $2s - b - c$ 13. $\{w: w > -6\}$ 14. $\sqrt{73}$
15. $-\frac{3}{4}$ 16. $y = -\frac{1}{3}x + 8$ 17. The diagram has three segments with a single arrow
head on each. They each start at $(0, 0)$; one goes to $(3, 4)$, one goes to $(5, -2)$ and
one goes to $(8, 2)$; $2\sqrt{17}$ 18. 35   19. 16   20. b

Chapter 6   1. 8   2. 9   3. a, c   4. U; W 5. a, c, d   6. $(0, -5)$ 7. $x = -1$; $(-1, -5)$
8. -12; Minimum   9. A parabola with a vertex of $(4, -1)$ and x intercepts of $(3, 0)$
and $(5, 0)$; $\{3, 5\}$. The parabola opens upward.   10. $\{2, -2\}$ 11. $\{18, -2\}$
12. $\{3, -\frac{1}{2}\}$ 13. One real number   14. 2; $\frac{8}{3}$

Chapter 7   1. One line passing through $(0, 4)$ and $(6, 0)$ and another line passing through
$(0, -1)$ and $(1, 0)$, intersecting at $(3, 2)$; $\{(3, 2)\}$ 2. $\{(\frac{1}{3}, -3)\}$ 3. $\{(1, \frac{1}{2})\}$
4. Consistent and dependent; One distinct line   5. Inconsistent; Two parallel lines
6. 16 and 22   7. A dotted line passing through $(0, 4)$ and $(4, 0)$ and the region
above and to the right of this line. Also a dotted line passing through $(0, -7)$ and
$(4, 1)$ and the region above and to the left of this line.   8. The interior of the triangular
region bounded by these three dotted lines: a dotted line through $(0, 4)$ and $(-4, 0)$;
a dotted line through $(-4, 0)$ and $(0, -2)$; a dotted line through $(3, 0)$ parallel to the
y axis.   9. $\{(3, -2, 2)\}$ 10. $\{(2, -3, \frac{1}{2})\}$

Cumulative Test (Chapters 1–7): Part I   1. $\sqrt{3}, \pi$ 2. $4y\sqrt{5}$ 3. $10\sqrt{3}$ 4. $-4\sqrt{3}$
5. $19 + 0i$ 6. $\frac{2}{3} + \frac{1}{3}i$ 7. a, b   8. $-2g^4 + 7g^3 - 8g^2$ 9. $4x^2 - 20x + 25$
10. $5y^3(3y - 7y^3 + 4)$ 11. 10   12. $\frac{3(y + 4)}{y(y - 3)}$ 13. $\frac{7b - 4a}{b(a - b)}$ 14. $\{6\}$ 15. $\{6\}$
16. $\{4\frac{1}{3}, -3\}$ 17. $\{w: w < -2\}$ 18. $2\frac{2}{5}$ hours   19. $11 + \sqrt{61}$ 20. $(1, 6)$

Cumulative Test (Chapters 1–7): Part II   **1.** 3   **2.** $y = -3x + 14$ **3.** A vector from (0, 0) to $(-8, 6)$; 10   **4.** Yes   **5.** $\{(3, 8), (3, 4), (5, 4), (5, 0), (-2, -1)\}$ **6.** -4 and 3   **7.** $\{(2, -3), (3, -1), (4, 0)\}$ **8.** 27   **9.** a, c   **10.** $x = 1$; $(1, -9)$ **11.** $\{6 \pm 3\sqrt{2}\}$ **12.** $\left\{\dfrac{2 \pm \sqrt{2}i}{3}\right\}$ **13.** $\left\{\left(-2, \dfrac{1}{3}\right)\right\}$ **14.** Inconsistent   **15.** A dotted line passing through (0, 5) and $(-5, 0)$ and the region below and to the right of it; also a dotted line passing through (0, 1) and $(2, -3)$ and the region above and to the right of it.   **16.** $\{(2, 3, 5)\}$

Chapter 8   **1.** 1   **2.** $\frac{4}{3}$ **3.** $\dfrac{5}{a^4}$ **4.** 6.4×10^6 **5.** 3.48×10^{-4} **6.** 284,000   **7.** $\dfrac{1}{x^6}$ **8.** $\dfrac{ab}{b(b + a)}$ **9.** $3a^{-2}b^3c^4d^{-1}$ **10.** 125   **11.** $x^{\frac{2}{3}}y^{\frac{4}{3}}$ **12.** $\sqrt{ab^3}$ **13.** $7\sqrt{2}$ **14.** $29\sqrt{2}$ **15.** $\sqrt[4]{3^3}$ **16.** $\{14\}$ **17.** $\{-27\}$ **18.** $\{5\}$ **19.** $\{\frac{4}{3}\}$ **20.** $\{-\frac{3}{2}\}$

Chapter 9   **1.** An exponential curve passing through $(-1, \frac{1}{3})$, (0, 1), (1, 3), and (2, 9)   **2.** 128   **3.** 4   **4.** 5   **5.** 0.2648   **6.** 2.35   **7.** 2.33   **8.** $7.4533 - 10$ **9.** 1.8122   **10.** 1.54   **11.** 0.5116   **12.** $2413   **13.** 7.3

Chapter 10   **1.** $(x - 3)^2 + (y + 4)^2 = 36$ **2.** $(5, -2)$; 4   **3.** $\dfrac{x^2}{36} + \dfrac{y^2}{16} = 1$ **4.** A parabola with vertex (0, 0), axis of symmetry the x axis, and focus (4, 0); (4, 0); (0, 0); $x = -4$ **5.** $y = -\dfrac{1}{20}x^2$ **6.** A hyperbola with x intercepts (3, 0) and $(-3, 0)$ and asymptotes $y = \frac{5}{3}x$ and $y = -\frac{5}{3}x$ **7. a.** Ellipse;   **b.** Parabola;   **c.** Hyperbola;   **d.** Line   **8.** $10\frac{2}{3}$ **9. b;** $\{(0, 3), (0, -3)\}$ **10.** $\{(3, 6), (\frac{33}{5}, -\frac{6}{5})\}$ **11.** $\{(\pm 1, \pm 3)\}$ **12.** The interior of a circular region with center at (0, 0) and radius of 3.

Cumulative Test (Chapters 6–10)   **1.** c, d   **2.** $x = 3$; $(3, -1)$ **3.** $\{6 \pm \sqrt{26}\}$ **4.** Two real, irrational roots   **5.** $\{(4, -1)\}$ **6.** Inconsistent; Two parallel lines   **7.** 12, 43   **8.** $\dfrac{6a^5c^3}{b^2}$ **9.** $\sqrt[12]{2^5}$ **10.** $\{8\}$ **11.** 2   **12.** $6.9365 - 10$ **13.** 2.664   **14.** $(x + 6)^2 + (y - 2)^2 = 25$ **15. a.** Hyperbola   **b.** Parabola   **c.** Circle   **d.** Line   **16.** An ellipse passing through (3, 0), $(-3, 0)$, (0, 4), $(0, -4)$ and its interior

Chapter 11   **1.** $a_n = 5 + 2(n - 1)$; 13, 15, 17   **2.** $a_n = 3(\frac{1}{3})^{n-1}$; $\frac{1}{27}$, $\frac{1}{81}$, $\frac{1}{243}$ **3.** 4, $3\frac{1}{2}$, 3, $2\frac{1}{2}$, 2   **4.** -32 **5.** 7.5, 8.8, 10.1   **6.** $3\sqrt{3}$, 9, $9\sqrt{3}$, 27   **7.** 400,000,000   **8.** 6, 9, $\dfrac{27}{2}$ or $-6, 9, -\dfrac{27}{2}$ **9.** 8   **10.** $819y$ **11.** 625   **12.** $\frac{665}{27}$ **13.** $\frac{64}{3}$ or $21\frac{1}{3}$ **14.** $\frac{2}{3}$

Chapter 12   **1.** 5040   **2.** 360   **3.** 15,120   **4.** 56   **5.** 1140   **6.** 658,008   **7.** $c^5 + 10c^4d + 40c^3d^2 + 80c^2d^3 + 80cd^4 + 32d^5$ **8.** $-252x^5y^5$ **9.** $\frac{2}{6}$, or $\frac{1}{3}$ **10.** $\dfrac{7}{29}$ **11.** $\frac{16}{52}$, or $\frac{4}{13}$ **12.** $\frac{14}{36}$, or $\frac{7}{18}$

Chapter 13

1. An angle whose initial side is the positive x axis and whose terminal side is in the third quadrant, making a 60° angle with the negative x axis. 2. The first quadrant 3. 0.6 4. $\frac{1}{2}$, or 0.5 5. -1 6. $\frac{24}{25}, \frac{24}{25}, \frac{24}{7}$ 7. 0.9525 8. 14 cm 9. $\frac{\sqrt{3}}{2}; -\frac{1}{2}; -\sqrt{3}$ 10. $-\cos\theta$ 11. $\frac{13}{5}, \frac{13}{12}, \frac{12}{5}$ 12. $\frac{20\sqrt{6}}{3}$ 13. 149

Chapter 14

1. $\frac{2}{3}\pi$ 2. 300° 3. $-\frac{1}{2}$ or $-.5$ 4. a; 3; π 5. b 6. $\cos^2\theta$ 7. $\frac{-\sqrt{6}-\sqrt{2}}{4}$ 8. $\frac{\sin^2\theta}{\cos\theta}+\frac{\cos\theta}{1}=\sec\theta; \frac{\sin^2\theta}{\cos\theta}+\frac{\cos^2\theta}{\cos\theta}=\sec\theta; \frac{\sin^2\theta+\cos^2\theta}{\cos\theta}=\sec\theta; \frac{1}{\cos\theta}=\sec\theta; \sec\theta=\sec\theta$ 9. $\frac{\sqrt{3}}{3}$ 10. $\{0, 2\pi\}$

Cumulative Test (Chapters 11–14) 1. 53 2. 6, 18, 54, or -6, 18, -54 3. 54 4. 720 5. $126a^5b^4$ 6. $\frac{1}{3}$ 7. 0.8 8. $\sqrt{3}$ 9. 0.7238 10. 27 m 11. 2; $\frac{-2\sqrt{3}}{3}$; $-\sqrt{3}$ 12. $18^2=22^2+27^2-2(22)(27)\cos D$ 13. $-\frac{1}{2}$ 14. c 15. -1 16. $\frac{2\sqrt{3}}{3}$

Cumulative Test (Chapters 8–14): Part I 1. $\frac{9}{4}$ 2. .000352 3. $x^{\frac{3}{4}}y^{\frac{5}{4}}$ 4. 2 5. $\left\{\frac{3}{2}\right\}$ 6. An exponential curve that includes the points $(-3, \frac{1}{8})$, $(-2, \frac{1}{4})$, $(-1, \frac{1}{2})$, $(0, 1)$, $(1, 2)$, $(2, 4)$, and $(3, 8)$. 7. 3 8. 4.66 9. 4.5159 10. 4.78 11. 0.2732 12. 4.0 13. $(-6, 3)$; 5 14. An ellipse with its center at the origin and having as intercepts $(0, 5)$, $(-3, 0)$, $(0, -5)$, and $(3, 0)$. 15. $y=\frac{1}{24}x^2$ 16. a. Hyperbola b. Circle c. Parabola d. Hyperbola 17. b; $\{(0, 6), (0, -6)\}$ 18. $\{(1, 3), (1, -3), (-1, 3), (-1, -3)\}$ 19. 15, $15\frac{2}{3}$, $16\frac{1}{3}$, 17 20. $33\frac{2}{3}$, $36\frac{1}{3}$

Cumulative Test (Chapters 8–14): Part II 1. x^3, x^5, x^7, x^9 2. -216 3. 12,288 4. $\frac{81}{2}$ or $40\frac{1}{2}$ 5. 60 6. 455 7. $792a^5b^7$ 8. $\frac{5}{36}$ 9. The third quadrant 10. $-\frac{1}{2}$ 11. $\frac{24}{26}$, or $\frac{12}{13}; \frac{24}{26}$, or $\frac{12}{13}; \frac{24}{10}$, or $\frac{12}{5}$ 12. $\frac{26}{10}$, or $\frac{13}{5}; \frac{26}{24}$, or $\frac{13}{12}; \frac{24}{10}$, or $\frac{12}{5}$ 13. 7 14. $25\sqrt{2}$ 15. $\frac{-\sqrt{3}}{3}$ 16. a 17. $\cos\theta$ 18. $\frac{\sqrt{6}+\sqrt{2}}{4}$ 19. $\frac{2\sqrt{3}}{3}$ 20. $\left\{\frac{\pi}{4}, \frac{3\pi}{4}, \frac{5\pi}{4}, \frac{7\pi}{4}\right\}$

Chapter 1   1. 1.35, $0.\overline{72}$, and -0.9 2. Distributive postulate   3. -9 4. $6, 7$ 5. $3y\sqrt{5}$
6. $24\sqrt{6}$ 7. $\dfrac{\sqrt{5}}{4}$ 8. $11\sqrt{x}$ 9. $7\sqrt{2}$ 10. $10i$ 11. $-2\sqrt{6}$ 12. $\dfrac{\sqrt{30}}{5}$

13. $12 - 20i$; 12; -20 14. $-\dfrac{4}{5} + 0i$ 15. $-13 + 2\sqrt{7}i$ 16. $-2\sqrt{3} + 3i$ 17. $58 + 0i$

18. $72 - 14\sqrt{3}i$ 19. $-5 - 3\sqrt{2}i$ 20. $-\frac{11}{53} - \frac{41}{53}i$

Chapter 2   1. a and d 2. 5; 4; Rational   3. $10x^3 + 16x^2 + 5x$ 4. $3y^3 - 5y^2 + y + 1$
5. $-28a^6b^5$ 6. $9n^2 - 48n + 64$ 7. $3x^3 + x^2 - 6x + 8$ 8. $(4a - 7b)(4a + 7b)$
9. $3ab^3(a - ab + 5)$ 10. $(x - 6y)^2$ 11. $(n - 7)(n + 5)$ 12. $(4x - 3)(x + 2)$
13. $(\sqrt{3}x + \sqrt{7}y)(\sqrt{3}x - \sqrt{7}y)$ 14. $-5a + 3ab - 8b$ 15. 2 16. Yes

17. $\{-5, -6\}$ 18. $\dfrac{3}{n}$ 19. $\dfrac{x}{3(x + 3)}$ 20. $\dfrac{n + 5}{n - 1}$ 21. $\dfrac{-2a - 5}{8}$ 22. $\dfrac{5x - 28}{9}$

23. $\dfrac{4x + 6}{x(x + 3)}$ 24. $n^3 - 12n^2 + 48n - 64$ 25. $66x^2y^{10}$

Chapter 3   1. $\{8\}$ 2. $\{-2\}$ 3. $\{7\}$ 4. $\{3\}$ 5. $\{1\}$ 6. $\{1, -\frac{1}{3}\}$ 7. $\{-1, 0\}$ 8. $m = \dfrac{grF}{V^2}$

9. $x = \dfrac{d + bc}{a - b}$ 10. $\{x\colon x < -16\}$ 11. $\{y\colon y \geq 4\}$ 12. 14 minutes   13. $\dfrac{8}{3}$

14. 6 cm   15. $\{y\colon 1 \leq y \leq 5\}$; The graph is a line segment between 1 and 5 inclusive.
The circles at 1 and 5 are filled.   16. $\{x\colon x > 15\} \cup \{x\colon x < -3\}$; The graph consists
of two arrows, one starting at 15 and going to the right, the other starting at -3 and
going to the left. The circles at 15 and -3 are empty.

Chapter 4   1. $(-3, 2)$ 2. The point is 4 units left of the y axis and 1 unit below the x axis.
3. $4\sqrt{5}$ 4. 30 5. $(3, -6)$ 6. $(12, 17)$ 7. $-\frac{2}{5}$ 8. The graph is a straight line
containing points $(0, 2)$ and $(-3, -2)$.   9. $\frac{4}{5}$ 10. $a = 2$ 11. $x + 3y - 6 = 0$
12. $4x - y - 6 = 0$ 13. The graph is a straight line containing points $(-1, -1)$ and
$(0, -4)$.   14. $3 - 2i$ 15. Using $(0, 0)$ as the initial point of the vector, the terminal
point is then at $(-6, -8)$; Length: 10   16. The first vector $(3 + 3i)$ is drawn from
$(0, 0)$ to $(3, 3)$. The second vector $(5 - 2i)$ is drawn from $(3, 3)$ to $(8, 1)$. Then the
vector for the sum $(8 + i)$ is drawn from $(0, 0)$ to $(8, 1)$; Sum: $8 + i$; Length: $\sqrt{65}$

Chapter 5   1. $\{2, 0, -2, -4\}$; $\{5, 3, 0\}$ 2. Real numbers   3. $\{5, 1, 11\}$ 4. No   5. F   6. $-\frac{8}{9}$
7. $\{(3, -3), (0, 1), (1, 1), (4, 1)\}$ 8. The x value -1 maps onto the y value 3,
0 maps onto 0, 1 maps onto -3, and -2 maps onto 6.   9. $\{\sqrt{4}, 0.3, 0, 6, 8.1\}$ 10. 90
11. 1 and -5 12. 7 and -2 13. $\{(1, 7), (2, -5), (3, -2)\}$; $\{1, 2, 3\}$; $\{7, -5, -2\}$
14. $2x^2 + 1$; $4x^2 + 12x + 8$ 15. Yes.   16. The graph of the function defined by
$y = \frac{1}{2}x$ is a straight line containing points $(0, 0)$ and $(2, 1)$. The graph of the inverse
is a straight line containing points $(0, 0)$ and $(1, 2)$; Yes.

Cumulative Test (Chapters 1–5)　　**1.** $-1.95, -\sqrt{25}, \frac{3}{4}$　　**2.** $30\sqrt{14}$　　**3.** $\frac{\sqrt{42}}{6}$

4. $3\sqrt{5} + 4i$　　**5.** $4n^3 - 2n^2 + 5n - 1$　　**6.** $10a^2 - 3ab - 4b^2$　　**7.** $(20x - 3y)(20x + 3y)$

8. $\{8, -5\}$　　**9.** $\frac{a + b}{2}$　　**10.** $\frac{12x + 18}{3x}$, or $\frac{4x + 6}{x}$　　**11.** $\{-5\}$　　**12.** $h = \frac{6V}{a + b + 4M}$

13. $\{n: n < 6\}$　　**14.** $\sqrt{85}$　　**15.** $\frac{1}{5}$　　**16.** $y = \frac{3}{5}x - 1$　　**17.** The first vector $(5 + 2i)$ is
drawn from $(0, 0)$ to $(5, 2)$. The second vector $(-2 + 4i)$ is drawn from $(5, 2)$ to
$(3, 6)$. Then the vector for the sum $(3 + 6i)$ is drawn from $(0, 0)$ to $(3, 6)$; $\sqrt{45}$ or $3\sqrt{5}$.
18. 18　　**19.** 25　　**20.** a

Chapter 6　　**1.** 150　　**2.** $b = 5$　　**3.** a, c, d　　**4.** D; S　　**5.** b, c　　**6.** $(0, 3)$　　**7.** $x = -3$; $(-3, -2)$
8. 8; Maximum　　**9.** The graph of $y = x^2 + 6x + 5$ is a parabola that opens upward and
crosses the x axis at $(-5, 0)$ and $(-1, 0)$ and has $(-3, -4)$ for its vertex; $\{-5, -1\}$
10. $\{10, -10\}$　　**11.** $\{2, -16\}$　　**12.** $\left\{-\frac{4}{3}, 1\right\}$　　**13.** Two imaginary numbers　　**14.** $\frac{5}{2}; -3$

Chapter 7　　**1.** $\{(-3, 2)\}$　　**2.** $\{(-11, 8)\}$　　**3.** $\{(-9, 4)\}$　　**4.** Inconsistent; two parallel lines
5. Consistent and independent; two intersecting lines　　**6.** 7 and 15　　**7.** The graph is
the interior of an angle whose vertex is $(\frac{3}{2}, -\frac{3}{2})$. One ray of the angle contains the
point $(0, 3)$; the other ray contains the point $(0, -3)$. The points of the graph are left
of both boundary lines, $x - y = 3$ and $3x + y = 3$. Neither boundary line is part of the
graph.　　**8.** The graph is the interior of a triangle whose vertices are $(-3, 6)$, $(-3, -2)$,
and $(3, 0)$. The boundary lines whose equations are $x = -3$, $y = \frac{1}{3}x - 1$, and $y = -x + 3$
are not part of the graph.　　**9.** $\{(5, -3, 2)\}$　　**10.** $\{(-2, 1, \frac{1}{3})\}$

Cumulative Test (Chapters 1–7): Part I　　**1.** $-\sqrt{12}, \sqrt{300}, \pi$　　**2.** $6x\sqrt{5}$　　**3.** $-2\sqrt{2}$
4. $-15\sqrt{2}$　　**5.** $9 + 0i$　　**6.** $\frac{3}{5} + \frac{1}{5}i$　　**7.** a, c　　**8.** $5n^5 - 4n^3 + 8n$　　**9.** $9x^2 + 66x + 121$
10. $8x^3(2x^4 - x + 3)$　　**11.** -2　　**12.** $\frac{b + 5}{4b^3(b + 3)}$　　**13.** $\frac{2x + 3y}{x(x - y)}$　　**14.** $\{6\}$　　**15.** $\{-1\}$
16. $\{2, -\frac{8}{5}\}$　　**17.** $\{n: n > 3\}$　　**18.** 3 hours　　**19.** $10 + 5\sqrt{2}$　　**20.** $(3, 7)$

Cumulative Test (Chapters 1–7): Part II　　**1.** 8　　**2.** $y = -x + 4$　　**3.** Using $(0, 0)$
as the initial point of the vector, the terminal point is then at $(4, -3)$; 5　　**4.** Yes.
5. $\{(-2, 5), (1, 0), (6, 0), (6, -1), (6, 4)\}$　　**6.** 21 and -2　　**7.** $\{(1, -1), (4, 0), (8, 6)\}$
8. 72　　**9.** c, d　　**10.** $x = -5$; $(-5, -7)$　　**11.** $\{3 + \sqrt{2}, 3 - \sqrt{2}\}$　　**12.** $\{\frac{1}{2} + i, \frac{1}{2} - i\}$
13. $\{(2, 7)\}$　　**14.** Consistent and independent　　**15.** The graph is the set of interior
points of an angle whose vertex is $(1, 3)$. One of the sides of the angle contains $(0, 6)$;
the other side contains $(5, 7)$. The boundary lines, which contain the sides of the
angle, have equations $y = x + 2$ and $y = -3x + 6$. Neither boundary line is part of the
graph.　　**16.** $\{(-2, 3, 1)\}$

Chapter 8 1. $\frac{1}{5}$ 2. $\frac{7}{12}$ 3. $\frac{3}{n^5}$ 4. 7.65×10^4 5. 3.8×10^{-5} 6. 1,630,000 7. a^2b^6 8. xy
9. $5v^2w^{-3}xy^{-4}$ 10. 1000 11. $x^4 \cdot y^4$ 12. $\sqrt[3]{xy^5}$ 13. $4\sqrt{3}$ 14. $29\sqrt{5}$
15. $\sqrt[6]{32}$ 16. $\{11\}$ 17. $\{-8\}$ 18. $\{3\}$ 19. $\left\{\frac{2}{5}\right\}$ 20. $\left\{-\frac{3}{4}\right\}$

Chapter 9 1. An exponential curve passing through $(-1, \frac{1}{4})$, $(0, 1)$, $(1, 4)$, and $(2, 16)$ 2. 4
3. -2 4. 2 5. 0.3075 6. 1.56 7. 2.28 8. $0.6739 - 2$, or $8.6739 - 10$
9. 2.5433 10. 2.06 11. 0.8158 12. $1775 13. 2.1

Chapter 10 1. $(x - 5)^2 + (x + 2)^2 = 9$ 2. $(-8, 3)$; 7 3. $\frac{x^2}{4} + \frac{y^2}{81} = 1$ 4. A parabola with
vertex $(0, 0)$, axis of symmetry the y axis, and focus $(0, 2)$. Some points on the graph
are $(\pm 1, \frac{1}{8})$, $(\pm 2, \frac{1}{2})$, and $(\pm 4, 2)$; $(0, 2)$; $(0, 0)$; $y = -2$ 5. $x = \frac{1}{12}y^2$ 6. A hyperbola
with x intercepts $(4, 0)$ and $(-4, 0)$ and asymptotes $y = \frac{3}{4}x$ and $y = -\frac{3}{4}x$.
7. a. Hyperbola; b. Ellipse c. Parabola d. Circle 8. 36 9. a; $\{(3, 0), (-3, 0)\}$
10. $\{(-6, -11), (2, 5)\}$ 11. $\{(6, 1), (-6, 1), (6, -1), (-6, -1)\}$ 12. The graph
is the set of points on and outside the circle with center at $(0, 0)$ and radius of 2.

Cumulative Test (Chapters 6–10) 1. a, b 2. $x = 5$; $(5, -4)$ 3. $\{2 + 3\sqrt{5}, 2 - 3\sqrt{5}\}$
4. One distinct real number. 5. $\{(3, -8)\}$ 6. Consistent and dependent; one
distinct line (or two coinciding lines) 7. 4 and 28 8. $\frac{5ac}{b^3}$ 9. $\sqrt{5}$ 10. $\{-27\}$
11. 12 12. $0.8525 - 3$, or $7.8525 - 10$ 13. 3.533 14. $(x + 5)^2 + (y + 1)^2 = 81$
15. a. Parabola; b. Line; c. Hyperbola; d. Ellipse 16. The interior of an
ellipse that passes through points $(6, 0)$, $(-6, 0)$, $(0, 2)$ and $(0, -2)$.

Chapter 11 1. $a_n = 7 + 4(n - 1)$; 23, 27, 31 2. $a_n = \frac{1}{8}(4)^{n-1}$; 32, 128, 512 3. 3, $1\frac{1}{2}$, 0, $-1\frac{1}{2}$,
-3, $-4\frac{1}{2}$, -6 4. -105 5. 3.2, 3.7, 4.2, 4.7 6. $5\sqrt{2}$, 10, $10\sqrt{2}$, 20
7. 0.0000083 8. 216, 72, 24, or -216, 72, -24 9. 250 10. $528x$ 11. 81
12. $\frac{511}{16}$, or $31\frac{15}{16}$ 13. 2 14. $\frac{12}{99}$, or $\frac{4}{33}$

Chapter 12 1. 720 2. 210 3. 30 4. 126 5. 1001 6. 19,600 7. $16x^4 - 32x^3y + 24x^2y^2$
$- 8xy^3 + y^4$ 8. $495x^8y^4$ 9. $\frac{3}{10}$ 10. $\frac{2}{3}$ 11. $\frac{1}{3}$ 12. $\frac{11}{20}$

Chapter 13 1. An angle whose initial side is the positive x axis and whose terminal side is in the
second quadrant, making a 60° angle with the negative x axis. 2. The third quadrant
3. $\frac{3}{5}$, or 0.6 4. 1 5. $-\frac{1}{2}$, or -0.5

6. $\dfrac{21}{29}, \dfrac{20}{29}, \dfrac{20}{21}$ **7.** 0.8368   **8.** 48 cm   **9.** $-\dfrac{\sqrt{3}}{2}; -\dfrac{1}{2}; \sqrt{3}$ **10.** $-\sin\theta$ **11.** $\dfrac{37}{35}, \dfrac{37}{12}, \dfrac{12}{35}$

12. $16\sqrt{3}$ **13.** 12

Chapter 14   **1.** $\dfrac{4\pi}{3}$ **2.** 40°   **3.** $-\dfrac{1}{2}$ **4.** c; 4; 4π, or 720°   **5.** b   **6.** $\sin\theta$ **7.** $\dfrac{\sqrt{2}+\sqrt{6}}{4}$

8. $\dfrac{(\sin\theta + \cos\theta)^2 - 1}{2} = \sin\theta \cdot \cos\theta;$

$\dfrac{\sin^2\theta + 2\sin\theta \cdot \cos\theta + \cos^2\theta - 1}{2} = \sin\theta \cdot \cos\theta;$

$\dfrac{1 + 2\sin\theta \cdot \cos\theta - 1}{2} = \sin\theta \cdot \cos\theta;$

$\dfrac{2\sin\theta \cdot \cos\theta}{2} = \sin\theta \cdot \cos\theta; \sin\theta \cdot \cos\theta = \sin\theta \cdot \cos\theta$

9. $\dfrac{13}{12}$ **10.** $\left\{\dfrac{\pi}{6}, \dfrac{5\pi}{6}, \dfrac{\pi}{2}\right\}$

Cumulative Test (Chapters 11–14)   **1.** -53 **2.** 15, 75   **3.** $2\frac{1}{2}$ **4.** 120

5. $3003a^5b^{10}$ **6.** $\dfrac{1}{4}$ **7.** $-\dfrac{12}{13}$ **8.** $-\sqrt{3}$ **9.** 0.7855   **10.** 67   **11.** $-2; \dfrac{2\sqrt{3}}{3};$

$-\sqrt{3}$ **12.** $5^2 = 6^2 + 8^2 - 2(6)(8)\cos T$ **13.** $-\dfrac{\sqrt{3}}{2}$ **14.** a   **15.** $\cos^2\theta$ **16.** $\dfrac{5}{4}$

Cumulative Test (Chapters 8–14): Part I   **1.** $\dfrac{100}{81}$ **2.** 0.00683   **3.** $x^{\frac{5}{3}}y^{\frac{2}{3}}$ **4.** 5

5. $\left\{-\dfrac{1}{2}\right\}$ **6.** An exponential curve passing through $\left(-1, \dfrac{1}{5}\right)$, (0, 1), (1, 5), and

(2, 25).   **7.** 5   **8.** 4.78   **9.** 2.9274   **10.** 53.4   **11.** 0.4559   **12.** 4.1

13. $(5, -1)$; 4   **14.** An ellipse passing through (4, 0), (0, 5), (−4, 0), and (0, −5).

15. $y = -\frac{1}{4}x^2$ **16. a.** Hyperbola;   **b.** Line;   **c.** Circle;   **d.** Parabola   **17.** b;

$\{(0, 2), (-4, 0)\}$ **18.** $\{(3, 2), (-3, 2), (3, -2), (-3, -2)\}$ **19.** $8, 8\frac{4}{5}, 9\frac{3}{5}, 10\frac{2}{5}$

20. $19\frac{3}{4}, 20\frac{1}{2}, 21\frac{1}{4}$

Cumulative Test (Chapters 8–14): Part II   **1.** $12x, 4x^2, \dfrac{4}{3}x^3, \dfrac{4}{9}x^4$ **2.** -1290

3. 1152   **4.** $8\frac{1}{3}$ **5.** 360   **6.** 22,100   **7.** $-56a^3b^5$ **8.** $\dfrac{5}{12}$ **9.** The second quadrant

10. $-\dfrac{\sqrt{2}}{2}$ **11.** $\dfrac{39}{89}, \dfrac{39}{89}, \dfrac{80}{39}$ **12.** $\dfrac{89}{39}, \dfrac{89}{80}, \dfrac{80}{39}$ **13.** 37   **14.** $20\sqrt{6}$ **15.** $-\sqrt{3}$

16. c   **17.** $\cos\theta$ **18.** $\dfrac{-\sqrt{6}-\sqrt{2}}{4}$ **19.** $\dfrac{5}{12}$ **20.** $\left\{\dfrac{\pi}{6}, \dfrac{5\pi}{6}, \dfrac{7\pi}{6}, \dfrac{11\pi}{6}\right\}$

Teacher's Notes

Teacher's Notes

Teacher's Notes

Teacher's Notes

Teacher's Notes

Teacher's Notes

Teacher's Notes

Teacher's Notes

Teacher's Notes

Teacher's Notes

Teacher's Notes

Teacher's Notes

Algebra Two

Third Edition

Joseph N. Payne

Arthur F. Coxford

Francis G. Lankford, Jr.

Floyd F. Zamboni

with Trigonometry

Harcourt Brace Jovanovich

New York   Chicago   San Francisco   Atlanta   Dallas   *and*   London

Regular Edition: **ISBN 0-15-353933-X**
With Alternate Answers: **ISBN 0-15-353934-8**

About the Authors

Joseph N. Payne
Professor of Mathematics Education
University of Michigan
Ann Arbor, Michigan

Arthur F. Coxford
Professor of Mathematics Education
University of Michigan
Ann Arbor, Michigan

Francis G. Lankford, Jr.
Professor Emeritus of Education
University of Virginia
Charlottesville, Virginia

Floyd F. Zamboni
Teacher of Mathematics
Jefferson County Schools
Jefferson County, Colorado

Contents —————————————————————————

REVIEW
of
ALGEBRA
One

The following section, Review of Algebra One, is designed to help you recall many of the basic ideas about algebra that you learned in your first course. First, work through the Diagnostic Test. For those problems in the test that you cannot do correctly, refer to the corresponding items (R-1, R-2, R-3, · · ·) in the Review Unit that follows. When you understand these items and can do the exercises correctly, you are ready for the Mastery Test. You can check your answers for all the exercises on pages 531-533.

Important terms are printed in **boldface** type. Be sure that you know the meanings of these terms.

Contents

R-1
R-2
R-3
R-4
R-5

1. Tell which name does not correctly describe the corresponding set of numbers.

a. Natural numbers $\{1, 2, 3, 4, \cdots\}$

b. Whole numbers $\{0, 1, 2, 3, \cdots\}$

c. Integers $\{\cdots, -3, -2, -1, 0, 1, 2, 3, \cdots\}$

d. Rational numbers $\left\{\begin{array}{l}\text{Numbers that can be written as the}\\ \text{ratio of two integers, } \frac{a}{b}, \text{ where } b \neq 0\end{array}\right\}$

e. Real numbers $\left\{\begin{array}{l}\text{Numbers that cannot be written as the}\\ \text{ratio of two integers, } \frac{a}{b}, \text{ where } b \neq 0\end{array}\right\}$

R-6

2. Let N represent the set of natural numbers, W, the set of whole numbers, $\mathscr{I}$, the set of integers, and $\varnothing$, the empty set.

Classify each statement as <u>True</u> or <u>False</u>.

a. $\{0\} \subset N$ **b.** $\{0\} \subset W$ **c.** $W \subset I$ **d.** $\varnothing \subset \{0\}$

R-2
R-3
R-4
R-5
R-7

3. Match each graph on the left with its corresponding set description on the right. Each variable represents a real number, unless indicated otherwise.

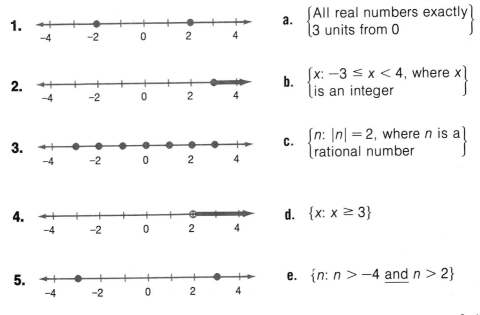

a. $\left\{\begin{array}{l}\text{All real numbers exactly}\\ \text{3 units from 0}\end{array}\right\}$

b. $\left\{\begin{array}{l}x: -3 \leq x < 4, \text{ where } x\\ \text{is an integer}\end{array}\right\}$

c. $\left\{\begin{array}{l}n: |n| = 2, \text{ where } n \text{ is a}\\ \text{rational number}\end{array}\right\}$

d. $\{x: x \geq 3\}$

e. $\{n: n > -4 \text{ <u>and</u> } n > 2\}$

*Use Postulates **A-E** in Exercises **4-6**.*

A. *Commutative Postulate*
B. *Associative Postulate*
C. *Distributive Postulate*
D. *Closure Postulate*
E. *Identity Postulate*

R-8
R-9

4. When adding or multiplying, tell which postulate allows you to <u>reverse</u> <u>the order</u> of the addends or factors and still get the same answer.

R-8
R-9

5. When adding or multiplying three numbers, tell which postulate allows you to <u>change the grouping</u> of the numbers and still get the same answer.

R-11

6. Tell which postulate states that $a(b + c) = ab + ac$.

R-10
R-11
R-12

7. Tell which postulate is incorrect for the given equation.

   a. $3 \cdot 1 = 3$ Multiplicative identity postulate

   b. $5(6 + 7) = 5 \cdot 6 + 5 \cdot 7$ Multiplication postulate

   c. $5 \cdot \frac{1}{5} = 1$ Multiplicative inverse postulate

   d. $\frac{1}{4} + (-\frac{1}{4}) = 0$ Additive inverse postulate

   e. $\sqrt{3} + 0 = \sqrt{3}$ Additive identity postulate

Review Unit 1: Real Numbers

R-1

One way to represent the set of **natural numbers** or **positive integers,** {1, 2, 3, 4, 5, $\cdots$}, is to match each number of the set with a point on the <u>number line.</u>

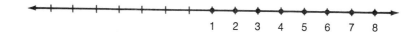

The set of points on the line is the **graph of the set.** Each number that is paired with a point is called the **coordinate** of the point.

Graph each set.

    a. {1, 3, 5}

    b. The set of odd natural numbers between 2 and 6

A-2   Review of Algebra One

c. The set of even natural numbers less than 5

d. The set of natural numbers greater than 2 and less than 6

e. The set of natural numbers greater than or equal to 1 and less than or equal to 3.

R-2   The set of **whole numbers,** or **nonnegative integers,** can also be shown on a number line.

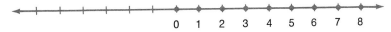

$$0 \quad 1 \quad 2 \quad 3 \quad 4 \quad 5 \quad 6 \quad 7 \quad 8$$

Similarly, the **negative integers** can be shown as points to the left of 0 on the number line.

$$-7 \quad -6 \quad -5 \quad -4 \quad -3 \quad -2 \quad -1 \quad 0 \quad 1 \quad 2 \quad 3 \quad 4 \quad 5 \quad 6 \quad 7$$

Write True or False to describe each sentence.

a. 0 is an integer.

b. All natural numbers and all whole numbers are integers.

c. The set of integers can be described as $\{\cdots, -2, -1, 0, 1, 2, \cdots\}$

R-3   The set of numbers that can be expressed as the ratio of two integers, $\dfrac{a}{b}$, where $b \neq 0$, is the set of **rational numbers.** The set of rational numbers can also be assigned to points on a number line. Some rational numbers are graphed below.

$$\begin{array}{cccccccc} & A & B & C & & D & & E \\ -6 & & -4\tfrac{1}{6} & -3 & -2.25 & 0 & 2 \ \sqrt{9} & 4 & 6 \end{array}$$

*Write the coordinate of each point, **A-E,** as a ratio of two integers.*

R-4   Numbers such as $\sqrt{2}$, $\sqrt{5}$, π and $-\sqrt{5}$ are **irrational numbers.** Irrational numbers <u>cannot</u> be expressed as the ratio of two integers.

Classify each set of numbers as rational or irrational.

a. The set of integers

b. $0, \dfrac{1}{2}, \dfrac{1}{3}, \dfrac{1}{4}, \dfrac{1}{5}$

c. $\sqrt{4}, \sqrt{9}, \sqrt{100}, \sqrt{1.21}$

d. $\sqrt{3}, \sqrt{7}, -\sqrt{7}, \sqrt{8}$

R-5   The rational numbers together with the irrational numbers form the set of **real numbers.** Every real number can be associated with a point on the number line and every point on the number line can be associated with a real number.

Tell whether each graph correctly represents the indicated set, where x is a real number.

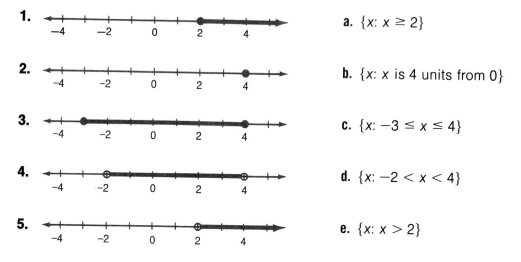

1.

2.

3.

4.

5.

a. $\{x: x \geq 2\}$

b. $\{x: x \text{ is 4 units from } 0\}$

c. $\{x: -3 \leq x \leq 4\}$

d. $\{x: -2 < x < 4\}$

e. $\{x: x > 2\}$

R-6   If A and B are two sets and every element of A is an element of B, then A is a subset of B (written A ⊂ B).

Example: $\{1, 2, 3,\} \subset \{1, 2, 3, 4, 5\}$

The **empty set,** Ø, is the set having no elements; it is a <u>subset</u> of <u>every set.</u>

Classify each sentence as <u>True</u> *or* <u>False</u>.
a. $\{2, 3, 5,\} \subset \{1, 2, 3, 5\}$ b. Ø ⊂ $\{0\}$
c. $\{0\} \subset$ Ø   d. $\{2, 4, 6\} \subset \{4, 2, 6\}$

R-7   Pairs of opposite numbers such as 2 and −2, 5 and −5 and 10 and −10, are equally distant from 0. Such numbers have the same <u>absolute value.</u> The **absolute value** of a real number x, written $|x|$, is a nonnegative real number. The absolute value of a positive number or 0 is the number itself. The absolute value of a negative number is the opposite of the number.

Examples: $|5| = 5$; $|0| = 0$; $|-7| = 7$

Classify each sentence as True or False.

a. $|-4| = 4$ **b.** $|7| = -7$ **c.** $-2 < |-3|$ **d.** $|0| > 0$

R-8   *Classify each sentence as True or False.*

a. $(-2)(3) = (3)(-2)$

b. $\dfrac{1}{3} = 0.3$

c. $\dfrac{9}{0} = 0$

d. $(6 + 7) + 8 = 6 + (7 + 8)$

e. $(64 + 26)$ names one and only one real number, 90.

R-9   The previous exercise suggests properties that are true for all real numbers. Each of these properties is stated as a <u>postulate</u>. A **postulate** is a basic statement that is accepted as true.

Postulate	Name
For all real numbers x and y, there is one and only one real number $x \cdot y$, and one and only one real number $x \cdot y$.	Closure postulate for addition Closure postulate for multiplication
$x + y = y + x$	Commutative postulate for addition
$x \cdot y = y \cdot x$	Commutative postulate for multiplication
$(x + y) + z = x + (y + z)$	Associative postulate for addition
$(x \cdot y) \cdot z = x \cdot (y \cdot z)$	Associative postulate for multiplication

Name the postulate that justifies each statement.

a. $2 \cdot (5 \cdot 9) = (2 \cdot 5) \cdot 9$

b. $\frac{1}{2}xy = \frac{1}{2}yx$

c. $\left(\dfrac{1}{3} + \dfrac{1}{4}\right) + \dfrac{1}{6} = \dfrac{1}{3} + \left(\dfrac{1}{4} + \dfrac{1}{6}\right)$

d. $2\sqrt{2} + \sqrt{3} = \sqrt{3} + 2\sqrt{2}$

e. $4\sqrt{5} + 2\sqrt{5}$ names one and only one real number, $6\sqrt{5}$.

R-10 Write *True* or *False* to describe each of the following.

a. $3(4 + 5) = 3 \cdot 4 + 3 \cdot 5$

b. $\pi + 0 = \pi$

c. $2 \cdot 1 = 2$

d. $\frac{1}{5} + (-\frac{1}{5}) = 0$

e. $4 \cdot \frac{1}{4} = 1$

R-11 The previous exercise suggests other postulates that are true for all real numbers x, y, and z.

Postulate	Name
$x(y + z) = xy + xz$	Distributive postulate
$x + 0 = x$	Additive identity postulate
$x \cdot 1 = x$	Multiplicative identity postulate
There exists one and only one real number, $-x$, such that $x + -x = 0$.	Additive inverse postulate
There exists one and only one real number, $\frac{1}{x}$, $x \neq 0$, such that $x \cdot \frac{1}{x} = 1$.	Multiplicative inverse postulate

Name the postulate that justifies each statement.

a. $3(x + 4) = 3x + 12$

b. $\frac{1}{2}\left(\frac{1}{8} + \left(-\frac{1}{8}\right)\right) = \frac{1}{2} \cdot 0$

c. $(x + y) \cdot 1 = x + y$

d. $6a + 0 = 6a$

e. $7 \cdot \frac{1}{7} = 1$

f. $\pi + (-\pi) = 0$

R-12 Name the postulate that justifies each statement.

a. $c + (-c) = 0$

b. $a(b + c) = ab + ac$

c. $5xy = 5yx$

d. $2x + (3x + 4y) = (2x + 3x) + 4y$

e. $a \cdot \frac{1}{a} = 1 \ (a \neq 0)$

f. $\frac{1}{2} \cdot 1 = \frac{1}{2}$

Mastery Test 1: Real Numbers

For Exercises 1–6, match each set with a set described in a–f.

1. Natural numbers, N

2. Whole numbers, W

3. Integers, $\mathscr{I}$

4. Rational numbers, Q

5. Irrational numbers, Ir

6. Real numbers, R

a. $\{\cdots -3, -2, -1, 0, 1, 2, 3, \cdots\}$

b. The set of rational numbers together with the set of irrational numbers

c. The set of numbers that can be written as the ratio of two integers, $\frac{a}{b}$, where $b \neq 0$

d. $\{1, 2, 3, 4, \cdots\}$

e. $\{0, 1, 2, 3, \cdots\}$

f. The set of real numbers that cannot be written as the ratio of two integers, $\frac{a}{b}$, where $b \neq 0$

Graph each set. Unless indicated otherwise, the replacement set is the set of real numbers.

7. $\{x: x > 1\}$

8. $\{n: -1 \leq n < 4\}$

9. $\{a: |a| = 3, \text{ where } a \text{ is an integer}\}$

10. The set of odd natural numbers between 4 and 10.

11. $\{x: -3 \leq x \leq 2, \text{ where } x \text{ is an integer}\}$

12. $\{n: -3 < n < 4\}$

Name the postulate that justifies each statement, where x, y, and z are real numbers.

13. $7 + 5 = 5 + 7$

14. $8(-3) = (-3)8$

15. $4 + 0 = 4$

16. $\frac{1}{2} \cdot 1 = \frac{1}{2}$

17. $(3+5) + 1 = 3 + (5+1)$

18. $(xy)z = x(yz)$

19. $\frac{3}{4} \cdot \frac{4}{3} = 1$

20. $-5(x-y) = -5x + 5y$

21. $2 \cdot 7 + (-2 \cdot 7) = 0$

22. $6 \cdot 9$ is one and only one real number.

Diagnostic Test 2: Operations, Equations, and Inequalities

R-1
R-2
R-3
R-4

1. Find the sum that is incorrect.

    a. $4 + 7 = 11$ **b.** $-9 + 3 = -12$
    c. $-7 + -3 = -10$ **d.** $-6 + 6 = 0$

R-5

2. Find the subtraction problem that is incorrectly rewritten.

    a. $8 - 2 = 8 + (-2)$ **b.** $7 - (-3) = 7 + 3$
    c. $-9 - 6 = -9 + (-6)$ **d.** $-5 - 4 = -5 + 4$

R-5
R-6

3. Find the incorrect sentence.

    a. $-5 - 9 = -14$ **b.** $8 - (-2) + 3 = 13$
    c. $-3 - (-2) = 1$ **d.** $-7 + (-5) - 6 = -18$

R-7
R-8

4. Find the product that is incorrect.

    a. $(-4)(-6) = 24$ **b.** $(-3)(7) = -21$
    c. $(8)(-2) = -16$ **d.** $(-5)(1) = 5$

R-9

5. Find the quotient that is incorrect.

    a. $\dfrac{8}{-2} = -4$ **b.** $\dfrac{-9}{-3} = -3$ **c.** $\dfrac{10}{5} = 2$ **d.** $\dfrac{1}{2} \div \dfrac{1}{8} = 4$

R-10
R-12
.
.
.
R-17
R-11

6. Find the pairs of sentences that are <u>not</u> equivalent. The replacement set is the set of real numbers.

    a. $6n = 18;\ \frac{1}{6}(6n) = \frac{1}{6}(18)$ **b.** $x - 7 = 3;\ x - 7 + 7 = 3 + 7$
    c. $\frac{1}{5}n = -1;\ 5(\frac{1}{5}n) = 5 + (-1)$ **d.** $a + 2 = 9;\ a + 2 - 2 = 9 - 2$

7. Tell which restrictions on replacements for x are correct.

    a. $\dfrac{3x^2}{x - 2},\ x \neq 2$ **b.** $\dfrac{3x^2}{x - 2},\ x \neq 0$

    c. $\dfrac{9}{x},\ x \neq 0$ **d.** $\dfrac{5x}{2x + 1},\ x \neq \dfrac{1}{2}$

R-13
R-15
R-16
R-18

8. If the replacement set is the set of real numbers, find the solution set for the equation $3x + 5(x - 2) = 22$.

    a. $\{3\}$ **b.** $\{8\}$ **c.** $\{4\}$ **d.** $\{-4\}$

R-19

9. Solve for w: $p = 2\ell + 2w$

    a. $w = p + 2\ell$ **b.** $w = \dfrac{p + 2\ell}{2}$

    c. $w = \dfrac{p - 2\ell}{2}$ **d.** $w = \dfrac{p}{2} - \ell$

10. If the replacement set is the set of real numbers, find the solution set for the inequality $-3x + 7 < -8$.

a. $x < \frac{5}{3}$　　　　**b.** $x > \frac{5}{3}$　　　　**c.** $x < 5$　　　　**d.** $x > 5$

11. Tell which sets are graphed incorrectly. The replacement set is the set of real numbers.

a. $\{x: x = 3\}$

b. $\{n: n \geq 3\}$

c. $\{a: 3 < a < 5\}$

d. $\{n: |n| = 4\}$

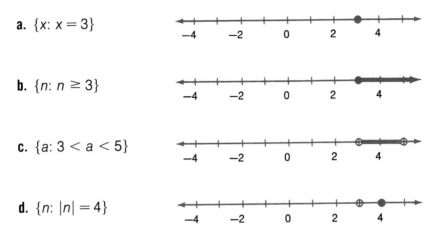

Review Unit 2: Operations, Equations, and Inequalities

Add.

a. $-6\frac{3}{4} + (-3\frac{1}{4})$　　　　**b.** $8 + (-3)$

c. $-9.9 + 3.4$　　　　**d.** $4 + (-4)$

Absolute value notation can be used to state the general rules for adding positive and negative real numbers.

$$\text{If } x \geq 0 \text{ and } y \geq 0, \text{ then } x + y = |x| + |y|.$$

Example: $5 + 3 = 8$

$$\text{If } x < 0 \text{ and } y < 0, \text{ then } x + y = -(|x| + |y|).$$

Example: $-5 + (-3) = -(|-5| + |-3|) = -8$

Add.

a. $3 + 8$　　　　**b.** $-\frac{3}{8} + (-\frac{1}{8})$

c. $7 + 26$　　　　**d.** $(-6.3) + (-8.9)$

R-3 To add a positive number and a negative number, use subtraction of positive numbers.

If $x > 0$ and $y < 0$ and $|x| \geq |y|$, then $x + y = |x| - |y|$.

Example: $2\frac{1}{3} + \left(-\frac{2}{3}\right) = \left|2\frac{1}{3}\right| - \left|-\frac{2}{3}\right| = 1\frac{2}{3}$

If $x > 0$ and $y < 0$ and $|y| \geq |x|$, then $x + y = -(|y| - |x|)$.

Example: $1.6 + (-5) = -(|-5| - |1.6|) = -3.4$

Add.

a. $9 + (-2)$ 　　　　　　　　　**b.** $8 + (-13)$

c. $-\dfrac{5}{8} + \dfrac{7}{8}$ 　　　　　　　**d.** $-77.1 + 4.3$

R-4 To find the sum of two or more negative numbers or of two or more positive numbers, first find the sum of all the positive numbers, and then find the sum of all the negative numbers. Then add these sums.

Example: $-4 + 8 + (-3) + 2 = -4 + (-3) + 8 + 2$

$$= -7 + 10$$

$$= 3$$

Add.

a. $-6 + 9 + (-8)$ 　　　　　　　**b.** $7.0 + (-0.3) + (4.5)$

c. $-6\frac{1}{4} + 5\frac{3}{4} - 7\frac{1}{2}$ 　　　　　　**d.** $5 + (-2) + 4 + (-6)$

R-5 Adding the opposite of a number is the same as subtracting the number. To subtract b from a, where a and b are real numbers, add the **opposite,** or **additive inverse,** of b to a.

$$a - b = a + (-b)$$

Examples: $5 - 3 = 5 + (-3)$ 　　　　$7 - (-2) = 7 + 2$

$$= 2 \qquad\qquad\qquad = 9$$

Subtract.

a. $-2 - 8$ 　　　　　　　　**b.** $\dfrac{3}{7} - \left(-\dfrac{2}{7}\right)$

c. $-3.4 - (-8.5)$ 　　　　　　**d.** $0 - (-7)$

R-6   *Perform the indicated operations.*

a. $-2 + (-5) - 3$

b. $3\frac{1}{2} + (-2\frac{1}{2}) - 1\frac{1}{2}$

c. $7.2 - (-1.6) - 1.8$

d. $18.32 - 14.78 - 2.37$

R-7   Study the following examples.

$8 \cdot 4 = 32$ ←—— The product of two positive numbers is positive.

$(-8) \cdot (-4) = +32$ ←—— The product of two negative numbers is positive.

$8 \cdot (-4) = -32$ ←—— The product of a positive number and a negative number is negative.

$(-8) \cdot 4 = -32$ ←—— The product of a negative number and a positive number is negative.

Multiply.

a. $(-8)(-2)$ **b.** $(\frac{3}{4}) \cdot (-\frac{1}{4})$ **c.** $5 \cdot 8$ **d.** $(-7.5) \cdot (3.4)$

R-8   *Replace* __?__ *by* $<, >,$ *or* $=$ *to make a true statement.*

a. If $x > 0$ and $y > 0$, then xy __?__ 0.
b. If $x > 0$ and $y < 0$, then xy __?__ 0.
c. If $x < 0$ and $y > 0$, then xy __?__ 0.
d. If $x < 0$ and $y < 0$, then xy __?__ 0.
e. If $x = 0$ and $y < 0$, then xy __?__ 0.

R-9   To divide two real numbers, multiply by the **multiplicative inverse,** or reciprocal, of the divisor.

Examples: $\dfrac{12}{3} = 4$ $\dfrac{-12}{-3} = 4$ $\dfrac{12}{-3} = -4$ $-12 \div \dfrac{1}{3} = -12 \times 3 = -36$

Divide.

a. $\dfrac{-21}{3}$ **b.** $\dfrac{15}{-3}$ **c.** $\dfrac{-1.8}{-2}$ **d.** $\dfrac{3}{4} \div \dfrac{1}{4}$

R-10   In algebra, you have learned to replace letters with numbers. These letters are called <u>variables</u>. In the **algebraic expression** $5x + 3$, x is a variable. A **variable** is a symbol that can represent any element in a given set. The given set is called the **replacement set** for the variable.

    The value of an expression for a particular number is found by replacing the variable with that number and simplifying.

Examples: When $x = 2$, $5x + 3 = 5(2) + 3$, or 13.
               When $x = -1$, $5x + 3 = 5(-1) + 3$, or -2.

Find the value of each expression when $x = 2$, when $x = 0$, and when $x = -3$.

a. $2x$ **b.** $3x - 4$ **c.** x^2 **d.** $x^2 - 2x$

R-11   Division by zero is <u>undefined</u>. Note the restriction on replacements for x so that the <u>denominator is not zero</u>.

Example: $\dfrac{5x + 3}{x - 4}$ Restriction: $x \neq 4$ Otherwise $x - 4 = 0$ and division by 0 is undefined.

Indicate the restrictions on replacements for x so that the denominator is not zero.

a. $\dfrac{6x + 2}{x}$ **b.** $\dfrac{5x^3}{x - 2}$ **c.** $\dfrac{3x^2 + 2x - 1}{2x + 8}$ **d.** $\dfrac{x^4}{x^2 - 9}$

R-12   A mathematical sentence that uses $=$ is an **equation.** Two equations are **equivalent** if they have the same solution set. The **solution set** of a sentence is the set of numbers that makes the sentence true.

Classify the following pairs of equations as <u>Equivalent</u> or <u>Not Equivalent</u>. The replacement set is the set of real numbers.

a. $2x = 4$; $3x = 6$ **b.** $x + 2 = 10$; $x + 5 = 12$

c. $\dfrac{x}{3} = 27$; $x = 81$ **d.** $2(x + 1) = 8$; $2x + 2 = 8$

R-13   The postulates used in solving equations are given below. The letters a, b, and c represent real numbers.

$a = b$ is equivalent to $a + c = b + c$.   Addition postulate

If $c \neq 0$, $a = b$ is equivalent to $ac = bc$.   Multiplication postulate

Name the postulate that produces the second equation when applied to the first equation.

First Equation	**Second Equation**
a. $x - 4 = 10$	$x - 4 + 4 = 10 + 4$
b. $3n = 15$	$\frac{1}{3}(3n) = \frac{1}{3}(15)$
c. $a + 2 = 7$	$a + 2 + (-2) = 7 + (-2)$
d. $\frac{n}{5} = 6$	$\frac{n}{5} \cdot \frac{5}{1} = 6 \cdot \frac{5}{1}$
e. $\frac{1}{3}w = 9$	$\left(\frac{1}{3}w\right) \cdot 3 = 9 \cdot 3$

R-14 To solve an equation such as $n + 14 = 55$ for n, add the opposite of 14 to both sides of the equation.

Example:
$$n + 14 = 55$$
$$n + 14 + (-14) = 55 + (-14)$$
$$n = 41$$

Check: $41 + 14 \overset{?}{=} 55$
$$55 = 55$$
Solution set: $\{41\}$

Solve each equation. The replacement set is the set of real numbers.

a. $x + 11 = 15$ **b.** $n + 5 = -8$

c. $7 = a + 3$ **d.** $14 + c = -19$

R-15 To solve $y - 3 = 8$, add 3 to both sides of the equation.

Example:
$$y - 3 = 8$$
$$y - 3 + 3 = 8 + 3$$
$$y = 11$$

Check: $11 - 3 \overset{?}{=} 8$
$$8 = 8$$
Solution set: $\{11\}$

Solve. The replacement set is the set of real numbers.

a. $x - 1 = 9$ **b.** $n - 6 = -4$

c. $10 = x - 2$ **d.** $y - 0.2 = 3.7$

R-16 To solve $2x = 3$, multiply both sides of the equation by $\frac{1}{2}$, the reciprocal of 2.

Example: $2x = 3$ **Check:** $2\left(\frac{3}{2}\right) \overset{?}{=} 3$ **Solution set:** $\{3\}$

$$\frac{1}{2}(2x) = \frac{1}{2} \cdot 3$$
$$\frac{6}{2} \overset{?}{=} 3$$

$$x = \frac{3}{2}$$
$$3 = 3$$

Solve. The replacement set is the set of real numbers.

a. $3n = 15$ **b.** $5x = 28$

c. $24 = -6m$ **d.** $1.6x = 4.8$

R-17 To solve $\frac{c}{3} = 7$, multiply both sides of the equation by 3.

Example: $\frac{c}{3} = 7$ **Check:** $\frac{21}{3} \overset{?}{=} 7$ **Solution set:** $\{21\}$

$$\frac{c}{3} \cdot \frac{3}{1} = 7 \cdot \frac{3}{1}$$
$$7 = 7$$

$$c = 21$$

Solve. The replacement set is the set of real numbers.

a. $\dfrac{x}{2} = 9$ **b.** $\dfrac{c}{4} = 16$

c. $\dfrac{n}{8} = 0.6$ **d.** $-17 = \dfrac{y}{-5}$

R-18   To solve an equation such as $2x + 3 = -9$, "undo" the addition first. Then "undo" the multiplication.

Example:

$$2x + 3 = -9$$
$$2x + 3 - 3 = -9 - 3$$
$$2x = -12$$
$$\frac{1}{2} \cdot (2x) = \frac{1}{2}(-12)$$
$$x = -6$$

Check:
$$2(-6) + 3 \overset{?}{=} -9$$
$$-12 + 3 \overset{?}{=} -9$$
$$-9 = -9$$

Solution set: $\{-6\}$

Solve. The replacement set is the set of real numbers.

a. $3n + 4 = 25$ **b.** $-46 = 4c - 13$

c. $10 = \dfrac{x}{6} + 4$ **d.** $\dfrac{a}{-8} - 0.3 = 4.7$

R-19   Formulas in science often involve equations that contain more than one variable. In solving such formulas, express one variable in terms of the other variables.

Example: In the distance formula $d = rt$, d represents the distance, r represents the speed or rate, and t represents the time. Solve for t.

$$d = rt$$
$$\frac{1}{r} \cdot d = \frac{1}{r}(rt)$$
$$\frac{d}{r} = t$$

Check:
$$d \overset{?}{=} r\left(\frac{d}{r}\right)$$
$$d \overset{?}{=} \frac{rd}{r}$$
$$d = d$$

Solution set: $\left\{\dfrac{d}{r}\right\}$

Solve for the indicated variable.

a. $p - a = b$, for p **b.** $A = bh$, for h

c. $\dfrac{x}{a} = b$, for x **d.** $p = 2\ell + 2w$, for w

An **inequality** is a mathematical sentence that uses $<$, $>$, or $\neq$.

When both sides of an inequality are <u>multiplied</u> or <u>divided</u> by a <u>negative</u> <u>number</u>, the <u>direction</u> of the inequality is <u>reversed</u>.

$$-3 < 6$$
$$(-2)(-3) < (-2)(6)$$
$$6 < -12 \quad \text{False}$$
$$6 > -12 \quad \text{True} \leftarrow \text{Reversing the direction of the inequality}$$
will give a true statement.

Examples

$n + 3 > 2$	$-3n < 9$	$\dfrac{x}{-2} > 5$
$n + 3 - 3 > 2 - 3$	$\dfrac{-3n}{-3} > \dfrac{9}{-3}$	$\dfrac{x}{-2}(-2) < 5(-2)$
$n > -1$	$n > -3$	$x < -10$

Solve. The replacement set is the set of real numbers.

a. $n + 5 > 4$ **b.** $x - 4 < -7$

c. $-2n > 8$ **d.** $\dfrac{x}{-3} > 2$

To **graph an inequality** means to graph its solution set.

Example: Solve and graph: $-2x + 3 > 5$

$$-2x + 3 > 5$$
$$-2x + 3 - 3 > 5 - 3$$
$$-2x > 2 \quad \longleftarrow \quad \text{Divide by } -2. \text{ Reverse the inequality.}$$
$$x < -1$$

Solution set: $\{x: x < -1\}$

Solve and graph each inequality.

a. $2n > -4$ **b.** $-4n < -8$

c. $\dfrac{-x}{3} > 1$ **d.** $3a - 1 < 2$

Mastery Test 2: Operations, Equations, and Inequalities

Add.

1. $3 + 6$

2. $11 + (-5)$

3. $7 + (-7)$

4. $-\dfrac{1}{2} + \left(-\dfrac{1}{2}\right)$

5. $\dfrac{7}{3} + \left(-\dfrac{1}{3}\right)$

6. $-8 + (-8)$

7. $3.6 + (-1.5)$

8. $-\dfrac{7}{2} + (-5\tfrac{1}{2})$

9. $37 + (-10) + (-7)$

Subtract.

10. $2 - 9$

11. $8 - (-3)$

12. $4 - (-4)$

13. $-7 - (-5)$

14. $2.6 - (-0.4)$

15. $(-0.12) - (-0.74)$

16. $-2.38 - 0.46$

17. $5\tfrac{1}{4} - 12\tfrac{3}{4}$

18. $0 - (0.32)$

Multiply.

19. $(4)(-8)$

20. $(-3)(-5)$

21. $(-7)(2)$

22. $\left(\dfrac{1}{2}\right)\left(\dfrac{3}{4}\right)$

23. $(5)(0)$

24. $(-4)(3)(-1)$

Divide.

25. $\dfrac{30}{6}$

26. $\dfrac{-24}{3}$

27. $\dfrac{42}{-7}$

28. $\dfrac{-6}{-6}$

29. $\dfrac{0}{-4}$

30. $68 \div (-17)$

31. $15 \div \left(\dfrac{1}{3}\right)$

32. $\left(\dfrac{1}{6}\right) \div \left(-\dfrac{3}{4}\right)$

33. $(-1.44) \div (-1.2)$

Complete the table by finding the value of $2x - 5$ for the given values of x.

34.

When x is	−4	−3	−1	0	2	4	7
2x − 5 is	−13	−11	?	?	?	?	?

35. Give the restriction on replacements for x to exclude division by zero in the expression $\dfrac{5x + 3}{2x - 9}$.

36. Tell what must be done to each side of the first equation to produce the second equation in each pair.

    a. $x + 2 = 8$; $x = 8 + (-2)$

    b. $y - 5 = 7$; $y = 7 + 5$

    c. $\frac{1}{2}a = 6$; $a = 2(6)$

    d. $6x = 48$; $x = \frac{1}{6}(48)$

Solve. The replacement set is the set of real numbers.

37. $n + 18 = 42$ **38.** $y - 15 = -36$

39. $13a = 39$ **40.** $\frac{1}{2}x = -4$

41. $6x - 10 = 2$ **42.** $\frac{2}{5}a + 3 = -12$

43. $c^2 = a^2 + b^2$, for a^2 **44.** $p = 2\ell + 2w$, for ℓ

45. $x - 7 > 2$ **46.** $n + 13 < -4$

47. $-2a > 10$ **48.** $4y < 12$

*Match each inequality in Exercises **49–52** with its corresponding graph in **a–d**. The replacement set is the set of real numbers.*

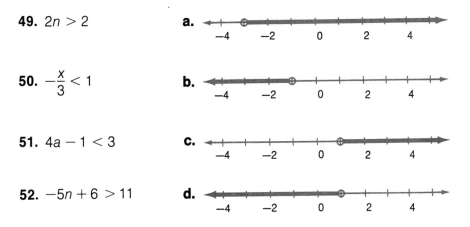

49. $2n > 2$ **a.**

50. $-\frac{x}{3} < 1$ **b.**

51. $4a - 1 < 3$ **c.**

52. $-5n + 6 > 11$ **d.**

Diagnostic Test 3: Exponents and Polynomial Expressions

R-1
R-4
R-6

1. One statement about the monomial x^3 is incorrect. Find that statement.

    a. x is the base.

    c. 3 is the exponent.

    c. The coefficient is 1 and the degree is 3.

    d. x^3 is equivalent to $3x$.

R-2

2. Tell which expression can be simplified directly by adding exponents.

    a. $x^2 \cdot x^3$ **b.** $\dfrac{x^6}{x^3}$ **c.** $(x^2)^3$ **d.** $x^3 - 2x^3$

R-2

3. Tell which expression can be simplified directly by subtracting exponents.

    a. $x^2 \cdot x^5$ **b.** $(x^4)^3$ **c.** $(3x^2)^3$ **d.** $\dfrac{x^8}{x^5}$

R-2

4. Tell which expression can be simplified directly by multiplying exponents.

    a. $x^4 \cdot x^3$ **b.** $(x^2)^3$ **c.** $(2x^3)(3x^4)$ **d.** $(x)^0 \cdot (x)^6$

R-2
R-3

5. Tell which statement is *false* where $x \neq 0$.

    a. $x^3 \cdot x^5 = x^8$ **b.** $x^0 = 1$ **c.** $(2x^2)^3 = 2x^6$ **d.** $\dfrac{x^{10}}{x^2} = x^8$

R-5
R-6
R-7

6. Find the sum of $5x^2 - 8y + 9$ and $-2x^2 + 4y - 3$.

    a. $7x^2 - 4y + 6$ **b.** $3x^2 - 4y + 6$

    c. $3x^2 - 12y + 6$ **d.** $7x^2 - 12y + 12$

R-5
R-6
R-7

7. Subtract: $6x^3 + 8y^2 - 2 - (4x^3 - 5y^2 + 6)$

    a. $2x^3 + 13y^2 - 8$ **b.** $-2x^3 - 13y^2 + 8$

    c. $-2x^3 + 13y^2 + 8$ **d.** $2x^3 - 13y^2 + 8$

R-8
R-9

8. Find the product that is incorrect.

    a. $(4x^3)(-3x^5) = -12x^8$ **b.** $(2a^2b)(3a^3b^2) = 6a^5b^3$

    c. $(2y)(3x)^2 = 6x^2y$ **d.** $2n^2(5n^3 + 3) = 10n^5 + 6n^2$

R-10
R-11

9. Find the product that is incorrect.

    a. $(x + 3)(x + 7) = x^2 + 10x + 21$

    b. $(2a - 1)(a + 2) = 2a^2 + 3a - 2$

    c. $(x - 3y)^2 = x^2 - 6y + 9y^2$

    d. $(3n + 4)^2 = 9n^2 + 12n + 16$

10. Find the quotient that is incorrect.

a. $\dfrac{14x^6y^4}{7x^2y} = 2x^4y^3$

b. $\dfrac{10a^3b^4}{20a^5b^2} = \dfrac{2b^2}{a^2}$

c. $\dfrac{9y^3 - 6y^2 + 15y}{3y} = 3y^2 - 2y + 5$

d. $\dfrac{x^2 + 6x + 8}{x + 2} = x + 4$

Review Unit 3: Exponents and Polynomial Expressions

In $x^3 \cdot x^2 = x^5$, x is the **base** in each of the exponential expressions, and 3, 2, and 5 are **exponents**. A positive integral exponent indicates the number of times the base is taken as a factor.

Example: $x^3 \cdot x^2 = x^5$

$$(x \cdot x \cdot x) \cdot (x \cdot x) = x \cdot x \cdot x \cdot x \cdot x$$

In x^2y, what is the exponent of x? of y? How is x^2 read? x^3?

Each of the following theorems is true for all real numbers x, and for the positive integers m and n.

i. $x^m \cdot x^n = x^{m+n}$ **iv.** $(x^m)^n = x^{mn}$

ii. $\dfrac{x^m}{x^n} = x^{m-n}$, $x \neq 0$ and $m > n$ **v.** $(xy)^n = x^ny^n$

iii. $\dfrac{x^m}{x^n} = \dfrac{1}{x^{n-m}}$, $x \neq 0$ and $n > m$ **vi.** $x^0 = 1$, $x \neq 0$

Examples: $x^5 \cdot x^3 = x^8$ $(x^3)^2 = (x^{3 \cdot 2}) = x^6$

$\dfrac{x^8}{x^3} = x^{8-3} = x^5$ $(mn)^4 = m^4n^4$

$\dfrac{x^2}{x^6} = \dfrac{1}{x^{6-2}} = \dfrac{1}{x^4}$ $6^0 = 1$

Use the exponent theorems to simplify each expression.

a. $x^5 \cdot x^3$ **b.** $\dfrac{x^8}{x^3}$ **c.** $\dfrac{x^2}{x^7}$ **d.** $(3x^2)^3$

R-3   *Simplify.*

a. $3^3 \cdot 3^7$ **b.** $\dfrac{5^6}{5^2}$ **c.** $(2^5)^3$ **d.** $(2+3)^0$

R-4   A **monomial** is an algebraic expression of the form ax^n, where a, the coefficient, is a real number and n, the degree, is a nonnegative integer.

Monomial	Coefficient	Degree
$2x^3$	2	3
$-3x^2$	-3	2
4	4	0

Indicate the coefficient and degree of each monomial.

a. $5x^4$ **b.** $-3x^6$ **c.** x^2 **d.** 8

R-5   A **polynomial** is an expression formed by adding or subtracting monomials a finite number of times. A monomial is also a polynomial.

Example: 3, $5x^2 - 2x$, and $4x^2 - 3x$ are all polynomials.

Sometimes a polynomial is described by the number of its terms.

Polynomial	Number of Terms	Description
$3x$	1	monomial
$5x^2 - 2x$	2	binomial
$4x^2 - 3x + 1$	3	trinomial

Classify each polynomial as a monomial, a binomial, or a trinomial.

a. $2x^3 - 4x$ **b.** $a + b + c$ **c.** $5m^3$ **d.** 6

R-6   To simplify polynomials, you use the distributive postulate to combine like terms. A monomial is a **term. Like terms,** such as $2x^2$ and $3x^2$, have the same variables with the same exponents.

Example: $2x^2 + 3x^2 = (2+3)x^2 = 5x^2$

The expressions $5x^2$ and $2x^2 + 3x^2$ are equivalent expressions. **Equivalent expressions** are expressions that name the same number for every replacement of the variable for which both expressions are defined.

Simplify each polynomial.

a. $5m^3 + 4m^3$

b. $a^2 + 2b^3 + 4a^2 + 6b^3$

c. $4x^2y - 3xy^2 + xy^2 - x^2y$

d. $-8x + 2y - 3x + 6y$

R-7

To add polynomials, add like terms. To subtract polynomials, write the additive inverse of the polynomial being subtracted. Then add. (To find the additive inverse of a polynomial write the opposite of each of its terms.)

Example: $(5x^2 + 2x) - (4x^2 - 3x + 1) = (5x^2 + 2x) + (-4x^2 + 3x - 1)$
$$= x^2 + 5x - 1$$

Add or subtract as indicated.

a. $(x^2 + 2x + 1) + (3x^2 - 6x + 4)$

b. $(3x^2 - 6x + 4) - (2x^2 + 3x - 7)$

c. $(b^3 - 2b^2 + 6b - 3) - (5b^3 + 4b^2 - b + 1)$

d. $(5x^3 + 2x^2 - 3x + 1) + (6x^3 - 4x^2 + 5x - 3)$

R-8

To multiply a monomial by a monomial, you use the commutative and associative postulates for real numbers.

Example: $(4x^2y)(-3xy^2) = (4)(-3)(x^2 \cdot x)(y \cdot y^2)$
$$= -12x^3y^3$$

Multiply.

a. $(2x^3)(7x)$ **b.** $(-2a^2b)(3ab^2)$ **c.** $(-2b)^2(3b)$ **d.** $(-y)^3(2y)$

R-9

Multiplication of a polynomial by a monomial uses the distributive, commutative, and associative postulates for real numbers.

Example: $2x(5x + 7) = 2x(5x) + 2x(7)$
$$= 10x^2 + 14x$$

Find each product.

a. $3x(6x - 3)$

b. $xy(2x - 3y)$

c. $-4a(7a^2 - 3a + 5)$

d. $2ax(-a^2 + 7ax - 3x^2)$

R-10 Two binomials can be multiplied by using the distributive postulate.

Example: $(a + 5)(a - 2) = (a + 5)a + (a + 5)(-2)$
$$= a^2 + 5a - 2a - 10$$
$$= a^2 + 3a - 10$$

Multiply.

a. $(x + 2)(x + 5)$ **b.** $(x + 3)(x + 1)$

c. $(m + 3)(m - 3)$ **d.** $(2c + 3)(c + 1)$

R-11 When you square a binomial (multiply it by itself), a simple pattern results.

$$(a + b)^2 = (a + b)(a + b) = a^2 + ab + ab + b^2$$
$$= a^2 + 2ab + b^2$$

Examples: $(x + 1)^2 = x^2 + 2x + 1$

$(x - 1)^2 = x^2 - 2x + 1$

Square each binomial.

a. $(a + 2)^2$ **b.** $(b - 3)^2$

c. $(5 - x)^2$ **d.** $(3y - 1)^2$

R-12 To divide a monomial by a monomial, use the division properties of exponents **ii** and **iii** from Exercise **R-2**.

Examples

$$\frac{x^5}{x^2} = x^{5-2} = x^3 \qquad\qquad \frac{n^4}{n^9} = \frac{1}{n^{9-4}} = \frac{1}{n^5}$$

$$\frac{10a^4b^3}{5a^2b} = \frac{10}{5} \cdot \frac{a^4}{a^2} \cdot \frac{b^3}{b} = 2a^3b^2 \qquad \frac{4x^6y^3}{8xy^5} = \frac{4}{8} \cdot \frac{x^6}{x} \cdot \frac{y^3}{y^5} = \frac{x^5}{2y^2}$$

Divide.

a. $\dfrac{y^8}{y^5}$ **b.** $\dfrac{12x^6}{2x^2}$

c. $\dfrac{n^3}{n^8}$ **d.** $\dfrac{24m^5n}{-3mn^4}$

R-13 You can use the distributive property to divide a polynomial by a monomial.

Example: $\dfrac{4n^3 - 12n^2 + 2n}{2n} = \dfrac{4n^3}{2n} - \dfrac{12n^2}{2n} + \dfrac{2n}{2n}$
$$= 2n^2 - 6n + 1$$

Divide.

a. $\dfrac{4x + 20}{4}$

b. $\dfrac{a^2b^3 - ab^2}{ab}$

c. $\dfrac{9x^4 - 12x^3 + 3x^2}{3x}$

d. $\dfrac{8m^3 - 4m^2n - 6m}{2m}$

R-14 Division of polynomials by a polynomial is similar to division of numbers.

Step 1. Divide the highest power of the dividend by the highest power of the divisor. Then multiply and subtract as shown. This leaves a polynomial of lesser degree.

$$
\begin{array}{r}
x \\
x - 2 \, \overline{)\, x^2 + 7x + 8} \\
\underline{x^2 - 2x} \\
9x + 8
\end{array}
$$

$\longleftarrow \quad x^2 \div x = x$

$\longleftarrow \quad x(x - 2)$

Step 2. Divide the highest power of this polynomial by the highest power in the divisor. Then multiply and subtract as shown. Continue until the remainder is a number.

$$
\begin{array}{r}
x + 9 \\
x - 2 \, \overline{)\, x^2 + 7x + 8} \\
\underline{x^2 - 2x} \\
9x + 8 \\
\underline{9x - 18} \\
26
\end{array}
$$

$\longleftarrow \quad 9x \div x = 9$

$\longleftarrow \quad 9(x - 2)$

$\longleftarrow \quad$ Remainder

Check: Dividend = (Divisor × Quotient) + Remainder

$$x^2 + 7x + 8 = (x - 2)(x + 9) + 26$$
$$= x^2 + 7x - 18 + 26$$
$$= x^2 + 7x + 8$$

Divide.

a. $(x^2 + 7x + 12) \div (x + 3)$

b. $(3a^2 + 5a - 8) \div (a + 1)$

c. $(x^2 - 5x - 14) \div (x - 7)$

d. $(2y^2 - 3y + 10) \div (y - 2)$

Mastery Test 3: Exponents and Polynomial Expressions

Simplify.

1. $x^3 \cdot x^6$ **2.** $a^2 \cdot a^5$ **3.** $\dfrac{n^7}{n^4}$ **4.** $\dfrac{y^2}{y^6}$

5. $x^2 \cdot x \cdot x^7$ **6.** $(x^5)^3$ **7.** $(2x^3)^2$ **8.** $(-3a^2)^3$

9. $(2x^2y)^4$ **10.** $4m^0$ **11.** $2^8 \div 2^5$ **12.** $(3^4)^3$

13. $4^3 \div 4^9$ **14.** $(2^3)^0$ **15.** $12y + 5y$ **16.** $-18x + 6y + 24x$

Give the coefficient and degree of each monomial.

17. $3x^4$ **18.** $-x^5$

Classify each polynomial as a monomial, a binomial, or a trinomial.

19. $2x^2 + 7x + 6$ **20.** $3mn$ **21.** 5 **22.** $18 + a^3$

Add or subtract as indicated.

23. $(3x + 2) + (4x + 7)$ **24.** $7a - 3 - (2a + 5)$

25. $(3x^2 - 5x + 9) + (-4x^2 + 8x - 2)$

26. $(5y^2 - 2y + 3) - (2y^2 + 5y + 6)$

Multiply.

27. $(5x^3)(-2x^4)$ **28.** $(2y)^3(-3y)^2$

29. $(-2xy)^3(xy)$ **30.** $3x(x - 5)$

31. $4y^2(y^3 - 3y + 4)$ **32.** $(x + 3)(x + 2)$

33. $(n - 2)(n + 7)$ **34.** $(y + 8)(y - 8)$

35. $(2a + 3)(a + 4)$ **36.** $(x - 2)(3x + 5)$

37. $(n + 4)^2$ **38.** $(y - 2)^2$

39. $(2m + 1)^2$ **40.** $(3a - 2)^2$

Divide.

41. $\dfrac{8x^{10}}{2x^4}$ **42.** $\dfrac{-24n^3}{3n^9}$ **43.** $\dfrac{6a^4b^3}{18ab^2}$ **44.** $\dfrac{15x^7y^3}{-3x^2y^4}$

45. $\dfrac{2x - 14}{2}$ **46.** $\dfrac{4m^3 - 8m^2 + 12m}{4m}$

47. $(x^2 + 7x + 10) \div (x + 2)$ **48.** $(2y^2 - 5y - 1) \div (y - 3)$

Diagnostic Test 4: Factoring

R-1
1. Tell which of the following shows the correct way of renaming 15 by factoring.
   a. $10 + 5$ **b.** $3 \cdot 5$
   c. $18 - 3$ **d.** $30 \div 2$

R-1
R-2
2. Tell which of the following is the prime factorization of 24.
   a. $4 \cdot 6$ **b.** $2 \cdot 12$
   c. $2 \cdot 2 \cdot 6$ **d.** $2 \cdot 2 \cdot 2 \cdot 3$

R-1
R-2
R-6
3. Factor completely: $6x^2 - 9x$
   a. $x(6x - 9)$ **b.** $3(2x^2 - 3x)$
   c. $3x(2x - 3)$ **d.** $(3x - 3)(2x + 3)$

R-2
R-3
R-6
4. Factor completely: $(x + 4)d + (x + 4)e$
   a. $(x + d)(x + e)$ **b.** $(x + e)(d + 4)$
   c. $(x + 4)(d + e)$ **d.** $(x + 4)d + e$

R-2
R-4
R-6
5. Factor completely: $ax + by + ay + bx$
   a. $a(x + y) + b(y + x)$ **b.** $(x + a)(y + b)$
   c. $(x + y)(a + b)$ **d.** $(x + b)(y + a)$

R-5
R-6
6. Factor completely: $x^2 - 36$
   a. $(x - 6)(x - 6)$ **b.** $(x + 6)(x - 6)$
   c. $(x + 6)(x + 6)$ **c.** $(x - 9)(x + 4)$

R-6
7. Factor completely: $6a^2 - 6b^2$
   a. $6(a + b)(a - b)$ **b.** $6(a - b)(a - b)$
   c. $(3a + 2b)(2a - 3b)$ **d.** $(6a - b)(a + 6b)$

R-6
R-7
8. Factor completely: $n^2 - 5n + 6$
   a. $(n + 3)(n - 2)$ **b.** $(n - 3)(n + 2)$
   c. $(n + 3)(n + 2)$ **d.** $(n - 3)(n - 2)$

9. Factor completely: $2x^2 + x - 6$

    a. $(2x + 3)(x - 2)$ **b.** $(2x - 3)(x + 2)$

    c. $(2x - 3)(x - 2)$ **d.** $(2x + 3)(x + 2)$

10. Factor the perfect square trinomial: $x^2 + 12x + 36$

    a. $(x + 6)^2$ **b.** $(x - 6)^2$

    c. $(x + 6)(x - 6)$ **d.** $(x + 12)(x + 3)$

Review Unit 4: Factoring

To **factor a polynomial,** rename it as the product of two or more polynomials. Since $5x + 5y = 5(x + y)$, 5 and $x + y$ are factors of $5x + 5y$. The first step in factoring a polynomial is to factor out any common factors. The <u>distributive postulate</u> is used to do this.

Example: Factor: $3x + 6y$

Polynomial	Common Monomial Factor	Factored Expression
$3x + 6y$	3	$3(x + 2y)$

Check: Does $3(x + 2y) = 3x + 6y$?   Yes

Factor.

a. $2x + 10y$ **b.** $5c - 30$ **c.** $ab + ac$ **d.** $3x^2 - 9x + 15$

The polynomials above are factored over the integers. To **factor a polynomial over the integers,** <u>each factor</u> of the polynomial <u>must have coefficients that are integers.</u>

Examples: $6x - 21 = 3(2x - 7)$ ⟵   Since 3, 2, and 7 are integers, $6x - 21$ is factored over the integers.

                $4x + 5 = 4(x + \frac{5}{4})$ ⟵   Since $\frac{5}{4}$ is not an integer, $4x + 5$ is <u>not</u> factored over the integers.

When $4x + 5$ is factored over the integers, its only polynomial factor over the integers is 1. A polynomial whose only polynomial factor over the integers is 1, is called a **prime polynomial over the integers.** Hence, $4x + 5$ is a prime polynomial over the integers. In this review, <u>all polynomials will be factored over the integers.</u>

Name the "prime" polynomials.

a. $3x + 3y - 3z$

b. $2c^2 + 6c - 8$

c. $3x^2 - 5x + 7$

d. $24x^2 - 10xy + 15y^2$

R-3 To factor $a(c + 5) - b(c + 5)$, note that $c + 5$ is a **common binomial factor.** Polynomials that have common binomial factors can be factored by the distributive postulate.

Example: $a(c + 5) - b(c + 5) = (c + 5)(a - b)$

Check: $(c + 5)(a - b) = (c + 5)a + (c + 5)(-b)$
$$= a(c + 5) - b(c + 5)$$

Factor each polynomial.

a. $2(a + b) - x(a + b)$

b. $a(4 - b) + c(4 - b)$

c. $m(x + y) - n(x + y)$

d. $x(3a - 2b) + y(3a - 2b)$

R-4 Polynomials with four or more terms are usually factored by rearranging and grouping terms.

Example: $ax + by + bx + ay = (ax + by) + (ay + by)$
$$= x(a + b) + y(a + b)$$
$$= (a + b)(x + y)$$

Factor each polynomial.

a. $cw + dw + ca + da$

b. $ab + 2c + 2b + ac$

c. $5x - 25 + ax - 5a$

d. $a^3 + a - a^2 - 1$

R-5 An expression such as $x^2 - 25$ is called a **difference of squares.** The factoring pattern for a difference of squares is $a^2 - b^2 = (a + b)(a - b)$.

Factor each polynomial. Write _Prime_ if a polynomial cannot be factored.

a. $x^2 - 16$

b. $m^2 - n^2$

c. $4a^2 - b^2$

d. $a^2 + b^2$

R-6 To **factor a polynomial completely** means to factor until all factors are prime.

Example: $2a^2 - 2b^2 = 2(a^2 - b^2)$ ⟵ $a^2 - b^2$ is not prime.
$$= 2(a + b)(a - b)$$ ⟵ Prime factors

Factor each polynomial completely. Write Prime if a polynomial cannot be factored.

a. $5x^2 - 5y^2$ **b.** $4x^2 - 16$ **c.** $y^2 + 1$ **d.** $12c^2 - 27$

R-7   Quadratic trinomials of the form $ax^2 + bx + c$, $a = 1$, are factored as the product of two binomials.

Examples: $x^2 - 5x + 6 = (x \quad)(x \quad)$ ←——— Factor x^2.

$$= (x - 3)(x - 2) \quad \text{←——— Find two factors of 6.}$$

$$2x^2 - 4x - 30 = 2(x^2 - 2x - 15) \quad \text{←——— Factor out the common factor, 2.}$$

$$= 2(x + 3)(x - 5) \quad \text{←——— Then factor as in Example 1.}$$

Factor completely.

a. $x^2 + 7x + 12$ **b.** $2c^2 + 10c + 12$

c. $x^2 - 10x + 21$ **d.** $3n^2 - 9n + 6$

R-8   A similar procedure is used to factor quadratic trinomials of the form $ax^2 + bx + c$, $a \neq 1$. For example, the factorization of $2x^2 + 5x - 12$ is $(2x - 3)(x + 4)$.

$$2x^2 + 5x - 12 = (2x \quad)(x \quad) \quad \text{←——— Factor } 2x^2.$$

$$= (2x - 3)(x + 4) \quad \text{←——— Factor } (-12).$$

The middle term, the sum of the outer and inner products, is found by a trial and error procedure.

Trial	Middle Term
$(2x - 6)(x + 2)$	$-2x$
$(2x - 2)(x + 6)$	$10x$
$(x - 2)(2x + 6)$	$2x$
$(2x + 4)(x - 3)$	$-2x$
$(2x - 3)(x + 4)$	$5x$ ←——— Correct

Example: $6n^2 - 19n + 10 = (3n - 2)(2n - 5)$ ←————— $-4n - 15n = -19n$

Check: $(3n - 2)(2n - 5) = 6n^2 - 15n - 4n + 10$
$$= 6n^2 - 19n + 10$$

Factor completely.

a. $2x^2 + 9x + 4$

b. $6x^2 - 13x + 6$

c. $4n^2 - 11n - 20$

d. $6a^2 - 19a + 3$

R-9 Trinomials such as $x^2 + 6x + 9$ are called perfect square trinomials. A **perfect square trinomial** has 3 characteristics.

1. It has three terms.

2. Its first and last terms are perfect squares.

3. Its second term is twice the product of the square roots of the first and last terms.

Example: $x^2 + 6x + 9$ is a perfect square trinomial since

      1. It has 3 terms.

      2. x^2 and 9 are perfect squares.

      3. $6x = 2(3x)$, twice the product of the square roots of x^2 and 9.

Name the perfect square trinomials.

a. $x^2 + 10x + 25$

b. $c^2 + 8c + 16$

c. $x^2 + 6x + 36$

d. $x^2 - 14x + 49$

R-10 A perfect square trinomial is factored as the <u>square of a binomial.</u>

Examples: $x^2 + 2xy + y^2 = (x + y)(x + y)$
$$= (x + y)^2$$
$$x^2 - 2xy + y^2 = (x - y)(x - y)$$
$$= (x - y)^2$$

Factor each perfect square trinomial.

a. $x^2 + 4x + 4$

b. $x^2 - 4x + 4$

c. $a^2 - 14a + 49$

d. $b^2 + 10b + 25$

Mastery Test 4: Factoring

*Identify the factor pattern, **A–D,** used to factor each polynomial. If the pattern is **A,** give the common factor and indicate whether it is a monomial or a binomial.*

Factoring Pattern	Name
A. $ax + ay = a(x + y)$	Common Factor
B. $x^2 - y^2 = (x + y)(x - y)$	Difference of Squares
C. $x^2 + 2xy + y^2 = (x + y)^2$	Perfect Square Trinomials
D. $x^2 - 2xy + y^2 = (x - y)^2$	

Example: $(n + 2)d + (n + 2)e$

Since $(n+2)d + (n+2)e = (n+2)(d-e)$, the answer is A, $n+2$, binomial.

1. $5x - 30$ **2.** $a^2 - 4$

3. $n^2 - 4n + 4$ **4.** $-3ax + 12\,ay$

5. $m(c+2) - n(c+2)$ **6.** $y^2 + 6y + 9$

Factor completely.

7. $8n - 2$ **8.** $3x^2 + 15x$

9. $6(a + b) - x(a + b)$ **10.** $x(m - n) + y(n - m)$

11. $5y - 10 + xy - 2x$ **12.** $cf + ab + af + bc$

13. $9m^2 - 1$ **14.** $y^2 - 9$

15. $4x^2 - 1$ **16.** $3n^2 - 12$

17. $a^2 + 5a + 6$ **18.** $y^2 - 5y - 24$

19. $2n^2 + 13n + 6$ **20.** $3x^2 - 2x - 8$

Chapter 1
Systems of Numbers

1-1 Real Numbers

The objectives for this section are on page 34.

Some sets of numbers used in mathematics can be represented by a set description.

Natural Numbers $N = \{1, 2, 3, \cdots\}$

Whole Numbers $W = \{0, 1, 2, \cdots\}$

Integers $\mathscr{I} = \{\cdots, -3, -2, -1, 0, 1, 2, 3, \cdots\}$

The set of integers is the <u>union</u>, symbolized by $\cup$, of W with the **additive inverses,** or **opposites,** of the natural numbers.

$$\mathscr{I} = W \cup \{\cdots, -3, -2, -1\}$$

<u>Set builder notation</u> is used to describe the set of rational numbers because there is no way to list them.

Rational Numbers $Q = \{x: x = \dfrac{a}{b}, a \in \mathscr{I}, b \in N\}$

The set-builder notation above is read, "The set of rational numbers is the set of numbers, x, such that $x = \dfrac{a}{b}$, where a is an element of the set of integers and b is an element of the set of natural numbers." The symbol, $\in$, means "is an element of."

Every rational number can also be expressed either as a <u>terminating decimal</u> or as a <u>nonterminating, repeating decimal</u>.

Example 1

Determine whether $\dfrac{1}{16}$ is a terminating decimal or a nonterminating, repeating decimal.

$$\begin{array}{r} .0625 \\ 16\overline{)1.0000} \end{array} \quad \longleftarrow \quad \frac{1}{16} = 16\overline{)1.0000}$$

Thus, $\dfrac{1}{16}$ is a terminating decimal.

Example 2 Determine whether $\frac{2}{11}$ is a terminating, or a nonterminating, decimal.

$$\begin{array}{r} .181818\cdots \\ 11\overline{)2.000000\cdots} \end{array} \qquad\longleftarrow\qquad \frac{2}{11}=11\overline{)2.000000}$$

Thus, $\frac{2}{11}$ is a nonterminating, repeating decimal.

The decimal .181818 $\cdots$ may also be written $.\overline{18}$. The bar indicates the repeating digits.

A number that cannot be written as the ratio of an integer and a natural number is an **irrational number.** Further, irrational numbers cannot be represented as terminating, or as nonterminating, repeating decimals.

$$\sqrt{2} \qquad \pi \qquad -\sqrt{7} \qquad \sqrt{50} \qquad -\sqrt{19}$$

The union of the set of rational numbers with the set of irrational numbers is R, the set of **real numbers.**

$$R = Q \cup Ir$$

The relationships between the set of real numbers, R, and its subsets are shown.

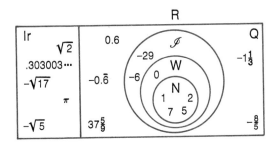

N: Natural numbers
W: Whole numbers
$\mathscr{I}$: Integers
Q: Rational numbers
Ir: Irrational numbers
R: Real numbers

For example, N is a **subset** of W, or

$$N \subset W \qquad\longleftarrow\qquad \text{Read: ``N is a subset of W.''}$$

because every element of N is also in W.

The basic *postulates for the addition and multiplication of real numbers* are reviewed below. The complete set of these postulates is found on page 560.

Real Number Postulate	Operations	
	Addition	**Multiplication**
Closure	$a + b$ is a real number.	ab is a real number.
Commutative	$a + b = b + a$	$ab = ba$
Associative	$a + (b + c) = (a + b) + c$	$a(bc) = (ab)c$
Identity	$a + 0 = a$	$a \cdot 1 = a$
Inverse	$a + (-a) = 0$	$a \cdot \dfrac{1}{a} = 1,\ a \neq 0$
Distributive	$a(b + c) = ab + ac$ or $(b + c)a = ba + ca$	

Try These Classify each sentence as *True (T)* or *False (F)*.

1. $\sqrt{3} \in R$ T

2. $\sqrt{3} \in N$ F

3. $\sqrt{3} \in \mathscr{I}$ F

4. $\sqrt{3} \in W$ F

5. $-\dfrac{2}{3} \in Q$ T

6. $-\dfrac{2}{3} \in Ir$ F

7. $0 \in N$ F

8. $0 \in Q$ T

Exercises

Use the $\in$ symbol to write true sentences that show each set to which the given number belongs.

Example: 5   **Answer:** $5 \in N, W, \mathscr{I}, Q, R$

1. 0 $0 \in W, I, Q, R$

2. -23 $-23 \in I, Q, R$

3. $\dfrac{1}{2}$ $\frac{1}{2} \in Q, R$

4. $\sqrt{5}$ $\sqrt{5} \in Ir, R$

5. $\sqrt{25}$ $\sqrt{25} \in N, W, I, Q, R$

6. $-\dfrac{2}{3}$ $-\frac{2}{3} \in Q, R$

7. $\sqrt{2}$ $\sqrt{2} \in Ir, R$

8. 0.85 $.85 \in Q, R$

The symbol $\not\subset$ means "is not a subset of." Replace each __?__ with $\subset$ or $\not\subset$ to make true sentences.

9. W __?__ N $\not\subset$

10. N __?__ W $\subset$

11. $\mathscr{I}$ __?__ R $\subset$

12. R __?__ $\mathscr{I}$ $\not\subset$

13. Ir __?__ Q $\not\subset$

14. Q __?__ Ir $\not\subset$

15. W __?__ Ir $\not\subset$

16. R __?__ W $\not\subset$

Determine whether each rational number is a terminating, or a nonterminating, repeating decimal.

17. $\frac{1}{5}$ Terminating

18. $-\frac{1}{6}$ Nonterminating

19. $\frac{2}{7}$ Nonterminating

20. $\frac{1}{11}$ Nonterminating

21. $\frac{7}{8}$ Terminating

22. $\frac{1}{9}$ Nonterminating

23. $-\frac{5}{3}$ Nonterminating

24. $1\frac{1}{13}$ Nonterminating

Tell whether each statement is True or False.

25. $N \cup \{0\} = W$ T

26. $Ir \cup Q = R$ T

27. $R = R \cup Ir$ T

28. $Ir = W \cup \mathscr{I}$ F

29. $W \cup N = \mathscr{I}$ F

30. $W \cup N = N$ F

31. $Q = \mathscr{I} \cup N$ F

32. $R = Ir \cup \mathscr{I}$ F

Tell which postulate for real numbers is illustrated by each exercise.

33. $-0.07 + 0.07 = 0$ Inverse, Addition

34. $\left(-\frac{5}{9}\right)\left(-\frac{6}{7}\right) = \left(-\frac{6}{7}\right)\left(-\frac{5}{9}\right)$ Commutative, Multiplication

35. $50(2 + \sqrt{3}) = 50 \cdot 2 + 50 \cdot \sqrt{3}$ Dist., Mult. over Add.

36. $50 \cdot (2 + \sqrt{3}) = (2 + \sqrt{3}) \cdot 50$ Commutative, Multiplication

37. $\frac{1}{\pi} \cdot 1 = \frac{1}{\pi}$ Identity, Multiplication

38. $5 + (15 + 65) = (5 + 15) + 65$ Associative, Addition

39. $\frac{7}{6} \cdot \left(\frac{2}{3} \cdot \frac{9}{16}\right) = \left(\frac{7}{6} \cdot \frac{2}{3}\right) \cdot \frac{9}{16}$ Associative, Multiplication

40. $-\sqrt{2} + 0 = -\sqrt{2}$ Ident., Addition

41. $\sqrt{5} \cdot \frac{1}{\sqrt{5}} = 1$ Inverse, Multiplication

42. $3 + \sqrt{5}$ is a real number. Closure, Addition

Write CA if the given set is closed under addition; write CM if it is closed under multiplication.

43. $\{-1, 0, 1\}$ CM

44. W CA, CM

45. Q CA, CM

46. Ir Neither

PUZZLE ────────────────────────────

Each of six sections of chain has four links.

What is the minimum cost of joining the six pieces into one chain
if the cost of cutting open one link is \$.50 and of welding it together is \$1.00? Cut open the four links of one section to weld together the remaining five sections. The cost is \$6.00.

1-2 Radicals and Variables

The objective for this section is on page 34.

Every positive real number has two square roots.
The square root of n is $\sqrt{n}$, and $\sqrt{n}$ is the principal square root of n. Thus,

$$\sqrt{25} = 5 \qquad -\sqrt{25} = -5 \longleftarrow \quad \text{These two statements can be combined thus: } \pm\sqrt{25} = \pm 5$$

The symbol $\sqrt{}$ is a radical sign; $\sqrt{25}$ is a **radical,** and 25 is the **radicand.**

Definition: If n is a real number and $a^2 = n$, then
$$a = \sqrt{n} \text{ or } a = -\sqrt{n}.$$

Square roots are irrational except when the radicand is a perfect square. A **perfect square** is the square of an integer. Thus,

$$\sqrt{2} \in \text{Ir since 2 is not a perfect square.}$$
$$\sqrt{3} \in \text{Ir since 3 is not a perfect square.}$$
$$\sqrt{4} \in \text{Q since 4 is a perfect square.}$$

In the sentence $\qquad x^2 = 25$

the letter x is a variable. A **variable** is a symbol that represents any element of a specified **replacement set.** Sentences with variables are **open sentences.** They may be true for all, some, or no replacements of the variables.

Open Sentence	Variable	Replacement Set	Solution
$x = x + 1$	x	R	No real number
$y = 2y$	y	R	$y = 0$
$t + t = 2t$	t	R	All real numbers
$\sqrt{25x^2} = 5x$	x	W	All whole numbers

Unless otherwise stated, variables represent real numbers.

The following sentence is not true for all numbers.

$$\sqrt{25x^2} = 5x$$

Example 1   Determine whether $\sqrt{25x^2} = 5x$ when $x = -2$.

$$
\begin{array}{c|c}
\sqrt{25x^2} \overset{?}{=} 5x & \\
\sqrt{25(-2)^2} & 5(-2) \\
\sqrt{25 \cdot 4} & -10 \\
\sqrt{100} & \\
10 &
\end{array}
$$

Thus, $\sqrt{25x^2} = 5x$ is not true for $x = -2$. Further, it is not true for $x < 0$.

To simplify $\sqrt{25x^2}$ and to emphasize that it is nonnegative, absolute value notation is used.

Definition: The **absolute value of x,** written $|x|$, is x if x is nonnegative and $-x$ if x is negative. That is,

$$|x| = \begin{cases} x, & \text{if } x \geq 0. \\ -x, & \text{if } x < 0. \end{cases}$$

Example 2   Name each of the following without radicals.

a. $\sqrt{25x^2}$ **b.** $\sqrt{16x^4}$ **c.** $\sqrt{x^6}$

a. $\sqrt{25x^2} = |5x|$, or $5|x|$ **b.** $\sqrt{16x^4} = 4|x^2|$, or $4x^2$ **c.** $\sqrt{x^6} = |x^3|$

Note that $\sqrt{16x^4}$ may be written as $4|x^2|$ or as $4x^2$. However, $\sqrt{x^6}$ <u>must</u> be written as $|x^3|$ and not as x^3 because $x^3 < 0$ if $x < 0$.

Name each of the following without using a radical sign.

1. $\sqrt{121}$ 11

2. $\sqrt{36x^2}$ $6|x|$

3. $\sqrt{100x^2}$ $10|x|$

4. $\sqrt{25x^{10}}$
            $5|x^5|$

Exercises

1. $1^2 = 1, 2^2 = 4, 3^2 = 9, 4^2 = 16, 5^2 = 25, 6^2 = 36, 7^2 = 49,$
$8^2 = 64, 9^2 = 81, 10^2 = 100;$ so the list is
$1, 4, 9, 16, 25, 36, 49, 64, 81, 100$

a

1. Write a list of the perfect squares from 1 to 100. See above.

Name each expression without using a radical sign.

2. $\sqrt{16}$ 4

3. $-\sqrt{25}$ -5

4. $\sqrt{36}$ 6

5. $\pm\sqrt{64}$ ±8

6. $-\sqrt{100}$ -10

7. $\sqrt{\frac{1}{4}}$ $\frac{1}{2}$

8. $\sqrt{\frac{9}{25}}$ $\frac{3}{5}$

9. $\sqrt{169}$ 13

10. $\pm\sqrt{196}$ ±14

11. $2 \cdot \sqrt{16}$ 8

12. $-4 \cdot \sqrt{36}$ -24

13. $\pm5 \cdot \sqrt{49}$
       ±35

Each number below is irrational. Replace each pair of question marks with a pair of consecutive integers to make a true statement. They will show the two integers closest to the irrational number.

Example: $\underline{\quad?\quad} < \sqrt{20} < \underline{\quad?\quad}$ **Solution:** 20 is between $4 \cdot 4$ and $5 \cdot 5$.
                                      Hence, $4 < \sqrt{20} < 5$.

14. $\underline{\quad?\quad}_3 < \sqrt{12} < \underline{\quad?\quad}_4$

15. $\underline{\quad?\quad}_5 < \sqrt{29} < \underline{\quad?\quad}_6$

16. $\underline{\quad?\quad}_7 < \sqrt{50} < \underline{\quad?\quad}_8$

17. $\underline{\quad?\quad}_8 < \sqrt{79} < \underline{\quad?\quad}_9$

Name each of the following without radicals. No denominator is zero.
                                                 $\frac{a^2}{8x^2|x|}$ ←

18. $\sqrt{x^2}$ $|x|$

19. $\sqrt{y^6}$ $|y^3|$

20. $\sqrt{x^4}$ x^2

21. $-\sqrt{y^{10}}$ $-|y^5|$

22. $\sqrt{4a^2}$ $2|a|$ or $|2a|$

23. $\sqrt{4a^4}$ $2a^2$

24. $\pm\sqrt{25a^4}$ $\pm5a^2$

25. $\sqrt{9b^8}$
         $3b^4$

b

26. $\sqrt{36b^{36}}$ $6b^{18}$

27. $\sqrt{\frac{1}{m^2}}$ $|\frac{1}{m}|$, or $\frac{1}{|m|}$

28. $\sqrt{\frac{36a^2b^4}{49m^6}}$ $\frac{6b^2|a|}{7m^2|m|}$

29. $\sqrt{\frac{a^4}{(2x)^6}}$

30. $\sqrt{\frac{(a+b)^4}{(a-b)^4}}$ $\frac{(a+b)^2}{(a-b)^2}$

31. $\sqrt{4x^{2a}}$ $2|x^a|$

32. $\sqrt{25a^{2x-4}}$ $5|a^{x-2}|$

33. $\sqrt{x^{8b-16}}$
       x^{4b-8}

Remember

Write each number as a perfect square times a natural number.

1. 40 $4 \cdot 10$

2. 72 $4 \cdot 18, 9 \cdot 8, 36 \cdot 2$

3. 200 $100 \cdot 2, 25 \cdot 8, 4 \cdot 50$

4. 32
            $16 \cdot 2, 4 \cdot 8$

The answers are on page 36.

1-3 Multiplication of Radicals

The objective for this section is on page 35.

The following example illustrates Theorem 1-1.

$$\sqrt{25} \cdot \sqrt{4} = 5 \cdot 2 = 10 = \sqrt{100} = \sqrt{25 \cdot 4}$$

Theorem 1-1: Multiplication Theorem for Radicals

For $a \geq 0$ and $b \geq 0$,

$$\sqrt{a} \cdot \sqrt{b} = \sqrt{ab}$$

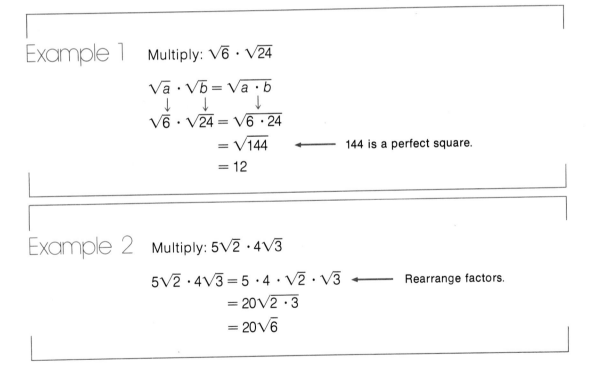

Example 1   Multiply: $\sqrt{6} \cdot \sqrt{24}$

$$\sqrt{a} \cdot \sqrt{b} = \sqrt{a \cdot b}$$
$$\downarrow \qquad \downarrow \qquad \qquad \downarrow$$
$$\sqrt{6} \cdot \sqrt{24} = \sqrt{6 \cdot 24}$$
$$= \sqrt{144} \quad \longleftarrow \quad \text{144 is a perfect square.}$$
$$= 12$$

Example 2   Multiply: $5\sqrt{2} \cdot 4\sqrt{3}$

$$5\sqrt{2} \cdot 4\sqrt{3} = 5 \cdot 4 \cdot \sqrt{2} \cdot \sqrt{3} \quad \longleftarrow \quad \text{Rearrange factors.}$$
$$= 20\sqrt{2 \cdot 3}$$
$$= 20\sqrt{6}$$

The radical $\sqrt{6}$ is expressed in simplest form because 6 is not a perfect square and none of its factors, other than 1, is a perfect square.

Example 3 Simplify $\sqrt{27}$.

$$\sqrt{27} = \sqrt{9 \cdot 3} \quad \longleftarrow \quad \text{Find the largest perfect square factor of 27.}$$
$$= \sqrt{9} \cdot \sqrt{3} = 3\sqrt{3}$$

When a radical involves variables, rewrite the radicand as a product. Then group the factors that are perfect squares.

Example 4 Simplify $4\sqrt{18x^8y^4}$.

$$4\sqrt{18x^8y^4} = 4\sqrt{9x^8y^4 \cdot 2} \quad \longleftarrow \quad \text{Find the largest perfect square}$$
$$= 4\sqrt{9x^8y^4} \cdot \sqrt{2} \qquad \text{factor of } 18x^8y^4.$$
$$= 4(3x^4y^2)\sqrt{2} = 12\sqrt{2}\,x^4y^2$$

The following example illustrates Theorem 1-2.

If $\dfrac{\sqrt{16}}{\sqrt{25}} = \dfrac{4}{5}$ and $\sqrt{\dfrac{16}{25}} = \dfrac{4}{5}$, then $\dfrac{\sqrt{16}}{25} = \sqrt{\dfrac{16}{25}}.$

Theorem 1-2: Division Theorem for Radicals

For any real numbers a and b where $a \geq 0$ and $b > 0$,

$$\frac{\sqrt{a}}{\sqrt{b}} = \sqrt{\frac{a}{b}}.$$

Example 5 Divide: $\sqrt{24} \div \sqrt{8}$

$$\frac{\sqrt{24}}{\sqrt{8}} = \sqrt{\frac{24}{8}} = \sqrt{3}$$

When simplifying a square root radical containing a fraction, it is sometimes necessary to multiply the fraction by the number 1 expressed in a form that will make the denominator of the fraction a perfect square. This is called **rationalizing the denominator.**

Example 6   Simplify $\sqrt{\dfrac{3}{2}}$.

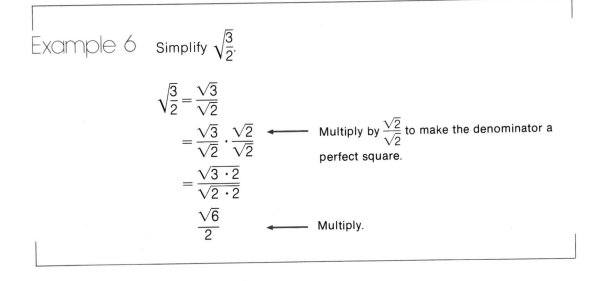

$$\sqrt{\dfrac{3}{2}} = \dfrac{\sqrt{3}}{\sqrt{2}}$$

$$= \dfrac{\sqrt{3}}{\sqrt{2}} \cdot \dfrac{\sqrt{2}}{\sqrt{2}} \longleftarrow \text{Multiply by } \dfrac{\sqrt{2}}{\sqrt{2}} \text{ to make the denominator a perfect square.}$$

$$= \dfrac{\sqrt{3 \cdot 2}}{\sqrt{2 \cdot 2}}$$

$$\dfrac{\sqrt{6}}{2} \longleftarrow \text{Multiply.}$$

Try These   *Rewrite each expression in a simpler form.*

1. $\sqrt{3} \cdot \sqrt{5}$ $\sqrt{15}$ **2.** $5\sqrt{2} \cdot 6\sqrt{3}$ $30\sqrt{6}$ **3.** $\sqrt{\dfrac{3}{8}}$ $\dfrac{\sqrt{6}}{4}$ **4.** $\sqrt{5\frac{5}{6}}$ $\frac{1}{6}\sqrt{210}$ **5.** $\dfrac{1}{2}\sqrt{\dfrac{3}{4}}$ $\frac{\sqrt{3}}{4}$

Exercises

Simplify.

1. $\sqrt{8}$ $2\sqrt{2}$ **2.** $\sqrt{20}$ $2\sqrt{5}$ **3.** $\sqrt{18}$ $3\sqrt{2}$ **4.** $\sqrt{27}$ $3\sqrt{3}$ **5.** $2\sqrt{12}$ $4\sqrt{3}$

6. $2\sqrt{24}$ $4\sqrt{6}$ **7.** $5\sqrt{32}$ $20\sqrt{2}$ **8.** $4\sqrt{63}$ $12\sqrt{7}$ **9.** $\sqrt{\dfrac{1}{2}}$ $\frac{1}{2}\sqrt{2}$ **10.** $\sqrt{\dfrac{1}{3}}$ $\frac{1}{3}\sqrt{3}$

11. $\sqrt{\dfrac{2}{3}}$ $\frac{1}{3}\sqrt{6}$ **12.** $\sqrt{\dfrac{3}{5}}$ $\frac{1}{5}\sqrt{15}$ **13.** $\sqrt{\dfrac{1}{8}}$ $\frac{1}{4}\sqrt{2}$ **14.** $\sqrt{\dfrac{5}{6}}$ $\frac{1}{6}\sqrt{30}$ **15.** $\sqrt{\dfrac{19}{24}}$ $\frac{1}{12}\sqrt{114}$

16. $\sqrt{2\frac{2}{5}}$ $\frac{2}{5}\sqrt{15}$ **17.** $\sqrt{x^6}$ $|x^3|$, or $x^2|x|$ **18.** $\sqrt{x^{10}}$ **19.** $\sqrt{a^2 b^{14}}$ **20.** $\sqrt{45x^6 y^2}$
$\qquad\qquad\qquad\qquad\qquad\qquad\qquad\qquad\quad$ $|x^5|$, or $x^4|x|$ $|ab^7|$, or $b^6|ab|$ $|3x^3 y|\sqrt{5}$, or $3x^2 |xy|\sqrt{5}$

Multiply. Simplify the product where possible.

21. $\sqrt{2} \cdot \sqrt{5}$ $\sqrt{10}$ **22.** $\sqrt{8} \cdot \sqrt{2}$ 4   **23.** $\sqrt{5} \cdot \sqrt{5}$ 5   **24.** $2\sqrt{2} \cdot 2\sqrt{6}$ $8\sqrt{3}$

25. $3\sqrt{2} \cdot 5\sqrt{2}$ 30   **26.** $5\sqrt{3} \cdot 3\sqrt{2}$ $15\sqrt{6}$ **27.** $6\sqrt{2} \cdot 2\sqrt{6}$ $24\sqrt{3}$ **28.** $(\sqrt{5})(-\sqrt{5})$ -5

Divide. Express denominators as rational numbers.

29. $\dfrac{\sqrt{6}}{\sqrt{3}}$ $\sqrt{2}$ **30.** $\dfrac{\sqrt{8}}{\sqrt{2}}$ 2   **31.** $\dfrac{\sqrt{18}}{\sqrt{2}}$ 3   **32.** $\dfrac{\sqrt{21}}{\sqrt{7}}$ $\sqrt{3}$

33. $\dfrac{\sqrt{27}}{\sqrt{3}}$ 3   **34.** $\dfrac{\sqrt{18}}{\sqrt{3}}$ $\sqrt{6}$ **35.** $\dfrac{\sqrt{60}}{\sqrt{20}}$ $\sqrt{3}$ **36.** $\dfrac{\sqrt{20}}{\sqrt{5}}$ 2

37. $\dfrac{\sqrt{40}}{\sqrt{5}}$ $2\sqrt{2}$ **38.** $\dfrac{8\sqrt{32}}{2\sqrt{50}}$ $\frac{16}{5}$, or $3\frac{1}{5}$ **39.** $\dfrac{\sqrt{78}}{\sqrt{18}}$ $\frac{1}{3}\sqrt{39}$ **40.** $\dfrac{\sqrt{44}}{\sqrt{99}}$ $\frac{2}{3}$

Multiply. Simplify the product where possible.

41. $(\sqrt{3})^2$ 3   **42.** $(4\sqrt{5})^2$ 80   **43.** $(-4\sqrt{2})^2$ 32   **44.** $-(4\sqrt{2})^2$ -32

Example: $\sqrt{3}(\sqrt{3} - \sqrt{2}) = \sqrt{3}\,\sqrt{3} - \sqrt{3}\,\sqrt{2} = 3 - \sqrt{6}$

45. $\sqrt{2}(\sqrt{2}+\sqrt{3})$ $2+\sqrt{6}$ **46.** $\sqrt{5}(\sqrt{3}+\sqrt{2})$ $\sqrt{15}+\sqrt{10}$ **47.** $\sqrt{7}(\sqrt{2}-\sqrt{7})$ $\sqrt{14}-7$ **48.** $5\sqrt{5}(5\sqrt{5}-3\sqrt{2})$ $125-15\sqrt{10}$

Divide and simplify.

49. $\dfrac{\sqrt{8}+\sqrt{50}}{\sqrt{2}}$ 7   **50.** $\dfrac{5\sqrt{12}-\sqrt{48}}{\sqrt{3}}$ 6   **51.** $\dfrac{5\sqrt{40}-7\sqrt{15}}{\sqrt{5}}$ $10\sqrt{2}-7\sqrt{3}$ **52.** $\dfrac{2\sqrt{48}-8\sqrt{12}}{\sqrt{6}}$ $-4\sqrt{2}$

53. $\sqrt{3} \div \sqrt{\frac{1}{3}}$ 3   **54.** $\sqrt{3} \div \sqrt{\frac{3}{4}}$ 2   **55.** $\sqrt{\frac{2}{3}} \div \dfrac{\sqrt{3}}{2}$ $\frac{2\sqrt{2}}{3}$ **56.** $\sqrt{1\frac{1}{4}} \div \sqrt{\frac{4}{5}}$ $\frac{5}{4}$, or $1\frac{1}{4}$

57. Is "$\sqrt{5^2 + 4^2} = \sqrt{5^2} + \sqrt{4^2}$" true? Explain. No.

58. Prove Theorem 1-1. (*Hint:* Show that $\sqrt{a} \cdot \sqrt{b}$ is the square root of ab.)
Prove that for $a \geq 0$ and $b \geq 0$, $\sqrt{a} \cdot \sqrt{b} = \sqrt{ab}$. The square of $\sqrt{ab}$ is ab, and $(\sqrt{a} \cdot \sqrt{b})^2 =$ $(\sqrt{a} \cdot \sqrt{b})(\sqrt{a} \cdot \sqrt{b}) = (\sqrt{a} \cdot \sqrt{a})(\sqrt{b} \cdot \sqrt{b}) = ab$.

59. Prove Theorem 1-2. (*Hint:* Show that $\left(\dfrac{\sqrt{a}}{\sqrt{b}}\right)^2 = \dfrac{a}{b}$.) Prove that for any real numbers a and b where $a \geq 0$, and $b \geq 0$, $\dfrac{\sqrt{a}}{\sqrt{b}} = \sqrt{\dfrac{a}{b}}$. The square of $\sqrt{\dfrac{a}{b}}$ is $\dfrac{a}{b}$, and $\left(\dfrac{\sqrt{a}}{\sqrt{b}}\right)^2 = \dfrac{(\sqrt{a})^2}{(\sqrt{b})^2} = \dfrac{\sqrt{a} \cdot \sqrt{a}}{\sqrt{b} \cdot \sqrt{b}} = \dfrac{a}{b}$.

Remember

Combine like terms.

1. $2x + 5x$ $7x$

2. $3x^2y - 7x^2y + x$ $-4x^2y + x$

3. $8ab + 7ab^2 + 9ab$ $17ab + 7ab^2$

4. $-7q^2 - 9q - 15q^2$ $-22q^2 - 9q$

The answers are on page 36.

1-4 Addition of Radicals

The objective for this section is on page 35.

The Distributive Postulate can be used to find the sum or difference of two or more radicals.

Distributive Postulate

For any real numbers a, b, and c,

$$ac + bc = (a + b)c$$

Example 1   Add: $3\sqrt{7} + 2\sqrt{7}$

$$ac + \quad bc = (a + b) \cdot c$$

$$3\sqrt{7} + 2\sqrt{7} = (3 + 2)\sqrt{7} \longleftarrow \text{Distributive postulate}$$

$$= 5\sqrt{7} \longleftarrow \text{Add.}$$

Sometimes the radicand must be simplified before applying the distributive property. Radicals must be exactly alike before they can be combined into one term.

Example 2   Add: $\sqrt{32} + 3\sqrt{2}$

$$\sqrt{32} + 3\sqrt{2} = \sqrt{16} \cdot \sqrt{2} + 3\sqrt{2} \longleftarrow \sqrt{32} = \sqrt{16 \cdot 2}.$$

$$= 4\sqrt{2} + 3\sqrt{2}$$

$$= (4 + 3)\sqrt{2} \longleftarrow \text{Distributive postulate}$$

$$= 7\sqrt{2}$$

The commutative and associative postulates are also useful in adding or subtracting radicals.

Example 3 Add or subtract as indicated: $\sqrt{8} - \sqrt{12} + 5\sqrt{2}$

$$\sqrt{8} - \sqrt{12} + 5\sqrt{2} = 2\sqrt{2} - 2\sqrt{3} + 5\sqrt{2} \quad \longleftarrow \quad \sqrt{8} = 2\sqrt{2}; \ \sqrt{12} = 2\sqrt{3}$$
$$= 2\sqrt{2} + 5\sqrt{2} - 2\sqrt{3} \quad \longleftarrow \quad \text{Commutative and associative postulates}$$
$$= (2\sqrt{2} + 5\sqrt{2}) - 2\sqrt{3} \quad \longleftarrow \quad \text{Associative postulate}$$
$$= (2 + 5)\sqrt{2} - 2\sqrt{3} \quad \longleftarrow \quad \text{Distributive postulate}$$
$$= 7\sqrt{2} - 2\sqrt{3}$$

Try These Add or subtract as indicated.

1. $5\sqrt{7} + 2\sqrt{7}$ $\ 7\sqrt{7}$

2. $17\sqrt{3} - \sqrt{3}$ $\ 16\sqrt{3}$

3. $\sqrt{8} + \sqrt{32}$ $\ 6\sqrt{2}$

4. $5\sqrt{7} - \sqrt{63}$ $\ 2\sqrt{7}$

5. $\sqrt{12} + 6\sqrt{3}$ $\ 8\sqrt{3}$

6. $\sqrt{\frac{1}{2}} + \sqrt{2}$ $\ \frac{3\sqrt{2}}{2}$

Exercises

Add or subtract as indicated.

a

1. $4\sqrt{3} - 2\sqrt{3}$ $\ 2\sqrt{3}$

2. $5\sqrt{2} + 3\sqrt{2}$ $\ 8\sqrt{2}$

3. $6\sqrt{a} - 5\sqrt{a}$ $\ \sqrt{a}$

4. $8\sqrt{2} + \sqrt{2}$ $\ 9\sqrt{2}$

5. $\sqrt{3} + \sqrt{27}$ $\ 4\sqrt{3}$

6. $\sqrt{20} + \sqrt{12}$ See below.

7. $\sqrt{2} + \sqrt{8}$ $\ 3\sqrt{2}$

8. $\sqrt{98} - \sqrt{50}$ $\ 2\sqrt{2}$

9. $2\sqrt{12} - 3\sqrt{48}$ $-8\sqrt{3}$

10. $32\sqrt{b^3} - 5\sqrt{b^5}$
    $(32\,|b| - 5b^2)\sqrt{b}$

11. $\sqrt{a^2b} + \sqrt{bc^2}$ See below.

12. $2\sqrt{99} - \sqrt{176}$ $2\sqrt{11}$

13. $2\sqrt{72} - 5\sqrt{20} - \sqrt{98}$
    $5\sqrt{2} - 10\sqrt{5}$

14. $\sqrt{\frac{3}{4}} + \sqrt{\frac{1}{3}} - \sqrt{\frac{1}{5}}$
    $\frac{5}{6}\sqrt{3} - \frac{1}{5}\sqrt{5}$

15. $6\sqrt{2} + 7\sqrt{3} + 5\sqrt{2}$
    $11\sqrt{2} + 7\sqrt{3}$

16. $2\sqrt{45} - \frac{2}{3}\sqrt{\frac{1}{5}}$ $\frac{88}{15}\sqrt{5}$

17. $5\sqrt{18} + 6\sqrt{2}$ $21\sqrt{2}$

18. $3\sqrt{45} - 2\sqrt{50}$ See below.

19. $6\sqrt{5} + 8\sqrt{20} - \sqrt{80}$ $\ 18\sqrt{5}$

20. $3 + 4\sqrt{2} - 5\sqrt{50}$
    $3 - 21\sqrt{2}$

21. $\frac{-3 + \sqrt{2}}{2} + \frac{-3 - \sqrt{2}}{2}$ -3

22. $\frac{5 + \sqrt{7}}{6} + \frac{5 - \sqrt{7}}{6}$ $\ \frac{5}{3}$

23. $\sqrt{\frac{y}{7}} + \sqrt{\frac{y}{28}}$ $\ \frac{3}{14}\sqrt{7y}$

24. $\sqrt{\frac{t}{3}} - \sqrt{\frac{t}{12}}$ $\ \frac{1}{6}\sqrt{3t}$

11. $(|a| + |c|)\sqrt{b}$

6. $2\sqrt{5} + 2\sqrt{3}$
18. $9\sqrt{5} - 10\sqrt{2}$

Multiply.

Example:

$$(\sqrt{3} + \sqrt{2})(2\sqrt{3} + 3\sqrt{2}) = \sqrt{3}(2\sqrt{3} + 3\sqrt{2}) + \sqrt{2}(2\sqrt{3} + 3\sqrt{2})$$
$$= \sqrt{3}(2\sqrt{3}) + \sqrt{3}(3\sqrt{2}) + \sqrt{2}(2\sqrt{3}) + \sqrt{2}(3\sqrt{2})$$
$$= 6 + 3\sqrt{6} + 2\sqrt{6} + 6$$
$$= 12 + 5\sqrt{6}$$

25. $(3\sqrt{2} + 2\sqrt{3})(5\sqrt{2} - \sqrt{3})$ $24 + 7\sqrt{6}$
26. $(\sqrt{6} + 8)(\sqrt{6} - 3)$ $-18 + 5\sqrt{6}$
27. $(5\sqrt{2} - 2\sqrt{3})^2$ $62 - 20\sqrt{6}$
28. $(a + b\sqrt{2})^2$ $a^2 + 2ab\sqrt{2} + 2b^2$

Example: $(\sqrt{7} + \sqrt{2})(\sqrt{7} - \sqrt{2}) = \sqrt{7}(\sqrt{7} - \sqrt{2}) + \sqrt{2}(\sqrt{7} - \sqrt{2})$
$$= 7 - \sqrt{14} + \sqrt{14} - 2 = 5$$

29. $(\sqrt{5} + 4)(\sqrt{5} - 4)$ -11
30. $(\sqrt{6} + \sqrt{3})(\sqrt{6} - \sqrt{3})$ 3
31. $(2\sqrt{3} - 3\sqrt{2})(2\sqrt{3} + 3\sqrt{2})$ -6
32. $(2\sqrt{7} - 5)(2\sqrt{7} + 5)$ 3
33. $(-\sqrt{3} - \sqrt{5})(-\sqrt{3} + \sqrt{5})$ -2
34. $(-3\sqrt{5} - 2\sqrt{3})(-3\sqrt{5} + 2\sqrt{3})$ 33
35. $\left(\dfrac{3 + 2\sqrt{5}}{2}\right)\left(\dfrac{3 - 2\sqrt{5}}{2}\right)$ $-\dfrac{11}{4}$
36. $\left(\dfrac{6 + 3\sqrt{2}}{4}\right)\left(\dfrac{6 - 3\sqrt{2}}{4}\right)$ $\dfrac{9}{8}$

1-5 Pure Imaginary Numbers

The objectives for this section are on pages 34-35.

Example 1   Solve the equation, $x^2 = -1$.

$$x^2 = -1$$
$$x = \sqrt{-1} \text{ or } x = -\sqrt{-1} \quad \longleftarrow \quad \text{Definition of square root}$$

There is no real number whose square is -1. To solve equations such as this, mathematicians invented the numbers i and $-i$.

Definition: $i^2 = -1$ and $(-i)^2 = -1$

By the definition of square root,

$$(\sqrt{-1})^2 = -1 \qquad \text{and} \qquad (-\sqrt{-1})^2 = -1.$$

So $\qquad i = \sqrt{-1} \qquad$ and $\qquad -i = -\sqrt{-1}.$

Note that i is <u>not a variable</u>; it names a number, $\sqrt{-1}$.
Numbers such as

$$\sqrt{-1} \qquad -\sqrt{-1} \qquad \sqrt{-5} \qquad -\sqrt{-\tfrac{1}{7}} \qquad -\sqrt{-49}$$

are <u>pure imaginary numbers</u>. A **pure imaginary number** is a square root of a negative number. Pure imaginary numbers are written as the product of a real number and i. This is called the <u>i-form</u> of the number.

Definition: For any real number a, where $-a < 0$,

$$\sqrt{-a} = i\sqrt{a} = \sqrt{a} \cdot i.$$

Notice that as a result of this definition, Theorem 1-1 on page 9 is also true if $b = -1$.

$$\text{For } a \geq 0 \text{ and } b = -1, \; \sqrt{a}\,\sqrt{b} = \sqrt{ab}.$$

Thus,

$$\sqrt{-5} = \sqrt{5 \cdot -1} = \sqrt{5} \cdot \sqrt{-1} = \sqrt{5} \cdot i = i\sqrt{5}.$$

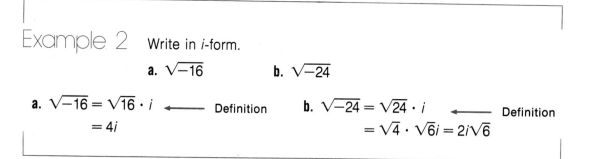

Example 2 Write in i-form.

a. $\sqrt{-16}$ b. $\sqrt{-24}$

a. $\sqrt{-16} = \sqrt{16} \cdot i \quad \longleftarrow \text{ Definition}$
$\quad = 4i$

b. $\sqrt{-24} = \sqrt{24} \cdot i \quad \longleftarrow \text{ Definition}$
$\quad = \sqrt{4} \cdot \sqrt{6}i = 2i\sqrt{6}$

To add, subtract, multiply, or divide pure imaginary numbers you must assume that they have all the properties of real numbers listed on page 4 (except closure).

Example 3   Add: $2i + 3i$.

$$2i + 3i = (2 + 3)i \quad \longleftarrow \quad \text{Distributive postulate}$$
$$= 5i \quad \longleftarrow \quad \text{Add.}$$

Before computing with pure imaginary numbers, always change to the i-form.

Example 4   Subtract: $\sqrt{-12} - \sqrt{-27}$

$$\sqrt{-12} - \sqrt{-27} = i\sqrt{12} - i\sqrt{27} \quad \longleftarrow \quad \text{Write in } i\text{-form.}$$
$$= i \cdot \sqrt{4} \cdot \sqrt{3} - i\sqrt{9} \cdot \sqrt{3}$$
$$= 2i\sqrt{3} - 3i\sqrt{3}$$
$$= (2i - 3i)\sqrt{3}$$
$$= -i\sqrt{3}$$

Example 5   Multiply: $\sqrt{-2} \cdot \sqrt{-3}$

$$\sqrt{-2} \cdot \sqrt{-3} = i\sqrt{2} \cdot i\sqrt{3} \quad \longleftarrow \quad \text{Write in } i\text{-form.}$$
$$= i^2\sqrt{6} \quad \longleftarrow \quad i \cdot i = i^2; \ \sqrt{2} \cdot \sqrt{3} = \sqrt{6}$$
$$= (-1)\sqrt{6} \quad \longleftarrow \quad i^2 = -1$$
$$= -\sqrt{6}$$

Note what would have happened if you had not changed to the i-form before computing.

$$\sqrt{-2} \cdot \sqrt{-3} \overset{?}{=} \sqrt{-2 \cdot -3} \overset{?}{=} \sqrt{6} \quad \longleftarrow \quad \text{This is not correct.}$$

This illustrates the fact that the rule $\sqrt{ab} = \sqrt{a}\sqrt{b}$ is <u>not</u> correct when a and b are <u>both</u> negative.

Example 6

Divide: $\sqrt{-2} \div \sqrt{-3}$. Express the denominator as a rational number.

$$\frac{\sqrt{-2}}{\sqrt{-3}} = \frac{i\sqrt{2}}{i\sqrt{3}} \quad \longleftarrow \quad \text{Write in } i\text{-form.}$$

$$= \frac{\sqrt{2}}{\sqrt{3}} \cdot \frac{\sqrt{3}}{\sqrt{3}} \quad \longleftarrow \quad \frac{i}{i} = 1. \text{ Multiply by } \frac{\sqrt{3}}{\sqrt{3}}.$$

$$= \frac{\sqrt{6}}{3}$$

Try These

Perform the indicated operations. Express each result in i-form.

1. $\sqrt{-25}$ 5i
2. $\sqrt{-3}$ $i\sqrt{3}$
3. $\sqrt{-8}$ $2i\sqrt{2}$
4. $3i + 5i$ 8i
5. $\sqrt{-1} - \sqrt{-4}$ $-i$
6. $\sqrt{-9} \cdot \sqrt{-4}$ -6
7. $\sqrt{-8} \div \sqrt{-4}$ $\sqrt{2}$
8. $\sqrt{-3} \div \sqrt{-2}$ $\frac{\sqrt{6}}{2}$

Exercises

Express each pure imaginary number in i-form.

1. $\sqrt{-12}$ $2i\sqrt{3}$
2. $\sqrt{-18}$ $3i\sqrt{2}$
3. $2\sqrt{-3}$ $2i\sqrt{3}$
4. $\sqrt{-32}$ $4i\sqrt{2}$

5. $3\sqrt{-24}$ $6i\sqrt{6}$
6. $\frac{1}{2}\sqrt{-\frac{3}{4}}$ $\frac{\sqrt{3}}{4}i$
7. $\sqrt{-\frac{2}{3}}$ $\frac{1}{3}i\sqrt{6}$
8. $\sqrt{-\frac{4}{9}}$ $\frac{2}{3}i$

9. $\sqrt{-121}$ $11i$
10. $-\sqrt{-5}$ $-i\sqrt{5}$
11. $-\sqrt{-72}$ $-6i\sqrt{2}$
12. $\sqrt{-300}$ $10i\sqrt{3}$

Perform the indicated operations.

13. $4\sqrt{-3} - \sqrt{-3}$ $3i\sqrt{3}$
14. $\sqrt{-20} + \sqrt{-8}$ $2(\sqrt{5} + \sqrt{2})i$
15. $\sqrt{-3} + \sqrt{-27}$ $4i\sqrt{3}$
16. $\sqrt{-20} + \sqrt{-12}$ $2(\sqrt{5} + \sqrt{3})i$
17. $\sqrt{-2} + \sqrt{-8}$ $3i\sqrt{2}$
18. $\sqrt{-98} - \sqrt{-50}$ $2i\sqrt{2}$
19. $2\sqrt{-12} - 3\sqrt{-48}$ $-8i\sqrt{3}$
20. $\sqrt{-4} + \sqrt{-16} - \sqrt{-25}i$ i
21. $\sqrt{-4} + \sqrt{-9} + \sqrt{-25}$ $10i$
22. $\sqrt{-\frac{3}{4}} + \sqrt{-\frac{1}{3}} - \sqrt{-\frac{4}{5}}$
23. $\sqrt{-3} \cdot \sqrt{-7}$ $-\sqrt{21}$
24. $\sqrt{-3} \cdot \sqrt{-5}$ $-\sqrt{15}$

22. $\left(\frac{5}{6}\sqrt{3} - \frac{2}{5}\sqrt{5}\right)i$

25. $\sqrt{-16} \cdot \sqrt{-9}$ _-12_ **26.** $(\sqrt{-3})^2$ _-3_ **27.** $\sqrt{-4} \cdot \sqrt{-5}$ _-2√5_ **28.** $3i \cdot 5i \cdot 2i$ _-30i_

29. $i^2 \cdot i^2$ _1_ **30.** $\sqrt{-\frac{1}{4}} \cdot \sqrt{-\frac{1}{9}}$ _-⅙_ **31.** $\sqrt{-\frac{9}{16}} \cdot \sqrt{-\frac{7}{25}}$ _-\frac{3\sqrt{7}}{20}_ **32.** $i^3 \cdot i$ _1_

Divide. Express denominators as rational numbers.

33. $\dfrac{\sqrt{-6}}{\sqrt{-2}}$ _√3_   **34.** $\dfrac{\sqrt{-15}}{\sqrt{-5}}$ _√3_   **35.** $\dfrac{\sqrt{-2}}{\sqrt{-8}}$ _½_   **36.** $\dfrac{-5\sqrt{-3}}{2\sqrt{-6}}$ _-\frac{5}{4}\sqrt{2}_

Simplify each power of i.

Example: $i^5 = i^4 \cdot i = i^2 \cdot i^2 \cdot i = (-1)(-1)i = i$

37. i^6 _-1_   **38.** i^7 _-i_   **39.** i^8 _1_   **40.** i^9 _i_

41. Find the repeating pattern in the values of i from i^1 to i^9. Write the pattern. _i, -1, -i, 1, i, -1, -i, 1, i_

Use the pattern of Exercise 41 to find each power of i.

42. i^{18} _-1_   **43.** i^{19} _-i_   **44.** i^{20} _1_   **45.** i^{21} _i_

46. Is $i \cdot i^2$ a <u>real</u> number or a <u>pure imaginary</u> number?   _Pure imaginary._

47. Is $i \cdot i$ a <u>real</u> number or a <u>pure imaginary</u> number?   _Real._

48. Is $i \cdot (-i)$ a <u>real</u> number or a <u>pure imaginary</u> number?   _Real._

49. Is the product of two pure imaginary numbers a <u>real</u> number or a <u>pure imaginary</u> number?   _Real._

50. Answer Exercises 46-49 for addition, subtraction, and division.   _See key._

PUZZLE

In each of these two tricks, do what the magician says. Can you tell how the magician knows what he claims to know?

A (1) Think of a number. **(2)** Triple it. **(3)** Add the number you started with. **(4)** Subtract 4. **(5)** Divide by 4. **(6)** Add 1. **(7)** Subtract the number you started with. I can tell what number you now have. (*Hint:* Use the language of algebra to trace his steps. **(1)** x **(2)** $3x$ **(3)** $4x$ **(4)** $4x-4$, and so on.) _You always get the original number._ $\left(\frac{4x-4}{4} + 1 = x\right)$

B (1) Write the last 2 digits of your birth year. **(2)** Multiply by 100. **(3)** Add 10,000. **(4)** Add 50. **(5)** Add the number of the month when you were born (1 for Jan., 2 for Feb., etc.) **(6)** Subtract 20. **(7)** Subtract 30. Give me your answer. I can tell your age and the month you were born. _Steps 1-7 give 10,000 + 100 (last two digits of birth year) + birth month. Example: March, 1968 gives 16803._

1-6 The Set of Complex Numbers

The objectives for this section are on pages 34-35.

A <u>complex number</u> is the sum of a real number and a pure imaginary number.

Definition: A **complex number** is a number of the form $a + bi$, where a and b are real numbers and $i = \sqrt{-1}$.

The form $a + bi$ is the <u>standard form of a complex number.</u>

Complex Number	Standard Form	a	b
$2 - 3i$	$2 + (-3i)$	2	-3
$7i$	$0 + 7i$	0	7
0	$0 + 0i$	0	0
$-\dfrac{1}{2}$	$\left(-\dfrac{1}{2}\right) + 0i$	$-\dfrac{1}{2}$	0
$i\sqrt{5}$	$0 + \sqrt{5}i$	0	$\sqrt{5}$
$6 + \sqrt{-2}$	$6 + \sqrt{2}i$	6	$\sqrt{2}$

Any complex number for which $b \neq 0$ is an **imaginary number.** A complex number for which $a = 0$ is a pure imaginary number. When $b = 0$, the number is a real number. Thus, every real number is also a complex number. The diagram below illustrates the relationships between the set of complex numbers and some of its subsets.

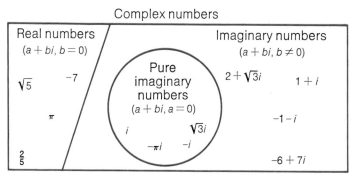

Complex numbers

Real numbers ($a + bi, b = 0$)   Imaginary numbers ($a + bi, b \neq 0$)

Pure imaginary numbers ($a + bi, a = 0$)

$\sqrt{5}$ -7 $2 + \sqrt{3}i$ $1 + i$

π $-1 - i$

i $\sqrt{3}i$

$-\pi i$ $-i$

$\dfrac{2}{5}$ $-6 + 7i$

The set of complex numbers is the union of the set of real numbers and the set of imaginary numbers. Since every real number is also a complex number, you should expect the definitions and properties of complex numbers to be true also for real numbers.

Definition: Two complex numbers, $a + bi$ and $c + di$, are equal if and only if $a = c$ and $b = d$.

Example 1   Tell whether each pair of numbers is equal or unequal. Give a reason for each answer.

     a. $4 + 5i,\ 4 - 5i$ **b.** $4 + 5i,\ 4 + \sqrt{-25}$

     a. $4 + 5i \neq 4 - 5i$ because $5 \neq -5$.

     b. $4 + 5i = 4 + \sqrt{-25}$ because $4 + \sqrt{-25} = 4 + 5i$.

Try These   *Simplify. Write each result in standard form.*

1. $2 + \sqrt{-3}$ $_{2+\sqrt{3}i}$ **2.** $\sqrt{-16}$ $_{0+4i}$ **3.** i^2 $_{-1+0i}$ **4.** $1 - \sqrt{-1}$ $^{1+(-1)i}$

5. $i - \sqrt{-4}$ $_{0+(-1i)}$ **6.** $-1 - \sqrt{-1}$ $_{-1+(-1i)}$ **7.** $\sqrt{5} + \sqrt{-5}$ $_{\sqrt{5}+\sqrt{5}i}$ **8.** $-i^2 + i$ $_{1+1i}$

Exercises

     Write each number in standard form if it is not already in that form. For each number, state the value of a and b.

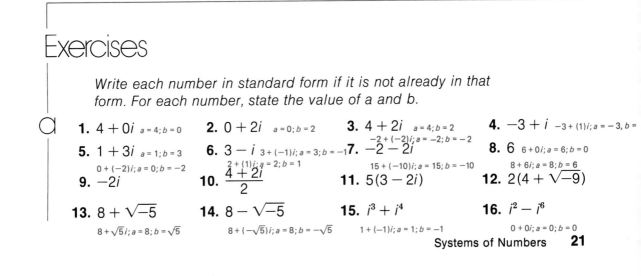

1. $4 + 0i$ $_{a=4;b=0}$ **2.** $0 + 2i$ $_{a=0;b=2}$ **3.** $4 + 2i$ $_{a=4;b=2}$ **4.** $-3 + i$ $_{-3+(1)i;\,a=-3,b=}$

5. $1 + 3i$ $_{a=1;b=3}$ **6.** $3 - i$ $_{3+(-1)i;\,a=3;b=-1}$ **7.** $-2 - 2i$ $^{-2+(-2)i;\,a=-2;b=-2}$ **8.** 6 $_{6+0i;\,a=6;b=0}$

9. $-2i$ $_{0+(-2)i;\,a=0;b=-2}$ **10.** $\dfrac{4 + 2i}{2}$ $_{2+(1)i;\,a=2;b=1}$ **11.** $5(3 - 2i)$ $_{15+(-10)i;\,a=15;b=-10}$ **12.** $2(4 + \sqrt{-9})$ $_{8+6i;\,a=8;b=6}$

13. $8 + \sqrt{-5}$ $_{8+\sqrt{5}i;\,a=8;b=\sqrt{5}}$ **14.** $8 - \sqrt{-5}$ $_{8+(-\sqrt{5})i;\,a=8;b=-\sqrt{5}}$ **15.** $i^3 + i^4$ $_{1+(-1)i;\,a=1;b=-1}$ **16.** $i^2 - i^6$ $_{0+0i;\,a=0;b=0}$

*For Exercises **17-21**, replace __?__ with ⊂ or ⊄ to make a true statement.*

17. The set of real numbers __?__ ⊂ the set of complex numbers.

18. The set of imaginary numbers __?__ ⊂ the set of complex numbers.

19. The set of real numbers __?__ ⊄ the set of imaginary numbers.

20. The set of pure imaginary numbers __?__ ⊂ the set of imaginary numbers.

21. The set of pure imaginary numbers __?__ ⊄ the set of real numbers.

Tell whether each pair of complex numbers is equal or unequal.

22. $2 + i; -2 - i$ *Unequal*   **23.** $2 + i; 2 - i$ *Unequal*   **24.** $2 + i; \sqrt{4} + \sqrt{-4}$ *Unequal*

25. $5i; \sqrt{25}i$ *Equal*   **26.** $-3i; 0 - \sqrt{-9}$ *Equal*   **27.** $\frac{1}{2}; \frac{1}{2} + 0i$ *Equal*

28. When is the complex number $a + bi$ a real number? *b = 0*

29. When is the complex number $a + bi$ an imaginary number? *b ≠ 0*

30. When is the complex number $a + bi$ a pure imaginary number? *a = 0, b ≠ 0*

$9\left(\frac{1}{3}i\right)^2 + 1 = 9\left(\frac{1}{9}\right)i^2 + 1 = -1 + 1 = 0; 9\left(-\frac{1}{3}i\right)^2 + 1 = 9\left(-\frac{1}{9}\right) + 1 = -1 + 1 = 0$

31. Use substitution to show that $\frac{3}{2}i$ is a member of the solution set of the equation $4x^2 + 9 = 0$. $4\left(\frac{3}{2}i\right)^2 + 9 = 4\left(\frac{9}{4}\right)i^2 + 9 = -9 + 9 = 0$

32. Show that the numbers $\frac{1}{3}i$ and $-\frac{1}{3}i$ satisfy the equation $9x^2 + 1 = 0$.

33. Show that i and $-i$ are reciprocals of each other; that is show that $i \cdot -i = 1$. $i \cdot -i = i\left((-1)i\right) = (-1)i^2 = (-1)(-1) = 1$

Remember

Add or subtract as indicated.

1. $(7 + 2\sqrt{5}) + (3 + 9\sqrt{5})$ $10 + 11\sqrt{5}$

2. $(-2 + 3\sqrt{3}) + (5 - 6\sqrt{3})$ $3 - 3\sqrt{3}$

3. $(-3 + 2\sqrt{7}) + (3 - 2\sqrt{7})$ 0

4. $(4 + 2\sqrt{2}) - (5 - 6\sqrt{2})$ $-1 + 8\sqrt{2}$

The answers are on page 36.

PUZZLE

In the figure below, find six dots such that no two of these six are on the same line segment.

Imagine the square as being part of the first quadrant of a coordinate plane, with the bottom left corner at the origin. Then the coordinates of one possible solution are (0, 1), (1, 3), (2, 5), (3, 0), (4, 2), and (5, 4).

1-7 Addition / Subtraction of Complex Numbers

The objectives for this section are on page 35.

The definition for the addition of complex numbers applies the commutative, associative, and distributive properties.

Definition: Addition of Complex Numbers

For all real numbers, $a, b, c,$ and d,
$$(a + bi) + (c + di) = (a + c) + (b + d)i.$$

The sum of two complex numbers is a complex number.

Example 1

Add: $(-2 + 3i) + (5 - 6i)$

$(-2 + 3i) + (5 - 6i) = (-2 + 5) + (3 - 6)i$ ⟵ Definition of addition
$$= 3 - 3i$$

The identity element for addition of complex numbers is zero. Recall that the sum of a number and the identity element is that number.

Example 2

Show that zero is the identity element for $a + bi$.

$$(a + bi) + (0 + 0i) = (a + 0) + (b + 0)i$$
$$= a + bi$$

Every complex number, $a + bi$, has an additive inverse, $-(a + bi)$ or $(-a - bi)$.

Example 3 Show that $3 - 2i$ is the additive inverse for $-3 + 2i$.

$$(-3 + 2i) + (3 - 2i) = (-3 + 3) + (2 - 2)i = 0 + 0i$$

Example 4 Find the additive inverse for $a + bi$. Show that you are correct.

The additive inverse of $a + bi$ is $-(a + bi)$ or $-a - bi$.

$$(a + bi) + (-a - bi) = (a - a) + (b - b)i = 0 + 0i$$

Subtraction of complex numbers is defined in terms of additive inverses, just as is subtraction of real numbers.

Definition

To subtract a complex number, $a + bi$, add its additive inverse, $-a - bi$, where a and b are real numbers.

Example 5 Subtract: $(4 + 2i) - (5 - 6i)$

$$(4 + 2i) - (5 - 6i) = (4 + 2i) + (-5 + 6i) \longleftarrow \text{ Definition of subtraction}$$
$$= (4 - 5) + (2 + 6)i = -1 + 8i$$

Try These *Add or subtract as indicated.*

1. $(3 + 2i) + (4 + 6i)$ ₇₊₈ᵢ 7 + 8i

2. $(3 + 5i) - (7 - 2i)$ -4 + 7i

3. $(-6 + 4i) + (-7 - 2i)$ -13 + 2i

4. $(-9 - 3i) - (12 - 8i)$ -21 + 5i

5. $(0 + 0i) + (2 - 6i)$ 2 - 6i

6. $(4 + \sqrt{-4}) - (2 - 6i)$ 2 + 8i

Exercises

Add.

a

1. $9+(6-2i)$ $15-2i$

2. $(6-3i)+4$ $10-3i$

3. $(1+5i)+3i$ $1+8i$

4. $(3-2i)+(3+2i)$ 6

5. $(4+i)+(-4+i)$ $2i$

6. $(2-3i)+(-2+3i)$ 0

7. $(6+5i)+(-6-6i)$ $-i$

8. $(-6-5i)+(-6+i)$ $-12-4i$

9. $(4+0i)+(7+0i)$ 11

10. $(\frac{2}{5}+0i)+(0+0i)$ $\frac{2}{5}$

11. $(\sqrt{2}+3i)+(\sqrt{3}-4i)$ $\sqrt{2}+\sqrt{3}-i$

12. $(2+\sqrt{-9})+(5-\sqrt{-9})$ 7

13. $(3+\sqrt{-7})+(18-\sqrt{-7})$ 21

14. $(-2+\sqrt{-25})+(-9+\sqrt{-36})$ $-11+11i$

15. $(a+bi)+(a-bi)$ $2a$

16. $(a+bi)+(-a-bi)$ 0

Subtract. Write each answer in standard form. $-2\sqrt{3}+(-3)i$

17. $(3-7i)-(6+2i)$ $-3+(-9)i$

18. $(\sqrt{3}+6i)-(\sqrt{3}-7i)$ $0+13i$

19. $(-2-\frac{1}{2}i)-(-7+6i)$ $5+(-6\frac{1}{2})i$

20. $(\sqrt{3}-i)-(3\sqrt{3}+2i)$

21. $(1-2i)-4i$ $1+(-6)i$

22. $7i-(6-3i\sqrt{2})$ $-6+(7+3\sqrt{2})i$

23. $(0+0i)-(2+5i)$ $-2+(-5)i$

24. $9-(6-2i)$ $3+2i$

25. $(3+11i)-(-3-11i)$ $6+22i$

26. $(18-2i)-24$ $-6+(-2)i$

Find a number that can be added to each given complex number such that the resulting sum is a real number. Is there just one such number in each case? No, there are an infinite number of possibilities in each case.

27. $4+3i$ $-3i$

28. $8-4i$ $4i$

29. $-2+6i$ $-6i$

30. $\sqrt{2}+13i$ $-13i$

31. $4+\sqrt{3}i$ $-\sqrt{3}i$

32. $-4i$ $4i$

33. $3+0i$
Any real number

34. $\sqrt{7}$
Any real number

35. What number should be added to each of the numbers in Exercises **27-34** so that the resulting sum will be zero? What are such pairs of numbers called?
See above.   Additive inverses

b

36. Use an example to show that addition of complex numbers is commutative. Use an example to show that the addition of complex numbers is associative.
Answers will vary.

37. Show that subtraction of complex numbers is not commutative.
$(4+3i)-(2+i) \neq (2+i)-(4+3i)$

38. Is subtraction of complex numbers associative? Give an example.
No. $[(2+i)-(3+2i)]-(1-i) \neq (2+i)-[(3+2i)-(1-i)]$

39. Is the set of complex numbers closed under addition? under subtraction? Why, or why not?
Yes, because the set of real numbers is closed under addition.
Yes, because subtraction is defined in terms of addition.

Systems of Numbers **25**

Tell which are real numbers.

1. $\sqrt{2}$ Yes   **2.** $2i$ No   **3.** $\sqrt{-9}$ No

Simplify.

4. $\sqrt{175}$ $5\sqrt{7}$ **5.** $\sqrt{20x^3y^2}$ $2\,|xy|\sqrt{5x}$ **6.** $(4\sqrt{2})^3$
$128\sqrt{2}$

Find each product.

7. $i \cdot i^2$ $-i$ **8.** $\sqrt{-4} \cdot \sqrt{-9}$ -6 **9.** $i^2\sqrt{-5} \cdot \sqrt{-5}$
5

The answers are on page 36.

1-8 Multiplication of Complex Numbers

The objectives for this section are on page 35.

To multiply two complex numbers, you use the distributive postulate twice.

Example 1   Multiply: $(5 - 2i)(4 + 3i)$

$$
\begin{aligned}
(5 - 2i)(4 + 3i) &= 5(4 + 3i) - 2i(4 + 3i) &&\longleftarrow \text{ Distributive postulate}\\
&= 5(4) + 5(3i) - 2i(4) - 2i(3i) &&\longleftarrow \text{ Distributive postulate}\\
&= 20 + 15i - 8i - 6i^2 &&\longleftarrow \text{ Multiply.}\\
&= 20 + 7i + 6 &&\longleftarrow \text{ } 15i - 8i = 7i;\ -6i^2 = 6\\
&= 26 + 7i
\end{aligned}
$$

The number 1, the identity element for multiplication of real numbers, is also the <u>identity element</u> for <u>multiplication</u> of complex numbers.

Example 2   For each complex number below, show that multiplying by
1 + 0i does not change the number.

    a. $(6 - 7i)$ **b.** $(a + bi)$

$$\begin{aligned}
\textbf{a.} \quad (6 - 7i)(1 + 0i) &= 6(1 + 0i) - 7i(1 + 0i) \\
&= 6 + 0i - 7i - 0i \\
&= 6 - 7i
\end{aligned}$$

$$\begin{aligned}
\textbf{b.} \quad (a + bi)(1 + 0i) &= a(1 + 0i) + bi(1 + 0i) \\
&= a + 0i + bi + 0i \\
&= a + bi
\end{aligned}$$

The multiplicative inverse, or reciprocal, of every nonzero complex
number, $a + bi$, is $\dfrac{1}{a + bi}$.

Example 3   Show that the product of each number below and its multiplicative inverse is 1.

    a. $-2 + 5i$ **b.** $a + bi$

$$\begin{aligned}
\textbf{a.} \quad (-2 + 5i)\left(\frac{1}{-2 + 5i}\right) &= \frac{-2 + 5i}{-2 + 5i} \\
&= 1
\end{aligned}$$

$$\begin{aligned}
\textbf{b.} \quad (a + bi)\left(\frac{1}{a + bi}\right) &= \frac{a + bi}{a + bi} \\
&= 1
\end{aligned}$$

Try These   *Multiply. Write each answer in standard form.*

1. $(2 + 3i)(4 + 5i)$ $-7 + 22i$ **2.** $(6 - 7i)(9 + 4i)$ $82 - 39i$ **3.** $(6 - 7i)(9 - 4i)$ $26 - 87i$

4. $(4 + 9i)(1 + 0i)$ $4 + 9i$ **5.** $\left(\frac{1}{5} + \frac{2}{5}i\right)(2 - 5i)$ $2\frac{2}{5} - \frac{1}{5}i$ **6.** $(-4 + \sqrt{-6})(7 - \sqrt{-3})$

                                                          $(-28 + 3\sqrt{2}) + (4\sqrt{3} + 7\sqrt{6})i$

Exercises

Multiply. Write each answer in standard form.

a

1. $(0 + i)(3 - 4i)$ ₄₊₃ᵢ — *4 + 3i* **2.** $(2 + 0i)(5 + 8i)$ — *10 + 16i (above)* **3.** $(0 + 0i)(3 - 2i)$ — *0 + 0i (above)*

4. $(4 + 8i)(2 - i)$ *16 + 12i* **5.** $(1 + i)(1 - i)$ *2 + 0i* **6.** $(7 + i)(7 + 7i)$ *42 + 56i*

7. $(3 - i)(6 - i)$ *17 − 9i* **8.** $(2 + 2i)(1 + 2i)$ *−2 + 6i* **9.** $(4 - 3i)(3 + 4i)$ *24 + 7i*

10. $(\sqrt{2} + 2i)(1 + 0i)$ *√2 + 2i* **11.** $(\frac{1}{2} + 2i)(\frac{1}{2} + 3i)$ *−²³⁄₄ + ⁵⁄₂i* **12.** $(\frac{1}{2} - i)(\frac{1}{2} + i)$ *⁵⁄₄ + 0i*

13. $(2 + 3i)(2 - 3i)$ *13 + 0i* **14.** $(a + bi)(a - bi)$ *a² + b² + 0i* **15.** $(5 + 2\sqrt{3}i)(5 + 2\sqrt{3}i)$ *13 + 20√3i*

Write the reciprocal of each number.

16. $2 + 3i$ $\frac{1}{2 + 3i}$ **17.** $3 - 2i$ $\frac{1}{3 - 2i}$ **18.** $-i$ $\frac{1}{-i}$, or $-\frac{1}{i}$

19. $-5 + i$ $\frac{1}{-5 + i}$ **20.** $-3 - 2i$ $\frac{1}{-3 - 2i}$ **21.** 3 $\frac{1}{3}$

Multiply.

b

22. $(2 + 3i)(\frac{2}{13} - \frac{3}{13}i)$ *1 + 0i* **23.** $(2 + 3i)^2$ *−5 + 12i* **24.** $(2 + 3i)^3$ *−46 + 9i*

25. How are the two numbers in Exercise 22 related? What is the name for two numbers that have this special product? *Product of 1.; They are multiplicative inverses.*

26. Use examples to show that multiplication of complex numbers is commutative and associative. *Answers will vary.*

27. Use examples to show that multiplication of complex numbers is distributive over addition. *Answers will vary.*

c

28. Use the definition of multiplication of complex numbers to show that the product of zero and any complex number $a + bi$ is zero. *See key.*

29. Prove that multiplication of complex numbers is commutative. *See key.*

For all $a,b,c,d \in R$, $(a + bi) \cdot (c + di) = (c + di) \cdot (a + bi)$.

30. Prove that multiplication of complex numbers is associative. *See key.*

For all $a,b,c,d,e,f \in R$, $[(a + bi) \cdot (c + di)] \cdot (e + fi) = (a + bi) \cdot [(c + di) \cdot (e + fi)]$.

31. Prove the distributive property for complex numbers. *See key.*

For all $a,b,c,d,e,f \in R$
$(a + bi) \cdot [(c + di) + (e + fi)] = (a + bi)(c + di) + (a + bi)(e + fi)$.

1-9 Division of Complex Numbers

The objective for this section is on page 35.

Two complex numbers of the form $a + bi$ and $a - bi$ are **conjugates**. Their product is a real number, $a^2 + b^2$.

Example 1   Find the product of $a + bi$ and its conjugate, $a - bi$.

$$(a + bi)(a - bi) = a(a - bi) + bi(a - bi)$$
$$= a^2 - abi + abi - b^2i^2 \quad \longleftarrow \quad -b^2i^2 = -b^2(-1) = b^2$$
$$= a^2 + b^2 \quad \longleftarrow \quad a^2 + b^2 \text{ is a real number.}$$

Each nonzero complex number has a <u>reciprocal</u> or <u>multiplicative inverse</u>.

$-\pi$ is the reciprocal of $-\dfrac{1}{\pi}$. $\dfrac{7}{5}$ is the reciprocal of $\dfrac{5}{7}$.

$\dfrac{1}{a + bi}$ is the reciprocal of $a + bi$.

Example 2   Write $\dfrac{1}{a + bi}$ in standard form.

$$\frac{1}{a + bi} = \frac{1}{a + bi} \cdot \frac{a - bi}{a - bi} \quad \longleftarrow \quad \text{The conjugate of } (a + bi) \text{ is } a - bi.$$
$$= \frac{a - bi}{(a + bi)(a - bi)}$$
$$= \frac{a - bi}{a^2 + b^2}$$
$$= \frac{a}{a^2 + b^2} + \frac{-b}{a^2 + b^2}i \quad \longleftarrow \quad \text{Standard form}$$

Example 3

Write the reciprocal of $1 - i$ in standard form.

$$\frac{1}{1-i} = \frac{1}{1-i} \cdot \frac{1+i}{1+i}$$ ⟵ The conjugate of $1 - i$ is $1 + i$.

$$= \frac{1+i}{1+1}$$

$$= \frac{1+i}{2}$$

$$= \frac{1}{2} + \frac{1}{2}i$$ ⟵ Standard form

Division of complex numbers is defined in terms of multiplying by a reciprocal.

Definition: For any real numbers a, b, c, and d where $c \neq 0$, $d \neq 0$,

$$(a + bi) \div (c + di) = (a + bi)\left(\frac{1}{c + di}\right), \text{ or}$$

$$(a + bi) \div (c + di) = (a + bi)\left(\frac{c}{c^2 + d^2} - \frac{d}{c^2 + d^2}i\right).$$

Example 4

Divide: $4 + 2i$ by $3 + 5i$

$$(4 + 2i) \div (3 + 5i) = (4 + 2i)\left(\frac{1}{3 + 5i}\right)$$ ⟵ Definition of division

$$= \frac{4 + 2i}{3 + 5i} \cdot \frac{3 - 5i}{3 - 5i}$$ ⟵ The conjugate of $3 + 5i$ is $3 - 5i$.

$$= \frac{4(3 - 5i) + 2i(3 - 5i)}{9 + 25}$$

$$= \frac{12 - 20i + 6i - 10i^2}{34}$$

$$= \frac{22 - 14i}{34},$$

$$= \frac{11 - 7i}{17}$$

$$= \frac{11}{17} + \frac{-7}{17}i \qquad \longleftarrow \text{Standard form}$$

Example 5 Divide: $(2 - 5i) \div (6 + 4i)$

$$\frac{2 - 5i}{6 + 4i} = \frac{2 - 5i}{6 + 4i} \cdot \frac{6 - 4i}{6 - 4i}$$

$$= \frac{2(6 - 4i) - 5i(6 - 4i)}{36 + 16}$$

$$= \frac{-8 - 38i}{52}$$

$$= \frac{-4 - 19i}{26}$$

$$= \frac{-2}{13} + \frac{-19}{26}i \qquad \longleftarrow \text{Standard form}$$

Try These   Write the quotients in standard form.

1. $\dfrac{1}{2 + i}$ $\frac{2}{5} - \frac{1}{5}i$

2. $\dfrac{5}{3i}$ $0 - \frac{5}{3}i$

3. $\dfrac{2 - 3i}{3 + 2i}$ $0 - 1i$

Exercises

Name the conjugate of each of the following.

1. $3 + 2i$ $3 - 2i$

2. $4 - 5i$ $4 + 5i$

3. $-3 + 6i$ $-3 - 6i$

4. $3 + \sqrt{2}i$ $3 - \sqrt{2}i$

5. $4 - \sqrt{7}i$ $4 + \sqrt{7}i$

6. $0 + 2i$

7. $-7i$ $7i$

8. $8 + 0i$ $8 - 0i$ or 8

9. 10 10

$\longrightarrow 0 - 2i$ or $-2i$

Systems of Numbers   **31**

Find each quotient. Express the result in standard form. $-\frac{13}{10} - \frac{9}{10}i$

10. $\dfrac{4+2i}{1+i}$ $3-i$

11. $\dfrac{6-5i}{2+3i}$ $-\frac{3}{13} - \frac{28}{13}i$

12. $\dfrac{3+5i}{2+i}$ $\frac{11}{5} + \frac{7}{5}i$

13. $\dfrac{-4+3i}{1-3i}$

14. $\dfrac{5-\sqrt{-2}}{5+\sqrt{-2}}$

15. $\dfrac{2+3\sqrt{-3}}{2-3\sqrt{-3}}$

16. $\dfrac{5-\sqrt{-2}}{3+\sqrt{-2}}$

17. $\dfrac{\sqrt{2}-\sqrt{-3}}{\sqrt{2}+\sqrt{-3}}$

$\frac{23}{27} - \frac{10}{27}\sqrt{2}i$ $-\frac{23}{31} + \frac{12}{31}\sqrt{3}i$ $\frac{13}{11} - \frac{8}{11}\sqrt{2}i$ $-\frac{1}{5} - \frac{2}{5}\sqrt{6}i$

18. Show that $(a+bi)\left(\dfrac{a}{a^2+b^2} + \dfrac{-b}{a^2+b^2}i\right)$ is $1 + 0i$, or 1.

Apply the definition of mult. of complex numbers.

Let $x = 2 - 3i$ and $y = -3 + 2i$ in each of the quotients of Exercises **19-26**. Express the result in standard form.

19. $\dfrac{xy}{5}$ $0 + \frac{13}{5}i$

20. $\dfrac{x^2 - y^2}{i}$ $0 + 10i$

21. $\dfrac{1}{x}$ $\frac{2}{13} + \frac{3}{13}i$

22. $\dfrac{1}{y}$ $-\frac{3}{13} - \frac{2}{13}i$

23. $\dfrac{2x}{y}$ $-\frac{24}{13} + \frac{10}{13}i$

24. $\dfrac{x^2}{y}$ $-\frac{9}{13} + \frac{46}{13}i$

25. $\dfrac{x}{2y}$ $-\frac{6}{13} + \frac{5}{26}i$

26. $\dfrac{x}{y^2}$ $\frac{46}{169} + \frac{9}{169}i$

27. Use the definition of multiplication of complex numbers to show that

Simply carry out the multiplication to show this.

$$\left[\dfrac{ac+bd}{c^2+d^2} + \dfrac{(bc-ad)}{c^2+d^2}i\right](c+di) = a+bi.$$

28. Examine the following statements. $\sqrt{-\frac{16}{4}} = 2i.$ It is necessary to name pure imaginary numbers in i form first in order to achieve consistent results.

$$\sqrt{-\frac{16}{4}} = \sqrt{\frac{-16}{4}} = \frac{\sqrt{-16}}{\sqrt{4}} = \frac{4i}{2} = 2i$$

$$\sqrt{-\frac{16}{4}} = \sqrt{\frac{16}{-4}} = \frac{\sqrt{16}}{\sqrt{-4}} = \frac{4}{2i} = -2i$$

Which is correct, $\sqrt{-\frac{16}{4}} = 2i$ or $\sqrt{-\frac{16}{4}} = -2i$? Explain your reasoning.

PUZZLE

Five friends are sitting in the same row of seats.

Pat, Bill, Jan, Dot, and Ruth

Neither Pat nor Bill is seated next to Dot. Neither Pat nor Bill is seated next to Ruth. Neither Dot nor Bill is seated next to Jan. Ruth is seated just to the right of Jan. Name the seating arrangement from left to right. Bill, Pat, Jan, Ruth, Dot

Mathematics and Finance

A COMMON element in many of the careers related to finance is an aptitude for mathematics. The amount of formal training in mathematics varies with the career choice.

Securities salesworkers handle investments in stocks, bonds, and mutual funds. Most are employed by brokerage firms, investments bankers, and insurance companies. Large firms offer training in security analysis, but require a college degree with courses in economics and finance.

The **accountant** prepares and analyzes financial reports. Specialized fields deal with auditing (reviewing a client's financial records and reports), investing, taxes, and budgets. A bachelor's degree in accounting or a related field is essential. Because of the growing use of computers, many accountants study computer operations and programming.

There are various types of **bank officers,** each being concerned with supervising financial services. The **loan officer** evaluates applications for loans. The **trust officer** advises on the investment of funds. The **operations officer** strives for bank efficiency. A business administration major in finance with a background in statistics is often a requirement for an officer training position.

Chapter
Objectives
and
Review

Objective: To know the meanings of the important mathematical terms of this chapter.

1. Here are many of the important terms used in this chapter. Be sure that you know their meanings and that you can use them correctly.

absolute value (p. 7)
additive inverse (p. 2)
complex conjugate (p. 29)
complex number (p. 20)
imaginary number (p. 20)
integer (p. 2)
irrational number (p. 3)
natural number (p. 2)
open sentence (p. 6)
opposite (p. 2)
perfect square (p. 6)

pure imaginary number (p. 16)
radical (p. 6)
radicand (p. 6)
rational number (p. 2)
rationalizing the denominator (p. 11)
real number (p. 3)
replacement set (p. 6)
standard form (p. 20)
subset (p. 3)
variable (p. 6)
whole number (p. 2)

Objective: To identify rational numbers, irrational numbers, real numbers, pure imaginary numbers, and complex numbers. (Sections 1-1, 1-5, 1-6)

Classify each number as rational, irrational, real, pure imaginary, or complex. More than one answer is possible.

2. $\frac{2}{3}$ Rational, real, complex

3. $2 + 3i$ Rational, real, complex
Complex

4. $-\sqrt{4}$

5. $-\sqrt{-4}$ Pure imaginary, complex

6. $\sqrt{8}$ Irrational, real, complex

7. $\pi + 0i$ Irr., real, complex

Objective: To identify the real number postulate illustrated by an example. (Section 1-1)

Write the name of the real number postulate illustrated by each equation.

8. $0 + 5 = 5 + 0$
Comm., add.

9. $\frac{2}{3}(5\pi) = (\frac{2}{3} \cdot 5)\pi$
Assoc., mult.

10. $5 + (-5) = 0$
Inverse, addition

Objective: To simplify radicals. (Section 1-2)

Simplify each radical.

11. $\sqrt{y^4}$ y^2

12. $\sqrt{125}$ $5\sqrt{5}$

13. $\sqrt{\dfrac{36}{25}}$ $\frac{6}{5}$

Objective: To multiply and divide with radicals. (Section 1-3)

Multiply or divide. Simplify where possible.

14. $\sqrt{6} \cdot \sqrt{8}$ $4\sqrt{3}$ **15.** $\sqrt{5} \cdot \sqrt{8}$ $2\sqrt{10}$ **16.** $\sqrt{3} \div \sqrt{\dfrac{3}{2}}$ $\sqrt{2}$ **17.** $\dfrac{\sqrt{42} - 4\sqrt{84}}{\sqrt{7}}$ $\sqrt{6} - 8\sqrt{3}$

Objective: To add and subtract with radicals. (Section 1-4)

Add or subtract. Simplify where possible.

18. $5\sqrt{2} - 2\sqrt{2}$ $3\sqrt{2}$ **19.** $6\sqrt{55} + \sqrt{176}$ $6\sqrt{55} + 4\sqrt{11}$ **20.** $\sqrt{20} - \sqrt{5}$ $\sqrt{5}$ **21.** $3\sqrt{28} + \sqrt{\dfrac{1}{7}}$ $\dfrac{43}{7}\sqrt{7}$

Objective: To add, subtract, multiply and divide with pure imaginary numbers.

Perform the indicated operations. Write your answer in i-form. (Section 1-5)

22. $\sqrt{-2} + 4\sqrt{-2}$ $5i\sqrt{2}$ **23.** $\sqrt{-24} + \sqrt{-16}$ $(2\sqrt{6} + 4)i$ **24.** $\sqrt{-4} \cdot \sqrt{-3}$ $-2\sqrt{3}$ **25.** $\dfrac{\sqrt{-16}}{\sqrt{-2}}$ $2\sqrt{2}$

Objective: To express complex numbers in standard form. (Section 1-6)

Write each complex number in standard form.

26. $\sqrt{-9}$ $0 + 3i$ **27.** $5 - \sqrt{-50}$ $5 + (-5\sqrt{2})i$ **28.** $\sqrt{-\dfrac{3}{8}}$ $0 + \dfrac{\sqrt{6}}{4}i$ **29.** $\sqrt{\dfrac{5}{6}}$ $\dfrac{\sqrt{30}}{6} + 0i$

Objective: To write the conjugate and the reciprocal of a complex number in standard form. (Section 1-8)

Write the conjugate and reciprocal of each number in standard form.

30. $2 - i$ $2 + i; \dfrac{2}{5} + \dfrac{1}{5}i$ **31.** i $0 + (-1)i; 0 + (-1)i$ **32.** 3 $3 + 0i; \dfrac{1}{3} + 0i$ **33.** $1 + 5i$ $1 + (-5)i; \dfrac{1}{26} + \left(-\dfrac{5}{26}\right)i$

Objective: To add, subtract, multiply, and divide complex numbers. (Sections 1-7, 1-8, 1-9)

Perform the indicated operations. Express your answer in standard form.

34. $(-4 - 6i) + (-10 - 12i)$ $-14 + (-18)i$ **35.** $(2 + 3i) + (-2 - 4i)$ $0 + (-1)i$

36. $(3 - 5i) - (2 + i)$ $1 + (-6)i$ **37.** $(0 + i) - (5 + 3i)$ $-5 + (-2)i$

38. $\sqrt{-16} \cdot \sqrt{-9}$ -12 **39.** $(5 - 2i)(3 + 3i)$ $21 + 9i$

40. $\sqrt{-4} \div 3i$ $\dfrac{2}{3}$ **41.** $(4 - 2i) \div (3 - 2i)$ $\dfrac{16}{13} + \dfrac{2}{13}i$

Chapter
Test

Complete each sentence.

1. The union of Q and Ir is ___R___.

2. The union of R and the set of imaginary numbers is ___the set of complex numbers___.

3. The conjugate of $2 - 6i$ is ___$2 + 6i$___.

4. The reciprocal of $3 + 2i$ expressed in standard form is ___$\frac{3}{13} - \frac{2}{13}i$___.

5. If $a + bi = 3 - 7i$, then $b =$ ___-7___.

Classify each sentence as True (T) or False (F).

6. The number $\frac{2}{9}$ is a complex number. T

7. The set of irrational numbers is a subset of the complex numbers. T

8. The number $5 - 3i$ is a pure imaginary number. F

9. $\sqrt{-1} = i$ T

10. The set of real numbers and the set of imaginary numbers have no elements in common. T

Simplify.

11. $\sqrt{36y^2}$ $6|y|$

12. $\sqrt{48}$ $4\sqrt{3}$

13. $\sqrt{15} \cdot \sqrt{18}$ $3\sqrt{30}$

14. $\sqrt{12} - \sqrt{27}$ $-\sqrt{3}$

15. $3\sqrt{2} - 3\sqrt{3} + \sqrt{50}$ $8\sqrt{2} - 3\sqrt{3}$

16. $i^2 \cdot i^2$ 1

Perform the indicated operations. Express your answers in standard form.

17. $(2 - 3i) + (-5 + 6i)$ $-3 + 3i$

18. $(5 + i) - (4 - 2i)$ $1 + 3i$

19. $(4 + i)(-2 - 3i)$ $-5 - 14i$

20. $(2 + 3i) \div (1 - i)$ $-\frac{1}{2} + \frac{5}{2}i$

Answers to Remember

Page 8:   **1.** $4 \cdot 10$ **2.** $9 \cdot 8$; $36 \cdot 2$; $4 \cdot 18$ **3.** $100 \cdot 2$; $50 \cdot 4$, $25 \cdot 8$ **4.** $16 \cdot 2$; $16 \cdot 2$

Page 12:   **1.** $7x$ **2.** $-4x^2y + x$ **3.** $17ab + 7ab^2$ **4.** $-22q^2 - 9q$

Page 22:   **1.** $10 + 11\sqrt{5}$ **2.** $3 - 3\sqrt{3}$ **3.** 0 **4.** $-1 + 8\sqrt{2}$

Page 26:   **1.** Yes   **2.** No   **3.** No   **4.** $5\sqrt{7}$ **5.** $2|xy|\sqrt{5x}$ **6.** $128\sqrt{2}$ **7.** $-i$ **8.** -6 **9.** 5

Chapter 2
Polynomials and Rational Expressions

2-1 Polynomial Expressions

The objectives for this section are on page 96.

The following algebraic expressions are <u>monomials</u>.

$$2y^5 \qquad \sqrt{5}x^3 \qquad -3 \qquad (2-i)z^2$$

A **monomial** is a term that consists only of the product of complex numbers and variables with exponents that are whole numbers. A **polynomial** is a monomial or the sum of monomials. Verify that each expression in the second column is not a polynomial.

Polynomials	Not Polynomials
$-7x^2$	$-7\sqrt{x}$
5	$\dfrac{1}{x}$
$(2+i)y^3 + 3y$	$2y^4 + 3y^{-5}$
$9x^0$	$x^{\sqrt{5}}$

Polynomials can be classified by the number of terms.

Polynomial	Number of terms	Name
$\frac{1}{2}x$	1	Monomial
$x^2 + y^2$	2	Binomial
$\sqrt{2}xy - \sqrt{7}x + 1$	3	Trinomial

The **degree of a term** of a polynomial is the sum of the exponents of its variables. The **degree of a polynomial** is the greatest degree of its terms.

Polynomial	Term of greatest degree	Degree of polynomial
$10x^2y^5$	$10x^2y^5$	$2+5=7$
$-x^4 + 10x^2y^5$	$10x^2y^5$	$2+5=7$
$-x^4 + 10x^2y^5 + y^9$	y^9	9
$x + 2xy + y$	$2xy$	$1+1=2$
5	5	0
$x^3 - y^3$	x^3 or y^3	3

Polynomials can also be classified by their coefficients.

Polynomials	Coefficients	Polynomial over the set of
$-5x^2 + 3y^2$	$-5, 3$	integers
$\frac{2}{3}x^2 - 6xy + \frac{1}{2}y^2$	$\frac{2}{3}, -6, \frac{1}{2}$	rational numbers
$\sqrt{3}z^2 - 5$	$\sqrt{3}, -5$	real numbers
$(2-i)x^2 + 3ix - 2$	$(2-i), 3i, -2$	complex numbers

Try These *Classify each expression as a polynomial or not a polynomial. Classify each polynomial according to its coefficients.*

1. $-5b^3$ Polynomial, integers

2. $2 + 5x^{-1}$ Not a polynomial

3. $\dfrac{4}{x} - y^2$ Not a polynomial

4. $iy^3 - i^2y$ Polynomial, complex

5. $\sqrt{5}z^5 - 1$ Polynomial, real numbers

6. $6 - 5y + 2z - 10x$ Polynomial, integers

Exercises

For each exercise, write P if the expression is a polynomial. Write NP if it is not.

1. 3 P

2. $\sqrt{3}$ P

3. $\sqrt{3x}$ NP

4. $2x^2$ P

5. $-3x^2$ P

6. $-\frac{1}{2}x^2 + 5xy + y^2$ P

7. $\dfrac{3}{x}$ NP

8. i^2 P

9. $2ix^2$ P

10. $\dfrac{5}{x^2}$ NP

11. $\dfrac{x-3}{x+3}$ NP

12. $5x^{-4} + x^3 - 1$ NP

13. $(3+i)x^2 + 5x - i$ P

14. $x^{\frac{2}{3}} + 6x$ NP

15. $3\frac{1}{3}x^2 - 4x + \sqrt{2}$ P

Write the degree of each polynomial.

16. $3x^3 - 2x^2 + 5x - 12$ 3

17. $xy + 5$ 2

18. $2x^5 + 7x^4y - 18x^3y^7$ 10

Classify each polynomial by its coefficients.

19. $2x^2 - 3xy + 12y^2$ Integers

20. $(5+3i)x^3 - 4i$ Complex

21. $\dfrac{x}{2} + 12$ Rational

22. $(6-4i)x^4$ Complex

23. $\sqrt{5}x^2 - 2$ Real

24. $\sqrt[3]{-27}$ Integers

Polynomials and Rational Expressions **39**

Determine the complex number named by each polynomial.

Example: $2x^2 + 3x$, when $x = i$ **Solution:** $2x^2 + 3x = 2(i^2) + 3i = -2 + 3i$

25. $-3x^2$ when $x = 2$ $\quad_{-12}$ **26.** $x^2 + x$ when $x = 1$ $\quad^2$ **27.** x^2 when $x = i$ $\quad^{-1}$ $\quad_{10 - 6\sqrt{3}}$

28. $2x^2$ when $x = \sqrt{2}$ $\quad^4$ **29.** $x^2 - 5x$ when $x = 3$ $\quad^{-6}$ **30.** $2x^2 - 6x + 4$ when $x = \sqrt{3}$

31. ix^3 when $x = -i$ $\quad^{-1}$ **32.** $x^2 + 2i$ when $x = -3i$ $\quad_{-9 + 2i}$ **33.** $x^2 - 2x + 1$ when $x = 2i$ $\quad_{-3 - 4i}$

Rewrite each polynomial as a sum or difference of terms with the term of highest degree listed first.

34. $x(x + 1)$ $\quad^{x^2 + x}$ **35.** $(x + 1)(x - 1)$ $\quad^{x^2 - 1}$ **36.** $(1 - x)(x + 2)$ $\quad^{-x^2 - x + 2}$

2-2 Addition and Subtraction of Polynomials

The objective for this section is on page 96.

Terms such as $3ab^2$, $7ab^2$, and $-\sqrt{5}ab^2$ are **like terms.** Their variable factors, ab^2, are exactly alike. To add polynomials with like terms, use the distributive postulate.

Example 1   Add: $2x^2y + 5x^2y$

$$2x^2y + 5x^2y = (2 + 5)x^2y \quad \longleftarrow \quad \text{Distributive postulate}$$
$$= 7x^2y \quad \longleftarrow \quad \text{Add.}$$

Example 2   Add: $(\sqrt{3}x^2 - 6xy + \sqrt{2}y^2) + (2\sqrt{3}x^2 + xy - 2\sqrt{2}y^2)$

$(\sqrt{3}x^2 - 6xy + \sqrt{2}y^2) + (2\sqrt{3}x^2 + xy - 2\sqrt{2}y^2)$
$$= \sqrt{3}x^2 + 2\sqrt{3}x^2 - 6xy + xy + \sqrt{2}y^2 - 2\sqrt{2}y^2 \quad \longleftarrow \quad \begin{array}{l}\text{Commutative and}\\\text{associative postulates}\end{array}$$
$$= (\sqrt{3} + 2\sqrt{3})x^2 + (-6 + 1)xy + (\sqrt{2} - 2\sqrt{2})y^2 \quad \longleftarrow \quad \text{Distributive postulate}$$
$$= 3\sqrt{3}x^2 - 5xy - \sqrt{2}y^2$$

To subtract two polynomials, add the additive inverse of the polynomial to be subtracted. The additive inverse of the polynomial can be found by multiplying it by -1.

$$(z^5 - 6z) - (-2z^5 + 3z) \text{ means } (z^5 - 6z) + (-1)(-2z^5 + 3z).$$
$$(z^5 - 6z) - (-2z^5 + 3z) \text{ means } (z^5 - 6z) + (2z^5 - 3z).$$

Example 3   Subtract $4a^4 - 2a^3 + 9$ from $9a^4 - 3a^3 - 6$.

$9a^4 - 3a^3 - 6 - (4a^4 - 2a^3 + 9)$

$= 9a^4 - 3a^3 - 6 + (-1)(4a^4 - 2a^3 + 9)$ ⟵ Add the additive inverse of $4a^4 - 2a^3 + 9$.

$= 9a^4 - 3a^3 - 6 - 4a^4 + 2a^3 - 9$

$= 9a^4 - 4a^4 - 3a^3 + 2a^3 - 6 - 9$ ⟵ Commutative and associative postulates

$= (9 - 4)a^4 + (-3 + 2)a^3 - 6 - 9$

$= 5a^4 - a^3 - 15$ ⟵ Add.

It is sometimes easier to add or subtract polynomials by arranging like terms in the same vertical column.

Example 4   Add: $(7z - 2z^3 - 1) + (10z^4 - 8 + z^3 - 5z^2)$.

$$
\begin{array}{l}
 -2z^3 + 7z - 1 \quad \longleftarrow \text{ Start with the term of highest degree.} \\
\underline{10z^4 + z^3 - 5z^2 - 8} \quad \longleftarrow \text{ Write like terms in the same column.} \\
10z^4 - z^3 - 5z^2 + 7z - 9 \quad \longleftarrow \text{ Add.}
\end{array}
$$

Example 5   Subtract: $ix^2 + 4iy^2 - (-2ix^2 + 7iy^2)$

First, write the like terms in the same column. ⟶

$$
\begin{array}{c}
ix^2 + 4iy^2 \\
- \underline{-2ix^2 + 7iy^2}
\end{array}
\qquad
\begin{array}{c}
ix^2 + 4iy^2 \\
+ \underline{2ix^2 - 7iy^2} \\
3ix^2 - 3iy^2
\end{array}
$$

⟵ Then, add the additive inverse of $-2ix^2 + 7iy^2$.

Add.

1. $(3x+5) + (-5x+2)$ $_{-2x+7}$

2. $(\sqrt{3}y^3 + \sqrt{7}y^2 + 5y) + (3\sqrt{3}y^3 - 3\sqrt{7}y^2)$
   $_{4\sqrt{3}y^3 - 2\sqrt{7}y^2 + 5y}$

Subtract. Remember to rewrite Exercises 5 and 6 as addition problems.

3. $(4x - 5y + 18) - (6x - 5y - 2)$ $_{-2x+20}$

4. $(5iz^2 + iz) - (6z^2 + iz)$ $_{(5i-6)z^2}$

5. $\begin{array}{r} c^3 - 3c^2 + 8c + 1 \\ -2c^3 + 5c^2 - 2c - 3 \\ \hline \scriptstyle 3c^3 - 8c^2 + 10c + 4 \end{array}$

6. $\begin{array}{r} 2x^4 \qquad - 3x^2 + 8x \\ 2x^4 - 4x^3 + 2x^2 \\ \hline \scriptstyle 4x^3 - 5x^2 + 8x \end{array}$

Exercises

Add.

1. $(3x^2) + (4x^2)$ $_{7x^2}$

2. $(2x^2) + (-5x^2)$ $_{-3x^2}$

3. $(2x+3) + (x+5)$ $_{3x+8}$

4. $(3x+2) + (-4x-3)$ $_{-x-1}$

5. $(7x+4) + (-4x-2)$ $_{3x+2}$

6. $(2x-1) + (x+4)$ $_{3x+3}$

7. $(5x^2 - 7x + 3) + (4x^2 + 2x)$ $_{9x^2 - 5x + 3}$

8. $(y^2 + 2y - 5) + (8y^2 - 5y + 9)$ $_{9y^2 - 3y + 4}$

9. $\begin{array}{r} y^2 + 9y + 6 \\ -5y^2 - 3y + 5 \\ \hline \scriptstyle -4y^2 + 6y + 11 \end{array}$

10. $\begin{array}{r} -4z^3 + 5z^2 - 2z + 3 \\ 2z^3 - z^2 + 7z - 8 \\ \hline \scriptstyle -2z^3 + 4z^2 + 5z - 5 \end{array}$

11. $\begin{array}{r} a^3 - a^2 + 1 \\ 5a^2 - 7 \\ \hline \scriptstyle a^3 + 4a^2 - 6 \end{array}$

12. $\begin{array}{r} 3b^4 - 2b^3 + 19b^2 + 3b - 13 \\ - b^3 - 12b^2 \qquad + 9 \\ \hline \scriptstyle 3b^4 - 3b^3 + 7b^2 + 3b - 4 \end{array}$

13. $(18a^3 - 5a^2 - 6a + 2) + (7a^3 - 8a + 9)$ $_{25a^3 - 5a^2 - 14a + 11}$

14. $(2x^4 - 3x^2 + 2 - 5x) + (4x^2 + 2x - 7x^4 + 6)$ $_{-5x^4 + x^2 - 3x + 8}$

15. $(x^2 + y^2 - z^2) + (3z^2 - 2x^2 - 4y^2) + (4x^2 - 5y^2 + z^2)$ $_{3x^2 - 8y^2 + 3z^2}$

16. $\begin{array}{r} 3ix^2y^5 \\ 5ix^2y^5 \\ -6ix^2y^5 \\ \hline \scriptstyle 2ix^2y^5 \end{array}$

17. $\begin{array}{r} \sqrt{5}x^2 - 3xy + \sqrt{2}y^2 \\ 3\sqrt{5}x^2 + 4xy - 2\sqrt{2}y^2 \\ 3\sqrt{5}x^2 - 8xy - 6\sqrt{2}y^2 \\ \hline \scriptstyle 7\sqrt{5}x^2 - 7xy - 7\sqrt{2}y^2 \end{array}$

18. $(23ix^2 - 35ixy - 18iy^2) + (9iy^2 - 7iy - 5ixy - 19ix^2)$ $_{4ix^2 - 40ixy - 7iy - 9iy^2}$

Subtract.

19. $(-5x - 7y + 9) - (2x + 4y - 3)$ $_{-7x - 11y + 12}$

20. $(7x^3 - 5y^2 - 2) - (5x^3 - 2y^2 + 4)$ $_{2x^3 - 3y^2 - 6}$

21. $(y^4 + 9y^2 - 11y) - (13y^3 - 5y^4 + 19y - 1)$ $_{6y^4 - 13y^3 + 9y^2 - 30y + 1}$

22. $(k^3 - 3k^2 + 6 + 5k) - (3k - 4k^2 + 2k^3 - 8)$ $\;\; {}_{-k^3 + k^2 + 2k + 14}$

23. $(3a^5 - 2a^3 + 4a^2 - 7) - (-2a^3 + 3a^5 - 7 + 4a^2)$ $\;\; {}_{0}$

24. $(9 + 3t^2 - t + 5t^4) - (2t - 3 + 8t^2 - 3t^4)$ $\;\; {}_{8t^4 - 5t^2 - 3t + 12}$

25. $(-x^2 - iy^2) - (-2x^2 + 3xy - 2iy^2)$ $\;\; {}_{x^2 - 3xy + iy^2}$

26. $(9x^2y^2 - 5ixy + 25iy^2) - (5x^2y^2 + 10ixy - 9iy^2)$ $\;\; {}_{4x^2y^2 - 15ixy + 34iy^2}$

Subtract. Remember to rewrite each subtraction problem as an addition problem.

27. $x^2 - 2x$ $\;\; {}_{-5x}$
$x^2 + 3x$

28. a^3 $\qquad -1$ $\;\; {}_{a^2 - 1}$
$\underline{a^3 - a^2}$

29. $y^3 - 2iy + 7i$
$\underline{\quad\; 5iy - 5i}$
$\;\;\; {}_{y^3 - 7iy + 12i}$

30. $\quad ix^2 + 7ix - 13$
$\underline{-9ix^2 + 3ix + 15}$
$\;\;\; {}_{10ix^2 + 4ix - 28}$

Perform the indicated operations.

31. $((3 + i)a^3 - 2ia^2 + 7) + (-5ia^2 + 8) + ((-4 + i)a^3 + 9ia^2)$ $\;\; {}_{(-1 + 2i)a^3 + 2ia^2 + 15}$

32. $((4 - i)a^4 + 6ia) + (8 - 2(4 - i)a^4 + 7ia^2) + (-5ia^2 - (i - 2)a^4)$ $\;\; {}_{-2a^4 + 2ia^2 + 6ia + 8}$

33. $(4\sqrt{3}x^2 - 8xy + 4\sqrt{2}y^2) - (3\sqrt{3}x^2 - 5xy + \sqrt{2}y^2)$ $\;\; {}_{\sqrt{3}x^2 - 3xy + 3\sqrt{2}y^2}$

34. From $x - 2iy$, take $-x + iy + z$. $\;\; {}_{2x - 3iy - z}$

35. Subtract $\sqrt{6}x^3 - 4x^2 + \sqrt{2}x - 5$ from 0. $\;\; {}_{-\sqrt{6}x^3 + 4x^2 - \sqrt{2}x + 5}$

36. Add $(0.5a^2 - 0.7b^2 - 0.3)$, $(1.7a^2 - 4.6b^2 - 0.9)$, and $(3a^2 + 4b^2 - 2)$. $\;\; {}_{5.2a^2 - 1.3b^2 - 3.2}$

37. From the sum of $(2x^2 + 3xy - 5y^2)$ and $(6y^2 - 4x^2)$, subtract $(8y^2 - 7xy)$. $\;\; {}_{-2x^2 + 10xy - 7y^2}$

38. By how much does $(\frac{3}{4}x^2 - 0.5x + 7)$ exceed $(\frac{1}{2}x^2 + \frac{1}{4}x - 5)$? $\;\; {}_{\frac{1}{4}x^2 - \frac{3}{4}x + 12}$

*The set of polynomials is a **commutative group under addition** because it satisfies the five postulates listed in Column II. Match each statement in Column I with a postulate from Column II. (P, Q, and R are polynomials and 0 is the zero polynomial.)*

Column I: Statements

39. $P + Q = Q + P$ $\;\; {}_{b.}$

40. $P + 0 = P$ $\;\; {}_{d.}$

41. $P + (-P) = 0$ $\;\; {}_{e.}$

42. $P + Q$ is a polynomial. $\;\; {}_{a.}$

43. $(P + Q) + R = P + (Q + R)$ $\;\; {}_{c.}$

Column II: Postulates

a. Closure

b. Commutativity

c. Associativity

d. Existence of an identity element

e. Existence of an additive inverse for each polynomial

44. Verify each statement in Exercises 39–43 on the previous page by using the polynomial $(3x + 5)$ for P, $(2x^2 - 4x + 4)$ for Q, and $(x^2 + 5x + 6)$ for R.

45. Give an example to show that the set of polymonials is not commutative under subtraction. <small>Answers will vary.</small>

46. Give an example to show that the set of polynomials is not associative under subtraction. <small>Answers will vary.</small>

Remember

Multiply and simplify the result.

1. $\sqrt{2} \cdot \sqrt{6}$ <small>$2\sqrt{3}$</small>

2. $\sqrt{6} \cdot \sqrt{12}$ <small>$6\sqrt{2}$</small>

3. $(i + 2)(i - 1)$ <small>$i - 3$</small>

4. $(1 - i)(3 + i)$ <small>$4 - 2i$</small>

The answers are on page 99.

2-3 Multiplication of Polynomials

The objective for this section is on page 97.

Since x^2 means $x \cdot x$ and x^3 means $x \cdot x \cdot x$,

$$x^2 \cdot x^3 = \underbrace{x \cdot x}_{2} \cdot \underbrace{x \cdot x \cdot x}_{3}$$

$$\underbrace{}_{\textbf{5 factors}}$$

Thus,

$$x^2 \cdot x^3 = x^{2+3} = x^5.$$

Theorem 2-1: Exponent Property for Multiplication

If m and n are positive integers and a is a complex number,

$$a^m \cdot a^n = a^{m+n}.$$

Theorem 2-1 can be used to multiply monomials. This is illustrated in the following examples.

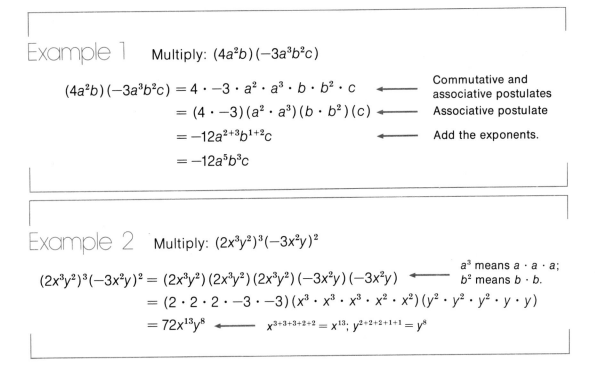

Example 1   Multiply: $(4a^2b)(-3a^3b^2c)$

$(4a^2b)(-3a^3b^2c) = 4 \cdot -3 \cdot a^2 \cdot a^3 \cdot b \cdot b^2 \cdot c$ ◄——— Commutative and associative postulates

$= (4 \cdot -3)(a^2 \cdot a^3)(b \cdot b^2)(c)$ ◄——— Associative postulate

$= -12a^{2+3}b^{1+2}c$ ◄——— Add the exponents.

$= -12a^5b^3c$

Example 2   Multiply: $(2x^3y^2)^3(-3x^2y)^2$

a^3 means $a \cdot a \cdot a$; b^2 means $b \cdot b$.

$(2x^3y^2)^3(-3x^2y)^2 = (2x^3y^2)(2x^3y^2)(2x^3y^2)(-3x^2y)(-3x^2y)$ ◄———

$= (2 \cdot 2 \cdot 2 \cdot -3 \cdot -3)(x^3 \cdot x^3 \cdot x^3 \cdot x^2 \cdot x^2)(y^2 \cdot y^2 \cdot y^2 \cdot y \cdot y)$

$= 72x^{13}y^8$ ◄——— $x^{3+3+3+2+2} = x^{13}$; $y^{2+2+2+1+1} = y^8$

To multiply a polynomial by a monomial, use the distributive postulate.

Example 3   Multiply: $-cd^2(c^2 + cd + d^2)$

$-cd^2(c^2 + cd + d^2)$
$= (-cd^2)(c^2) + (-cd^2)(cd) + (-cd^2)(d^2)$ ◄——— Distributive postulate

$= (-c \cdot c^2 \cdot d^2) + (-c \cdot c \cdot d^2 \cdot d) + (-c \cdot d^2 \cdot d^2)$

$= -c^3d^2 - c^2d^3 - cd^4$

You can find the product of two binomials by using the distributive postulate twice. This is illustrated in the example at the top of the next page.

Example 4   Multiply: $(5x - 4)(2x + 7)$

$(5x - 4)(2x + 7)$

$= 5x(2x + 7) - 4(2x + 7)$ ⟵ Distributive postulate

$= 5x \cdot 2x + 5x \cdot 7 + (-4)(2x) + (-4)(7)$ ⟵ Distributive postulate

$= 10x^2 + 35x - 8x - 28$ ⟵ Multiply.

$= 10x^2 + 27x - 28$ ⟵ Combine like terms.

Example 5   Multiply by inspection: $(5x - 4)(2x + 7)$

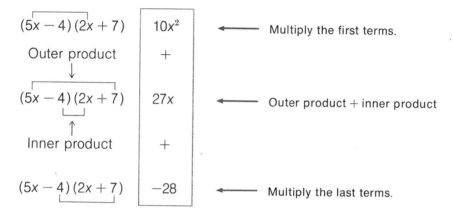

$(5x - 4)(2x + 7)$	$10x^2$	⟵ Multiply the first terms.
Outer product	$+$	
$(5x - 4)(2x + 7)$	$27x$	⟵ Outer product + inner product
Inner product	$+$	
$(5x - 4)(2x + 7)$	-28	⟵ Multiply the last terms.

Thus, $(5x - 4)(2x + 7) = 10x^2 + 27x - 28$.

Example 6   Multiply by inspection:

     a. $(4x + 5)(x - 9)$ **b.** $(6x^2 - 2)(3x + 4)$

     a. $(4x + 5)(x - 9) = 4x^2 - 36x + 5x - 45 = 4x^2 - 31x - 45$

     b. $(6x^2 - 2)(3x + 4) = 18x^3 + 24x^2 - 6x - 8$

The square of a binomial can also be found by inspection.

Example 7 Find $(a + b)^2$.

$$(a + b)^2 = (a + b)(a + b)$$

$$= (a + b)(a + b) \quad \boxed{\begin{array}{c} a^2 \\ + \end{array}} \quad \longleftarrow \quad \text{Multiply the first terms.}$$

Outer product

$\downarrow$

$$= (a + b)(a + b) \quad 2ab \quad \longleftarrow \quad \text{Outer product + inner product}$$

$\uparrow$

Inner product

$+$

$$= (a + b)(a + b) \quad b^2 \quad \longleftarrow \quad \text{Multiply the last terms.}$$

Thus, $(a + b)^2 = a^2 + 2ab + b^2$.

It is sometimes convenient to use a vertical form.

Example 8   Multiply: $(x^2 + 2x + i)(5x - i)$.

$$
\begin{array}{r}
x^2 + 2x \; + i \\
5x \; - i \\
\hline
-ix^2 - 2ix - i^2 \quad \longleftarrow \quad -i(x^2 + 2x + i) \\
5x^3 + 10x^2 + 5ix \quad \longleftarrow \quad 5x(x^2 + 2x + i) \\
\hline
5x^3 + (10 - i)x^2 + 3ix + 1 \quad \longleftarrow \quad \text{Add. } -i^2 = 1
\end{array}
$$

Try These   *Multiply.*

1. $(-2xy)(3x^2y^3)$ **2.** $7c(9 - 6d)$ **3.** $(2x + 1)(3x - 2)$ **4.** $(x - 2i)(x + 3i)$

    $-6x^3y^4$ $63c - 42cd$ $6x^2 - x - 2$ $x^2 + ix + 6$

Polynomials and Rational Expressions   **47**

Exercises

Multiply.

1. $2x^3(-3x^7)$ $\quad$ $-6x^{10}$

2. $a^3 \cdot 4a^2$ $\quad$ $4a^5$

3. $7s^2t^5(-8st^2)$ $\quad$ $-56s^3t^7$

4. $5a^7 \cdot \sqrt{2}a^5 \cdot a^3$ $\quad$ $5\sqrt{2}a^{15}$

5. $(-3mn^2)(2m^2n)$ $\quad$ $-6m^3n^3$

6. $(-5c^4d^3)(-2c^2d)$ $\quad$ $10c^6d^4$

7. $(3x^2y)(-4xy)(5xy^2)$ $\quad$ $-60x^4y^4$

8. $(-3a^2b)(-2ab^2)(-a^2b^2)$ $\quad$ $-6a^5b^5$

9. $(-2c^2)(3cd)^2$ $\quad$ $-18c^4d^2$

10. $(2mn)(-3n)^3$ $\quad$ $-54mn^4$

11. $(5t^3)^2(-2s^2)^3$ $\quad$ $-200t^6s^6$

12. $(2x^2yz^3)^2(-3xy^3z^2)^3$ $\quad$ $-108x^7y^{11}z^{12}$

13. $5xy^2(2x - 3y)$ $\quad$ $10x^2y^2 - 15xy^3$

14. $mn(5m - 3n)$ $\quad$ $5m^2n - 3mn^2$

15. $-r^2t^2(r^3t - rt^5)$ $\quad$ $-r^5t^3 + r^3t^7$

16. $cd(7c + 4d)$ $\quad$ $7c^2d + 4cd^2$

17. $i(6ix - 7iy^2)$ $\quad$ $-6x + 7y^2$

18. $-2(a^2 + 6a + 10)$ $\quad$ $-2a^2 - 12a - 20$

19. $4xy^2(3xy - x^2y + 5)$ $\quad$ $12x^2y^3 - 4x^3y^3 + 20xy^2$

20. $2ab(9a^3b^4 + 3a^2b - 2b^4)$ $\quad$ $18a^4b^5 + 6a^3b^2 - 4ab^5$

21. $(2x + 5)(3x + 4)$ $\quad$ $6x^2 + 23x + 20$

22. $(2x + 5)(3x - 4)$ $\quad$ $6^2 + 7x - 20$

23. $(2x - 5)(3x - 4)$ $\quad$ $6x^2 - 23x + 20$

24. $(5x - 2)(2x - 3)$ $\quad$ $10x^2 - 19x + 6$

25. $(a^2 + b^2)(a^2 - 2b^2)$ $\quad$ $a^4 - a^2b^2 - 2b^4$

26. $(n + 6)^2$ $\quad$ $n^2 + 12n + 36$

27. $(2m - 7)^2$ $\quad$ $4m^2 - 28m + 49$

28. $(x + y)^2$ $\quad$ $x^2 + 2xy + y^2$

29. $(2x - 5y)^2$ $\quad$ $4x^2 - 20xy + 25y^2$

30. $(7t - 3r)^2$ $\quad$ $49t^2 - 42rt + 9r^2$

31. $-(2a - 3b)^2$ $\quad$ $-4a^2 + 12ab - 9b^2$

32. $(x - y)(x + y)$ $\quad$ $x^2 - y^2$

33. $(3m + 4n)(3m - 4n)$ $\quad$ $9m^2 - 16n^2$

34. $(3c - 7d)(2c + d)$ $\quad$ $6c^2 - 11cd - 7d^2$

35. $(x - 3i)(7x - 9i)$ $\quad$ $7x^2 - 30ix - 27$

36. $(a - 3)(a^2 - 5a + 6)$ $\quad$ $a^3 - 8a^2 + 21a - 18$

37. $(x - 2)(x^2 + 6x - 9)$ $\quad$ $x^3 + 4x^2 - 21x + 18$

38. $(2m + 3)(m^2 + 4m - 1)$

39. $(2a - 3b)(2a + 3b)(4a^2 + 9b^2)$ $\quad$ $16a^4 - 81b^4$

40. $(i^3 - 1)(i + 1)(2i + 1)$ $\quad$ $4 - 2i$

41. $(2m + n)^3$ $\quad$ $8m^3 + 12m^2n + 6mn^2 + n^3$

42. $(\frac{2}{3}x - \frac{3}{5})(\frac{2}{3}x + \frac{3}{5})(4x^2 + 9)$ $\quad$ See below.

$\rightarrow$ 2m^3 + 11m^2 + 10m - 3

43. The set of polynomials is not a commutative group under multiplication. (See page 43.) Which of the following postulates for a commutative group does not hold for polynomials? $\quad$ *e*

$\quad$ **42.** $\frac{16}{9}x^4 + \frac{64}{25}x^2 - \frac{81}{25}$

$\quad$ **a.** Closure under multiplication

$\quad$ **b.** Commutativity under multiplication

$\quad$ **c.** Associativity under multiplication

$\quad$ **d.** Existence of a multiplicative identity

$\quad$ **e.** Existence of a multiplicative inverse for each nonzero polynomial

The objective for this section is on page 97.

Renaming a polynomial as the product of two or more polynomials is called **factoring**. The patterns shown in the following table are useful for factoring polynomials.

Finding Products	Finding Factors
Monomial $\times$ Binomial	**Common monomial factor**
1. $a(b+c) = ab + ac$	**1.** $ab + ac = a(b+c)$
$3x(x^2 - 6) = 3x^3 - 18x$	$3x^3 - 18x = 3x(x^2 - 6)$
	Common binomial factor
2. $a(b+c) + d(b+c) = ab + ac + db + dc$	**2.** $ab + ac + db + dc = a(b+c) + d(b+c)$
	$ = (b+c)(a+d)$
$x(x+y) + 2(x+y) = x^2 + xy + 2x + 2y$	$x^2 + xy + 2x + 2y = x(x+y) + 2(x+y)$
	$ = (x+y)(x+2)$
Sum $\times$ Difference	**Difference of squares**
3. $(a+b)(a-b) = a^2 - b^2$	**3.** $a^2 - b^2 = (a+b)(a-b)$
$(x+2)(x-2) = x^2 - 4$	$x^2 - 4 = (x+2)(x-2)$
Square of a sum	**Perfect square trinomial**
4. $(a+b)^2 = a^2 + 2ab + b^2$	**4.** $a^2 + 2ab + b^2 = (a+b)^2$
$(x+7)^2 = x^2 + 14x + 49$	$x^2 + 14x + 49 = (x+7)^2$
$(2 \cdot 7)x$	$(2 \cdot 7)x$
Square of a difference	**Perfect square trinomial**
5. $(a-b)^2 = a^2 - 2ab + b^2$	**5.** $a^2 - 2ab + b^2 = (a-b)^2$
$(x-7)^2 = x^2 - 14x + 49$	$x^2 - 14x + 49 = (x-7)^2$
$2(-7)x$	$2(-7)x$

To factor a polynomial, first look for common monomial factors. Then look for one of the patterns in the table on page 49.

Example 1   Factor $2x^4y^3 - 6x^3y^3 - 10x^2y^4$.

$2x^4y^3 - 6x^3y^3 - 10x^2y^4 = 2x^2y^3 \cdot x^2 - 2x^2y^3 \cdot 3x - 2x^2y^3 \cdot 5y$ ← The common factor
$$= 2x^2y^3(x^2 - 3x - 5y)$$ is $2x^2y^3$.

The polynomial $x^2 - 3x - 5y$ has no polynomial factors other than itself, its opposite, and ± 1. Hence, it is a **prime polynomial.**

A polynomial is **prime over the integers** when it cannot be factored further into monomials or polynomials with terms that have integral coefficients.

Example 2   Factor $25x^2 - 49y^2$ over the integers.

$$25x^2 - 49y^2 = (5x)^2 - (7y)^2$$ ← Difference of squares
$$= (5x + 7y)(5x - 7y)$$ ← Prime polynomials

Example 3   Factor $9y^2 - 24y + 16$ over the integers.

$$9y^2 - 24y + 16 = (3y)^2 - 2(3y)(4) + (4)^2$$ ← Perfect square trinomial
$$= (3y - 4)^2$$ ← Prime polynomial

Example 4   Factor $a^2(b + 1) + 2(b + 1)$ over the integers.

$$a^2(b + 1) + 2(b + 1) = (b + 1)(a^2 + 2)$$ ← $(b + 1)$ is a common binomial factor.

Example 5 Factor $4a^4 - 4b^4$ over the integers.

$$4a^4 - 4b^4 = 4(a^4 - b^4)$$
$$= 4[(a^2)^2 - (b^2)^2] \qquad \longleftarrow \quad \text{Difference of squares}$$
$$= 4(a^2 + b^2)(a^2 - b^2) \qquad \longleftarrow \quad \begin{array}{l}(a^2 - b^2) \text{ is the difference} \\ \text{of squares.}\end{array}$$
$$= 4(a^2 + b^2)(a + b)(a - b) \qquad \longleftarrow \quad \text{Prime polynomials}$$

Try These   Classify each statement as True (T) or False (F).

1. $a^2 - b^2 = (a + b)(a - b)$ T

2. $3x^3 + 6x^2 - 9x = 3x(x^2 + 2x - 3)$ T

3. $4x^2 - 12x + 9 = (2x - 3)^2$ T

4. $x^2 + 6x - x - 6 = (x + 6)(x - 1)$ T

5. $4x^2 + 12x + 4 = (2x + 2)^2$ F

6. $25x^2 - y^2 = (5x - y)^2$ F

Exercises

Factor over the integers. One factor is written for you.

1. $4ab + b = \underline{\ ?\ }(4a + 1)$ $_{b(4a + 1)}$

2. $3ab - 6ab^2 + 9b = \underline{\ ?\ }(a - 2ab + 3)$ $^{3b(a - 2ab + 3)}$

3. $3x^2 - x = x(\underline{\ ?\ } - \underline{\ ?\ })$ $_{x(3x - 1)}$

4. $a^3 + 3a^2b + ab^2 = a(\underline{\ ?\ } + \underline{\ ?\ } + \underline{\ ?\ })$ $_{a(a^2 + 3ab + b^2)}$

Factor the following polynomials over the integers.

5. $8y + 16b$ $_{8(y + 2b)}$

6. $7x - 7$ $_{7(x - 1)}$

7. $5ax - 5a^2x$ $_{5ax(1 - a)}$

8. $3a^2 + 3a$ $_{3a(a + 1)}$

9. $2x^2 + 8$ $_{2(x^2 + 4)}$

10. $2x^3 + 4$ $_{2(x^3 + 2)}$

11. $3a^3 - 3a^2b - 3ab^3$ $_{3a(a^2 - ab - b^3)}$

12. $3a^2b + 3ab^2 + 3b^4$ $_{3b(a^2 + ab + b^3)}$

13. $2x^2 + 3x^3 + 4x^4y$ $_{x^2(2 + 3x + 4x^2y)}$

14. $24a - 16b + 24c$ $_{8(3a - 2b + 3c)}$

Factor by finding the common binomial factor.

15. $a(x + y) - b(x + y)$ $_{(x + y)(a - b)}$

16. $x(a - b) + y(a - b)$ $_{(a - b)(x + y)}$

17. $3(2x - 5) - a(2x - 5)$ $_{(2x - 5)(3 - a)}$

18. $3a(b + c) - 5(b + c)$ $_{(b + c)(3a - 5)}$

19. $cx + cy + bx + by$ $_{(x + y)(c + b)}$

20. $y^3 + 2y^2 + 3y + 6$ $_{(y^2 + 3)(y + 2)}$

21. $1 - y + y^2 - y^3$ $_{(1 - y)(1 + y^2)}$

22. $b^3 + b^2 + b + 1$ $_{(b + 1)(b^2 + 1)}$

Factor as the difference of squares. Inspect for a common monomial factor first.

23. $x^2 - 4 = (x+2)(\underline{} - \underline{})$ $(x+2)(x-2)$

24. $4a^2 - 144b^2 = 4(\underline{} + \underline{})(\underline{} - \underline{})$ $4(a+6b)(a-6b)$

25. $9x^2 - b^2$ $(3x+b)(3x-b)$

26. $16b^2 - 9$ $(4b+3)(4b-3)$

27. $45x^2 - 20$ $5(3x+2)(3x-2)$

28. $25 - x^2y^2$ $(5+xy)(5-xy)$

29. $x^4 - y^2$ $(x^2+y)(x^2-y)$

30. $z^2 - 16x^2y^2$ $(z+4xy)(z-4xy)$

31. $25a^4 - 4$ $(5a^2+2)(5a^2-2)$

32. $2a^2 - 50b^2$ $2(a+5b)(a-5b)$

33. $169 - 49x^2$ $(13+7x)(13-7x)$

34. $400 - 25y^2$ $25(4+y)(4-y)$

35. $x^4 - y^4$ $(x^2+y^2)(x+y)(x-y)$

36. $16x^4 - y^4$ $(4x^2+y^2)(2x+y)(2x-y)$

37. The area of the shaded part of the figure at the right is $S^2 - s^2$. Write this in factored form and then find the area of the shaded part when S is 1.5 meters and s is 0.6 meter.   1.89 m²

38. The diagram at the right is the plan for a square metal box without a cover. The small squares at the corners are to be cut from the original square piece of metal before the sides are bent up. Find the number of square inches of metal that is used for the box if the original piece is 10.5 inches on a side and each small square is 2.5 inches on a side. Use $A = x^2 - 4a^2$.   85.25 sq. in.

Factor over the integers.

39. $x^2 - 10xy + 25y^2 = (x - \underline{})^2$ $(x-5y)^2$

40. $4a^2 + 4a + 1 = (\underline{} + 1)^2$ $(2a+1)^2$

41. $9a^2 - 12ay + 4y^2$ $(3a-2y)^2$

42. $25x^2 - 60x + 36$ $(5x-6)^2$

43. $25x^2 - 25x - 36$ $(5x-9)(5x+4)$

44. $a^2 + 4ab + 4b^2$ $(a+2b)^2$

45. $s^2 - 8st + 16t^2$ $(s-4t)^2$

46. $4x^2 + 20x + 25$ $(2x+5)^2$

47. $25x^2 - 40xz + 16z^2$ $(5x-4z)^2$

48. $49x^2 + 112xy + 64y^2$ $(7x+8y)^2$

49. $b^2(b+1) + (b+1)$ $(b+1)(b^2+1)$

50. $(a-b)^2 - (a+b)(a-b)$

51. $x^3 + x^2y - xy^2 - y^3$ $(x+y)(x+y)(x-y)$

52. $3ax - 6ay - 8by + 4bx$

53. $a(x-y) - b(y-x)$ $(x-y)(a+b)$

54. $3(4x-2) - b(2-4x)$

55. $a(x+y) - b(y+x)$ $(x+y)(a-b)$

56. $5a(x-3y) - 2b(3y-x)$

57. $(a+b)^2 - c^2$ $(a+b+c)(a+b-c)$

58. $a^2 - (b+c)^2$ $(a+b+c)(a-b-c)$

59. $(2x+3y)^2 - 9z^2$ $(2x+3y+3z)(2x+3y-3z)$

60. $(2a-b)^2 - c^2$ $(2a-b+c)(2a-b-c)$

61. $(m^2 + 2mn + n^2) - a^2$ $(m+n+a)(m+n-a)$

62. $(a^2 + 6a + 9) - 9b^2$

63. $1 - x^2 - 2xy - y^2$ $(1+x+y)(1-x-y)$

64. $36x^2 - 9y^2 + 6y - 1$

50. $(a-b)(-2b)$ 52. $(x-2y)(3a+4b)$ 54. $(4x-2)(3+b)$ 56. $(x-3y)(5a+2b)$

62. $(a+3+3b)(a+3-3b)$ 64. $(6x+3y-1)(6x-3y+1)$

Factoring Quadratic Trinomials

The objective for this section is on page 97.

A trinomial such as $x^2 + 5x + 6$ is a **quadratic trinomial** because the degree of the polynomial is 2. In general, quadratic trinomials are factored by finding two binomial factors.

Finding Products

$$(x + 3)(x + 2) = x(x + 2) + 3(x + 2)$$
$$= x^2 + 2x + 3x + 6$$
$$= x^2 + (2 + 3)x + 6$$
$$= x^2 + 5x + 6$$

Finding Factors

$$x^2 + 5x + 6 = x^2 + (2 + 3)x + 2 \cdot 3$$
$$= (x + 2)(x + 3)$$

The key step in factoring $x^2 + 5x + 6$ is in identifying two integers whose product is 6 and whose sum is 5.

Example 1   Factor over the integers: $x^2 + 3x - 10$

$x^2 + 3x - 10 = (x \qquad)(x \qquad)$ ⟵——— Factor x^2.

-10	10	-5	5	⟵——— Find two integers whose
1	-1	2	-2	product is -10 and whose
$\overline{-9}$ No	$\overline{9}$ No	$\overline{-3}$ No	$\overline{3}$ Yes	sum is 3.

$x^2 + 3x - 10 = (x + 5)(x - 2)$ ⟵——— Write the factors.

Check: $(x + 5)(x - 2) = x^2 + 5x - 2x - 10$
$$= x^2 + 3x - 10$$

A similar procedure can be used to factor quadratic trinomials of the form $ax^2 + bx + c$, where $a \neq 1$ and $a \neq 0$.

Polynomials and Rational Expressions   **53**

Example 2 Factor over the integers: $3x^2 - 10x + 8$

$$3x^2 - 10x + 8 = (3x \qquad)(x \qquad) \longleftarrow \text{Factor } 3x^2.$$

Since $-10x$ is negative, both factors of 8 must be negative. Write possible pairs of factors.

Trial Factors	Outer Product	+ Inner Product	= Middle Term	
$(3x - 8)(x - 1)$	$-3x$	$-8x$	$-11x$	No
$(3x - 1)(x - 8)$	$-24x$	$-x$	$-25x$	No
$(3x - 2)(x - 4)$	$-12x$	$-2x$	$-14x$	No
$(3x - 4)(x - 2)$	$-6x$	$-4x$	$-10x$	Yes

$$3x^2 - 10x + 8 = (3x - 4)(x - 2)$$

Check by multiplying the factors to see whether you obtain the original trinomial.

Example 3 Factor over the integers: $6y^2 - 5y - 25$

$$6y^2 - 5y - 25 = (\qquad)(\qquad) \longleftarrow \begin{array}{l} \text{The factors of } 6y^2 \text{ could be} \\ 6y \cdot y \text{ or } 3y \cdot 2y. \end{array}$$

Trial Factors	Outer Product	+ Inner Product	= Middle Term	
$(6y + 5)(y - 5)$	$-30y$	$5y$	$-25y$	No
$(6y - 5)(y + 5)$	$30y$	$-5y$	$25y$	No
$(3y + 5)(2y - 5)$	$-15y$	$10y$	$-5y$	Yes

$$6y^2 - 5y - 25 = (3y + 5)(2y - 5)$$

Some quadratic trinomials cannot be factored over the integers.

Example 4 Factor over the integers: $3 + 2x^2 + 4x$

$$3 + 2x^2 + 4x = 2x^2 + 4x + 3 \quad \longleftarrow \text{Write in descending powers of } x.$$
$$= (2x \quad)(x \quad)$$

Trial Factors	Outer Product + Inner Product = Middle Term			
$(2x + 3)(x + 1)$	$2x$	$3x$	$5x$	No
$(2x + 1)(x + 3)$	$6x$	x	$7x$	No

Since $2x^2 + 4x + 3$ has no other possible factors with integral coefficients, it is a prime polynomial.

Try These Factor over the integers.

1. $x^2 + 8x + 15$ $\quad (x + 3)(x + 5)$

2. $2n^2 + 7n - 4$ $\quad (2n - 1)(n + 4)$

3. $3a^2 + 7a + 2$ $\quad (3a + 1)(a + 2)$

4. $12y^2 - 7y + 1$ $\quad (3y - 1)(4y - 1)$

5. $10c^2 - 7c - 12$ $\quad (2c - 3)(5c + 4)$

6. $3w^2 - 16w - 12$ $\quad (w - 6)(3w + 2)$

Exercises

Factor over the integers. If a polynomial is prime, write *Prime*.

1. $x^2 + x - 6 = \overset{(x + 3)(x - 2)}{(x + 3)}(x - \underline{\ ?\ })$

2. $x^2 + 10x + 24$ $\quad \overset{(x + 6)(x + 4)}{}$

3. $r^2 - 15r + 54$ $\quad (r - 6)(r - 9)$

4. $a^2 + 12a + 35$ $\quad (a + 7)(a + 5)$

5. $x^2 - x - 42$ $\quad (x - 7)(x + 6)$

6. $c^2 + 4c - 21$ $\quad (c + 7)(c - 3)$

7. $c^2 - 12 + 4c = c^2 + 4c - 12 = (c + \underline{\ ?\ })(c - \underline{\ ?\ })$ $\quad (c + 6)(c - 2)$

8. $-8x + x^2 - 20$ $\quad (x - 10)(x + 2)$

Polynomials and Rational Expressions   55

9. $e + e^2 - 90$ $(e + 10)(e - 9)$

10. $-2a - 63 + a^2$ $(a - 9)(a + 7)$

11. $2y^2 - 3y - 5 = (2y - 5)(y + \underline{\ ?\ })$ $(2y - 5)(y + 1)$

12. $3x^2 - 10x + 8$ $(3x - 4)(x - 2)$

13. $3a^2 + 10a - 8$ $(3a - 2)(a + 4)$

14. $6c^2 - c - 15$ $(3c - 5)(2c + 3)$

15. $2c^2 + 7c - 30$ $(2c - 5)(c + 6)$

16. $e^2 - 18e + 81$ $(e - 9)^2$

17. $3b^2 + 5b + 2$ $(3b + 2)(b + 1)$

18. $2b^2 + 3 - 7b$ $(2b - 1)(b - 3)$

19. $n^2 + 7n - 6$ Prime.

20. $2y^2 - y - 15$ $(2y + 5)(y - 3)$

21. $3x^2 + 5x + 2$ $(3x + 2)(x + 1)$

22. $a^2 + 18 - 9a$ $(a - 6)(a - 3)$

23. $ax^2 + 7ax - 78a = a(x^2 + 7x - 78)$
$a(x + 13)(x - 6)$ $= a(x + 13)(x - \underline{\ ?\ })$

24. $2bx^2 - bx - 15b$
$b(2x + 5)(x - 3)$

25. $3mx^2 + 2m + 5mx$ $m(3x + 2)(x + 1)$

26. $4b^2 - 8ab - 12a^2$
$4(b + a)(b - 3a)$

27. $x^4 - x^2y - 6y^2 = (x^2 + 2y)(x^2 - \underline{\ ?\ })$

28. $a^6 + 3a^3 - 28$ $(a^3 + 7)(a^3 - 4)$

29. $a^4 - 2a^2y^2 - 3y^4$ $(a^2 - 3y^2)(a^2 + y^2)$

30. $4y^6 - 17y^3 - 15$ $(4y^3 + 3)(y^3 - 5)$

31. $x^8 + 4x^4 - 21$ $(x^4 + 7)(x^4 - 3)$

32. $m^{16} - 18m^8 + 81$ $(m^4 + 3)^2(m^4 - 3)^2$

27. $(x^2 + 2y)(x^2 - 3y)$

Factor over the rational numbers.

33. $x^2 + \frac{3}{4}x + \frac{1}{8}$ $\left(x + \frac{1}{4}\right)\left(x + \frac{1}{2}\right)$

34. $\frac{1}{4} - 3x + 9x^2$ $\left(\frac{1}{2} - 3x\right)^2$

35. $x^2 + 0.5x + 0.06$ $(x + 0.3)(x + 0.2)$

36. $a^{2m} + 6a^m - 16,\ m \in N$
$(a^m + 8)(a^m - 2)$

37. $a^2 + 0.5a - 0.24$ $(a + 0.8)(a - 0.3)$

38. $2y^{2x} - 3y^x - 5,\ x \in N$
$(2y^x - 5)(y^x + 1)$

39. $x^2 + (a + b)x + ab,\ a,\ b \in Q$ $(x + a)(x + b)$

40. $x^2 - rx + sx - rs,\ r,\ s \in Q$
$(x + s)(x - r)$

Factor over the integers.

41. $(x + y)^2 + 6(x + y) - 72$
$(x + y + 12)(x + y - 6)$

42. $(c + d)^2 - 7(c + d) - 18$
$(c + d - 9)(c + d + 2)$

43. $a^{2m} + 6a^{m-16},\ m \in N$ $a^{m-16}(a^{m+16} + 6)$

44. $2y^{2x} - 3y^x - 5,\ x \in N$

45. $18x^{4t} - 15x^{2t} - 12,\ t \in N$
$(6x^{2t} + 3)(3x^{2t} - 4)$

44. $(2y^x - 5)(y^x + 1)$

46. $57 - 22c^{3n} + c^{6n},\ n \in N$
$(3 - c^{3n})(19 - c^{3n})$

Remember

Perform the indicated operations.

1. $(i - 3) + (2i - 1)$ $3i - 4$

2. $i \cdot i^2$ $-i$

3. $i^5 \cdot i^3$ 1

4. $(i + 1)(i - 1)$ -2

5. $(i + 1)^2$ $2i$

6. $\sqrt{-2} \cdot \sqrt{-2}$ -2

7. $\sqrt{2} \cdot \sqrt{-2}$ $2i$

8. $(-\sqrt{2})(-\sqrt{2})$ 2

The answers are on page 99.

2-6 Factoring over Real and Complex Numbers

The objective for this section is on page 97.

The table below shows binomials factored over different sets of numbers. Multiply to verify each factorization.

Binomial	Integers	Real Numbers	Complex Numbers
$a^2 - b^2$	$(a+b)(a-b)$	$(a+b)(a-b)$	$(a+b)(a-b)$
$x^2 - 3$	Prime	$(x+\sqrt{3})(x-\sqrt{3})$	$(x+\sqrt{3})(x-\sqrt{3})$
$4x^2 - 11$	Prime	$(2x+\sqrt{11})(2x-\sqrt{11})$	$(2x+\sqrt{11})(2x-\sqrt{11})$
$a^2 + b^2$	Prime	Prime	$(a+bi)(a-bi)$
$4x^2 + 5$	Prime	Prime	$(2x+\sqrt{5}i)(2x-\sqrt{5}i)$

The sum of two squares such as $a^2 + b^2$ is always prime over the integers and over the real numbers. It can be factored only over the complex numbers.

Example

Factor $x^4 - y^4$ over the complex numbers.

$$x^4 - y^4 = (x^2)^2 - (y^2)^2 \quad \longleftarrow \text{Difference of squares}$$
$$= (x^2 + y^2)(x^2 - y^2) \quad \longleftarrow \text{Not prime over the complex numbers.}$$
$$= (x^2 + y^2)(x+y)(x-y)$$
$$= (x+iy)(x-iy)(x+y)(x-y)$$

Try These

Factor over the real numbers. Write _Prime_ if the polynomial cannot be factored over the real numbers.

1. $x^2 + 5$ Prime

2. $5z^2 + 5$ $5(z^2 + 1)$

3. $9y^2 - 10$
$(3y + \sqrt{10})(3y - \sqrt{10})$

Factor over the complex numbers.

4. $x^2 + 9$ $(x + 3i)(x - 3i)$

5. $6x^2 + 24$ $6(x + 2i)(x - 2i)$

6. $5a^2 + 5$
$5(a + i)(a - i)$

Polynomials and Rational Expressions   **57**

Exercises

Factor over the real numbers. Write <u>Prime</u> if a polynomial cannot be factored over the real numbers.

1. $x^2 - 3$ $(x + \sqrt{3})(x - \sqrt{3})$
2. $x^4 - 3x^2 - 40$ $(x + 2\sqrt{2})(x - 2\sqrt{2})(x^2 + 5)$
3. $2x^2 - 9$ $(\sqrt{2}x + 3)(\sqrt{2}x - 3)$

4. $5y^2 - 4$ $(\sqrt{5}y - 2)(\sqrt{5}y + 2)$
5. $7y^2 - 11b^2$ $(\sqrt{7}y + \sqrt{11}b)(\sqrt{7}y - \sqrt{11}b)$
6. $5a^2 - 5b^2$ $5(a + b)(a - b)$

7. $9x^2 - 36$ $9(x + 2)(x - 2)$
8. $3ax - 6ay + 12\,az$ $3a(x - 2y + 4z)$
9. $x^2 + x + 1$ Prime

10. $x^2 + y^2$ Prime
11. $7x^2 - 7y^2$ $7(x + y)(x - y)$
12. $x^3 + x^2 - 12x$ $x(x - 3)(x + 4)$

13. $4x^2 - 11$ $(2x + \sqrt{11})(2x - \sqrt{11})$
14. $2a^2 + 10ab + 12b^2$ $2(a + 2b)(a + 3b)$
15. $6a^3 + a^2 - 15a$ $a(2a - 3)(3a + 5)$

16. $4a^2 + 16b^2$ $4(a^2 + 4b^2)$
17. $18x^3 - 3x^2y - 36xy^2$
18. $4ax^2 + 4ax + a$ $a(2x + 1)(2x + 1)$

19. $r^2 - 144b^4$ $(r + 12b^2)(r - 12b^2)$
20. $x^4 - 81$ $3x(2x - 3y)(3x + 4y)$ $(x^2 + 9)(x + 3)(x - 3)$
21. $144x^4 - 81y^4$

$9(4x^2 + 3y^2)(2x + \sqrt{3}\,y)(2x - \sqrt{3}\,y)$

Factor over the complex numbers.

$(x + y)(x - y)(x + yi)(x - yi)$

22. $x^2 + y^2$ $(x + yi)(x - yi)$
23. $x^4 - 1$ $(x + 1)(x - 1)(x + i)(x - i)$
24. $x^4 - y^4$

$(1 + 4y)(1 - 4y)(1 + 4yi)(1 - 4yi)$

25. $1 - 256y^4$
26. $7x^2 + 7y^2$ $7(x + yi)(x - yi)$
27. $9x^2 + 36$ $9(x + 2i)(x - 2i)$

28. $abx^2 - 9ab$ $ab(x + 3)(x - 3)$
29. $a^2x^4 - a^3$ $a^2(x + \sqrt[4]{a})(x - \sqrt[4]{a})(x + i\sqrt[4]{a})(x - i\sqrt[4]{a})$
30. $ax^2 + bx^4$

31. $(a^2 - b^2) - 3(a + b)$ $(a + b)(a - b - 3)$

30. $x^2(\sqrt{a} + x\sqrt{b}\,i)(\sqrt{a} - x\sqrt{b}\,i)$

32. $(x - y)(x^2 + y^2) + 2xy(x - y)$ $(x + y)^2(x - y)$

33. $(2a + 1)(a^2 + 2) - 3a(2a + 1)$ $(2a + 1)(a - 1)(a - 2)$

34. $(a^2 - b^2) + (a - b)(b - a)$ $2b(a - b)$

35. $(a^2 - b^2) - (a^2 - 6ab + 5b^2)$ $6b(a - b)$

36. $x^2 - y^2 - (x^2 - 2xy + y^2)$ $2y(x - y)$

PUZZLE

One coin out of 12 is counterfeit. It is lighter or heavier than the other 11, all of which weigh the same. How can you find the coin in 3 weighings on a platform balance and tell whether it is heavier or lighter than the other 11?

(HINT: Start by balancing one group of 4 coins with another group of 4 coins.) See key.

2-7 Division of Polynomials

The objective for this section is on page 97.

The following examples illustrate the basic exponent theorems for division.

Multiplication	Division
$\dfrac{x^5}{x^2} = \dfrac{x^2}{x^2} \cdot \dfrac{x^3}{1} = x^3$	$\dfrac{x^5}{x^2} = x^{5-2} = x^3$
$\dfrac{x^{10}}{x^{12}} = \dfrac{x^{10}}{x^{10}} \cdot \dfrac{1}{x^2} = \dfrac{1}{x^2}$	$\dfrac{x^{10}}{x^{12}} = \dfrac{1}{x^{12-10}} = \dfrac{1}{x^2}$
$\dfrac{x^{12}}{x^{12}} = 1$	$\dfrac{x^{12}}{x^{12}} = x^{12-12} = x^0 = 1$

Theorems 2-3, 2-4, 2-5: Exponent Properties for Division

For nonnegative integers m and n, and for any nonzero complex number, x,

2-3 $\qquad\qquad \dfrac{x^m}{x^n} = x^{m-n}$, where $m > n$;

2-4 $\qquad\qquad \dfrac{x^m}{x^n} = \dfrac{1}{x^{n-m}}$, where $m < n$;

2-5 $\qquad\qquad \dfrac{x^m}{x^m} = x^0 = 1$.

The exponent theorems can be used to divide a monomial by a monomial.

Example 1 Divide: $\dfrac{3x^5}{x^2}$

$$\frac{3x^5}{x^2} = \frac{3}{1} \cdot x^{5-2} = 3x^3 \qquad \longleftarrow \text{ Subtract the exponents.}$$

Example 2

Divide: **a.** $\dfrac{-8x^2}{x^7}$ **b.** $\dfrac{12a^7}{-2a^4}$

a. $\dfrac{-8x^2}{x^7} = \dfrac{-8}{1} \cdot \dfrac{x^2}{x^7} = \dfrac{-8}{x^{7-2}} = -\dfrac{8}{x^5}$ **b.** $\dfrac{12a^7}{-2a^4} = \dfrac{12}{-2} \cdot \dfrac{a^7}{a^4} = -6a^{7-4} = -6a^3$

In general, you divide a polynomial by a monomial by dividing each term of the polynomial by the monomial.

Example 3

Divide $x^3 + x^2 - 2x + 8$ by x.

$$\dfrac{x^3 + x^2 - 2x + 8}{x} = \dfrac{1}{x}(x^3 + x^2 - 2x + 8)$$

$$= \dfrac{1}{x}(x^3) + \dfrac{1}{x}(x^2) + \dfrac{1}{x}(-2x) + \dfrac{1}{x}(8) \longleftarrow \text{Distributive postulate}$$

$$= x^2 + x - 2 + \dfrac{8}{x}$$

Example 4

Divide $x^2 + 5x + 4$ by $x + 1$.

$$
\begin{array}{r}
x \\
x + 1 \overline{)\,x^2 + 5x + 4} \\
\underline{x^2 + x} \\
4x + 4
\end{array}
$$

$\longleftarrow$ $x^2 \div x = x$. Write x in the quotient.

$\longleftarrow$ $x(x + 1) = x^2 + x$

$\longleftarrow$ $(x^2 + 5x + 4) - (x^2 + x) = 4x + 4$

$$
\begin{array}{r}
x + 4 \\
x + 1 \overline{)\,x^2 + 5x + 4} \\
\underline{x^2 + x} \\
4x + 4 \\
\underline{4x + 4} \\
0
\end{array}
$$

$\longleftarrow$ $4x \div x = 4$. Write 4 in the quotient.

$\longleftarrow$ $4(x + 1) = 4x + 4$

$\longleftarrow$ $(4x + 4) - (4x + 4) = 0$

Thus, $(x^2 + 5x + 4) \div (x + 1) = x + 4$.

As Example 4 shows, dividing by a binomial resembles division in arithmetic. You can check the answer, $x + 4$, by using the following fact from arithmetic.

$$\text{divisor} \times \text{quotient} + \text{remainder} = \text{dividend}$$

Here is the check for Example 4.

$$(x + 1)(x + 4) + 0 = x^2 + 5x + 4 + 0 = x^2 + 5x + 4$$

Example 5   Divide $2a - 5a^2 + 4a^4 - 10$ by $2a - 3$.

$4a^4 + 0a^3 - 5a^2 + 2a - 10$ ◄—— Arrange the terms in descending powers of a. Give missing terms a coefficient of 0.

$$\begin{array}{r} 2a^3 + 3a^2 + 2a + 4 \\ 2a - 3 \overline{\smash{\big)}\, 4a^4 + 0a^3 - 5a^2 + 2a - 10} \\ \underline{4a^4 - 6a^3} \\ 6a^3 - 5a^2 + 2a - 10 \\ \underline{6a^3 - 9a^2} \\ 4a^2 + 2a - 10 \\ \underline{4a^2 - 6a} \\ 8a - 10 \\ \underline{8a - 12} \\ 2 \end{array}$$

◄—— $4a^4 \div 2a = 2a^3$. Write $2a^3$ in the quotient.

◄—— $2a^3(2a - 3)$
◄—— $6a^3 \div 2a = 3a^2$. Write $3a^2$ in the quotient.

$3a^2(2a - 3)$ ——►

$2a(2a - 3)$ ——►   ◄—— $4a^2 \div 2a = 2a$. Write $2a$ in the quotient.

◄—— $8a \div 2a = 4$. Write 4 in the quotient.

$4(2a - 3)$ ——►

◄—— Remainder

Thus, $4a^4 - 5a^2 + 2a - 10 \div 2a - 3 = 2a^3 + 3a^2 + 2a + 4 + \dfrac{2}{2a - 3}$,

or $4a^4 - 5a^2 + 2a - 10 = (2a - 3)(2a^3 + 3a^2 + 2a + 4) + 2$.

Try These   Divide. No denominator is 0.

1. $\dfrac{x^7}{x^4}$ x^3

2. $\dfrac{-a^{10}}{a^7}$ $-a^3$

3. $\dfrac{m^{15}}{m^{20}}$ $\dfrac{1}{m^5}$

4. $\dfrac{15a^6}{-5a^2}$ $-3a^4$

5. $\dfrac{3x^2 + 9x}{3x}$ $x + 3$

6. $\dfrac{a^2 - ab}{a}$ $a - b$

Polynomials and Rational Expressions   **61**

Exercises

Divide. No denominator is 0.

a **1.** $\dfrac{45m^9}{-5m}$ $_{-9m^8}$

2. $\dfrac{42x^5y^2}{-6x^4y^2}$ $_{-7x}$

3. $\dfrac{5x^7 - 10x^5}{5x^5}$ $_{x^2 - 2}$

4. $\dfrac{5x^2y^2 - 15xy^3}{5xy}$ $_{xy - 3y^2}$

5. $\dfrac{36a^5 + 16a^2b^3 - 12a^2b^2}{-4a^2}$ $_{-9a^3 - 4b^3 + 3b^2}$

6. $(y^2 - 5y - 24) \div (y + 3)$ $_{y - 8}$

7. $(x^2 + 6x - 55) \div (x - 5)$ $_{x + 11}$

8. $(3a^2 + 14a + 15) \div (a + 3)$ $_{3a + 5}$

9. $(9x^2 - 16) \div (3x - 4)$ $_{3x + 4}$

10. $(2b^2 + 13b - 24) \div (2b - 5)$ $_{b + 9, R = 21}$

11. $(6m^2 - 11m + 7) \div (3m - 4)$ $_{2m - 1, R = 3}$

12. $(8b^2 - 35 - 6b) \div (4b + 7)$ $_{2b - 5}$

13. $(12a^2 - 11a - 10) \div (3a - 5)$ $_{4a + 3, R = 5}$

14. $(2y + 24y^2 - 15) \div (4y - 3)$ $_{6y + 5}$

15. $(x^3 + 8) \div (x + 2)$ $_{x^2 - 2x + 4}$

16. $(3x^3 - 10x^2 + 5x - 6) \div (x - 3)$ $_{\text{See below.}}$

17. $(15y^3 - y^2 - 18y + 8) \div (3y - 2)$ $_{5y^2 + 3y - 4}$

18. $(2n^3 - 13n + 15) \div (n + 3)$ $_{\text{See below.}}$

19. $(a^3 - 3a^2 + 5a + 1) \div (a - 2)$ $_{a^2 - a + 3, R = 7}$ **20.** $(3x^3 - 13x^2 + 6x - 8) \div (x - 4)$ $_{3x^2 - x + 2}$

21. $(2m^4 - 2m^3 - m^2 + 4m + 1) \div (m + 1)$ $_{2m^3 - 4m^2 + 3m + 1}$

22. $(6b^4 - 31b^3 + 6b^2 + 4b - 5) \div (b - 5)$
$_{6b^3 - b^2 + b + 9, R = 40}$

$_{\text{16. } 3x^2 - x + 2}$
$_{\text{18. } 2n^2 - 6n + 5}$

Divide to determine whether the second polynomial is a factor of the first.

b **23.** $6x^3 + 5x^2 - x + 4$, $3x + 4$ $_{\text{Yes, } 2x^2 - x + 1}$

24. $n^4 - n^2 - 42$, $n^2 + 6$ $_{\text{Yes, } n^2 - 7}$

25. $8y^3 + 125$, $5 + 2y$ $_{\text{Yes, } 4y^2 - 10y + 25}$

26. $3(x + y)^2 - 5(x + y)$, $x + y$ $_{\text{Yes, } 3x + 3y - 5}$

27. $-2n^4 - 5n^3 + 10n^2 + 16$, $n + 4$ $_{\text{No, } -2n^3 + 3n^2 - 2n + 8, R = -16}$

28. $(6r^4s^3t^2)^3 - 8r^3s^4t^2 + 16r^3s^5$, $(2rs)^3$ $_{\text{Yes, } 27r^9s^6t^6 - st^2 + 2s^2}$

Find the value of k that makes the second polynomial a factor of the first.

c **29.** $2s^3 - 10s^2 + ks + 66$, $s - 3$ $_{k = -10}$

30. $-6t^4 + kt^3 + 3t^2 - t + 2$, $t + 2$ $_{k = -10}$

31. $kn^5 - 3n^4 + n^3 - 2n + 5$, $n - 1$ $_{k = -1}$

Divide.

32. $(a^3 + b^3 + c^3) \div (a + b + c)$ $\quad a^2 - (b+c)a + (b+c)^2 - \frac{3b^2c + 3bc^2}{a+b+c}$

33. $(2x^{3a} - 6x^{2a}y^a + 6x^a y^{2a} - 2y^{3a}) \div (2x^a - 2y^a)$ $\quad x^{2a} - 2x^a y^a + y^{2a}$

34. $(x^{4a} + x^{2a}y^{2b} + y^{4b}) \div (x^{2a} + x^a y^b + y^{2b})$ $\quad x^{2a} - x^a y^b + y^{2b}$

35. $(2x^5 - x^4) \div (x^2 - 2x + 1)$ $\quad 2x^3 + 3x^2 + 4x + 5 + \frac{6x - 5}{x^2 - 2x + 1}$

36. $x^5 \div (x^2 + 2x + 1)$ $\quad x^3 - 2x^2 + 3x - 4 + \frac{5x + 4}{x^2 + 2x + 1}$

Remember

Find the greatest common factor of each pair of numbers.

1. 39 and 24 $\quad$ 3

2. 39 and 71 $\quad$ NO COMMON FACTOR

Rewrite each division problem as a statement involving multiplication and addition

3. $\overset{\displaystyle 6 \quad \text{Remainder } 2}{5)\overline{32}}$ $\quad$ 5 X 6 + 2 = 32

4. $\overset{\displaystyle 5 \quad \text{Remainder } 6}{7)\overline{41}}$ $\quad$ 7 X 5 + 6 = 41

Find each product.

5. $(x + y)(x^2 - xy + y^2)$ $\quad x^3 + y^3$

6. $(x - y)(x^2 + xy + y^2)$ $\quad x^3 - y^3$

The answers are on page 99.

PUZZLE

What do you see in this picture? Name at least two different things that you see.

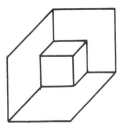

1. a small cube in a corner
2. a large rectangular solid with a small cubical slice removed

Polynomials and Rational Expressions **63**

2-8 The Remainder and Factor Theorems

The objectives for this section are on page 97.

Compare the remainder obtained in the division problem on the left with the value of the polynomial when $x = 3$.

$$
\begin{array}{r}
3x - 1 \\
x - 3 \overline{\smash{)}3x^2 - 10x + 8} \\
\underline{3x^2 - 9x} \\
-x + 8 \\
\underline{-x + 3} \\
5
\end{array}
\qquad
\begin{array}{l}
3x^2 - 10x + 8 \\
3(3)^2 - 10(3) + 8 \\
27 - 30 + 8 \\
5
\end{array}
$$

Now check whether the remainder equals the value of the polynomial when $x = 3$ by replacing x with 3 in the following equation.

(divisor $\times$ quotient) + remainder = polynomial or dividend

$$
\begin{array}{llll}
(x - 3) \cdot (3x - 1) + & 5 & = 3x^2 - 10x + 8 \\
0 \cdot (8) + & 5 & = 27 - 30 + 8 \\
0 + & 5 & = 35 - 30 \\
& 5 & = 5
\end{array}
$$

The relationship is stated in the Remainder Theorem.

Theorem 2-6: Remainder Theorem

When a polynomial in x is divided by $(x - a)$, the remainder is equal to the value of the polynomial when $x = a$.

Example 1   Find the remainder when $x^3 + 2x^2 - 6x + 7$ is divided by $x + 3$.

$$
\begin{array}{l}
 x - a \\
 \downarrow \downarrow \searrow \\
x + 3 = x - (-3) \quad \longleftarrow \quad \text{Write } x + 3 \text{ in the form } x - a. \\
a = -3 \qquad\qquad \longleftarrow \quad \text{Find } a.
\end{array}
$$

For $x = -3$, $x^3 + 2x^2 - 6x + 7 = (-3)^3 + 2(-3)^2 - 6(-3) + 7$ ◄——— Replace x with -3.

$\qquad\qquad\qquad\quad = -27 + 18 + 18 + 7$

$\qquad\qquad\qquad\quad = -27 + 43$

$\qquad\qquad\qquad\quad = 16$ ◄——— Remainder

The remainder is 16.

A special application of the Remainder Theorem occurs when the remainder is 0.

Example 2   Determine whether $(x - 2)$ is a factor of $3x^2 - 10x + 8$.

$x - a$
$\quad\downarrow$
$x - 2$ ◄——— Find a.
$a = 2$

For $x = 2$, $3x^2 - 10x + 8 = 3(2)^2 - 10(2) + 8$ ◄——— Replace x with 2.

$\qquad\qquad\qquad\qquad = 12 - 20 + 8$

$\qquad\qquad\qquad\qquad = 0$ ◄——— Remainder

Since the remainder is 0,

$(x - 2)(\text{quotient}) = 3x^2 - 10x + 8$,

and $(x - 2)$ is a factor of $3x^2 - 10x + 8$.

The principle illustrated in Example 2 is stated in the <u>Factor Theorem</u>.

Theorem 2-7: Factor Theorem
The binomial $(x - a)$ is a factor of a polynomial in x if and only if the value of the polynomial is 0 when $x = a$.

Example 3

Determine whether $x + 4$ is a factor of $x^3 + 10x^2 + 29x + 20$.

$$x - a = x - (-4); a = -4 \qquad \longleftarrow \text{Find } a.$$

$$x^3 + 10x^2 + 29x + 20 = (-4)^3 + 10(-4)^2 + 29(-4) + 20 \qquad \longleftarrow \text{Replace } x \text{ with } (-4).$$

$$= -64 \quad +160 \qquad -116 \qquad +20$$

$$= -180 + 180$$

$$= 0 \qquad \longleftarrow \text{Remainder}$$

Thus, $(x + 4)$ is a factor of $x^3 + 10x^2 + 29x + 20$.

It can also be shown, either by division or by repeated use of the Factor Theorem, that $(x + 1)$ and $(x + 5)$ are the remaining factors.

$$x^3 + 10x^2 + 29x + 20 = (x + 4)(x + 1)(x + 5)$$

$$\longrightarrow 4 \cdot 1 \cdot 5 = 20$$

The following principle will help you find a trial factor of a polynomial.

If $x - a$ is a factor of a polynomial, then a must be a factor of the constant term provided that the polynomial has integral coefficients and that the coefficient of the highest power of x is 1.

Example 4

Factor $x^3 - 9x^2 + 24x - 20$.

$$\pm 1, \pm 2, \pm 4, \pm 5, \pm 10, \pm 20 \qquad \longleftarrow \text{Write the possible factors of 20.}$$

$$x^3 - 9x^2 + 24x - 20 = (1)^3 - 9(1)^2 + 24(1) - 20 \neq 0 \qquad \longleftarrow \text{Replace } x \text{ with 1.}$$

$$(-1)^3 - 9(-1)^2 + 24(-1) - 20 \neq 0 \qquad \longleftarrow \text{Replace } x \text{ with } -1.$$

$(2)^3 - 9(2)^2 + 24(2) - 20 = 0$ ⟵ Replace x with 2.

$(x-2)(\qquad)$ ⟵ $(x-2)$ is one factor.

$(x-2)(x^2-7x+10)$ ⟵ Divide $x^3-9x^2+24x-20$ by $(x-2)$ to find the other factor.

$(x-2)(x-2)(x-5)$ ⟵ Factor $x^2-7x+10$.

Thus, $x^3 - 9x^2 + 24x - 20 = (x-2)(x-2)(x-5)$.

The polynomial x^3+8 is the sum of two cubes; x^3-8 is the difference of two cubes. The pattern for factoring these binomials is given below.

Sum and Difference of Two Cubes

$$a^3 + b^3 = (a+b)(a^2 - ab + b^2)$$
$$a^3 - b^3 = (a-b)(a^2 + ab + b^2)$$

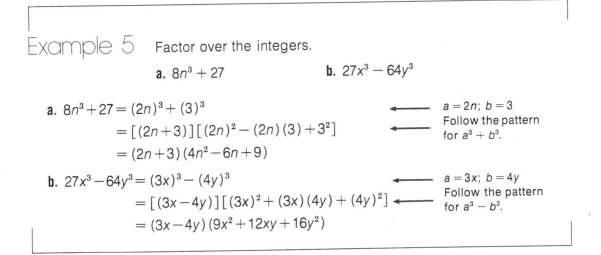

Example 5   Factor over the integers.

a. $8n^3 + 27$ b. $27x^3 - 64y^3$

a. $8n^3 + 27 = (2n)^3 + (3)^3$ ⟵ $a = 2n;\ b = 3$ Follow the pattern for $a^3 + b^3$.

$= [(2n+3)][(2n)^2 - (2n)(3) + 3^2]$

$= (2n+3)(4n^2 - 6n + 9)$

b. $27x^3 - 64y^3 = (3x)^3 - (4y)^3$ ⟵ $a = 3x;\ b = 4y$ Follow the pattern for $a^3 - b^3$.

$= [(3x-4y)][(3x)^2 + (3x)(4y) + (4y)^2]$

$= (3x-4y)(9x^2 + 12xy + 16y^2)$

Try These   Tell whether the second polynomial is a factor of the first.

1. $y^3 - 8y^2 + 19y - 12,\ y - 4$ Yes

2. $z^3 - 27z + 10,\ z + 5$ No

3. $x^3 - 8,\ x - 2$ Yes

4. $a^4 - 27a^2 + 14a + 120,\ a - 12$ No

5. $y^3 + 81,\ y + 3$ No

6. $m^4 - 8m^2 + 16,\ m + 2$ Yes

Exercises

Use the Remainder Theorem to find the remainders.

1. $(x^3 + 2x^2 - 3x + 1) \div (x - 1)$ ^{1}

2. $(5n^3 - 2n^2 + n + 4) \div (n + 1)$ $^{-4}$

3. $(4t^3 - 3t^2 + 2t + 1) \div (t - 2)$ ^{25}

4. $(2a^3 - 4a^2 - 3a + 2) \div (a + 4)$ $^{-178}$

5. $(m^4 - 3m^3 - 2m^2 + m + 5) \div (m + 2)$ ^{35}

6. $(2x^4 - 4x^3 + x^2 + x + 1) \div (x - 3)$ $_{67}$

Use the Factor Theorem to determine whether the second polynomial is a factor of the first.

7. $y^3 - 8y^2 + 19y - 12,\ y - 3$ ^{Yes}

8. $a^3 + 5a^2 + 8a + 4,\ a + 2$ ^{Yes}

9. $3x^4 - 2x^3 + 5x^2 - 2x + 1,\ x - 1$ ^{No}

10. $n^4 - 27n^2 + 14n + 120,\ n - 4$ ^{Yes}

11. $2m^3 + 3m^2 - 7m - 3,\ m - 2$ ^{No}

12. $6x^4 - 7x^3 + 3x^2 - 7x - 9,\ x + 1$ ^{No}

Determine whether the second polynomial is a factor of the first. If it is, divide to find the quotient. Then factor the quotient.

$x^2 - 9x + 18 = (x - 6)(x - 3)$

13. $x^3 - 10x^2 + 27x - 18,\ x - 1$

$s^2 - 1 = (s + 1)(s - 1)$

14. $s^3 - 2s^2 - s + 2,\ s - 2$

$z^2 - 5z + 6 = (z - 2)(z - 3)$

15. $z^3 - 8z^2 + 21z - 18,\ z - 3$

$y^2 + 6y + 5 = (y + 1)(y + 5)$

16. $y^3 + 10y^2 + 29y + 20,\ y + 4$

Factor completely over the integers.

$(y - 3)(y - 4)(y - 1)$

17. $y^3 - 8y^2 + 19y - 12$

$(a + 2)(a + 2)(a + 1)$

18. $a^3 + 5a^2 + 8a + 4$

19. $y^3 - 11y^2 + 31y - 21$ $(y - 3)(y - 7)(y - 1)$

20. $s^3 + 6s^2 + 11s - 6$ $^{(s - 3)(s - 1)(s - 2)}$

21. $x^4 - 8x^2 + 16$ $(x - 2)(x - 2)(x + 2)(x + 2)$

22. $x^3 - 27x + 10$ $(x - 5)(x^2 + 5x - 2)$

23. $x^4 - 27x^2 + 14x + 120$ $(x + 2)(x - 3)(x - 4)(x + 5)$

24. $x^4 - 10x^3 + 35x^2 - 50x + 24$ $(x - 1)(x - 2)(x - 3)(x - 4)$

25. $a^3 + 1$ $(a + 1)(a^2 - a + 1)$ **26.** $m^3 - n^3$ $(m - n)(m^2 + mn + n^2)$

27. $c^3 - 1$ $(c - 1)(c^2 + c + 1)$ **28.** $b^3 + 8c^3$ See below.

29. $a^3 - 27b^3$ **30.** $27x^3 + 8y^3$ See below. **31.** $a^3b^3 + 27c^3$ **32.** $64 - x^3$ See below.

$(a - 3b)(a^2 + 3ab + 9b^2)$ $(ab + 3c)(a^2b^2 - 3abc + 9c^2)$

Find the value of k that makes the second polynomial a factor of the first.

Example: $x^3 - 2x^2 - x + k,\ x - 2$

$(2)^3 - 2(2)^2 - 2 + k = 0$ ⟵ When $x = 2$, $x^3 - 2x^2 - x + k = 0$.

$8 - 8 - 2 + k = 0$

28. $(b + 2c)(b^2 - 2bc + 4c^2)$
30. $(3x + 2y)(9x^2 - 6xy + 4y^2)$
32. $(4 - x)(16 + 4x + x^2)$

$-2 + k = 0$

$k = 2$

33. $x^3 + 3x^2 - x + k$, $x - 2$ −18

34. $kx^3 - 2x^2 + x - 6$, $x + 3$ −1

35. $n^4 - kn^2 + 5n - 1$, $n - 1$ 5

36. $a^3 - ka^2 + 2a + k - 3$, $a + 2$ −5

37. $k^2c^3 + 4kc - 5$, $c - 1$ −5 or 1

38. $n^4 - 2n^3 + kn^2 - k^2n + k - 6$, $n + 1$
1 or −3

Factor over the integers.

$(a^2 + b^2)(a^4 - a^2b^2 + b^4)$
39. $a^6 + b^6$

$(n^2 + 2)(n^4 - 2n^2 + 4)$
40. $n^6 + 8$

$(a + b)(a^2 - ab + b^2)(a - b)(a^2 + ab + b^2)$
42. $a^6 - b^6$

41. $16c^4 + 2cd^3$
$2c(2c + d)(4c^2 - 2cd + d^2)$

43. $16x^5 + 54x^2y^3$

$2x^2(2x + 3y)(4x^2 - 6xy + 9y^2)$

44. $1 + x^{3a}$, $a \in N$ $(1 + x^a)(1 - x^a + x^{2a})$, or
$(x^a + 1)(x^{2a} - x^a + 1)$

2-9 Solving Polynomial Equations by Factoring

The objective for this section is on page 98.

Some polynomial equations of the second and third degree can be solved by factoring. The method applies the following theorem.

Theorem 2-8: **Zero Product Theorem**
If a and b are complex numbers and $a \cdot b = 0$, then either $a = 0$ or $b = 0$, or both a and b equal 0.

Example 1   Solve $x^2 + 5x + 6 = 0$.

$(x + 3)(x + 2) = 0$ ←——— Factor.

$x + 3 = 0$ or $x + 2 = 0$ ←——— If $a \cdot b = 0$, then $a = 0$ or $b = 0$.

$x = -3$ or $x = -2$ ←——— Solve for x.

Check: $(-3)^2 + 5(-3) + 6 \overset{?}{=} 0$ $(-2)^2 + 5(-2) + 6 \overset{?}{=} 0$

$9 - 15 + 6 \overset{?}{=} 0$ $4 - 10 + 6 \overset{?}{=} 0$

$0 = 0$ $0 = 0$

The two numbers that make $x^2 + 5x + 6 = 0$ true are −3 and −2.

The **solution set** of an equation is the set of numbers from a replacement set that makes the equation true. Thus, $\{-3, -2\}$ is the solution set for the equation of Example 1. Unless otherwise stated, the replacement set is the set of complex numbers.

Example 2 Solve $x^3 - 4x^2 + x + 6 = 0$.

$$x^3 - 4x^2 + x + 6 = 0$$
$$(x - 2)(x + 1)(x - 3) = 0 \longleftarrow \text{Factor. Use the Factor theorem.}$$

$x - 2 = 0$	or	$x + 1 = 0$	or	$x - 3 = 0$
$x = 2$	or	$x = -1$	or	$x = 3$

Check in the original equation.

Solution set: $\{2, -1, 3\}$

Try These   *Solve.*

1. $x^2 - 2x - 63 = 0$ $\{-7, 9\}$ 2. $y^2 - 9 = 0$ $\{3, -3\}$ 3. $y^2 + 9 = 0$ $\{3i, -3i\}$

4. $16x^2 - 1 = 0$ $\{\frac{1}{4}, -\frac{1}{4}\}$ 5. $16x^2 + 1 = 0$ $\{\frac{1}{4}i, -\frac{1}{4}i\}$ 6. $6x^2 - 7x - 5 = 0$ $\{\frac{5}{3}, -\frac{1}{2}\}$

Exercises

Solve.

a

1. $x^2 - x - 6 = 0$ $\{3, -2\}$ 2. $x^2 - 4 = 0$ $\{-2, 2\}$ 3. $x^2 + 4 = 0$ $\{-2i, 2i\}$

4. $x^2 - 9x + 20 = 0$ $\{4, 5\}$ 5. $x^2 - 9ix - 20 = 0$ $\{5i, 4i\}$ 6. $x^2 - 5x - 14 = 0$ $\{7, -2\}$

7. $4x^2 - 1 = 0$ $\{\frac{1}{2}, -\frac{1}{2}\}$ 8. $9x^2 + 1 = 0$ $\{\frac{i}{3}, -\frac{i}{3}\}$ 9. $2x^2 + 9x - 5 = 0$ $\{\frac{1}{2}, -5\}$

10. $x^2 + 6x - 27 = 0$ $\{3, -9\}$ 11. $x^2 - 121 = 0$ $\{11, -11\}$ 12. $x^2 + 81 = 0$ $\{-9i, 9i\}$

13. $3x^2 - 4x - 15 = 0$ $\{3, -\frac{5}{3}\}$ 14. $2x^2 + ix + 1 = 0$ $\{-i, \frac{i}{2}\}$ 15. $6x^2 + 7x + 2 = 0$ $\{-\frac{2}{3}, -\frac{1}{2}\}$

16. $x^3 - 6x^2 + 11x - 6 = 0$ $\{1, 2, 3\}$ 17. $x^3 - 7x - 6 = 0$ $\{-1, -2, 3\}$

18. $x^3 + 6x^2 + 11x + 6 = 0$ $\{-1, -2, -3\}$ 19. $x^3 - 2x^2 - x + 2 = 0$ $\{1, -1, 2\}$

20. $x^3 + 7x^2 + 7x - 15 = 0$ $\{1, -3, -5\}$ 21. $x^3 - x^2 - 4x + 4 = 0$ $\{1, -2, 2\}$

b

22. $2x^2 + (2 - i)x - i = 0$ $\{-1, \frac{i}{2}\}$ 23. $3x^2 + (4 - 6i)x - 8i = 0$ $\{2i, -\frac{4}{3}\}$

Synthetic Division

Synthetic division shortens the process of finding the quotient and remainder when a polynomial is divided by $x - a$.

Find $4x^4 + 3x^2 - 2x + 1 \div x - 2$ by synthetic division.

Coefficients ⟶
$$\begin{array}{rrrrr|r}
4 & 0 & 3 & -2 & 1 & \underline{2} \quad\longleftarrow\quad a = 2 \\
  & 8 & 16 & 38 & 72 & \\
\hline
4 & 8 & 19 & 36 & 73 &
\end{array}$$

Quotient: $4x^3 + 8x^2 + 19x + 36$ Remainder: 73

Recall that if a polynomial is divided by $x - a$ and the remainder is zero, then $x - a$ is a factor of the polynomial. You can use the factors of the constant term to find the factors of a polynomial whose leading coefficient is 1.

Factor $x^3 - 9x^2 + 24x - 20$.

$\pm1, \pm2, \pm4, \pm5, \pm10, \pm20$ ⟵ Factors of -20.

$1 - 9 + 24 - 20 = -4$ ⟵ Try $+1$ by substitution. Since the remainder is -4, $x - 1$ is not a factor.

$$\begin{array}{rrrr|r}
1 & -9 & 24 & -20 & \underline{2} \\
  & 2 & -14 & 20 & \\
\hline
1 & -7 & 10 & 0 &
\end{array}$$
⟵ Try $+2$ by synthetic division.

⟵ The remainder is 0. Thus, $x - 2$ is a factor.

This quotient, $x^2 - 7x + 10$, is called a **depressed polynomial.**

$(x^2 - 7x + 10) = (x - 5)(x - 2)$ ⟵ Factor the depressed polynomial.

Thus, $x^3 - 9x^2 + 24x - 20 = (x - 2)(x - 5)(x - 2)$.

Use synthetic division to solve Exercises 7–12 on page 68.

2-10 Simplifying Rational Expressions

The objective for this section is on page 98.

Expressions written as the ratio of two polynomials are called rational expressions. For example,

$$\frac{x-1}{x+1}, \; x \neq -1 \qquad \frac{2a^2 - 5a + 1}{a + 6}, \; a \neq -6 \qquad \frac{2m - 7}{1}$$

are all rational expressions.

Definition: A **rational expression** is an expression of the form

$$\frac{P}{Q},$$

where P and Q are polynomials and $Q \neq 0$.

A rational expression is simplified when its numerator and denominator have no common factors except ± 1. To simplify a rational expression, factor its numerator and denominator and look for common factors.

Example 1

Simplify: $\dfrac{10x^4yz^2}{16xy^2z^2}$

$$\frac{10x^4yz^2}{16xy^2z^2} = \frac{(2xyz^2)(5x^3)}{(2xyz^2)(8y)} \qquad \longleftarrow \quad \text{Factor both numerator and denominator.}$$

$$= \frac{2xyz^2}{2xyz^2} \cdot \frac{5x^3}{8y^2}$$

$$= 1 \cdot \frac{5x^3}{8y}$$

$$= \frac{5x^3}{8y}$$

Example 2

Simplify: $\dfrac{x^2 - 9}{x^2 + 5x + 6}$

$$\dfrac{x^2 - 9}{x^2 + 5x + 6} = \dfrac{(x+3)(x-3)}{(x+3)(x+2)} \quad \longleftarrow \quad \text{Factor.}$$

$$= 1 \cdot \dfrac{x-3}{x+2} = \dfrac{x-3}{x+2}$$

Example 3

Simplify: $\dfrac{a^2 - 1}{1 - a}$

$$\dfrac{a^2 - 1}{1 - a} = \dfrac{(a+1)(a-1)}{1-a} \quad \longleftarrow \quad \text{Factor.}$$

$$= \dfrac{(a+1)(a-1)}{-(a-1)} \quad \longleftarrow \quad 1 - a = -(a-1)$$

$$= \dfrac{(a+1)}{-1}$$

$$= -a - 1$$

Try These

The following set of exercises contains errors made by students in simplifying rational expressions. Find the error in each exercise and give the correct answer.

1. $\dfrac{3(a+b)}{z+2(a+b)} = \dfrac{3}{z+2}$ Cannot be simplified.

2. $\dfrac{x+y}{x^2+y^2} = \dfrac{1}{x+y}$ Cannot be simplified.

3. $\dfrac{a+b+c}{a+b} = c$ Cannot be simplified.

4. $\dfrac{(x+y)}{(x+y)(x+y)} = x+y$ $\frac{1}{x+y}$

5. $\dfrac{2a+b}{a+b} = 2$ Cannot be simplified.

6. $\dfrac{x^2+a^2}{z^2+a^2} = \dfrac{x^2}{z^2}$ Cannot be simplified.

7. $\dfrac{a+b}{x+y} \cdot \dfrac{x+y}{a+b} = 0$ 1

8. $\dfrac{x}{x+y} = \dfrac{1}{1+y}$ Cannot be simplified.

9. $\dfrac{a-b}{b-a} = 1$ -1

10. $\dfrac{a-b}{(b-a)(a+b)} = \dfrac{1}{a+b}$ $-\frac{1}{a+b}$

Exercises

Simplify each rational expression or indicate that it cannot be simplified.

a

1. $\dfrac{12}{20}$ $\frac{3}{5}$

2. $\dfrac{ax}{ay}$ $\frac{x}{y}$

3. $\dfrac{ax^2y}{ax^2z}$ $\frac{y}{z}$

4. $\dfrac{c(x+y)}{d(x+y)}$ $\frac{c}{d}$

5. $\dfrac{r(x-y)^2}{t(x-y)}$ $\frac{r(x-y)}{t}$

6. $\dfrac{-3x^2y^3}{6x^3y^2}$ $\frac{-y}{2x}$

7. $\dfrac{12(a+b)}{3(2a+b)}$ $\frac{4(a+b)}{2a+b}$

8. $\dfrac{6abx}{9a^2x^2}$ $\frac{2b}{3ax}$

9. $\dfrac{2a^3b^2x^3}{6a^2b^2x}$ $\frac{ax^2}{3}$

10. $\dfrac{10x^4yz^2}{16xy^2z^2}$ $\frac{5x^3}{8y}$

11. $\dfrac{60x^2yz^4}{24x^2z^4}$ $\frac{5y}{2}$

12. $\dfrac{ax+ay}{bx+by}$ $\frac{a}{b}$

13. $\dfrac{x^2-y^2}{x^2+2xy+y^2}$ $\frac{x-y}{x+y}$

14. $\dfrac{x^2-16}{x^2+6x+8}$ $\frac{x-4}{x+2}$

15. $\dfrac{x^2-5x}{x^2-7x+10}$ $\frac{x}{x-2}$

16. $\dfrac{(x-2)(x+3)(x+4)}{(x-2)(x+3)(x+4)}$ 1

17. $\dfrac{(x-2)(x+3)+(x-4)}{(x-2)(x+3)(x-4)}$ Cannot simplify

18. $\dfrac{-x-y}{-(x+y)}$ 1

19. $\dfrac{ax-ay}{y-x}$ $-a$

20. $\dfrac{a^2-1}{a^2+3a+2}$ $\frac{a-1}{a+2}$

21. $\dfrac{a^2-b^2}{b-a}$ $-a-b$

22. $\dfrac{3a^2-12}{a^2-4a+4}$ $\frac{3(a+2)}{a-2}$

23. $\dfrac{(x+y)(2x-2y)}{(x-y)(3x+3y)}$ $\frac{2}{3}$

24. $\dfrac{a(a^2-b^2)}{(a-b)^2}$ $\frac{a(a+b)}{a-b}$

25. $\dfrac{a^2-b^2}{(b-a)^2}$ $\frac{a+b}{a-b}$

26. $\dfrac{2x^2-8}{x^3-8}$ $\frac{2(x+2)}{x^2+2x+4}$

27. $\dfrac{3ix}{6x}$ $\frac{1}{2}i$

28. $\dfrac{3x+6}{x^4-16}$ $\frac{3}{(x^2+4)(x-2)}$

29. $\dfrac{a^2-b^2}{a^3+b^3}$ $\frac{a-b}{a^2-ab+b^2}$

30. $\dfrac{ad+bd}{a^2+2ab+b^2}$ $\frac{d}{a+b}$

b

31. $\dfrac{2x+3(x-2)}{4x+5(x-2)}$ $\frac{5x-6}{9x-10}$

32. $\dfrac{16x+3x^2-35}{33x+5x^2-14}$ $\frac{3x-5}{5x-2}$

33. $\dfrac{3x^3+3y^3}{2x^3-2x^2y+2xy^2}$ $\frac{3(x+y)}{2x}$

34. $\dfrac{(2+4i)x^2}{(1+2i)x}$ $2x$

35. $\dfrac{x^5+y^5}{x^3+y^3}$ $\frac{x^4-x^3y+x^2y^2-xy^3+y^4}{x^2-xy+y^2}$

36. $\dfrac{x^3-5x^2-2x-8}{x^2-4x+4}$

cannot simplify

Multiplication of Rational Expressions

The objective for this section is on page 98.

Recall how to multiply two rational numbers.

$$\frac{2}{3} \cdot \frac{5}{7} = \frac{2 \cdot 5}{3 \cdot 7} = \frac{10}{21}$$

Rational expressions are multiplied in the same way.

Definition: Multiplication of Rational Expressions

If $\dfrac{P}{Q}$ and $\dfrac{R}{S}$ are rational expressions, then

$$\frac{P}{Q} \cdot \frac{R}{S} = \frac{P \cdot R}{Q \cdot S}$$

Example 1   Multiply. **a.** $\dfrac{3a}{b} \cdot \dfrac{c}{2d}$ **b.** $\dfrac{3x}{4y} \cdot \dfrac{9y^2}{12x^3}$

a. $\dfrac{3a}{b} \cdot \dfrac{c}{2d} = \dfrac{3a \cdot c}{b \cdot 2d}$ ⟵ Definition

$\phantom{\dfrac{3a}{b} \cdot \dfrac{c}{2d}} = \dfrac{3ac}{2bd}$

b. $\dfrac{3x}{4y} \cdot \dfrac{9y^2}{12x^3} = \dfrac{3x \cdot 9y^2}{4y \cdot 12x^3}$ ⟵ Definition

$\phantom{\dfrac{3x}{4y} \cdot \dfrac{9y^2}{12x^3}} = \dfrac{(3xy)(3y)}{(3xy)(16x^2)}$ ⟵ The numerator and denominator have a common factor, $3xy$.

$\phantom{\dfrac{3x}{4y} \cdot \dfrac{9y^2}{12x^3}} = 1 \cdot \dfrac{3y}{16x^2}$

$\phantom{\dfrac{3x}{4y} \cdot \dfrac{9y^2}{12x^3}} = \dfrac{3y}{16x^2}$

Polynomials and Rational Expressions   **75**

Example 2   Multiply: $\dfrac{ab^2 - b^3}{a^3 + a^2b} \cdot \dfrac{a^2 - ab - 2b^2}{a^2 - 2ab + b^2}$

$$= \dfrac{(ab^2 - b^3)(a^2 - ab - 2b^2)}{(a^3 + a^2b)(a^2 - 2ab + b^2)} \quad \longleftarrow \quad \text{Definition}$$

$$= \dfrac{b^2(a - b)(a + b)(a - 2b)}{a^2(a + b)(a - b)(a - b)} \quad \longleftarrow \quad \text{Factor.}$$

$$= \dfrac{(a - b)(a + b)b^2(a - 2b)}{(a - b)(a + b)a^2(a - b)} \quad \longleftarrow \quad \begin{array}{l}\text{The factors } (a - b) \text{ and } (a + b) \\ \text{are common to the numerator} \\ \text{and the denominator.}\end{array}$$

$$= \dfrac{b^2(a - 2b)}{a^2(a - b)}, \text{ or } \dfrac{ab^2 - 2b^3}{a^3 - a^2b}$$

Try These   *Multiply.*

1. $1\frac{2}{3} \cdot 3\frac{3}{4}$ $\frac{25}{4}$

2. $\dfrac{1}{3} \cdot \dfrac{x - 3}{2}$ $\frac{x-3}{6}$

3. $\dfrac{5}{b^2} \cdot \dfrac{6}{10}$ $\frac{3}{b^2}$

4. $\dfrac{9}{2} \cdot \dfrac{3x - 5}{3}$ $\frac{9x-15}{2}$

5. $\dfrac{2a}{3b} \cdot \dfrac{27b^3}{16a}$ $\frac{9b^2}{8}$

6. $\dfrac{y^2 - 9}{y + 4} \cdot \dfrac{y^2 - 16}{y + 3}$
$(y - 3)(y - 4) = y^2 - 7y + 12$

Exercises

Write each product as a rational expression in simplest form. No denominator is 0.

1. $\dfrac{4}{a^2} \cdot \dfrac{a}{8}$ $\frac{1}{2a}$

2. $\dfrac{4}{5} \cdot \dfrac{-5n}{2}$ $-2n$

3. $3 \cdot \dfrac{x + 3}{5}$ $\frac{3(x+3)}{5}$

4. $\dfrac{2}{5} \cdot \dfrac{x + 2}{4}$ $\frac{x+2}{10}$

5. $\dfrac{3x^2}{2} \cdot \dfrac{3x - 5}{3x}$ $\frac{x(3x-5)}{2}$

6. $12a^3x \cdot \dfrac{2a + 3}{4a}$
$3a^2x(2a + 3)$

7. $\dfrac{6}{8} \cdot \left(\dfrac{2a}{3} + 1\right)$ $\frac{2a+3}{4}$

8. $12 \cdot \left(\dfrac{x}{2} + 5\right)$ $6(x + 10)$

9. $\dfrac{6x}{5} \cdot \left(-\dfrac{10 - x}{3}\right)$

10. $\dfrac{2ab}{3c^2} \cdot \dfrac{a^2}{c}$ $\frac{2a^3b}{3c^3}$

11. $\dfrac{a^3y^2}{2x^3} \cdot 4x^3$ $2a^3y^2$

12. $\dfrac{7a}{3b} \cdot \dfrac{4b}{14a^2}$ $\frac{2}{3a}$

$\frac{2x(x - 10)}{5}$

13. $\dfrac{4a^2}{3bc} \cdot \dfrac{12b^2c}{6a^3}$ $\frac{8b}{3a}$

14. $\dfrac{3x^4}{4a^2y^2} \cdot \dfrac{8a^6y^3}{6x^6}$ $\frac{a^4y}{x^2}$

15. $\dfrac{7x^2y}{3a^2b} \cdot \dfrac{6a}{14x^2}$ $\frac{y}{ab}$

16. $(x^2 - 16) \cdot \dfrac{3(x+4)^3}{x-4}$ $3(x+4)^4$

17. $\dfrac{9 - d^2}{d+3} \cdot \dfrac{d}{d-3}$ $-d$

18. $\dfrac{c^2 - 3c - 10}{(c-2)^2} \cdot \dfrac{c-2}{c-5}$ $\frac{c+2}{c-2}$

19. $\dfrac{x^4 - y^4}{(x-y)^2} \cdot \dfrac{y-x}{x^2+y^2}$ $-x-y$

20. $\dfrac{e^2 - 24 - 2e}{e^2 - 30 - e} \cdot \dfrac{(e+5)^2}{e^2-16}$ $\frac{e+5}{e-4}$

21. $\dfrac{x^3 + y^3}{(x+y)^3} \cdot \dfrac{x^2 - y^2}{x^3 - y^3}$ $\frac{x^2 - xy + y^2}{(x+y)(x^2+xy+y^2)}$

22. $\dfrac{a^2 - b^2}{(a+b)^2} \cdot \dfrac{3a + 3b}{6a(b-a)}$ $-\frac{1}{2a}$

23. $\dfrac{a^2 - 1}{a^2 + 2a + 1} \cdot \dfrac{1+a}{1-a}$ -1

24. $\dfrac{9 - a^2}{12 + a - a^2} \cdot \dfrac{a-4}{a-3}$ 1

25. $\dfrac{a^2 - b^2}{2a + 2b} \cdot \dfrac{a^2 + ab}{(b-a)^2}$ $\frac{a(a+b)}{2(a-b)}$

26. $\dfrac{2x + 4i}{x^2 + 1} \cdot x - i$ $\frac{2(x+2i)}{(x+i)}$

27. $\dfrac{ab^2 - b^3}{a^3 + a^2b} \cdot \dfrac{a^2 - ab - 2b^2}{a^2 - 2ab + b^2}$ $\frac{b^2(a-2b)}{a^2(a-b)}$

28. $\dfrac{x^2 + 7xy + 10y^2}{x^2 + 6xy + 5y^2} \cdot \dfrac{x+y}{x^2 + 4xy + 4y^2} \cdot \dfrac{x+2y}{1}$ 1

29. $\dfrac{x^2 - y^2}{x^3 - 3x^2y + 2xy^2} \cdot \dfrac{xy - 2y^2}{y^2 + xy} \cdot \dfrac{x(x-y)}{(x-y)^2}$ $\frac{1}{x-y}$

Classify as <u>True</u> *or* <u>False</u> *for all replacements for the variables.*

30. $\dfrac{x}{x} = 1,\ x \neq 0$ True.

31. $(a + x)^2 = a^2 + x^2$ False.

32. $\dfrac{x + x}{2} = x^2$ False.

33. $\dfrac{1 + (x - 1)}{x - 1} = 1,\ x \neq 1$ False.

PUZZLE

$\begin{array}{r} 573 \\ 215\overline{)123195} \\ \underline{1075} \\ 1569 \\ \underline{1505} \\ 645 \\ \underline{645} \end{array}$

A six-digit number is divided by a three-digit number to give a three–digit number.

Find the missing digits. (There is only one solution.)

$\begin{array}{r} xxx \\ xxx\overline{)xxxxxx} \\ x0xx \\ \underline{} \\ xxxx \\ x50x \\ \underline{} \\ xxx \\ x4x \\ \underline{} \end{array}$

2-12 Division by a Rational Expression

The objective for this section is on page 98.

Division by a rational expression is similar to division by a rational number.

Theorem 2-9: Division of Rational Expressions

If $\dfrac{P}{Q}$ and $\dfrac{R}{S}$ are rational expressions, then

$$\frac{P}{Q} \div \frac{R}{S} = \frac{P}{Q} \cdot \frac{S}{R} = \frac{PS}{QR}$$

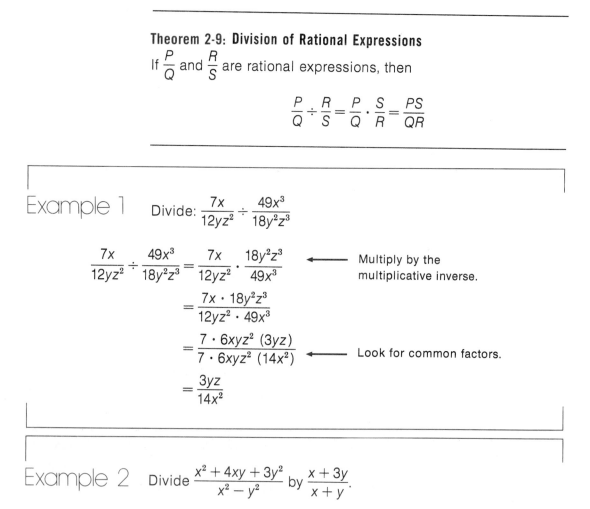

Example 1   Divide: $\dfrac{7x}{12yz^2} \div \dfrac{49x^3}{18y^2z^3}$

$$\frac{7x}{12yz^2} \div \frac{49x^3}{18y^2z^3} = \frac{7x}{12yz^2} \cdot \frac{18y^2z^3}{49x^3}$$ ⟵ Multiply by the multiplicative inverse.

$$= \frac{7x \cdot 18y^2z^3}{12yz^2 \cdot 49x^3}$$

$$= \frac{7 \cdot 6xyz^2 \,(3yz)}{7 \cdot 6xyz^2 \,(14x^2)}$$ ⟵ Look for common factors.

$$= \frac{3yz}{14x^2}$$

Example 2   Divide $\dfrac{x^2 + 4xy + 3y^2}{x^2 - y^2}$ by $\dfrac{x + 3y}{x + y}$.

$$\frac{x^2 + 4xy + 3y^2}{x^2 - y^2} \div \frac{x + 3y}{x + y} = \frac{x^2 + 4xy + 3y^2}{x^2 - y^2} \cdot \frac{x + y}{x + 3y}$$

78   Chapter 2

$$= \frac{(x^2 + 4xy + 3y^2)(x + y)}{(x^2 - y^2)(x + 3y)}$$

$$= \frac{(x + 3y)(x + y)(x + y)}{(x + y)(x - y)(x + 3y)}$$

$$= \frac{(x + 3y)(x + y)(x + y)}{(x + 3y)(x + y)(x - y)}$$

$$= \frac{x + y}{x - y}$$

Try These *Divide. No denominator is 0.*

1. $\dfrac{2 \cdot 4}{5} \div \dfrac{3 \cdot 6}{15}$ $\frac{4}{3}$

2. $\dfrac{7b}{6c} \div \dfrac{9bc}{4}$ $\frac{14}{27c^2}$

3. $\dfrac{5(x - 3)}{2x} \div \dfrac{x^2 - 9}{x}$ $\frac{5}{2(x + 3)}$

4. $\dfrac{y^2 + 3y + 2}{y^5} \div \dfrac{y + 2}{y^3}$ $\frac{y + 1}{y^2}$

Exercises

Divide. No denominator is 0.

a 1. $\dfrac{x^2y^4}{6a^2} \div \dfrac{x^4y}{10a^2}$ $\frac{5y^3}{3x^2}$

2. $\dfrac{14x^2}{10b^2} \div \dfrac{21x^2}{15b^2}$ 1

3. $\dfrac{5a}{12yz^2} \div \dfrac{15a^2}{18y^2z^2}$ $\frac{y}{2a}$

4. $\dfrac{34a}{4x^2y} \div \dfrac{17a^3}{2xy}$ $\frac{1}{a^2x}$

5. $\dfrac{25x^2}{(3yz)^2} \div \dfrac{100x^3}{18yz^3}$ $\frac{z}{2yx}$

6. $\dfrac{(2a)^3}{(4yz)^2} \div \dfrac{16a}{8y^2z^3}$ $\frac{a^2z}{4}$

7. $\dfrac{(d - b)(a + b)}{(x - y)(x + y)} \div \dfrac{d - b}{x + y}$ $\frac{a + b}{x - y}$

8. $\dfrac{-4(a - 2)}{-2(x + 5)} \div \dfrac{3(a - 2)}{(x - 5)(x + 5)}$ $\frac{2(x - 5)}{3}$

9. $\dfrac{3(x + 5)}{7x} \div \dfrac{(x - 5)(x + 5)}{49x}$ $\frac{21}{x - 5}$

10. $4(n - 3) \div \dfrac{12(n - 3)}{100}$ $\frac{100}{3}$

11. $\dfrac{3y^5}{2c - 8} \div \dfrac{-18y}{c - 4}$ $-\frac{y^4}{12}$

12. $\dfrac{3d + 15}{10d} \div \dfrac{2d + 10}{100}$ $\frac{15}{d}$

13. $\dfrac{x^2 + 2x}{y^2 - 9} \div \dfrac{x + 2}{y + 3}$ $\frac{x}{y - 3}$

14. $\dfrac{x^2y^3 - x^2y^2}{a + b} \div \dfrac{3y - 3}{(a + b)^2}$ $\frac{x^2y^2(a + b)}{3}$

Polynomials and Rational Expressions **79**

15. $\dfrac{c^2 - b^2}{x^2 - y^2} \div \dfrac{c + b}{y - x}$ $\frac{b-c}{x+y}$

16. $\dfrac{a^2 - 16}{a + 7} \div \dfrac{3a - 12}{a^2 - 49}$ $\frac{(a+4)(a-7)}{3}$

17. $\dfrac{10x^2}{(x + y)^2} \div \dfrac{5x}{x + y}$ $\frac{2x}{x+y}$

18. $\dfrac{5}{2a + 3b} \div \dfrac{10}{4a^2 - 9b^2}$ $\frac{2a-3b}{2}$

19. $\dfrac{2c}{d - 5} \div \dfrac{16c^5}{5 - d}$ $-\frac{1}{8c^4}$

20. $\dfrac{8a^2}{a^2 - 16} \div \dfrac{4a}{4 - a}$ $\frac{-2a}{a+4}$

21. $\dfrac{7y^2 - 21y}{x + 5} \div \dfrac{9 - y^2}{(x + 5)^2}$ $\frac{-7y(x+5)}{y+3}$

22. $\dfrac{x^2 - 9}{x^2 - x - 2} \div \dfrac{x - 3}{x^2 + x - 6}$ $\frac{(x+3)^2}{x+1}$

23. $\dfrac{x^2 + 5x + 6}{3x + 12} \div \dfrac{x + 3}{x^2 + 4x}$ $\frac{x(x+2)}{3}$

24. $\dfrac{3a^2 + 30a + 75}{a - 5} \div \dfrac{a}{a^2 - 25}$ $\frac{3(a+5)^3}{a}$

25. $\dfrac{x^2 + 2x + 1}{x^2 - 4} \div \dfrac{x^2 - x - 2}{x + 2}$ $\frac{x+1}{(x-2)^2}$

26. $\dfrac{d^2 + 6d}{d^2 + 2d - 8} \div \dfrac{d^2 - 36}{d + 4}$ $\frac{d}{(d-2)(d-6)}$

27. $\dfrac{x^2 - x - 2}{x^2 - x - 6} \div \dfrac{2x - x^2}{2x + x^2}$ $\frac{-x-1}{x-3}$

28. $\dfrac{y^3 + 1}{x^2 - 4y^2} \div \dfrac{y^2 - y + 1}{x - 2y}$ $\frac{y+1}{x+2y}$

29. $\dfrac{x^2 - 1}{x^2 - 2x + 1} \div \dfrac{1 - x}{5 + x}$ $\frac{-(x+1)(5+x)}{(x-1)^2}$

30. $\dfrac{(a - b)(b - c)}{c - a} \div \dfrac{c - b}{a - c}$ $a-b$

31. $\dfrac{3ix}{11} \div \dfrac{7x}{2i}$ $-\frac{6}{77}$

32. $\dfrac{2z + 3i}{3z - 2i} \div \dfrac{3z + 2i}{2z - 3i}$ $\frac{4z^2+9}{9z^2+4}$

33. $\dfrac{(5 - 3i)z + 1}{(5 - 3i)z + 2} \div \dfrac{5z - 3i}{4iz^2}$ $\frac{4iz^2[(5-3i)z+1]}{(5z-3i)[(5-3i)z+2]}$

34. $\dfrac{x^2 + 6xy + 5y^2}{x^2 + 4xy + 4y^2} \div \dfrac{x + y}{x + 2y}$ $\frac{x+5y}{x+2y}$

35. $\dfrac{x^3 - 6x^2 + 8x}{x^2 - 8x + 16} \div \dfrac{2x - 4}{10x^2 - 40x}$ $5x^2$

36. $\dfrac{8x^3 - 27y^3}{2x + 3y} \div \dfrac{4x^2 + 6xy + 9y^2}{4x^2 - 9y^2}$ $(2x-3y)^2$

37. Prove the theorem for division by a rational expression, using the pattern established in Examples 1 and 2 of this section. See key.

Remember

Perform the indicated operations.

1. $\dfrac{3}{4} + \dfrac{2}{4}$ $1\frac{1}{4}$

2. $\dfrac{2}{5} - \dfrac{3}{5}$ $-\frac{1}{5}$

3. $\dfrac{2}{3} + \dfrac{3}{5}$ $1\frac{4}{15}$

4. $\dfrac{7}{8} - \dfrac{1}{6}$ $\frac{17}{24}$

The answers are on page 99.

2-13 Addition/Subtraction: Like Denominators

The objective for this section is on page 98.

Addition and subtraction of rational expressions follow the same pattern as addition and subtraction of rational numbers.

Theorem 2-10: Addition and Subtraction of Rational Expressions

If $\dfrac{P}{Q}$ and $\dfrac{R}{Q}$ are rational expressions, then

$$\frac{P}{Q} + \frac{R}{Q} = \frac{P+R}{Q} \qquad \text{and} \qquad \frac{P}{Q} - \frac{R}{Q} = \frac{P-R}{Q}.$$

Example 1

Add: $\dfrac{5}{n} + \dfrac{3}{n}$

$$\frac{5}{n} + \frac{3}{n} = \frac{5+3}{n}, \text{ or } \frac{8}{n}$$

The theorem can be extended to more than two expressions.

Example 2

$$\frac{x+2}{x-4} + \frac{2x-9}{x-4} - \frac{3x-4}{x-4} = \underline{}$$

$$\frac{x+2}{x-4} + \frac{2x-9}{x-4} - \frac{3x-4}{x-4} = \frac{(x+2)+(2x-9)-(3x-4)}{x-4}$$

$$= \frac{x+2+2x-9-3x+4}{x-4} \qquad \longleftarrow \quad -(3x-4) = -3x+4$$

$$= \frac{-3}{x-4} \qquad \longleftarrow \quad \text{Combine like terms.}$$

Polynomials and Rational Expressions **81**

Try These   *Perform the indicated operations.*

1. $\dfrac{2x-11}{2}+\dfrac{2x+11}{2}$ $2x$

2. $\dfrac{2x-11}{2}-\dfrac{2x+11}{2}$ -11

3. $\dfrac{10x-4y}{x+y}-\dfrac{8x-y}{x+y}$ $\dfrac{2x-3y}{x+y}$

Exercises

Perform the indicated operations. No denominator is zero.

1. $\dfrac{3}{4}+\dfrac{7}{4}$ $\tfrac{10}{4}$, or $\tfrac{5}{2}$

2. $\dfrac{8}{7}-\dfrac{3}{7}$ $\tfrac{5}{7}$

3. $\dfrac{6}{5}-\dfrac{5}{5}$ $\tfrac{1}{5}$

4. $\dfrac{15}{10}-\dfrac{6}{10}$ $\tfrac{9}{10}$

5. $\dfrac{3}{4}+\dfrac{7}{4}+\dfrac{9}{4}$ $\tfrac{19}{4}$

6. $\dfrac{8}{10}-\dfrac{1}{10}+\dfrac{3}{10}$ $\tfrac{10}{10}$, or 1

7. $\dfrac{3}{a}+\dfrac{7}{a}$ $\tfrac{10}{a}$

8. $\dfrac{15}{y}-\dfrac{16}{y}$ $-\tfrac{1}{y}$

9. $\dfrac{19}{a}-\dfrac{17}{a}$ $\tfrac{2}{a}$

10. $\dfrac{2}{a-b}+\dfrac{3}{a-b}$ $\tfrac{5}{a-b}$

11. $\dfrac{4}{x+y}-\dfrac{1}{x+y}$ $\tfrac{3}{x+y}$

12. $\dfrac{9}{x-y}-\dfrac{13}{x-y}$ $-\tfrac{4}{x-y}$

13. $\dfrac{2x}{x-y}-\dfrac{5x}{x-y}$ $\tfrac{-3x}{x-y}$

14. $\dfrac{8m}{m^2-n^2}-\dfrac{17m}{m^2-n^2}$ $\tfrac{-9m}{m^2-n^2}$

15. $\dfrac{x}{y}-\dfrac{10}{y}$ $\tfrac{x-10}{y}$

16. $\dfrac{3n-7}{5}-\dfrac{9n-9}{5}$ $\tfrac{-6n+2}{5}$

17. $\dfrac{6m-8}{9}-\dfrac{7m-9}{9}$ $\tfrac{-m+1}{9}$

18. $\dfrac{x-7y}{12}-\dfrac{x-9y}{12}$ $\tfrac{y}{6}$

19. $\dfrac{2x-15}{26}-\dfrac{2x-19}{26}$ $\tfrac{4}{26}$ or $\tfrac{2}{13}$

20. $\dfrac{4a-2}{a^2}+\dfrac{3a-7}{a^2}$ $\tfrac{7a-9}{a^2}$

21. $\dfrac{19a-2}{b^2}-\dfrac{a+7}{b^2}$ $\tfrac{18a-9}{b^2}$

22. $\dfrac{2a-1}{a^2}-\dfrac{a}{a^2}+\dfrac{3a-7}{a^2}$ $\tfrac{4a-8}{a^2}$

23. $\dfrac{4a-9}{b^2}-\dfrac{3a-6}{b^2}$ $\tfrac{a-3}{b^2}$

24. $\dfrac{2x-y}{x+y}+\dfrac{x-7y}{x+y}$ $\tfrac{3x-8y}{x+y}$

25. $\dfrac{3}{x-2}-\dfrac{3x}{x-2}$ $\tfrac{3-3x}{x-2}$

26. $\dfrac{3-3y}{x^2}+\dfrac{1}{x^2}-\dfrac{y+1}{x^2}$ $\tfrac{3-4y}{x^2}$

27. $\dfrac{4a-3}{a^2-4}-\dfrac{3a-2}{a^2-4}$ $\tfrac{a-1}{a^2-4}$

Remember

Find the least common multiple of each of the following.

1. 3, 2, 5   30

2. 4, 5, 6   60

3. x, x^2, x^3 x^3

The answers are on page 99.

The objective for this section is on page 99.

The least common multiple, LCM, of two or more numbers is used to add or subtract rational expressions with unlike denominators. To find the LCM, first find the greatest common factor, GCF.

Example 1   Find the LCM of 36 and 54.

$36 = 2 \cdot \underline{2 \cdot 3} \cdot 3$ ◀——— Factor. Find the GCF.

$54 = \underline{2 \cdot 3} \cdot 3 \cdot 3$

Greatest common factor (GCF)
↓
LCM: $\underline{2 \cdot 3} \cdot 3 \cdot \underline{2 \cdot 3} = 108$ ◀——— **LCM = (GCF)(other factors)**
↑
Other factors

Example 2   Find the LCM of $3(x^2 - 4)$ and $9(x^2 - 4x + 4)$.

$3(x^2 - 4) = 3 \cdot \underline{(x - 2)} \cdot (x + 2)$ ◀——— Factor. Find the GCF.

$9(x^2 - 4x + 4) = 3 \cdot \underline{3 \cdot (x - 2)} \cdot (x - 2)$

GCF   **Other factors**
↓   ↓
LCM: $\underline{3(x-2)}\ \underline{(x+2)3(x-2)}$, or $9(x+2)(x-2)^2$ ◀——— **LCM = (GCF)(other factors)**

When you have three or more numbers, you can find their LCM by working with two of the numbers at a time. This is illustrated in Example 3 on the top of the next page.

Polynomials and Rational Expressions   **83**

Example 3   Find the LCM of 22, 24, and 60.

GCF of 22 and 24   Other factors of 22 and 24

LCM of 22 and 24 = $2 \cdot 2 \cdot 2 \cdot 3 \cdot 11$

$= 264$

GCF of 264 and 60   Other factors of 264 and 60

LCM of 264 and 60 = $2 \cdot 2 \cdot 3 \cdot 2 \cdot 5 \cdot 11$

$= 1320 \longleftarrow$ LCM of 22, 24, and 60

Sometimes the LCM can be found by direct inspection.

Example 4   Find the LCM of 12, 5, and 60.

60 is a common multiple of 12, 5, and 60, and no number smaller than 60 is a multiple of 60. Thus, 60 is the least common multiple of 12, 5, and 60.

When the denominators of rational expressions are unlike, the **least common denominator, LCD,** is used to rewrite the expressions so that their denominators are the same. The LCD of two or more rational expressions is the least common multiple, LCM, of their denominators.

Example 5 $\dfrac{4a - 3}{4} - \dfrac{2a + 7}{5} + \dfrac{a + 2}{2} = \underline{\quad ? \quad}$

LCD: 20 $\longleftarrow$ Find the LCD of 4, 5, 2.

$\dfrac{4a - 3}{4} - \dfrac{2a + 7}{5} + \dfrac{a + 2}{2}$

$= \dfrac{4a - 3}{4} \cdot \dfrac{5}{5} - \dfrac{2a + 7}{5} \cdot \dfrac{4}{4} + \dfrac{a + 2}{2} \cdot \dfrac{10}{10}$ $\longleftarrow$ Multiply each expression by a name for 1 to make each denominator 20.

$= \dfrac{5(4a - 3)}{20} - \dfrac{4(2a + 7)}{20} + \dfrac{10(a + 2)}{20}$

$$= \frac{5(4a-3) - 4(2a+7) + 10(a+2)}{20} \quad \longleftarrow \quad \frac{P}{Q} + \frac{R}{Q} = \frac{P+R}{Q}$$

$$= \frac{20a - 15 - 8a - 28 + 10a + 20}{20} \quad \longleftarrow \quad \text{Multiply.}$$

$$= \frac{22a - 23}{20} \quad \longleftarrow \quad \text{Combine like terms.}$$

Example 6 $\quad \dfrac{7m}{6a^2b^4} + \dfrac{5}{9a^3b^2} = \dfrac{?}{\underline{}}$

LCD: $18a^3b^4$

$$\frac{7m}{6a^2b^4} + \frac{5}{9a^3b^2} = \frac{7m}{6a^2b^4} \cdot \frac{3a}{3a} + \frac{5}{9a^3b^2} \cdot \frac{2b^2}{2b^2} \quad \longleftarrow$$

Multiply each expression by a name for 1 to make each denominator $18a^3b^4$.

$$= \frac{7m(3a)}{18a^3b^4} + \frac{5(2b^2)}{18a^3b^4}$$

$$= \frac{7m(3a) + 5(2b^2)}{18a^3b^4}$$

$$= \frac{21am + 10b^2}{18a^3b^4}$$

Example 7 $\quad \dfrac{3a-4}{a^2-9} - \dfrac{2a-3}{a^2-a-6} = \dfrac{?}{\underline{}}$

LCD: $(a-3)(a+3)(a+2)$

$$\frac{3a-4}{a^2-9} - \frac{2a-3}{a^2-a-6} = \frac{3a-4}{(a-3)(a+3)} \cdot \frac{(a+2)}{(a+2)} - \frac{2a-3}{(a-3)(a+2)} \cdot \frac{(a+3)}{(a+3)}$$

$$= \frac{(3a-4)(a+2) - (2a-3)(a+3)}{(a-3)(a+3)(a+2)}$$

$$= \frac{(3a^2+2a-8) - (2a^2+3a-9)}{(a-3)(a+3)(a+2)} \quad \longleftarrow \quad \textit{LCD: } (a-3)(a+3)(a+2)$$

$$= \frac{3a^2+2a-8-2a^2-3a+9}{(a-3)(a+3)(a+2)} \quad \longleftarrow \quad \begin{array}{l} -(2a^2+3a-9) = \\ -2a^2-3a+9 \end{array}$$

$$= \frac{a^2-a+1}{(a-3)(a+3)(a+2)}$$

Try These   Rewrite each pair of rational expressions so that they have the same denominator.

1. $\dfrac{2}{3a}, \dfrac{3}{5a^2}$ $\dfrac{10a}{15a^2}, \dfrac{9}{15a^2}$

2. $\dfrac{a+b}{3a^3b^2}, \dfrac{5}{4a^4b}$ $\dfrac{4a(a+b)}{12a^4b^2}, \dfrac{15b}{12a^4b^2}$

3. $\dfrac{x+2}{4}, \dfrac{x-5}{5}$ $\dfrac{5(x+2)}{20}, \dfrac{4(x-5)}{20}$

4. $\dfrac{x-2}{(x+2)^2}, \dfrac{5}{3(x+2)}$ $\dfrac{3(x-2)}{3(x+2)^2}, \dfrac{5(x+2)}{3(x+2)^2}$

5. $\dfrac{2x-3}{2x-5}, \dfrac{25x^2}{4x^2-25}$ $\dfrac{(2x-3)(2x+5)}{(2x-5)(2x+5)}, \dfrac{25x^2}{(2x-5)(2x+5)}$

6. $\dfrac{2}{1-x}, \dfrac{2x}{x^2-1}$ $\dfrac{-2(x+1)}{(x-1)(x+1)}, \dfrac{2x}{(x-1)(x+1)}$

Exercises

Perform the indicated operations. No denominator is 0.

1. $\dfrac{5}{b} - \dfrac{3}{c}$ $\dfrac{5c-3b}{bc}$

2. $\dfrac{a}{x^2y} + \dfrac{b}{xy^2}$ $\dfrac{ay+bx}{x^2y^2}$

3. $\dfrac{r}{m+n} - \dfrac{s}{m-n}$ $\dfrac{r(m-n)-s(m+n)}{m^2-n^2}$

4. $\dfrac{2}{9} + \dfrac{4}{3} - \dfrac{1}{2}$ $\dfrac{19}{18}$

5. $\dfrac{1}{4} - \dfrac{2}{5} + \dfrac{5}{6}$ $\dfrac{41}{60}$

6. $\dfrac{3x}{4} + \dfrac{2x}{3} - \dfrac{x}{12}$ $\dfrac{4x}{3}$

7. $\dfrac{5}{2c} + \dfrac{1}{6c} - \dfrac{4}{3c}$ $\dfrac{4}{3c}$

8. $\dfrac{5a}{b^2} - \dfrac{3a}{b} + \dfrac{7a}{b^3}$ $\dfrac{5ab-3ab^2+7a}{b^3}$

9. $\dfrac{3}{8mn^2} - \dfrac{5}{4m^2n} + \dfrac{2}{3mn}$ $\dfrac{9m-30n+16mn}{24m^2n^2}$

10. $\dfrac{2a+b}{8} + \dfrac{3a-4b}{8}$ $\dfrac{5a-3b}{8}$

11. $\dfrac{5m-n}{3} - \dfrac{2m-n}{3}$ m

12. $\dfrac{3a-b}{6} - \dfrac{3a-2b}{4}$ $\dfrac{4b-3a}{12}$

13. $\dfrac{3x-5}{9} + \dfrac{2x+7}{6}$ $\dfrac{12x+11}{18}$

14. $\dfrac{5a+2}{a} + \dfrac{3b+1}{b}$ $\dfrac{8ab+2b+a}{ab}$

15. $\dfrac{2s-t}{s} - \dfrac{5s+2t}{t}$ $\dfrac{-5s^2-t^2}{st}$

16. $\dfrac{3m-1}{2} - \dfrac{4m+5}{3} + \dfrac{6m+7}{5}$ $\dfrac{41m-23}{30}$

17. $\dfrac{4n^2+1}{8p} + \dfrac{n^2+3}{2p} - \dfrac{2n^2-1}{3p}$ $\dfrac{8n^2+47}{24p}$

18. $\dfrac{3}{y+2} + \dfrac{5}{y-4}$ $\dfrac{8y-2}{(y+2)(y-4)}$

19. $\dfrac{6}{x+4} + \dfrac{4}{x+8}$ $\dfrac{10x+64}{x^2+12x+32}$

20. $\dfrac{3}{m-2} - \dfrac{2}{m+5}$ $\dfrac{m+19}{m^2+3m-10}$

21. $\dfrac{4}{3a-6}+\dfrac{7}{5a-10}$ $\qquad$ $\frac{41}{15(a-2)}$ or $\frac{41}{15a-30}$

22. $\dfrac{5}{3c+12}-\dfrac{3}{7c+28}$ $\qquad$ $\frac{26}{21(c+4)}$ or $\frac{26}{21c+84}$

23. $\dfrac{a}{a+b}+\dfrac{b}{b+a}$ $\qquad$ $\frac{a+b}{a+b}$ or 1

24. $\dfrac{2m}{m-n}+\dfrac{n}{n-m}$ $\qquad$ $\frac{2m-n}{m-n}$

25. $\dfrac{10}{2t-1}-\dfrac{6}{1-2t}$ $\qquad$ $\frac{16}{2t-1}$

26. $\dfrac{2}{c^2-4}-\dfrac{3}{2-c}$ $\qquad$ $\frac{3c+8}{c^2-4}$

27. $\dfrac{x}{x-y}-\dfrac{2x}{x+y}+\dfrac{2xy}{x^2-y^2}$ $\qquad$ $\frac{-x^2+5xy}{x^2-y^2}$

28. $\dfrac{3}{t^2-4}-\dfrac{4}{t^2-3t+2}$ $\qquad$ $\frac{-t-11}{(t-2)(t+2)(t-1)}$

29. $\dfrac{3a}{a+b}-\dfrac{3b}{a-b}+\dfrac{a^2+b^2}{a^2-b^2}$ $\qquad$ $\frac{4a^2-6ab-2b^2}{a^2-b^2}$

30. $\dfrac{n+5}{n^2-8n+16}-\dfrac{n-4}{n^2-2n-8}$ $\qquad$ $\frac{15n-6}{(n-4)^2(n+2)}$

31. $\dfrac{2}{x^2-y^2}+\dfrac{2}{(x+y)^2}+\dfrac{2}{(x-y)^2}$ $\qquad$ $\frac{6x^2+2y^2}{(x+y)^2(x-y)^2}$

32. $\dfrac{n+2}{6n^2-n-12}+\dfrac{3n+4}{2n^2+n-6}$ $\qquad$ $\frac{10n^2+28n+20}{(2n-3)(3n+4)(n+2)}$

Use Method 1 or Method 2 to express each numerator and denominator as a rational expression. Then simplify.

Method I

$$\dfrac{a+\dfrac{ab}{c}}{\dfrac{a^2}{d}-a}=\dfrac{\dfrac{ac+ab}{c}}{\dfrac{a^2-ad}{d}}$$

$$=\dfrac{a(c+b)}{c}\div\dfrac{a(a-d)}{d}$$

$$=\dfrac{a(c+b)}{c}\cdot\dfrac{d}{a(a-d)}$$

$$=\dfrac{d(c+b)}{c(a-d)}, \text{ or } \dfrac{cd+bd}{ac-dc}$$

Method II

$$\dfrac{a+\dfrac{ab}{c}}{\dfrac{a^2}{d}-a}=\dfrac{cd\left(a+\dfrac{ab}{c}\right)}{cd\left(\dfrac{a^2}{d}-a\right)}$$

$$=\dfrac{cda+dab}{ca^2-cda}$$

$$=\dfrac{a(cd+db)}{a(ca-cd)}$$

$$=\dfrac{cd+db}{ca-cd}$$

33. $\dfrac{\dfrac{1}{2}+\dfrac{1}{3}}{\dfrac{1}{2}-\dfrac{1}{3}}$ $\quad$ 5

34. $\dfrac{2-\dfrac{1}{6}}{3+\dfrac{1}{4}}$ $\quad$ $\frac{22}{39}$

35. $\dfrac{1+\dfrac{x}{y}}{1-\dfrac{x}{y}}$ $\quad$ $\frac{y+x}{y-x}$

36. $\dfrac{2-\dfrac{m}{3}}{5+\dfrac{m}{8}}$ $\quad$ $\frac{8(6-m)}{3(40+m)}$

37. $\dfrac{\dfrac{1}{x}-1}{1+\dfrac{1}{y}}$ $\quad$ $\frac{y(1-x)}{x(1+y)}$

38. $\dfrac{a+\dfrac{a}{b}}{1-\dfrac{1}{b^2}}$ $\quad$ $\frac{ab}{b-1}$

39. $\dfrac{\dfrac{m}{n}-1}{\dfrac{1}{m}+\dfrac{1}{n}}$ $\quad$ $\frac{m(m-n)}{m+n}$

40. $\dfrac{c-d}{c-\dfrac{d^2}{c}}$ $\quad$ $\frac{c}{c+d}$

41. $\dfrac{\dfrac{y}{x-y}-1}{2-\dfrac{x}{x-y}}$ -1

42. $\dfrac{1}{\dfrac{1}{a}+\dfrac{1}{b}+\dfrac{1}{c}}$ $\frac{abc}{bc+ac+ab}$

43. $\dfrac{1-\dfrac{r^2}{s^2}}{1-\dfrac{2r}{s}+\dfrac{r^2}{s^2}}$ $\frac{s+r}{s-r}$

Perform the indicated operations.

C **44.** $\dfrac{3x+y}{6x^2-5xy-6y^2}-\dfrac{x-3y}{8x^2-14xy+3y^2}$ $\frac{9x^2+8xy+5y^2}{(3x+2y)(2x-3y)(4x-y)}$

45. $\dfrac{m+1}{m^2+9m+14}-\dfrac{m-2}{m^2-3m-10}+\dfrac{m+2}{m^2+2m-35}$ $\frac{m^2-5m+13}{(m+2)(m+7)(m-5)}$

46. $\dfrac{3a-b}{4a^2-11ab-3b^2}+\dfrac{a+b}{a^2-4ab+3b^2}+\dfrac{5a+b}{4a^2-3ab-b^2}$ $\frac{12a^2-13ab-b^2}{(4a+b)(a-3b)(a-b)}$

47. Prove that if $\dfrac{P}{Q}$ and $\dfrac{R}{S}$ are rational expressions, $\dfrac{P}{Q}+\dfrac{R}{S}=\dfrac{PS+QR}{QS}$. See key.

2-15 The Binomial Theorem

The objective for this section is on page 99.

A product or power rewritten as a sum is called an **expansion**. Here are some expansions of $(a+b)^n$.

$$n=0: \quad (a+b)^0 = 1$$
$$n=1: \quad (a+b)^1 = a+b$$
$$n=2: \quad (a+b)^2 = a^2 + 2ab + b^2$$
$$n=3: \quad (a+b)^3 = a^3 + 3a^2b + 3ab^2 + b^3$$
$$n=4: \quad (a+b)^4 = a^4 + 4a^3b + 6a^2b^2 + 4ab^3 + b^4$$

The expansion of a binomial has patterns such as the following that simplify finding $(a+b)^n$.

$$a+b \ =$$
$$(a+b)^2 =$$
$$(a+b)^3 =$$
$$(a+b)^4 = \quad a^4 + 4a^3b + 6a^2b^2 + 4ab^3 + b^4$$

The numerical coefficients form a triangular array of numbers that is called **Pascal's Triangle.**

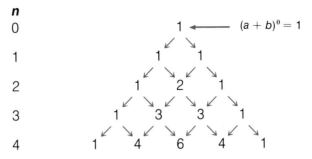

Note that the first and last number of each row is 1.
Each of the other numbers is found by adding the numbers that are above it and just to its left and to its right. For example, the first 4 in the fifth row is the sum of the 3 and 1 above, and on either side of, the 4.

Example 1   Use Pascal's triangle to write the coefficients for $(a + b)^5$.

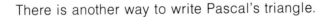

Write the coefficients for the fifth row.
Write 1 for the first and last numbers. Add to find the other numbers.

There is another way to write Pascal's triangle.

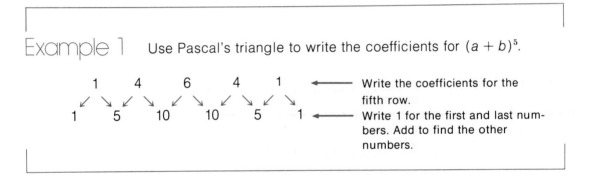

Using this method, you can write the coefficients for any row without writing the previous rows.

Polynomials and Rational Expressions   **89**

Summary for Finding the Coefficients of $(a + b)^n$

1. The coefficient of the first and last term is 1.
2. The number of terms in the expansion of $(a + b)^n$ is one more than n. Thus, there are $(n + 1)$ *terms*.
3. The coefficient of the second term is a fraction with $(2 - 1)$, or 1 factor in the numerator and denominator; the third term has $(3 - 1)$, or 2 factors, in the numerator and denominator. That is, the coefficient of the rth term has $(r - 1)$ factors in the numerator and denominator.

Example 2 Write the coefficients for the expansion of $(a + b)^5$.

Term	1	2	3	4	5	6
	1	$\dfrac{5}{1}$	$\dfrac{5 \cdot 4}{1 \cdot 2}$	$\dfrac{5 \cdot 4 \cdot 3}{1 \cdot 2 \cdot 3}$	$\dfrac{5 \cdot 4 \cdot 3 \cdot 2}{1 \cdot 2 \cdot 3 \cdot 4}$	$\dfrac{5 \cdot 4 \cdot 3 \cdot 2 \cdot 1}{1 \cdot 2 \cdot 3 \cdot 4 \cdot 5}$
	$\downarrow$	$\downarrow$	$\downarrow$	$\downarrow$	$\downarrow$	$\downarrow$
	1	5	10	10	5	1

The pattern for the variable factors of each term is easy to see.

Variable factors for the expansion of $(a + b)^n$

n						
1			a	b		
2		a^2	ab	b^2		
3	a^3	a^2b	ab^2	b^3		
4	a^4	a^3b	a^2b^2	ab^3	b^4	
5	a^5	a^4b	a^3b^2	a^2b^3	ab^4	b^5

The pattern is summarized below.

1. For the first term, the exponent of a *is* n.
2. The exponent of a decreases by 1 for each term. In the last, or $(n + 1)$st term the exponent for a is 0. Since $a^0 = 1$, the a does not usually appear in the last term.
3. The exponent of b starts with b^0 for the first term, and increases by 1 for each term. The exponent of b for the rth term is $r - 1$.
4. In any term, the sum of the exponents is n.

Example 3 Write the variable factors for each term in the expansion of $(a+b)^5$

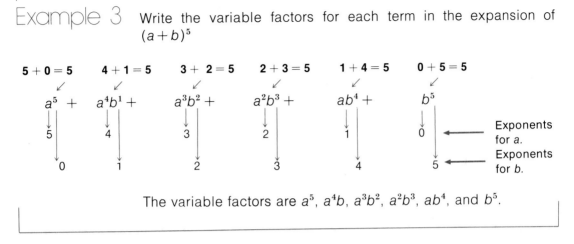

5 + 0 = 5 **4 + 1 = 5** **3 + 2 = 5** **2 + 3 = 5** **1 + 4 = 5** **0 + 5 = 5**

$a^5 +$ $a^4b^1 +$ $a^3b^2 +$ $a^2b^3 +$ $ab^4 +$ b^5

5   4   3   2   1   0 ← Exponents for a.

0   1   2   3   4   5 ← Exponents for b.

The variable factors are a^5, a^4b, a^3b^2, a^2b^3, ab^4, and b^5.

These patterns for coefficients and variable factors suggest the Binomial Theorem.

Theorem 2-1: Binomial Theorem

For any positive integer n,

$$(a+b)^n = a^n + \frac{n}{1}a^{n-1}b + \frac{n(n-1)}{1 \cdot 2}a^{n-2}b^2 + \frac{n(n-1)(n-2)}{1 \cdot 2 \cdot 3}a^{n-3}b^3 + \cdots + b^n$$

Example 4 Write the expansion of $(2x+y)^5$. Simplify.

$a^5 + 5a^4b + 10a^3b^2 + 10a^2b^3 + 5ab^4 + b^5$ ← Write the expansion of $(a+b)^5$.

$(2x)^5 + 5(2x)^4y + 10(2x)^3y^2 + 10(2x)^2y^3 + 5(2x)y^4 + y^5$ ← Replace a with $2x$ and b with y.

$32x^5 + 80\ x^4y + 80x^3y^2 + 40x^2y^3 + 10xy^4 + y^5$ ← Simplify.

Thus, $(2x+y)^5 = 32x^5 + 80x^4y + 80x^3y^2 + 40x^2y^3 + 10xy^4 + y^5$.

Example 5 Write the expansion of $(m - 2n)^4$. Simplify.

$a^4 + 4a^3b \qquad + 6a^2b^2 \qquad + \qquad 4ab^3 \qquad + \qquad b^4$ ⟵ Write the expansion of $(a + b)^4$.

$m^4 + 4m^3(-2n) + 6m^2(-2n)^2 + 4m(-2n)^3 + (-2n)^4$ ⟵ Replace a with m and b with $(-2n)$.

$m^4 - 8m^3n + 24m^2n^2 - 32mn^3 + 16n^4$ ⟵ Simplify

Consider the third term of each expansion in the table.

| $(a + b)^n$ | Third Term | Exponent | | Number of Factors in the | |
		b	a	Denominator	Numerator
$(a + b)^3$	$\dfrac{3 \cdot 2}{1 \cdot 2}ab^2$	2	$(3 - 2)$	2	2
$(a + b)^4$	$\dfrac{4 \cdot 3}{1 \cdot 2}a^2b^2$	2	$(4 - 2)$	2	2
$(a + b)^5$	$\dfrac{5 \cdot 4}{1 \cdot 2}a^3b^2$	2	$(5 - 2)$	2	2

Note that the exponent of b is simply the number of the term minus one. Knowing the exponent for b, how can you find the exponent for a?

Example 6 Find the fifth term of $(x - y)^9$.

$\underline{\quad ? \quad} x^?(-y)^?$ ⟵ Replace a with x and b with $(-y)$.

$\underline{\quad ? \quad} x^5(-y)^4$ ⟵ For the 5th term, the exponent of b is 4; the exponent of a is $9 - 4$.

$\dfrac{9 \cdot 8 \cdot 7 \cdot 6}{1 \cdot 2 \cdot 3 \cdot 4}x^5y^4$ ⟵ There are 4 factors in the denominator and 4 in the numerator.

$126x^5y^4$ ⟵ Simplify.

Try These   *Write the fourth term of each binomial.*

1. $(x + y)^6$ $20x^3y^3$ **2.** $(x - y)^6$ $-20x^3y^3$ **3.** $(2x + y)^6$ $160x^3y^3$ **4.** $(x - \frac{1}{2}y)^6$
$-\frac{5}{2}x^3y^3$

Exercises

See key for Exercises 1-12.

Use the Binomial Theorem to write each expansion. Then simplify.

a

1. $(x + y)^4$ **2.** $(r + s)^7$ **3.** $(c - d)^3$ **4.** $(m - n)^6$

5. $(x + 3)^5$ **6.** $(2r + 1)^4$ **7.** $(w - 4)^3$ **8.** $(3m + 2)^5$

9. $(2x - 3)^4$ **10.** $(3x + 2y)^4$ **11.** $(2a - 3b)^5$ **12.** $(x + .2)^3$

Find the required term.

13. 5th term of $(a + b)^7$ $35a^3b^4$ **14.** 4th term of $(m + n)^6$ $20m^3n^3$

15. 5th term of $(r - s)^7$ $35r^3s^4$ **16.** 4th term of $(2x + y)^{10}$ $15,360x^7y^3$

$243s^{10} + 405s^8t + 270s^6t^2 + 90s^4t^3 + 15s^2t^4 + t^5$

Use the Binomial Theorem to write each expansion. Simplify.

b

17. $(3s^2 + t)^5$ **18.** $(1 + i)^7$ $8 - 8i$

19. $(1 - i)^7$ $8 + 8i$ **20.** $(4x^2 - 3y^2)^5$ See key

21. $(x + \frac{1}{2})^4$ $x^4 + 2x^3 + \frac{3}{2}x^2 + \frac{1}{2}x + \frac{1}{16}$ **22.** $(2y - \frac{1}{2})^5$ $32y^5 - 40y^4 + 20y^3 - 5y^2 + \frac{5}{8}y - \frac{1}{32}$

23. $\left(\frac{a}{b} + \frac{b}{a}\right)^6$ **24.** $\left(1 - \frac{m}{n}\right)^4$ $1 - 4\left(\frac{m}{n}\right) + 6\left(\frac{m}{n}\right)^2 - 4\left(\frac{m}{n}\right)^3 + \left(\frac{m}{n}\right)^4$

$\left(\frac{a}{b}\right)^6 + 6\left(\frac{a}{b}\right)^4 + 15\left(\frac{a}{b}\right)^2 + 20 + 15\left(\frac{b}{a}\right)^2 + 6\left(\frac{b}{a}\right)^4 + \left(\frac{b}{a}\right)^6$

25. Find the 8th term of $(2x^2 - y)^9$. $_{-144x^4y^7}$ **26.** Find the 4th term of $\left(\frac{x}{2} + 4y\right)^8$. $112x^5y^3$

27. Find the middle term of $(2a - b)^6$.   **28.** Find the term with n^{10} in $(m + n^2)^5$. n^{10}
$-160a^3b^3$

Use the Binomial Theorem to find the first four terms. Simplify.

c   **29.** $(1.04)^5$ **30.** $(2.03)^6$ **31.** $(3 + n)^n$ **32.** $(2 - n)^n$

1.21664   69.98032   See key.   See key.

PUZZLE

Look for a pattern below. Try to write the next 5 lines.

$3^2 - 1^2 = 8 = 2^3$ $6^2 - 3^2 = 27 = (?)^3$

Do the squares of successive terms differ by a cube always?

$10^2 - 6^2 = 4^3$
$15^2 - 10^2 = 5^3$
$21^2 - 15^2 = 6^3$
$28^2 - 21^2 = 7^3$
$36^2 - 28^2 = 8^3$

Yes. For explanation, see key.

Polynomials and Rational Expressions   **93**

Mathematics and
Data Analysis

WHEN the results of surveys and tests are graphed, a bell-shaped curve often results. This curve is called the <u>normal distribution curve</u>.

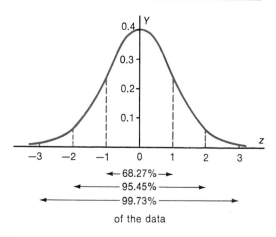

— 68.27% —
— 95.45% —
— 99.73% —
of the data

Persons working in the fields shown here use statistics and the normal curve to help them analyze and interpret data, and to make predictions based on this analysis.

Most **sociologists** are employed in research and teaching at the college level. Sociological research involves the collection of information, preparation of case studies, testing, and the supervision of surveys and experiments. A master's degree is the minimum educational requirement.

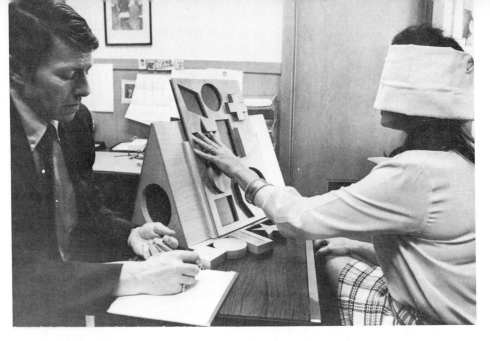

A master's degree is the minimum educational requirement for a **psychologist**. Persons who qualify may administer and interpret psychological tests, collect and analyze data, conduct research experiments, teach in colleges, or work as school psychologists and counselors.

Actuaries design insurance and pension plans that can be maintained on a sound financial basis. The minimum requirement for beginning jobs in actuarial work is a bachelor's degree with a major in mathematics, statistics, economics, or business administration.

Market research workers analyze data on products and sales, make surveys, and conduct interviews. They prepare sales forecasts and make recommendations on product design and advertising. A bachelor's degree is the usual requirement for trainees.

Chapter Objectives and Review

Objective: To know the meanings of the important mathematical terms of this chapter.

1. Here are many of the mathematical terms used in this chapter. Be sure that you know their meanings and that you can use them correctly.

degree of a polynomial (p. 38)
degree of a term (p. 38)
expansion of a binomial (p. 88)
factoring polynomials (p. 49)
greatest common factor, GCF (p. 83)
least common denominator, LCD (p. 84)
least common multiple, LCM (p. 83)
like terms (p. 40)

monomial (p. 38)
Pascal's triangle (p. 89)
polynomial (p. 38)
prime polynomial (p. 50)
quadratic trinomial (p. 53)
rational expression (p. 71)
solution set (p. 70)

Objective: To identify polynomials. (Section 2-1)

For each expression, write P if it is a polynomial. Write NP if it is not.

2. $\dfrac{5}{x} + 2$ *NP*

3. $(1 + i)x^4 - (2 - i)x$ *P*

4. $a^{-1} + a^7$
NP

Objective: To classify a polynomial according to its degree, the number of terms and the nature of its coefficients. (Section 2-1)

Determine the degree, the number of terms, and the nature of the coefficients of each polynomial.

5. $4x^2 + xy + 5xy^3$
4th degree trinomial over
the set of integers.

6. $(5 + i)x^2 - x$
2nd degree binomial over
the set of complex numbers.

7. $\frac{2}{3}x^5 y$
6th degree monomial over
the set of rational numbers.

Objectives: To add and subtract polynomials. (Section 2-2)

Perform the indicated operations.

8. $(5m^2n + 3mn - 4mn^2) + (3m^2n - 2mn + 7mn^2)$ $8m^2n + mn + 3mn^2$

9. $(2a^3 - 3a^2 + 5a - 7) - (4a^3 + 3a^2 - 5a + 2)$ $-2a^3 - 6a^2 + 10a - 9$

10. What polynomial decreased by $4x^2 - 5a + 2$ equals $3x^2 + 7a - 4$? $7x^2 + 2a - 2$

Objective: To multiply polynomials. (Section 2-3)

Multiply.

11. $(2x^4y)(-3x^5y^2)$ $-6x^9y^3$

12. $3m(5m^2 - 2m + 10)$ $15m^3 - 6m^2 + 30m$

13. $(5s^2 - 3t)(5s^2 + 3t)$ $25s^4 - 9t^2$

14. $(x + 2y)^2$ $x^2 + 4xy + 4y^2$

15. $(3x + 2y)(5x - 4y)$ $15x^2 - 2xy - 8y^2$

16. $(2a - 5b)(2a^2 - 3ab + b^2)$
$4a^3 - 16a^2b + 17ab^2 - 5b^3$

Objective: To factor a given polynomial over the integers. (Sections 2-4 and 2-5)

Factor over the integers.

17. $3ax + 6a^2xy$ $3ax(1 + 2ay)$

18. $2a^2 - 128$ $2(a + 8)(a - 8)$

19. $n^2 - 2n - 15$ $(n - 5)(n + 3)$

20. $10m^2 - 11m - 6$ $(5m + 2)(2m - 3)$

21. $9c^2 - 24c + 16$ $(3c - 4)(3c - 4)$

22. $4a^2 + 12ab + 9b^2$ $(2a + 3b)(2a + 3b)$

23. $3(a - b) - 4x(a - b)$ $(a - b)(3 - 4x)$

24. $27x^3 + 64y^3$ $(3x + 4y)(9x^2 - 12xy + 16y^2)$

Objective: To factor a given polynomial over the real numbers or over the complex numbers. (Section 2-6)

Factor over the real numbers.

25. $x^2 - 11$ $(x - \sqrt{11})(x + \sqrt{11})$

26. $3a^2 - 9$ $3(a - \sqrt{3})(a + \sqrt{3})$

Factor over the complex numbers.

27. $t^4 - 1$ $(t + 1)(t - 1)(t + i)(t - i)$

28. $m^4 - n^4$ $(m + n)(m - n)(m + in)(m - in)$

Objective: To find the quotient of two given polynomials. (Section 2-7)

Find each quotient.

29. $\dfrac{9x^3y^2 - 15x^2y + 12x^2y^2}{3x^2y}$ $3xy - 5 + 4y$

30. $(x^2 + 9x + 8) \div (x + 3)$ $x + 6 - \dfrac{10}{x + 3}$

Objective: To use the Remainder Theorem (Section 2-8)

Use the Remainder Theorem to find each remainder.

31. $x^3 + 4x^2 - 7x + 3 \div x - 1$ 1

32. $m^4 + 2m^3 + m^2 + m - 6 \div m + 3$
27

Objective: To use the Factor Theorem (Section 2-8)

Determine whether the second polynomial is a factor of the first. If it is, divide to find the quotient. Then factor the quotient.

33. $s^3 - 4s^2 - s - 4$, $s + 4$

No. Remainder is −128.

34. $y^3 + 6y^2 - 13y - 42$, $y - 3$

Yes. $y^2 + 9y + 14 = (y + 2)(y + 7)$

Objective: To solve polynomial equations by factoring. (Section 2-9)

Solve.

35. $x^2 - 2x - 63 = 0$ {9, −7}

36. $x^3 - 2x^2 - 5x + 6 = 0$ {1, −2, 3}

Objective: To simplify rational expressions. (Section 2-10)

Simplify.

37. $\dfrac{mx + my}{nx + ny}$ $\frac{m}{n}$

38. $\dfrac{a^3 + 2a^2b + ab^2}{a^2 - b^2}$ $\frac{a(a+b)}{(a-b)}$

39. $\dfrac{x^3 - y^3}{x^2 - 2xy + y^2}$ $\frac{x^2 + xy + y^2}{x - y}$

40. $\dfrac{2c^2 - 5c + 3}{6c^2 - c - 12}$ $\frac{c-1}{3c+4}$

Objective: To multiply rational expressions. (Section 2-11)

Multiply.

41. $\dfrac{x^2y}{a^2b} \cdot \dfrac{ab^2}{x^3y^2}$ $\frac{b}{axy}$

42. $\dfrac{a^2 - 6a + 8}{a^2 - a - 2} \cdot \dfrac{a^2 - 1}{a^2 - 8a + 16}$ $\frac{a-1}{a-4}$

Objective: To divide rational expressions. (Section 2-12)

Divide.

43. $\dfrac{5x^2yz^2}{30p} \div \dfrac{15xy^2z}{20mp}$ $\frac{2xzm}{9y}$

44. $\dfrac{m^2 - mn}{mn - n^2} \div \dfrac{m^2 - n^2}{mn^2 - n^3}$ $\frac{mn}{m+n}$

Objective: To add or subtract rational expressions with like denominators. (Section 2-13)

Add or subtract as indicated.

45. $\dfrac{2}{x} + \dfrac{y}{x}$ $\frac{2+y}{x}$

46. $\dfrac{3}{a+b} - \dfrac{1}{a+b}$ $\frac{2}{a+b}$

47. $\dfrac{3a + 1}{12} + \dfrac{4a - 7}{12}$ $\frac{7a-6}{12}$

48. $\dfrac{5x - 4}{7} - \dfrac{3 + 5x}{7}$ −1

Objective: To add or subtract rational expressions with unlike denominators. (Section 2-14)

Add or subtract as indicated.

49. $\dfrac{1}{a-b} - \dfrac{1}{a+b}$ $\frac{2b}{a^2-b^2}$

50. $\dfrac{2c}{c^2+2cd+d^2} + \dfrac{5}{c+d}$ $\frac{7c+5d}{c^2+2cd+d^2}$

51. $\dfrac{2r+8}{3} - \dfrac{5r-4}{2}$ $\frac{-11r+28}{6}$

52. $\dfrac{6}{x^2-9} - \dfrac{3}{x-3}$ $\frac{-3x-3}{x^2-9}$

Objectives: To use the Binomial Theorem and to find a given term in the expansion of a binomial. (Section 2-15)

$a^4 + 4a^3b + 6a^2b^2 + 4ab^3 + b^4 ; x^4 + 8x^3y + 24x^2y^2 + 32xy^3 + 16y^4$

53. Write the expansions of $(a+b)^4$ and $(x+2y)^4$.

54. Find the 7th term of $(a+b)^9$ and of $(2x-y)^9$. $84a^3b^6 ; 672x^3y^6$

1. Add: $(x^3 - 5x^2 - 6x + 7) + (2x^2 - 14 + 3x - x^3)$ $-3x^2 - 3x - 7$

2. Subtract: $(3m^4 - 2m^3 + 6m + 1) - (2m^4 - 3m^2 + 8m - 5)$ $m^4 - 2m^3 + 3m^2 - 2m + 6$

Factor completely over the integers.

3. $9x^2 - 144$ $(3x + 12)(3x - 12) = 9(x - 4)(x + 4)$

4. $15m^2 + 41m + 14$ $(5m + 2)(3m + 7)$

5. $2a^3 + 54$ $2(a + 3)(a^2 - 3a + 9)$

6. $36s^2 + 60st + 25t^2$ $(6s + 5t)^2$

7. $50 - 20y + 2y^2$ $2(y - 5)^2$

8. $n^3 - 125$ $(n - 5)(n^2 + 5n + 25)$

9. Factor $4x^2 - 5$ over the real numbers. $(2x - \sqrt{5})(2x + \sqrt{5})$

10. Factor $a^4 - b^4$ over the complex numbers. $(a - b)(a + b)(a + bi)(a - bi)$

11. Use the Remainder Theorem to find the remainder when $3x^4 - 2x^2 + x - 1$ is divided by $x + 2$. 37

12. Use the Factor Theorem to determine whether $x - 3$ is a factor of $x^3 + 2x^2 - 9x - 18$. Yes.

Find each quotient.

13. $\dfrac{6x^2y^3 + 12xy^2 - 18xy}{3xy}$ $2xy^2 + 4y - 6$

14. $(2y^3 + y^2 - 18y - 9) \div (y + 3)$ $2y^2 - 5y - 3$

Perform the indicated operations. Simplify your answers if possible.

15. $\dfrac{x^2 - 3x - 10}{(x - 2)^2} \cdot \dfrac{x - 2}{x - 5}$ $\frac{x + 2}{x - 2}$

16. $\dfrac{10a^3}{(a + b)^2} \div \dfrac{2a}{a + b}$ $\frac{5a^2}{a + b}$

17. $\dfrac{3m}{m^2 - mn} + \dfrac{5}{n}$ $\frac{-2n + 5m}{n(m - n)}$

18. $\dfrac{c}{cd - d^2} - \dfrac{d}{c^2 - cd}$ $\frac{c + d}{cd}$

19. Expand $(a - 2b)^4$. $a^4 - 8a^3b + 24a^2b^2 - 32ab^3 + 16b^4$

20. Find the third term of $(2m + n^2)^7$. $672m^5n^4$

Chapter 3
Linear Equations
and Inequalities

3-1 Solving Equations

The objective for this section is on page 130.

To solve some equations, you use the addition and multiplication properties of equations.

Addition and Multiplication Properties of Equations

If the same real number is added to both sides of an equation, or if both sides of an equation are multiplied by the same non-zero real number, the result is an equation with the same solution set.

Equations that have the same solution set are **equivalent equations.**

Example 1

Solve: $-4x + 7 = -5$

$$-4x + 7 = -5$$

$$-4x + 7 + (-7) = -5 + (-7)$$ ⟵ Add -7, the opposite of 7, to both sides of the equation.

$$-4x = -12$$

$$-\frac{1}{4}(-4x) = -\frac{1}{4}(-12)$$ ⟵ Multiply both sides by $-\frac{1}{4}$, the reciprocal of -4.

$$x = 3$$

Check: $-4(3) + 7 \overset{?}{=} -5$ ⟵ Check in the original equation.

$$-12 + 7 \overset{?}{=} -5$$

$$-5 = -5$$

Solution set: $\{3\}$

When terms containing variables occur on both sides of an equation, write an equivalent equation with the variables only on one side of the equation.

102 Chapter 3

Example 2

Solve: $5m - 7 = 2m + 3$

$$5m - 7 = 2m + 3$$
$$5m - 2m - 7 = 2m - 2m + 3 \quad \longleftarrow \quad \text{Add } -2m \text{ to both sides.}$$
$$3m - 7 = 3 \quad \longleftarrow \quad \text{Add 7 to both sides.}$$
$$3m = 10 \quad \longleftarrow \quad \text{Multiply both sides by } \frac{1}{3}.$$
$$m = \frac{10}{3}$$

Check: $5(\frac{10}{3}) - 7 \overset{?}{=} 2(\frac{10}{3}) + 3$ **Solution set:** $\{\frac{10}{3}\}$

$$\frac{50}{3} - \frac{21}{3} \overset{?}{=} \frac{20}{3} + \frac{9}{3}$$
$$\frac{29}{3} = \frac{29}{3}$$

To solve an equation containing parentheses, write an equivalent equation without parentheses as the first step.

Example 3

Solve $5(2x + 3) = 28 - 3x$.

$$5(2x + 3) = 28 - 3x$$
$$5 \cdot 2x + 5 \cdot 3 = 28 - 3x \quad \longleftarrow \quad \text{Distributive postulate}$$
$$10x + 15 = 28 - 3x \quad \longleftarrow \quad \text{Add the opposite of } -3x.$$
$$13x + 15 = 28$$
$$13x = 13$$
$$x = 1$$

Check: $5(2 \cdot 1 + 3) \overset{?}{=} 28 - 3 \cdot 1$ **Solution set:** $\{1\}$

$$5(5) = 25$$

Try These

Solve.

1. $7c - 3 = 25$ {4}

2. $-5 - 3x = 16$ {-7}

3. $\frac{4}{3}n + 10 = 2$ {-6}

4. $3y + 2y = -20$ {-4}

5. $12 = 5c - 9c$ {-3}

6. $3x - 2 = 8 + 2x$
{10}

Linear Equations and Inequalities   **103**

Exercises

Solve each equation.

a

1. $m + 2 = -13$ {-15}

2. $\frac{1}{4}c = 8$ {32}

3. $5a = 3$ $\{\frac{3}{5}\}$

4. $3y = y - 24$ {-12}

5. $-5n - 7 = 28$ {-7}

6. $3x + x = 1$ $\{\frac{1}{4}\}$

7. $3x - 7x = 48$ {-12}

8. $2m = 18 - m$ {6}

9. $17 - 6c = 11$ {1}

10. $\frac{3}{4}a = -2.4$ {-3.2}

11. $\frac{2}{3}m = -2$ {-3}

12. $5m = -8 - 6$ $\{-\frac{14}{5}\}$

13. $2x - 3 = 15$ {9}

14. $8 = 0.3y - 10$ {60}

15. $4n = n + 4.5$ {1.5}

16. $5x + 3 - 14x = 30$ {-3}

17. $7(x + 3) = -28$ {-7}

18. $3(2y - 5) = 9$ {4}

19. $7c + 16 = 2$ {-2}

20. $2a + 0.7 = 2.0$ {0.65}

21. $7x - 8 = 0$ $\{\frac{8}{7}\}$

22. $3n - 2 - 5n = 3n - 7$ {1}

23. $6x + 14 - 3x + 18 = 7x + 8 - 2x$ {12}

24. $2.5x = 0.4x - 16.8$ {-8}

25. $5a - 9a - 12 = 28 - 3a$ {-40}

26. $10 + 2(3m + 4) = 5m + 14$ {-4}

27. $5(3 - 2n) = 5n$ {1}

28. $4(3c - 2) + 2c = 6$ {1}

29. $3n - 4 = 15(\frac{1}{3}n + \frac{2}{5})$ {-5}

30. $6y - \frac{1}{2}(2y - 8) = 11$ $\{\frac{7}{5}\}$

b

31. $3a - 0.2(4a - 1) = 8$ $\{3\frac{6}{11}\}$

32. $x - 25 = \frac{11}{3}$ $\{28\frac{2}{3}\}$

33. $6 - c = 2 - 5(2c - 7)$ $\{\frac{31}{9}\}$

34. $5(2y - 3) = -2(3y + 4)$ $\{\frac{7}{16}\}$

35. $3(5a - 2) = 4(7 + a) - 1$ {3}

36. $10(0.6 - m) = 2(7m + 0.6)$ {0.2}

37. $0.2(3x - 4) = 2(19.7 + 7x)$ {-3}

38. $3(1 - 2n) + 10 = -4(2n - 3)$ $\{-\frac{1}{2}\}$

39. $3m(2m + 3) + 2(m - 3) = m(6m + 1) - 7$ $\{-\frac{1}{10}\}$

40. $0.4(3 - 2x) = 2.4 - 6(x - 5)$ {6}

c

41. $(x - 5)(x + 2) - (x + 3)(x - 2) = 0$ {-1}

42. $(2n - 3)(n + 1) = (n - 3)(2n + 1)$ {0}

43. $2(3y - 4) - y(2y + 3) = 2y(5 - 4y) + 8$ $\left\{\frac{7 \pm \sqrt{433}}{12}\right\}$

Remember

Find the least common multiple for each pair.

1. 24 and 42 168

2. 5 and 17 85

3. ab^2 and b^2c^2 ab^2c^2

4. $(x - 3)$ and $(x + 1)(x - 3)(x - 2)$ $(x + 1)(x - 3)(x - 2)$

The answers are on page 132.

3-2 Equations with Rational Expressions

The objective for this section is on page 130.

To solve an equation containing rational expressions, write an equivalent equation involving polynomials. This can be done by multiplying both sides of the equation by the lowest common denominator, LCD, of the rational expressions. For such equations, assume that no denominator equals 0.

Example 1 Solve: $\dfrac{1}{3z} + \dfrac{1}{8} = \dfrac{4}{3z}$.

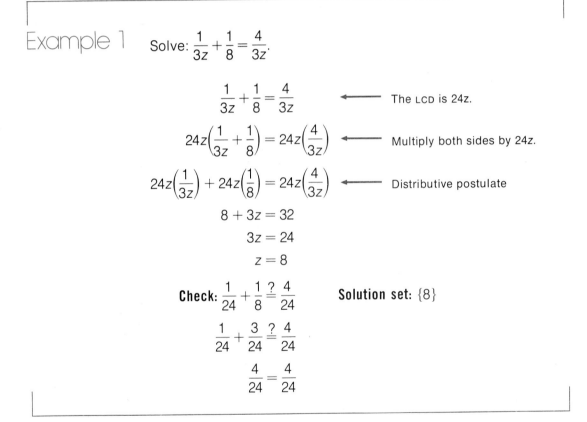

$$\frac{1}{3z} + \frac{1}{8} = \frac{4}{3z} \qquad \longleftarrow \qquad \text{The LCD is } 24z.$$

$$24z\left(\frac{1}{3z} + \frac{1}{8}\right) = 24z\left(\frac{4}{3z}\right) \qquad \longleftarrow \qquad \text{Multiply both sides by } 24z.$$

$$24z\left(\frac{1}{3z}\right) + 24z\left(\frac{1}{8}\right) = 24z\left(\frac{4}{3z}\right) \qquad \longleftarrow \qquad \text{Distributive postulate}$$

$$8 + 3z = 32$$

$$3z = 24$$

$$z = 8$$

Check: $\dfrac{1}{24} + \dfrac{1}{8} \overset{?}{=} \dfrac{4}{24}$ **Solution set:** $\{8\}$

$$\frac{1}{24} + \frac{3}{24} \overset{?}{=} \frac{4}{24}$$

$$\frac{4}{24} = \frac{4}{24}$$

Sometimes the number obtained as a solution to an equation does not check in the original equation. The number is then only an **apparent solution** (not a solution at all). Thus, it is important to check all solutions. This is illustrated in Example 2 on the next page.

Linear Equations and Inequalities   **105**

Example 2

Solve: $\dfrac{2x+3}{x-1} - \dfrac{2x-3}{x+1} = \dfrac{10}{x^2-1}$

$$\frac{2x+3}{x-1} - \frac{2x-3}{x+1} = \frac{10}{x^2-1}$$ ← The LCD is $(x+1)(x-1)$.

$$(x+1)(x-1)\left(\frac{2x+3}{x-1} - \frac{2x-3}{x+1}\right) = (x+1)(x-1)\left(\frac{10}{x^2-1}\right)$$ ← Multiply both sides by the LCD.

$$(x+1)(2x+3) - (x-1)(2x-3) = 10$$ ← Distributive postulate

$$2x^2+5x+3 - (2x^2-5x+3) = 10$$ ← Multiply.

$$2x^2+5x+3 - 2x^2+5x-3 = 10$$ ← Solve for x.

$$10x = 10$$

$$x = 1$$

Check: $\dfrac{2+3}{0} - \dfrac{2-3}{2} \overset{?}{=} \dfrac{10}{0}$

Since no denominator can be zero, the number 1 is an apparent solution. The solution set is the empty set, or ∅.

Try These

Give the least number by which to multiply both sides of each equation in order to eliminate fractions.

1. $\dfrac{x}{2} + \dfrac{x}{3} = 12$ ₆   6

2. $\dfrac{n}{6} - \dfrac{n}{4} = 9$ 12

3. $\dfrac{3}{a} + \dfrac{5}{7} = 2$ 7a

4. $5 = \dfrac{3}{m} \cdot \dfrac{(m+14)}{9}$ 9m

5. $\dfrac{2}{3y} - 6 = \dfrac{5}{y}$ 3y

6. $\dfrac{3}{c} = \dfrac{5}{4c} + 1$ 4c

Exercises

Solve and check.

1. $\dfrac{n}{3} + \dfrac{n}{4} = 21$ {36}

2. $\dfrac{2n}{3} + \dfrac{3n}{4} = 51$ {36}

3. $\dfrac{x}{4} - \dfrac{3}{2} = \dfrac{x}{6}$ {18}

4. $\dfrac{1}{2}x - \dfrac{1}{6}x = x - 16$ {24}

5. $\dfrac{n}{3} - \dfrac{2n}{3} + \dfrac{7}{6} = \dfrac{13}{6}$ $\{-3\}$

6. $\dfrac{2n}{3} + \dfrac{5n}{12} - \dfrac{n}{6} - \dfrac{5n}{9} = \dfrac{13}{2}$ $\{18\}$

7. $\dfrac{3n}{8} - \dfrac{1}{4} = \dfrac{n}{3} - \dfrac{11}{24}$ $\{-5\}$

8. $\dfrac{1}{9} + \dfrac{1}{15} = \dfrac{1}{n}$ $\left\{\dfrac{45}{8}\right\}$

9. $\dfrac{3x}{4} - 12 = \dfrac{3(x-12)}{5}$ $\{32\}$

10. $\dfrac{3}{10}x + 8 = \dfrac{5}{12}(x+8)$ $\{40\}$

11. $4m - \dfrac{6m+3}{2} = 8$ $\left\{\dfrac{19}{2}\right\}$

12. $\dfrac{3x+1}{2} - \dfrac{3x-4}{3} = \dfrac{3x+1}{4}$ $\left\{\dfrac{19}{3}\right\}$

13. $4x - \dfrac{5(3-2x)}{3} = 17$ $\{3\}$

14. $\dfrac{10}{x} - 2 = \dfrac{5-x}{4x}$ $\{5\}$

15. $\dfrac{x}{x+5} = \dfrac{1}{2}$ $\{5\}$

16. $\dfrac{5}{2x} = \dfrac{9-2x}{8x} + 3$ $\left\{\dfrac{1}{2}\right\}$

17. $\dfrac{z}{z-3} = 2$ $\{6\}$

18. $\dfrac{a-2}{a+3} = \dfrac{3}{8}$ $\{5\}$

19. $\dfrac{a-2}{a+3} = \dfrac{3}{5}$ $\left\{\dfrac{19}{2}\right\}$

20. $\dfrac{11-x}{12+2x} = \dfrac{4}{7}$ $\left\{\dfrac{29}{15}\right\}$

21. $\dfrac{x-1}{x-2} = 1.5$ $\{4\}$

22. $\dfrac{9}{x-3} = \dfrac{7}{x-5}$ $\{12\}$

23. $\dfrac{6}{x-2} = \dfrac{5}{x-3}$ $\{8\}$

24. $\dfrac{x-1}{2} - \dfrac{3x-4}{2} = \dfrac{5x-3}{8}$ $\left\{\dfrac{15}{13}\right\}$

25. $\dfrac{8x-5}{3} + 7 = \dfrac{3x+6}{4} - \dfrac{3x-7}{6} + \dfrac{1}{4}$ $\{-1\}$

26. $40 - x + \dfrac{5}{6}(40-x) = 2x - 11$ $\{22\}$

27. $\dfrac{2y-1}{2} - \dfrac{y+2}{2y+5} = \dfrac{6y-5}{6}$ $\{-1\}$

28. $\dfrac{3}{x^2-4} = \dfrac{-2}{5x+10}$ $\left\{-\dfrac{11}{2}\right\}$

29. $\dfrac{3}{x+2} + \dfrac{12}{x^2-4} = \dfrac{-1}{x-2}$ $\varnothing$

30. $\dfrac{3n-1}{3} - \dfrac{2n+3}{2} = \dfrac{n-3}{15}$ $\left\{-\dfrac{49}{2}\right\}$

31. $3\left(\dfrac{15x}{4} - 2\right) = 5x - \dfrac{7}{2}$ $\left\{\dfrac{2}{5}\right\}$

32. $\dfrac{x+3}{x-5} + \dfrac{6+2x^2}{x^2-7x+10} = \dfrac{3x}{x-2}$ $\{0\}$

33. $\dfrac{n-5}{n+5} + \dfrac{n+15}{n-5} = \dfrac{25}{25-n^2} + 2$ $\left\{-\dfrac{35}{2}\right\}$

34. $\dfrac{x}{12} = \dfrac{1}{3}\left(17 - \dfrac{2x}{3}\right) - \dfrac{1}{3}\left(15 - \dfrac{3x}{4}\right)$ $\{12\}$

35. $\dfrac{2x}{x+7} - 1 = \dfrac{x}{x+3} + \dfrac{1}{x^2+10x+21}$ $\{-2\}$

36. $\dfrac{ix}{x-1} = \dfrac{-x}{ix+4}$ $\{0\}$

37. $\dfrac{z+1}{z-1} = 1 - 2i$ $\{1+i\}$

38. $\dfrac{ix}{x+3} = \dfrac{-x}{ix-5}$ $\{0\}$

39. $\dfrac{2}{3}\left(\dfrac{x}{a} - 1\right) = \dfrac{3}{4}\left(\dfrac{x}{a} + 1\right)$. Solve for x. $\{x: x = -17a\}$

40. $\dfrac{x}{a-x} - \dfrac{a-x}{x} = \dfrac{a}{x}$. Solve for x. $\left\{x: x = \dfrac{2a}{3}\right\}$

Remember

Find each product.

1. $i^2 \cdot i$ $-i$

2. $\sqrt{-5} \cdot \sqrt{-5}$ -5

3. $(-\sqrt{3})^2$ 3

4. $(-\sqrt{-3})^2$ -3

Factor over the complex numbers.

5. $x^2 - y^2$ $(x+y)(x-y)$ **6.** $x^2 + y^2$ $(x+iy)(x-iy)$

$(x-y)(x+y)(x-iy)(x+iy)$

7. $x^4 - y^4$

8. $a^3 - b^3$
$(a-b)(a^2+ab+b^2)$

The answers are on page 132.

PUZZLE

Find x. (The dots mean the pattern continues without end.) $\frac{3}{2}$

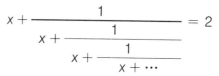

$$x + \cfrac{1}{x + \cfrac{1}{x + \cfrac{1}{x + \cdots}}} = 2$$

3-3 Solving Equations for Variables

The objective for this section is on page 130.

Equations such as those below have more than one variable.

$$d = rt \qquad\qquad A = \tfrac{1}{2}(b_1 + b_2)h$$

Example 1

Solve $an + bn - cn = c - d + e$ for n.

$an + bn - cn = c - d + e$

$n(a + b - c) = c - d + e$ ⟵ n is a common factor.

$n = \dfrac{c - d + e}{a + b - c},\ a + b - c \neq 0$ ⟵ Multiply both sides by $\dfrac{1}{a + b - c}$.

Example 2   Solve $ax - b(x + 2b) = a^2 - 3ab$ for x.

$$ax - b(x + 2b) = a^2 - 3ab$$

$$ax - bx - 2b^2 = a^2 - 3ab \qquad \longleftarrow \quad \text{Distributive postulate}$$

$$ax - bx = a^2 - 3ab + 2b^2 \qquad \longleftarrow \quad \text{Add } 2b^2 \text{ to both sides.}$$

$$x(a - b) = (a - b)(a - 2b) \qquad \longleftarrow \quad \text{Factor.}$$

$$x = \frac{(a - b)(a - 2b)}{(a - b)}, \ a \neq b \qquad \longleftarrow \quad \text{Multiply both sides by } \frac{1}{a - b}.$$

$$x = a - 2b, \ a \neq b$$

Example 3   The formula expressing <u>Celsius</u> temperature in terms of Fahrenheit temperature is $C = \frac{5}{9}(F - 32)$. Find F in terms of C.

$$C = \frac{5}{9}(F - 32)$$

$$9C = 9 \cdot \frac{5}{9}(F - 32)$$

$$9C = 5F - 160$$

$$9C + 160 = 5F$$

$$\frac{9C + 160}{5} = F, \text{ or}$$

$$F = \frac{9}{5}C + 32$$

C	F
100°	212°
37°	98.6°
20°	68°
0°	32°
−17.8°	0°
−40°	−40°

Try These   Solve each equation for x.

1. $2ax + 2bx = 4ab$ $x = \frac{2ab}{a+b}, a \neq -b$

2. $ax - a^3 + 2a^2 = 8x - 48$ $x = \frac{a^3 - 2a^2 - 48}{a - 8}, a \neq 8$

3. $x(a + b) = cx - 2$ $x = \frac{-2}{a+b-c}, a+b-c \neq 0$

4. $\frac{x}{a} = \frac{b}{c}$ $x = \frac{ab}{c}, c \neq 0$

Linear Equations and Inequalities   **109**

Exercises

11. $x = \frac{m^2 + n^2}{m + n}, m \neq -n$

7. $x = \frac{a^2b - ac + b}{a + b}, a + b \neq 0$

Solve each equation for x in terms of the other variables.

$x = \frac{b+c}{a-b+c}, a-b+c \neq 0$

a

1. $ax - bx = 2c$ $x = \frac{2c}{a-b}, a \neq b$

2. $ax - bx + cx = b + c$

3. $ax - b = cx + d$ $x = \frac{b+d}{a-c}, a \neq c$

4. $x + ax = b$ $x = \frac{b}{1+a}, a \neq -1$

5. $4x - 3c = ax - ac$ $x = \frac{c(3-a)}{4-a}, a \neq 4$

6. $ax + 2x = 4x - a + 2c$ $x = \frac{2c-a}{a-2}, a \neq 2$

7. $ac + ax - b = a^2b - bx$ See above.

8. $a(a - x) = b(b + x)$ $x = a - b, a \neq -b$

9. $a^2 - bx = b^2 + ax$ $x = a - b, a \neq -b$

10. $cx - c^2d = cd^2 - dx$ $x = cd, c \neq -d$

11. $m^2 - nx = mx - n^2$ See above

12. $mx + 9 = m^2 + 3x$ $x = m + 3, m \neq 3$

13. $ax - 8 = a^2 - 4x + 6a$ $x = a + 2, a \neq -4$

14. $m(x - m) = n(x - m)$ $x = m, m \neq n$

15. $\frac{x}{a} = \frac{b}{c}$ $x = \frac{ab}{c}, c \neq 0$

16. $\frac{x}{a} - 1 = b$ $x = a(b+1)$

17. $\frac{a}{x} = \frac{5}{e}$ $x = \frac{ae}{5}$

18. $a(x - a) = b(b + 2a - x)$ $x = a + b, a \neq -b$

Solve for the variables indicated.

19. $E = mc^2$, for m $m = \frac{E}{c^2}, c \neq 0$

20. $R = \frac{EI}{M}$, for E $E = \frac{MR}{I}, I \neq 0$

21. $C = \frac{Ka - b}{a}$, for K $K = \frac{aC + b}{a}, a \neq 0$

22. $r = \frac{v^2pL}{a}$, for a $a = \frac{v^2pL}{r}, r \neq 0$

$a = rl - s(r - l)$

23. $s = \frac{r\ell - a}{r - \ell}$, for a, for ℓ and for r
$l = \frac{sr + a}{r + s}, r \neq -s; r = \frac{a - sl}{l - s}, l \neq s$

24. $R = \frac{WL - x}{L}$, for W and for L
$W = \frac{RL + x}{L}, L \neq 0; L = \frac{x}{W - R}, W \neq R$

25. $S = \frac{n}{2}(a + \ell)$, for a and for n
$a = \frac{2S - nl}{n}, n \neq 0; n = \frac{2S}{a + l}, a \neq -l$

26. $L = \frac{Mt - g}{t}$, for M and for g
$M = \frac{Lt + g}{t}, t \neq 0; g = t(M - L)$

27. $E^2 = \frac{JWhr}{t}$, for h
$h = \frac{E^2t}{JWr}, J, W, r \neq 0$

28. $V = 2\pi r(r + h)$, for h
$h = \frac{V - 2\pi r^2}{2\pi r}, r \neq 0$

b

29. $V = \frac{1}{6}h(b + c + 4m)$, for h and for m
$h = \frac{6V}{b + c + 4m}, b + c + 4m \neq 0; m = \frac{6V - h(b + c)}{4h}, h \neq 0$

30. $\frac{1}{O} + \frac{1}{M} = \frac{1}{F}$, for M $M = \frac{OF}{O - F}, O \neq F$

31. $ax - bx = a^2 - 2ab + b^2$, for x
$x = a - b, a \neq b$

32. $T = mg - mf$, for m $m = \frac{T}{g - f}, g \neq f$

33. $A = p + prt$, for p $p = \frac{A}{1 + rt}, 1 + rt \neq 0$

34. $S(r - 1) = r\ell - a$, for r $r = \frac{S - a}{S - l}, S \neq l$

35. $S = \frac{n}{2}[2a + (n - 1)d]$, for a and for d
$a = \frac{2S - nd(n - 1)}{2n}; n \neq 0; d = \frac{2(S - an)}{n(n - 1)}, n \neq 0 \text{ or } n \neq 1$

36. $\frac{1}{D} + \frac{1}{d} = \frac{1}{f}$, for d $d = \frac{Df}{D - f}, D \neq f$

110   Chapter 3

37. $wt = \left(\dfrac{w}{k} - 1\right)f$, for w $\quad w = \frac{fk}{f-kt}; f-kt \neq 0$

38. $R = \dfrac{gs}{g+s}$, for s $\quad s = \frac{Rg}{g-R}; g \neq R$

Solve for x.

39. $\dfrac{x}{a+b} - b = a$ $\quad x = (a+b)^2$

40. $\dfrac{ax}{b} + \dfrac{bx}{a} = 2$ $\quad x = \frac{2ab}{a^2+b^2}$

41. $\dfrac{x}{m} = \dfrac{a-x}{m} - d$ $\quad x = \frac{1}{2}(a - dm)$

42. $\dfrac{p^2}{qx} + \dfrac{p}{q} = \dfrac{q}{x} + \dfrac{q}{p}$ $\quad x = -p, p \neq \pm q$

The **mass ratio,** R of a space vehicle is defined as

$$R = \dfrac{S + F + P}{S + P}$$

where S is the weight of the vehicle, F is the weight of the fuel, and P is the weight of the payload.

C **43.** Express S in terms of R, F, and P. $\quad S = \frac{F - P(R-1)}{R-1}, R \neq 1$

44. Express F and P in terms of the other variables. $\quad F = (S + P)(R-1), P = \frac{F - S(R-1)}{R-1}, R \neq 1$

Remember

For each value of x, find $|x - 7|$.

1. $x = 7$ $\quad$ 0

2. $x = -7$ $\quad$ 14

3. $x = 5$ $\quad$ 2

4. $x = 9$ $\quad$ 2

5. Complete the following.

$|x| = \underline{\ ?\ }$ for $x \geq 0$ and $|x| = \underline{\ ?\ }$ for $x < 0$. $\quad$ x, -x

The answers are on page 132.

PUZZLE

A car accelerates uniformly from rest to $8p$ kilometers per hour in $\dfrac{p}{5}$ minutes. It continues at that speed for p minutes, then decelerates uniformly and takes another $\dfrac{p}{5}$ minutes to come to rest, having traveled exactly $p - 1$ kilometers. The trip took a whole number of minutes. How many? $\quad$ The trip took 7 minutes; $p = 5$

3-4 Equations with Absolute Value

The objective for this section is on page 131.

The absolute value of a number gives the distance of that number from zero on a number line. An equation involving absolute value usually has two solutions that can be written as an equivalent **compound sentence.** For example,

$$\text{"}|x| = 6\text{" is equivalent to "}x = 6 \text{ or } x = -6.\text{"}$$

The solution set of the equation $|x| = 6$ is $\{6, -6\}$. Notice that the compound sentence, "$x = 6$ or $x = -6$," has the same solution set as "$|x| = 6$."

Example 1

Solve: $|2x + 5| = 11$

$$|2x + 5| = 11$$

$2x + 5 = 11$ or $2x + 5 = -11$ ⟵ Write the equivalent compound sentence.

$\quad 2x = 6$ or $\qquad 2x = -16$ ⟵ Solve for x.

$\qquad x = 3$ or $\qquad\quad x = -8$

Check: $|2(3) + 5| \overset{?}{=} 11 \qquad |2(-8) + 5| \overset{?}{=} 11 \qquad$ **Solution set:** $\{3, -8\}$

$\qquad\quad |6 + 5| \overset{?}{=} 11 \qquad\quad\; |-16 + 5| \overset{?}{=} 11$

$\qquad\qquad\; 11 = 11 \qquad\qquad\qquad 11 = 11$

Example 2

Solve: $3|6m| - 8 = 1$

$$3|6m| - 8 = 1$$

$$3|6m| = 9 \qquad\qquad ⟵ \text{ Add 8 to both sides.}$$

$$|6m| = 3 \qquad\qquad ⟵ \text{ Multiply both sides by } \tfrac{1}{3}.$$

$6m = 3 \quad$ or $\quad 6m = -3$ ⟵ Write the equivalent compound sentence.

$\; m = \tfrac{1}{2} \quad$ or $\quad\; m = -\tfrac{1}{2}$

112 Chapter 3

Check: $3\left|6 \cdot \dfrac{1}{2}\right| - 8 \overset{?}{=} 1$ $\qquad$ $3\left|6 \cdot -\dfrac{1}{2}\right| - 8 \overset{?}{=} 1$

$\qquad\qquad$ $3|3| - 8 \overset{?}{=} 1$ $\qquad\qquad$ $3|-3| - 8 \overset{?}{=} 1$

$\qquad\qquad\qquad$ $1 = 1$ $\qquad\qquad\qquad\qquad$ $1 = 1$

Solution set: $\left\{\dfrac{1}{2}, -\dfrac{1}{2}\right\}$

It is possible to obtain <u>apparent solutions</u> to an absolute value equation. Therefore, it is <u>important to check all solutions</u> in the original equation.

Example 3 Solve: $|3a + 14| = 5a + 2$

$$|3a + 14| = 5a + 2$$

$3a + 14 = 5a + 2$ $\quad$ or $\quad$ $3a + 14 = -(5a + 2)$

$\qquad$ $14 = 2a + 2$ $\quad$ or $\quad$ $3a + 14 = -5a - 2$

$\qquad\qquad$ $12 = 2a$ $\quad$ or $\qquad\qquad$ $8a = -16$

$\qquad\qquad\qquad$ $6 = a$ $\quad$ or $\qquad\qquad\qquad$ $a = -2$

Check: $|3(6) + 14| \overset{?}{=} 5(6) + 2$ $\qquad$ $|3(-2) + 14| \overset{?}{=} 5(-2) + 2$

$\qquad\qquad$ $|18 + 14| \overset{?}{=} 32$ $\qquad\qquad$ $|-6 + 14| \overset{?}{=} -10 + 2$

$\qquad\qquad\qquad$ $|32| \overset{?}{=} 32$ $\qquad\qquad\qquad$ $|8| \overset{?}{=} -8$

$\qquad\qquad\qquad$ $32 = 32$ $\qquad\qquad\qquad$ $8 \neq -8$

Solution set: $\{6\}$

Try These *Write each absolute value equation as an equivalent compound sentence. Do not solve.*

1. $|x| = 2$ $\qquad$ **2.** $|3y| = 9$ $\qquad$ **3.** $|n + 7| = 3$ $\qquad$ **4.** $|n - 4| = 2$

$\;\;$ $x = 2$ or $x = -2$ $\qquad$ $3y = 9$ or $3y = -9$ $\qquad$ $n + 7 = 3$, or $n + 7 = -3$ $\qquad$ $n - 4 = 2$ or $n - 4 = -2$

Solve each compound sentence.

5. $2m - 1 = 5$ <u>or</u> $2m - 1 = -5$ $\;$ $\{3, -2\}$ $\qquad$ **6.** $\dfrac{1}{2}k + 1 = 8$ <u>or</u> $\dfrac{1}{2}k + 1 = -8$ $\;$ $\{14, -18\}$

Exercises

Solve and check.

a

1. $|n| = 7$ $\{7, -7\}$

2. $|3w| = 5$ $\{\frac{5}{3}, -\frac{5}{3}\}$

3. $|-4k| = 8$ $\{2, -2\}$

4. $|x + 6| = 2$ $\{-4, -8\}$

5. $|3y - 5| = 4$ $\{3, \frac{1}{3}\}$

6. $|8 - 2t| = 6$ $\{1, 7\}$

7. $|\frac{1}{2}y - 7| = 2$ $\{10, 18\}$

8. $|\frac{3}{4} + c| = \frac{1}{6}$ $\{-\frac{7}{12}, -\frac{11}{12}\}$

9. $|\frac{1}{3}(6k - 2)| = 6$ $\{-\frac{8}{3}, \frac{10}{3}\}$

10. $|4x - 3| = \frac{1}{2}$ $\{\frac{5}{8}, \frac{7}{8}\}$

11. $\left|\frac{5k + 1}{3}\right| = 7$ $\{4, -\frac{22}{5}\}$

12. $\left|\frac{3(4m - 1)}{5}\right| = 6$ $\{\frac{11}{4}, -\frac{9}{4}\}$

13. $|2w + 7| = 3w$ $\{7\}$

14. $|4k + 9| = 3k + 5$ $\emptyset$

15. $|3x + 10| = 5x + 6$ $\{2\}$

16. $|2(3y - 2)| = 3y - 8$ $\emptyset$

17. $|3 - 8n| = -1.3$ $\emptyset$

18. $|2x - 15 + x| = 2x$ $\{15, 3\}$

19. $|5c - 2| = 2c + 7$ $\{3, -\frac{5}{7}\}$

20. $|3(2n + 3)| = \frac{1}{2}n$ $\emptyset$

21. $\frac{1}{3} - |7y + 1| = \frac{1}{3}$ $\{-\frac{1}{7}\}$

22. $|1.4t - 3| = 1.2$ $\{3, \frac{9}{7}\}$

List and graph the elements in each of the following sets. The replacement set is {real numbers}.

b

23. $\{x: |\frac{1}{3}x + 4| = -7\}$ $\emptyset$; there are no points in the graph.

24. $\{y: |7y - 3| = 4y + 6\}$ $\{3, -\frac{3}{11}\}$

25. $\left\{k: \left|\frac{2k}{3} - 6\right| = 1\right\}$ $\{\frac{21}{2}, \frac{15}{2}\}$

26. $\left\{t: \left|\frac{2t - 1}{5}\right| = 5\right\}$ $\{13, -12\}$

27. $\{x: 0.3|x + 2x| - 1.6 = 3.8\}$ $\{6, -6\}$

28. $\left\{m: \left|\frac{4(3m - 1)}{6}\right| = 2\right\}$ $\{\frac{4}{3}, -\frac{2}{3}\}$

Use the definition of absolute value and the separate cases, $x \geq 0$ and $x < 0$, to prove the theorems below for all real numbers, x.

c

29. $|x| = |-x|$ If $x \geq 0$, $|x| = x$ and $|-x| = x$.
    If $x < 0$, $|x| = -x$ and $|-x| = -x$. Therefore $|x| = |-x|$.

30. $|x|^2 = x^2$ $|x|^2 = |x||x|$
    If $x \geq 0$, $|x||x| = (x)(x) = x^2$.
    If $x < 0$, $|x||x| = (-x)(-x) = (-1)^2 x^2 = x^2$.

Remember

Write new inequalities by multiplying each side of the given inequality by 3, by -5, and by $\frac{1}{4}$.

$6y \leq 12x, -10y \geq -20x, \frac{1}{2}y \leq x$

1. $3 < 5$ **2.** $x > 3$ **3.** $2y \leq 4x$ **4.** $8a \geq 4b$

$9 < 15, -15 > -25, \frac{3}{4} < \frac{5}{4}$ $3x > 9, -5x < -15, \frac{1}{4}x > \frac{3}{4}$ $24a \geq 12b, -40a \leq -20b, 2a \geq b$

The answers are on page 132.

3-5 Solving Linear Inequalities

The objective for this section is on page 131.

The mathematical model of some situations is an <u>inequality</u>. An **inequality** is a mathematical sentence that uses $>$, $<$, or $\neq$. Postulates similar to those properties used to solve equations are used to find the solution set of an inequality.

Postulate: Addition Postulate for Inequalities

For all real numbers, a, b, c, if $a < b$, then $a + c < b + c$.

Postulate: Multiplication Postulate for Inequalities ($c > 0$)

For all real numbers, a, b, c, if $a < b$ and $c > 0$, then $ac < bc$.

Example 1   Solve $2x + 3 = 7$ and $2x + 3 < 7$. Graph each solution set.

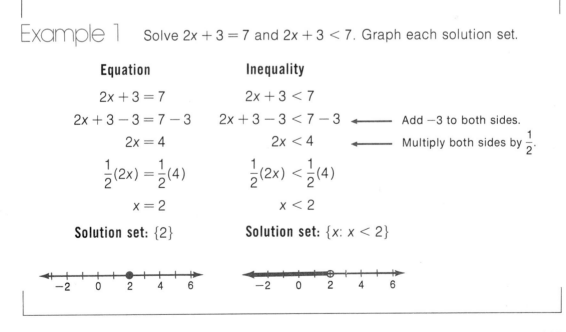

Equation

$$2x + 3 = 7$$
$$2x + 3 - 3 = 7 - 3$$
$$2x = 4$$
$$\frac{1}{2}(2x) = \frac{1}{2}(4)$$
$$x = 2$$

Solution set: $\{2\}$

Inequality

$$2x + 3 < 7$$
$$2x + 3 - 3 < 7 - 3 \quad \longleftarrow \quad \text{Add } -3 \text{ to both sides.}$$
$$2x < 4 \quad \longleftarrow \quad \text{Multiply both sides by } \frac{1}{2}.$$
$$\frac{1}{2}(2x) < \frac{1}{2}(4)$$
$$x < 2$$

Solution set: $\{x \colon x < 2\}$

The following table suggests that multiplying both sides of an inequality by a negative number <u>reverses the order of the inequality.</u>

Inequality	Multiply by 2	Multiply by −2	Multiply by −1
$5 < 7$	$10 < 14$	$-10 > -14$	$-5 > -7$
$-7 < 5$	$-14 < 10$	$14 > -10$	$7 > -5$
$-7 < -5$	$-14 < -10$	$14 > 10$	$7 > 5$

Postulate: Multiplication Postulate for Inequalities (c < 0)

For all real numbers a, b, c, if $a < b$ and $c < 0$, then $ac > bc$.

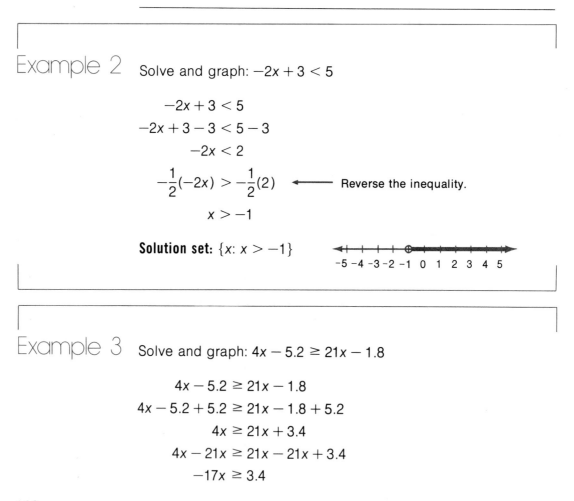

Example 2   Solve and graph: $-2x + 3 < 5$

$$-2x + 3 < 5$$
$$-2x + 3 - 3 < 5 - 3$$
$$-2x < 2$$
$$-\frac{1}{2}(-2x) > -\frac{1}{2}(2) \quad \longleftarrow \quad \text{Reverse the inequality.}$$
$$x > -1$$

Solution set: $\{x: x > -1\}$

-5 -4 -3 -2 -1 0 1 2 3 4 5

Example 3   Solve and graph: $4x - 5.2 \geq 21x - 1.8$

$$4x - 5.2 \geq 21x - 1.8$$
$$4x - 5.2 + 5.2 \geq 21x - 1.8 + 5.2$$
$$4x \geq 21x + 3.4$$
$$4x - 21x \geq 21x - 21x + 3.4$$
$$-17x \geq 3.4$$

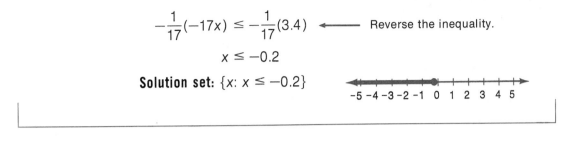

$$-\frac{1}{17}(-17x) \le -\frac{1}{17}(3.4) \qquad \longleftarrow \text{Reverse the inequality.}$$

$$x \le -0.2$$

Solution set: $\{x\colon x \le -0.2\}$

-5 -4 -3 -2 -1 0 1 2 3 4 5

Try These *Write "Same" or "Reverse" to describe the direction of an inequality after each operation is performed.*

1. Add -6.
Same.

2. Multiply by 2.
Same.

3. Multiply by $-\frac{1}{3}$.
Reverse.

4. Multiply by -1.
Reverse.

Exercises

Solve each inequality, and graph its solution set.

1. $x - 3 > 10$ $\{x\colon x > 13\}$

2. $y + 4 \le -1$ $\{y\colon y \le -5\}$

3. $3a < 12$ $\{a\colon a < 4\}$

4. $\frac{c}{4} > 8$ $\{c\colon c > 32\}$

5. $\frac{1}{3}n \ge 2$ $\{n\colon n \ge 6\}$

6. $-5t < 25$ $\{t\colon t > -5\}$

7. $\frac{w}{-6} > -2$ $\{w\colon w < 12\}$

8. $\frac{x}{1000} < \frac{1}{100}$ $\{x\colon x < 10\}$

9. $3m - 4 > 11$ $\{m\colon m > 5\}$

10. $4(c + 3) \ge 12$ $\{c\colon c \ge 0\}$

11. $-8 - 2c \ge 12$ $\{c\colon c \le -10\}$

12. $4a - 5 < 6a + 3$ $\{a\colon a > -4\}$

13. $-4n + \frac{1}{8} < 2\frac{1}{8}$ $\{n\colon n > -\frac{1}{2}\}$

14. $4(x - 7) \ge x + 2$ $\{x\colon x \ge 10\}$

15. $-3(4 - 3n) > 3 - 6n$ $\{n\colon n > 1\}$

16. $3a < 4(2a + 5)$ $\{a\colon a > -4\}$

17. $2m - 10 + 4m > -8$ $\{m\colon m > \frac{1}{3}\}$

18. $6x - 3(4 - 3x) \le 3$ $\{x\colon x \le 1\}$

19. $-4c - 5 \ge 7(4c - 3)$ $\{c\colon c \le \frac{1}{2}\}$

20. $2(y - 1) - 4 \le 8y$ $\{y\colon y \ge -1\}$

21. $-5w + \frac{1}{2} \le -3w - \frac{1}{4}$ $\{w\colon w \ge \frac{3}{8}\}$

22. $\frac{x}{3} - 5 > \frac{x}{2} - 1$ $\{x\colon x < -24\}$

23. $-2(n - 3) > 6n - 10$ $\{n\colon n < 2\}$

24. $6 < 26 + \frac{2a}{5}$ $\{a\colon a > -50\}$

25. $10y - 8.5 < y - 4$ $\{y\colon y < \frac{1}{2}\}$

26. $\frac{7}{10}n + 1 > 4$ $\{n\colon n > \frac{30}{7}\}$

27. $(4 - 2t) - (4 - t) < (2t - 1) + (t - 3)$ $\quad \{t : t > 1\}$

28. $7(2n + 5) - 6(n + 8) > 7$ $\quad \{n : n > 2\frac{1}{2}\}$

$\{w : w \le -6\frac{1}{2}\}$

29. $w - 2(5 - 2w) \ge 6w - 3\frac{1}{2}$

30. $6x^2 - 8 > 2x(3x - 4)$ $\quad \{x : x > 1\}$

31. $-\frac{2}{3}(3c - 12) < 6 - \frac{1}{2}(4c + 8)$ $\quad \emptyset$

Illustrate each theorem with a numerical example. Then prove each theorem for all real numbers.

If $x > 0$, $x^2 = x \cdot x = |x| \cdot |x| > 0$. Thus, $x^2 > 0$.

32. *If $x \ne 0$, then $x^2 > 0$.* (Hint: Consider two cases: $x > 0$ and $x < 0$.)

If $x < 0$, $x^2 = x \cdot x = (-|x|)(-|x|) = (-1)^2 |x|^2 = 1 |x|^2 = |x|^2 > 0$.

33. *If $x > 0$, then $\frac{1}{x} > 0$.* (Hint: Use an indirect proof. That is, assume $\frac{1}{x} \not> 0$ and show that this leads to a contradiction.) Can you state a similar theorem when $x < 0$?

If $\frac{1}{x} \not> 0$, then $\frac{1}{x} \le 0$. However, $\frac{1}{x} \ne 0$ since $x > 0$. If $\frac{1}{x} < 0$, then $|\frac{1}{x}| = -\frac{1}{x}$. But $|\frac{1}{x}| = \frac{1}{|x|} = \frac{1}{x}$ since $x > 0$.

This is a contradiction. Thus, $\frac{1}{x} \not> 0$ is false and $\frac{1}{x} > 0$.

34. *If $x > y > 0$, then $\frac{1}{x} < \frac{1}{y}$.* (Hint: Use the theorem in Exercise 33 to show that

$x > 0, y > 0$ therefore $xy > 0$ and $\frac{1}{xy} > 0$.

$\frac{1}{xy} > 0$. Then use the hypothesis.)

Since $x > y$, $\frac{1}{xy}x > \frac{1}{xy}y$.

Then, $\frac{1}{y} > \frac{1}{x}$, or $\frac{1}{x} < \frac{1}{y}$.

Remember

Perform the indicated operations.

1. $\dfrac{p}{3} + \dfrac{p}{7}$ $\quad \frac{10p}{21}$

2. $\dfrac{q}{5} - \dfrac{q}{3}$ $\quad \frac{-2q}{15}$

3. $\dfrac{x}{5} - \dfrac{2}{x}$ $\quad \frac{x^2 - 10}{5x}$

4. $\dfrac{5}{x} + \dfrac{2}{y}$

$\frac{5y + 2x}{xy}$

The answers are on page 132.

PUZZLE

Two of these are FALSE. Which one is TRUE? The second equation is true.

$1 \sqrt{\dfrac{1}{3}} = \sqrt{1\dfrac{1}{3}}$ $\qquad 2 \sqrt{\dfrac{2}{3}} = \sqrt{2\dfrac{2}{3}}$ $\qquad 3 \sqrt{\dfrac{2}{3}} = \sqrt{3\dfrac{2}{3}}$

Can you show that

$\sqrt{x + \dfrac{x}{x^2 - 1}} = x\sqrt{\dfrac{x}{x^2 - 1}}$ $\qquad \sqrt{x + \dfrac{x}{x^2 - 1}} = \sqrt{\dfrac{x(x^2 - 1) + x}{x^2 - 1}} = \sqrt{\dfrac{x^2 \cdot x}{x^2 - 1}} = x\sqrt{\dfrac{x}{x^2 - 1}}$

is an identity? ($x > 1$, of course)

3-6 Mathematical Models for Problems

The objective for this section is on page 131.

The idea of <u>rate</u> is important in many everyday situations.

Unit Rate	×	Number of Units	=	Amount
10 km / hour	×	5 hours	=	50 kilometers
50 pages / day	×	3 days	=	150 pages
15 trout / day	×	$\frac{1}{3}$ day	=	5 trout
$\frac{1}{4}$ field / week	×	4 weeks	=	1 field
300,000 km / second	×	$\frac{1}{15}$ second	=	20,000 kilometers

Example 1   Steve can mow $\frac{1}{4}$ of a golf course in a day.

a. What is Steve's mowing rate?
b. How many days will it take him to mow the Glen Shores course?
c. After 3 days of mowing, how much of the course remains to be mowed?

a. Steve's rate is $\frac{1}{4}$ golf course / day.

b.
$$\begin{array}{ccc}
\text{(Unit} & \text{(Number} & \\
\text{rate)} \times & \text{of units)} = & \text{Amount}
\end{array}$$

$\frac{1}{4} \times t = 1$ ⟵ $r = \frac{1}{4}$; time = t; A(amount) = 1 golf course

$t = 4$ ⟵ Multiply by 4.

It will take Steve 4 days to mow the entire golf course.

c.
$$\begin{array}{ccc}
\text{(Unit} & \text{(Number} & \\
\text{rate)} \times & \text{of units)} = & \text{Amount}
\end{array}$$

$\frac{1}{4} \times t = A$ ⟵ $r = \frac{1}{4}$; time = t; A = amount mowed.

$\frac{1}{4} \times 3 = A$ ⟵ Let $t = 3$.

$\frac{3}{4} = A$

After 3 days, $\frac{3}{4}$ of the course is mowed and $\frac{1}{4}$ remains to be mowed.

Equations or mathematical models of situations involving rate can also have the form

$$r_1 t_1 + r_2 t_2 + r_3 t_3 + \cdots = \text{Amount}$$

where t_1, t_2, t_3, $\cdots$ represent different times and r_1, r_2, r_3, $\cdots$ represent their corresponding rates.

Example 2   Babs can mow $\frac{1}{4}$ of a golf course in one day and Jill can mow $\frac{1}{3}$ of the course in one day.

    a. Write an equation that shows the number of golf courses they can mow in t days by working together.
    b. How much can they mow in one day by working together?

  a. (Amount   (Amount   Total
     by Babs) + by Jill) = Amount

$$\frac{1}{4}t \quad + \quad \frac{1}{3}t \quad = \quad A \qquad\longleftarrow \qquad t = \text{time}; r(\text{Babs}) = \frac{1}{4};$$

$$\uparrow \qquad\qquad \uparrow \qquad\qquad\qquad\qquad r(\text{Jill}) = \frac{1}{3}; A =$$

t is the same for   amount done.
both.

  b.

$$\frac{1}{4}t + \frac{1}{3}t = A \qquad\longleftarrow \qquad \text{Write the equation.}$$

$$\frac{1}{4}(1) + \frac{1}{3}(1) = A \qquad\longleftarrow \qquad \text{Let } t = 1.$$

$$\frac{7}{12} = A$$

Working together, they can mow $\frac{7}{12}$ of a golf course in 1 day.

Example 3   How long would it take Babs and Jill together to mow one golf course?

$$\frac{1}{4}t + \frac{1}{3}t = A \qquad\longleftarrow \qquad \text{Write the equation from Example 2.}$$

$$\frac{1}{4}t + \frac{1}{3}t = 1 \qquad\longleftarrow \qquad \text{Let } A = 1.$$

$$\frac{7}{12}t = 1$$

$$t = \frac{12}{7}$$

It would take them $\frac{12}{7}$ or $1\frac{5}{7}$ days.

Try These *Write an equation to represent each situation. Let t = time, r = rate, and A = amount done.*

1. Ted plants $\frac{1}{6}$ of a field in a day. How much can he plant in t days? $A = \frac{1}{6}t$

2. Martina can address envelopes at the rate of $\frac{1}{5}$ box per hour. How many can she do in t hours? $A = \frac{1}{5}t$

3. If Sue can address envelopes at the rate of $\frac{1}{4}$ box per hour, how many envelopes can Mary and Sue address in t hours by working together? $A = \frac{1}{5}t + \frac{1}{4}t$

4. The rates for filling a tank with oil from 3 different pipes are $\frac{1}{4}$ tank / hour, $\frac{1}{5}$ tank / hour, and $\frac{1}{6}$ tank / hour. How much of the tank is filled after t hours?

5. How many hours will it take the 3 pipes in Exercise 4 to fill 2 tanks?

$$\frac{1}{4}t + \frac{1}{5}t + \frac{1}{6}t = 2 \qquad\qquad A = \frac{1}{4}t + \frac{1}{5}t + \frac{1}{6}t$$

Exercises

Write an equation for each problem. Let t = time, r = rate, and A = amount done. Use the equation to answer the specific questions asked in each exercise.

1. Fred can sweep the snow from a sidewalk in 4 minutes while Sarah can do it in 3 minutes. Working together, how long will it take them to sweep the sidewalk?

   Fred's rate is $\frac{1}{4}$ sidewalk / minute. Sarah's rate is $\frac{1}{3}$ sidewalk / minute. The equation is

   $$\frac{1}{4}t + \frac{1}{3}t = A. \qquad \frac{12}{7} \text{ minutes}$$

   Complete the solution.

2. If Ann can sweep the leaves from a yard in 6 minutes and Grace can do it in 8 minutes, how much can they get done working together for 1 minute? for 3 minutes? $\frac{7}{24} \cdot \frac{7}{8}$

3. Jonne can paint a house in 6 days. It would take Tom 9 days to do the same work. If Jonne works alone for 2 days and then is joined by Tom, how long would it take to paint the house? The equation is

   $$\frac{1}{6}t_1 + \left(\frac{1}{6}t_2 + \frac{1}{9}t_2\right) = A \qquad 4\frac{2}{5} \text{ days}$$

   where t_1 is the time Jonne works alone, t_2 is the time Tom and Jonne work together, and A is the amount done. Complete the solution.

4. Mr. Chu can plow one of his fields with a tractor in 4 days. It takes his neighbor 12 days to plow the same field. How long will it take Mr. Chu if his neighbor helps him? 3 days

5. Ruth can mow a certain strip of our lawn with her mower in 20 minutes, and Jane can mow it with hers in 30 minutes. How long would it take if they did this work together?   12 minutes

6. If one pipe can fill a tank in 3 hours, a second pipe in 4 hours, and a third in 5 hours, how long will it take to fill the tank if all three pipes are being used? $1\frac{13}{47}$ hours

7. Mr. Ellers, working alone, can paint our house in 12 days. If he has Mr. Gallup to help him, it takes only 4 days. How long would it take Mr. Gallup alone?
6 days

8. Art can do a piece of work alone in 8 days. After he has been working alone for 2 days, he is joined by Pete, who is a faster worker. They finish the job together in 2 more days. How long would it have taken Pete to do the work alone? 4 days

9. A large pipe can fill a tank in 5 hours and a smaller pipe can fill it in 8 hours. A third pipe can empty the tank in 10 hours. How long would it take to fill the tank if all three pipes are open? $4\frac{4}{9}$ hours

10. Ellen can drive her car over a route in 4 hours, and Lila can drive her car over the same route in $3\frac{1}{2}$ hours. How long will it take them to meet if they start at opposite ends at the same time? $1\frac{13}{15}$ hours

11. Steve, José, and Clyde can do a piece of work in 4 hours. If Steve can do the same piece of work in 10 hours, and José in 12 hours, how many hours will it take Clyde to do the work? 15 hours

12. Sue's, Lucy's, and Helen's rates of work are $\frac{1}{10}$ job / hr, $\frac{1}{12}$ job / hr and $\frac{1}{13}$ job / hr. Set up the model for Sue and Lucy if they work together for 3 hours, and then are joined by Helen. How long will they take to complete the job?   1.73 hours

Remember

Write an algebraic expression to represent each condition.

1. The sum of an unknown number and 3. $n + 3$

2. Eight less than six times an unknown number. $6n - 8$

3. Five times the difference when a number is decreased by 6. $5(n - 6)$

4. The quotient obtained when an unknown number is divided by 8. $\frac{n}{8}$

The answers are on page 132.

3-7 More Problems

The objective for this section is on page 131.

The equation or mathematical model for a problem situation must reflect all the conditions essential to the problem. Identifying these conditions is an important step in writing the equation.

Example 1

The sum of two rational numbers is $\frac{3}{4}$. One number is $\frac{1}{2}$ the other. Find the numbers.

Let q = one number.   ⟵   Represent the numbers.
Then $\frac{1}{2}q$ = the other number,

$$q + \tfrac{1}{2}q = \tfrac{3}{4}$$ ⟵   Write the equation.

$$4(q + \tfrac{1}{2}q) = 4 \cdot \tfrac{3}{4}$$ ⟵   The LCD is 4.

$$4q + 2q = 3$$ ⟵   Solve for q.

$$6q = 3$$

$$q = \tfrac{1}{2}$$

$$\tfrac{1}{2}q = \tfrac{1}{4}$$ ⟵   Find $\frac{1}{2}q$.

Check: Does $\frac{1}{2} + \frac{1}{4} = \frac{3}{4}$? Yes.   Is one number $\frac{1}{2}$ the other? Yes.

The numbers are $\frac{1}{2}$ and $\frac{1}{4}$.

Always check answers in the original statement of the problem.

Linear Equations and Inequalities   **123**

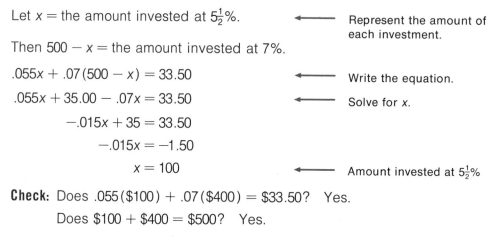

Example 2   Paula Hatcher invested $500 part at $5\frac{1}{2}\%$ in savings and part at 7% in bonds. Her income from this in one year was $33.50. How much did she invest at $5\frac{1}{2}\%$?

Let $x =$ the amount invested at $5\frac{1}{2}\%$.   ← Represent the amount of each investment.

Then $500 - x =$ the amount invested at 7%.

$.055x + .07(500 - x) = 33.50$ ← Write the equation.

$.055x + 35.00 - .07x = 33.50$ ← Solve for x.

$-.015x + 35 = 33.50$

$-.015x = -1.50$

$x = 100$ ← Amount invested at $5\frac{1}{2}\%$

Check: Does $.055(\$100) + .07(\$400) = \$33.50$?   Yes.

Does $\$100 + \$400 = \$500$?   Yes.

Paula invested $100 at $5\frac{1}{2}\%$.

Exercises

Write an equation to represent the conditions of each problem. Then solve and check each equation.

1. The sum of two rational numbers is $\frac{7}{16}$, and one of them is $\frac{2}{5}$ of the other. What are the two numbers? $\frac{5}{16}$ and $\frac{1}{8}$

2. The difference between two positive rational numbers is $\frac{3}{8}$. One number is $\frac{2}{5}$ of the other. Find the two numbers. $\frac{5}{8}$ and $\frac{1}{4}$

3. The numerator of a fraction exceeds its denominator by 2. If 1 is added to the denominator and 3 is subtracted from the numerator, the fraction you get names $\frac{1}{2}$. What is the original fraction? $\frac{5}{3}$

4. What number must be subtracted from the numerator and the denominator of the fraction $\frac{5}{8}$ in order that the fraction obtained names $\frac{1}{2}$? 2

5. Separate 80 into two parts so that one part will be $\frac{2}{3}$ of the other part.

32 and 48.

6. One man can lay a sidewalk in 4 days and another can do it in 4.5 days. How long does it take them when they work together? $2\frac{2}{17}$ days

7. Sauna has invested $475, part at 5% and the remainder at 8%. If she receives dividends of $27.50 at the end of one year, how much does she invest at each rate? $350 at 5%; $125 at 8%

8. Mr. Romero invests $2500 at 4%. How much should he invest at 6% in order to have a 5% annual return on the total investment? $2500

9. A boy bought apples at 3 for 5 cents and sold them at 2 for 5 cents. By doing this he made a profit of one dollar. How many apples did he buy? 120 apples

10. What is the price of eggs per dozen, if a decrease of 32 cents per dozen would make it possible to buy 9 dozen for the same amount that would buy 6 dozen at the original price? 96 cents

11. The length of a rectangular picture, not including the frame, is 6 centimeters more than its width. The area of the frame, $2\frac{1}{2}$ centimeters wide on all sides, is 155 square centimeters. What are the dimensions of the picture? 10 cm × 16 cm

12. Mae Chung drives to a certain place at the rate of 90 kilometers an hour. She returns by a road that is 10 kilometers longer at the rate of 80 kilometers an hour and takes 1 hour longer to return. How long is each road? (One *time* is an hour longer than the other.) 630 km and 640 km

13. A man has $3\frac{1}{3}$ hours in which to show some visitors the surrounding countryside. How far from his house can he drive if he plans to go at the rate of 50 kilometers per hour and return at the rate of 75 kilometers per hour? 100 km

14. Separate $139 into three charity donations so that the first donation is twice the second donation and the third donation exceeds the sum of the other two donations by one dollar. $46, $23, $70

15. Find the measure of each angle of a triangular rose garden, if the measure of the second angle is one half the first and the measure of the third angle is 15 more than the first. 66°, 33°, 81°

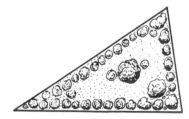

16. The ages of three cousins are three consecutive even integers such that the sum of the first and last is 28. Find the age of each. 12, 14, 16

17. Lee Chuen received $2.50 on his 4th birthday. When he put the money in his bank, he put one more dime than quarters and two more nickels than quarters and dimes together. How many coins of each kind did he put in his bank? 5 quarters, 6 dimes, 13 nickels

18. Tracey can drive her car over a route in 6 hours and Sam can drive his car over the same route in 5 hours. How long would it take them to meet if they started from opposite ends of the route at the same time? $2\frac{8}{11}$ hours

19. In how many minutes after 3 o'clock will the hands of the clock first be together? (Treat this as a problem in time, rate, and distance. What is the rate of each hand in minute-spaces per hour? The equation will make a statement about the distances the hands travel.) $16\frac{4}{11}$ minutes

20. In how many minutes after 12 o'clock will the hands of a clock first be 20 minute-spaces apart? $21\frac{9}{11}$ minutes

C **21.** Joe does $\frac{2}{3}$ of a job in 4 hours. Kara can do $\frac{3}{4}$ of what remains to be done in 1 hour, and Gloria can finish the job in 20 minutes. What is each person's rate of work? How long would it take the three people to do the job if they worked together? $1\frac{1}{2}$ hours

22. A stream can carry a floating object from point A to point B in 4 hours. Lea could paddle a canoe in still water from A to B in one hour. How long would it take Lea to paddle a canoe upstream from point B to point A?

$\frac{4}{3}$ hours

Remember

Solve for x.

1. $|x| = 2$ {−2, 2}   **2.** $|x| = 0$ {0}   **3.** $|x| - 1 = 0$ {−1, 1}   **4.** $|x - 1| = 2$

The answers are on page 132.

{−1, 3}

3-8 Solving Inequalities with Absolute Value

The objective for this section is on page 131.

The solution set of $|x| < 2$ contains those points less than two units from zero on a number line. Thus, the solution set is the intersection of $\{x : x > -2\}$ with $\{x : x < 2\}$.

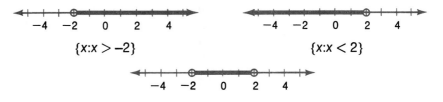

$\{x:x > -2\}$ $\{x:x < 2\}$

Solution set: $\{x : x > -2\} \cap \{x : x < 2\}$

The solution set of $|x| > 2$ contains those points greater than two units from zero on a number line. Thus, the solution set is the union of $\{x : x < -2\}$ with $\{x : x > 2\}$.

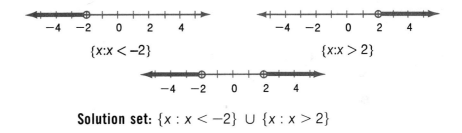

$\{x:x < -2\}$ $\{x:x > 2\}$

Solution set: $\{x : x < -2\} \cup \{x : x > 2\}$

Example 1   Solve and graph: $|2n - 3| < 7$

$$|2n - 3| < 7 = \{n : 2n - 3 > -7\} \cap \{n : 2n - 3 < 7\}$$
$$= \{n : 2n > -4\} \cap \{n : 2n < 10\} \quad \longleftarrow \text{ Solve for } n.$$
$$= \{n : n > -2\} \cap \{n : n < 5\}$$

Solution set: $\{n : -2 < n < 5\}$

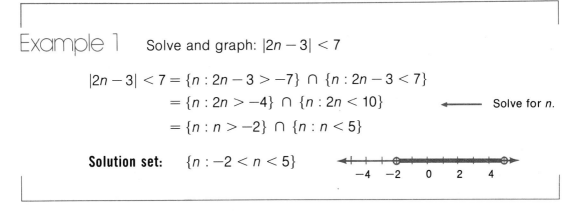

Example 2   Solve and graph: $|5y - 8| \geq 22$

$$|5y - 8| \geq 22 = \{y : 5y - 8 \leq -22\} \cup \{y : 5y - 8 \geq 22\}$$
$$= \{y : 5y \leq -14\} \cup \{y : 5y \geq 30\} \quad \longleftarrow \quad \text{Solve for } y.$$
$$= \{y : y \leq -\tfrac{14}{5}\} \cup \{y : y \geq 6\}$$

Solution set: $\{y : y \leq -\tfrac{14}{5}\} \cup \{y : y \geq 6\}$

Try These   *Write as the intersection, or as the union, of two sets.*

1. $|x| < 4$ $\{x : x > -4\} \cap \{x : x < 4\}$

2. $|y| > 2$ $\{y : y > 2\} \cup \{y : y < -2\}$

3. $|c - 3| \leq 5$ $\{c : c \geq -2\} \cap \{c : c \leq 8\}$

4. $|n - 6| \geq 8$ $\{n : n \leq -2\} \cup \{n : n \geq 14\}$

Exercises

Solve and graph. The replacement set for the variable is the set of real numbers.

a

1. $|n| > 6$ $\{n : n < -6\} \cup \{n : n > 6\}$

2. $|y| < 8$ $\{y : -8 < y < 8\}$

3. $|x - 3| < 1$ $\{x : 2 < x < 4\}$

4. $|t + 4| > 2$ $\{t : t < -6\} \cup \{t : t > -2\}$

5. $|6 - m| < 4$ $\{m : 2 < m < 10\}$

6. $|2a + 3| \leq 1$ $\{a : -2 \leq a \leq -1\}$

7. $|3c - 7| \geq 2$ $\{c : c \leq \tfrac{5}{3}\} \cup \{c : c \geq 3\}$

8. $|5 - 2t| \leq 3$ $\{t : 1 \leq t \leq 4\}$

9. $|4x + 3| > 6$ $\{x : x < -\tfrac{9}{4}\} \cup \{x : x > \tfrac{3}{4}\}$

10. $|3 - 2y| > 10$ $\{y : y < -3\tfrac{1}{2}\} \cup \{y : y > 6\tfrac{1}{2}\}$

b

11. $|\tfrac{2}{3}d - 1| > 5$ $\{d : d < -6\} \cup \{d : d > 9\}$

12. $|1 - (3 - t)| < 2$ $\{t : 0 < t < 4\}$

13. $|4 - (m - 1)| \leq 7$ $\{m : -2 \leq m \leq 12\}$

14. $|-2 - 5w| \geq 8$ $\{w : w \geq \tfrac{6}{5}\} \cup \{w : w \leq -2\}$

15. $|3n + 5| < 4$ $\{n : -3 < n < -\tfrac{1}{3}\}$

16. $|6 - a| < 2a$ $\{a : a > 2\}$

17. $|2c - 1| \leq 3 - c$ $\{c : -2 \leq c \leq \tfrac{4}{3}\}$

18. $|3w + 4| \geq w + 7$ $\{w : w \leq -\tfrac{11}{4}\} \cup \{w : w \geq \tfrac{3}{2}\}$

Use absolute value notation to describe each set.

19. $\{t : t > -3\} \cap \{t : t < 3\}$ $|t| < 3$

20. $\{a : a < -4\} \cup \{a : a > 4\}$ $|a| > 4$

21. $\{n : n \geq -6\} \cap \{n : n \leq 6\}$ $|n| \leq 6$

22. $\{c : 3c + 4 \leq -1\} \cup \{c : 3c + 4 \geq 1\}$ $|3c + 4| \geq 1$

23. $\{m : m \geq 3\} \cap \{m : m \leq 7\}$ $|m - 5| \leq 2$

24. $\{x : x > -9\} \cap \{x : x < 1\}$ $|x + 4| < 5$

If and Only If

Statement **a** is a **conditional statement,** because it is in if–then form. The symbol for a conditional is $p \rightarrow q$, where the $\rightarrow$ connects the if–part, p, and the then–part, q.

a. If the square of a number is even, then the number is even.

By interchanging the p and q parts, you form the **converse** of the statement. The converse of $p \rightarrow q$ is $q \rightarrow p$.

b. If a number is even, then its square is even.

Theorems that contain the phrase if and only if are biconditionals.

> **Theorem:** For all real numbers a and b,
> $ab = 0$ if and only if $a = 0$ or $b = 0$.

A biconditional is really two theorems. Each theorem must be proved.

1. If $ab = 0$, then $a = 0$ or $b = 0$. (Conditional: $p \rightarrow q$)
2. If $a = 0$ or $b = 0$, then $ab = 0$. (Converse: $q \rightarrow p$)

The biconditional is written $p \leftrightarrow q$. All definitions are biconditionals, although they are not always written in if and only if form.

Can You Solve These?

Combine each pair of statements to form a conditional. Then write the converse and the biconditional.

1. p: A number is an integer.
   q: The number is a real number.

2. p: A number is divisible by 4.
   q: The number is an even number.

3. Classify each conditional, converse, and biconditional in Exercises 1 and 2 as True or False.

Objective: To know the meanings of the important mathematical terms of this chapter.

1. Here are many of the mathematical terms used in this chapter. Be sure that you know their meanings and that you can use them correctly.

apparent solution (p. 105)   equivalent equations (p. 102)
compound sentence (p. 112)   inequality (p. 115)

Objective: To solve equations. (Section 3-1)

Solve and check.

2. $3n - 5 = 13$ {6}

3. $3y - 9 = y + 2$ $\{\frac{11}{2}\}$

4. $7 - 3a = 5a + 14$ $\{-\frac{7}{8}\}$

5. $8c - 5 = 3c + c + 15$ {5}

6. $\frac{1}{2}x - \frac{3}{4} = x - 7$ $\{12\frac{1}{2}\}$

7. $0.8t + 11 = .78t + 13$ {100}

8. $3(4k - 1) = 9$ {1}

9. $15 - (3a - 30) = 15a - 9$ {3}

10. $5(2d - 3) - 6(d + 2) = -7$ {5}

11. $\frac{1}{2}(p - 2) = \frac{1}{3}(p + 2)$ {10}

Objective: To solve equations involving rational expressions (Section 3-2)

Solve and check.

12. $\dfrac{3a - 7}{4} = 2$ {5}

13. $\dfrac{w}{4} + \dfrac{w}{3} = \dfrac{2}{3}$ $\{\frac{8}{7}\}$

14. $\dfrac{c - 1}{2} - \dfrac{c + 1}{3} = \dfrac{3}{4}$ $\{\frac{19}{2}\}$

15. $\dfrac{4n + 7}{5} = \dfrac{2n + 3}{4}$ $\{-\frac{13}{6}\}$

16. $\dfrac{x + 6}{2x} = \dfrac{-10}{x} - 6$ {-2}

17. $\dfrac{2}{y^2 - 1} = \dfrac{5}{y - 1} - \dfrac{4}{y + 1}$ {-7}

Objective: To solve an equation for one variable in terms of the remaining variables. (Section 3-3)

Solve each equation for the variable indicated.

18. $ax + b = c$; x $x = \frac{c-b}{a}$ **19.** $25g = w(v - u)$; u $u = \frac{wv - 25g}{w}$ **20.** $I = \dfrac{NE}{Nr + R}$; N

$N = \frac{RI}{E - rI}$

Objective: To solve equations involving absolute value. (Section 3-4)

Solve and check.

21. $|5t| = 30$ $\{6, -6\}$ **22.** $|3a - 2| = 7$ $\{3, -\frac{5}{3}\}$ **23.** $|4n + 6| = 2n$

ϕ

Objective: To solve an inequality and graph its solution set. (Section 3-5)

Solve. Then graph the solution set.

24. $2a + 4 < 12$ $\{a: a < 4\}$ **25.** $3 - 4y > 27$ $\{y: y < -6\}$ **26.** $\dfrac{k}{2} \leq 12 + 2k$

$\{k: k \geq -8\}$

Objective: To solve word problems. (Sections 3-6 and 3-7)

Write an equation to represent each problem. Then solve the problem.

27. The denominator of a fraction is 5 more than the numerator. If 17 is added to the numerator, you get the fraction, $\frac{2}{1}$. What is the original fraction? $\frac{7}{12}$

28. The combined ages of Hank's father and mother are 75. His mother is $\frac{7}{8}$ the age of his father. What is the age of each?   Father, 40 years; Mother, 35 years.

29. The length of the altitude of a triangle is 8 centimeters more than the base. Another triangle has an altitude that is 3 centimeters shorter than the first, and a base that is 4 centimeters longer than the first. The area of the second is 16 square centimeters more than the first. Find the base and altitude of each triangle.   First triangle: base 12 cm; altitude, 20 cm; Second triangle: base 16 cm; altitude, 17 cm.

30. A water tank can be filled using a small pipe in 48 hours and in 16 hours using a large pipe. Using the one drain pipe, it can be emptied in 24 hours. Starting with an empty tank, will it ever be filled using all three pipes? If so, how long will it take?   24 hours

Objective: To solve and graph inequalities with absolute value. (Section 3-8)

Solve and graph.

31. $|2x + 5| \geq 15$

$\{x: x \leq -10\} \cup \{x: x \geq 5\}$

32. $|3y - 1| < 8$

$\{y: -\frac{7}{3} < y < 3\}$

33. $|3n| \leq 21$

$\{n: n \geq -7\} \cap \{n: n \leq 7\}$

Chapter Test

Solve each equation.

1. $-3n - 7 = 14$ $_{-7}$

2. $4 - 5a = 2a + 11$ $_{-1}$

3. $1.3t - 0.6 = 0.4 - 0.7t$ $_{\frac{1}{2}}$

4. $7(2m + 5) - 6(m + 8) = 7$ $_{\frac{5}{2}}$

5. $\frac{4}{3}(x + 1) = x + 4$ $_{8}$

6. $\frac{1}{2}c + \frac{1}{3}c + \frac{1}{6}c = 5$ $_{5}$

7. $\dfrac{3n}{2} - \dfrac{2n}{3} = \dfrac{5}{2}$ $_{3}$

8. $0.05x + 0.03(x + 4.5) = 0.455$ $_{4}$

9. $\dfrac{d - 1}{3} + 3 = \dfrac{d + 14}{9}$ $_{-5}$

10. $\dfrac{1}{K + 3} + \dfrac{12}{K^2 - 9} = \dfrac{2}{K + 3}$ $_{15}$

11. $|2y + 7| = 13$ $\{3, -10\}$

12. $|5a - 6| = 3a$ $\{3\frac{3}{4}\}$

13. $a(r - s) = t$, for r $r = s + \frac{t}{a}$

14. $S = \dfrac{ar^n - a}{r - 1}$, for a. $a = \frac{S(r - 1)}{r^n - 1}$

Solve each inequality and graph its solution set. The replacement set is the set of real numbers.

15. $-3(2x - 1) < 15$ $x > -2$

16. $7y - 2 \le 4y + 13$ $y \le 5$

17. The length of a rectangular rock garden is 2 meters more than its width. If each dimension were increased by 3 meters, the area would be increased by 33 square meters. Find the original dimensions. 5m by 3m

18. A truck traveling at the rate of 70 kilometers per hour is followed 3 hours later by a passenger car traveling at the rate of 100 kilometers per hour. In how many hours will the car overtake the truck? 7 hours

Answers to Remember

Page 104: **1.** 168 **2.** 85 **3.** ab^2c^2 **4.** $(x + 1)(x - 3)(x - 2)$

Page 108: **1.** $-i$ **2.** -5 **3.** 3 **4.** 3 **5.** $(x - y)(x + y)$ **6.** $(x + iy)(x - iy)$
7. $(x - y)(x + y)(x - iy)(x + iy)$ **8.** $(a - b)(a^2 + ab + b^2)$

Page 111: **1.** 0 **2.** 14 **3.** 2 **4.** 2 **5.** $x; -x$

Page 114: **1.** $9 < 15; -15 > -25; \frac{3}{4} < \frac{5}{4}$ **2.** $3x > 9; -5x < -15; \frac{1}{4}x > \frac{3}{4}$ **3.** $6y \le 12x; -10y \ge -20x; \frac{1}{2}y \le x$
4. $24a \ge 12b; -40a \le -20b; 2a \ge b$

Page 118: **1.** $\dfrac{10p}{21}$ **2.** $-\dfrac{2q}{15}$ **3.** $\dfrac{x^2 - 10}{5x}$ **4.** $\dfrac{5y + 2x}{xy}$

Page 123: **1.** $n + 3$ **2.** $6n - 8$ **3.** $5(n - 6)$ **4.** $\dfrac{n}{8}$

Page 126: **1.** $\{-2, 2\}$ **2.** $\{0\}$ **3.** $\{-1, 1\}$ **4.** $\{-1, 3\}$

Chapter 4
Coordinate Geometry

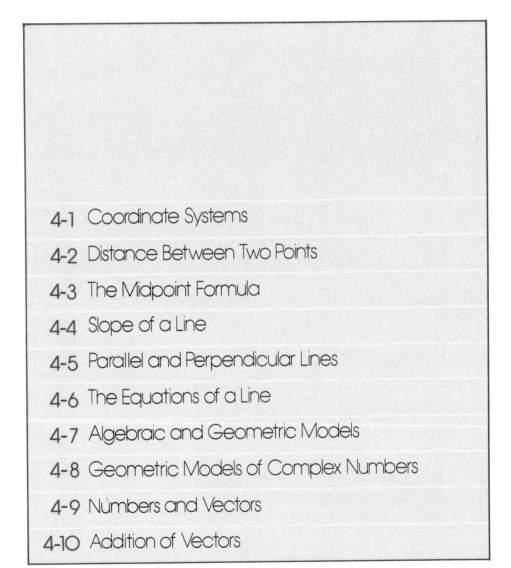

4-1 Coordinate Systems

The objective for this section is on page 174.

Two perpendicular lines are the **axes** of the **coordinate plane.** The point of intersection is the origin, 0. The points of the plane can be placed in one-to-one correspondence with ordered pairs of real numbers (x,y). The first number, x, is the **abscissa** and the second number, y, is the **ordinate.** The two numbers are the **coordinates** of the point. You locate a point by identifying x, its horizontal distance from 0, and y, its vertical distance from the x axis.

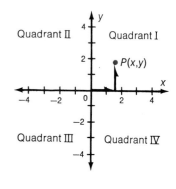

Example

Graph the points associated with each ordered pair. Tell in which quadrant each point lies.

$A(-2, 4)$ $B(4, -2)$ $C(0, -3)$

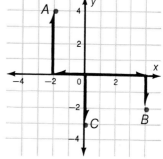

$A(-2, 4)$: 2 units to the left of 0 and 4 units upward from the x axis.   Quadrant II

$B(4, -2)$: 4 units to the right of 0 and 2 units downward from the x axis.   Quadrant IV

$C(0, -3)$: On the y axis, 3 units downward. It is not in any quadrant.

Try These

1. In which quadrant would you find the point (3,4)? (−3, −4)? (3, −4)? (−3, 4)?   I, III, IV, II

2. What is the abscissa of the point (4,6)? What is its ordinate?   4, 6

134   Chapter 4

3. In which quadrant are abscissas and ordinates both positive? both negative? the abscissa positive and the ordinate negative? the abscissa negative and the ordinate positive? <small>I, III, IV, II</small>

4. Points on the coordinate axes do <u>not</u> lie in quadrants. On which axis is the point (0, 3)? (3, 0)? (−3, 0)? (0, −3)? <small>y axis, x axis, x axis, y axis</small>

5. What are the coordinates of the origin? <small>(0, 0)</small>

Exercises :

Write the coordinates of each point on the graph.

1. A <small>(3, 5)</small>   **2.** B <small>(−4, −4)</small>

3. C <small>(−7, 3)</small>   **4.** D <small>(7, 2½)</small>

5. E <small>(−4, 5½)</small>   **6.** F <small>(−6½, −6)</small>

7. G <small>(2½, −5½)</small>   **8.** H <small>(−6, 0)</small>

9. I <small>(0, −4)</small>   **10.** J <small>(5, 0)</small>

11. K <small>(0, 3)</small>   **12.** L <small>(3, −2)</small>

Graph the following points on the same pair of coordinate axes.

<small>For Ex. 13-24, start at origin and move the given number of units in the given direction.</small>

13. A(3, 5) <small>3 right, 5 up</small>   **14.** B(−2, 1) <small>2 left, 1 up</small>   **15.** C(3, −2) <small>3 right, 2 down</small>   **16.** D(−1, −4) <small>1 left, 4 down</small>

17. E(6, 0) <small>6 right</small>   **18.** F(0, −5) <small>5 down</small>   **19.** G(0, 0) <small>G is the origin.</small>   **20.** H(−3, 0) <small>3 left</small>

21. I(0, 4) <small>4 up</small>   **22.** J(2, 3) <small>2 right, 3 up</small>   **23.** K(−4, 3/2) <small>4 left, 1½ up</small>   **24.** L(4, −4) <small>4 right, 4 down</small>

25. Locate several points on the x axis. What is the ordinate, or y value, of these points? What is the ordinate of every point on the x axis? <small>0; 0</small>

26. Locate several points on the y axis. What is the abscissa, or x value, of these points? What is the abscissa of every point on the y axis? <small>0; 0</small>

27. Describe the graph of the set of all ordered pairs of real numbers whose ordinates are 8; whose ordinates are −2; whose ordinates are 0. <small>Straight line parallel to, and 8 units above x axis; straight line parallel to, and 2 units below x axis; x axis.</small>

28. Describe the graph of the set of ordered pairs of real numbers whose abscissas are 3; whose abscissas are −1; whose abscissas are 0. <small>Straight line parallel to, and 3 units right of y axis; straight line parallel to, and 1 unit left of y axis; y axis.</small>

29. Describe the graph of the set of ordered pairs of real numbers whose abscissas and ordinates are equal. <small>Straight line through (0, 0) and (1, 1).</small>

30. Describe the graph of the set of ordered pairs of real numbers whose abscissas and ordinates are additive inverses of each other. <small>Straight line through (0, 0) and (1, −1).</small>

In each of Exercises 31-34, the given coordinates represent the three vertices of a quadrilateral. Find the coordinates of the fourth vertex, D, so that ABCD is the required kind of quadrilateral. In Exercise 33, there are three possible locations for D. In Exercise 34, there are two possible locations for D.

31. $A(2, 2)$, $B(5, 2)$, $C(5, 4)$, rectangle $D(2, 4)$

32. $A(-2, -1)$, $B(-4, -1)$, $C(-4, -3)$ square $D(-2, -3)$

33. $A(-2, 4)$, $B(-4, 2)$, $C(-6, 2)$, parallelogram $D(-4, 4)$, $(0, 4)$, $(-8, 0)$

34. $A(3, 3)$, $B(5, 1)$, $C(8, 1)$, isosceles trapezoid $D(10, 3)$, $(3, 6)$

35. What are the coordinates of the point of intersection of the line passing through $(-2, -3)$ and $(4,3)$ and the line passing through $(3,0)$ and $(5, 2)$? No point of intersection.

36. Graph several ordered pairs of real numbers in Quadrant I and Quadrant II, such that the ordinate of each point equals the square of its abscissa. Connect the points with a smooth curve. Describe the graph. Parabola

37. Graph several ordered pairs of real numbers in Quadrant I and Quadrant II, such that the ordinate of each point equals the absolute value of its abscissa. Connect the points to the origin. Describe the graph.

38. What are the coordinates of the intersection point of lines ℓ_1 and ℓ_2, when ℓ_1 is parallel to the x axis and 5 units above it and ℓ_2 is parallel to the y axis and 6 units to the left of it? $(-6, 5)$

37. Two rays starting at the origin, one passing through $(1, 1)$ and the other passing through $(-1, 1)$.

Remember

Solve for x.

1. $|2x| = 5$ $\pm 2\frac{1}{2}$

2. $|x - 5| = 0$ 5

3. $|2x - 1| < 3$ $-1 < x < 2$

Simplify.

4. i^7 $-i$

5. $(3i - 1)(i + 2)$ $-5 + 5i$

6. $\sqrt{9 + 36}$ $3\sqrt{5}$

Tell which statements are true and which are false.

7. $\sqrt{7^2} = 7$ True

8. $\sqrt{a^2} = |a|$ True

9. $\sqrt{5} + \sqrt{7} = \sqrt{12}$ False

The answers are on page 176.

The objective for this section is on page 174.

The distance between points A and B on a number line is the length of $\overline{AB}$ (read: line segment AB or segment AB). The symbol AB represents the distance between A and B or the length of $\overline{AB}$. Since distance (or length) does not involve direction, it is always a nonnegative number.

Definition: The **distance between two points** P_1 and P_2, with real coordinates x_1 and x_2 on a real number line, is $|x_1 - x_2|$ or $|x_2 - x_1|$. That is,

$$P_1 P_2 = |x_1 - x_2| \quad \text{or} \quad |x_2 - x_1|.$$

Example 1   Find AB, BA, and AC.

A: 3
B: 11
C: −7

$AB = |3 - 11| = 8$
$BA = |11 - 3| = 8$
$AC = |3 - (-7)| = 10$

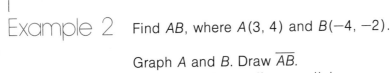

This definition and the Pythagorean Theorem can be used to find the distance between two points in the coordinate plane.

Example 2   Find AB, where $A(3, 4)$ and $B(-4, -2)$.

Graph A and B. Draw $\overline{AB}$. Through B, draw a line parallel to the x axis. Through A, draw a line parallel to the y axis. The intersection of these two lines is $C(3, -2)$.

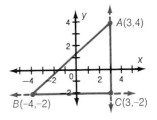

Coordinate Geometry   **137**

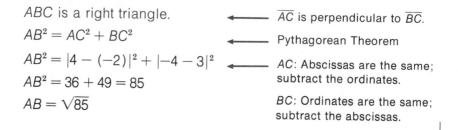

ABC is a right triangle. ⟵ —— $\overline{AC}$ is perpendicular to $\overline{BC}$.

$AB^2 = AC^2 + BC^2$ ⟵ —— Pythagorean Theorem

$AB^2 = |4 - (-2)|^2 + |-4 - 3|^2$ ⟵ —— AC: Abscissas are the same; subtract the ordinates.

$AB^2 = 36 + 49 = 85$

$AB = \sqrt{85}$ BC: Ordinates are the same; subtract the abscissas.

The example is generalized in the following theorem.

Theorem 4-1: Distance Formula for Two-Space

The distance between two points $P_1(x_1, y_1)$ and $P_2(x_2, y_2)$ is given by the formula.

$$P_1P_2 = \sqrt{(x_1 - x_2)^2 + (y_1 - y_2)^2}$$

Try These   *Find the distance between the points with these coordinates.*

1. $A(-2, 5)$, $B(-2, 0)$ 5
2. $A(7, -1)$, $B(-3, -1)$ 10
3. $A(7, -1)$, $B(-3, -11)$ $10\sqrt{2}$
4. $A(a, b)$, $B(3, 3)$ $\sqrt{(a-3)^2 + (b-3)^2}$

Exercises

Find the distance between the points with these coordinates.

1. $A(1, 2)$; $B(4, 3)$ $\sqrt{10}$
2. $A(-4, 1)$; $B(-5, 4)$ $\sqrt{10}$
3. $P(2, -6)$; $Q(7, -5)$ $\sqrt{26}$
4. $P(3, 6)$; $Q(-1, -2)$ $4\sqrt{5}$
5. $C(4, -3)$; $D(-4, 3)$ 10
6. $E(-3, 3)$; $F(0, -4)$ $\sqrt{58}$
7. $A(7, 1)$; $B(6, 2)$ $\sqrt{2}$
8. $H(5, 2)$; $I(2, 2)$ 3
9. $P(-2, -5)$; $Q(-2, 4)$ 9
10. $M(4, -3)$; $N(-1, -3)$ 5
11. $R(a, b)$; $S(c, d)$ $\sqrt{(a-c)^2 + (b-d)^2}$
12. $T(a, b)$; $U(c, b)$ $\sqrt{(a-c)^2}$, or $|a-c|$

Find the perimeter of each triangle whose vertices have the following coordinates.

13. $A(0, 8)$, $B(-6, 0)$, $C(15, 0)$ 48

14. $A(-3, -1)$, $B(1, 2)$, $C(1, -1)$ 12

15. $QR + RP \overset{?}{>} PQ$
$3\sqrt{5} + 3\sqrt{5} \overset{?}{>} 3\sqrt{10}$
$6\sqrt{5} > 3\sqrt{10}$
$QR = RP = 3\sqrt{5}$

15. Use the distance formula to show that $P(-4, 1)$, $Q(5, 4)$ and $R(2, -2)$ are the vertices of an isosceles triangle. See above.

16. Use the distance formula and the Pythagorean theorem to show that $A(-4, 1)$, $B(5, 4)$, and $C(2, -2)$ are the vertices of a right triangle.
$BC = \sqrt{45}; CA = \sqrt{45}; AB = \sqrt{90}; (BC)^2 + (CA)^2 \overset{?}{=} (AB)^2; 45 + 45 = 90$

17. Determine whether the triangle whose vertices are $C(-2, 3)$, $D(1, -1)$ and $E(3, 3)$ is isosceles, equilateral, or both. Isosceles

18. Determine whether the triangle whose vertices are $F(7, 3)$, $H(6, 9)$ and $L(2, 3)$ is isosceles or scalene. Scalene

19. Find the length of the diameter of a circle whose end points have the coordinates $A(3, 5)$ and $B(7, -4)$. $\sqrt{97}$

20. Find the length of the radius of a circle that has a center $O(-3, 4)$ and passes through $P(2, -5)$. $\sqrt{106}$

21. Find the lengths of the diagonals of a rectangle with vertices $P(-6, -5)$, $Q(5, -5)$, $R(5, -8)$ and $S(-6, -8)$. $PR = \sqrt{130}; SQ = \sqrt{130}$

22. Find the lengths of the diagonals of an isosceles trapezoid whose vertices are $A(-1, 5)$, $B(2, 5)$, $C(5, 2)$, and $D(-4, 2)$. $AC = \sqrt{45}; DB = \sqrt{45}$

23. Use the distance formula to show that $P(-1, -3)$, $Q(2, 1)$ and $R(5, 5)$ lie on a straight line. (HINT: Show that the longest distance is the sum of the two shorter distances.) $PQ = 5; QR = 5; RP = 10; PQ + QR = RP$. Therefore, P, Q, and R lie on a straight line.

24. Use the distance formula to show that the points $P(-2, 1)$, $Q(2, 2)$ and $R(-1, -1)$ do not lie on the same straight line. $RP = \sqrt{5}; PQ = \sqrt{17}; QR = \sqrt{18};$
$RP + PQ \neq QR$. Therefore P, Q, and R do not lie on a straight line.

25. Use the distance formula to show that $M(-1, 4)$, $N(-5, 3)$, $R(1, -3)$, and $Q(5, -2)$ are the vertices of a parallelogram. $NM = \sqrt{17}; RQ = \sqrt{17};$ thus, $NM = RQ$.
$NR = 6\sqrt{2}; MQ = 6\sqrt{2};$ thus $NR = MQ$. Since the opposite sides are equal, it is a parallelogram.

26. Write an equation to describe all points $P(x, y)$ in a plane that are r units from the origin. $\sqrt{x^2 + y^2} = r$

27. Prove that the lengths of the diagonals of a rectangle are equal. (HINT: Use $(0, 0)$, $(a, 0)$, (a, b), and $(0, b)$ as the consecutive vertices of the rectangle.) $D_1 = \sqrt{(0-a)^2 + (0-b)^2} = \sqrt{a^2 + b^2}; D_2 = \sqrt{(0-a)^2 + (b-0)^2} = \sqrt{a^2 + b^2}$. Therefore, $D_1 = D_2$

28. Show that the point $P_3\left(\dfrac{a+c}{2}, \dfrac{b+d}{2}\right)$ is equidistant from the points $P_1(a, b)$ and $P_2(c, d)$. $P_3P_1 = \frac{1}{2}\sqrt{a^2 + b^2 + c^2 + d^2 - 2ac - 2bd}; P_3P_2 = \frac{1}{2}\sqrt{a^2 + b^2 + c^2 + d^2 - 2ac - 2bd}$.
Since $P_3P_1 = P_3P_2$, P_3 is equidistant from P_1 and P_2.

Coordinate Geometry **139**

4-3 The Midpoint Formula

The objective for this section is on page 174.

The point on a line segment equidistant from the end points of the segment is the **midpoint** of the segment.

Example 1   Find the coordinates of M, the midpoint of $\overline{AB}$, given $A(-6, 0)$ and $B(3, 0)$.

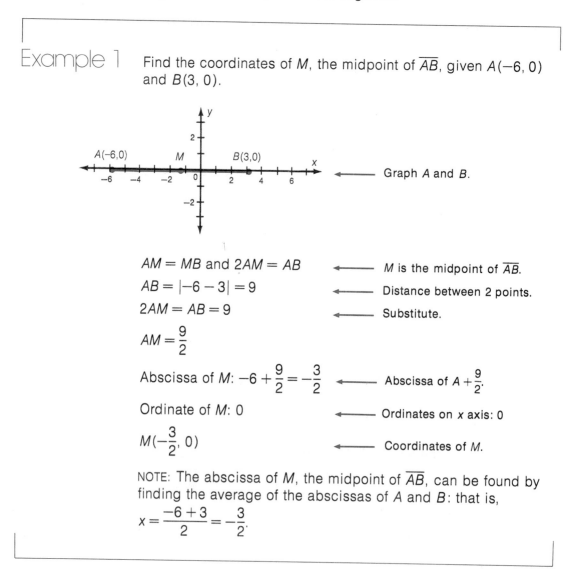

	Graph A and B.
$AM = MB$ and $2AM = AB$	M is the midpoint of $\overline{AB}$.
$AB = |-6 - 3| = 9$	Distance between 2 points.
$2AM = AB = 9$	Substitute.
$AM = \dfrac{9}{2}$	
Abscissa of M: $-6 + \dfrac{9}{2} = -\dfrac{3}{2}$	Abscissa of $A + \dfrac{9}{2}$.
Ordinate of M: 0	Ordinates on x axis: 0
$M(-\dfrac{3}{2}, 0)$	Coordinates of M.

NOTE: The abscissa of M, the midpoint of $\overline{AB}$, can be found by finding the average of the abscissas of A and B: that is,
$$x = \frac{-6 + 3}{2} = -\frac{3}{2}.$$

Example 2   Find the coordinates of M, the midpoint of $\overline{CD}$.

$CM = MD$ and $2MD = CD$ ◄——— M is the midpoint of $\overline{CD}$.

$CD = |7 - (-3)| = 10$ ◄——— Distance between 2 points.

$2MD = CD$ ◄——— Substitute.

$MD = \dfrac{10}{2} = 5$

Abscissa of M: 0 ◄——— Abscissas on y axis: 0

Ordinate of M: $-3 + 5 = 2$ ◄——— Ordinate of $M =$ Ord. of $D + 5$

$M(0, 2)$ ◄——— Coordinates of M.

NOTE: The ordinate of M is the average of the ordinates of the endpoints, C and D; that is, $y = \dfrac{7 + (-3)}{2} = 2.$

The following theorem from geometry is used in Example 3.

If a line is parallel to one side of a triangle and intersects the second side at its midpoint, it intersects the third side at its midpoint.

Example 3   Find the midpoint, $M(x, y)$, of $\overline{AB}$.

M_1 is the midpoint of $\overline{AC}$.

For M_1, $x_1 = 2$, $y_1 = \dfrac{8 + (-1)}{2} = \dfrac{7}{2}$.

M_2 is the midpoint of $\overline{BC}$.

For M_2, $x_2 = \dfrac{-6 + 2}{2} = -2$, $y_2 = -1$.

Draw $\overline{M_1 M}$ parallel to $\overline{BC}$, and $\overline{M_2 M}$ parallel to $\overline{AC}$.

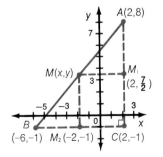

By the given theorem from geometry, $M(x, y)$ is the midpoint of $\overline{AB}$. The abscissa of M is the abscissa of M_2, and the ordinate of M is the ordinate of M_1. Thus the coordinates of the midpoint are:

$$M\left(-2, \frac{7}{2}\right)$$

Theorem 4-2: Midpoint Formula

The coordinates of the midpoint $M(x, y)$ of the line segment with endpoints $P_1(x_1, y_1)$ and $P_2(x_2, y_2)$ are

$$x = \frac{x_1 + x_2}{2} \qquad \text{and} \qquad y = \frac{y_1 + y_2}{2}.$$

Example 4 Find the coordinates of $M(x, y)$, the midpoint of the segment with endpoints $A(3, -5)$ and $B(-5, 11)$.

$$x = \frac{3 + (-5)}{2} = -1 \text{ and } y = \frac{-5 + 11}{2} = 3 \quad \longleftarrow \quad \text{Theorem 4-2.}$$

$M(-1, 3)$ $\quad\quad\quad\quad\quad\quad\quad\quad \longleftarrow \quad$ Coordinates of M.

Exercises

Find the coordinates of the midpoint of the segment with the given endpoints.

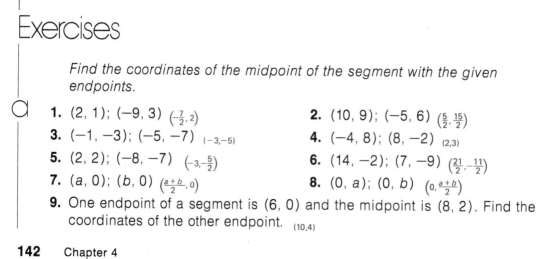

1. $(2, 1); (-9, 3)$ $\left(-\frac{7}{2}, 2\right)$
2. $(10, 9); (-5, 6)$ $\left(\frac{5}{2}, \frac{15}{2}\right)$
3. $(-1, -3); (-5, -7)$ $(-3,-5)$
4. $(-4, 8); (8, -2)$ $(2,3)$
5. $(2, 2); (-8, -7)$ $\left(-3,-\frac{5}{2}\right)$
6. $(14, -2); (7, -9)$ $\left(\frac{21}{2},-\frac{11}{2}\right)$
7. $(a, 0); (b, 0)$ $\left(\frac{a+b}{2},0\right)$
8. $(0, a); (0, b)$ $\left(0, \frac{a+b}{2}\right)$
9. One endpoint of a segment is $(6, 0)$ and the midpoint is $(8, 2)$. Find the coordinates of the other endpoint. $(10,4)$

10. One endpoint of a segment is $(-8, -12)$ and the midpoint is $(-4, -2)$. Find the coordinates of the other endpoint. $(0,8)$

11. Find the coordinates of the center of a circle, when the endpoints of one of its diameters are $(-8, 2)$ and $(10, -4)$. $(1,-1)$

12. If the center of a circle is $(3, 2)$ and one endpoint of a diameter is $(6, 6)$, what are the coordinates of the other endpoint? $(0,-2)$

13. Show that the diagonals of the parallelogram whose vertices are $P(1, 2)$, $Q(4, 2)$, $R(-4, -3)$, and $S(-1, -3)$ bisect each other. (HINT: Show that the midpoints of the diagonals coincide.) The midpoint of $\overline{RQ}$ and $\overline{PS}$ is $\left(0, -\frac{1}{2}\right)$. Thus, the diagonals bisect each other.

14. The vertices of a triangle are $A(4, 6)$, $B(-2, -4)$, and $C(-8, 2)$. Show that the length of the line segment that connects the midpoints of $\overline{AC}$ and $\overline{AB}$ is $\frac{1}{2}BC$. The midpoint of $\overline{AC}$ is $P(-2, 4)$. The midpoint of $\overline{AB}$ is $Q(1, 1)$. $PQ = 3\sqrt{2}$; $\frac{1}{2}BC = 3\sqrt{2}$. Thus, $PQ = \frac{1}{2}BC$.

15. Find the perimeter of the triangle formed by joining the midpoints of the sides of triangle ABC given $A(-3, 0)$, $B(5, 0)$ and $C(1, 8)$. $4(1+\sqrt{5})$

16. The vertices of a trapezoid are $A(2, 3)$, $B(-1, 3)$, $C(5, -1)$, and $D(-4, -1)$. Show that the length of the segment that joins the midpoints of the nonparallel sides is equal to one half the sum of the lengths of the parallel sides. The midpoint of $\overline{AC}$ is $M\left(\frac{7}{2}, 1\right)$. The midpoint of $\overline{BD}$ is $N\left(-\frac{5}{2}, 1\right)$. $NM = 6$. $BA = 3$; $DC = 9$; $\frac{1}{2}(BA + DC) = 6$. Thus, $MN = \frac{1}{2}(BA + DC)$.

17. Find the value of a and b if the coordinates of the endpoints of a segment are $(a - 3, b + 1)$ and $(a + 7, b + 17)$ and its midpoint is $(3, 3)$. $a = 1; b = -6$

18. The vertices of a triangle are $A(2, 3)$, $B(6, 9)$ and $C(10, -5)$. Find the length of the median from A to side BC. $\sqrt{37}$

19. Find the coordinates of a point P that divides the segment from $A(2, 3)$ to $B(12, 8)$ so that the ratio $\dfrac{AP}{PB} = \dfrac{2}{3}$. Check by using the distance formula.

(HINT: Consider $\overline{AB}$ the hypotenuse of right triangle ABC whose legs are parallel to the axes. The line that contains P and is parallel to the x axis intersects $\overline{BC}$ at some point $E(12, y)$. The line through P parallel to the y axis intersects $\overline{AC}$ at $D(x, 3)$. Then $\dfrac{AD}{DC} = \dfrac{2}{3}$ and $\dfrac{CE}{EB} = \dfrac{2}{3}$. $(6, 5)$

20. What are the coordinates of $P(x, y)$ that divides the segment from $C(5, 2)$ to $D(12, 16)$ so that the ratio $\dfrac{PC}{PD} = \dfrac{3}{4}$? Use the distance formula to check your answer. $(8, 8)$

21. Find the coordinates of $P(x, y)$ that divides the segment from $E(2, -4)$ to $F(9, 3)$ so that $\dfrac{PE}{PF} = \dfrac{2}{5}$. Check your answer by using the distance formula. $(4, -2)$

Mathematics and the Biological Sciences

PERSONS interested in careers in the biological sciences should have strong backgrounds in biology, chemistry, physics, and mathematics.

Biomedical engineers apply engineering principles to the solving of medical and health problems. They work closely with life scientists, chemists, and medical doctors in studying the engineering aspects of the biological systems of people and animals. Biomedical engineers have helped in the development of artificial hearts and kidneys, and of devices such as lasers and cardiac pacemakers.

Biochemists study the chemical composition of organisms and the changes caused by genetic and environmental factors. They apply the methods and techniques of biochemistry to other areas such as medicine or agriculture. A bachelor's degree with a major in biochemistry or chemistry is necessary for entry jobs in this field.

Biological oceanographers, or marine biologists, study plant and animal life in the ocean. They investigate the life processes of marine animals, particularly with respect to determining the effects of radioactivity and pollution on fish. A college degree in oceanography or biology is generally the minimum requirement for work in this field.

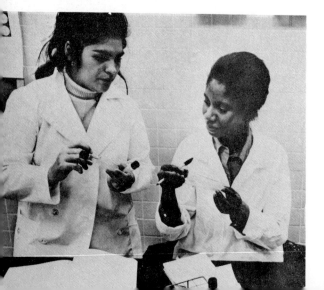

4-4 Slope of a Line

The objective for this section is on page 174.

Example 1   Find the grade of a road bed that rises 5 meters over a horizontal distance, or run, of 50 meters.

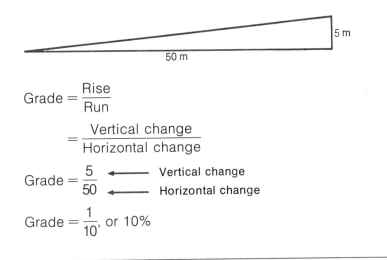

50 m   5 m

$$\text{Grade} = \frac{\text{Rise}}{\text{Run}}$$

$$= \frac{\text{Vertical change}}{\text{Horizontal change}}$$

$$\text{Grade} = \frac{5}{50} \quad \longleftarrow \text{Vertical change} \\ \longleftarrow \text{Horizontal change}$$

$$\text{Grade} = \frac{1}{10}, \text{ or } 10\%$$

In mathematics, the measure of the slant of a line is called **slope**. The slope of a line is a ratio calculated in much the same way as the grade of a road bed. In coordinate geometry, it is useful to give the slope of a line in terms of any two points on the line.

Definition: The **slope, m, of a line** that contains the points $P_1(x_1, y_1)$ and $P_2(x_2, y_2)$ is

$$m = \frac{y_2 - y_1}{x_2 - x_1}, \quad \text{or}$$

$$m = \frac{y_1 - y_2}{x_1 - x_2}, \quad x_1 \neq x_2.$$

Coordinate Geometry   **145**

Example 2 Find the slope of the line that contains the points $P_1(-2, 9)$ and $P_2(-5, -6)$.

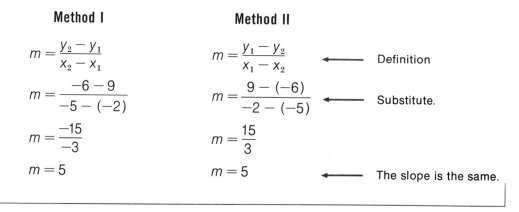

Method I | **Method II** |
$m = \dfrac{y_2 - y_1}{x_2 - x_1}$ | $m = \dfrac{y_1 - y_2}{x_1 - x_2}$ | ← Definition
$m = \dfrac{-6 - 9}{-5 - (-2)}$ | $m = \dfrac{9 - (-6)}{-2 - (-5)}$ | ← Substitute.
$m = \dfrac{-15}{-3}$ | $m = \dfrac{15}{3}$ |
$m = 5$ | $m = 5$ | ← The slope is the same.

The symbol Δy ("delta y") is generally used to represent the change in y, and Δx is used to represent the change in x.

$$m = \frac{y_2 - y_1}{x_2 - x_1} = \frac{\Delta y}{\Delta x} \quad \text{or} \quad m = \frac{y_1 - y_2}{x_1 - x_2} = \frac{\Delta y}{\Delta x}$$

Example 3 Find the slope of line q whose graph is given at the right.

Choose any 3 points on q.

$P_1(0,0) \qquad P_2(2,-1) \qquad P_3(-6,3)$

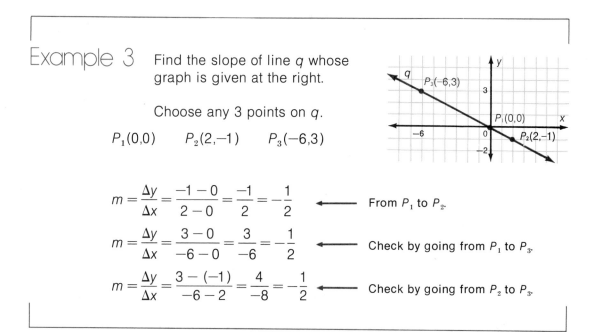

$m = \dfrac{\Delta y}{\Delta x} = \dfrac{-1 - 0}{2 - 0} = \dfrac{-1}{2} = -\dfrac{1}{2}$ ← From P_1 to P_2.

$m = \dfrac{\Delta y}{\Delta x} = \dfrac{3 - 0}{-6 - 0} = \dfrac{3}{-6} = -\dfrac{1}{2}$ ← Check by going from P_1 to P_3.

$m = \dfrac{\Delta y}{\Delta x} = \dfrac{3 - (-1)}{-6 - 2} = \dfrac{4}{-8} = -\dfrac{1}{2}$ ← Check by going from P_2 to P_3.

Example 4

Graph the line that has a slope of $-\dfrac{2}{3}$ and contains the point $R(-3, -1)$.

Graph $R(-3, -1)$.

$m = \dfrac{\Delta y}{\Delta x} = \dfrac{-2}{3}$.

Start at R. Move 2 units down; then 3 units to the right. Name this point $Q(0, -3)$.

Start at Q. Move 2 units down; then 3 units to the right. Name this point $P(3, -5)$.

Join P, Q, and R.

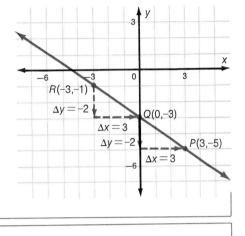

Example 5

Find the slope of line AB; of line CD.

Line AB: $m = \dfrac{\Delta y}{\Delta x} = \dfrac{2 - 0}{3 - 3} = \dfrac{2}{0}$

Line CD: $m = \dfrac{\Delta y}{\Delta x} = \dfrac{3 - 3}{-4 - 0} = 0$

The slope of the y axis or of a line parallel to the y axis is undefined. The slope of the x axis or of a line parallel to the x axis is zero.

Exercises

Find the slope of the line that contains the two given points.

1. $(6,3)$; $(4,1)$ ₁   **2.** $(3,4)$; $(9,12)$ $\frac{4}{3}$ **3.** $(-2,5)$; $(-4,11)$ -3 **4.** $(8,-3)$; $(-2,7)$ -1

5. $(-4,-6)$; $(2,-3)$ $\frac{1}{2}$ **6.** $(5,8)$; $(-3,-4)$ $\frac{3}{2}$ **7.** $(-3,5)$; $(4,7)$ $\frac{2}{7}$ **8.** $(2,-6)$; $(-1,9)$ -5

$m_1 = \frac{1}{5}, m_2 = \frac{3}{4}, m_3 = \frac{5}{3}, m_4 = 3, m_5$ is undefined, $m_6 = -3, m_7 = -\frac{5}{4}, m_8 = -\frac{2}{3}, m_9 = -\frac{1}{3}, m_{10} = -\frac{1}{7}$

Use the figure at the right for Exercises 9-13.

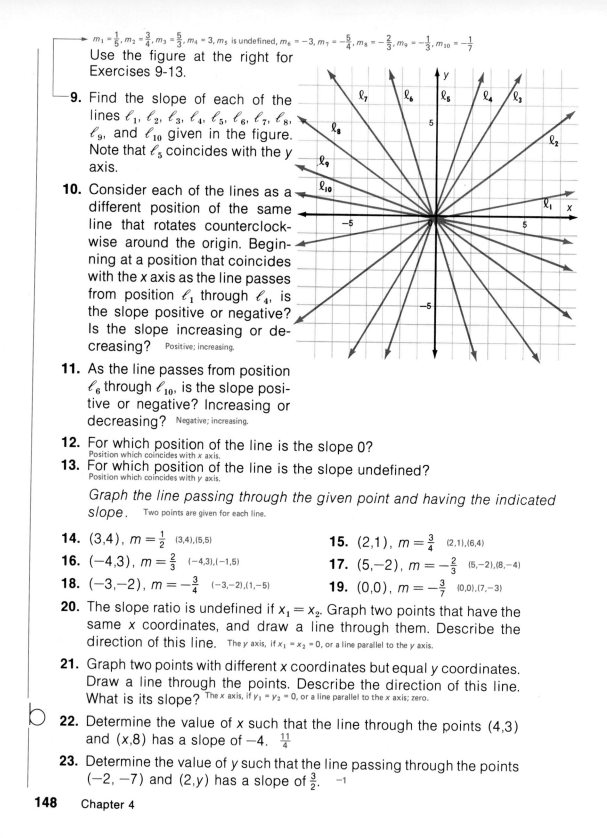

9. Find the slope of each of the lines $\ell_1, \ell_2, \ell_3, \ell_4, \ell_5, \ell_6, \ell_7, \ell_8,$ $\ell_9,$ and ℓ_{10} given in the figure. Note that ℓ_5 coincides with the y axis.

10. Consider each of the lines as a different position of the same line that rotates counterclockwise around the origin. Beginning at a position that coincides with the x axis as the line passes from position ℓ_1 through ℓ_4, is the slope positive or negative? Is the slope increasing or decreasing? Positive; increasing.

11. As the line passes from position ℓ_6 through ℓ_{10}, is the slope positive or negative? Increasing or decreasing? Negative; increasing.

12. For which position of the line is the slope 0?
Position which coincides with x axis.

13. For which position of the line is the slope undefined?
Position which coincides with y axis.

Graph the line passing through the given point and having the indicated slope. Two points are given for each line.

14. $(3,4)$, $m = \frac{1}{2}$ (3,4),(5,5)

15. $(2,1)$, $m = \frac{3}{4}$ (2,1),(6,4)

16. $(-4,3)$, $m = \frac{2}{3}$ (-4,3),(-1,5)

17. $(5,-2)$, $m = -\frac{2}{3}$ (5,-2),(8,-4)

18. $(-3,-2)$, $m = -\frac{3}{4}$ (-3,-2),(1,-5)

19. $(0,0)$, $m = -\frac{3}{7}$ (0,0),(7,-3)

20. The slope ratio is undefined if $x_1 = x_2$. Graph two points that have the same x coordinates, and draw a line through them. Describe the direction of this line. The y axis, if $x_1 = x_2 = 0$, or a line parallel to the y axis.

21. Graph two points with different x coordinates but equal y coordinates. Draw a line through the points. Describe the direction of this line. What is its slope? The x axis, if $y_1 = y_2 = 0$, or a line parallel to the x axis; zero.

22. Determine the value of x such that the line through the points $(4,3)$ and $(x,8)$ has a slope of -4. $\frac{11}{4}$

23. Determine the value of y such that the line passing through the points $(-2, -7)$ and $(2,y)$ has a slope of $\frac{3}{2}$. -1

Find the slope of the line that contains the following points.

24. $(a, b + c); (a + b, b + c)$ $\quad 0$ **25.** $(a, b); (a, b + c)$ $\quad$ *m is undefined*

26. $(a + b, c + d); (a - b, -c - d)$ $\frac{c+d}{b}$ **27.** $(2a, 3b); (a, -b)$ $\frac{4b}{a}$

28. Find the slopes of the sides of the triangle formed by joining the midpoints of the sides of a triangle whose vertices are $A(2,4)$, $B(6, -4)$, and $C(-4, -2)$. $\quad 1; -2; -\frac{1}{5}$

C **29.** Find x such that the points $A(-3, -4)$ $B(1, -2)$ and $C(x, 3)$ are collinear. $\quad 11$

4-5 Parallel and Perpendicular Lines

The objective for this section is on page 175.

Example 1   Show that the slopes of lines ℓ_1 and ℓ_2 are equal.

Choose two points on ℓ_1.
$P_1(-4,3) \qquad P_2(2,7)$
Through P_1 and P_2 draw lines parallel
to the y axis. These lines intersect
ℓ_1 and ℓ_2 at P_3 and P_4, respectively.
Find $P_3(x_3,y_3)$ and $P_4(x_4,y_4)$.
$P_1P_3P_4P_2$ is a parallelogram.
Thus, $P_1P_3 = P_2P_4$.
Let P_1P_3 and $P_2P_4 = c$.

$P_3(-4,3 - c); P_4(2,7 - c)$

$$m_1 = \frac{7 - 3}{2 - (-4)} = \frac{4}{6} = \frac{2}{3} \quad \longleftarrow \quad \text{Slope of } \ell_1$$

$$m_2 = \frac{7 - c - (3 - c)}{2 - (-4)}$$

$$m_2 = \frac{7 - c - 3 + c}{2 + 4} = \frac{4}{6} = \frac{2}{3} \quad \longleftarrow \quad \text{Slope of } \ell_2$$

Thus, $m_1 = m_2$, and the nonvertical parallel lines have the same slope.

Coordinate Geometry   **149**

Theorem 4-3

If two nonvertical lines are parallel, they have the same slope. Conversely, if two nonvertical lines have the same slope, they are parallel.

Example 2 Show that line, ℓ_1, which contains $A(-3, -4)$ and $B(5, -2)$ is parallel to line, ℓ_2, which contains $C(2,6)$ and $D(6,7)$.

$A(-3, -4)$ $B(5, -2)$ ⟵ Points on ℓ_1

$m_1 = \dfrac{-2 - (-4)}{5 - (-3)} = \dfrac{-2 + 4}{5 + 3} = \dfrac{2}{8} = \dfrac{1}{4}$ ⟵ Slope of ℓ_1

$C(2, 6)$ $D(6, 7)$ ⟵ Points on ℓ_2

$m_2 = \dfrac{7 - 6}{6 - 2} = \dfrac{1}{4}$ ⟵ Slope of ℓ_2

Since $m_1 = m_2$, line ℓ_1 is parallel to line ℓ_2.

Two numbers are **negative reciprocals** of each other if their product is -1. Since $-1 \times 1 = -1$, 1 and -1 are negative reciprocals.

Example 3 Two nonvertical perpendicular lines, ℓ_1 and ℓ_2, intersect at $P_1(4, 4)$. Show that their slopes are negative reciprocals.

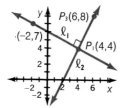

$m_1 = \dfrac{7 - 4}{-2 - 4} = \dfrac{3}{-6} = -\dfrac{1}{2}$ ⟵ Slope of ℓ_1.

$m_2 = \dfrac{8 - 4}{6 - 4} = \dfrac{4}{2} = 2$ ⟵ Slope of ℓ_2.

$m_1 \cdot m_2 = -\dfrac{1}{2} \cdot 2 = -1$ ⟵ Find $m_1 \cdot m_2$.

Thus, the slopes of the perpendicular lines are negative reciprocals.

Theorem 4-4

If two nonvertical lines are perpendicular, their slopes are negative reciprocals of each other. Conversely, if the slopes of two lines are negative reciprocals of each other, the lines are perpendicular.

Example 4   Show that line ℓ_1, which contains $A(0, 3)$ and $B(4, 0)$, is perpendicular to line ℓ_2, which contains $C(0, -2)$ and $D(3, 2)$.

$$m_1 = \frac{0-3}{4-0} = -\frac{3}{4} \quad \longleftarrow \quad \text{Slope of } \ell_1$$

$$m_2 = \frac{2-(-2)}{3-0} = \frac{4}{3} \quad \longleftarrow \quad \text{Slope of } \ell_2$$

$$m_1 \cdot m_2 = -\frac{3}{4} \cdot \frac{4}{3} = -1 \quad \longleftarrow \quad \text{Find } m_1 \cdot m_2.$$

Since $m_1 \cdot m_2 = -1$, the lines are perpendicular.

Try These   *Find the slope of all lines parallel to ℓ_1 and of all lines perpendicular to ℓ_1, if ℓ_1 contains the following points.*

1. $(2, 0)$; $(-4, 1)$ **2.** $(7, -3)$; $(4, 2)$ **3.** $(-4, 3)$; $(1, 7)$ **4.** $(0, 0)$; (a, b)

$m_1 = -\frac{1}{6}, m_2 = 6$ $m_1 = -\frac{5}{3}, m_2 = \frac{3}{5}$ $m_1 = \frac{4}{5}, m_2 = -\frac{5}{4}$ $m_1 = \frac{b}{a}, m_2 = -\frac{a}{b}$

Exercises

Classify the lines determined by the two pairs of points as parallel, perpendicular, or neither parallel nor perpendicular.

1. $(-2, 7)$, $(3, 6)$ and $(4, 2)$, $(9, 1)$ Parallel   **2.** $(0, 0)$, $(-5, 3)$ and $(5, 2)$, $(0, 5)$ Parallel

3. $(2, 5)$, $(8, 7)$ and $(-3, 1)$, $(-2, -2)$ Perpendicular   **4.** $(5, 3)$, $(-5, -2)$ and $(6, -2)$, $(4, 5)$ Neither

5. Determine y so that the slope of the line through $P(4, -2)$ and $Q(3, y)$ is -2. $y = 0$

6. Find the value of x so that the slope of the segment with endpoints at $M(x, 5)$ and $N(3, -1)$ is 4. $x = \frac{9}{2}$

7. The line that contains $E(a, 3)$ and $F(2, 0)$ is parallel to the line that contains $D(2, 8)$ and $C(-3, -4)$. Find a. $a = \frac{13}{4}$

8. Show that $P(-9, 3)$, $Q(2, 1)$, $R(8, 9)$, and $S(-3, 11)$ are the vertices of a parallelogram. The slope of $\overline{PQ}$ and $\overline{RS}$ is $-\frac{2}{11}$. The slope of $\overline{QR}$ and $\overline{PS}$ is $\frac{4}{3}$. Thus, the opposite sides are parallel.

9. Find the value of k if the line through $R(5, -3)$ and $S(0, k)$ is perpendicular to the line through $T(-3, 2)$ and $V(-2, -5)$. $k = -\frac{26}{7}$

10. Show that the triangle whose vertices have the coordinates $A(3, 2)$, $B(8, 16)$ and $C(11, 4)$ is a right triangle. (HINT: Prove that two of its sides lie on perpendicular lines.) The slope $\overline{BC}$ is -4; and for $\overline{AC}$ it is $\frac{1}{4}$. Since, the slopes are negative reciprocals, $\overline{BC}$ and $\overline{AC}$ are perpendicular.

11. Show that $P(-3, -1)$, $Q(-1, -3)$, $R(4, 2)$ and $S(2, 4)$ are the vertices of a rectangle. The slope of $\overline{PQ}$ and $\overline{RS}$ is -1. The slope of $\overline{QR}$ and $\overline{PS}$ is 1. Thus, the opposite sides are parallel, and are perpendicular since $-1 \times 1 = -1$.

12. Show that $A(2, 4)$, $B(1, 1)$ and $C(4, 0)$ are the vertices of an isosceles right triangle. $AB = \sqrt{10}$; $BC = \sqrt{10}$. Thus $AB = BC$. The slope of $\overline{AB}$ is 3, and $-\frac{1}{3}$ for $\overline{BC}$. Thus $\overline{AB}$ is perpendicular to $\overline{BC}$.

13. Determine the values of y so that $Q(0, y)$ is the vertex of the right angle of a right triangle whose other vertices are $S(-3, 1)$ and $R(-4, 8)$. $y = 4$ or $y = 5$

14. Show that $B(7, 1)$, $C(3, -4)$, $D(-2, 0)$, and $E(2, 5)$ are the vertices of a square. $BC = CD = DE = EB = \sqrt{41}$; The slope of $\overline{BC}$ and $\overline{DE}$ is $\frac{5}{4}$; for $\overline{DC}$ and $\overline{EB}$ it is $-\frac{4}{5}$. Thus, the four sides are equal and adjacent sides are perpendicular.

15. Show that $L(-3, 5)$, $Q(0, 2)$, $T(-2, -5)$, and $V(-10, 3)$ are the vertices of an isosceles trapezoid. Two opposite sides, $\overline{LQ}$ and $\overline{VT}$, are parallel, and the non-parallel sides, $\overline{TQ}$ and $\overline{VL}$, have the same length, $\sqrt{53}$.

16. Prove that the line segment joining the midpoints of two sides of a triangle is parallel to the third side and one half as long as the third side. Use $(0, 0)$, $(a, 0)$, and (b, c) as coordinates of the vertices of the triangle. See key.

17. Prove that the line segments that join the midpoints of consecutive sides of any quadrilateral form a parallelogram. See key.

18. Complete the following proof by supplying the missing reasons. See key.

Given: $\ell_1 \parallel \ell_2$, and m_1 the slope of ℓ_1, m_2 the slope of ℓ_2.
Conclusion: $m_1 = m_2$

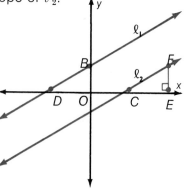

1. $\ell_1 \parallel \ell_1$
2. Construct $\overline{FE}$ perpendicular to the x axis at E.
3. $\angle ODB \cong \angle ECF$
4. $\triangle BOD$ and $\triangle FEC$ are right triangles.
5. $\triangle BOD \sim \triangle FEC$
6. $\dfrac{OB}{OD} = \dfrac{EF}{EC}$
7. $m_1 = m_2$

Remember

Simplify.

1. $a^2b^3 \div ab^4x$ $\frac{a}{bx}$

2. $2a^4b \cdot \dfrac{5b^3}{a}$ $10a^3b^4$

3. $\dfrac{5xy^2z}{2x^2y^2z^5}$

The answers are on page 176.

4-6 The Equations of a Line

The objective for this section is on page 175.

When you know the slope of a line and the coordinates of a point on the line, you can write the equation that defines the line.

Example 1   Write the equation of the line passing through the point $P(1, 2)$ and having a slope of 3.

$P(1, 2)$ ⟵   Given point.

$R(x, y)$ ⟵   Represent any other point.

$m = \dfrac{y - 2}{x - 1}$ ⟵   Write the slope.

$3 = \dfrac{y - 2}{x - 1}$ ⟵ $m = 3$; substitute.

$3(x - 1) = y - 2$, or $y - 2 = 3(x - 1)$

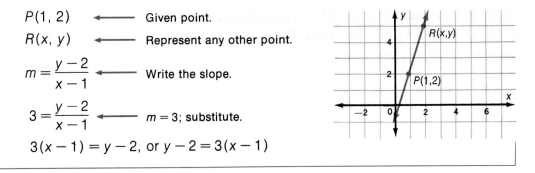

Theorem 4-5: Point-Slope Form of a Linear Equation

If the slope of a line is a real number, m, and a point $P_1(x_1, y_1)$ lies on the line, the equation of the line is

$$y - y_1 = m(x - x_1) \text{ for all } x, y \in R.$$

Conversely, $y - y_1 = m(x - x_1)$ where $x, y \in R$, defines a line whose slope is m and which contains the point $P_1(x_1, y_1)$.

Coordinate Geometry   **153**

Example 2 Write the equation of the line that contains the point $P(2, -3)$ and has slope $-\frac{1}{2}$. Graph the line.

$$y - y_1 = m(x - x_1)$$ ⟵ Theorem 4-5

$$y - (-3) = -\frac{1}{2}(x - 2)$$ ⟵ Substitute.

$$y + 3 = -\frac{1}{2}(x - 2)$$ ⟵ Simplify.

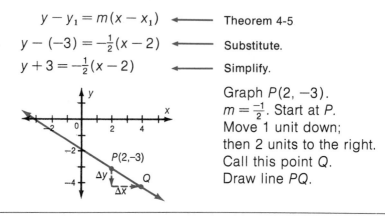

Graph $P(2, -3)$.
$m = \frac{-1}{2}$. Start at P.
Move 1 unit down;
then 2 units to the right.
Call this point Q.
Draw line PQ.

Two convenient points to determine and graph are the points in which a line intersects the x axis and the y axis. These are called the **x intercept** and the **y intercept,** respectively.

Example 3 Write the equation of the line that has slope m and y intercept at $(0, b)$.

$$P(0, b); \text{slope} = m$$ ⟵ P and m are given.

$$y - y_1 = m(x - x_1)$$ ⟵ Theorem 4-5.

$$y - b = m(x - 0)$$ ⟵ Substitute.

$$y = mx + b$$ ⟵ Solve for y.

Theorem 4-6: Slope-Intercept Form of a Linear Equation
If the slope of a line is m and its y intercept is $(0, b)$, the equation of the line is

$$y = mx + b, \text{ for } x, y, b \in R.$$

Conversely, $y = mx + b$ where $x, y, b \in R$ defines a line with slope m and y intercept $(0, b)$.

Example 4   Find the slope and y intercept of the line defined by $2x + 3y = 6$.
Graph the line.

$$2x + 3y = 6$$
$$3y = -2x + 6$$
$$y = -\tfrac{2}{3}x + 2 \qquad \longleftarrow \quad \text{Solve for } y.$$
$$y = \quad mx + b$$

Slope of the line: $-\dfrac{2}{3}$; y intercept: $(0, 2)$ $\longleftarrow$ $m = -\dfrac{2}{3}$; $b = 2$

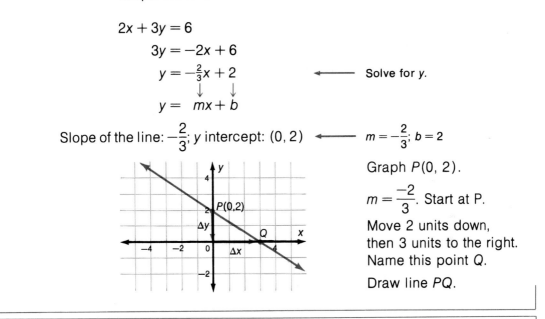

Graph $P(0, 2)$.

$m = \dfrac{-2}{3}$. Start at P.

Move 2 units down,
then 3 units to the right.
Name this point Q.

Draw line PQ.

Example 5   Write the equation of the line containing the points $R(1, 1)$
and $Q(5, 9)$.

$R(1, 1)$; $Q(5, 9)$ $\longleftarrow$ Given points

$m = \dfrac{9 - 1}{5 - 1} = \dfrac{8}{4} = 2$ $\longleftarrow$ Find m.

$y - y_1 = m(x - x_1)$ $\longleftarrow$ Theorem 4-5

$y - 9 = 2(x - 5)$ $\longleftarrow$ Substitute. $m = 2$; $Q(5, 9)$

$y - 9 = 2x - 10$ $\longleftarrow$ Solve for y.

$y = 2x - 1$ $\longleftarrow$ Slope-intercept form

The same equation would have been obtained if point $R(1, 1)$
had been used.

The equation of any line in the coordinate plane can be written
in **standard form**.

Theorem 4-7: Standard Form of a Linear Equation

Any line in the xy plane can be defined by an equation of the form

$Ax + By + C = 0$, where A, B, C, $\in R$ and A and B not both zero.

Conversely, $Ax + By + C = 0$, where A, B, C, $\in R$ and A and B not both zero, defines a line.

Try These

Use the given point and slope to write the equation of the line in slope-intercept form.

1. $P(0, 5)$; $m = -3$
$y = -3x + 5$

2. $(0, 0)$; $m = -\dfrac{3}{5}$
$y = -\frac{3}{5}x$

3. $(1 - 1)$; $m = 3$
$y = 3x - 4$

Rewrite each equation in slope-intercept form. Give the slope and y intercept of each line.

4. $3x - y = 5$
$y = 3x - 5; m = 3; (0,-5)$

5. $x - y = 0$
$y = x; m = 1; (0,0)$

6. $x + 2y - 5 = 0$
$y = -\frac{1}{2}x + \frac{5}{2}; m = -\frac{1}{2}; \left(0, \frac{5}{2}\right)$

Exercises

Use the given point and slope to write the equation of the line in slope-intercept form.

1. $P(5, 2)$; $m = 3$
$y = 3x - 13$

2. $Q(3, -5)$; $m = 2$
$y = 2x - 11$

3. $Q(-2, 7)$; $m = -3$
$y = -3x + 1$

4. $R(0, 3)$; $m = \dfrac{2}{3}$
$y = \frac{2}{3}x + 3$

5. $P(-2, 3)$; $m = -\dfrac{3}{2}$
$y = -\frac{3}{2}x$

6. $T(-3, 0)$; $m = -5$
$y = -5x - 15$

7. $A(3, -4)$; $m = 0$
$y = -4$

8. $S(-1, -5)$; $m = \dfrac{3}{4}$
$y = \frac{3}{4}x - \frac{17}{4}$

9. $T(-2, 4)$; $m = -\dfrac{4}{3}$
$y = -\frac{4}{3}x + \frac{4}{3}$

Rewrite each equation in slope-intercept form. Give the slope and y intercept of each line and draw the graph. Two points are given.

10. $2x + y = 4$
$y = -2x + 4; (0,4); (2,0)$

11. $3x - y = 8$
$y = 3x - 8; (0,-8); \left(\frac{8}{3}, 0\right)$

12. $x - 2y = 0$
$y = \frac{1}{2}x; (0,0); (2, 1)$

13. $2x + 3y = -6$
$y = -\frac{2}{3}x - 2; (0,-2); (-3,0)$

14. $3x + 4y = 12$
$y = -\frac{3}{4}x + 3; (0,3); (4,0)$

15. $2x - 6y = 2$
$y = \frac{1}{3}x - \frac{1}{3}; \left(0, -\frac{1}{3}\right); (1,0)$

Write the equation of the line containing each of the following pairs of points. Write your answer in the standard form, $Ax + By + C = 0$.

16. $A(3, 1)$; $B(5, 6)$
$5x - 2y - 13 = 0$

17. $P(-5, 3)$; $Q(8, 1)$
$2x + 13y - 29 = 0$

18. $R(-5, -2)$; $S(7, 5)$
$7x - 12y + 11 = 0$

19. $S(0, 0)$; $R(6, 8)$ $\frac{4}{3}x - y = 0$

20. $C(0, 0)$; $F(-5, 1)$
$\frac{1}{5}x + y = 0$

21. $F(0, 8)$; $C(8, 0)$
$x + y - 8 = 0$

22. $D(-5, -3)$; $G(0, 0)$
$\frac{3}{5}x - y = 0$

23. $B(5, 3)$; $D(5, 9)$
$x - 5 = 0$

24. $M(8, 0)$; $N(-4, 1)$
$x + 12y - 8 = 0$

Classify the graphs of the following pairs of equations as parallel (P), perpendicular (D), or neither parallel nor perpendicular (N).

25. $2x - 3y = 6$ and $10x - 15y = 6$ ^{P}

26. $5x + 4y = 0$ and $8x - 10y = 7$ ^{D}

27. $2x + 3y = 0$ and $x = \frac{2}{3}y$ ^{D}

28. $2x + 4y - 1 = 0$ and $x + 4y = 17$ ^{N}

Show that the graphs of the following pairs of equations are parallel.

29. $y = 2x + 8$ and $y - 2x = 5$
$m = 2$ for both

30. $3x + y = 0$ and $6x + 2y = 9$
$m = -3$

Show that the graphs of the following pairs of equations are perpendicular.

31. The slopes of the two lines are negative reciprocals, 2 and $-\frac{1}{2}$.

31. $y = 2x + 8$ and $2y + x = 1$

32. The slopes are negative reciprocals, -3 and $\frac{1}{3}$.

32. $3x + y = 4$ and $x - 3y = 4$

33. Write the equation of the line that contains the origin and is parallel to the line defined by the equation $2x + 3y = 5$. $y = -\frac{2}{3}x$

34. Write the equation of the line that contains $(3, -5)$ and is parallel to the graph of $3x + 4y = 12$. $y = -\frac{3}{4}x - \frac{11}{4}$

35. Write the equation of the line that contains $(-4, -7)$ and is perpendicular to the graph of $2x - 3y = 6$. $y = -\frac{3}{2}x - 13$

36. Write the equation of the line that contains the point $(3, 2)$ and is parallel to the x axis. $y = 2$

37. Write the equation of the line that is parallel to the y axis and contains the point $P(3, 2)$. $x = 3$

38. Write the equation of the line that is parallel to the x axis and 3 units below it. $y = -3$

39. Write the equation of the line parallel to the y axis and 7 units to the left of it. $x = -7$

40. Write the equations of 2 lines, both of which are equidistant from the x and y axes. $y = x, y = -x$

Let $A(3, -1)$, $B(-5, 5)$, and $C(2, 6)$ be the vertices of triangle ABC.

41. Find the equations of $\overleftrightarrow{AB}$, $\overleftrightarrow{BC}$, and $\overleftrightarrow{AC}$. $y = -\frac{3}{4}x + \frac{5}{4}; y = \frac{1}{7}x + \frac{40}{7}; y = -7x + 20$

42. What is the equation of the line parallel to $\overleftrightarrow{BC}$ through point A? $y = \frac{1}{7}x - \frac{10}{7}$

43. What is the equation of the line perpendicular to $\overleftrightarrow{AC}$ through point B? $y = \frac{1}{7}x + \frac{40}{7}$

44. What is the equation of the line perpendicular to $\overleftrightarrow{AB}$ through point C? $y = \frac{4}{3}x + \frac{10}{3}$

45. Write the equation of the median from vertex C to side AB. $y = \frac{4}{3}x + \frac{10}{3}$

46. Prove that the line in the xy plane whose x intercept is $(a, 0)$ and whose y intercept is $(0, b)$ is defined by

$$\frac{x}{a} + \frac{y}{b} = 1,$$

where $x, y, a, b \in R$ and $a \neq 0, b \neq 0$. This is the **intercept form** of the linear equation. The slope of the line is $-\frac{b}{a}$. Thus, $y - 0 = -\frac{b}{a}(x - a)$, or $y = -\frac{b}{a}x + b$ or $\frac{x}{a} + \frac{y}{b} = 1$.

Let the vertices of triangle ABC be A(3, 3), B(6, 2), and C(8, −2).

47. Find the equations of the lines that contain the altitudes of triangle ABC. $y = 3x - 26; y = \frac{1}{2}x + \frac{3}{2}; y = x - 4$

48. Find the equations of the perpendicular bisectors of the sides of triangle ABC. $y = 3x - 11; y = \frac{1}{2}x - \frac{7}{2}; y = x - 5$

Write each of the following in the standard form, Ax + By + C = 0. In each case, identify A, B, and C.

49. $y = mx + b$

$mx - y + b = 0$
$A = m, B = -1, C = b$

50. $\dfrac{y - y_1}{x - x_1} = m$

$mx - y - mx_1 + y_1 = 0$
$A = m, B = -1, C = -mx_1 + y_1$

51. $\dfrac{x}{a} + \dfrac{y}{b} = 1$

$bx + ay - ab = 0$
$A = b, B = a, C = -ab$

Remember

1. Write the expansion for $(a + b)^4$. $a^4 + 4a^3b + 6a^2b^2 + 4ab^3 + b^4$

2. Find the fourth term of $(x + y)^7$. $35x^4y^3$

3. Write the fifth term of $(a - b)^8$. $70a^4b^4$

The answers are on page 176.

PUZZLE

Hope and Winkie Peabody are both 90 years old. Katherine Hill, on the other hand, is one and a half times as old as she was when she was one and a half times as old as she was when she lacked 5 years of being half as old as she is now. How old is Katherine? 90

4-7 Algebraic and Geometric Models

The objective for this section is on page 175.

Example 1 Graph the compound sentence $x \geq 2$ <u>and</u> $y \geq \frac{1}{2}x - 3$.

Graph $x = 2$.
All points on the line $x = 2$ <u>and</u>
all points in the half-plane to
the right of $x = 2$ make $x \geq 2$ true.

Graph $y = \frac{1}{2}x - 3$.
Test for $y > \frac{1}{2}x - 3$. Try $(0, 0)$.
Is $0 > \frac{1}{2}(0) - 3$? Yes. Then
$y > \frac{1}{2}x - 3$ is the half-plane
above the line.

All points on the line $y = \frac{1}{2}x - 3$
<u>and</u> all points in the half-plane
above the line make $y \geq \frac{1}{2}x - 3$
true.

Graph $x \geq 2$ <u>and</u> $y \geq \frac{1}{2}x - 3$ on
the same set of axes.
The graph is the intersection
of the shaded regions.

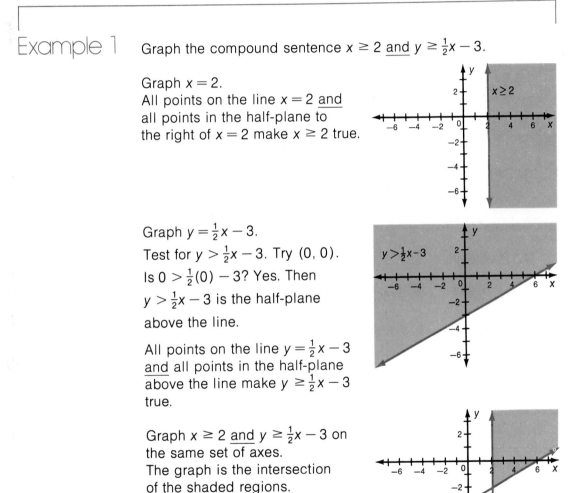

Both algebraic and geometric models can be found to represent word descriptions of some physical problems.

Example 2 Find a geometric and an algebraic model to represent all points in Quadrant I of the coordinate plane.

Draw the coordinate axes.

Shade Quadrant I. Neither the x axis nor the y axis belongs to the graph. The positive x and y axes are dashed to show this.

The algebraic model can be written in several ways.

$x > 0$ and $y > 0$ ◄────── Compound sentence.
$\{(x, y): x > 0$ and $y > 0\}$ ◄────── Set-builder notation.
$\{(x, y): x > 0\} \cap \{(x, y): y > 0\}$ ◄────── Intersection of sets.

► **6.** The set of all points in the coordinate plane that are 3 units or more below the x axis.

Try These *Write an algebraic model for each set of points.*

1. The set of all points in the coordinate plane that are 2 units to the left of the y axis. $x = -2$

2. The set of all points in the coordinate plane that are 3 units above the x axis. $y = 3$

3. The set of all points in the coordinate plane that are 3 or more units above the x axis. $y \geq 3$

4. The set of all points in Quadrant II of the coordinate plane. $x < 0$ and $y > 0$

5. The set of all points in Quadrant III of the coordinate plane. $x < 0$ and $y < 0$

7. The set of all points in the coordinate plane that are 3 units or more to the right of the y axis.

Give a word description of the geometric models in Exercises 6-8.

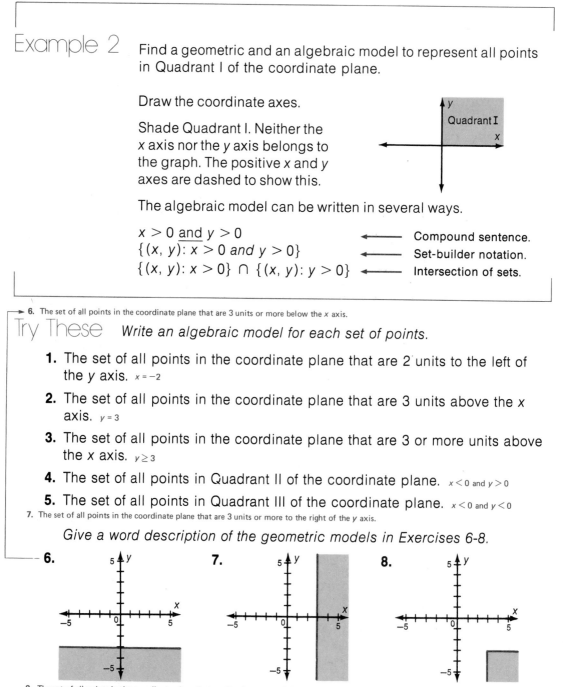

6. **7.** **8.**

8. The set of all points in the coordinate plane that are 3 units or more below the x axis and 3 units or more to the right of the y axis.

Exercises

In Exercises 1-20, draw a geometric model to represent each algebraic model. See key for Exercises 1-20.

1. $x = 2$

2. $y = 3$

3. $x \geq -2$

4. $y \leq -4$

5. $y = x$

6. $y = -x$

7. $y \geq 0$

8. $x \leq 0$

9. $y = 3x - 2$

10. $y = -2x + 5$

11. $x + 2y = 4$

12. $2x + y = 6$

13. $x + 3y < 6$

14. $-2x + y > 8$

15. $y \geq 2x - 3$

16. $y \leq -4x + 7$

17. $x \geq 3$ and $y \leq -2$

18. $x < -1$ and $y \geq 4$

19. $x + 3y \leq 6$ and $2x + y \geq 4$

20. $2x - y \leq 8$ and $x - 2y \geq -2$

In Exercises 21-28, draw a geometric model to represent each set of points.

21. The set of all points in the coordinate plane that are 4 units from the origin. All points on a circle of radius 4, centered on the origin.

22. The set of all points in the coordinate plane in the interior of the circle whose center is the origin and whose radius is 5 units. The interior of a circle of radius 5, centered on the origin.

23. The set of all points in the coordinate plane that are 6 units from the point $(3, -4)$. All points on a circle of radius 6 and centered on the point $(3,-4)$.

24. The set of all points in the coordinate plane with x coordinates between 1 and 4 and with y coordinates between 1 and 6. The interior of the rectangle whose sides are defined by the equations $x = 1$, $x = 4$, $y = 1$, $y = 6$.

25. The set of all points in the coordinate plane equidistant from the points $P(-4, 6)$ and $R(2, 6)$. All points on the line 1 unit left of the y axis.

26. The set of all points in the coordinate plane equidistant from the points $A(-2, 5)$ and $C(2, 1)$. All points on the line passing through the points $(0,3)$ and $(-3,0)$.

27. The set of all points in the coordinate plane that lie below the line on which the coordinates of every point are additive inverses. All points below the line passing through $(-1,1)$ and $(0,0)$.

28. The set of all points on a line that contains $Q(2, -3)$ and has a slope of $\frac{2}{5}$. All points on the line passing through $Q(2,-3)$ and $R(7,-1)$.

Coordinate Geometry **161**

Write an algebraic model for each of the following.

29. The points described in Exercise 21.
(HINT: The equation of a circle with center at the origin and radius r is $x^2 + y^2 = r^2$.) $\quad$ $x^2 + y^2 = 4^2$

30. The points described in Exercise 23.
(HINT: The equation of a circle with center at (h, k) and radius r is $(x - h)^2 + (y - k)^2 = r^2$.) $\quad$ $(x-3)^2 + (y+4)^2 = 6^2$

31. The points described in Exercise 25. $\quad$ $x = -1$

32. The points described in Exercise 26. $\quad$ $y = x + 3$

33. The points described in Exercise 27. $\quad$ $x + y < 0$

34. The points described in Exercise 28. $\quad$ $y = \frac{2}{5}x - \frac{19}{5}$

Remember

1. Simplify and rewrite in standard form: $i + 3 - 2i + 5$ $\quad$ $8 - i$

2. Write another name for $\sqrt{-1}$. $\quad$ i

3. Simplify: i^3 $\quad$ $-i$

4. Is it true that $3i + 1 = 3 + i$? $\quad$ No

The answers are on page 176.

PUZZLE

What is the smallest whole number which,
when divided by 10 leaves a remainder of 9,
when divided by 9 leaves a remainder of 8,
when divided by 8 leaves a remainder of 7,
when divided by 7 leaves a remainder of 6,
when divided by 6 leaves a remainder of 5,
when divided by 5 leaves a remainder of 4,
when divided by 4 leaves a remainder of 3,
when divided by 3 leaves a remainder of 2, and
when divided by 2 leaves a remainder of 1? $\quad$ 2519

4-8 Geometric Models of Complex Numbers

The objectives for this section are on page 175.

Every complex number can be written in standard form, $a + bi$, where a and b are real numbers. Every complex number can also be represented by an ordered pair of real numbers, (a, b), where a is the real number part of the complex number and b is the real number coefficient of i.

Standard Form	Ordered Pair Form
$3 + 4i$	$(3, 4)$
$1 - 5i$	$(1, -5)$
$-7 + i$	$(-7, 1)$
$0 + 6i$	$(0, 6)$
$6 + 0i$	$(6, 0)$
$x + yi$	(x, y)

The definitions stated in Chapter 1 can be written using ordered pair notation.

Definitions: For all real numbers a, b, c, and d,

$(a, b) = (c, d)$ if and only if $a = c$ and $b = d$;

$(a, b) + (c, d) = (a + c, b + d)$;

$(a, b) - (c, d) = (a - c, b - d)$;

$(a, b) \cdot (c, d) = (ac - bd, ad + bc)$;

$(a, b) \div (c, d) = \dfrac{(a, b)}{(c, d)} = \left(\dfrac{ac + bd}{c^2 + d^2}, \dfrac{bc - ad}{c^2 + d^2} \right)$

Example 1

Perform the indicated operations on the complex numbers.

a. $(3, 5) + (7, -8) = (3 + 7, 5 + (-8)) = (10, 5 - 8) = (10, -3)$

b. $(2, 3) \div (-3, 4) = \left(\dfrac{2(-3) + 3 \cdot 4}{(-3)^2 + (4)^2}, \dfrac{3(-3) - 2 \cdot 4}{(-3)^2 + (4)^2} \right) = \left(\dfrac{6}{25}, \dfrac{-17}{25} \right)$

Each point on the coordinate plane is associated with an ordered pair of real numbers and each ordered pair of real numbers can be associated with a complex number. Therefore, each point on the coordinate plane can be associated with a complex number.

Example 2   Name the complex number associated with each point on the **complex number plane.** The **real axis** represents complex numbers of the form $(a, 0)$. The **imaginary axis** represents complex numbers of the form $(0, b)$.

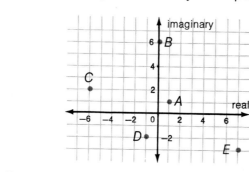

Coordinate	Complex Number
$P(1, 5)$	$1 + 5i$ or $(1, 5)$
$Q(3, -4)$	$3 - 4i$ or $(3, -4)$
$R(-4, 0)$	$-4 + 0i$ or $(-4, 0)$
$T(0, 3)$	$0 + 3i$ or $(0, 3)$

Try These

1. Write an ordered pair to identify each point.

$A(1,1)$
$B(0,6)$
$C(-6,2)$
$D(-1,-2)$
$E(7,-3)$

In Exercises 2–9, find the value of the variable that makes the sentence true.

2. $(x, 2) = (3, 2)$ $\quad x = 3$

3. $(-3, 5) = (-3, y)$ $\quad y = 5$

4. $(x, y) = (6, -2)$ $\quad x = 6, y = -2$

5. $(-2, y) = (x, -3)$ $\quad x = -2, y = -3$

6. $(5, 12) = (x, y) + (5, 12)$ $\quad x = 0, y = 0$

7. $(-3, y) + (x, 4) = (0, 0)$
$\quad x = 3, y = -4$

8. $(3, 6) \cdot (1, 0) = (3, y)$ $\quad y = 0$

9. $(2, 7) \cdot (x, 0) = (-2, -7)$ $\quad x = -1$

Exercises

Perform the indicated operations

a
1. $(5, 2) + (4, 3)$ (9, 5)

2. $(-6, 3) + (-2, -3)$ (-8, 0)

3. $(-1, 4) - (3, -6)$ (-4, 10)

4. $(-1, 6) + (3, -2)$ (2, 4)

5. $(25, 36) + (-16, 42)$ (9, 78)

6. $(2, 10) - (-2, -10)$ (4, 20)

7. $(4, 3) - (-3, -4)$ (7, 7)

8. $(5, -4) + (6, 2)$ (11, -2)

9. $(5, 3) \cdot (1, 1)$ (2, 8)

10. $(1, 2) \cdot (2, 3)$ (-4, 7)

11. $(1, -1) \cdot (2, 1)$ (3, -1)

12. $(1, 0) \cdot (0, 1)$ (0, 1)

13. $(0, 1) \cdot (0, 1)$ (-1, 0)

14. $(0, 1) \cdot (0, 1) \cdot (0, 1)$ (0, -1)

15. $(0, 1) \cdot (0, 1) \cdot (0, 1) \cdot (0, 1)$ (1, 0)

16. $(2, 1) \div (1, 2)$ $\left(\frac{4}{5}, -\frac{3}{5}\right)$

17. $(-1, 2) \cdot (2, -2)$ (2, 6)

18. $(3, 4) \cdot (-3, 1)$ (-13, -9)

19. $(x, y) \cdot (c, d)$ (cx− dy, cy + dx)

20. $(-1, -6) \div (2, 3)$ $\left(-\frac{20}{13}, -\frac{9}{13}\right)$

Write each complex number graphed below in a + bi form.

21. A A(3, 2); 3 + 2i

22. B B(−5, 1); −5 + 1 · i

23. C C(15, −5); 15 − 5i

24. D D(0, 6); 0 + 6i

25. E E(−13, −4); −13 − 4i

26. F F(11, 0); 11 + 0i

27. G G(−8, 5); −8 + 5i

28. H H(7, −6); 7 − 6i

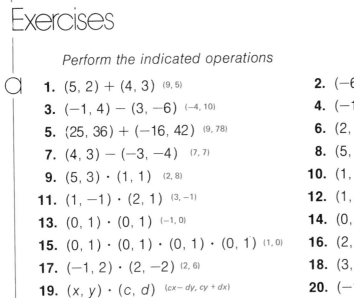

Graph each of the following on the complex plane. For Ex. 29-40, move the given number of units in the given directions, starting at the origin.

29. $(2, 4)$ 2 right; 4 up

30. $(3, -5)$ 3 right; 5 down

31. $(-1, 2)$ 1 left; 2 up

32. $5 + 2i$ 5 right; 2 up

33. $2 - 7i$ 2 right; 7 down

34. $-4 + 6i$ 4 left; 6 up

35. $(-3, -3)$ 3 left; 3 down

36. $-7 - i$ 7 left; 1 down

37. $(0, 8)$ 8 up

38. 8 8 right

39. $2i$ 2 up

40. 0 0 = 0 + 0i; graph is origin

b
41. What ordered pairs of real numbers represent the additive and multiplicative identity element of set C, the set of complex numbers? Add. ident. element is (0, 0); Mult. ident. element is (1, 0).

42. What ordered pair of real numbers represents the imaginary unit? (0, 1)

4-9 Numbers and Vectors

The objectives for this section are on page 175.

Numbers, both real and complex, can be represented by **directed line segments,** or **vectors.**

Example 1

Represent −3 as a vector in one-space.

Draw a number line.

Start at 0.
Move 3 units to the left.

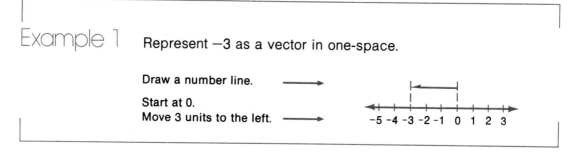

Vector a (symbolized as $\vec{a}$), vector b, and vector c each represent the number −3.

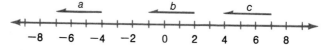

Therefore, $\vec{a}$, $\vec{b}$, and $\vec{c}$ are **equivalent,** as they are models of the same number.

Any complex number, $a + bi$, can be represented by the vector whose **initial point** is the origin and whose **terminal point** is the graph of the ordered pair (a, b).

Example 2

Represent $3 + 4i$ as a vector in the complex plane.

Graph $P(3, 4)$.

Join the origin to P.

The vector is named by its initial and terminal points as $\overrightarrow{OP}$, or as $\vec{z}$, or simply as $(3, 4)$.

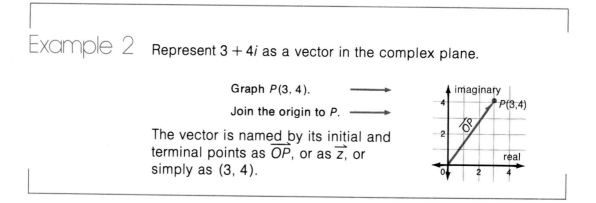

In the complex number plane also, equivalent vectors are models of the same number. Equivalent vectors can have different initial and terminal points. However, they must have the same direction.

Example 3 Find the complex number that each vector in the figure represents. Tell which vectors are equivalent.

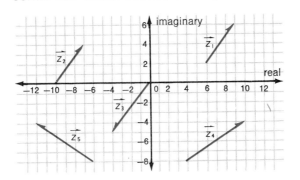

Vector	Initial Point	Terminal Point	Horizontal Change	Vertical Change	Complex Number
$\vec{z}_1$	(6, 2)	(9, 6)	3	4	(3, 4)
$\vec{z}_2$	(−10, 0)	(−7, 4)	3	4	(3, 4)
$\vec{z}_3$	(0, 0)	(−4, −5)	−4	−5	(−4, −5)
$\vec{z}_4$	(4, −8)	(10, −4)	6	4	(6, 4)
$\vec{z}_5$	(−6, −8)	(−12, −4)	−6	4	(−6, 4)

Equivalent vectors: $\vec{z}_1$ and $\vec{z}_2$

Example 4 Find the length of the vector (3, 4). Use the distance formula.

Graph the relation.
Initial point: $O(0, 0)$
Terminal point: $P(3, 4)$

Length of $\overrightarrow{OP}$:
$$\sqrt{(4-0)^2 + (3-0)^2} = \sqrt{16 + 9} = 5$$

The symbol $|3 + 4i|$, read "the absolute value of $3 + 4i$," represents the length of the vector $3 + 4i$. Thus, $|3 + 4i| = 5$. In general, if $a + bi$ is a complex number whose geometric model is the vector (a, b),

$$\text{length of } (a, b) = \sqrt{a^2 + b^2} = |a + bi|.$$

Remember! Vectors are equivalent if and only if they have the same length <u>and</u> direction.

Example 5

Find which complex number each vector in the figure represents. Find the length of each vector.

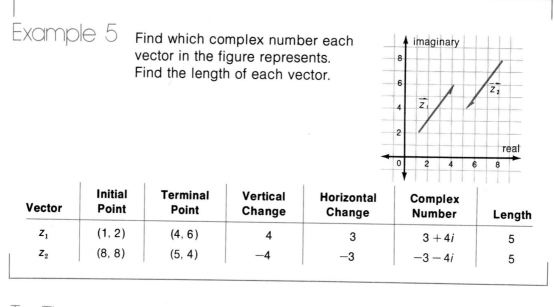

Vector	Initial Point	Terminal Point	Vertical Change	Horizontal Change	Complex Number	Length
z_1	(1, 2)	(4, 6)	4	3	$3 + 4i$	5
z_2	(8, 8)	(5, 4)	−4	−3	$-3 - 4i$	5

Try These

Graph each pair of vectors. Classify each pair as equivalent (E), having the same length (L), or having the same direction (D).

1. $(5, -2); (15, -6)$ D

2. $(2, 1); (-2, 1)$ L

3. $(8, 6); (10, 0)$ L

4. $(3, -2); (3, -2)$ L, D, E

5. $(-9, 12); (-6, 8)$ D

6. $(15, 0); (9, 12)$ L

Exercises

Using the origin as the initial point, graph the following complex numbers as vectors.   A vector from (0,0) to:

1. $3 - 7i$ (3,−7)   **2.** $-2 + 6i$ (−2,6)   **3.** $3i$ (0,3)   **4.** -3 (−3,0)   **5.** $-4i$ (0,−4)   **6.** $-2 - 5i$ (−2,−5)

7. Beginning at $P(-2, 1)$, graph a vector model of each of the complex numbers of Exercises 1–6. A vector from $(-2,1)$ to: $(1,-6)$; $(-4,7)$; $(-2,4)$; $(-5,1)$; $(-2,-3)$; $(-4,-4)$

In Exercises 8–13, graph a vector beginning at (0, 0) that is equivalent to the vector from A to B. Write the complex number represented by your vector in a + bi form. The terminal point is given.

8. $A(2, -3)$; $B(4, -7)$ $(2, -4); 2 - 4i$
9. $A(-3, -5)$; $B(2, 1)$ $(5, 6); 5 + 6i$
10. $A(2, 1)$; $B(-3, -2)$ $(-5, -3); -5 - 3i$

11. $A(3, -5)$; $B(3, -2)$ $(0, 3); 0 + 3i$
12. $A(1, 2)$; $B(-4, 3)$ $(-5, 1); -5 + i$
13. $A(2, -5)$; $B(-3, -5)$ $(-5, 0); -5 + 0i$

Determine the complex number associated with each vector. Then find the length of the vector.

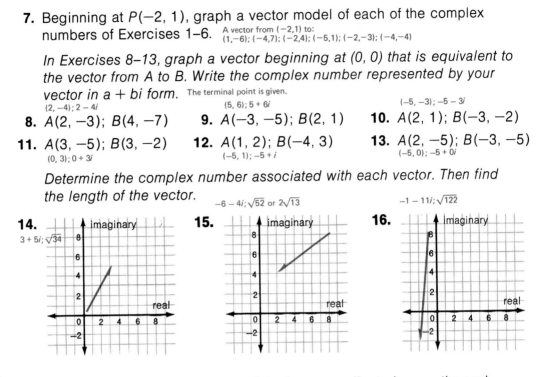

14. $3 + 5i; \sqrt{34}$

15. $-6 - 4i; \sqrt{52}$ or $2\sqrt{13}$

16. $-1 - 11i; \sqrt{122}$

17. Given a vector that starts at a point whose coordinate is a on the real number line and that ends at a point whose coordinate is b, tell the real number with which it is associated. $b - a$

18. Given a vector starting at a point (a, b) on the complex plane, and ending at a point with coordinates (c, d). Find the complex number with which it is associated. $(c - a, d - b)$

19. The slope of a vector is the slope of the line containing the vector. Determine formulas for the magnitude and slope of any vector associated with (x, y). Magnitude $= \sqrt{x^2 + y^2}$; Slope $= \frac{y}{x}$.

20. The vectors (a, b) and (c, d) have the same magnitude and slope, but different directions. Write a formula for c and d in terms of a and b. $(c, d) = (-a, -b)$

Remember

Simplify.

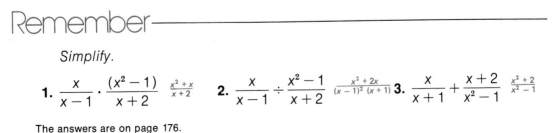

1. $\dfrac{x}{x - 1} \cdot \dfrac{(x^2 - 1)}{x + 2}$ $\frac{x^2 + x}{x + 2}$

2. $\dfrac{x}{x - 1} \div \dfrac{x^2 - 1}{x + 2}$ $\frac{x^2 + 2x}{(x - 1)^2 (x + 1)}$

3. $\dfrac{x}{x + 1} + \dfrac{x + 2}{x^2 - 1}$ $\frac{x^2 + 2}{x^2 - 1}$

The answers are on page 176.

4-10 Addition of Vectors

The objective for this section is on page 175.

Example 1 Find the sum of the complex numbers (5, 3) and (2, 6).

$$(5, 3) + (2, 6) = (5 + 2, 3 + 6) \longleftarrow \text{Definition}$$
$$= (7, 9)$$

Addition of vectors is defined to obtain the same result.

Example 2 Use vectors to find the sum of the complex numbers (5, 3) and (2, 6).

Graph $P(5, 3)$. Draw $\overrightarrow{OP}$.

$\overrightarrow{OP}$ represents (5, 3).

Start at P. Move 2 units to the right and 6 units up. Call the point Q.
$\overrightarrow{PQ}$ represents (2, 6).

Draw $\overrightarrow{OQ}$. $\overrightarrow{OQ}$ represents $\overrightarrow{OP} + \overrightarrow{PQ}$.

$\overrightarrow{OP} + \overrightarrow{PQ} = \overrightarrow{OQ} \longrightarrow (5, 3) + (2, 6) = (7, 9)$

Check: Is $\overrightarrow{OQ}$ the vector (7, 9)? Yes.

Definition: To <u>add two vectors</u>, place the initial point of the second vector at the terminal point of the first. The sum of two vectors so placed is the vector with the same initial point as the first vector and with the same terminal point as the second vector.

---

170   Chapter 4

Example 3   Use vectors to find $(9, 7) + (-6, 2)$.

Graph $P(9, 7)$. *Draw* $\overrightarrow{OP}$.

$\overrightarrow{OP}$ represents $(9, 7)$.

Start at P. Move 6 units to
the left and 2 units up.
Call the point Q.
$\overrightarrow{PQ}$ represents $(-6, 2)$.

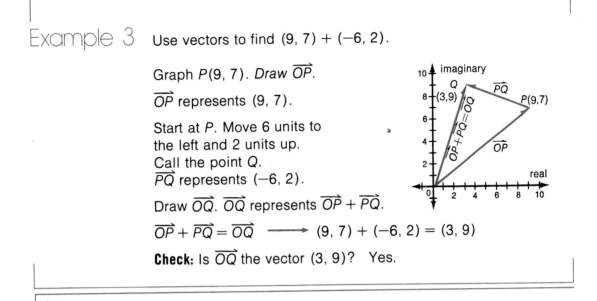

Draw $\overrightarrow{OQ}$. $\overrightarrow{OQ}$ represents $\overrightarrow{OP} + \overrightarrow{PQ}$.

$\overrightarrow{OP} + \overrightarrow{PQ} = \overrightarrow{OQ}$ ⟶ $(9, 7) + (-6, 2) = (3, 9)$

Check: Is $\overrightarrow{OQ}$ the vector $(3, 9)$?   Yes.

Exercises

1. Draw the first vector, (3,2), from (0,0) to (3,2). Draw the second vector, (−1,5), from (3,2); it will terminate at (−1 + 3, 5 + 2), or (2,7). Thus, (3 + 2i) + (−1 + 5i) = 2 + 7i. The length of the vector for the sum is $\sqrt{2^2 + 7^2} = \sqrt{53}$.

Use vectors to find each sum. Find the length of the vector for each sum.

a
1. $(3 + 2i) + (-1 + 5i)$
2. $(-6 - 3i) + (-3 + 6i)$ $^{-9 + 3i;\ 3\sqrt{10}}$
3. $(5 - 6i) + (-4 + 2i)$ $^{1 - 4i;\ \sqrt{17}}$
4. $(10 + 3i) + (2 - 5i)$ $^{12 - 2i;\ 2\sqrt{37}}$
5. $(-4 - 2i) + (6i)$ $^{-4 + 4i;\ 4\sqrt{2}}$
6. $(-8 + 7i) + (5 - 4i)$ $^{-3 + 3i;\ 3\sqrt{2}}$
7. $(3, -1) + (-4, 0)$ $^{(-1,-1);\ \sqrt{2}}$
8. $(2, -3) + (4, -6)$ $^{(6,-9);\ 3\sqrt{13}}$
9. $(-7, 5) + (7, 5)$ $^{(0,10);\ 10}$
10. $(6, -1) + (-6, 1)$ $^{(0,0);\ 0}$
11. $(6, -1) + (-12, 1)$ $^{(-6,0);\ 6}$
12. $(9, 2) + (7, 6)$ $^{(16,8);\ 8\sqrt{5}}$
13. $(1, 0) + (-5, 0)$ $^{(-4,0);\ 4}$
14. $(2, 0) + (3, 0)$ $^{(5,0);\ 5}$
15. $(-3, 0) + (-1, 0)$ $^{(-4,0);\ 4}$
16. $(-3, 0) + (3, 4)$ $^{(0,4);\ 4}$
17. $(4, -3) + (-4, 3)$ $^{(0,0);\ 0}$
18. $(0 + 2i) + (0 - 5i)$ $^{0 - 3i;\ 3}$
19. $(0 + 0i) + (-2 - 4i)$ $^{(-2 - 4i);\ 2\sqrt{5}}$
20. $(2 - 3i) + (2 + 3i)$ $^{4 + 0i;\ 4}$

Find each sum geometrically.

b
21. What vector is the additive identity element? In which of Exercises 13–20 is this vector shown?   (0,0); Exercise 19

22. Show geometrically how to add the complex numbers $(2, 3)$, $(-1, -5)$, and $(2, -1)$.   See key.

Coordinate Geometry   **171**

Coordinate Geometry in Three-Space

In three-space, three mutually perpendicular axes, *x*, *y*, and *z*, determine three planes: the *xy* plane, the *xz* plane, and the *yz* plane. (See Figure 1.)

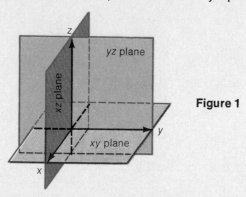

Figure 1

You use an **ordered triple,** (*x*, *y*, *z*), to locate a point in three-space. To graph points *A* and *B* in Figure 2, follow these steps.

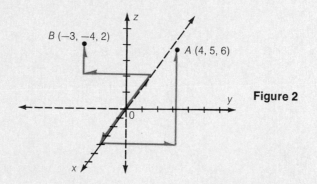

Figure 2

A(4, 5, 6)	*B*(−3, −4, 2)
1. Move 4 units from 0 along the positive *x* axis.	1. Move 3 units from 0 along the negative *x* axis.
2. Move 5 units in the direction of the positive *y* axis.	2. Move 4 units in the direction of the negative *y* axis.
3. Move 6 units in the direction of the positive *z* axis.	3. Move 2 units in the direction of the positive *z* axis.

You use the following formula to find the distance between two points $P_1(x_1, y_1, z_1)$ and $P_2(x_2, y_2, z_2)$ in three-space.

$$P_1P_2 = \sqrt{(x_2 - x_1)^2 + (y_2 - y_1)^2 + (z_2 - z_1)^2}$$

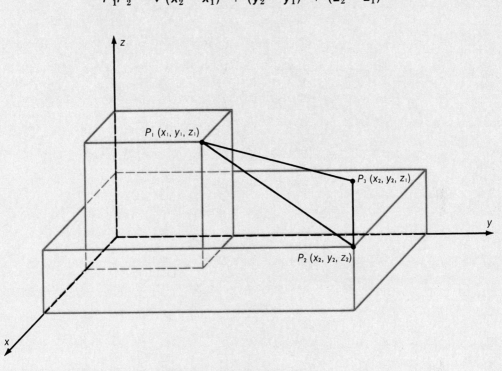

Figure 3

Can You Solve These?

Graph the following points in three-space.

1. $A(3, 4, 5)$ **2.** $B(-2, 4, -3)$ **3.** $C(-1, -6, 6)$

4. In Figure 2, verify that $AB = 12.1$ (to the nearest tenth).

5. In the xy plane, which coordinate is always zero?

6. Use Figure 3 to verify the distance formula for three-space.
(HINT: First find P_1P_3 in a plane parallel to the xy plane.)

Chapter Objectives and Review

Objective: To know the meanings of the important mathematical terms of this chapter.

1. Here are many of the mathematical terms used in this chapter. Be sure that you know their meanings and that you can use them correctly.

abscissa (p. 134)
absolute value of a
   complex number (p. 168)
addition of vectors (p. 170)
complex number plane (p. 164)
coordinate (p. 134)
distance formula (p. 138)
equivalent vectors (p. 166)
imaginary axis (p. 164)
initial point (p. 166)
midpoint formula (p. 142)

ordinate (p. 134)
point-slope form of
   the linear equation (p. 153)
real axis (p. 164)
slope (p. 145)
slope-intercept form of
   the linear equation (p. 154)
standard form of the
   linear equation (p. 156)
terminal point (p. 166)
vector (p. 166)

Objectives: To write the coordinates of a point in two-space, and to graph a point in two-space. (Section 4-1) For Ex. 2-5, start at the origin and move the given number of units in the given direction.

Graph the following points on the same set of coordinates.

2. $A(-3, 5)$ **3.** $B(2, -3\frac{1}{2})$ **4.** $C(0, -3)$ **5.** $D(7, 0)$
  3 left, 5 up   2 right, $3\frac{1}{2}$ down   3 down   7 right

Objective: To find the distance between two points in the coordinate plane. (Section 4-2)

Find the distance between the points with these coordinates.

6. $(7, 3)$; $(-1, -3)$ **7.** $(-11, 5)$; $(-16, 5)$ **8.** $(-3, -3)$; $(1, 2)$ **9.** $(0, 5)$; $(5, 0)$
    10   5 $\sqrt{41}$ $5\sqrt{2}$

Objective: To find the coordinates of the midpoint of a segment given the coordinates of its endpoints. (Section 4-3)

Find the coordinates of the midpoint of the segment with the given endpoints.

10. $(2, 5)$; $(-4, 3)$ **11.** $(-2, -3)$; $(1, -4)$ **12.** $(-3, 2)$; $(-3, 5)$ **13.** $(0, 4)$; $(5, 0)$
  (−1,4)   See below.   See below.   See below.

Objective: To find the slope of a line given two points. (Section 4-4)

11. $\left(-\frac{1}{2}, -\frac{7}{2}\right)$ **12.** $\left(-3, \frac{7}{2}\right)$ **13.** $\left(\frac{5}{2}, 2\right)$

Find the slope of the line that contains the two given points.

14. $(-3, 2)$; $(5, -7)$ $-\frac{9}{8}$ **15.** $(-7, 2)$; $(3, 2)$ $_0$ **16.** $(\frac{1}{2}, 3)$; $(\frac{3}{4}, 2)$ $_{-4}$ **17.** $(3, -4)$; $(3, -7)$ undefined

Objective: To use the relation between the slopes of parallel lines and of perpendicular lines. (Section 4-5)

18. The slope of line p is 3. What is the slope of line q and line r if lines q and r are parallel and line r is perpendicular to line p?

slope of r is $-\frac{1}{3}$; slope of q is also $-\frac{1}{3}$

Objective: To determine an equation of a line and to write it in standard form given **(a)** a point on the line and the slope of the line, or **(b)** two points on the line, or **(c)** the slope and y intercept of the line. (Section 4-6)

For each exercise, use the given data to determine an equation of line q. Write the equation in standard form.

19. The point $(2, -3)$ is on line q and the slope of line q is 3. $3x - y - 9 = 0$

20. Line q contains the points $(3, -3)$ and $(6, 1)$. $4x - 3y - 21 = 0$

21. The y intercept of the graph of line q is at $(0, 6)$ and the slope is $\frac{1}{2}$. $x - 2y + 12 = 0$

Objective: To graph linear equations and inequalities. (Section 4-7)

Draw the graph of each sentence. The points on the line passing through $(0,3)$ and $(1,5)$, to the right of, and including, the point $(-2,-1)$.

22. $y \geq 2x - 1$ and $y \leq -3x - 1$ **23.** $y = 2x + 3$ and $y \geq -\frac{1}{2}x - 2$

see below

Objective: To add, subtract, multiply, and divide two complex numbers given as ordered pairs. (Section 4-8)

Perform the indicated operation.

24. $(-12, 4) + (5, -1)$ $(-7,3)$ **25.** $(5, -2) \div (1, 3)$ $\left(-\frac{1}{10}, -\frac{17}{10}\right)$

Objective: To graph complex numbers as a point or as a vector in the complex plane. (Sections 4–8 and 4–9)

Graph each complex number as a point in the complex plane. Then graph each as a vector in another complex plane.

2 right, 3 down

26. $2 - 3i$ **27.** $-5 + 6i$ 4 left, 2 down **28.** $-4 - 2i$ **29.** $5 + 2i$

5 left, 6 up   5 right, 2 up

Objective: To find the length of a vector (a, b). (Section 4-9)

Find the length of each vector.

30. $(3, 2)$ $\sqrt{13}$ **31.** $(3, -2)$ $\sqrt{13}$ **32.** $(-5, 4)$ $\sqrt{41}$ **33.** $(-6, -3)$ $3\sqrt{5}$

Objective: To add vectors. (Section 4-10)

Use vectors to find each sum.

34. $(5 - 2i) + (-2 + 3i)$ $(3 + i)$ **35.** $(2, -5) + (0, -3)$ $(2,-8)$

22. All points on or above the line passing through $(0,-1)$ and $(1,1)$ and on or below the line passing through $(0,-1)$ and $(-1,2)$.

Coordinate Geometry   **175**

Complete each statement.

1. The abscissa of the point $A(2, -5)$ is _____2_____.

2. The slope of the line defined by $y = 3x - 5$ is _____3_____.

3. The coordinates of the y intercept of $y = -2x + 1$ are _____(0, 1)_____.

4. Two-dimensional vectors are a model for the set of ____complex____ numbers.

5. The axes on the complex coordinate plane are called the ____real____ axis and the ____imaginary____ axis.

6. Find the distance between the points $P(-3, 2)$ and $Q(5, -2)$. $4\sqrt{5}$

7. Find the midpoint of $\overline{AB}$ if its endpoints are $A(-3, 1)$ and $B(5, 7)$. $(1, 4)$

8. Give the slope of the line that contains the points $(-6, 5)$ and $(2, -3)$. -1

9. Find the slope of the line that is parallel to the line defined by $2x - y + 3 = 0$. 2

10. Find the slope of the line that is perpendicular to $3x + 2y + 4 = 0$. $\frac{2}{3}$

11. Write the equation of the line that contains the points $(2, 6)$ and $(4, 10)$. $y = 2x + 2$

12. Write the equation of the line that contains $(4, -1)$ and has a slope of 2. $y = 2x - 9$

13. Write the equation of the line having a slope of -3 and with its y intercept at $(0, 5)$. $y = -3x + 5$

14. Name the complex number represented by each vector in the figure at the right. $\overrightarrow{AB} = 1 + 3i,$ $\overrightarrow{OC} = -3 + i,$ $\overrightarrow{DE} = -1 - 5$

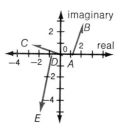

15. Graph $y = 2x$. A line that contains (0, 0) and (1, 2)

16. Graph $y > 2x - 6$. The half plane above the line defined by $y = 2x - 6$. The line is not included.

Answers to Remember

Page 136: **1.** $\pm 2\frac{1}{2}$ **2.** 5 **3.** $-1 < x < 2$ **4.** $-i$ **5.** $-5 + 5i$ **6.** $3\sqrt{5}$ **7.** True **8.** True **9.** False

Page 153: **1.** $\dfrac{a}{bx}$ **2.** $10a^3b^4$ **3.** $\dfrac{5}{2xz^4}$

Page 158: **1.** $a^4 + 4a^3b + 6a^2b^2 + 4ab^3 + b^4$ **2.** $35x^4y^3$ **3.** $70a^4b^4$

Page 162: **1.** $8 - i$ **2.** i **3.** $-i$ **4.** No

Page 169: **1.** $\dfrac{x^2 + x}{x + 2}$ **2.** $\dfrac{x^2 + x}{(x + 1)(x - 1)^2}$ **3.** $\dfrac{x^2 + 2x}{x^2 - 1}$

Cumulative Review

Write the letter of the response that best answers each question.

1. Name the set that does not contain $-\sqrt{4}$ as an element.

    a. Q   **b.** Ir   **c.** $\mathcal{I}$ **d.** R

2. Name the real number postulate illustrated by

$$\tfrac{2}{3}(5\pi - \sqrt{2}) = \tfrac{2}{3} \cdot 5\pi - \tfrac{2}{3} \cdot \sqrt{2}$$

    a. Multiplicative identity postulate   **b.** Distributive postulate
    c. Commutative postulate for addition   **d.** Additive inverse postulate

3. Choose the pure imaginary number.

    a. $-\sqrt{2}$ **b.** $-\sqrt{-x}$, $x < 0$ **c.** $\sqrt{-4}$ **d.** $\sqrt{6}$

4. Tell which number is rational.

    a. $\sqrt{2} + \sqrt{3}$ **b.** $\sqrt{2} \cdot \sqrt{3}$ **c.** $\sqrt{3} \cdot \sqrt{27}$ **d.** $\sqrt{6} \div \sqrt{2}$

5. Write $\sqrt[3]{x^2} \cdot \sqrt[3]{x^3}$ in its simplest radical form:

    a. $x^3 \sqrt[6]{x}$ **b.** $x\sqrt[3]{x^2}$ **c.** $\sqrt[5]{x^6}$ **d.** $\sqrt[5]{x^2}$

6. Add: $(4 + 5i) + (-2 - 3i)$

    a. 4   **b.** $2 + 2i$ **c.** $4 + 2i$ **d.** $4i$

7. Tell which statements are <u>not</u> true for the set of complex numbers.

    a. The additive identity element is $(0 + 0i)$.
    b. The multiplicative identity element is $1 + i$.
    c. The additive inverse of $c + di$ is $-c - di$.
    d. The multiplicative inverse of $a + bi$ is $\dfrac{a - bi}{a^2 + b^2}$.

8. Name the polynomial in x over the rational numbers.

    a. $\dfrac{x^2 + x - 3}{2}$ **b.** $\sqrt{x^3} + 5xy$ **c.** $|3 + 5x|$ **d.** $\dfrac{3y^2 - 7}{x}$

9. Multiply: $(3 - 2i)(3 - 2i)$

    a. 5   **b.** $6 - 4i$ **c.** $6 + 4i$ **d.** $5 - 12i$

10. Give the degree of the polynomial $6x^2y - 3x^2y^2 + y^3$.

    a. 2   **b.** 4   **c.** 3   **d.** 10

11. Multiply and simplify: $\left(\dfrac{9xy}{2x^2y^2}\right)\left(\dfrac{5xy^4}{3x}\right)$

    a. $\dfrac{45x^2y^5}{6x^3y^2}$ **b.** $\dfrac{15y^3}{2x}$ **c.** $\dfrac{45y^3}{6x}$ **d.** $\dfrac{15y^2}{2x^2}$

12. Name the expression that is the expansion of $(2x^2 - 3)^3$.

    a. $(2x^2)^3 + 6(2x^2)^2(-3) + 12(2x^2)(-3)^2 + 8(2x^2)^0(-3)^3$.

    b. $2x^6 + 6x^5(-3) + 15x^4(-3)^2 + 20x^3(-3)^3 + 15x^2\ (-3)^4 + 6x^3(-3)^5 + (-3)^6$.

    c. $(2x^2)^3 + 3(2x^2)^2(-3) + 3(2x^2)(-3)^2 + (-3)^3 = 8x^5 - 36x^4 + 54x^2 - 27$.

    d. $8x^6 - 36x^4 + 54x^2 - 27$.

13. Name the greatest common factor over the integers of $(x^3 - 8)$ and $(x^4 - 16)$.

    a. $x - 2$ **b.** $(x - 2)^2$ **c.** $(x + 2)^2$ **d.** $(x + 2)^3$

14. Solve: $|2x + 5| = 11$

    a. $\{3\}$ **b.** $\{-8\}$ **c.** $\{3, -8\}$ **d.** $\{-3, 8\}$

15. Find the coordinates of the midpoint of a line segment whose endpoints have coordinates $(-3, 7)$ and $(-5, -1)$.

    a. $(1, 4)$ **b.** $(-4, 3)$ **c.** $(-8, 6)$ **d.** $(1, 2)$

16. Find the value of y if the line that contains $(3, 4)$ and $(4, 2)$ is perpendicular to the line that contains $(6, y)$ and $(22, 3)$.

    a. -5 **b.** 35 **c.** 11 **d.** -29

17. If $A(-1, 2)$ and $B(4, 2)$ are the coordinates of two vertices of a quadrilateral, choose the pair of points that would <u>not</u> make the resulting quadrilateral a parallelogram.

    a. $C(0, 4); D(5, 4)$ **b.** $C(0, 7); D(5, 7)$

    c. $C(0, -2); D(3, -2)$ **d.** $C(-1, -3); D(4, -3)$

18. Choose the binomial that is a factor of $2x^3 - x^2 - 15x + 18$.

    a. $x - 3$ **b.** $x + 2$ **c.** $2x + 3$ **d.** $2x - 3$

19. Give the first term of the quotient when $6x^3y - 19x^2y + 10$ is divided by $(-2x + 5)$.

    a. $-3x^2y$ **b.** $-3x^3y^2$ **c.** $3x^2y$ **d.** $-3x^3y^2$

20. Name the complex conjugate of $6 - 3i$.

    a. $6 + 3i$ **b.** $-6 + 3i$ **c.** $6 - 3i$ **d.** $-3 + 6i$

Chapter 5
Relations
and Functions

5-1 Relations

The objective for this section is on page 208.

Recall the following definition from your first course in algebra.

Definition: A **relation** is a set of ordered pairs.

A set of ordered pairs consists of a set of first elements and a set of second elements.

$$\{(-4, 4), (-3, 1), (-2, 2), (-1, 1), (0, 0), (2, 1), (3, 3), (4, 5)\}$$
First elements: $\{-4, -3, -2, -1, 0, 1, 2, 3, 4\}$
Second elements: $\{0, 1, 2, 3, 4, 5\}$

Definitions: For a relation, the set of its first elements is the **domain**; the set of its second elements is the **range.** The variable associated with the domain is the independent variable; the variable associated with the range is the dependent variable.

The domain and range can be listed as a set or in tabular form.

Example 1

Find the range of the relation $2x = y - 4$ for the domain $\{-2, -1, 0, 1\}$.

$$y = 2x + 4 \longleftarrow \text{Solve the relation for } y.$$

x	y
−2	?
−1	?
0	?
1	?

$y = 2(-2) + 4 = 0$
$y = 2(-1) + 4 = 2$
$y = 2(0) + 4 = 4$
$y = 2(1) + 4 = 6$

x	y
−2	0
−1	2
0	4
1	6

Range: $\{0, 2, 4, 6\}$.

If the domain is not specified, consider it to be the set of real numbers.

Example 2 Graph the relation $y = 3x + 2$. Find three ordered pairs that belong to the relation.

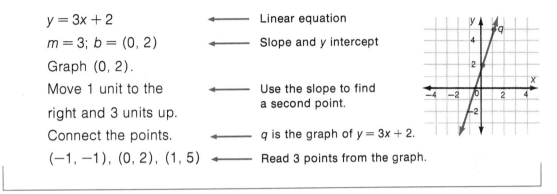

$y = 3x + 2$	←——— Linear equation
$m = 3; b = (0, 2)$	←——— Slope and y intercept
Graph $(0, 2)$.	
Move 1 unit to the right and 3 units up.	←——— Use the slope to find a second point.
Connect the points.	←——— q is the graph of $y = 3x + 2$.
$(-1, -1)$, $(0, 2)$, $(1, 5)$	←——— Read 3 points from the graph.

Try These   *Identify the domain and range of each relation.*

D: {1,2,5,8}; R: {4,3,6,13}   D: {4,6,2,−2}; R: {3,−3,−1}

1. $\{(1, 4), (2, 3), (5, 6), (8, 13)\}$ **2.** $\{(4, 3), (6, -3), (2, -1), (-2, -1)\}$

3. $\{(-1, 1), (2, 4), (-1, 7), (2, 9)\}$ **4.** $\{(0, 1), (0, 0), (5, 3), (-2, 6)\}$

D: {−1,2}; R: {1,4,7,9}   D: {0,5,−2}; R: {1,0,3,6}

Exercises
1. $D = \{-4, -2, -1, 1, 2\}$, $R = \{-4, -2, 1, 2, 4\}$
2. $D = \{x : x = 3\}$, $R = \{\text{real numbers}\}$
3. $D = \{x : 0 \le x \le 3\}$, $R = \{y : 0 \le y \le 3\}$

Identify the domain and range of each relation.

1.

2.

3.

Find the range of each relation for its given domain.

Relation **Domain**

4. $y = 7x$ $\{1, 2, 3\}$ {7, 14, 21}

5. $y = 12 - 5x$ $\{-6, -5, -4, -3\}$ {42, 37, 32, 27}

6. $y = 8 - 3x$ $\{0, 1, 2, 3\}$ {8, 5, 2, −1}

7. $y = 2x + 4$ $\{-6, -5, -4, -3\}$ {−8, −6, −4, −2}

8. $y = 3x$ $\{x: 0 < x < 4, x \in I\}$ {3, 6, 9}

9. $y = -4x$ $\{x: 0 < x < 4, x \in I\}$ {−4, −8, −12}

10. $y = 0 \cdot x - 9$ $\{0, 1, 2, 3, \cdots\}$ {−9}

11. $y = x^2$ Real numbers {y: y ≥ 0}

12. $y = -x^2$ Real numbers {y: y ≤ 0}

13. $y = \sqrt{x}$ $\{1, 4, 9, 16\}$ {1, 2, 3, 4}

14. $y = -\sqrt{x}$ $\{1, 4, 9, 16\}$ {−1, −2, −3, −4}

15. $y = |x|$ $\{-5, -4, -3, -2, -1, 0, 1, 2, 3, 4, 5\}$ {0, 1, 2, 3, 4, 5}

16. $y = -|x|$ $\{-4, -2, 0, 2, 4\}$ {−4, −2, 0}

17. $y > 2x$ $\{4\}$ {y: y > 8}

18. $y > -5x$ $\{3\}$ {y: y > −15}

19. $y > x - 9$ $\{-2\}$ {y: y > −11}

Two points are given for Exercises 20-23.

Determine several ordered pairs that are elements of each relation. Plot the points located by the ordered pairs, and draw the graph of each relation.

(0, −3), (1, −1) (0, 3), (1, 4) (0, 0), (1, 1) (0, 10), (10, 0)

20. $y = 2x - 3$ **21.** $y = x + 3$ **22.** $y = x$ **23.** $x + y = 10$

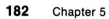

24. $y = x^2$ See key. **25.** $y < x$ See key. **26.** $y \geq x + 5$ See key. **27.** $y \leq 2x - 3$
See key.

28. Let d represent the number of dozens determined by e, the number of eggs. Then $e = 12d$ defines a relation in which d is the independent variable. Which of $0, \frac{1}{12}, \frac{1}{13}, \frac{1}{2}, 2, 2\frac{1}{5}, -8, 25$ are in the domain of the relation? In general, what is the domain? What is the range? $0, \frac{1}{12}, \frac{1}{2}, 2, 25;$

Domain: $\{d: d \geq 0$ and $12d \in I\}$, Range: $\{e: e \geq 0$ and $e \in I\}$

Write the inequalities that define the relations graphed below.

29.
$x > 2$

30.
$y < -\frac{3}{2}$

31.
$y > x$

For Exercises 32–37, write an equation in two variables with a solution that includes the given relation.

32. $\{(-1, 1), (-2, 2), (-3, 3), (-4, 4), (5, -5), (6, -6)\}$ $y = -x$

33. $\{(1, 1), (2, 8), (3, 27), (4, 64), (5, 125)\}$ $y = x^3$

34. $\{(25, 5), (36, 6), (49, 7), (81, 9), (100, 10)\}$ $y = \sqrt{x}$

35. $\{(-1, -3), (0, -1), (1, 1), (2, 3), (3, 5)\}$ $y = 2x - 1$

36. $\{(2, 5), (2, 3), (2, 1), (2, 0), (2, -1), (2, -3), (2, -5)\}$ $x = 2$

37. $\{(2, 0), (0, 0), (1, 0), (-1, 0), (-3, 0), (-7, 0)\}$ $y = 0$

38. Graph $y = |x| + 3$, $x \in R$. What is the range of the relation?
Two rays, both starting at (0,3) one passing through (2,5), the other through (−2,5). Range: $\{y : y \geq 3\}$

39. Graph $y = -3 - |x|$, for $x \in R$. What is the range of the relation?
Two rays, both starting at (0,−3), one passing through (2,−5) the other through (−2,−5). Range: $\{y : y \leq -3\}$

Remember

Find the value of the polynomial $3x^2 - 2x + 1$ for each value of x.

1. 2   9

2. −3   34

3. $a + 1$ $3a^2 + 4a + 2$

4. $b - 3$
$3b^2 - 20b + 34$

The answers are on page 210.

5-2 Functions

The objectives for this section are on page 208.

In the following relation, each element of the domain is paired with only one element of the range.

$$\{(-2, 4), (-1, 1), (0, 0), (1, 1), \ldots, (x, x^2)\}$$

Definition: A **function** is a relation such that for every element of the domain there is <u>one and only one</u> element of the range.

The graph of a relation tells whether or not it is a function. Move a vertical line across the graph. If it intersects the graph anywhere in more than one point, the relation is not a function. This **Vertical Line Test** is a direct application of the definition of function.

Example 1

Tell which relations graphed below represent functions.

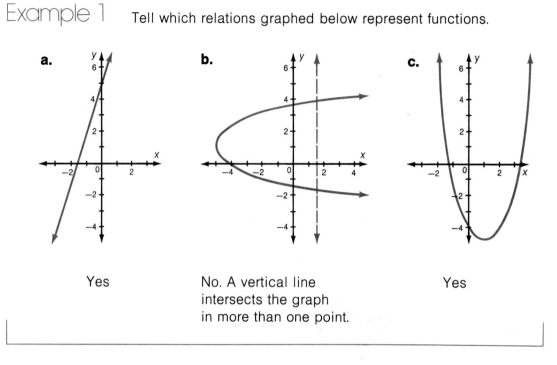

a.

b.

c.

Yes

No. A vertical line
intersects the graph
in more than one point.

Yes

The letters f, g, and h are often used to represent functions. If x represents an element in the domain of a function f, then

$$f(x), \text{ read “}f \text{ at } x\text{”,}$$

is the corresponding element of the range. Thus, the ordered pairs of a function can be written as

$$(x, f(x)) \quad \text{or as} \quad (x, y)$$

Example 2

For the function f defined by $y = 3x$, find $f(a + b)$.

$y = 3x \quad$ or $\quad f(x) = 3x$ ←———— **Represent the function.**

$f(a + b) = 3(a + b)$ ←———— **Substitute $(a + b)$ for x.**

$f(a + b) = 3a + 3b$

Example 3 State the rule for the function graphed below.

1. When $x > 0$, $y = 1$.
2. When $x = 0$, $y = 0$.
3. When $x < 0$, $y = -1$.

$$f(x) = \begin{cases} 1, & \text{for } x > 0 \\ 0, & \text{for } x = 0 \\ -1, & \text{for } x < 0 \end{cases}$$

This function is called a piece function because it is defined by different equations on different parts of the domain. The domain for this function is the set of real numbers. The range is $\{-1, 0, 1\}$.

Try These

Determine which relations are functions. If a relation is not a function, tell why it is not.

1. $\{(1, 2), (2, 3), (3, 4), (4, 5)\}$ Function.

2. $\{(2, 1), (2, 7), (3, -1), (4, 5)\}$ Not a function.

3. $\{(0, 2), (2, 0), (3, 3), (-3, 3)\}$ Function.

4. $\{(3, 4), (-1, 2), (5, 4), (-1, 3)\}$ Not a function.

5. If f is a function defined by $y = 6 - 4x$, find $f(0)$, $f(-6)$, $f(8)$. 6, 30, −26

6. If f is a function defined by $f(x) = 8 - 3x^2$, find $f(0)$, $f(-2)$, and $f(3)$. 8, −4, −19

Exercises

Determine which relations are functions. If a relation is not a function, tell why it is not.

Function
1. $\{(1, 3), (2, 3), (-1, 4), (-6, 4)\}$

Function
2. $\{(-4, -4), (-1, -1), (0, 0), (1, 1), (4, 4)\}$

Function
3. $\{(-4, 4), (-1, 1), (0, 0), (1, -1), (4, -4)\}$

Not a Function
4. $\{(-1, -4), (-1, 0), (-1, 2), (-1, 4)\}$

Function
5. $\{(-3, -2), (-1, -2), (0, -2), (3, -2)\}$

Not a Function
6. $\{(4, -2), (1, -1), (0, 0), (1, 1), (4, 2)\}$

Classify each graph as a function (F) or as a relation that is not a function (NF).

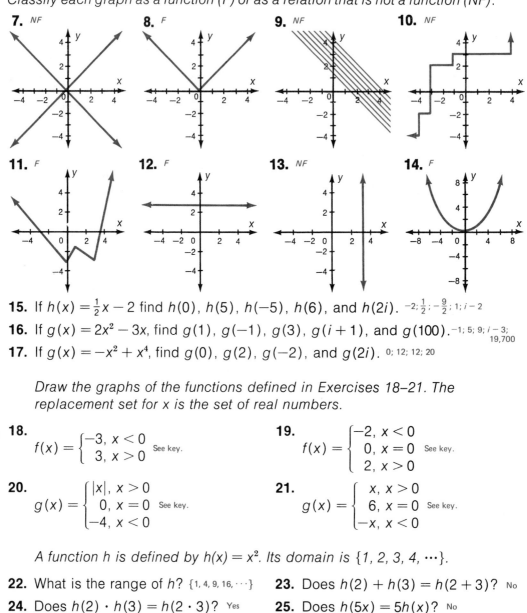

7. *NF* **8.** *F* **9.** *NF* **10.** *NF*

11. *F* **12.** *F* **13.** *NF* **14.** *F*

15. If $h(x) = \frac{1}{2}x - 2$ find $h(0)$, $h(5)$, $h(-5)$, $h(6)$, and $h(2i)$. $\quad$ $-2; \frac{1}{2}; -\frac{9}{2}; 1; i - 2$

16. If $g(x) = 2x^2 - 3x$, find $g(1)$, $g(-1)$, $g(3)$, $g(i + 1)$, and $g(100)$. $\quad$ $-1; 5; 9; i - 3;$ $19{,}700$

17. If $g(x) = -x^2 + x^4$, find $g(0)$, $g(2)$, $g(-2)$, and $g(2i)$. $\quad$ $0; 12; 12; 20$

Draw the graphs of the functions defined in Exercises 18–21. The replacement set for x is the set of real numbers.

18.
$$f(x) = \begin{cases} -3, & x < 0 \\ 3, & x > 0 \end{cases}$$ See key.

19.
$$f(x) = \begin{cases} -2, & x < 0 \\ 0, & x = 0 \\ 2, & x > 0 \end{cases}$$ See key.

20.
$$g(x) = \begin{cases} |x|, & x > 0 \\ 0, & x = 0 \\ -4, & x < 0 \end{cases}$$ See key.

21.
$$g(x) = \begin{cases} x, & x > 0 \\ 6, & x = 0 \\ -x, & x < 0 \end{cases}$$ See key.

A function h is defined by $h(x) = x^2$. Its domain is $\{1, 2, 3, 4, \cdots\}$.

22. What is the range of h? $\{1, 4, 9, 16, \cdots\}$ **23.** Does $h(2) + h(3) = h(2 + 3)$? No

24. Does $h(2) \cdot h(3) = h(2 \cdot 3)$? Yes **25.** Does $h(5x) = 5h(x)$? No

If $f(x) = 2x^2 + 3$, $g(x) = 3x^2 + 4x + 1$, and $h(x) = 3x - 1$, find:

26. $f[g(x)]$ (HINT: Replace x in $f(x)$ with $3x^2 + 4x + 1$ and simplify.) $\quad$ $18x^4 + 48x^3 + 44x^2 + 16x + 5$

27. $g[f(x)]$ $12x^4 + 44x^2 + 40$ **28.** $h[f(x)]$ $6x^2 + 8$

29. $g[h(x)]$ $27x^2 - 6x$ **30.** $h[g(x)]$ $9x^2 + 12x + 2$

Mappings

The objective for this section is on page 209.

When you want to graph a relation, it is useful to think of the relation as a set of ordered pairs. When you want to emphasize the rule of a relation, it is sometimes useful to think of it as a **mapping.** Geometric models of mappings use arrow diagrams.

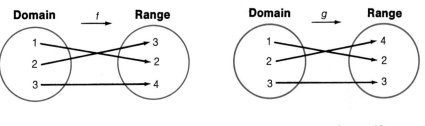

f: x maps onto $(x + 1)$.

f: $x \longrightarrow (x + 1)$

g: x maps onto $-\frac{3}{2}x^2 + \frac{13}{2}x - 3$

g: $x \longrightarrow -\frac{3}{2}x^2 + \frac{13}{2}x - 3$

Example 1   Give the rule for the mapping f shown below. Tell whether the mapping is a function.

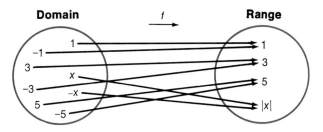

Some ordered pairs: $\{(-1, 1), (1, 1), (3, 3), (-3, 3), (-5, 5), \ldots (x, |x|)\}$
Algebraic rule: f: x maps onto $|x|$.

Since each element of the domain is paired with only one element of the range, f is a function.

Function notation: $f(x) = |x|$ or f: $x \longrightarrow |x|$

Relations and Functions   **187**

Example 2 Give the rule for the mapping *h* shown in the diagram. Tell whether *h* is a function.

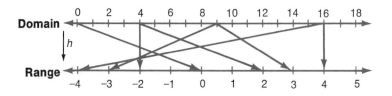

Some ordered pairs: $\{(0, 0), (4, 2), (4, -2), (9, 3), (9, -3), \cdots, (x, \pm\sqrt{x})\}$

Algebraic rule: *x* maps onto $\pm\sqrt{x}$, or $x \longrightarrow \pm\sqrt{x}$.

Since each element of the domain is <u>not</u> paired with only one element of the range, *h* is not a function.

Try These *Find the range for each domain and mapping.*

Domain $\{-3, -2, -1, 0, 1, 2, 3\}$ **Mapping**

1. $\{1, 2, 3, 4, 5\}$ *x* maps onto $2x + 1$. $\{3, 5, 7, 9, 11\}$

2. $\{-3, -2, -1, 0, 1, 2, 3\}$ *x* maps onto its absolute value. $\{0, 1, 2, 3\}$

3. $\{-3, -2, -1, 0, 1, 2, 3\}$ *x* maps onto its square. $\{0, 1, 4, 9\}$

4. $\{-3, -2, -1, 0, 1, 2, 3\}$ *x* maps onto its additive inverse.

5. $\{-3, -\frac{1}{2}, -\frac{1}{3}, 1, 5\}$ *x* maps onto its multiplicative inverse. $\{-\frac{1}{3}, -2, -3, 1, \frac{1}{5}\}$

Exercises

Represent each mapping as a set of ordered pairs.

1. $\{(1, 2), (3, 5)\}$

2. $\{(1, 6), (2, 6), (4, 6)\}$

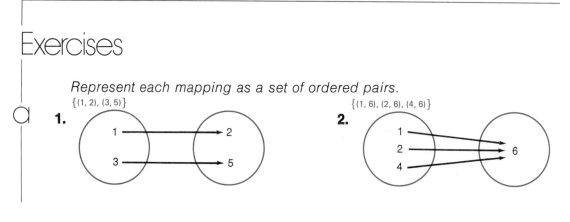

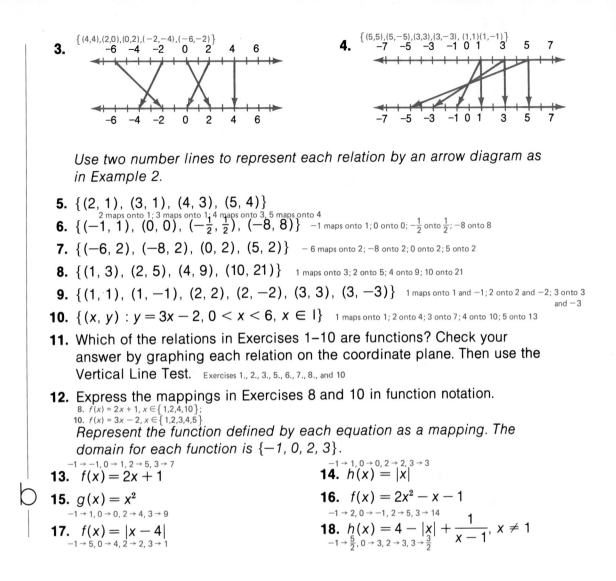

3. $\{(4,4),(2,0),(0,2),(-2,-4),(-6,-2)\}$

4. $\{(5,5),(5,-5),(3,3),(3,-3), (1,1)(1,-1)\}$

Use two number lines to represent each relation by an arrow diagram as in Example 2.

5. $\{(2, 1), (3, 1), (4, 3), (5, 4)\}$
2 maps onto 1; 3 maps onto 1; 4 maps onto 3, 5 maps onto 4

6. $\{(-1, 1), (0, 0), (-\frac{1}{2}, \frac{1}{2}), (-8, 8)\}$ −1 maps onto 1; 0 onto 0; $-\frac{1}{2}$ onto $\frac{1}{2}$; −8 onto 8

7. $\{(-6, 2), (-8, 2), (0, 2), (5, 2)\}$ − 6 maps onto 2; −8 onto 2; 0 onto 2; 5 onto 2

8. $\{(1, 3), (2, 5), (4, 9), (10, 21)\}$ 1 maps onto 3; 2 onto 5; 4 onto 9; 10 onto 21

9. $\{(1, 1), (1, -1), (2, 2), (2, -2), (3, 3), (3, -3)\}$ 1 maps onto 1 and −1; 2 onto 2 and −2; 3 onto 3 and −3

10. $\{(x, y) : y = 3x - 2, 0 < x < 6, x \in I\}$ 1 maps onto 1; 2 onto 4; 3 onto 7; 4 onto 10; 5 onto 13

11. Which of the relations in Exercises 1–10 are functions? Check your answer by graphing each relation on the coordinate plane. Then use the Vertical Line Test. Exercises 1., 2., 3., 5., 6., 7., 8., and 10

12. Express the mappings in Exercises 8 and 10 in function notation.
8. $f(x) = 2x + 1, x \in \{1,2,4,10\}$;
10. $f(x) = 3x - 2, x \in \{1,2,3,4,5\}$
Represent the function defined by each equation as a mapping. The domain for each function is $\{-1, 0, 2, 3\}$.

13. $f(x) = 2x + 1$
−1 → −1, 0 → 1, 2 → 5, 3 → 7

14. $h(x) = |x|$
−1 → 1, 0 → 0, 2 → 2, 3 → 3

15. $g(x) = x^2$
−1 → 1, 0 → 0, 2 → 4, 3 → 9

16. $f(x) = 2x^2 - x - 1$
−1 → 2, 0 → −1, 2 → 5, 3 → 14

17. $f(x) = |x - 4|$
−1 → 5, 0 → 4, 2 → 2, 3 → 1

18. $h(x) = 4 - |x| + \dfrac{1}{x - 1}, x \neq 1$
−1 → $\frac{5}{2}$, 0 → 3, 2 → 3, 3 → $\frac{3}{2}$

Remember

Perform the indicated operations. Simplify where possible.

1. $(3x^4 - 2x^2 + 1) - (2x^4 + x^3 - 3x^2 + 5)$ $x^4 - x^3 + x^2 - 4$

2. $(3 - 2i)^2$ $5 - 12i$

3. $\dfrac{x}{2x + 5} + \dfrac{x + 1}{x}$ $\frac{3x^2 + 7x + 5}{2x^2 + 5x}$

4. $(5 - 3i)(5 + 3i)$ 34

The answers are on page 210.

The objective for this section is on page 209.

The following functions occur often in mathematics.

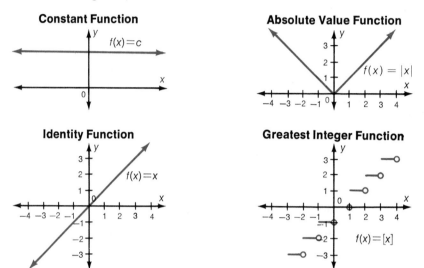

Constant Function

$f(x) = c$

Absolute Value Function

$f(x) = |x|$

Identity Function

$f(x) = x$

Greatest Integer Function

$f(x) = [x]$

Example 1   Give the domain and range for each function shown above.

Constant function: For all real x, x maps onto c.
Domain: {real numbers}   Range: {c}

Absolute value function: For all real x, x maps onto $|x|$.
Domain: {real numbers}   Range: {nonnegative real numbers}

Identify function: For all real x, x maps onto x.
Domain: {real numbers}   Range: {real numbers}

Greatest integer function: For all real x, x maps onto the
greatest integer less than or equal
to x.
Domain: {real numbers}   Range: {integers}

The constant function and the identity function are examples of linear functions. Every **linear function** can be expressed as

$$y = mx + b, \quad \text{or} \quad f(x) = mx + b.$$

For the constant function, $f(x) = b$, $m = 0$; for the identity function, $f(x) = x$, $b = 0$ and $m = 1$. The graph of a linear function whose domain is the set of real numbers is a straight line.
    Whenever $b = 0$ and $m \neq 0$, $y = mx + b$ becomes

$$y = mx \quad \text{or} \quad m = \frac{y}{x}.$$

The function $y = mx$ expresses **direct variation.** The constant m, sometimes called k, is called a **constant of variation.**

Example 2   Show that $\{(4, -2), (5, -2\frac{1}{2})\ (6, -3)\ (7, -3\frac{1}{2}), (8 - 4)\}$ is an example of direct variation. Find the constant of variation, and write the variation as a function.

$$\{(4, -2),\ (5, -2\tfrac{1}{2}),\ (6, -3),\ (7, -3\tfrac{1}{2}),\ (8, -4)\} \longleftarrow \text{Ordered pairs}$$

$$\frac{y}{x} = \frac{-2}{4} = \frac{-2\frac{1}{2}}{5} = \frac{-3}{6} = \frac{3\frac{1}{2}}{7} = \frac{-4}{8} = -\frac{1}{2} \qquad \longleftarrow \quad k = \frac{y}{x}$$

$$k = -\frac{1}{2} \qquad \longleftarrow \text{Constant of variation}$$

$$f(x) = -\frac{1}{2}x \qquad \longleftarrow \quad f(x) = kx$$

Example 3   If y varies directly as x and $y = -9$ when $x = 3$, find the constant of variation. Find y when $x = -4$.

Model: $y = kx$ $\longleftarrow$ y varies directly as x.
$\quad\quad\quad -9 = 3k$ $\longleftarrow$ When $x = 3$, $y = -9$.
$\quad\quad\quad -3 = k$ $\longleftarrow$ Constant of variation
$\quad\quad\quad f(x) = -3x$ $\longleftarrow$ Function
$\quad\quad\quad f(x) = -3(-4)$ $\longleftarrow$ Substitute $x = -4$.
$\quad\quad\quad f(x) = 12$

Exercises

Using the given domain and type of function, determine the range of the function.

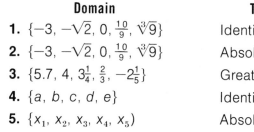

Domain	Type of Function
1. $\{-3, -\sqrt{2}, 0, \frac{10}{9}, \sqrt[3]{9}\}$	Identity function $\{-3, -\sqrt{2}, 0, \frac{10}{9}, \sqrt[3]{9}\}$
2. $\{-3, -\sqrt{2}, 0, \frac{10}{9}, \sqrt[3]{9}\}$	Absolute value function $\{3, \sqrt{2}, 0, \frac{10}{9}, \sqrt[3]{9}\}$
3. $\{5.7, 4, 3\frac{1}{4}, \frac{2}{3}, -2\frac{1}{5}\}$	Greatest integer function $\{5, 4, 3, 0, -3\}$
4. $\{a, b, c, d, e\}$	Identity function $\{a, b, c, d, e\}$
5. $\{x_1, x_2, x_3, x_4, x_5)$	Absolute value function
	$\{|x_1|, |x_2|, |x_3|, |x_4|, |x_5|\}$

Indicate which of the mappings below are functions. If the mapping illustrates a special function, name it.

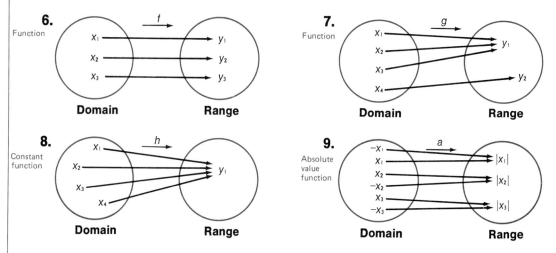

6. Function — f — Domain, Range

7. Function — g — Domain, Range

8. Constant function — h — Domain, Range

9. Absolute value function — a — Domain, Range

In Exercises 10-14, y varies directly as x.

10. If $y = -6$ when $x = 3$, find y when $x = 8$. -16

11. If $y = 2$ when $x = 10$, find y when $x = 27$. $\frac{27}{5}$

12. If $y = -1$ when $x = 3$, find y when $x = -8$. $\frac{8}{3}$

13. If $y = 3.5$ when $x = 14$, find y when $x = 8.4$. 2.1

14. If $y = 7\frac{1}{2}$ when $x = 2\frac{1}{4}$, find y when $x = 2\frac{2}{5}$. 8

15. If $y = kx$ and $k > 0$, does y increase or decrease as x increases? as x decreases? Increases; decreases

16. If $y = kx$ and $k < 0$, does y increase or decrease as x increases? as x decreases?   Decreases; increases.

*Write an equation for each of the following examples of direct variation.
Use k as the constant of variation.*

17. The total cost of gasoline, T, varies directly as the number of gallons, g. $T = kg$
18. The distance, d, traveled in a given number of hours varies directly as the
average rate, r. $d = kr$
19. The total cost, c, of a given number of candy bars varies directly as the price
per bar, p. $c = kp$
20. For rectangles of the same base, the area, A, varies directly as the height, h.
$A = kh$

Graph each function.   See key.

21. $y = x$ 22. $y = -x$ 23. $y = 3$

24. $y = -3$ 25. $y = |x|$ 26. $y = -|x|$

27. $y = [x]$ 28. $y = -[x]$ 29. $y = \frac{1}{2}x$

30. If $f(x) = |x|$, compute $f(2)$, $f(-1)$, $f(3.5)$, $f(-\sqrt{2})$, $f(-6.3)$ 2; 1; 3.5; $\sqrt{2}$; 6.3
31. If $f(x) = [x]$, compute $f(-\pi)$. $f(\sqrt{2})$, $f(0)$, $f(-2.1)$, $f(3.7)$. -4; 1; 0; -3; 3

*Write the equation that defines each relation. Tell which relations are also
functions.*

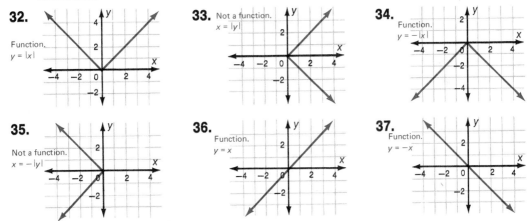

32. Function. $y = |x|$

33. Not a function. $x = |y|$

34. Function. $y = -|x|$

35. Not a function. $x = -|y|$

36. Function. $y = x$

37. Function. $y = -x$

38. Let $f(x) = |x| - x + [x]$. Find $f(1)$, $f(-1)$, $f(\sqrt{2})$, $f(\pi)$, $f(-2.3)$.
   1; 1; 1; 3; 1.6
   *The six special functions of this section are $f(x) = c$, $f(x) = x$, $f(x) = |x|$,
   $f(x) = [x]$, $f(x) = kx$ and $f(x) = mx + b$.*
   $f(x) = x$ and $f(x) = kx$
39. For which of these functions is it true that $f(x_1) + f(x_2) = f(x_1 + x_2)$?
40. For which of these functions is it true that $f(x_1) \cdot f(x_2) = f(x_1 \cdot x_2)$?
   $f(x) = x$ and $f(x) = |x|$

Zeros of a Function

The objective for this section is on page 209.

The points in which the graph of a function intersects the x axis identify the values of x for which $f(x) = 0$. These values of x are called the **zeros of the function.**

Definition: A **zero of a function** f is any number a, for which $f(a) = 0$.

Example 1

Identify the zeros of $f(x) = 2x - 4$ and of $g(x) = -x^2 + 9$.

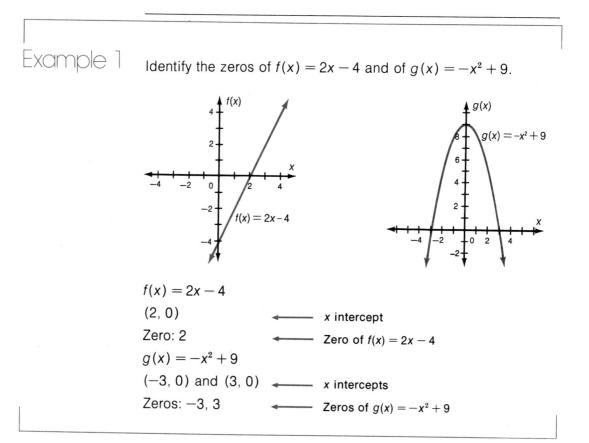

$f(x) = 2x - 4$

$(2, 0)$ ⟵ x intercept

Zero: 2 ⟵ Zero of $f(x) = 2x - 4$

$g(x) = -x^2 + 9$

$(-3, 0)$ and $(3, 0)$ ⟵ x intercepts

Zeros: $-3, 3$ ⟵ Zeros of $g(x) = -x^2 + 9$

The zeros of a function can also be found by solving the equation $f(x) = 0$.

Example 2 Find the zeros of $f(x) = 2x^2 - x$.

$$f(x) = 2x^2 - x$$
$$2x^2 - x = 0 \qquad \longleftarrow \quad \text{Let } f(x) = 0.$$
$$x(2x - 1) = 0 \qquad \longleftarrow \quad \text{Factor.}$$
$$x = 0 \quad \text{or} \quad 2x - 1 = 0 \quad \longleftarrow \quad \text{Solve.}$$
$$\text{Then} \quad x = 0 \quad \text{or} \quad x = \frac{1}{2} \quad \longleftarrow \quad \text{Zeros: } 0, \frac{1}{2}$$

Try These   *Find the zeros of each function.*

1. $f(x) = 2x - 3$ $\frac{3}{2}$

2. $g(x) = 5x + 1$ $-\frac{1}{5}$

3. $h(x) = x^2 - 5x + 6$ 2, 3

4. $t(x) = x^3 - 4x$ 0, −2, 2

Exercises

Read the zeros of each function from its graph.

1. −3, 3

2. −4, −2

3. 3

4. −5, 0, 5

5. −4, 4

6. −3, −1, 1, 3

7. No zeros.

8. 0

Find the zeros of each function.

9. $f(x) = 3x - 1$
$3x - 1 = 0, x = \frac{1}{3}$; zero is $\frac{1}{3}$

10. $g(x) = 2x + 6$ -3

11. $h(x) = -5x + 2$ $\frac{2}{5}$

12. $f(x) = -2x - 3$ $-\frac{3}{2}$

13. $g(x) = x^2 - 9$ -3 and 3

14. $f(x) = x^2 + x - 12$ -4 and 3

15. $h(x) = 2x^2 - x - 36$ $\frac{9}{2}$ and -4

16. $h(x) = x^2 + x - 20$ -5 and 4

17. $h(x) = 3x^2 - x$ 0 and $\frac{1}{3}$

18. $g(x) = 2x^2 - 8$ -2 and 2

19. Which of the numbers 1, 2, 3, and 6 are zeros of $f(x) = x^3 - 6x^2 + 11x - 6$?
1, 2, and 3

Use the zeros of each function to aid in graphing the function.
See key for Exercises 20-25.

20. $f(x) = 5x + 10$

21. $h(x) = 2x - 3$

22. $g(x) = 4x^2 - 1$

23. $f(x) = x^2 - 6x$

24. Explain why the function defined by $f(x) = a^x$, $a \neq 1$, $a > 0$, called an exponential function, has no zeros.

25. Show that the function defined by $f(x) = ax^2 + bx + c$, $a \neq 0$, called a quadratic function, has the zeros See key.

$$\frac{-b + \sqrt{b^2 - 4ac}}{2a} \quad \text{and} \quad \frac{-b - \sqrt{b^2 - 4ac}}{2a}.$$

Remember

Find the value of the polynomial in Column A when $x = 2$. Then substitute the Column A value in the polynomial in Column B.

Column A	Column B
1. $x^2 + 2$ 6	$x + 7$ 13
2. $x^2 + 2x - 5$ 3	$2x - 9$ -3
3. $3x^2 - 7x - 6$ -8	$x^2 - 5$ 59

The answers are on page 210.

PUZZLE

Write a digit for each letter. Find one solution.

$$(1)(AM)(NOT) = SURE$$

or $1 \times 26 \times 345 = 8970$
$2 \times 14 \times 307 = 8596$

5-6 Composite Functions

The objective for this section is on page 209.

In the diagram below *f* maps {1, 2, 3} onto {0, 2, 4}, while *g* maps {0, 2, 4} onto {−1, 3, 7}. The set {0, 2, 4} plays two roles; it is both the range of *f* and the domain of *g*.

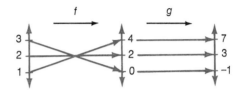

When one set is the range of one function and the domain of a second function, a third function is defined. In the diagram,

3 maps onto 0 and 0 maps onto −1, so 3 maps onto −1;

2 maps onto 2 and 2 maps onto 3, so 2 maps onto 3;

1 maps onto 4 and 4 maps onto 7, so 1 maps onto 7.

The new function maps {3, 2, 1} onto {−1, 3, 7}, where the set {0, 2, 4} is the link between sets A and C. The new function is called the <u>composite function</u> of *g* and *f*. It is written *g* ∘ *f* and is read "*g* composition *f*" or "the composite of *g* and *f*."

Example 1   If $f = \{(1, 2), (2, 3), (3, 4), (4, 5)\}$ and $g = \{(2, 5), (3, 4), (4, 2), (5, 1)\}$, use an arrow diagram to show *g* ∘ *f* and name its ordered pairs.

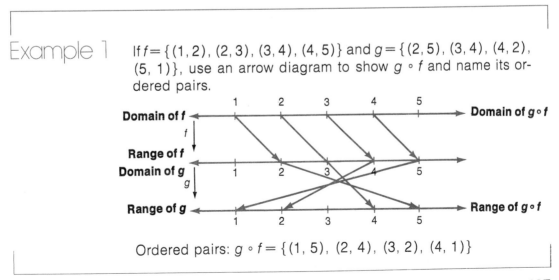

Ordered pairs: $g \circ f = \{(1, 5), (2, 4), (3, 2), (4, 1)\}$

Relations and Functions   **197**

Example 2 Let f be a function that maps kilometers onto liters of gasoline, such that $f(k) = \dfrac{k}{4}$, where k represents the number of kilometers.

Let h be a function that maps liters onto cost in cents, such that $h(\ell) = 16\ell$, where ℓ represents the number of liters. Find the equation of the function mapping kilometers onto cost.

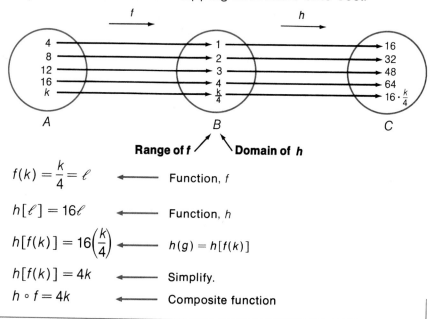

$f(k) = \dfrac{k}{4} = \ell$ ⟵ Function, f

$h[\ell] = 16\ell$ ⟵ Function, h

$h[f(k)] = 16\left(\dfrac{k}{4}\right)$ ⟵ $h(g) = h[f(k)]$

$h[f(k)] = 4k$ ⟵ Simplify.

$h \circ f = 4k$ ⟵ Composite function

Definition: If f is a function with range B and g is a function with domain contained in B, then the **composite of g and f** is the function $g \circ f = g(f)$.

Example 3 If $f(x) = 6 - 2x$ and $g(t) = t^2 - 1$, find $g \circ f$ and $f \circ g$.

$g \circ f = g[f(x)]$

$g \circ f = g(6 - 2x)$ ⟵ Replace $f(x)$ with $6 - 2x$.

$g \circ f = (6 - 2x)^2 - 1$ ⟵ $g(t) = t^2 - 1; t = 6 - 2x$

$g \circ f = 35 - 24x + 4x^2$

$$f \circ g = f[g(t)] \qquad \longleftarrow \quad f(x) = 6 - 2x. \text{ Replace } x \text{ with } g(t).$$

$$f \circ g = f(t^2 - 1) \qquad \longleftarrow \quad \text{Replace } g(t) \text{ with } t^2 - 1.$$

$$f \circ g = 6 - 2(t^2 - 1) \qquad \longleftarrow \quad f(x) = 6 - 2x; \; x = t^2 - 1$$

$$f \circ g = 8 - 2t^2$$

Notice the $f \circ g$ need not equal $g \circ f$. Thus, the operation of composition of functions is <u>not</u> commutative. In certain instances, however $f \circ g$ can equal $g \circ f$.

Example 4   If $h(x) = 4x - 3$ and $p(x) = \dfrac{x+3}{4}$, find $h[p(-2)]$ and $p[h(-2)]$.

$$p(-2) = \frac{-2+3}{4} = \frac{1}{4} \qquad \longleftarrow \quad \text{Let } x = -2.$$

$$h[p(-2)] = h\left(\frac{1}{4}\right) = 4\left(\frac{1}{4}\right) - 3 \qquad \longleftarrow \quad h(p(-2)) = h\left(\frac{1}{4}\right)$$

$$h(p(-2)) = 1 - 3 = -2$$

$$h(x) = 4x - 3$$

$$h(-2) = 4(-2) - 3 = -11 \qquad \longleftarrow \quad \text{Let } x = -2.$$

$$p[h(-2)] = p(-11) = \frac{-11+3}{4} \qquad \longleftarrow \quad p(h(-2)) = p(-11)$$

$$p[h(-2)] = \frac{-8}{4} = -2$$

Thus, $h[p(-2)] = p[h(-2)]$.

Try These   Use sets A, B, and C, to write the functions f and g as sets of ordered pairs, where f maps A onto B and g maps B onto C. Then write g(f).

1. $A = \{1, 2, 3\}$, $B = \{3, 5, 7\}$ $C = \{3, 5, 7\}$, $f(1) = 3$, $f(2) = 5$, $f(3) = 7$, $g(3) = 7$, $g(5) = 5$, $g(7) = 3$.

   $f = \{(1,3), (2,5), (3,7)\} ; g = \{(3,7), (5,5), (7,3)\} ; g(f) = \{(1,7), (2,5), (3,3)\}$

2. $A = \{1, 2, 3\}$, $B = \{4, 5\}$, $C = \{6, 7\}$, $f(1) = 4$, $f(2) = 5$, $f(3) = 4$, $g(4) = 6$, $g(5) = 7$.

   $f = \{(1,4), (2,5), (3,4)\} ; g = \{(4,6), (5,7)\} ; g(f) = \{(1,6), (2,7), (3,6)\}$

Exercises

Write the indicated composite function as a set of ordered pairs and state its domain and range.

1. Given $f = \{(2, 3), (5, 6), (7, 9)\}$ and $g = \{(6, 8), (3, 11), (9, 4)\}$, find $g(f)$. $\{(2, 11), (5, 8), (7, 4)\}; D = \{2, 5, 7\}; R = \{11, 8, 4\}$

2. Given $g = \{(1, 4), (-2, 6), (3, -8)\}$ and $h = \{(-8, 10), (6, -3), (4, 7)\}$, find $h(g)$. $\{(1, 7), (-2, -3), (3, 10)\}; D = \{1, -2, 3\}; R = \{7, -3, 10\}$

3. Given $f = \{(-5, 2), (1, -4), (2, -7)\}$ and $g = \{(-6, 1), (7, -5), (0, 2)\}$, find $f(g)$. $\{(-6, -4), (7, 2), (0, -7)\}; D = \{-6, 7, 0\}; R = \{-4, 2, -7\}$

4. Given $g = \{(6, -5), (3, 1), (-2, -3)\}$ and $h = \{(1, 3), (-5, 6), (-3, -2)\}$, find $g(h)$. $\{(1, 1), (-5, -5), (-3, -3)\}; D = \{1, -5, -3\}; R = \{-1, -5, -3\}$

5. Given that $f(1) = 7$, $f(2) = 6$, $f(3) = 8$, $f(4) = 5$ and that $g(5) = 9$, $g(7) = -1$, $g(6) = 0$ and $g(8) = 11$, draw a mapping diagram to illustrate $g \circ f$. State the domain and range of the composite function.
$1 \to 7 \to -1; 2 \to 6 \to 0; 3 \to 8 \to 11; 4 \to 5 \to 9; D = \{1, 2, 3, 4\}; R = \{-1, 0, 11, 9\}$

In Exercises 6–11, $f(x) = 1 - x^2$ and $g(x) = 2x + 5$.

6. Find $f(1)$ and $g[f(1)]$. $0, 5$

7. Find $f(2)$ and $g[f(2)]$. $-3, -1$

8. Find $g[f(x)]$. $7 - 2x^2$

9. Find $g(1)$ and $f[g(1)]$. $7, -48$

10. Find $g(2)$ and $f[g(2)]$. $9, -80$

11. Find $f[g(x)]$. $-4x^2 - 20x - 24$

Write the equations that define $g(f)$ and $f(g)$.

12. $f(x) = 2x - 1$ $g(f) = 6x + 1;$
$g(x) = 3x + 4$ $f(g) = 6x + 7$

13. $f(x) = x$ $g(f) = -x;$
$g(x) = -x$ $f(g) = -x$

14. $f(x) = \frac{1}{2}x + 3$ $g(f) = x + 1;$
$g(x) = 2x - 5$ $f(g) = x + \frac{1}{2}$

15. $f(x) = 5x + 2$ $g(f) = -10x - 7;$
$g(x) = -2x - 3$ $f(g) = -10x - 13$

16. $f(x) = x^2$ $g(f) = x^2 + 1;$
$g(x) = x + 1$ $f(g) = x^2 + 2x + 1$

17. $f(x) = x^2 - x - 1$ $g(f) = 2x^2 - 2x - 2;$
$g(x) = 2x$ $f(g) = 4x^2 - 2x - 1$

18. $f(x) = 2x^2 - x + 1$ $g(f) = 6x^2 - 3x + 7;$
$g(x) = 3x + 4$ $f(g)$ $18x^2 + 45x + 29$

19. $f(x) = |x|$ $g(f) = x^2 - 9;$
$g(x) = x^2 - 9$ $f(g) = |x^2 - 9|$

Draw the graphs of the indicated composite function. The domain is the set of real numbers.

20. $g[h(x)]$, where $g(x) = -x + 4$ and $h(x) = 2x - 5$. $g[h(x)] = -2x + 9$; A line through $(0, 9)$ and $(2, 5)$.

21. $f[g(x)]$, where $f(x) = x$ and $g(x) = x^2$. $f[g(x)] = x^2$; A parabola with vertex at $(0, 0)$ passing through $(1, 1)$ and $(-1, 1)$.

5-7 Inverse Relations

The objective for this section is on page 209.

Let M be a mapping that maps $A = \{0, 1, 2, 3\}$ onto $B = \{3, 4, 7, 12\}$.

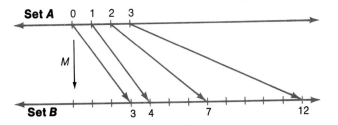

The ordered pairs of M are $\{(0, 3), (1, 4), (2, 7), (3, 12)\}$. Interchange the elements of the ordered pairs. The resulting set defines a mapping from B onto A.

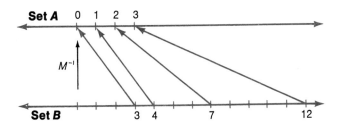

This mapping is called the **inverse** of M and is written M^{-1}. The ordered pairs of M^{-1} are $\{(3, 0), (4, 1), (7, 2), (12, 3)\}$.

Definition: Relations Q and Q^{-1} are **inverse relations** if and only if for every ordered pair (x, y) in Q, there is an ordered pair (y, x) in Q^{-1}.

Example 1   Let $Q = \{(2, 1), (3, 2), (4, 2), (5, 3)\}$. Find Q^{-1}. Determine whether Q and Q^{-1} are functions.

$Q = \{(2, 1), (3, 2), (4, 2), (5, 3)\}$ ←——— Q is a function.

$Q^{-1} = \{(1, 2), (2, 3), (2, 4), (3, 5)\}$ ←——— Interchange the elements of the ordered pairs of Q.

Q^{-1} is not a function. ←——— (2, 3) and (2, 4) have the same first member.

Example 1 illustrates an important fact: The inverse of a function is not always a function.

In the figure at the right, P is the midpoint of $\overline{AB}$, and line q is perpendicular to $\overline{AB}$ at P. Then line q is the perpendicular bisector of $\overline{AB}$ and points A and B are said to be symmetric with respect to line q.

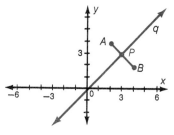

Definition: Two points A and B are said to be **symmetric with respect to a line** q if and only if q is the perpendicular bisector of line segment AB.

Example 2   Find the midpoint of the segment determined by $A(2, 4)$ of a relation and the corresponding point $B(4, 2)$ of the inverse relation. Show that the midpoint lies on the line $y = x$.

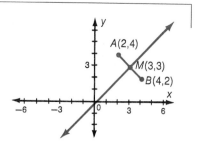

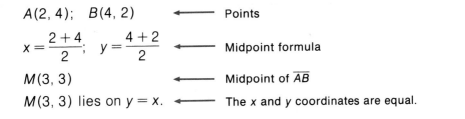

$A(2, 4); \quad B(4, 2)$ ← Points

$x = \dfrac{2 + 4}{2}; \quad y = \dfrac{4 + 2}{2}$ ← Midpoint formula

$M(3, 3)$ ← Midpoint of $\overline{AB}$

$M(3, 3)$ lies on $y = x$. ← The x and y coordinates are equal.

To show that $\overline{AB}$ is perpendicular to the line $y = x$, show that the product of their slopes is -1.

$$m_1 = \frac{2 - 4}{4 - 2} = -\frac{2}{2} = -1$$ ← Slope of $\overline{AB}$

$$m_2 = 1$$ ← Slope of $y = x$

$$m_1 \cdot m_2 = -1$$ ← Product of the slopes.

Since the line $y = x$ is perpendicular to, and bisects, $\overline{AB}$, points A and B are symmetric with respect to the line $y = x$.

A point on the graph of a relation and the corresponding point on the graph of its inverse relation are symmetric with respect to the line $y = x$.

Example 3   Graph $f(x) = 2x + 1$. Then graph the inverse, f^{-1}.

Graph f.

Write some ordered pairs of f:

$\{(0, 1), (-1, -1), (2, 5), \cdots\}$

Write corresponding ordered pairs of f^{-1}:

$\{(1, 0), (-1, -1), (5, 2), \cdots\}$

Graph the points of f^{-1}.

Join the points of f^{-1}.

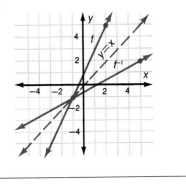

If a function is defined by an equation, the equation of the inverse is obtained by interchanging "x" and "y" in the original equation.

Example 4   The function f is defined by $y = 2x + 1$. Find the equation of f^{-1}.

$$y = 2x + 1$$

$x = 2y + 1$ ⟵——— Interchange x and y.

$y = \dfrac{x - 1}{2}$ ⟵——— Solve for y.

$y = \dfrac{1}{2}x - \dfrac{1}{2}$ ⟵——— Equation of f^{-1}

Try These   *Write the inverse of each function. Indicate whether the inverse is a function.*

1. $\{(1, 1), (2, 3), (3, 4), (4, 5)\}$
$\{(1, 1), (3, 2), (4, 3), (5, 4)\}$; function

2. $\{(0, 2), (2, 2), (3, 4), (1, 5)\}$
$\{(2, 0), (2, 2), (4, 3), (5, 1)\}$; not a function

Exercises   The inverse of each function in Ex. 1-10 is formed by interchanging x and y in the equation.

Write the equation that defines the inverse of each function.

1. $y = x + 2$ $x = y + 2$, or $y = x - 2$

2. $y = -x$ $x = -y$, or $y = -x$

3. $y = 2x$ $x = 2y$, or $y = \frac{1}{2}x$

4. $y = -x + 1$ $x = -y + 1$, or $y = -x + 1$

5. $y = -3x - 4$ $x = -3y - 4$, or $y = -\frac{1}{3}x - \frac{4}{3}$

6. $y = 5x + 6$ $x = 5y + 6$, or $y = \frac{1}{5}x - \frac{6}{5}$

7. $y = \frac{1}{2}x$ $x = \frac{1}{2}y$, or $y = 2x$

8. $y = \frac{1}{2}x + 3$ $x = \frac{1}{2}y + 3$, or $y = 2x - 6$

9. $y = 3$ $x = 3$

10. $y = 0$ $x = 0$

Indicate whether the following pairs of functions are inverses of each other.

11. $y = x + 2; y = x - 2$ Yes

12. $y = 2x + 3; y = \frac{1}{2}x + 3$ No

13. $y = 3x + 1; y = 3x - \frac{1}{3}$ No

14. $y = 5x + 4; y = \frac{1}{5}x - \frac{4}{5}$ Yes

15. $y = x; y = -x$ No

16. $y = 2x - 1; y = \frac{1}{2}x + \frac{1}{2}$ Yes

17. $y = 2x - 3; y = -2x + 3$ No

18. $y = \frac{1}{2}x; y = 2x$ Yes

19. $y = x + \frac{1}{2}; y = x - \frac{1}{2}$ Yes

20. $y = cx + b; y = \dfrac{1}{c}x - \dfrac{b}{c}$ Yes

Graph each function, f, and its inverse, f⁻¹, on the same set of coordinate axes. See key for Exercises 21-29.

21. $f = \{(2, 1), (1, 3), (5, -2), (-3, -4)\}$ **22.** $f(x) = -x$

23. $f(x) = 2x - 3$ **24.** $f(x) = -3x + 5$

25. $f(x) = x^2$ **26.** $f(x) = x$

27. $f(x) = |x|$ **28.** $f(x) = \pm\sqrt{x},\ x \geq 0$

29. If a relation is a function, then no vertical line intersects the graph of the relation in more than one point. How can you tell from the graph of a relation whether the inverse is a function?

Determine whether the inverse of each relation whose graph is given is a function.

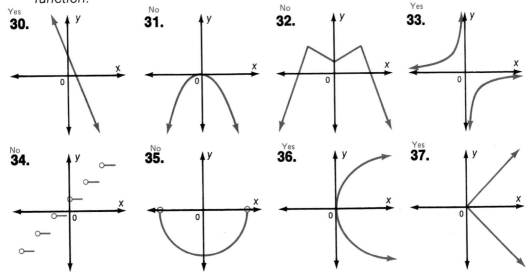

Yes
30.

No
31.

No
32.

Yes
33.

No
34.

No
35.

Yes
36.

Yes
37.

Determine whether this pair of graphs defines inverse functions. Justify your answer.

38.

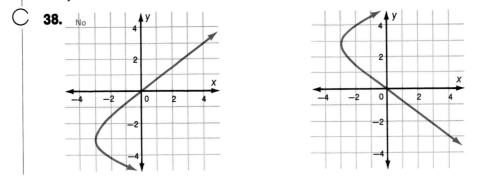

No

Determine whether each pair of graphs defines inverse functions. Justify your answer.

39. No

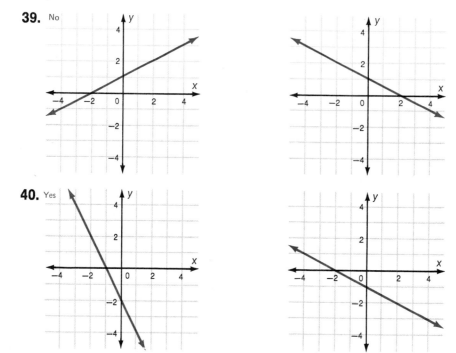

40. Yes

41. Give an example to show that if two functions are inverses of each other, then $f[f^{-1}(x)] = x$ and $f^{-1}[f(x)] = x$. See key.

42. Prove that the line $y = x$ is the perpendicular bisector of the line segment that joins the points (a, b) and (b, a) by using the distance formula.
See key.

PUZZLE

Which is true?

$$\sqrt[10]{10} > \sqrt[3]{2} \quad \text{or} \quad \sqrt[10]{10} < \sqrt[3]{2}$$

$\sqrt[10]{10} < \sqrt[3]{2}$

Inverse and Contrapositive

A **conditional statement** is formed by combining two simple statements.

p: A number is divisible by 6 q: The number is an even number.

$p \rightarrow q$: If a number is divisible by 6,   ⟵——— True
     then the number is an even number.

The converse of this statement, however, is false.

$q \rightarrow p$: If a number is an even number,   ⟵——— False
     then the number is divisible by 6.

If both parts of a conditional are <u>negated</u>, the **inverse** is formed.

$\sim p \rightarrow \sim q$: If a number is <u>not</u> divisible by 6,   ⟵——— False
     then the number is <u>not</u> an even number.

The **contrapositive** of $p \rightarrow q$ is formed by interchanging the $\sim p$ and $\sim q$ of its inverse. If a conditional is true, its contrapositive is also true. Similarly, if $p \rightarrow q$ is false, then $\sim q \rightarrow \sim p$ is false.

$\sim q \rightarrow \sim p$: If a number is <u>not</u> an even number,   ⟵——— True
     then it is <u>not</u> divisible by 6.

Can You Solve These?

Write the inverse and contrapositive of each conditional.

1. If a number is divisible by 9, then it is a multiple of 3.

2. If a number is an integer, then it is a rational number.

3. Classify each inverse and contrapositive as <u>True</u> or <u>False</u>.

Chapter Objectives and Review

Objective: To define the important mathematical terms of this chapter.

1. Here are many of the mathematical terms used in this chapter. Be sure that you know their meanings and that you can use them correctly.

absolute value function (p. 190)
composite function (p. 198)
constant function (p. 190)
constant of variation (p. 191)
direct variation (p. 191)
domain (p. 180)
function (p. 183)
greatest integer function (p. 190)

identity function (p. 190)
inverse relation (p. 202)
linear function (p. 191)
mapping (p. 187)
range (p. 180)
relation (p. 180)
symmetry of two points (p. 202)
Vertical Line Test (p. 183)
zero of a function (p. 194)

Objective: To identify the domain and range of a relation. (Section 5-1)

For each relation, identify the domain and the range.

2. $\{(2, 3), (-3, 2), (1, -3)\}$
   $D: \{2, -3, 1\}; R: \{3, 2, -3\}$

3. $\{(1, 2), (2, 2), (3, 2)\}$
   $D: \{1, 2, 3\}; R: \{2\}$

For each relation, specify the range for the given domain.

4. $y = 3x$; Domain: $\{1, 2, 3, 4\}$
   $R: \{3, 6, 9, 12\}$

5. $y = |2x|$; Domain: $\{-3, -2, -1, 0, 1\}$
   $R: \{0, 2, 4, 6\}$

Objective: To use graphs to distinguish between relations and functions. (Section 5-2)

Graph each relation. Tell which relations are functions.

6. $\{(1, 2), (2, 4), (4, 8)\}$ Function

7. $y = 3x - 2$; Domain: $\{-2, -1, 0, 1, 2\}$ Function

8. $\{(2, 5), (3, 5), (4, 5), (5, 4)\}$ Function

9. $y < x + 1, x \in R$ Not a function

Objective: To evaluate a function that is stated in function notation. (Section 5-2)

10. If $f(x) = 2x - 3$, find $f(-1)$, $f(2)$, and $f(0)$. $-5, 1, -3$

11. If $h(x) = -5x + 2$, find $h(4)$, $h(-4)$, and $h(-2)$. $-18, 22, 12$

Objective: To use mapping diagrams to represent relations. (Section 5-3)

Draw a mapping diagram for each relation.

12. $h: x \longrightarrow x - 3$; Domain: $\{-3, -2, -1, 0\}$ $\quad$ $-3 \to -6, -2 \to -5, -1 \to -4, 0 \to -3$

13. $g: x \longrightarrow 2$; Domain: $\{-3, -1, 1, 3\}$ $\quad$ $-3 \to 2, -1 \to 2, 1 \to 2, 3 \to 2$

14. $f: x \longrightarrow |x|$; Domain: $\{-3, -1, 1, 3\}$ $\quad$ $-3 \to 3, -1 \to 1, 1 \to 1, 3 \to 3$

Objective: To solve problems in direct variation. (Section 5-4)

In the following exercises, y varies directly as x. Find the constant of variation, and find y when x = 2.

15. When $x = -5$, $y = 2$. $\quad -\frac{2}{5}, -\frac{4}{5}$

16. When $x = -\frac{1}{3}$, $y = -3$. $\quad$ 9, 18

17. When $x = 8$, $y = 4$. $\quad \frac{1}{2}, 1$

18. When $x = 2\frac{1}{4}$, $y = 7\frac{1}{2}$. $\quad \frac{10}{3}, \frac{20}{3}$

Objective: To find the zeros of a function. (Section 5-5)

Determine the zeros of each function.

19.

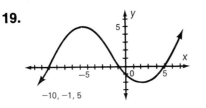

$-10, -1, 5$

20.

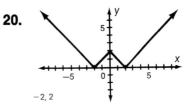

$-2, 2$

21. $f(x) = -3x - 2$ $\quad -\frac{2}{3}$

22. $g(x) = x^2 - 2x$ $\quad$ 0, 2

Objective: To find the equations for the composite functions $h(g)$ and $g(h)$, when the functions g and h are known. (Section 5-6)

$h(g) = 2x^2 - 1; g(h) = 4x^2 - 4x + 1$

23. If $h(x) = 2x - 1$ and $g(x) = x^2$, write the equations for $h(g)$ and $g(h)$.

24. If $f(x) = -x - 3$ and $g(x) = x + 3$, write the equations for $f(g)$ and $g(f)$.

$f(g) = -x - 6; g(f) = -x$

Objective: To find the inverse of a given function. (Section 5-7)

Write the equation that defines the inverse of each function.

25. $y = 2x$ $\quad y = \frac{1}{2}x$

26. $y = 3x + 4$ $\quad y = \frac{1}{3}x - \frac{4}{3}$

Graph each function, f, and its inverse, f^{-1}, on the same set of coordinate axes. (Section 5-7)

f: The straight line passing through $(0,-2)$ and $(1,1)$. f^{-1}: The line through $(-2,0)$ and $(1,1)$.

27. $f(x) = 3x - 2$

28. $f(x) = |x|$ $\quad$ See below.

28. f: See Ex. 32, on page 193. f^{-1}: x = |y| ; See Ex. 33, on page 193.

Relations and Functions $\quad$ **209**

Chapter
Test

Complete these statements.

1. A relation is <u>a set of ordered</u> pairs.

2. The function defined by the equation $y = x$ is called the _____<u>identity</u>_____ function.

3. If f is a function, the symbol used to represent its inverse is ____<u>f^{-1}</u>____.

4. The range of the function, $\{(1, 2), (2, 3)\}$ is ____<u>$\{2, 3\}$</u>____.

5. The equation, $y = 3x + 2$, defines a _____<u>linear</u>_____ function.

6. Specify the range of the function, $g(x) = -\frac{1}{3}x + 5$, where the domain is the set $A = \{-6, -3, 0, 3, 6\}$. <u>$\{7, 6, 5, 4, 3\}$</u>

7. If $f(x) = \frac{1}{2}x - 1$, find $f(-2)$ and $f(1)$. $f(-2) = -2; f(1) = -\frac{1}{2}$

8. Draw a mapping diagram that illustrates a constant function. Answers will vary.

9. Graph the function, $f(x) = x - 3$, where the domain is $\{-2, -1, 0, 2, 4\}$.

10. If y varies directly as x and $y = 1$ when $x = -3$, find y when $x = 2$. $-\frac{2}{3}$

11. Find the zeros of the function, $g(x) = 5x - 2$. $\frac{2}{5}$

12. Find the zeros of the function, $h(x) = 2x^2 - x$. $0, \frac{1}{2}$

13. If $g(x) = 2x - 3$ and $h(x) = 3x + 2$, determine the equation for $g(h)$. $g(h) = 6x + 1$

14. If $h(x) = 3x - 2$, find $h^{-1}(x)$. $h^{-1}(x) = \frac{1}{3}x + \frac{2}{3}$

9. The graph consists of the set of points, $\{(-2,-5), (-1,-4), (0,-3), (2,-1), (4,1)\}$.

Answers to Remember

Page 183: **1.** 9 **2.** 34 **3.** $3a^2 + 4a + 2$ **4.** $3b^2 - 20b + 34$

Page 189: **1.** $x^4 - x^3 + x^2 - 4$ **2.** $5 - 12i$ **3.** $\dfrac{3x^2 + 7x + 5}{2x^2 + 5x}$ **4.** 34

Page 196: **A: 1.** 6 **2.** 3 **3.** -8 **B: 1.** 13 **2.** -3 **3.** 59

Page 201: **1.** $\left(\frac{1}{2}, 0\right)$ **2.** $\left(-3, \frac{1}{2}\right)$ **3.** $-\frac{1}{5}$ **4.** $y = \frac{2}{3}x - \frac{5}{3}$; $x = \frac{3}{2}y + \frac{5}{2}$

Chapter 6
Quadratic Functions

6-1 Variation as the Square

The objective for this section is on page 252.

The equation $A = \pi r^2$ indicates that the area of a circular region varies **directly** as the square of its radius, r. The general equation for a <u>direct variation</u> of this kind is

$$y = kx^2,$$

where k is the <u>constant of variation</u>.

Example 1

If y varies directly as x^2 and $y = 12$ when $x = 2$, find y when $x = 5$.

$y = kx^2$ ← Model

$12 = k(2)^2$ ← When $x = 2$, $y = 12$.

$3 = k$

$y = 3x^2$ ← Equation

$y = 3(5)^2 = 75$ ← When $x = 5$.

<u>Variation as the square</u> can also be expressed as a <u>proportion</u>.

Example 2

If y varies directly as x^2 and $y = 12$ when $x = 2$, find y when $x = 5$.

$y = kx^2$ or $k = \dfrac{y}{x^2}$ ← Model

$\dfrac{y_1}{x_1^{\,2}} = \dfrac{y_2}{x_2^{\,2}}$ ← Ratio of y to x^2 is always the same.

$\dfrac{12}{2^2} = \dfrac{y_2}{5^2}$ ← $x_1 = 2$; $y_1 = 12$ $x_2 = 5$; $y_2 = \underline{\ ?\ }$

$4y_2 = 25 \times 12$ ← Solve for y_2.

$y_2 = 75$

Try These   *For each exercise, y varies directly as the square of x.*

1. If $y = 12$ when $x = 5$, find y when $x = 10$.   48

2. If $y = -5$ when $x = 4$, find y when $x = 8$.   −20

3. If $y = 27$ when $x = 3$, find y when $x = -5$.   75

4. If $y = 8$ when $x = 2$, find y when $x = 7$.   98

Exercises

In Exercises 1–4, write each statement as an equation. Use k as the constant of variation.

a

1. The area of a circle, A, varies directly as the square of its radius, r. $A = kr^2$

2. The distance, d, that an object falls varies directly as the square of the time, t. $d = kt^2$

3. The kinetic energy, E, of a moving object varies directly as the square of its velocity, v. $E = kv^2$

4. The surface area of a sphere, S, varies directly as the square of the radius, r. $S = kr^2$

5. The formula for the kinetic energy of a moving object is $E = KV^2$. Write this formula as a proportion using (E_1, V_1) and (E_2, V_2). $\frac{E_1}{V_1^2} = \frac{E_2}{V_2^2}$

6. The area of a square varies directly as the side of the square, $A = ks^2$. Write this relation as a proportion. $\frac{A_1}{S_1^2} = \frac{A_2}{S_2^2}$

7. If y varies directly as the square of x and $y = 4$ when $x = 6$, find y when $x = 9$.   9

8. If a varies directly as the square of b and $a = 1$ when $b = 8$, find b when $a = 4$.   ±16

9. If r varies directly as the square of t and $t = 6$ when $r = 9$, find t when $r = 4$.   ±4

10. If P varies directly as the square of q and if $P = 5$ when $q = 4$, find P when $q = 8$.   20

11. In the formula $A = \pi r^2$, how does the value of A change when r increases? when r decreases? when r is multiplied by 3?   increase; decreases; multiplied by 9

12. If an object is dropped from a height, the approximate distance it will fall in any number of seconds is expressed by the formula $d = 16t^2$. How does d change if t is doubled? tripled? halved?

d is multiplied by 4; d is multiplied by 9; d is divided by 4.

13. The formula for the surface area of a sphere is $S = 4\pi r^2$. If the value of r is tripled, how does S change? If the value of r is divided by 4, by what is the value of S divided? S is multiplied by 9; 16.

14. The area of one circular region is 20 square inches. Find the area of a second circular region if the ratio of the radius of the first circle to that of the second is 2 to 3. 45 sq. in.

15. Stopping distance after brakes are applied varies directly as the square of the velocity. How many times as great is the stopping distance when the velocity is 60 miles per hour than when it is 30 miles per hour? If the velocity is doubled, how is the stopping distance changed?
4 times as great; multiplied by 4

16. Is a circular pizza pie with a 16-centimeter diameter worth twice the price of a pizza with a 10-centimeter diameter? No, it is worth more.

17. Make a table of ordered pairs that satisfy $y = kx^2$. Use integral values from −5 to 5 for x.

x	−5	−4	−3	−2	−1	0	1	2	3	4	5
y	$25k$	$16k$	$9k$	$4k$	k	0	k	$4k$	$9k$	$16k$	$25k$

18. Use the table of Exercise 17 to find the difference between successive values for kx^2. Are the differences the same?
No; $9k$; $7k$; $5k$; $3k$; k; $-k$; $-3k$; $-5k$; $-7k$; $-9k$

19. Find the difference between the successive values obtained in Exercise 18. Are these "second differences" the same? Each difference is $2k$.

20. As x increases by 1 in $y = kx^2$, what generalization can you make about how the second differences change for y? They do not change; each is $2k$.

Remember

1. Find the equation of the line containing the point $A(2, -1)$ and having a slope of −3. $y = 3x + 5$

2. What is the slope of the line defined by the equation $2y - 5x = 5$? $\frac{5}{2}$

3. Two distinct lines are defined by the equations $4y - 3x = 7$ and $6y + 8x = 5$. How are the graphs of these lines related? They are perpendicular to each other.

The answers are on page 254.

PUZZLE

Express 5 with exactly two 2's and standard mathematical symbols. $(\sqrt{.2}\,)^{-2}$

6-2 Quadratic Functions

The objective for this section is on page 252.

In general, a **quadratic function** is a function that may be defined by

$$y = ax^2 + bx + c,$$

where a, b, and c are complex number constants, and $a \neq 0$. The restriction $a \neq 0$ assures that $y = ax^2 + bx + c$ defines a <u>nonlinear function</u>. When the domain is the set of real numbers, the graph of a quadratic function is a **parabola.**

Example 1

Graph the quadratic function

$$y = x^2.$$

Make a table.

x	−3	−2	−1	0	1	2	3
y	9	4	1	0	1	4	9

Plot each point.

Join the points with a smooth curve.

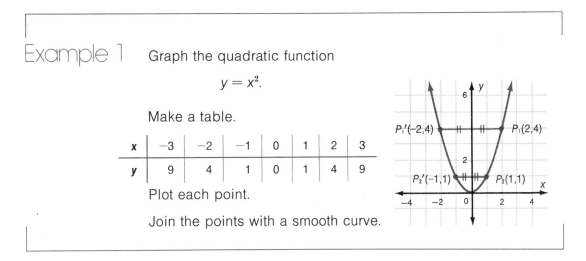

The graph of $y = x^2$ is a curve that is symmetric with respect to the y axis. For each point P on the graph, there is a corresponding point P' such that the y axis is the perpendicular bisector of segment PP'. When this is so, the points P and P' are said to be **mirror images** of each other. Every parabola is symmetric with respect to some line. This line is called the **axis of symmetry.** The axis of symmetry intersects the parabola in a single point called the **turning point,** or **vertex,** of the parabola. The vertex is its own mirror image with respect to the axis of symmetry. The vertex is the lowest, or **minimum** point of the parabola if the parabola opens upward; it is the highest, or **maximum,** point if the parabola opens downward.

Example 2 The equation of a parabola is $y = x^2 + 2x + c$. Find the value of c if the graph of the parabola contains $(1, -3)$.

$$y = x^2 + 2x + c \qquad \longleftarrow \text{Function}$$

$$-3 = (1)^2 + 2(1) + c \qquad \longleftarrow \text{Replace } x \text{ with 1 and } y \text{ with } -3.$$

$$-3 = 3 + c \qquad \longleftarrow \text{Solve for } c.$$

$$-6 = c$$

Thus, $c = -6$ and the equation of the parabola is $y = x^2 + 2x - 6$.

Try These Classify each function as linear (L) or quadratic (Q).

1. $f(x) = 2x + 7$ L

2. $f(x) = x^2 + 2x + 7$ Q

3. $f(x) = 2x$ L

4. $f(x) = 2x^2 + x$ Q

5. $f(x) = 6x^2 + 1$ Q

6. $f(x) = (a - x)^2$ Q

Exercises

Each figure below is the graph of a quadratic function.

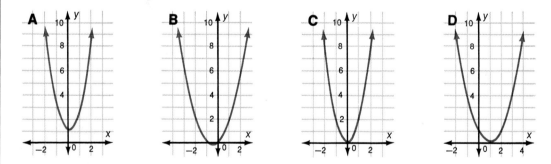

Identify the function graphed above that contains each of the following sets of ordered pairs.

1. $\{(-2, 8), (-1, 2), (0, 0), (1, 2), (2, 8)\}$ C

2. $\{(-2, 9), (-1, 3), (0, 1), (1, 3), (2, 9)\}$ A

3. $\{(-2, 9), (-1, 4), (0, 1), (1, 0), (2, 1)\}$ D

4. $\{(-2, 2), (-1, 0), (0, 0), (1, 2), (2, 6)\}$ B

For each function, make a table of values for integral values of x, −5 ≤ x ≤ 5.
Use the table to graph each function. See below for Exercises 5, 6, 7.

5. $y = x^2 + 1$ 　　　　　 **6.** $y = x^2 + 2x + 1$ 　　　　　 **7.** $y = x^2 - 5x + 6$

In Exercises 8-11, the equation of a parabola and a point through which
the graph of the parabola passes are given. For each parabola, find the
value of the specified coefficient.

8. $y = x^2 + bx - 9$; $A(-2, -5)$; $b = \underline{\ ?\ }$ 0

9. $y = 2x^2 + 3x + c$; $H(1, 0)$; $c = \underline{\ ?\ }$ −5

10. $y = ax^2 + 3x - 2$; $J(2, 24)$; $a = \underline{\ ?\ }$ 5

11. $y = x^2 + bx + 3$; $N(-1, 8)$; $b = \underline{\ ?\ }$ −4

In Exercises 12-13, graph the given quadratic functions on the same set
of coordinate axes. Compare the graphs by indicating the axis of symmetry
and the vertex of each parabola. Tell whether the parabolas are the same
size and shape.

12. $y = x^2$;　$y = x^2 - 4$;　$y = x^2 - 8x + 12$　See key.

13. $y = 2x^2$;　$y = 2x^2 - 8x + 8$;　$y = 2x^2 - 8x + 10$　See key.

14. For $f(x) = ax^2 + bx + c_1$ and $g(x) = ax^2 + bx + c_2$, a and b have the same
value in both functions. How do the graphs of the functions compare?
See key.

15. For $f(x) = a_1x^2 + c$ and $g(x) = a_2x^2 + c$, c has the same value for both
functions and $b = 0$. How do the graphs of the functions compare?
See key.

16. The distance an object will fall in t seconds is given approximately by
$d = 4.9t^2$. A ball is dropped from a 200-meter cliff. How long will it take to
hit the water below?   6.4 seconds

17. The height of a rocket t seconds after being given an upward velocity
of 80 meters per second is $s = 80t - 4.9t^2$. Sketch a graph of this function.
How many seconds after firing does the rocket hit the ground? What is its
highest altitude above the ground? See key.

x	−5	−4	−3	−2	−1	0	1	2	3	4	5
5. y	26	17	10	5	2	1	2	5	10	17	26
6. y	16	9	4	1	0	1	4	9	16	25	36
7. y	56	42	30	20	12	6	2	0	0	2	6

PUZZLE

Two sisters own a herd of cattle which they sell for as many
dollars each as there are heads of cattle. They use the income
from this sale to buy sheep at $10 each and one lamb. They then
divide equally the number of animals purchased. How much did
the lamb cost? $6

6-3 The Role of a in $y = ax^2$

The objectives for this section are on pages 252-253.

Example 1   Use the graph below to compare $y = x^2$ and $y = -x^2$.

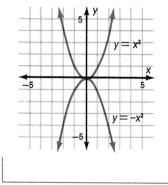

Graph of	
$y = x^2$	$y = -x^2$
Opens upward.	Opens downward.
Vertex: (0, 0)	Vertex: (0, 0)
Vertex is a minimum point.	Vertex is a maximum point.

The graphs have the same size and shape; that is, the parabolas are **congruent**.

Now compare the graphs of $y = ax^2$ and $y = -ax^2$ when $|a|$ equals $\frac{1}{2}$, 1, 2, and 3. Each graph is symmetric with respect to the y axis and each has its vertex at the origin. Some parabolas are "steeper" than others, but, for a given value for a, the graphs of $y = ax^2$ and $y = -ax^2$ are congruent.

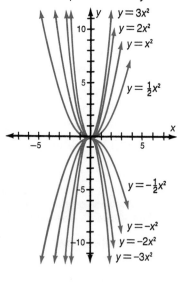

Value of a	Graph of $y = ax^2$
$a > 0$	Opens upward. Vertex: (0, 0) Vertex is a minimum.
$a < 0$	Opens downward Vertex: (0, 0) Vertex is a maximum.
$|a| > 1$	Steeper than $y = x^2$.
$|a| < 1$	Less steep than $y = x^2$.

Example 2 Without graphing, classify the graphs of $y = 3x^2$, $y = -\frac{1}{4}x^2$, $y = -2x^2$, $y = -7x^2$, and $y = \frac{1}{8}x^2$ as opening upward or opening downward. Then list the functions in order of the steepness of their graphs, beginning with the least steep.

Opens upward: $y = 3x^2$, $y = \frac{1}{8}x^2$ ⟵ $a > 0$

Opens downward: $y = -\frac{1}{4}x^2$, $y = -2x^2$, $y = -7x^2$ ⟵ $a < 0$

Steepness: $y = \frac{1}{8}x^2$, $y = -\frac{1}{4}x^2$, $y = -2x^2$, $y = 3x^2$, $y = -7x^2$ ⟵ $|\frac{1}{8}| < |\frac{1}{4}| < |-2| < |3| < |-7|$

Example 3 Sketch the graph of $y = \frac{1}{8}x^2$. Identify its axis of symmetry and the coordinates of its vertex. Tell whether the vertex is a maximum point or a minimum point.

Make a table.

x	−4	−2	−1	0	1	2	4
y	2	$\frac{1}{2}$	$\frac{1}{8}$	0	$\frac{1}{8}$	$\frac{1}{2}$	2

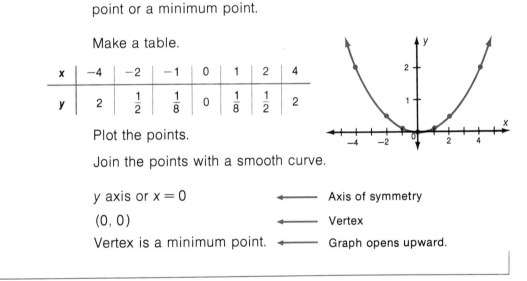

Plot the points.

Join the points with a smooth curve.

y axis or $x = 0$ ⟵ Axis of symmetry

$(0, 0)$ ⟵ Vertex

Vertex is a minimum point. ⟵ Graph opens upward.

Try These Classify the graph of each function as opening upward (U) or opening downward (D).

1. $y = 5x^2$ u

2. $y = \frac{1}{3}x^2$ u

3. $y = -\frac{1}{2}x^2$ d

4. $y + 2x^2 = 0$ d

5. $f(x) = 10x^2$ u

6. $f(x) = -1\frac{1}{2}x^2$ d

Quadratic Functions **219**

Exercises

a

1. Which graph is steeper, that of $y = x^2$ or that of $y = 2x^2$? $_{y = 2x^2}$

2. Which graph is wider, that of $y = 2x^2$ or that of $y = \frac{1}{2}x^2$? $_{y = \frac{1}{2}x^2}$

3. Which graph opens downward, that of $y = 3x^2$ or that of $y = -3x^2$? $_{y = -3x^2}$

4. State in your own words how to determine whether a parabola is "wide" or "narrow" and whether it opens upward or downward.

5. Arrange the following functions in order of the steepness of their graphs, beginning with the least steep. $_{e, c, f, d, a, b}$
   a. $f_1(x) = 3x^2$ **b.** $f_2(x) = 24x^2$ **c.** $f_3(x) = -\frac{1}{2}x^2$
   d. $f_4(x) = -2x^2$ **e.** $f_5(x) = \frac{1}{4}x^2$ **f.** $f_6(x) = -x^2$

6. For what values of a will the graph of $y = ax^2$ have a maximum point? $_{a < 0}$

7. What is the minimum point of the graph of $y = 4x^2$? of $y = 4x^2 + 6$? $_{(0, 0), (0, 6)}$

8. What is the maximum point of the graph of $y = -4x^2$? of $y = -4x^2 + 3$?
   $_{(0, 0), (0, 3)}$

9. Compare the graphs of $y = 2x^2$ and $y = -2x^2$. $_{\text{See below.}}$

10. Do the graphs of $y = -3x^2$ and $y = 3x^2$ have the same size and shape? Explain. $_{\text{Yes, since } |-3| = |3|. \text{ However, they open in opposite directions.}}$

Graph the functions defined by the following equations. Identify the axis of symmetry of each parabola, give the coordinates of its vertex, and indicate whether the vertex is a maximum point or a minimum point.

11. $y = 4x^2$ $_{x = 0; (0, 0); \text{ minimum}}$ 12. $y = \frac{1}{4}x^2$ $_{x = 0; (0, 0); \text{ minimum}}$ $_{x = 0; (0, 0); \text{ maximum}}$
13. $y = -\frac{1}{4}x^2$

14. $y = -4x^2$ $_{x = 0; (0, 0); \text{ maximum}}$ 15. $y = -2x^2$ $_{x = 0; (0, 0); \text{ maximum}}$ 16. $y = -\frac{1}{2}x^2$
   $_{x = 0; (0, 0); \text{ maximum}}$

b

17. Sketch a parabola that contains the points $(2, 6)$ *and* $(-3, 13\frac{1}{2})$ and has its vertex at the origin. $_{\text{Axis of symmetry: } y \text{ axis. Graph contains } (-2, 6) \text{ and } (3, 13\frac{1}{2}).}$

18. Sketch a parabola that has its minimum point at the origin and contains the point $(1, 5)$. $_{\text{Axis of symmetry: } y \text{ axis. } (-1, 5) \text{ is also on the graph.}}$

19. Sketch a parabola that contains the points $(1, 5)$ and $(2, 8)$ and has its vertex at the point $(0. 4)$. $_{\text{Axis of symmetry: } y \text{ axis. Graph contains } (-1, 5) \text{ and } (-2, 8).}$

20. Sketch a parabola that has a maximum point at $(0, -3)$ and contains the point $(-3, -7)$. $_{\text{Axis of symmetry: } y \text{ axis. } (3, -7) \text{ is also on the graph.}}$

c

21. Using y, x, and a, write a general equation for the parabola whose vertex is at the origin and whose axis of symmetry is the x axis. For which values of a will the parabolas open to the right? to the left? $_{x = ay^2; a > 0; a < 0}$

9. Each vertex is at $(0, 0)$. The y axis is the axis of symmetry. They have the same size and shape, but open in opposite directions.

The Role of c in $y = ax^2 + bx + c$

The objectives for this section are on pages 252-253.

Example 1. Use the graph at the right to compare these functions.

$$f(x) = \frac{1}{2}x^2$$

$$g(x) = \frac{1}{2}x^2 + 7$$

$$h(x) = \frac{1}{2}x^2 - 5$$

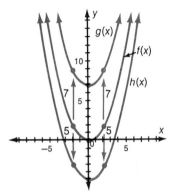

$f(x) = \frac{1}{2}x^2$	$g(x) = \frac{1}{2}x^2 + 7$	$h(x) = \frac{1}{2}x^2 - 5$
Opens upward	Opens upward	Opens upward
Vertex: (0, 0)	Vertex: (0, 7)	Vertex: (0, −5)
Vertex is a minimum point.	Vertex is a minimum point.	Vertex is a minimum point.
Axis of symmetry: $x = 0$	Axis of symmetry: $x = 0$	Axis of symmetry: $x = 0$

Example 2 Use the graph of $f(x) = x^2 - 2x$ at the right to sketch the graph of $g(x) = f(x) + 3$. Write an equation that defines $g(x)$.

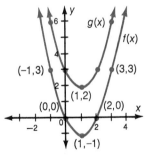

x	−1	0	1	2	3
f(x)	3	0	−1	0	3
f(x) + 3	6	3	2	3	6

$g(x) = f(x) + 3$ ⟵——— Equation of $g(x)$.
$g(x) = x^2 - 2x + 3$ ⟵——— Replace $f(x)$ with $x^2 - 2x$.

Quadratic Functions   **221**

In Example 1, the three graphs are <u>congruent</u>. Thus, for each point $(x, f(x))$ on $f(x) = \frac{1}{2}x^2$, there is a corresponding point $(x, f(x) + 7)$ on $g(x) = \frac{1}{2}x^2 + 7$ and a corresponding point $(x, f(x) - 5)$ on $h(x) = \frac{1}{2}x^2 - 5$.

Given a graph of a function, $f(x) = ax^2 + bx$, $a \neq 0$, and the graph of a function, $g(x) = ax^2 + bx + c$, $a \neq 0$, where a and b are the same in f and g, then

1. the graphs of $f(x)$ and $g(x)$ are congruent, and
2. each point on the graph of $g(x)$ is c units directly above or below the corresponding point of $f(x)$.

Example 3   The vertex of $f(x) = -3x^2 + 6x$ is at $V(1, 3)$. Determine the co-ordinates of the vertex, V', of $g(x) = -3x^2 + 6x - 3$.

Functions are congruent. ⟵⟶ For each function, $a = -3$, $b = 6$.
$V'(1, 0)$ ⟵ V' is 3 units below V.

Example 4   If $f(x) = ax^2 + bx + c$, find its y intercept.

$f(x) = ax^2 + bx + c$
$f(0) = 0 + 0 + c$ ⟵ For the y intercept, $x = 0$.
$f(0) = c$
$(0, c)$ ⟵ y intercept

Try These   *The graphs of each of the following functions are parabolas.*

$f_1(x) = 2x^2$ $f_2(x) = -3x^2 + 1$ $f_3(x) = \frac{1}{2}x^2$
$f_4(x) = -2x^2 - 1$ $f_5(x) = 2x^2 + 6$ $f_6(x) = 3x^2 + 4$

1. Which parabolas are congruent? f_1, f_5, f_4, f_2, f_6
2. Which parabolas open in the same direction? f_1, f_3, f_5 and f_6; f_2 and f_4
3. For each parabola, determine the coordinates of its vertex.
   $f_1:(0,0), f_2:(0,1), f_3:(0,0), f_4:(0,-1), f_5:(0,6), f_6:(0,4)$

Exercises

The function $f_2(x)$ is defined by the equation $y = \frac{1}{2}x^2$. The graphs of the functions $f_1(x)$ and $f_3(x)$ are congruent to the graph of $f_2(x)$.

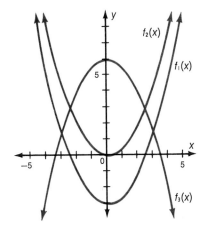

(0,−3); (0,0); (0,6)
1. List the coordinates of the vertex of each parabola.
2. Write the equation that defines $f_1(x)$ and $f_3(x)$.

$f_1(x) = \frac{1}{2}x^2 - 3;$

$f_2(x) = \frac{1}{2}x^2;$

$f_3(x) = -\frac{1}{2}x^2 + 6$

For Exercises 3-6, list the coordinates of the y intercept of the graph of each function.

3. $\overset{(0,-4)}{y = 2x^2 + 7x - 4}$ 4. $\overset{(0,0)}{y = 5x^2}$ 5. $\overset{(0,8)}{y = -3x^2 + 2x + 8}$ 6. $\overset{(0,0)}{y = x^2 + 2x}$

7. Are the graphs of the parabolas $y = 3x^2$, $y = -3x^2 + 2$ and $y = 3x^2 + 5$ congruent? Explain.   Yes, since |3| = |−3| = 3.

Sketch the graphs of $y = x^2$ and $y = -x^2$ on the same set of coordinate axes. Then sketch each of the following functions on the same set of axes. Give the coordinates of the vertex of each parabola.

8. $\overset{(0,2);\ upward}{y = x^2 + 2}$ 9. $\overset{(0,-3);\ upward}{y = x^2 - 3}$ 10. $\overset{(0,-4);\ downward}{y = -x^2 - 4}$

11. $y = x^2 + 6$ 12. $y = -x^2 + 1$ 13. $y = -x^2 - \frac{1}{2}$

(0,6); upward   (0,1); downward $(0,-\frac{1}{2})$; downward

Sketch the graph of $g(x)$ in Exercises 14-17 by moving the function f the required number of units up or down on its axis of symmetry. Write the equation that defines $g(x)$.

$g(x) = x^2 - 4x + 2$
14. $f(x)$ is moved up 2 units.

$g(x) = x^2 - 6x - 4$
15. $f(x)$ is moved down 4 units.

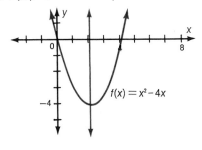

$f(x) = x^2 - 4x$

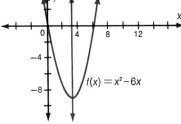

$f(x) = x^2 - 6x$

Quadratic Functions   **223**

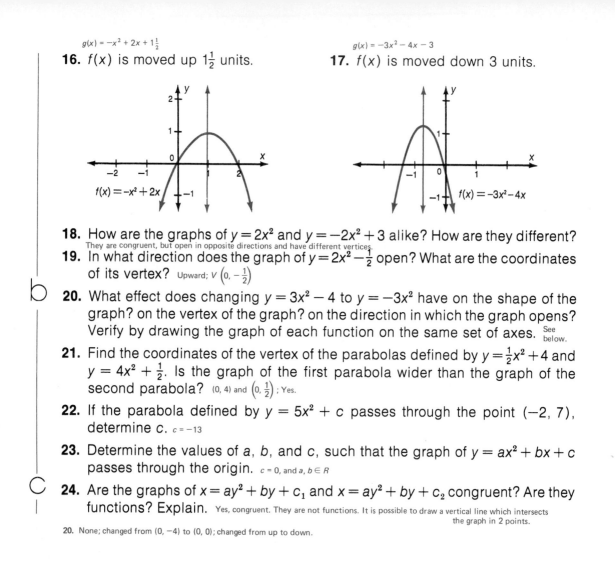

$g(x) = -x^2 + 2x + 1\frac{1}{2}$

16. $f(x)$ is moved up $1\frac{1}{2}$ units.

$f(x) = -x^2 + 2x$

$g(x) = -3x^2 - 4x - 3$

17. $f(x)$ is moved down 3 units.

$f(x) = -3x^2 - 4x$

18. How are the graphs of $y = 2x^2$ and $y = -2x^2 + 3$ alike? How are they different?
They are congruent, but open in opposite directions and have different vertices.

19. In what direction does the graph of $y = 2x^2 - \frac{1}{2}$ open? What are the coordinates of its vertex? Upward; $V\left(0, -\frac{1}{2}\right)$

20. What effect does changing $y = 3x^2 - 4$ to $y = -3x^2$ have on the shape of the graph? on the vertex of the graph? on the direction in which the graph opens? Verify by drawing the graph of each function on the same set of axes. See below.

21. Find the coordinates of the vertex of the parabolas defined by $y = \frac{1}{2}x^2 + 4$ and $y = 4x^2 + \frac{1}{2}$. Is the graph of the first parabola wider than the graph of the second parabola? $(0, 4)$ and $\left(0, \frac{1}{2}\right)$; Yes.

22. If the parabola defined by $y = 5x^2 + c$ passes through the point $(-2, 7)$, determine c. $c = -13$

23. Determine the values of a, b, and c, such that the graph of $y = ax^2 + bx + c$ passes through the origin. $c = 0$, and $a, b \in R$

24. Are the graphs of $x = ay^2 + by + c_1$ and $x = ay^2 + by + c_2$ congruent? Are they functions? Explain. Yes, congruent. They are not functions. It is possible to draw a vertical line which intersects the graph in 2 points.

20. None; changed from $(0, -4)$ to $(0, 0)$; changed from up to down.

6-5 The Role of b in $y = ax^2 + bx + c$

The objectives for this section are on pages 252-253.

When the term bx is included in $y = ax^2 + bx + c$, the axis of symmetry of the graph is no longer the y axis, but a line parallel to the y axis. The vertex of the parabola lies on the axis of symmetry.

Compare the graphs of $y = x^2$, $y = x^2 + 6x$, and $y = x^2 + 6x + 12$.

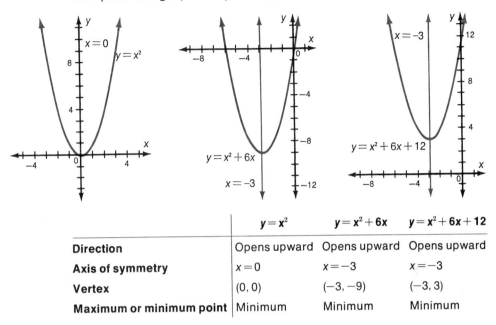

	$y = x^2$	$y = x^2 + 6x$	$y = x^2 + 6x + 12$
Direction	Opens upward	Opens upward	Opens upward
Axis of symmetry	$x = 0$	$x = -3$	$x = -3$
Vertex	$(0, 0)$	$(-3, -9)$	$(-3, 3)$
Maximum or minimum point	Minimum	Minimum	Minimum

Note that the parabolas are congruent.

Example 1 Find the equation of the axis of symmetry for $y = ax^2 + bx$.

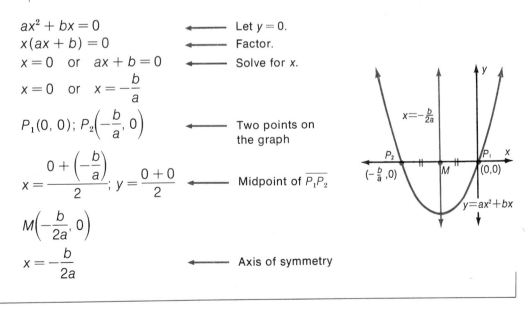

$ax^2 + bx = 0$ ⟵ Let $y = 0$.

$x(ax + b) = 0$ ⟵ Factor.

$x = 0$ or $ax + b = 0$ ⟵ Solve for x.

$x = 0$ or $x = -\dfrac{b}{a}$

$P_1(0, 0);\ P_2\left(-\dfrac{b}{a}, 0\right)$ ⟵ Two points on the graph

$x = \dfrac{0 + \left(-\dfrac{b}{a}\right)}{2};\ y = \dfrac{0 + 0}{2}$ ⟵ Midpoint of $\overline{P_1 P_2}$

$M\left(-\dfrac{b}{2a}, 0\right)$

$x = -\dfrac{b}{2a}$ ⟵ Axis of symmetry

Since c merely raises or lowers the parabola, the axis of symmetry is the same for $y = ax^2 + bx + c$.

Theorem 6-1: The equation of the axis of symmetry of a parabola defined by $y = ax^2 + bx + c$, $a \neq 0$, is

$$x = -\frac{b}{2a}.$$

Example 2   Find the equation of the axis of symmetry and the coordinates of the vertex of $y = 4x^2 - 8x - 5$. Tell whether the parabola has a maximum or a minimum point. Give the maximum or minimum value of the function. Find two other points on the parabola. Then sketch the parabola.

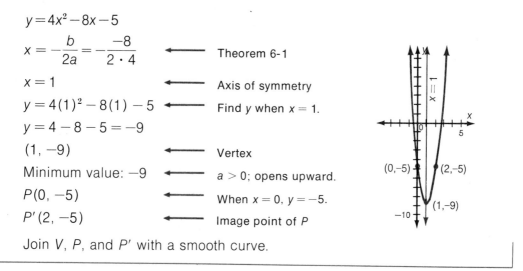

$y = 4x^2 - 8x - 5$

$x = -\dfrac{b}{2a} = -\dfrac{-8}{2 \cdot 4}$ ←—— Theorem 6-1

$x = 1$ ←—— Axis of symmetry

$y = 4(1)^2 - 8(1) - 5$ ←—— Find y when $x = 1$.

$y = 4 - 8 - 5 = -9$

$(1, -9)$ ←—— Vertex

Minimum value: -9 ←—— $a > 0$; opens upward.

$P(0, -5)$ ←—— When $x = 0$, $y = -5$.

$P'(2, -5)$ ←—— Image point of P

Join V, P, and P' with a smooth curve.

Try These   For each parabola, find the equation of the axis of symmetry.

1. $y = x^2$ $x = 0$ **2.** $y = -x^2 + 7x$ $x = \frac{7}{2}$ **3.** $y = x^2 - 4x - 5$
                                                                                    $x = 2$

For each parabola, determine the coordinates of the vertex. Indicate whether the point is a maximum or a minimum.

4. $y = 3x^2 + 1$ **5.** $y = -5x^2 + 4$ **6.** $y = -2x^2 + x - 3$
(0,1), minimum   (0,4) maximum $\left(\frac{1}{4}, -\frac{23}{8}\right)$, maximum

Exercises

For each function, determine the equation of the axis of symmetry and the coordinates of the vertex. Tell whether the function has a maximum or a minimum value.

1. $x = \frac{1}{2}; V\left(\frac{1}{2}, -\frac{9}{4}\right)$; minimum
   $y = x^2 - x - 2$

2. $x = -\frac{5}{2}; V\left(-\frac{5}{2}, -\frac{1}{4}\right)$; minimum
   $y = x^2 + 5x + 6$

3. $x = 0; V(0,4)$; min.
   $f(x) = x^2 + 4$

4. $x = 1; V(1,16)$; max.
   $f(x) = 15 + 2x - x^2$

5. $x = -\frac{1}{4}; V\left(-\frac{1}{4}, -\frac{25}{8}\right)$; min.
   $y = 2x^2 + x - 3$

6. $x = -\frac{1}{2}; V\left(-\frac{1}{2}, -\frac{9}{4}\right)$; min.
   $y = x^2 + x - 2$

7. $x = 0; V(0,4)$; max.
   $g(x) = 4 - x^2$

8. $x = -\frac{1}{6}; V\left(-\frac{1}{6}, \frac{25}{12}\right)$; max.
   $g(x) = 2 - x - 3x^2$

9. $x = 0; V(0,0)$; min.
   $f(x) = x^2$

10. $x = -1; V(-1,-2)$; min.
    $g(x) = 3x^2 + 6x + 1$

11. $x = -1; V(-1,-7)$; min.
    $y = 2x^2 + 4x - 5$

12. $x = \frac{3}{10}, V\left(\frac{3}{10}, \frac{29}{20}\right)$; max.
    $y = -5x^2 + 3x + 1$

Sketch each parabola by graphing (a) the axis of symmetry, (b) the vertex, (c) the zeros (x intercepts) of the function, (d) one other point on the parabola and the point symmetric to it with respect to the axis of the parabola (image point). See key for Exercises 13-19.

13. $y = x^2 + x - 6$

14. $y = x^2 - 4x$

15. $y = x^2 - 7x + 6$

16. $y = 2x^2 - 2x - 12$

17. $y = 6x^2 - 9x - 6$

18. $y = 4x^2 - 4x - 3$

19. How is the graph of $y = x^2 - 4x + 1$ like the graph of $y = 4x - x^2 - 1$? How is it different?

20. If b is changed from -8 to 8 in $y = 2x^2 - 8x + 1$, while a and c remain the same, how does this affect the position of the axis of symmetry? the position of the vertex? changed from $x = 2$ to $x = -2$; changed from $(2,-7)$ to $(-2,-7)$

21. The graph of a parabola is congruent to the graph of $y = 2x^2 - 8x + 3$, opens in the same direction, has the same y intercept, and is 2 units to the left of $y = 2x^2 - 8x + 3$. Write the equation of the parabola. $y = 2x^2 + 3$

22. The graph of a parabola is congruent to the graph of $y = 3x^2 - 6x + 4$, has the same y intercept, opens downward, and is 3 units to the right of $y = 3x^2 - 6x + 4$. Write the equation of the parabola. $y = -3x^2 + 24x + 4$

23. Show that if the abscissa of the vertex of the parabola defined by $y = ax^2 + bx + c$ is $-\dfrac{b}{2a}$, then the ordinate of the vertex is $-\dfrac{b^2}{4a} + c$.

24. Show that $y = a(x - h)^2 + k$ defines a parabola whose vertex is at (h, k). See key.

25. The equation $x = ay^2 + by + c$ defines a parabola with an axis of symmetry defined by $y = -\dfrac{b}{2a}$. Illustrate this by sketching the graphs of $x = y^2 - 4y + 2$ and $x = -y^2 - 4y + 2$. See key.

23. Replace x by $-\frac{b}{2a}$ in $y = ax^2 + bx + c$.

Find the solution set.

1. $3x - 2 = 5$ $\{\frac{7}{3}\}$

2. $4x + 2 = -6$ $\{-2\}$

3. $2x - 5 = 4$ <u>or</u> $2x - 5 = -4$ $\{4\frac{1}{2}, \frac{1}{2}\}$

Simplify.

4. $\sqrt{6} \cdot \sqrt{8} \cdot \sqrt{3}$ 12

5. $\dfrac{\sqrt{4 + 24}}{4}$ $\frac{\sqrt{7}}{2}$

6. $\dfrac{x}{2x - 5} - \dfrac{5}{2x + 5}$ $\frac{2x^2 - 5x + 25}{4x^2 - 25}$

The answers are on page 254.

6-6 Applications: Maximum and Minimum

The objective for this section is on page 253.

Quadratic functions can be useful models in situations where it is desirable to maximize or minimize the use of materials.

Example

A rain gutter is made by bending up the edges of a piece of aluminum 25 centimeters wide so that the cross-sectional area is a maximum. Find how much the edges of the piece should be bent to maximize the area.

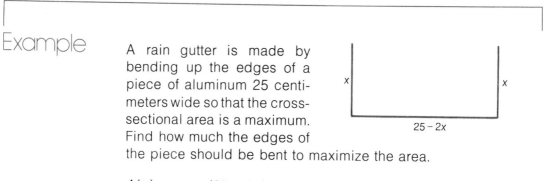

$25 - 2x$

$A(x) = y = x(25 - 2x)$ $\longleftarrow$ Model for cross sectional area

$\quad\quad y = 25x - 2x^2$

Graph opens downward; $\longleftarrow$ $a < 0$
thus, the vertex is a
maximum point

$x = -\dfrac{25}{-4} = 6.25$ $\longleftarrow$ Axis of symmetry: $x = -\dfrac{b}{2a}$

$V(6.25, f(6.25))$ $\longleftarrow$ Coordinates of vertex

$V(6.25, 78.125)$ $\longleftarrow$ Find y when $x = 6.25$.

Thus, the maximum cross-sectional area of 78.125 square centimeters occurs when the edge of the 25-centimeter strip is bent up 6.25 centimeters.

Try These   *Find the maximum or minimum value for each function.*

1. $f(x) = x^2 + x$

$-\frac{1}{4}$, minimum

2. $-x^2 + 3x = h(x)$

$2\frac{1}{4}$, maximum

3. $5x - x^2 = p(x)$

$6\frac{1}{4}$ maximum

Write a quadratic equation that can be a model for each situation.

4. The area of a rectangular field is 221 square meters and one side is 4 meters longer than the other. $(x + 4)x = 221$ or $x^2 + 4x = 221$

5. The area of a circular disc with radius, r, is 440 square centimeters. $\pi r^2 = 440$

Exercises

Find the maximum or minimum value of each function. State whether the value is a maximum or minimum.

1. $f(x) = 2x^2 - x$ min. of $-\frac{1}{8}$

2. $f(x) = 2x^2 + x$ min. of $-\frac{1}{8}$

3. $f(x) = -2x^2 + x$ max. of $\frac{1}{8}$

4. $-2x^2 - x = f(x)$ max. of $\frac{1}{8}$

5. $g(x) = \frac{1}{4}x^2 - 2x$ min. of -4

6. $g(x) = 2x^2 - \frac{1}{4}x$ min. of $-\frac{1}{128}$

7. A rectangular garden is to be enclosed on three sides by fencing; the fourth side is a side of the house. What is the largest garden that can be enclosed by 30 meters of fencing? (Write the area as a function of x and find the maximum value of the function.)   area at $x = \frac{15}{2}$ is $\frac{225}{2}$ square meters

House

x x

$30 - 2x$

8. If you throw a ball vertically with a velocity of v meters per second, its distance in meters, s, above the starting point in t seconds is shown by experiment to be $s = vt - 4.9t^2$. If the ball is thrown with an initial velocity of 30 meters per second, this formula becomes $s = 30t - 4.9t^2$. Is the graph of this quadratic function a parabola that opens downward or upward? How many seconds will it take the ball to reach its highest point? How high will it go?   downward, 3.1 sec.; 45.9 meters

9. How high will a bullet rise if fired vertically with an initial velocity of 300 meters per second? (See the formula in Exercise 8.) How long will it take the bullet to reach its maximum height?   4592 meters; 30.6 sec.

Quadratic Functions   **229**

10. A farmer's daughter wishes to fence in a rectangular poultry yard. She has 200 meters of fencing and wants to enclose the maximum area. What should be the dimensions of the yard so that the enclosed region has a maximum area? 50 m X 50 m

11. Find two numbers such that their sum is 20 and the sum of their squares is a minimum. 10 and 10

12. Find two numbers whose sum is 10 and whose product is a maximum. 5 and 5

13. Find two numbers such that their sum is 30 and the sum of their squares is a minimum. 15 and 15

14. Jon has two dogs. He wants to make two pens so that each dog will have the same size pen and as much ground space as possible. If Jon has 200 meters of fencing and the pens are to be rectangular, what should the dimensions be? (Part of the fencing is to be used to separate the two pens.) $33\frac{1}{3}m$ X 50m; $33\frac{1}{3}m$ is also dimension of the fence separating the two pens.

15. A tinsmith wishes to make a double gutter for two liquids from a strip of tin 26 centimeters wide by folding up the edges and folding in the middle. The cross sections of the parts are to be rectangular and have the same area. Find the dimensions that will give maximum carrying capacity. Each gutter is 3cm high and the width of each gutter is 6cm.

16. If, in Exercise 15, the center wall is to be one centimeter higher than the outer edges, what dimensions will produce the maximum carrying capacity? Gutter is $2\frac{3}{4}$ cm deep and $5\frac{1}{2}$ cm wide with center wall of $3\frac{3}{4}$ cm.

17. Given a fixed perimeter, P, of a rectangle, what are the dimensions of the sides that will give the greatest possible area? Each side is $\frac{P}{4}$

18. An open box is to be made from a rectangular sheet of metal by cutting 2-centimeter squares from each of its corners. If the perimeter of the base of the box must be 40 centimeters, what is the maximum possible volume of the box? 200 cubic centimeters

PUZZLE

A puppy was priced six consecutive weeks at $1.25, $1.89, $5.13, $5.94, $9.18, and was finally sold for $12.42. How were the prices figured? Add the square of the sum of the digits to the previous price. For example, 1 + 2 + 5 = 8; $8^2 = 64$; 1.25 + .64 = 1.89.

Solving Quadratic Equations Graphically

The objective for this section is on page 253.

When the graph of a quadratic function,

$$f(x) = ax^2 + bx + c,$$

intersects the x axis in two points, the **quadratic equation**,

$$ax^2 + bx + c = 0, \; x \in C,$$

has two real solutions or roots. When the graph of the function is tangent to the x axis, there is one real root. There are no real roots if the graph of the function does not intersect the x axis.

Example 1   Use the graphs below to determine the real roots of

$$x^2 + 6 = 0, \; x^2 - 6x + 9 = 0, \text{ and } x^2 - x - 6 = 0.$$

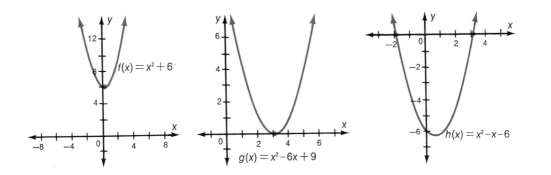

	$f(x) = x^2 + 6$	$g(x) = x^2 - 6x + 9$	$h(x) = x^2 - x - 6$
x intercepts	None	(3, 0)	(−2, 0) and (3, 0)
Zeros of the function	None	3	−2 and 3
Roots of the equation	None	3	−2 and 3

Example 2

Solve $-x^2 - 3x + 10 = 0$ graphically. First graph $y = -x^2 - 3x + 10$.

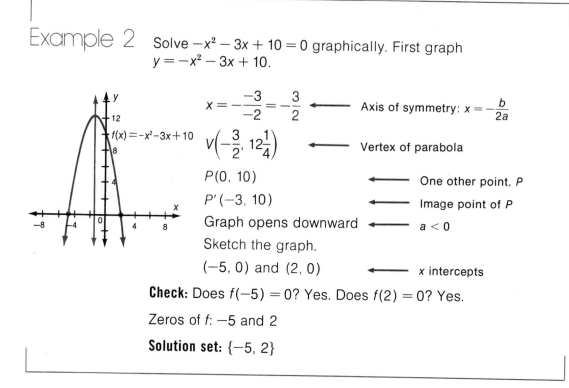

$$x = -\frac{-3}{-2} = -\frac{3}{2}$$ ⟵ Axis of symmetry: $x = -\frac{b}{2a}$

$$V\left(-\frac{3}{2}, 12\frac{1}{4}\right)$$ ⟵ Vertex of parabola

$P(0, 10)$ ⟵ One other point, P

$P'(-3, 10)$ ⟵ Image point of P

Graph opens downward ⟵ $a < 0$

Sketch the graph.

$(-5, 0)$ and $(2, 0)$ ⟵ x intercepts

Check: Does $f(-5) = 0$? Yes. Does $f(2) = 0$? Yes.

Zeros of f: -5 and 2

Solution set: $\{-5, 2\}$

Try These

The figure below includes the graphs for

$$f(x) = x^2 - 9$$
$$g(x) = x^2 - 14x + 50$$
$$h(x) = -x^2 + 2x - 1$$

1. How many real solutions are there for   Two.
$x^2 - 9 = 0$?

2. How many real solutions are there for   None.
$x^2 - 14x + 50 = 0$?

3. How many real solutions are there for   One.
$-x^2 + 2x - 1 = 0$?

4. Find the solution set of $-x^2 + 2x - 1 = 0$. $\{1\}$
Check it by substitution.

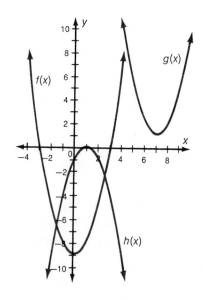

Exercises

Find the solution set of each quadratic equation graphically and check it by substitution. The replacement set for x is the set of real numbers.

a

1. $x^2 - x - 12 = 0$ {-3, 4}

2. $x^2 + 2x - 24 = 0$ {-6, 4}

3. $x^2 + x = 12$ {-4, 3}

4. $x^2 - 12 = -4x$ {2, -6}

5. $x^2 - 2x - 24 = 0$ {6, -4}

6. $x^2 - 10x + 24 = 0$ {6, 4}

7. $-3x^2 = 0$ {0}

8. $-x^2 + 4 = 0$ {2, -2}

9. $x^2 - 3x = 0$ {0, 3}

10. $x^2 + 2x - 6 = 9$ {-5, 3}

11. $x^2 - 4x + 4 = 0$ {2}

12. $-x^2 + x + 12 = 0$ {-3, 4}

Find each solution set graphically. Estimate solutions to the nearest tenth.

b

13. $2x^2 + 5x - 1 = 0$ {0.2, -2.7}

14. $-x^2 + 2x + 5 = 0$ {-1.4, 3.4}

15. $4x^2 - 7x + 2 = 0$ {0.4, 1.4}

16. $9x^2 + 9x - 10 = 0$ {-1.7, 0.7}

c

17. $(2x - 3)(2x + 3) = 11$ {-2.2, 2.2}

18. $2x^2 - 3 = 4x$ {-0.6, 2.6}

19. $\dfrac{4}{x^2} - \dfrac{1}{x} = 2 - \dfrac{3}{x}$ {2, -1}

20. $(2x - 3)^2 + 2x - 15 = 0$ $\{3, -\frac{1}{2}\}$

21. Draw the graph of the function defined by $y = x^2 + 3x - 4$ and use it to identify the solution sets of $x^2 + 3x - 4 = 0$, $x^2 + 3x - 4 > 0$, and $x^2 + 3x - 4 < 0$. {-4, 1}; {x: x > 1 or x < -4}; {x: -4 < x < 1}

22. Draw the graph of the function defined by $y = -x^2 - 3x + 4$ and use it to identify the solution sets of $-x^2 - 3x + 4 = 0$, $-x^2 - 3x + 4 > 0$, and $-x^2 - 3x + 4 < 0$. {-4, 1}; {x: -4 < x < 1}; {x: x > 1 or x < -4}

Remember

Simplify.

1. $\sqrt{3 - 12}$ $3i$

2. $(i - 1) \div (2i + 1)$ $\frac{1 + 3i}{5}$

3. $(2i + 5) - (3i + 7)$ $-(2 + i)$

4. $x^3yz^2 \div x^4y^2z$ $\frac{z}{xy}$

5. $4 \pm \sqrt{-48}$ $4 \pm 4i\sqrt{3}$

6. $i^2 \cdot i^3 \cdot i^5$ -1

The answers are on page 254.

Quadratic equations such as $x^2 = 9$ and $5x^2 - 24 = 0$ are **incomplete quadratics** because they do not contain an x term. Incomplete quadratics can be solved by applying the definition of square root.

Example 1

Solve: $x^2 = 9$

$x^2 = 9$	Of the form $x^2 = k$
$x = 3$ <u>or</u> $x = -3$	Definition of square root
$\{3, -3\}$	Solution set

Check: $x^2 = 9$ Replace x with 3 and -3.

$$(3)^2 = 9$$
$$(-3)^2 = 9$$

Many quadratic equations that are not of the form $x^2 = k$ can be expressed in this form. The solution set for each example should be checked in the original equation.

Example 2

Solve: $5x^2 - 24 = 0$

$5x^2 = 24$	⟵ Add 24 to each side.
$x^2 = \dfrac{24}{5}$	⟵ Of the form $x^2 = k$
$x = \pm\dfrac{2\sqrt{6}}{\sqrt{5}} = \pm\dfrac{2\sqrt{30}}{5}$	⟵ Definition of square root
$\left\{\dfrac{2\sqrt{30}}{5}, -\dfrac{2\sqrt{30}}{5}\right\}$	⟵ Solution set

234   Chapter 6

Example 3

Solve: $3x^2 + 5 = x^2 + 29$

$$2x^2 + 5 = 29 \qquad \longleftarrow \text{Add } -x^2 \text{ to each side.}$$
$$2x^2 = 24 \qquad \longleftarrow \text{Add } -5 \text{ to each side.}$$
$$x^2 = 12 \qquad \longleftarrow \text{Of the form } x^2 = k$$
$$x = \pm\sqrt{12} = \pm2\sqrt{3} \qquad \longleftarrow \text{Definition of square root.}$$
$$\{2\sqrt{3}, -2\sqrt{3}\} \qquad \longleftarrow \text{Solution set}$$

Example 4

Solve: $(x - 1)^2 - 16 = 0$.

$$(x - 1)^2 = 16 \qquad \longleftarrow \text{Of the form } x^2 = k$$
$$x - 1 = \pm4 \qquad \longleftarrow \text{If } x^2 = k, \ x = \pm\sqrt{k}.$$
$$x - 1 = 4 \ \underline{\text{or}} \ x - 1 = -4 \qquad \longleftarrow \text{Solve for } x.$$
$$x = 5 \ \underline{\text{or}} \qquad x = -3$$

Solution set: $\{5, -3\}$

Example 5

Solve: $(t + 2)^2 + 18 = 0$

$$(t + 2)^2 + 18 = 0$$
$$(t + 2)^2 = -18 \qquad \longleftarrow \text{Of the form } x^2 = k$$
$$(t + 2) = \pm\sqrt{-18} \qquad \longleftarrow \text{If } x^2 = k, \ x = \pm\sqrt{k}.$$
$$(t + 2) = \pm3i\sqrt{2}$$
$$t + 2 = 3i\sqrt{2} \ \underline{\text{or}} \ t + 2 = -3i\sqrt{2} \qquad \longleftarrow \text{Solve for } t.$$
$$t = -2 + 3i\sqrt{2} \ \underline{\text{or}} \ t = -2 - 3i\sqrt{2}$$

Solution set: $\{-2 + 3i\sqrt{2}, -2 - 3i\sqrt{2}\}$

Try These

Solve each equation.

1. $x^2 - 25 = 0$ $\{5, -5\}$

2. $2x^2 = 32$ $\{4, -4\}$

3. $p^2 + 2 = 0$ $\{i\sqrt{2}, -i\sqrt{2}\}$

4. $2x^2 - 7 = x^2 + 3$ $\{\sqrt{10}, -\sqrt{10}\}$

5. $4x^2 + 3 = 3$ $\{0\}$

6. $(t - 3)^2 = 4$ $\{5, 1\}$

Exercises

Solve each of the following equations. The replacement set for each variable is the set of complex numbers.

1. $2x^2 = 32$ {4, −4}

2. $3x^2 = 27$ {3, −3}

3. $x^2 = -7$ $\{i\sqrt{7}, -i\sqrt{7}\}$

4. $2x^2 = 22$ $\{\sqrt{11}, -\sqrt{11}\}$

5. $4x^2 = 36$ {3, −3}

6. $7x^2 = 42$ $\{\sqrt{6}, -\sqrt{6}\}$

7. $b^2 - 7 = 29$ {6, −6}

8. $a^2 + 30 = 5$ {5i, −5i}

9. $p^2 - 42 = 7$ {7, −7}

10. $m^2 - 5 = 59$ {8, −8}

11. $x^2 + 2 = 3$ {1, −1}

12. $y^2 - 5 = -6$ {i, −i}

13. $x^2 - 7 = 12$ $\{\sqrt{19}, -\sqrt{19}\}$

14. $-x^2 + 41 = 0$ $\{\sqrt{41}, -\sqrt{41}\}$

15. $2x^2 + 1 = 3$ {1, −1}

16. $-4x^2 - 16 = 0$ {2i, −2i}

17. $3x^2 - 5 = 2x^2 + 7$ $\{2\sqrt{3}, -2\sqrt{3}\}$

18. $8x^2 + 9 = 3x^2 + 24$ $\{\sqrt{3}, -\sqrt{3}\}$

19. $x^2 + 4 = 0$ {2i, −2i}

20. $3x^2 = -21$ $\{i\sqrt{7}, -i\sqrt{7}\}$

21. $4x^2 + 5 = x^2 - 4$ $\{i\sqrt{3}, -i\sqrt{3}\}$

22. $\dfrac{x}{5} = \dfrac{-8}{x}$ $\{2i\sqrt{10}, -2i\sqrt{10}\}$

23. $\dfrac{x^2}{4} = -4$ {4i, −4i}

24. $(x - 5)^2 = 4$ {7, 3}

25. $(x + 3)^2 = 16$ {1, −7}

26. $(x + 1)^2 = 9$ {2, −4}

27. $(2x + 3)^2 = 36$ $\{\frac{3}{2}, -\frac{9}{2}\}$

28. $(x - 5)^2 = 36$ {11, −1}

29. $(x + 2)^2 = 16$ {2, −6}

30. $\left(x - \dfrac{3}{2}\right)^2 = \dfrac{25}{4}$ {4, −1}

31. $\left(x + \dfrac{1}{2}\right)^2 = \dfrac{9}{4}$ {1, −2}

32. $0.03x^2 = 1.23$ $\{\sqrt{41}, -\sqrt{41}\}$

33. $0.4x^2 = 6.4$ {4, −4}

34. $0.2x^2 + 1.2 = 3.4$ $\{\sqrt{11}, -\sqrt{11}\}$

35. $\dfrac{3}{x} = \dfrac{x}{2}$ $\{\sqrt{6}, -\sqrt{6}\}$

36. $\dfrac{x}{2} = \dfrac{5}{x}$ $\{\sqrt{10}, -\sqrt{10}\}$

37. $(x - 2)^2 + 9 = 0$ $\{2 + 3i, 2 - 3i\}$

38. $\left(x + \dfrac{3}{4}\right)^2 = \dfrac{25}{16}$ $\{\frac{1}{2}, -2\}$

39. $(x - 5)^2 = -27$ $\{5 + 3i\sqrt{3}, 5 - 3i\sqrt{3}\}$

40. $\left(x + \dfrac{1}{2}\right)^2 = -\dfrac{1}{4}$ $\{-\frac{1}{2} + \frac{1}{2}i, -\frac{1}{2} - \frac{1}{2}i\}$

41. $(x + 1)^2 + 18 = 0$ $\{-1 + 3i\sqrt{2}, -1 - 3i\sqrt{2}\}$

42. $\dfrac{x^2}{a} = b$ (Solve for x.) $\{\sqrt{ab}, -\sqrt{ab}\}$

43. $(2x - 1)(3x - 2) = (x - 5)(x - 2)$ $\{\frac{2}{5}\sqrt{10}, -\frac{2}{5}\sqrt{10}\}$

44. $(x + 2)^2 + (x - 2)^2 = 3(x + 2)(x - 2)$ $\{2\sqrt{5}, -2\sqrt{5}\}$

45. $x(3x + 2) = (x + 1)^2$ $\{\frac{\sqrt{2}}{2}, -\frac{\sqrt{2}}{2}\}$

46. $x^2 + 5x - 7 = (2x + 1)(x + 2)$ {3i, −3i}

Express each equation in the form $(x + h)^2 = k$ and solve. The replacement set for each variable is the set of complex numbers.

47. $p^2 + 2p + 1 = 4$ {1, −3}

48. $t^2 + 6t + 9 = 16$ {1, −7}

49. $4t^2 + 12t + 9 = 100$ $\{\frac{7}{2}, -\frac{13}{2}\}$

Solving Quadratics: Completing the Square

The objective for this section is on page 253.

When the left side of a quadratic equation is not a perfect square, a technique called **completing the square** can be used to solve the equation.

Example 1   Find a number n such that $x^2 + 8x + n$ is a perfect square trinomial. Express the trinomial as a perfect square.

$x^2 + 8x +$ ___?___

Coefficient of x is 8; $\left(\dfrac{1}{2} \cdot 8\right) = 4$ ⟵   Find $\dfrac{1}{2}$ the coefficient of x.

$\left(\dfrac{1}{2} \cdot 8\right)^2 = 4^2 = 16$ ⟵   Find the square of $\left(\dfrac{1}{2} \cdot 8\right)$.

$x^2 + 8x + 16$ ⟵   Add 16 to $x^2 + 8x$.

$x^2 + 8x + 16 = (x + 4)^2$ ⟵   Express as a perfect square.

Example 2   Find a number P such that $z^2 - 7z + P$ is a perfect square trinomial. Express the trinomial as a perfect square.

$z^2 - 7z +$ ___?___

Coefficient of z is -7; $\left(\dfrac{1}{2} \cdot -7\right) = -\dfrac{7}{2}$ ⟵   Find $\dfrac{1}{2}$ the coefficient of z.

$\left(\dfrac{1}{2} \cdot -7\right)^2 = \left(-\dfrac{7}{2}\right)^2 = \dfrac{49}{4}$ ⟵   Find the square of $\left(\dfrac{1}{2} \cdot -7\right)$

$z^2 - 7z + \dfrac{49}{4}$ ⟵   Add $\dfrac{49}{4}$ to $z^2 - 7z$.

$z^2 - 7z + \dfrac{49}{4} = \left(z - \dfrac{7}{2}\right)^2$ ⟵   Express as a perfect square.

To solve a quadratic equation by the method of completing the square, add the square of one-half the coefficient of the x term to both sides of the equation.

Example 3 Solve $x^2 + 4x = 5$ by completing the square.

$$x^2 + 4x = 5$$

$$x^2 + 4x + \left(\frac{1}{2} \cdot 4\right)^2 = 5 + \left(\frac{1}{2} \cdot 4\right)^2 \qquad \longleftarrow \quad \text{Add } \left(\frac{1}{2} \cdot 4\right)^2 \text{ to each side.}$$

$$x^2 + 4x + 4 = 5 + 4$$

$$(x + 2)^2 = 9 \qquad \longleftarrow \qquad x^2 + 4x + 4 = (x + 2)^2$$

$$x + 2 = \pm 3 \qquad \longleftarrow \qquad \text{If } x^2 = k, \ x = \pm\sqrt{k}.$$

$$x + 2 = 3 \quad \underline{\text{or}} \quad x + 2 = -3 \qquad \longleftarrow \qquad \text{Solve for } x.$$

$$x = 1 \quad \underline{\text{or}} \qquad x = -5$$

Solution set: $\{1, -5\}$

A quadratic equation must be expressed in the form $x^2 + bx = k$ before applying the technique of completing the square.

Example 4 Solve $x^2 - 6x - 20 = 0$

$$x^2 - 6x - 20 = 0$$

$$x^2 - 6x = 20 \qquad \longleftarrow \qquad \text{Add 20 to each side.}$$

$$x^2 - 6x + \left(\frac{1}{2} \cdot -6\right)^2 = 20 + \left(\frac{1}{2} \cdot -6\right)^2 \qquad \longleftarrow \quad \text{Add } \left(\frac{1}{2} \cdot -6\right)^2 \text{ to each side.}$$

$$x^2 - 6x + 9 = 20 + 9$$

$$(x - 3)^2 = 29 \qquad \longleftarrow \qquad x^2 - 6x + 9 = (x - 3)^2$$

$$x - 3 = \pm\sqrt{29} \qquad \longleftarrow \qquad \text{If } x^2 = k, \ x = \pm\sqrt{k}.$$

$$x - 3 = \sqrt{29} \quad \underline{\text{or}} \quad x - 3 = -\sqrt{29} \qquad \longleftarrow \qquad \text{Solve for } x.$$

$$x = 3 + \sqrt{29} \quad \underline{\text{or}} \quad x = 3 - \sqrt{29}$$

Solution set: $\{3 + \sqrt{29}, \ 3 - \sqrt{29}\}$

When the coefficient of the x^2 term of a quadratic equation is not 1, each term of the equation must be divided by that coefficient.

Example 5   Solve: $3x^2 - 21 = 2x$

$$3x^2 - 21 = 2x$$

$$3x^2 - 2x = 21 \qquad \longleftarrow \quad \text{Add } (-2x + 21) \text{ to each side.}$$

$$x^2 - \frac{2}{3}x = 7 \qquad \longleftarrow \quad \text{Divide by 3.}$$

$$x^2 - \frac{2}{3}x + \left(\frac{1}{2} \cdot -\frac{2}{3}\right)^2 = 7 + \left(\frac{1}{2} \cdot -\frac{2}{3}\right)^2 \qquad \longleftarrow \quad \text{Add } \left(\frac{1}{2} \cdot -\frac{2}{3}\right)^2 \text{ to each side.}$$

$$x^2 - \frac{2}{3}x + \frac{1}{9} = 7 + \frac{1}{9}$$

$$\left(x - \frac{1}{3}\right)^2 = \frac{64}{9} \qquad \longleftarrow \quad x^2 - \frac{2}{3}x + \frac{1}{9} = \left(x - \frac{1}{3}\right)^2.$$

$$x - \frac{1}{3} = \pm\frac{8}{3} \qquad \longleftarrow \quad \text{If } x^2 = k,\ x = \pm\sqrt{k}.$$

$$x - \frac{1}{3} = \frac{8}{3} \quad \text{or} \quad x - \frac{1}{3} = -\frac{8}{3} \qquad \longleftarrow \quad \text{Solve for } x.$$

$$x = 3 \quad \text{or} \qquad x = -\frac{7}{3}$$

Solution set: $\left\{3, -\frac{7}{3}\right\}$

Steps for Completing the Square

1. Write an equivalent equation with only the x^2 term and the x term on the left side of the equation. The coefficient of the x^2 term must be 1.
2. Add the square of one-half the coefficient of the x term to both sides of the equation.
3. Express the left side of the equation as a perfect square.
4. Solve for x.

Solutions should be checked in the original equation.

Try These   Complete the square to form a perfect square trinomial. Express the trinomial as the square of a binomial.

1. $x^2 + 14x$ $_{+49}$ **2.** $a^2 - 16a$ $_{+64}$ **3.** $x^2 + 12x$ $_{+36}$ **4.** $x^2 + 5x$ $^{+\frac{25}{4}}$

$(x+7)^2$ $(a-8)^2$ $(x+6)^2$ $\left(x+\frac{5}{2}\right)^2$

Exercises

8. $x^2 + \frac{b}{a}x + \left(\frac{1}{2} \cdot \frac{b}{a}\right)^2 = x^2 + \frac{b}{a}x + \frac{b^2}{4a^2} = \left(x + \frac{b}{2a}\right)^2$

Complete the square to form a perfect square trinomial. Express the trinomial as the square of a binomial.

a

1. $x^2 - 2x$
$x^2 - 2x + \left(\frac{-2}{2}\right)^2$ or $x^2 - 2x + 1 = (x-1)^2$

2. $n^2 - 6n$ $n^2 - 6n + 9;\ (n-3)^2$

3. $y^2 + y$ $y^2 + y + \frac{1}{4};\ \left(y + \frac{1}{2}\right)^2$

4. $x^2 - 10x$
$x^2 - 10x + 25;\ (x-5)^2$

5. $x^2 + 3x$
$x^2 + 3x + \frac{9}{4};\ \left(x + \frac{3}{2}\right)^2$

6. $c^2 + \frac{3}{2}c$
$c^2 + \frac{3}{2}c + \frac{9}{16};\ \left(c + \frac{3}{4}\right)^2$

7. $x^2 - 2bx$
$x^2 - 2bx + b^2;\ (x-b)^2$

8. $x^2 + \frac{b}{a}x$ See above

9. $x^2 - \frac{b}{a}x$
$x^2 - \frac{b}{a}x + \frac{b^2}{4a^2};\ \left(x - \frac{b}{2a}\right)^2$

Solve each equation by completing the square. Check your solutions.

10. $x^2 + 10x = -24$ $_{\{-4,\,-6\}}$ **11.** $r^2 + 4r = 21$ $_{\{-7,\,3\}}$ **12.** $x^2 - 2x = 15$ $^{\{5,\,-3\}}$

13. $x^2 - 8x = 48$ $_{\{12,\,-4\}}$ **14.** $x^2 = 8x - 15$ $_{\{5,\,3\}}$ **15.** $x^2 - 9 = -8x$ $^{\{1,\,-9\}}$

16. $10a = 24 - a^2$ $_{\{2,\,-12\}}$ **17.** $x^2 - 6x + 5 = 0$ $_{\{1,\,5\}}$ **18.** $b^2 - 2b = 48$ $^{\{8,\,-6\}}$

19. $y^2 = 6y + 7$ $_{\{-1,\,7\}}$ **20.** $x^2 - 9x = -20$ $_{\{4,\,5\}}$ **21.** $x^2 + x = 20$ $^{\{4,\,-5\}}$

22. $c^2 - 9c = -18$ $_{\{3,\,6\}}$ **23.** $x^2 + 3x = 18$ $_{\{3,\,-6\}}$ **24.** $x^2 - 5x = 50$ $^{\{10,\,-5\}}$

b

25. $x^2 - \frac{x}{3} = \frac{2}{3}$ $_{\{1,\,-\frac{2}{3}\}}$ **26.** $x^2 + \frac{x}{2} = \frac{3}{2}$ $_{\{1,\,-\frac{3}{2}\}}$ **27.** $4x^2 + x = 60$ $^{\{\frac{15}{4},\,-4\}}$

28. $4x^2 + 12x = 7$ $_{\{\frac{1}{2},\,-\frac{7}{2}\}}$ **29.** $6x^2 + x - 2 = 0$ $_{\{\frac{1}{2},\,-\frac{2}{3}\}}$ **30.** $2x^2 + x - 6 = 0$ $^{\{-2,\,\frac{3}{2}\}}$

31. $3n^2 + 2n - 8 = 0$ $_{\{-2,\,\frac{4}{3}\}}$ **32.** $4n^2 + 19n - 5 = 0$ $_{\{-5,\,\frac{1}{4}\}}$ **33.** $6x^2 + 5x = 6$ $^{\text{See below}}$

34. $6x^2 - 7x = -1$ $_{\{1,\,\frac{1}{6}\}}$ **35.** $x^2 - x - 1 = 0$ $_{\left\{\frac{1+\sqrt{5}}{2},\,\frac{1-\sqrt{5}}{2}\right\}}$ **36.** $x^2 + 3x - 5 = 0$ $^{\text{See below}}$

37. $2a^2 + 7a + 6 = 0$ $_{\{-2,\,-\frac{3}{2}\}}$ **38.** $2a^2 - 7a + 6 = 0$ $_{\{2,\,\frac{3}{2}\}}$ **39.** $x^2 + \frac{7x}{4} - \frac{1}{2} = 0$

33. $\{\frac{2}{3}, -\frac{3}{2}\}$ **36.** $\left\{\frac{-3+\sqrt{29}}{2}, \frac{-3-\sqrt{29}}{2}\right\}$

$\{-2, \frac{1}{4}\}$

PUZZLE

$\frac{3+\sqrt{33}}{6}$

Find the radius of a spherical pearl if by the time the radius of the pearl has increased by 1 millimeter, the surface area (in square millimeters) will have increased as much as the volume (in cubic millimeters). HINT: Surface area $= 4\pi r^2$ and Volume $= \frac{4}{3}\pi r^3$.

240   Chapter 6

The Quadratic Formula

The objective for this section is on page 253.

The solution set of any quadratic equation can be found by completing the square. When this method is applied to the general quadratic equation,

$$ax^2 + bx + c = 0,$$

the solutions are also general and can be used as a formula to determine the solutions of any quadratic equation.

Example 1   Solve: $ax^2 + bx + c = 0$

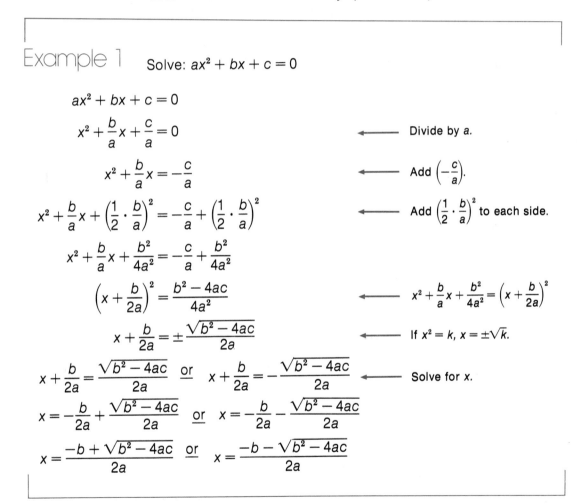

$$ax^2 + bx + c = 0$$

$$x^2 + \frac{b}{a}x + \frac{c}{a} = 0 \qquad \longleftarrow \quad \text{Divide by } a.$$

$$x^2 + \frac{b}{a}x = -\frac{c}{a} \qquad \longleftarrow \quad \text{Add } \left(-\frac{c}{a}\right).$$

$$x^2 + \frac{b}{a}x + \left(\frac{1}{2}\cdot\frac{b}{a}\right)^2 = -\frac{c}{a} + \left(\frac{1}{2}\cdot\frac{b}{a}\right)^2 \qquad \longleftarrow \quad \text{Add } \left(\frac{1}{2}\cdot\frac{b}{a}\right)^2 \text{ to each side.}$$

$$x^2 + \frac{b}{a}x + \frac{b^2}{4a^2} = -\frac{c}{a} + \frac{b^2}{4a^2}$$

$$\left(x + \frac{b}{2a}\right)^2 = \frac{b^2 - 4ac}{4a^2} \qquad \longleftarrow \quad x^2 + \frac{b}{a}x + \frac{b^2}{4a^2} = \left(x + \frac{b}{2a}\right)^2$$

$$x + \frac{b}{2a} = \pm\frac{\sqrt{b^2 - 4ac}}{2a} \qquad \longleftarrow \quad \text{If } x^2 = k, \ x = \pm\sqrt{k}.$$

$$x + \frac{b}{2a} = \frac{\sqrt{b^2 - 4ac}}{2a} \quad \text{or} \quad x + \frac{b}{2a} = -\frac{\sqrt{b^2 - 4ac}}{2a} \qquad \longleftarrow \quad \text{Solve for } x.$$

$$x = -\frac{b}{2a} + \frac{\sqrt{b^2 - 4ac}}{2a} \quad \text{or} \quad x = -\frac{b}{2a} - \frac{\sqrt{b^2 - 4ac}}{2a}$$

$$x = \frac{-b + \sqrt{b^2 - 4ac}}{2a} \quad \text{or} \quad x = \frac{-b - \sqrt{b^2 - 4ac}}{2a}$$

Quadratic Functions   **241**

Thus, for any quadratic equation, $ax^2 + bx + c = 0$,

$$x = \frac{-b + \sqrt{b^2 - 4ac}}{2a} \quad \underline{\text{or}} \quad x = \frac{-b - \sqrt{b^2 - 4ac}}{2a}.$$

This is the **quadratic formula.**

Example 2   Use the quadratic formula to solve $x^2 + 5x = 6$.

$x^2 + 5x - 6 = 0$ ←——— Express in standard form.

$a = 1;\ b = 5;\ c = -6$ ←——— Determine a, b, and c.

$x = \dfrac{-5 \pm \sqrt{25 - 4(1)(-6)}}{2(1)}$ ←——— Substitute in the formula.

$x = \dfrac{-5 + \sqrt{49}}{2} = 1,\ x = \dfrac{-5 - \sqrt{49}}{2} = -6$ **Solution set:** $\{1,\ -6\}$

Example 3   Solve: $2x^2 - 3x = 7$

$2x^2 - 3x - 7 = 0$ ←——— Express in standard form.

$a = 2;\ b = -3;\ c = -7$ ←——— Determine a, b, and c.

$x = \dfrac{-(-3) \pm \sqrt{(-3)^2 - 4(2)(-7)}}{2(2)}$ ←——— Substitute in the formula.

$x = \dfrac{3 \pm \sqrt{9 + 56}}{4}$ ←——— Solve for x.

$x = \dfrac{3 + \sqrt{65}}{4},\ x = \dfrac{3 - \sqrt{65}}{4}$ **Solution set:** $\left\{\dfrac{3 + \sqrt{65}}{4},\ \dfrac{3 - \sqrt{65}}{4}\right\}$

Using a table of square roots, $\sqrt{65}$ is approximately equal to 8.062. Thus, $x \approx 2.77$ $\underline{\text{or}}$ $x \approx -1.27$.

Try These   *For each quadratic equation, give the value of a, b, and c.*

1. $2x^2 + 5x - 6 = 0$ $_{a=2,\,b=5,\,c=-6}$ **2.** $x^2 + 2x + 3 = 0$ $_{a=1,\,b=2,\,c=3}$ **3.** $5x^2 + 3x = 4$

4. $2y^2 = 5y + 12$ $_{a=2,\,b=-5,\,c=-12}$ **5.** $3a - a^2 = 5$ $_{a=-1,\,b=3,\,c=-5}$ **6.** $b^2 = 14 + 5b$ $^{a=5,\,b=3,\,c=-4}$

$_{a=1,\,b=-5,\,c=-14}$

Exercises

Use the quadratic formula to solve each equation. Leave irrational solutions in simplest radical form.

$\left\{\frac{-3+\sqrt{5}}{2}, \frac{-3-\sqrt{5}}{2}\right\}$ 9. $\left\{\frac{7+\sqrt{5}}{2}, \frac{7-\sqrt{5}}{2}\right\}$ $\{5, -2\}$

1. $x^2 - 5x + 6 = 0$ $\{3, 2\}$ **2.** $x^2 - 8x + 15 = 0$ $\{5, 3\}$ **3.** $x^2 - 3x - 10 = 0$

4. $x^2 - 4x - 12 = 0$ $\{6, -2\}$ **5.** $x^2 + 4x - 12 = 0$ $\{2, -6\}$ **6.** $a^2 + 8a + 16 = 0$
                                                                       $\{-4\}$

7. $y^2 - 3y = 2$ $\left\{\frac{3+\sqrt{17}}{2}, \frac{3-\sqrt{17}}{2}\right\}$ **8.** $y^2 + 3y + 1 = 0$ **9.** $y^2 = 7y - 11$

10. $y^2 - 5y + 5 = 0$ $\left\{\frac{5+\sqrt{5}}{2}, \frac{5-\sqrt{5}}{2}\right\}$ **11.** $x^2 + 6x = -9$ $\{-3\}$ **12.** $2a^2 + 3a = 1$

13. $6x^2 - x - 12 = 0$ $\left\{\frac{3}{2}, -\frac{4}{3}\right\}$ **14.** $9x^2 + 3x - 2 = 0$ $\left\{\frac{1}{3}, -\frac{2}{3}\right\}$ **15.** $a^2 + a - 1 = 0$

16. $2x^2 + 5x + 2 = 0$ $\left\{-2, -\frac{1}{2}\right\}$ **17.** $3b^2 = 3b + 1$ $\left\{\frac{3+\sqrt{21}}{6}, \frac{3-\sqrt{21}}{6}\right\}$ **18.** $4x^2 + 12x = -9$ $\left\{-\frac{3}{2}\right\}$

   12. $\left\{\frac{-3+\sqrt{17}}{4}, \frac{-3-\sqrt{17}}{4}\right\}$ 15. $\left\{\frac{-1+\sqrt{5}}{2}, \frac{-1-\sqrt{5}}{2}\right\}$

Solve the following equations. Approximate irrational solutions to the nearest hundredth. (Use the table when the radicand appears in the table; otherwise, find the square root by computation.)

                                                               $\{1.16, -5.16\}$

19. $2x^2 - 3x + 1 = 0$ $\left\{1, \frac{1}{2}\right\}$ **20.** $4a^2 = 3 - 4a$ $\left\{\frac{1}{2}, -\frac{3}{2}\right\}$ **21.** $x^2 + 4x - 6 = 0$

22. $x^2 - 2x - 4 = 0$ $\{3.24, -1.24\}$ **23.** $x^2 + 3x + 1 = 0$ $\{-2.62, -0.38\}$ **24.** $x^2 + 8x + 5 = 0$
                                                                          $\{-0.68, -7.32\}$

25. One side of a right triangle is 2 centimeters more than the other and 2 centimeters less than the hypotenuse. How long are the three sides?

Let one side $= x$ and
the other side $= x - 2$.
hypotenuse $= x + 2$
$x^2 + (x - 2)^2 = (x + 2)^2$

Solve for x and check by substituting
both solutions of the equation in the problem.   8 cm; 6 cm; 10 cm

26. The length of a rectangle is 5 centimeters greater than its width. Its diagonal is 25 centimeters. Find the dimensions. $w = 15$ cm, $w + 5 = 20$ cm

Solve each equation. Leave irrational numbers in radical form.

27. $3x^2 - 3x - 1 = 0$ $\left\{\frac{3+\sqrt{21}}{6}, \frac{3-\sqrt{21}}{6}\right\}$ **28.** $2x^2 + 0.1x - 0.03 = 0$ $\{.1, -.15\}$

29. $(x^2 - 1) - (3x - 7)(x - 2) = 0$ $\left\{5, \frac{3}{2}\right\}$ **30.** $(2x - 8)(x - 8) = (x - 4)^2$ $\{12, 4\}$

31. $\dfrac{x^2 - 4x}{6} - \dfrac{x - 3}{3} = 1$ $\{0, 6\}$ **32.** $2x + 1 = \dfrac{1}{x - 1}$ $\left\{\frac{1+\sqrt{17}}{4}, \frac{1-\sqrt{17}}{4}\right\}$

33. $\dfrac{2}{x + 1} = \dfrac{x}{x + 1}$ $\{2\}$ **34.** $\dfrac{2x + 10}{5x} = \dfrac{10}{x}$ $\{20\}$

35. If the area of a rectangular region is 200 square centimeters and its length is 4 centimeters more than its width, find its dimensions to the nearest tenth of a centimeter. $w = 12.3\,cm; \ell = 16.3\,cm$

36. Find the number that is $\frac{21}{10}$ greater than its reciprocal. (HINT: Reciprocal is another name for multiplicative inverse.) $x = \frac{5}{2}$ or $x = -\frac{2}{5}$

37. If a playground, which measures 40 meters by 60 meters, is to be doubled in area by extending each side an equal amount, how much should each side be extended? Each side must be extended 20 meters.

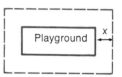

38. One side of a right triangle is 3 meters less than the hypotenuse and 3 meters more than the other side. How long is it? 12 meters

39. If the length of a rectangle is 4 meters more than twice the width, and the diagonal is 26 meters, what are the dimensions of the rectangle? $w = 10$ meters and $2w + 4 = 24$ meters

Solve each sentence. Be sure to check for apparent solutions that are not in the solution set.

40. $\dfrac{5x - 2}{2} - \dfrac{19x + 6}{2x} = \dfrac{3x - 2}{4}$ $\left\{6, -\frac{2}{7}\right\}$

41. $\dfrac{1}{2 - x} - 1 = \dfrac{x - 6}{x^2 - 4} - \dfrac{1}{x + 2}$ $\{-3\}$

42. $\dfrac{4}{c + 3} + \dfrac{1}{3} = \dfrac{4}{c - 3}$ $\{9, -9\}$

43. $\dfrac{3y}{y + 2} - \dfrac{y - 12}{y^2 + y - 2} = \dfrac{2y}{y - 1}$ $\{6, 2\}$

44. $\dfrac{x - 3}{x^2 - 4} = \dfrac{1}{x - 2} - 1$ $\{3, -3\}$

45. The sum of a fraction and its reciprocal is $3\frac{1}{24}$. If the denominator is five more than the numerator, what is the fraction? $\frac{3}{8}$

46. The square of one number is 14 more than twice the square of another number. If the second number is three less than the first, what are the two numbers? There are two different solutions. 5 and 8 or 1 and 4

Remember

Name all the sets, N, W, $\mathscr{I}$, Q, Ir, R, and C, to which each number belongs.

1. $\sqrt[3]{8}$ **2.** $\sqrt[3]{-8}$ **3.** $\sqrt{8}$ **4.** $\sqrt{-8}$ **5.** $5 - \sqrt{8 - 12}$

N, W, I, Q, R, C   I, Q, R, C   Ir, C   C   C

The answers are on page 254.

The Nature of the Solutions

The objective for this section is on page 253.

Since the solution set for every quadratic equation is

$$\left\{ \frac{-b + \sqrt{b^2 - 4ac}}{2a}, \frac{-b - \sqrt{b^2 - 4ac}}{2a} \right\},$$

the solutions can be expressed as

$$r_1 = \frac{-b}{2a} + \frac{\sqrt{b^2 - 4ac}}{2a} \qquad \underline{or} \qquad r_2 = \frac{-b}{2a} - \frac{\sqrt{b^2 - 4ac}}{2a}.$$

The expression $b^2 - 4ac$ is called the **discriminant** because it determines the nature of the solutions of a quadratic equation.

---

1. If $b^2 - 4ac = 0$, then $r_1 = r_2$ and the equation will have one real root.

2. If $b^2 - 4ac > 0$, then r_1 and r_2 will be two distinct real numbers, and the equation will have two, unequal, real roots. If $b^2 - 4ac$ is also a perfect square, these roots will be rational; otherwise, they will be irrational.

3. If $b^2 - 4ac < 0$, then r_1 and r_2 will be two distinct imaginary numbers, and the equation will have no real roots.

Example 1   Use the discriminant to determine the nature of the solutions of $4x^2 + 4x + 1 = 0$. Verify your answer.

$4x^2 + 4x + 1 = 0$

$b^2 - 4ac = 4^2 - 4(4)(1) = 0$ ←———— Discriminant

One real solution ←———— $b^2 - 4ac = 0$

Check: $x = \dfrac{-4 \pm \sqrt{16 - 4(4)(1)}}{2(4)} = -\dfrac{1}{2}$ **Solution set:** $\left\{ -\dfrac{1}{2} \right\}$

Example 2

Compare the nature of the solutions of $2x^2 + x - 3 = 0$ and $2x^2 + 2x - 3 = 0$.

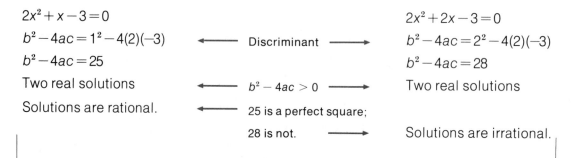

$2x^2 + x - 3 = 0$

$b^2 - 4ac = 1^2 - 4(2)(-3)$ ◄——— Discriminant ———►

$b^2 - 4ac = 25$

Two real solutions ◄——— $b^2 - 4ac > 0$ ———►

Solutions are rational. ◄——— 25 is a perfect square;

28 is not. ———►

$2x^2 + 2x - 3 = 0$

$b^2 - 4ac = 2^2 - 4(2)(-3)$

$b^2 - 4ac = 28$

Two real solutions

Solutions are irrational.

Example 3

Use the discriminant to determine the nature of the solutions of $x^2 + 2x + 5 = 0$. Verify your answer.

$x^2 + 2x + 5 = 0$

$b^2 - 4ac = 2^2 - 4(1)(5) = -16$ ◄——— Discriminant

Solutions are imaginary numbers ◄——— $b^2 - 4ac < 0$

Check: $x = \dfrac{-2 \pm \sqrt{-16}}{2}$

$= \dfrac{-2 \pm 4i}{2} = -1 \pm 2i$

Solution set: $\{-1 + 2i, -1 - 2i\}$

The table summarizes the algebraic and geometric properties determined by the discriminant of a quadratic equation.

Discriminant	Solutions to $ax^2 + bx + c = 0$ $a, b, c \in \mathbf{R}, x \in \mathbf{C}$	Graph of $y = ax^2 + bx + c$, $a, b, c \in \mathbf{R}$
$b^2 - 4ac = 0$	One real number	Tangent to x axis.
$b^2 - 4ac > 0$	Two real numbers	Intersects x axis in 2 distinct points.
$b^2 - 4ac < 0$	Two imaginary numbers	Does not intersect the x axis.

Find the discriminant of each equation.

1. $x^2 + 3x - 4 = 0$ 25

2. $4y^2 - 12y + 9 = 0$ 0

3. $4m = 2 - 3m^2$ 40

4. Use the discriminant to describe the nature of the roots of the quadratic equations in Exercises 1–3. 1,3. Two unequal, real roots 2. One real root

---

Exercises

Use the discriminant to determine the nature of the solutions of each equation. Tell whether the real solutions are rational or irrational.

a

1. Real, two, irrational
$x^2 + 5x - 2 = 0$

2. Real, two, rational
$n^2 - 6n + 8 = 0$

3. Real, one, rational
$y^2 - 6y + 9 = 0$

4. $m^2 - 6m + 12 = 0$

5. $x^2 - 6x + 1 = 0$

6. $x^2 + 2x - 15 = 0$

7. Two, imaginary
$4a^2 + 1 = 4a$

8. Real, two, irrational
$2 = 5y + y^2$

9. Real, two, rational
$2d^2 + 7d + 6 = 0$

10. Real, one, rational
$3m^2 - 7m = 2$

11. Real, two, irrational
$2n^2 + 3 = 5n$

12. Real, two, rational
$4x^2 - 10x - 6 = 0$

13. Real, two, irrational
$3d^2 - 6d = 8$

14. Real, two, rational
$6x^2 - 7x + 3 = 0$

15. Real, two, rational
$2a^2 - 3a = 5$

16. Real, two, irrational Two, imaginary
Describe the graph of $y = ax^2 + bx + c$ for $a, b, c \in R$ in terms of the number of points in which it intersects the x axis when $b^2 - 4ac = 0$; when $b^2 - 4ac > 0$; when $b^2 - 4ac < 0$. one point; two points; does not intersect

17. Determine, without graphing, whether the graph of $y = -4x^2 + 12x - 9$ intersects the x axis in exactly one point, in two points, or not at all.

$b^2 - 4ac = 144 - 4(-4)(-9) = 0$, therefore, the graph intersects the x axis in exactly one point.

Determine the value of k that will give the indicated solution set.

b

18. $y^2 - 6y + k = 0$; one real number $k = 9$

19. $y^2 + ky + 16 = 0$; two distinct real numbers $k > 8$ or $k < -8$

20. $kn^2 - 10n + 5 = 0$; two imaginary numbers $k > 5$

21. $3n^2 - 12n + 2k = 0$; two imaginary numbers $k > 6$

22. $2x^2 - 20x + k = 0$; two distinct real numbers $k < 50$

23. $ka^2 + 8a + k = 0$; two distinct real numbers $-4 < k < 4$

24. $y^2 = -4ky - 1$; one real number $k = \pm\frac{1}{2}$

25. $k^2x^2 + 40x + 25 = 9$; two distinct real numbers $-5 < k < 5$

c

26. Find k in $12x^2 + 4kx + k = 0$ such that the graph of $y = 12x^2 + 4kx + k$
 (a) is tangent to the x axis; $k = 0$ or $k = 3$
 (b) intersects the x axis in two points; $k < 0$ or $k > 3$
 (c) has no intersection with the x axis. $0 < k < 3$

6-12 Sum and Product of Solutions

The objective for this section is on page 253.

Example 1 Find an expression for the sum, $r_1 + r_2$, and for the product, $r_1 \cdot r_2$, of the solutions of a quadratic equation.

$$r_1 = \frac{-b + \sqrt{b^2 - 4ac}}{2a} \qquad r_2 = \frac{-b - \sqrt{b^2 - 4ac}}{2a} \qquad \longleftarrow \text{Solutions}$$

$$r_1 + r_2 = \frac{-b + \sqrt{b^2 - 4ac} - b - \sqrt{b^2 - 4ac}}{2a} = -\frac{b}{a} \qquad \longleftarrow \text{Sum}$$

$$r_1 \cdot r_2 = \left(-\frac{b}{2a} + \frac{\sqrt{b^2 - 4ac}}{2a}\right)\left(-\frac{b}{2a} - \frac{\sqrt{b^2 - 4ac}}{2a}\right)$$

$$r_1 \cdot r_2 = \left(-\frac{b}{2a}\right)^2 - \left(\frac{\sqrt{b^2 - 4ac}}{2a}\right)^2 \qquad \longleftarrow (x+y)(x-y) = x^2 - y^2$$

$$r_1 \cdot r_2 = \frac{b^2}{4a^2} - \frac{b^2 - 4ac}{4a^2} = \frac{4ac}{4a^2} = \frac{c}{a} \qquad \longleftarrow \text{Product}$$

Theorem 6-2: If r_1 and r_2 are the roots of the quadratic equation, $ax^2 + bx + c = 0$, then

$$r_1 + r_2 = -\frac{b}{a} \qquad \text{and} \qquad r_1 \cdot r_2 = \frac{c}{a}.$$

Example 2 Find the sum and product of the solutions of $x^2 - 6x + 8 = 0$.

$$r_1 + r_2 = -\frac{-6}{1} = 6 \qquad \longleftarrow r_1 + r_2 = -\frac{b}{a}$$

$$r_1 \cdot r_2 = \frac{8}{1} = 8 \qquad \longleftarrow r_1 \cdot r_2 = \frac{c}{a}$$

248 Chapter 6

Example 3   Find a quadratic equation for which $r_1 + r_2 = \frac{5}{2}$ and $r_1 \cdot r_2 = \frac{6}{2}$.

$$ax^2 + bx + c = 0$$

$$x^2 + \frac{b}{a}x + \frac{c}{a} = 0 \quad \longleftarrow \quad \text{Divide by a.}$$

$$x^2 - \frac{5}{2}x + \frac{6}{2} = 0 \quad \longleftarrow \quad r_1 + r_2 = -\frac{b}{a} \text{ and } r_1 \cdot r_2 = \frac{c}{a}; \text{ substitute.}$$

$$2x^2 - 5x + 6 = 0 \quad \longleftarrow \quad \text{Multiply by 2.}$$

There are many other quadratic equations for which $r_1 + r_2 = \frac{5}{2}$ and $r_1 \cdot r_2 = \frac{6}{2}$. Any equivalent equation will have the same solutions.

Exercises

Find the sum and product of the solutions of each equation.

1. $x^2 + 7x - 10 = 0$ $-7; -10$
3. $y^2 - 2y + 9 = 0$ $2; 9$
5. $3n^2 + 2n - 3 = 0$ $-\frac{2}{3}; -1$
7. $a^2 + a + 1 = 0$ $-1; 1$

2. $8x^2 - 6x + 1 = 0$ $\frac{3}{4}; \frac{1}{8}$
4. $m^2 - 4m + 1 = 0$ $4; 1$
6. $2t^2 - 3t - 5 = 0$ $\frac{3}{2}; -\frac{5}{2}$
8. $5x^2 - 7x + 3 = 0$ $\frac{7}{5}; \frac{3}{5}$

Write a quadratic equation whose solutions have the given sum and product. Write the equation with integral coefficients.

$\rightarrow x^2 + 13x + 40 = 0$
9. Sum: 3; product: -40 $x^2 - 3x - 40 = 0$
11. Sum: -13; product: 40
13. Sum: $\frac{1}{2}$; product: $-\frac{3}{16}$

$\rightarrow x^2 + x - 30 = 0$
10. Sum: 0; product: -9 $x^2 - 9 = 0$
12. Sum: -1; product: -30
14. Sum: $-\frac{7}{10}$; product: -8

$16x^2 - 8x - 3 = 0$ $10x^2 + 7x - 80 = 0$

Write a quadratic equation having the given solutions and having integral coefficients.

15. 3 and 5 $x^2 - 8x + 15 = 0$

16. -2 and 7 $x^2 - 5x - 14 = 0$

17. 2 and $-\dfrac{3}{4}$ $4x^2 - 5x - 6 = 0$

18. -4 and $+4$ $x^2 - 16 = 0$

19. $3i$ and $-3i$ $x^2 + 9 = 0$

20. $2 + \sqrt{7}$ and $2 - \sqrt{7}$ $x^2 - 4x - 3 = 0$

21. $\frac{1}{2}$ and $\frac{2}{3}$ $6x^2 - 7x + 2 = 0$

22. $\dfrac{3 + i\sqrt{2}}{4}$ and $\dfrac{3 - i\sqrt{2}}{4}$

$16x^2 - 24x + 11 = 0$

Mathematics and
Engineering

THE BASIC high school requirements for entrance into a degree program in any field of engineering are courses in mathematics and the physical sciences. The first two years of the college program emphasize mathematics and the physical sciences. The remaining years of study are devoted primarily to the engineering specialty.

Mechanical engineers design and develop various types of engines (gas, steam, jet, turbine) and machines. Since they are employed in a wide range of industries, their work varies with the industry. Among their specialities are motor vehicles, aircraft, petroleum, rubber, and plastics.

Civil engineers design and direct the building of roads, tunnels, harbors, bridges, water supply systems, and sewerage systems.

Industrial engineers are sometimes called efficiency experts since they are concerned with determining the most efficient ways of using people, machines, and materials. They design production plans and systems for coordinating the various steps involved in a manufacturing process.

Aerospace engineers develop aerospace products (satellites, manned space capsules, airplanes) from the initial planning and design stage to the final assembly and testing.

Chemical engineers design plants and equipment for the manufacture of chemicals.

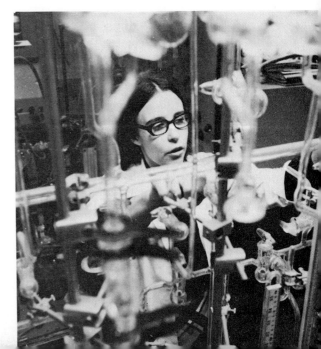

Chapter
Objectives
and
Review

Objective: To define the important mathematical terms in this chapter.

1. Here are many of the mathematical terms used in this chapter. Be sure that you know their meanings and that you can use them correctly.

axis of symmetry (p. 215)
completing the square (p. 237)
discriminant (p. 245)
incomplete quadratic (p. 234)
maximum point (p. 215)
minimum point (p. 215)

parabola (p. 215)
quadratic equation (p. 231)
quadratic formula (p. 242)
quadratic function (p. 215)
variation as the square (p. 212)
vertex (p. 215)

Objective: To solve problems in which one variable varies directly as the square of a second variable. (Section 6-1)

For each exercise, y varies directly as the square of x.

2. If $y = 9$ when $x = 3$, find y when $x = 5$.   25
3. If $y = \frac{1}{3}$ when $x = 3$, find y when $x = \frac{1}{3}$. $\frac{1}{243}$

Objective: To describe and identify quadratic functions. (Section 6-2)

4. What conditions must be satisfied by the coefficients a, b, and c, for $y = ax^2 + bx + c$ to define a quadratic function?   *a, b,* and *c* must be complex number constants, but a ≠ 0.
   Identify each function as quadratic, linear, or neither.

5. $f(x) = 2x^2 - x + 3$ quadratic
6. $g(x) = 2x - x^2$ quadratic
7. $h(x) = x^3 - 3x^2 + 1$ neither
8. $f(x) = 2x + 3$ linear

Objective: To sketch the graph of a quadratic function. (Sections 6-3, 6-4, 6-5)

For each exercise, sketch the given quadratic functions on the same set of coordinate axes. The domain is the set of real numbers.

9. $y = 3x^2$; $y = 3x^2 + 2x$; $y = 3x^2 + 2x + 6$ See key.
10. $y = -\frac{1}{2}x^2$; $y = -\frac{1}{2}x^2 + 2x$; $y = -\frac{1}{2}x^2 + 2x - 3$ See key.

252   Chapter 6

Objective: To identify the equation of the axis of symmetry and the coordinates of the vertex of a parabola from its equation. (Sections 6-3, 6-4, 6-5)

For each parabola, write the equation of its axis of symmetry and the coordinates of its vertex.

11. $y = 3x^2$
$x = 0; (0, 0)$

12. $y = -\frac{1}{2}x^2$
$x = 0; (0, 0)$

13. $y = 3x^2 + 2x$
$x = -\frac{1}{3}, \left(-\frac{1}{3}, -\frac{1}{3}\right)$

14. $y = 3x^2 + 2x + 6$
$x = -\frac{1}{3}, \left(-\frac{1}{3}, 5\frac{2}{3}\right)$

Objective: To solve problems that involve a maximum or a minimum. (Section 6-6)

15. What is the largest rectangular pen that can be enclosed with 200 meters of fencing?   50 meters by 50 meters

16. A tinsmith has a 40-cm strip of material he wishes to fold into an open rectangular gutter. How should he fold it to allow for maximum volume?
10 cm high, 20 cm wide

Objective: To solve quadratic equations by graphing. (Section 6-7)

Use a graph to determine the solutions of each equation.

17. $3x^2 - x - 2 = 0$ $\left\{1, -\frac{2}{3}\right\}$

18. $-x^2 + 5x - 4 = 0$ $\{1, 4\}$

Objective: To solve quadratic equations by taking square roots. (Section 6-8)

Solve.

19. $2x^2 = 72$ $\{6, -6\}$ **20.** $x^2 - 4 = 0$ $\{2, -2\}$ **21.** $(x - 2)^2 = 49$ $\{9, -5\}$ **22.** $(x + 4)^2 = 81$
$\{5, -13\}$

Objective: To solve quadratic equations by completing the square. (Section 6-9)

Solve each equation by completing the square.

23. $x^2 - 6x + 1 = 0$ $\{3 + \sqrt{8}, 3 - \sqrt{8}\}$

24. $4x^2 - 4x - 3 = 0$ $\left\{\frac{3}{2}, -\frac{1}{2}\right\}$

Objective: To solve quadratic equations by using the quadratic formula. (Section 6-10) $\left\{\frac{3 + \sqrt{21}}{6}, \frac{3 - \sqrt{21}}{6}\right\}$

Use the quadratic formula to find the solutions for each equation.

25. $3x^2 - 3x - 1 = 0$

26. $0 = x^2 + 4x + 1$ $\{-2 + \sqrt{3}, -2 - \sqrt{3}\}$

Objective: To use the discriminant to determine the nature of the solutions of a quadratic equation. (Section 6-11)

Use the discriminant to determine the nature of the solutions of each quadratic equation.

27. $x^2 - 6x + 9 = 0$ one, real, rational solution **28.** $x^2 - 6x + 10 = 0$ two, imaginary

Objective: To find the sum and the product of the roots of a quadratic equation. (Section 6-12)

Find the sum and product of the solutions of each equation.

29. $x^2 + 4x - 60 = 0$ $-4; -60$

30. $3x^2 - 5x + 3 = 0$ $\frac{5}{3}; 1$

Chapter
Test

Complete each statement.

1. The equation of the axis of symmetry of $y = ax^2 + bx + c$ is $\underline{\quad x = -\frac{b}{2a} \quad}$.

2. The solutions of $ax^2 + bx + c = 0$ are $\underline{\quad\quad}$. $x = \frac{-b \pm \sqrt{b^2 - 4ac}}{2a}$

3. If $a < 0$ for the parabola $y = ax^2 + bx + c$, the curve opens $\underline{\quad downward \quad}$.

4. If the discriminant of a quadratic equation is less than zero, then the solutions of the equation are $\underline{\quad imaginary \quad}$ numbers.

5. If y varies directly as the square of x and $y = 18$ when $x = 6$, find y when $x = 4$. $y = 8$

6. Solve $x^2 + 2x + 3 = 0$ by completing the square. $\{-1 \pm i\sqrt{2}\}$

7. Solve $2x^2 + 5x - 3 = 0$ by graphing. $\{\frac{1}{2}, -3\}$

8. Solve $x^2 + 6x + 6 = 0$ by the quadratic formula. $\{-3 \pm \sqrt{3}\}$

For the function defined by $y = 2x^2 - 4x + 1$, find each of the following.

9. The equation of its axis of symmetry. $x = 1$

10. The y intercept of its graph. $(0, 1)$

11. The coordinates of its vertex. $V(1, -1)$

12. Find two numbers whose sum is 10 such that the sum of their squares is a minimum. $5, 5$

13. For what values of k are the solutions of $x^2 + 5kx + 4 = 0$ two unequal real numbers? two imaginary numbers? $k > \frac{4}{5}$ or $k < -\frac{4}{5}$; $-\frac{4}{5} < k < \frac{4}{5}$

Answers to Remember

Page 214: **1.** $y = -3x + 5$ **2.** $\frac{5}{2}$ **3.** They are perpendicular to each other.

Page 228: **1.** $\{\frac{7}{3}\}$ **2.** $\{-2\}$ **3.** $\{4\frac{1}{2}, \frac{1}{2}\}$ **4.** 12 **5.** $\frac{\sqrt{7}}{2}$ **6.** $\frac{2x^2 - 5x + 25}{4x^2 - 25}$

Page 233: **1.** $3i$ **2.** $\frac{1 + 3i}{5}$ **3.** $-(2 + i)$ **4.** $\frac{z}{xy}$ **5.** $4 \pm 4i\sqrt{3}$ **6.** -1

Page 244: **1.** N, W, $\mathscr{I}$, Q, R, C **2.** $\mathscr{I}$, Q, R, C **3.** Ir, C **4.** C **5.** C

Chapter 7
Systems of Sentences

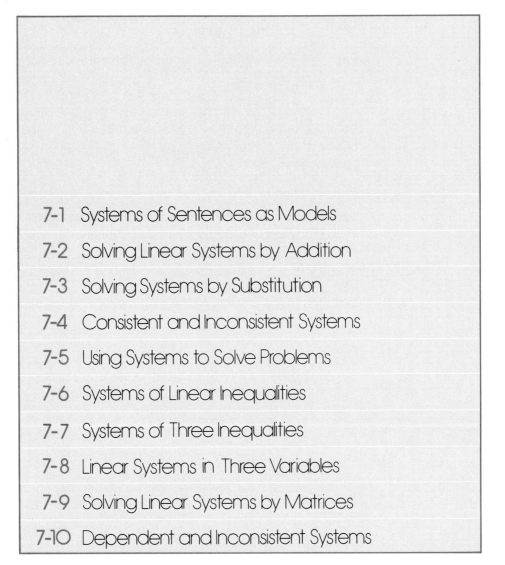

7-1 Systems of Sentences as Models

The objective for this section is on page 288.

Sets of two or more sentences are <u>systems of sentences</u>.

Systems of Equations		**System of Inequalities**

$$\begin{cases} x + y + 1 = 0 \\ 2x + y + 2 = 0 \end{cases} \qquad \begin{cases} x + 2y + z = 8 \\ 2x - 2y + z = 4 \\ -x + y + z = -1 \end{cases} \qquad \begin{cases} x - y < 8 \\ x + 2y > 6 \end{cases}$$

Each system is actually a <u>compound sentence</u>.

$$\begin{cases} x + y + 1 = 0 \\ 2x - y + 2 = 0 \end{cases} \quad \text{means} \quad x + y + 1 = 0 \ \underline{\text{and}}\ 2x - y + 2 = 0$$

Because the connective <u>and</u> means intersection, the solution set of one of the sentences must also be the solution set of the other sentences in the system.

Definition: The **solution set of a system of two equations in two variables** is the set of ordered pairs that makes both equations true.

Geometrically, the solution set of a system is the set of points, common to the graphs of the sentences of the system.

Example 1   Use a graph to solve the following system.

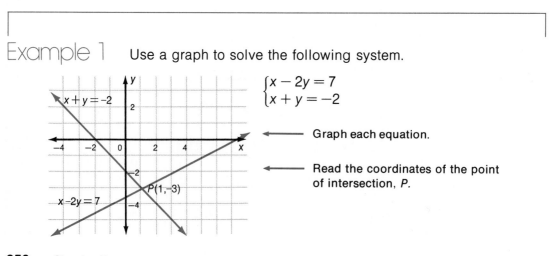

$$\begin{cases} x - 2y = 7 \\ x + y = -2 \end{cases}$$

Graph each equation.

Read the coordinates of the point of intersection, *P*.

256   Chapter 7

Check: $x - 2y = 7$ $x + y = -2$ ←———— Replace x with 1 and y
           $1 - 2(-3) \overset{?}{=} 7$ $1 + (-3) \overset{?}{=} -2$ with -3 in each equation.
           $1 + 6 = 7$ $1 - 3 = -2$ **Solution set:** $\{(1, -3)\}$

Example 2   The sum of two numbers, x and y, is 9 and their difference is 3.
             Write a system of equations to describe the relationship. Use a
             graph to solve the system.

$$\begin{cases} x + y = 9 \\ x - y = 3 \end{cases}$$ ←———— The sum of x and y is 9.
                                   ←———— The difference is 3.

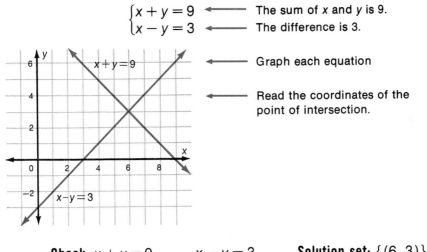

←———— Graph each equation

←———— Read the coordinates of the
       point of intersection.

Check: $x + y = 9$ $x - y = 3$ **Solution set:** $\{(6, 3)\}$
           $6 + 3 \overset{?}{=} 9$ $6 - 3 \overset{?}{=} 3$

Try These   *Check whether the given ordered pair satisfies both equations
             of the system.*

1. $\{(-2, 2)\}$
   $\begin{cases} x + 3y = 3 \quad \text{No.} \\ 2x + y = -4 \end{cases}$

2. $\{(-2, 2)\}$
   $\begin{cases} x + 2y - 2 = 0 \quad \text{Yes.} \\ x = -2 \end{cases}$

3. $\{(-4, 1)\}$
   $\begin{cases} x + 6y + 6 = 0 \\ y + x = 5 \quad \text{No.} \end{cases}$

Write a system of equations in two variables to describe each relationship.

4. The sum of two numbers, x and y, is 14; their difference is 4. $\begin{cases} x + y = 14 \\ x - y = 4 \end{cases}$

5. The product of two numbers, x and y, is 6. The difference of twice the
   second and the first is 1. $\begin{cases} xy = 6 \\ 2y - x = 1 \end{cases}$

Exercises

Use a graph to solve each system.

1. $\begin{cases} x + y = 0 \\ x - y = 3 \end{cases}$ $\{(\frac{3}{2}, -\frac{3}{2})\}$

2. $\begin{cases} y = x + 4 \\ y = 2x + 4 \end{cases}$ $\{(0, 4)\}$

3. $\begin{cases} y = 6 \\ 2x + y = -2 \end{cases}$ $\{(-4, 6)\}$

4. $\begin{cases} y = \frac{1}{2}x - 3 \\ x = 0 \end{cases}$ $\{(0, -3)\}$

5. $\begin{cases} x + 3 = 0 \\ y - 7 = 0 \end{cases}$ $\{(-3, 7)\}$

6. $\begin{cases} x = y \\ 2y + 3x = -10 \end{cases}$ $\{(-2, -2)\}$

7. $\begin{cases} 4x + 3y = 0 \\ 2x - 6y = 5 \end{cases}$ $\{(\frac{1}{2}, -\frac{2}{3})\}$

8. $\begin{cases} 4x + 2y = 6 \\ 3x - 4y = 10 \end{cases}$ $\{(2, -1)\}$

9. $\begin{cases} 2x + y = -2 \\ 4x + 2y = -1 \end{cases}$

11. $\begin{cases} n_1 + n_2 = 12 \\ n_1 - n_2 = 3 \end{cases}$; $\{(7\frac{1}{2}, 4\frac{1}{2})\}$

14. $\begin{cases} x + y = 87 \\ x - y = 19 \end{cases}$; $\{(53, 34)\}$

ϕ

Write a system of equations to describe each relationship in Exercises 10-16. Use a graph to solve each system in Exercises 10, 11, 13, and 14.

10. Two numbers, x and y; their sum is 5 and their difference is 1. $\begin{cases} x + y = 5 \\ x - y = 1 \end{cases}$; $\{(3, 2)\}$

11. Two numbers, n_1 and n_2; their sum is 12 and their difference is 3. See above.

12. Two numbers, a and b; the sum of their reciprocals is 24 and the difference is 4. See below.

13. Two numbers, p and q; the sum of the first and twice the second is 34, while the difference of the first and four times the second is 4. See below.

14. Two acute angles, x and y; their sum is 87° and their difference is 19°. See above.

15. Two numbers, r and s; the difference of their squares is 0 and the sum of the numbers is 0. $\begin{cases} r^2 - s^2 = 0 \\ r + s = 0 \end{cases}$; $\{(r, s): s = -r\}$

16. Two numbers, a and b; their product is 6, while the difference of the first and twice the second is 1. $\begin{cases} ab = 6 \\ a - 2b = 1 \end{cases}$; $\{(-3, -2), (4, \frac{3}{2})\}$

12. $\begin{cases} \frac{1}{a} + \frac{1}{b} = 24 \\ \frac{1}{a} - \frac{1}{b} = 4 \end{cases}$; $\{(\frac{1}{14}, \frac{1}{10})\}$

13. $\begin{cases} p + 2q = 34 \\ p - 4q = 4 \end{cases}$; $\{(24, 5)\}$

Write a system of equations to describe each relationship.

17. The dimensions of a field with area A are ℓ and w. The area increases by 1050 square meters when the length is increased by 10 meters and the width by 5 meters. The area decreases by 1050 square meters when the length is decreased by 5 meters and the width by 10 meters. $\begin{cases} 2w + \ell = 200 \\ w + 2\ell = 220 \end{cases}$

18. Rowing downstream, a person travels 6 kilometers in 1 hour. The return trip takes 2 hours. The person's rowing rate is r and the rate of the stream is s. $\begin{cases} r + s = 6 \\ 2r - 2s = 6 \end{cases}$

19. A three-digit number can be written in the form $100h + 10t + u$. The sum of the three digits of a certain three-digit number is 13; the sum of the units and tens digits is 10; and the number is increased by 99 if the digits are reversed. $\begin{cases} u + t + h = 13 \\ u + t = 10 \\ h - u = -1 \end{cases}$

20. Three trucks together haul a total of 78 cubic meters, 81 cubic meters, and 69 cubic meters in 3 successive days. Find the capacity of each truck if they haul the following number of loads each day. First day: 4, 3 and 5 loads; Second day: 5, 4 and 4 loads; Third day: 3, 5, and 3 loads.

21. In a three-digit number, the difference between each succeeding pair of digits is 1 and the sum of the digits is 15. <small>See below.</small>

22. Entrance to a school gym requires a half dollar from adults, a quarter from high schoolers and a dime from grade schoolers. For 320 admissions, $76.00 was collected. There were twice as many dimes as quarters. How many adults, high schoolers, and grade schoolers were admitted? <small>See below.</small>

→ Let x, y, and z represent the capacities of the three trucks. $\begin{cases} 4x + 3y + 5z = 78 \\ 5x + 4y + 4z = 81 \\ 3x + 5y + 3z = 69 \end{cases}$

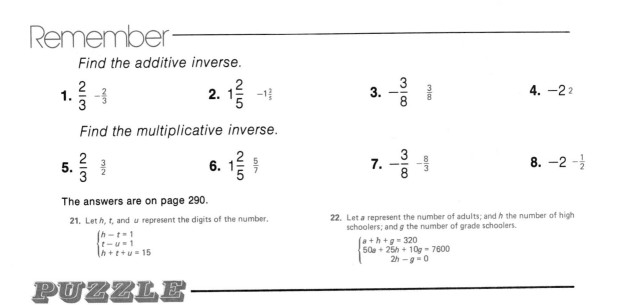

Remember

Find the additive inverse.

1. $\dfrac{2}{3}$ $\quad -\frac{2}{3}$

2. $1\dfrac{2}{5}$ $\quad -1\frac{2}{5}$

3. $-\dfrac{3}{8}$ $\quad \frac{3}{8}$

4. -2 $\quad 2$

Find the multiplicative inverse.

5. $\dfrac{2}{3}$ $\quad \frac{3}{2}$

6. $1\dfrac{2}{5}$ $\quad \frac{5}{7}$

7. $-\dfrac{3}{8}$ $\quad -\frac{8}{3}$

8. -2 $\quad -\frac{1}{2}$

The answers are on page 290.

21. Let h, t, and u represent the digits of the number.
$\begin{cases} h - t = 1 \\ t - u = 1 \\ h + t + u = 15 \end{cases}$

22. Let a represent the number of adults; and h the number of high schoolers; and g the number of grade schoolers.
$\begin{cases} a + h + g = 320 \\ 50a + 25h + 10g = 7600 \\ 2h - g = 0 \end{cases}$

PUZZLE

A man had three children. His will stated that his favorite riding horses should be divided among his children so that one child was to get half of them, the second child one-third of them, and the third child one-ninth of them. When the father died, he left 17 horses. How were they divided? <small>See key.</small>

7-2 Solving Linear Systems by Addition

The objective for this section is on page 288.

The solution set of the following system is $\{(1, -3)\}$.

$$\begin{cases} x - 2y = 7 & \quad 1 \\ x + y = -2 & \quad 2 \end{cases}$$

If you add the equations, right side to right side and left side to left side, you get equation .

$$(x - 2y) + (x + y) = 7 + (-2)$$
$$2x - y = 5 \qquad\qquad 3$$

Verify that $\{(1, -3)\}$ is also the solution set of equation **3**.

Three systems of <u>pairs</u> of equations can be formed using equations **1**, **2**, and **3**. These are **equivalent systems** because they have the same solution set $\{(1, -3)\}$.

System I
$$\begin{cases} x - 2y = 7 \\ x + y = -2 \end{cases}$$

System II
$$\begin{cases} x - 2y = 7 \\ 2x - y = 5 \end{cases}$$

System III
$$\begin{cases} x + y = -2 \\ 2x - y = 5 \end{cases}$$

Example 1

Use multiplication and addition to solve System I.

$$\begin{array}{ll} 2x - 4y = 14 & 2 \times 1 \\ \underline{x + y = -2} & 2 \\ 3x - 3y = 12 & 3 \end{array}$$ ⟵ Multiply $x - 2y = 7$ by 2. Add this to Equation 2.

$$\begin{array}{ll} x - 2y = 7 & 1 \\ \underline{2x + 2y = -4} & 2 \times 2 \\ 3x = 3, \text{ or} \\ x = 1 & 4 \end{array}$$ ⟵ Multiply Equation 2 by 2. Add this to Equation 1.

$$\begin{array}{ll} -x + 2y = -7 & -1 \times 1 \\ \underline{x + y = -2} \\ 3y = -9, \text{ or} & 2 \\ y = -3 & 5 \end{array}$$ ⟵ Multiply Equation 1 by −1. Add this to Equation 2.

The graphs of equations **1–5** verify that $\{(1, -3)\}$ is the solution set for each system made of pairs of equations **1–5**.

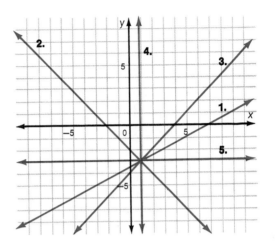

Example 1 suggests the following theorem.

Theorem 7.1

If the graphs of two linear equations, $A_1x + B_1y = C_1$ and $A_2x + B_2y = C_2$, intersect in $P(a, b)$, then the sum of any multiples of these equations is a line that passes through $P(a, b)$.

In finding the equations $x = 1$ and $y = -3$ in Example 1, one of the variables was eliminated in the original system. Further, the solution set $\{(1, -3)\}$ of the original system can be read from these equations. This suggests a method for solving a pair of linear equations, the <u>addition method</u>.

Addition Method for Solving Linear Systems

Choose multiples of the equations that eliminate one of the variables when the equations are added.

To eliminate one of the variables, the coefficients of that variable in both equations must be additive inverses.

Example 2 Solve the following system by eliminating the y term.

$$\begin{cases} 2x + y = 1 & \quad 1 \\ x + 3y = 13 & \quad 2 \end{cases}$$

$$\begin{array}{ll} -6x - 3y = -3 & \qquad \longleftarrow \text{Multiply 1 by } -3. \\ \underline{x + 3y = 13} & \\ -5x \quad\;\; = 10 & \qquad \longleftarrow \text{Solve for } x. \\ \quad\;\; x = -2 \end{array}$$

$$\begin{array}{ll} 2x + y = 1 & \qquad \longleftarrow \text{Solve for } y \text{ by replacing } x \\ 2(-2) + y = 1 & \qquad \text{with } -2 \text{ in one of the} \\ -4 + y = 1 & \qquad \text{original equations.} \\ y = 5 \end{array}$$

Check: $\quad x + 3y \overset{?}{=} 13 \qquad \longleftarrow$ Replace x with -2 and y with

$-2 + 3(5) \overset{?}{=} 13 \qquad\quad$ 5 in the other equation.

$13 = 13 \qquad\qquad$ **Solution set:** $\{(-2, 5\}$

Example 3 Solve the following system by eliminating the x term.

$$\begin{cases} 3x + 2y = 5 & \quad 1 \\ 4x + 4y = 10 & \quad 2 \end{cases}$$

$$\begin{array}{l} -4(3x + 2y = 5) \\ 3(4x + 4y = 10) \end{array} \longrightarrow \begin{array}{ll} -12x - 8y = -20 & \qquad \longleftarrow \text{Multiply 1 by } -4. \\ \underline{12x + 12y = 30} & \qquad \longleftarrow \text{Multiply 2 by 3.} \\ 4y = 10 \\ y = 2\tfrac{1}{2} \end{array}$$

$$\begin{array}{ll} 3x + 2y = 5 & \\ 3x + 2(2\tfrac{1}{2}) = 5 & \qquad \longleftarrow \text{Solve for } x \text{ by replacing } y \text{ with} \\ 3x + 5 = 5 & \qquad 2\tfrac{1}{2} \text{ in one of the original equations.} \\ 3x = 0 & \\ x = 0 \end{array}$$

Check: $4x + 4y = 10$ $\qquad\qquad\qquad$ **Solution set:** $\{(0, 2\tfrac{1}{2})\}$

$4(0) + 4(2\tfrac{1}{2}) \overset{?}{=} 10$

$10 = 10$

Try These *By what numbers could the equations in each system be multi-plied for their sum to be an equation with no y term?*

1. $\begin{cases} 3x - 5y = 7 & \text{2} \\ x + 10y = 0 & \text{1} \end{cases}$

2. $\begin{cases} x - 4y = 2 & \text{5} \\ 2x + 5y = 1 & \text{4} \end{cases}$

$\frac{1}{-7}$ or $\frac{-1}{7}$ **3.** $\begin{cases} 7y - 2x = 6 \\ x + y = -3 \end{cases}$

By what numbers could the equations in each system be multiplied for their sum to be an equation with no x term?

4. $\begin{cases} 2x + y = 6 \\ x - 3y = 4 \end{cases}$ $\frac{1}{-2}$ or $\frac{-1}{2}$

5. $\begin{cases} 3x - y = 1 \\ 2x + 3y = 2 \end{cases}$ $\frac{2}{-3}$ or $\frac{-2}{3}$

6. $\begin{cases} 2y = 6x - 4 & \text{1} \\ 3x - y = 2 & \text{2} \end{cases}$

Exercises

Solve each system by the addition method.

a

1. $\begin{cases} 4x + 3y = 17 \\ 2x + 3y = 13 \end{cases}$ $\{(2, 3)\}$

2. $\begin{cases} 5x + y = 14 \\ 2x + y = 5 \end{cases}$ $\{(3, -1)\}$

$\{(-2, -3)\}$
3. $\begin{cases} x - 3y = 7 \\ x - 5y = 13 \end{cases}$

4. $\begin{cases} 3x + y = 15 \\ 3x + 7y = 15 \end{cases}$ $\{(5, 0)\}$

5. $\begin{cases} x + y = 9 \\ 5x - y = 3 \end{cases}$ $\{(2, 7)\}$

6. $\begin{cases} 4a + b = 14 \\ 6a + b = 16 \end{cases}$ $\{(1, 10)\}$

7. $\begin{cases} a + 3b = 7 \\ a + b = 5 \end{cases}$ $\{(4, 1)\}$

8. $\begin{cases} m + 5n = 11 \\ m - n = 5 \end{cases}$ $\{(6, 1)\}$

9. $\begin{cases} 2x - 3y = -7 \\ 4x - 5y = -9 \end{cases}$ $\{(4, 5)\}$

10. $\begin{cases} 2x + 3y = -6 \\ 3x + 2y = 1 \end{cases}$ $\{(3, -4)\}$

11. $\begin{cases} 2x + 5y = 0 \\ 3x - 2y = -19 \end{cases}$ $\{(-5, 2)\}$

12. $\begin{cases} 8x + 5y = -13 \\ 3x - 2y = -1 \end{cases}$ $\{(-1, -1)\}$

13. $\begin{cases} 2x + y = 1 \\ 3x - 2y = 8 \end{cases}$ $\{(\frac{10}{7}, -\frac{13}{7})\}$

14. $\begin{cases} 4x + 3y = 0 \\ 2x - 6y = 5 \end{cases}$ $\{(\frac{1}{2}, -\frac{2}{3})\}$

15. $\begin{cases} 3x + 2y = 9 \\ 2x - 6y = 6 \end{cases}$ $\{(3, 0)\}$

b

16. $\begin{cases} 6ix - 5iy = -25 \\ 8ix + 2iy = 10 \end{cases}$ $\{(0, -5i)\}$

17. $\begin{cases} 8x + 6y = 6 + 8i \\ 5x + 2iy = 7i \end{cases}$ $\{(i, 1)\}$

18. $\begin{cases} 2ix - 5iy = 6 \\ 4ix - 3iy = 8 \end{cases}$ $\{(-\frac{11}{7}i, \frac{4}{7}i)\}$

Solve the following compound sentences.

19. $2x + 3y = -1$ <u>and</u> $5x + 6y = -3$ $\{(-1, \frac{1}{3})\}$

20. $9x + 2y = -12$ <u>and</u> $3x - 4y = -11$ $\{(-\frac{5}{3}, \frac{3}{2})\}$

21. $\{(x, y) : 3x + 2y = 5 \text{ <u>and</u> } 6x - 4y = -2\}$ $\{(\frac{2}{3}, \frac{3}{2})\}$

22. $\{(x, y) : 6x - 3y = -14 \text{ <u>and</u> } 3x + 12y = 38\}$ $\{(-\frac{2}{3}, \frac{10}{3})\}$

Consider the system

$$\begin{cases} 4x + 2y - 8 = 0 \\ -3x - 4y + 1 = 0. \end{cases}$$

The set of all sums of multiples of two linear equations have as graphs a **family of lines** *with a common point. The family of lines related to this system may be defined by the equation m(4x + 2y − 8) + n(−3x − 4y + 1) = 0, where m and n are any real numbers not both zero.*

23. Graph the original pair of equations. See key.

24. On the same pair of axes, graph the equation you get by letting See key.

    a. $m = 1$ and $n = 1$.

    b. $m = 2$ and $n = 1$.

    c. $m = 2$ and $n = 3$.

25. Do the lines in Exercise **24** have a point in common? Yes; (3, −2)

26. Let (x_1, y_1) be the point common to both $4x + 2y - 8 = 0$ and $-3x - 4y + 1 = 0$. Make a convincing argument that no matter what m and n are (not both zero) the resulting line contains the point (x_1, y_1). See key.

Solve the following system for x and y in terms of a and b.

Example: Solve the following system for x and y in terms of a and b.

$$\begin{cases} ax + by = 2ab & \quad \textbf{1} \\ bx + ay = a^2 + b^2 & \quad \textbf{2} \end{cases}$$

$abx + b^2y = 2ab^2$ ⟵   Multiply **1** by b.

$-abx - a^2y = -a^3 - ab^2$ ⟵   Multiply **2** by −a.

$(b^2 - a^2)y = a(-a^2 + b^2)$ ⟵   Add and factor.

$y = a$ (when $a \neq \pm b$)   ⟵   Solve for y.

$ax + ab = 2ab$ ⟵   Substitute for y in **1** and solve for x.

$x = b$ (when $a \neq 0$)

Check: Does $ab + ba = 2ab$? Yes.   **Solution set:** $\{(a, b)\}$

             Does $b^2 + a^2 = a^2 + b^2$? Yes.

27. $\begin{cases} x + y = m + n \\ x - y = m - n \end{cases}$ $\{(m, n)\}$

28. $\begin{cases} x + y = a \\ x - y = b \end{cases}$ $\{(\frac{a+b}{2}, \frac{a-b}{2})\}$

29. $\begin{cases} 3x + 2y = m \\ x - y = n \end{cases}$ $\{(\frac{m+2n}{5}, \frac{m-3n}{5})\}$

30. $\begin{cases} 2x + 3y = 13a \\ 3x - 4y = -6a \end{cases}$ $\{(2a, 3a)\}$

31. $\begin{cases} a_1x + b_1y = c_1 \\ a_2x + b_2y = c_2 \end{cases}$ $\{(\frac{b_2c_1 - b_1c_2}{a_1b_2 - a_2b_1}, \frac{a_2c_1 - a_1c_2}{a_2b_1 - a_1b_2})\}$

32. $\begin{cases} ax + by = r \\ cx - dy = 1 \end{cases}$ $\{(\frac{rd+b}{ad+bc}, \frac{rc-a}{bc+ad})\}$

Remember

Substitute 2 − 3x for y. Then solve for x.

1. $x + y = 2$ o

2. $2x + 3y = 12$ $-\frac{6}{7}$

3. $5x - 7y = 14$ $\frac{14}{13}$

The answers are on page 290.

7-3 Solving Systems by Substitution

The objective for this section is on page 288.

To solve a system of equations by the **substitution method,** solve one equation for one of the variables. Then substitute this value in the other equation.

Example

Solve the following system.

$$\begin{cases} 2x - 3y = 13 & \textbf{1} \\ 3x + y = 3 & \textbf{2} \end{cases}$$

$y = 3 - 3x$ ⟵ Solve for y in **2.**

$2x - 3(3 - 3x) = 13$ ⟵ Replace y in Equation **1** with $3 - 3x$.

$2x - 9 + 9x = 13$

$11x = 22$ ⟵ Solve for x.

$x = 2$

$3x + y = 3$ ⟵ To find possible values of x and y

$3(2) + y = 3$ that are the same for both equations,

$6 + y = 3$ substitute 2 for x in Equation **2**

$y = -3$ and solve for y.

Check: Does $2(2) - 3(-3) = 13$? (Equation **1**) Yes.

Solution set: $\{(2, -3)\}$ Does $3(2) + (-3) = 3$? (Equation **2**) Yes.

Try These

Solve for y in terms of x.

1. $y + x = 6$ $y = 6 - x$

2. $2x + y = -4$ $y = -4 - 2x$

Solve for x in terms of y.

3. $x - y = 8$ $x = y + 8$

4. $2x + y = 6$ $x = \frac{6-y}{2}$, or $x = 3 - \frac{y}{2}$

Exercises

Solve by the substitution method.

a

1. $\begin{cases} 2x + y = 7 \\ y = 3 \end{cases}$ $\{(2, 3)\}$

2. $\begin{cases} y = 2x + 4 \\ x = -2 \end{cases}$ $\{(-2, 0)\}$

3. $\begin{cases} x - 2y = 8 \\ x = 5 - y \end{cases}$ $\{(6, -1)\}$

4. $\begin{cases} x = 3y \\ x - y = 8 \end{cases}$ $\{(12, 4)\}$

5. $\begin{cases} 2x + 7y = 1 \\ 2x = 10 + 2y \end{cases}$ $\{(4, -1)\}$

6. $\begin{cases} 5x + y = 7 \\ 3x + 2y = 0 \end{cases}$ $\{(2, -3)\}$

7. $\begin{cases} x + y = 6 \\ 2x - 3y = 2 \end{cases}$ $\{(4, 2)\}$

8. $\begin{cases} 2x + y = -4 \\ 3x + 2y = -5 \end{cases}$ $\{(-3, 2)\}$

9. $\begin{cases} 3x - 2y = -16 \\ 2x + y = -9 \end{cases}$

Rewrite each equation to have integral coefficients. Then solve the system by any method you choose, and check.

$\{(-\frac{34}{7}, \frac{5}{7})\}$

b

10. $\begin{cases} \dfrac{x}{2} + \dfrac{y}{3} = 4 \\ \dfrac{2x}{3} + \dfrac{3y}{2} = 11\frac{2}{3} \end{cases}$ $\{(4, 6)\}$

11. $\begin{cases} \dfrac{3x}{2} + \dfrac{y}{4} = 7 \\ \dfrac{x}{5} - \dfrac{2y}{3} = 2\frac{1}{3} \end{cases}$ $\{(5, -2)\}$

12. $\begin{cases} \dfrac{x}{3} + \dfrac{y}{5} = -\dfrac{1}{5} \\ \dfrac{2x}{3} - \dfrac{3y}{4} = -5 \end{cases}$ $\{(-3, 4)\}$

13. $\begin{cases} \dfrac{a}{2} - \dfrac{2b}{3} = 2\frac{1}{3} \\ \dfrac{3a}{2} + 2b = -25 \end{cases}$ $\{(-6, -8)\}$

14. $\begin{cases} 2x - 1.5 = y \\ 2y + 0.5 = 3x \end{cases}$ $\{(2.5, 3.5)\}$

15. $\begin{cases} 2x - 3y = 0.1 \\ 5y - 0.3 = 3x \end{cases}$

$\{(1.4, 0.9)\}$

16. $\begin{cases} x - 2.3 = -5y \\ 3y = 2x - 2 \end{cases}$

$\{(1.3, 0.2)\}$

17. $\begin{cases} 10x + 5y = 3.5 \\ 3x + 0.6 = 4y \end{cases}$

$\{(0.2, 0.3)\}$

18. $\begin{cases} a - \dfrac{7b}{3} = -21 \\ a + \dfrac{b}{5} = 17 \end{cases}$

$\{(14, 15)\}$

c

19. Find an equation of the line which passes through $P(3, 2)$ and through the point of intersection of $y = \frac{1}{4}x + \frac{1}{2}$ and $x + \frac{3}{2}y = -\frac{1}{2}$. $x - 5y = -7$

20. Find an equation of the line which passes through $Q(1, 3)$ and through the point of intersection of $y = 2 - 4x$ and $2x - 3y = 8$. $x = 1$

Consistent and Inconsistent Systems

The objective for this section is on page 289.

The addition and substitution methods are based on the assumption that the solution set of a system contains at least one ordered pair. (See Figure 1.)

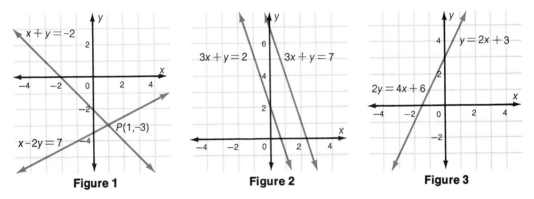

| Figure 1 | Figure 2 | Figure 3 |

When a system consists of equations that define two parallel lines, its solution set is the <u>empty set</u>. (See Figure 2.)

Definitions: A system of equations or inequalities whose solution set is the empty set is called an **inconsistent system**. A system of equations or inequalities whose solution set has one or more elements is called a **consistent system**.

Example 1   Solve the following system by the addition method.

$$\begin{cases} 3x + y = 7 \quad \textbf{1} \\ 3x + y = 2 \quad \textbf{2} \end{cases} \longrightarrow \begin{aligned} 3x + y &= 7 \\ -3x - y &= -2 \\ \hline 0 &= 5 \end{aligned} \longleftarrow \text{Multiply } \textbf{2} \text{ by } -1.$$

The result is a false statement. The solution set is ∅. The graph of this system shows two parallel lines. (See Figure 2.) The system is <u>inconsistent</u>.

If a system is inconsistent, then using algebraic methods leads to a false statement. Conversely, if using algebraic methods to solve a system leads to a false statement, then the system is inconsistent.

Equations 1 and 2 of the following system are equivalent.

$$\begin{cases} y = 2x + 3 & \quad 1 \\ 2y = 4x + 6 & \quad 2 \end{cases}$$

Their graphs have the same slope and the same y intercept. Thus, the graphs coincide. (See Figure 3.)

Definitions: A consistent system of linear equations whose solution set is infinite is called a **dependent system.** A consistent system of linear equations whose solution set has exactly one element is an **independent system,** or a **simultaneous system.**

Using algebraic methods to solve a dependent system results in an identity. For example, replacing y with $2x + 3$ in equation 2 gives

$$2(2x + 3) = 4x + 6.$$

If a system is dependent, then using algebraic methods leads to an identity. Conversely, if using algebraic methods to solve a system leads to an identity, then the system is dependent.

Exercises

Solve the following systems. Classify each system as Consistent, Inconsistent, Dependent, or Independent.

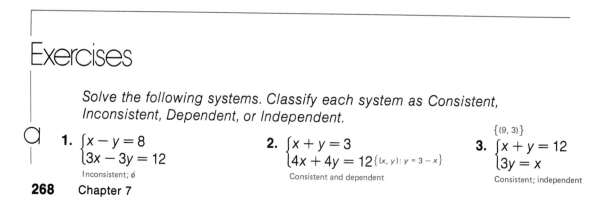

1. $\begin{cases} x - y = 8 \\ 3x - 3y = 12 \end{cases}$

   Inconsistent; ∅

2. $\begin{cases} x + y = 3 \\ 4x + 4y = 12 \end{cases}$ $\{(x, y): y = 3 - x\}$

   Consistent and dependent

3. $\begin{cases} x + y = 12 \\ 3y = x \end{cases}$

   $\{(9, 3)\}$

   Consistent; independent

4. $\begin{cases} 6x + 5y = 7 \\ 3x - 7y = 13 \end{cases}$ $\{(2,-1)\}$

Consistent, independent

5. $\begin{cases} 2x + 3y = 2 \\ y = -\dfrac{3x}{4} \end{cases}$ $\{(-8,6)\}$

Consistent, independent

6. $\begin{cases} x = 4y \\ \dfrac{x}{4} + y = 20 \end{cases}$ $\{(40, 10)\}$

Consistent, independent

Graph each system. Classify each system as Consistent, Inconsistent, Dependent, or Independent.

7. $\begin{cases} x - y = 4 \\ 3x = 4 + 2y \end{cases}$ $\{(-4,-8)\}$

Consistent, independent

8. $\begin{cases} x - y = 4 \\ 3x + 3y = 12 \end{cases}$ $\{(4,0)\}$

Consistent, independent

9. $\begin{cases} x - y = 4 \\ -2y = 4 - 2x \end{cases}$

Inconsistent; $\emptyset$

Solve by any method you choose.

10. $\begin{cases} \dfrac{x}{2} - \dfrac{y}{9} = 3 \\ y = \dfrac{9}{2}x - 27 \end{cases}$ $\{(x,y) : 9x - 2y = 54\}$

11. $\begin{cases} \dfrac{5a}{2} + \dfrac{2b}{3} = -21 \\ \dfrac{a}{3} - \dfrac{b}{9} = -1 \end{cases}$ $\{(-6,-9)\}$

12. $\begin{cases} \dfrac{2x}{5} + \dfrac{3y}{4} = -4\dfrac{1}{5} \\ \dfrac{3x}{5} = \dfrac{3y + 2}{4} + \dfrac{7}{10} \end{cases}$ $\{(-3,-4)\}$

13. $\begin{cases} 2x + \dfrac{y}{3} = 6\dfrac{1}{3} \\ 2x - \dfrac{y}{3} = 1\dfrac{2}{3} \end{cases}$ $\{(2,7)\}$

14. $\begin{cases} \dfrac{6a - 1}{3} + \dfrac{3b + 1}{2} = \dfrac{5}{3} \\ \dfrac{1 - 5b}{4} + \dfrac{a + 3}{7} = \dfrac{1}{3} \end{cases}$ $\{(\frac{1}{2},\frac{1}{3})\}$

15. $\begin{cases} \dfrac{a}{3} + 3b = 15 \\ \dfrac{a}{4} + 4b = 13 \end{cases}$ $\{(36,1)\}$

16. $\begin{cases} \dfrac{2x}{3} + \dfrac{3y}{4} = -10 \\ y + 34 = \dfrac{5x}{6} \end{cases}$ $\{(12,-24)\}$

17. $\begin{cases} \dfrac{3}{2}x - \dfrac{4}{3}y = \dfrac{11}{3} \\ \dfrac{1}{4}x - \dfrac{2}{3}y = -\dfrac{7}{6} \end{cases}$ $\{(6,4)\}$

Write a simpler name for each set intersection. Indicate whether each system is consistent or inconsistent.

18. $\{(x, y) : 2x + y = 10\} \cap \{(x, y) : 2x + y = 5\}$ $\emptyset$; inconsistent

19. $\{(x, y) : x + 3y = 7\} \cap \{(x, y) : 2x + 6y = 14\}$ Consistent; $\{(x,y) : x + 3y = 7\}$

20. If a numerator of $\frac{3}{4}$ is increased by two and the corresponding denominator is decreased by six, the result is $\frac{5}{6}$ of the reciprocal of the original number. Find the original number. $\frac{18}{24}$

21. The denominator of a fraction is three more than the numerator. If the numerator is increased by five and the denominator is multiplied by three, the resulting fraction is $\frac{1}{2}$. Find the original fraction. $\frac{1}{4}$

7-5 Using Systems to Solve Problems

The objective for this section is on page 289.

Example 1   When Robin Huche opened her bank, thirty of the coins she found were dimes and nickels. Their combined value was $2.10. How many coins of each kind did she have?

Let x = the number of nickels. ◄――― Represent each unknown by
Let y = the number of dimes.   a different letter.

$\begin{cases} x + y = 30 \\ 5x + 10y = 210 \end{cases}$

◄――― Condition 1: Number of coins is 30.
◄――― Condition 2: Value in cents is 210.

$x = 18; \; y = 12$ ◄――― Solve the system.

Check: Does $18 + 12 = 30$? Yes.   **Solution:**
            Does $18(.05) + 12(.10) = 2.10$? Yes.   18 nickels and 12 dimes

Example 2   The sum of the numbers represented by the two digits of a numeral is 11. If the digits are reversed, they represent a number that is 20 less than twice the original number. What is the original number.

Let t = tens digit. ◄――― Represent each unknown by
Let u = units digit.   a different letter.

Original number: $10t + u$ ◄――― Represent the original number.
New number: $10u + t$ ◄――― Represent the new number.

$\begin{cases} t + u = 11 \\ 10u + t = 2(10t + u) - 20 \end{cases}$

◄――― Condition 1: Sum of digits is 11.
◄――― Condition 2: The new number is
              20 less than twice
              the original number.

$t = 4, \; u = 7$ ◄――― Solve the system.

Check: Does $4 + 7 = 11$? Yes.   **Solution:**
            Does $19(4) - 8(7) = 20$? Yes.   The number $10t + u$ is 47.

Try These   *Express the following algebraically. In Exercises 1 and 2, use x to represent the first number and y to represent the second number.*

1. Twice a certain number exceeds a second number by 25. $2x - y = 25$

2. The sum of three times a certain number and 24 is 18 more than twice a second number. $3x + 24 = 2y + 18$

3. The value in cents of x nickels and y dimes. $5x + 10y$

4. The value of x nickels and y dimes is $7.50. $5x + 10y = 750$

In Exercises 5-7, let t represent the tens digit and u represent the units digit of a two-digit number.

5. Write an expression for the number. $10t + u$

6. Write an expression for the new number formed by reversing the digits. $10u + t$

Use x and y to write algebraic statements that represent each given set of facts.

7. The amount of butterfat in x liters of cream testing 30% butterfat and y liters of milk testing 4% butterfat. $0.3x + 0.04y$

8. For a given year, the total income from x dollars invested at 6% and y dollars invested at 8% is $370. The total amount invested was $5000.
$0.06x + 0.08y = 370, \; x + y = 5000$

Exercises

Use two variables to solve the following problems.

1. The sum of two numbers is 52. If twice the first number exceeds the second number by 17, what are the numbers? 23 and 29

2. Twice one number is 28 more than a second number. If 23 is added to the second number, the result is 12 less than three times the first number. What are the numbers? 7 and −14

3. One complementary angle is 36° more than twice the other. Find each angle. 72° and 18°

4. One supplementary angle is 28° less than three times the other. Find each angle. 128° and 52°

Systems of Sentences   **271**

5. A collection of coins consisting of dimes and quarters amounts to $5.35. Twice the number of dimes exceeds the number of quarters by 5. Find the number of each kind of coin. 11 dimes and 17 quarters

6. Jim Youngblood invested part of $8,000 at 6 per cent annually and the rest at 5 per cent. His total annual income from these investments is $452. How much did he invest at each rate? $5200 was invested at 6% and $2800 at 5%

7. Mrs. Velez invests a sum of money, part at 5 per cent and the rest at 8 per cent. Her total interest per year was $784. If the amount invested at 8 per cent was $2,000 more than the amount at 5 per cent, find the amount invested at each rate. $4800 was invested at 5% and $6800 at 8%

8. How many kilograms of candy worth $0.85 a kilogram and how many kilograms of candy worth $0.60 a kilogram must be used to make a 140 kilogram mixture to sell at $0.75 a kilogram? 84 kilograms of candy worth $0.85 a kilogram and 56 kilograms of candy worth $0.60 a kilogram.

9. A dairy has milk testing 4 per cent butterfat and cream testing 30 per cent butterfat. If a 39 liter mixture testing 20 per cent butterfat is desired, how many liters of each should be used? 15 liters of 4% butterfat milk and 24 liters of 30% butterfat cream.

10. A chemist has two solutions of acid, one containing 10 per cent acid and the other 25 per cent acid. How many cubic centimeters of each solution are needed to make 90 cubic centimeters of a new solution that is 18 per cent acid? 42 cubic centimeters of 10% acid solution and 48 cubic centimeters of 25% acid solution.

11. The tens digit of a two-digit number is three less than twice the units digit. If the sum of the numbers named by the digits is 12, find the number. 75

12. The sum of the numbers named by the digits of a two-digit numeral is 7. If you reverse the digits, the new number is two more than twice the original number. What is the original number? 25

13. The units digit of a two-digit number is 2 more than four times the tens digit. If the digits are reversed, the new number exceeds three times the original number by 13. Find the original number. 16

14. The perimeter of a rectangular swimming pool is 84 meters. If the width is $\frac{3}{4}$ the length, find the dimensions of the pool. length is 24 meters and width is 18 meters

15. In a small town election, 34 people voted. The number of women who voted was less than two-thirds the number of men. How many men and how many women voted? x = the number of men who voted and y = the number of women who voted. $\{(x, y): x + y = 34\} \cap \{x : x \geq 21\}, x, y \in W$

16. Two women can do a piece of work together in 15 days. After they have both worked together for 6 days, one leaves and the other finishes it in 12 days. How many days would it take each alone? 60 days and 20 days

7-6 Systems of Linear Inequalities

The objective for this section is on page 289.

The solution set of the system of inequalities

$$\begin{cases} x - y < 0 \\ 2x + y > 4, \end{cases}$$

is the same as the solution set of $x - y < 0$ <u>and</u> $2x + y > 4$.

Example 1

Graph the solution set of the above system.

1. To graph $x - y < 0$, first graph the related equation $x - y = 0$. This line is dashed to show that it is <u>not</u> in the solution set of $x - y < 0$.

2. Substitute the coordinates of at least two points to find the half-plane where $x - y < 0$ is true.

Test	Result	
(2, 0)	$x - y < 0$; $2 - 0 < 0$ is false.	◄――― The half-plane below.
(−2, 0)	$x - y < 0$; $-2 - 0 < 0$ is true.	◄――― The half-plane above.

Conclusion: Shade the half-plane <u>above</u> the line for $x - y = 0$. (Figure 1)

The graph for $2x + y > 4$ is found in the same way. (Figure 2) The solution set of the system is the <u>intersection</u> of these two graphs. (Figure 3)

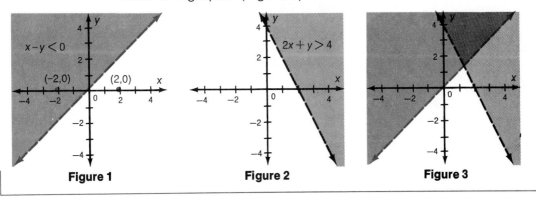

Figure 1   Figure 2   Figure 3

Example 2 Graph the solution set of the following system.

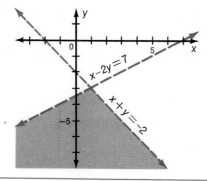

$$\begin{cases} x + y < -2 \\ x - 2y > 7 \end{cases}$$

The solution set is the intersection of the half-planes satisfying
$x + y < -2$ <u>and</u> $x - 2y > 7$.

Example 3 Graph the solution set of the following system.

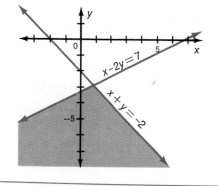

$$\begin{cases} x + y \le -2 \\ x - 2y \ge 7 \end{cases}$$

The solution is the same as that in Example 2 except that the lines for $x + y = -2$ and $x - 2y = 7$ <u>are</u> part of the solution set of each inequality. Therefore, these lines are <u>not</u> dashed.

The <u>union</u> of a line and one of its half-planes, such as the graph of $x + y \le 2$, is a <u>closed</u> <u>half-plane</u>.

Exercises

Solve each system of inequalities by graphing. See key for Exercises 1-12.

1. $\begin{cases} x + 2y \le 5 \\ x - 3y \le 2 \end{cases}$

2. $\begin{cases} 3x - 2y \ge 4 \\ x + y \ge 4 \end{cases}$

3. $\begin{cases} 2x - y < 2 \\ x + 3y > 3 \end{cases}$

4. $\begin{cases} 5x - y < 5 \\ x - y > -2 \end{cases}$

5. $\begin{cases} x + 3y < 1 \\ 2x + 6y < 4 \end{cases}$

6. $\begin{cases} x + 3y < 1 \\ 2x + 6y > 4 \end{cases}$

7. $\begin{cases} x + y > 4 \\ x - y > 6 \end{cases}$

8. $\begin{cases} x + y > 2 \\ x - y < 5 \end{cases}$

9. $\begin{cases} x + y > 8 \\ 2x - y > 4 \end{cases}$

10. $\begin{cases} 2x + 3y \le 8 \\ 5x - 4y \ge 10 \end{cases}$

11. $\begin{cases} 4y + 3x \ge 0 \\ 3y - 2x \le 4 \end{cases}$

12. $\begin{cases} 2y + 3x \ge -4 \\ 5y - x \le 6 \end{cases}$

7-7 Systems of Three Inequalities

The objective for this section is on page 289.

Example 1   Graph the solution set of the following system.

$$\begin{cases} x \ge 0 \\ y \ge 1 \\ x + y \le 4 \end{cases}$$

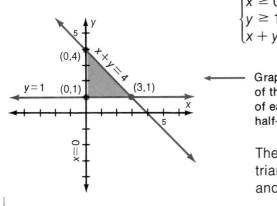

Graph each of the inequalities of the system. The solution set of each inequality is a closed half-plane.

The solution set can be described as the triangle whose vertices are (0, 1), (3, 1), and (0, 4) together with its interior.

The solution set of the system in Example 1 is a <u>polygonal convex set</u>.

Definition: A **polygonal convex set** is the nonempty intersection of a finite number of closed half-planes.

Example 2   Find the solution set of the following system.

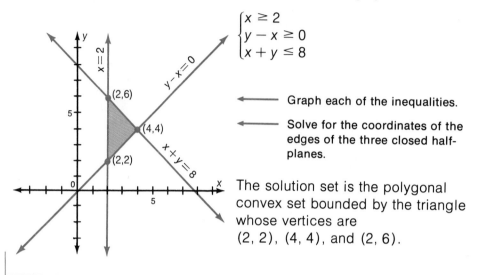

$$\begin{cases} x \geq 2 \\ y - x \geq 0 \\ x + y \leq 8 \end{cases}$$

⟵   Graph each of the inequalities.

⟵   Solve for the coordinates of the edges of the three closed half-planes.

The solution set is the polygonal convex set bounded by the triangle whose vertices are (2, 2), (4, 4), and (2, 6).

Exercises

Solve each system of inequalities by graphing. See key for Exercises 1-12.

a

1. $\begin{cases} x \geq 1 \\ y \geq 1 \\ x + y \leq 5 \end{cases}$

2. $\begin{cases} x \geq 1 \\ y \leq 1 \\ x - y \leq 7 \end{cases}$

3. $\begin{cases} x \leq -1 \\ y \geq 1 \\ 2y - x \leq 6 \end{cases}$

4. $\begin{cases} x \leq 0 \\ y \leq 0 \\ x + 2y \geq -6 \end{cases}$

5. $\begin{cases} x \leq 0 \\ 3y + 2x \geq 0 \\ 3y - 2x \leq 12 \end{cases}$

6. $\begin{cases} 2y - x \leq 5 \\ y + 4x \leq 25 \\ 5y + 2x \geq 17 \end{cases}$

7. $\begin{cases} 5y - x \leq 8 \\ y + 5x \leq 12 \\ 3y + 2x \geq -3 \end{cases}$

8. $\begin{cases} x \geq 0 \\ 2y + 3x \leq 8 \\ 4y - 5x \geq 24 \end{cases}$

9. $\begin{cases} x + y \geq 4 \\ x - y \leq 1 \\ x + 2y \leq 8 \end{cases}$

b

10. $\begin{cases} x + y \geq 7 \\ x + y \geq 2 \\ x \geq 0 \\ y \geq 0 \end{cases}$

11. $\begin{cases} x \geq 0 \\ y \geq 0 \\ y + x \leq 6 \\ y + 3x \leq 12 \end{cases}$

12. $\begin{cases} x \geq 0 \\ 2y - x \leq 8 \\ 4y + 3x \leq 36 \\ 8y - 3x \geq 0 \end{cases}$

Linear Systems in Three Variables

The objective for this section is on page 289.

Consider a linear system of three equations in three variables.

$$\begin{cases} x + y + z = 10 & \longleftarrow \text{Figure 1} \\ x - y = 0 & \longleftarrow \text{Figure 2} \\ z = 5 & \longleftarrow \text{Figure 3} \end{cases}$$

Each equation has a plane in three-space as its graph.

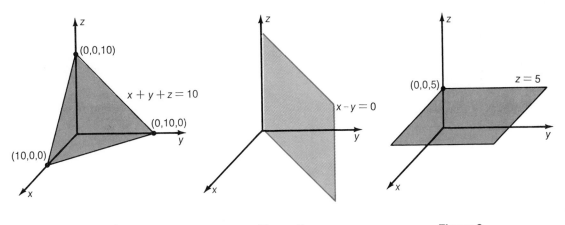

Figure 1　　　　**Figure 2**　　　　**Figure 3**

The solution to the system is represented geometrically by the intersection of the three planes. If that intersection is a single point, then the coordinates of that point, an <u>ordered triple</u>, satisfy each equation of the system. Thus, the solution set of such a system consists of a single ordered triple.

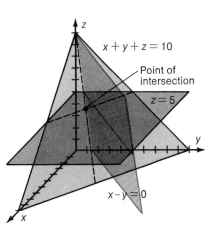

Two methods are shown in Example 1 for finding the coordinate of the point of intersection of this system.

Example 1　Solve the following system of equations.

$$\begin{cases} x+y+z=10 & 1 \\ x-y=0 & 2 \\ z=5 & 3 \end{cases}$$

Method 1

$2x+z=10$　$4 \leftarrow$ Add 1 and 2.

$z=5$　　　3

Equations **3** and **4** form a system equivalent to the original system.

$2x+5=10$　$\longleftarrow$　Substitute 3 in 4.

$x=2\frac{1}{2}$　$\longleftarrow$　Solve for x.

$y=2\frac{1}{2}$　$\longleftarrow$　Find y and z.

$z=5$

Check: $2\frac{1}{2}+2\frac{1}{2}+5\overset{?}{=}10$　Yes.

$2\frac{1}{2}-2\frac{1}{2}\overset{?}{=}0$　Yes.

$5\overset{?}{=}5$　Yes.

Method 2

$x+y+5=10$　$4 \leftarrow$ Substitute 3 in 1.

$x-y=0$　　2

Equations **4** and **2** form a system equivalent to the original system.

$2x=5$　$\longleftarrow$　Add 2 + 4.

$x=2\frac{1}{2}$　$\longleftarrow$　Solve for x.

$y=2\frac{1}{2}$　$\longleftarrow$　Find y and z.

$z=5$

Solution set: $\{(2\frac{1}{2}, 2\frac{1}{2}, 5)\}$

In general, the solution set of a system of three linear equations in three variables is the set of ordered triples that satisfy all three equations. It contains

(i) One ordered triple when the three planes intersect in one point.

(ii) Infinitely many ordered triples when the three planes intersect in one line or when they coincide.

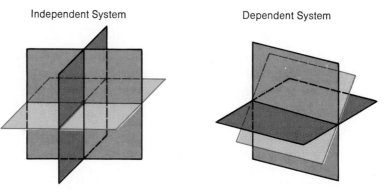

Independent System　　　　　Dependent System

(iii) No ordered triples when the three planes are parallel or intersect in two or three distinct lines.

Inconsistent System   Inconsistent System   Inconsistent System

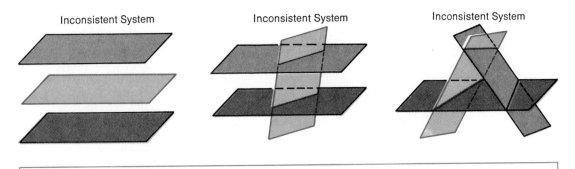

Example 2   Solve the following system of equations.

$$\begin{cases} x - 2y + 3z = -3 & \mathbf{1} \\ 2x - 3y - z = 7 & \mathbf{2} \\ 3x + y - 2z = 6 & \mathbf{3} \end{cases}$$

1. Eliminate any one variable to obtain an equivalent system in two variables.

Eliminate y from **1** and **3.**

$$\begin{array}{ll} x - 2y + 3z = -3 & \mathbf{1} \\ 6x + 2y - 4z = 12 & \mathbf{2 \times 3} \\ \hline 7x \qquad - z = 9 & \mathbf{4} \end{array}$$

Eliminate y from **2** and **3.**

$$\begin{array}{ll} 2x - 3y - z = 7 & \mathbf{2} \\ 9x + 3y - 6z = 18 & \mathbf{3 \times 3} \\ \hline 11x \qquad - 7z = 25 & \mathbf{5} \end{array}$$

$$\begin{cases} 7x - z = 9 & \mathbf{4} \\ 11x - 7x = 25 & \mathbf{5} \end{cases}$$

2. Eliminate z from the new system, and solve for x. Then use equation **4** to determine z.

$$\begin{array}{ll} -49x + 7z = -63 & \mathbf{-7 \times 4} \\ 11x - 7z = 25 & \mathbf{5} \\ \hline -38x \qquad = -38 \\ \qquad x = 1 \end{array}$$

$$\begin{array}{l} 7x - z = 9 \qquad \mathbf{4} \\ 7(1) - z = 9 \\ 7 - z = 9 \\ z = -2 \end{array}$$

3. Substitute $x = 1$ and $z = -2$ in **1, 2,** or **3** to determine y.

$$\begin{array}{l} 1 - 2y + 3(-2) = -3 \\ -2y = 2 \\ y = -1 \end{array}$$

Check: $2(1) - 3(-1) - (-2) \overset{?}{=} 7$ Yes.   **Solution set:** $\{(1, -1, -2)\}$
$3(1) + (-1) - 2(-2) \overset{?}{=} 6$ Yes.

Exercises

Solve the following systems. Check.

a

1. $\begin{cases} 2x - 3y - 4z = -21 \\ -4x + 2y - 3z = -14 \\ -3x - 4y + 2z = -10 \end{cases}$ $\{(2, 3, 4)\}$

2. $\begin{cases} 6x - y - 3z = 2 \\ -3x + y - 3z = 1 \\ -2x + 3y + z = -6 \end{cases}$ $\{(-\frac{1}{3}, -2, -\frac{2}{3})\}$

3. $\begin{cases} 3x + 2y = z - 7 \\ 5x + 3y = -12 + 2z \\ 2x + 3y = -5 + z \end{cases}$ $\{(-2, 0, 1)\}$

4. $\begin{cases} 2x + 5y = -5 + 3z \\ 3x + 7z = 15 - 2y \\ 5x + 6z = 34 + 4y \end{cases}$ $\{(4, -2, 1)\}$

5. $\begin{cases} 2x + 3y + 4z = 8 \\ 4x + 9y + 8z = 17 \\ 6x + 12y + 16z = 31 \end{cases}$ $\{(\frac{1}{2}, \frac{1}{3}, \frac{3}{2})\}$

6. $\begin{cases} 2x + 3y = -2 \\ 4y + 2z = -10 \\ 3x + 5z = 1 \end{cases}$ $\{(2, -2, -1)\}$

7. $\begin{cases} 3x + 4z = 22 \\ y - \dfrac{z}{2} = 1 \\ 5x + 3y = 19 \end{cases}$ $\{(2, 3, 4)\}$

8. $\begin{cases} x + y + z = 180 \\ \dfrac{x}{4} + \dfrac{y}{2} + \dfrac{z}{3} = 60 \\ 2y + 3z = 330 \end{cases}$ $\{(60, 30, 90)\}$

b

9. $\begin{cases} 0.5x + 0.8y + 0.9z = 32 \\ x + 0.6y + 0.4z = 26 \\ 2x + 0.3y + 0.2z = 31 \end{cases}$ $\{(12, 10, 20)\}$

10. $\begin{cases} 0.5a + 0.3b = 2.2 \\ 1.2c - 8.5b = -24.4 \\ 3.3c + 1.3a = 29 \end{cases}$ $\{(2, 4, 8)\}$

11. $\begin{cases} 3x + 2y + z = 7.7 \\ 2x - y - z = 3.3 \\ 5x - 4y - 2z = 5.5 \end{cases}$ $\{(1.9, 1.5, -1)\}$

12. $\begin{cases} 3x - 6y + 3z = 4 \\ x - 2y + z = 1 \\ 2x - 4y + 2z = 5 \end{cases}$ ϕ

13. The sum of the digits of a certain three-digit number is 13. The sum of the units digit and tens digit is 10. If the number is increased by 99 when the digits are reversed, what is the original number? (HINT: A three-digit number may be written as $100h + 10t + u$. The number reversed is written $100u + 10t + h$.) 364

14. Three trucks together haul 78 cubic meters, 81 cubic meters, and 69 cubic meters in three days. Find the capacity of each truck if they haul the following number of loads each day. First day: 4, 3, and 5 loads; Second day: 5, 4, and 4 loads; Third day: 3, 5, and 3 loads. 5 cubic meters; 6 cubic meters; 8 cubic meters

c

15. The sum of the digits of a certain three-digit number is 20. If 300 is subtracted from the number, the hundreds digit and the units digit of the new number will be the same. The number representing the units digit is equal to one third the sum of the numbers representing the hundreds and tens digit. What is the number? 875

Solving Linear Systems by Matrices

The objective for this section is on page 289.

A system of linear equations in two or more variables can be solved by writing the system as a matrix. A **matrix** is a rectangular array of numbers. Here are some examples.

a. 2×2

$$\begin{bmatrix} 1 & 2 \\ -1 & 4 \end{bmatrix}$$

b. 3×3

$$\begin{bmatrix} 1 & 0 & 0 \\ 0 & 1 & 0 \\ 0 & 0 & 1 \end{bmatrix}$$

c. column

$$\begin{bmatrix} 1 \\ -8 \\ 6\frac{1}{2} \end{bmatrix}$$

d. row

$$[-7, 3, -2\tfrac{2}{3}]$$

The matrix for a system of three variables is a 3×4 matrix.

$$\begin{cases} 12x - y + 12z = 6 \\ 2x + y - 2z = -4 \\ 9x + 2y + 3z = 3 \end{cases} \longrightarrow \begin{bmatrix} 12 & -1 & 12 & 6 \\ 2 & 1 & -2 & -4 \\ 9 & 2 & 3 & 3 \end{bmatrix}$$

Each row of the matrix corresponds to an equation. Each column designates the coefficient of a given variable or the constant term.

Three operations are permitted. They produce equivalent matrices, because the related linear systems are equivalent.

Row Operations for a Matrix

1. A row may be multiplied by a nonzero real number. (This corresponds to multiplying both sides of an equation by that number.)
2. Any two rows can be added by adding corresponding numbers of the rows. (This can be compared to the addition method for solving systems.)
3. Any two rows can be interchanged.

The goal is to get an equivalent matrix that is in the **triangular form.**

$$\begin{bmatrix} a_1 & 0 & 0 & C_1 \\ b_1 & b_2 & 0 & C_2 \\ c_1 & c_2 & c_3 & C_3 \end{bmatrix} \quad \text{or} \quad \begin{bmatrix} a_1 & a_2 & a_3 & C_1 \\ b_1 & b_2 & 0 & C_2 \\ c_1 & 0 & 0 & C_3 \end{bmatrix}$$

Systems of Sentences   **281**

Example

Solve the following system by the matrix method.

$$\begin{cases} 12x - y + 12z = 6 \\ 2x + y - 2z = -4 \\ 9x + 2y + 3z = 3 \end{cases}$$

$$\begin{bmatrix} 12 & -1 & 12 & 6 \\ 2 & 1 & -2 & -4 \\ 9 & 2 & 3 & 3 \end{bmatrix} \begin{matrix} 1 \\ 2 \\ 3 \end{matrix}$$ ◄——— Rewrite as a matrix.

$$\begin{bmatrix} 24 & 5 & 0 & -18 \\ 2 & 1 & -2 & -4 \\ 9 & 2 & 3 & 3 \end{bmatrix} \begin{matrix} 1 \\ 2 \\ 3 \end{matrix}$$ ◄——— To eliminate the second 12 in Row 1, multiply Row 2 by 6 and add this to Row 1. Replace Row 1 with the result.

$$\begin{bmatrix} 24 & 5 & 0 & -18 \\ 24 & 7 & 0 & -6 \\ 9 & 2 & 3 & 3 \end{bmatrix} \begin{matrix} 1 \\ 2 \\ 3 \end{matrix}$$ ◄——— To eliminate the −2 in Row 2, multiply Row 2 by 3 and Row 3 by 2. Add these products. Replace Row 2 with the result.

$$\begin{bmatrix} 48 & 0 & 0 & -96 \\ 24 & 7 & 0 & -6 \\ 9 & 2 & 3 & 3 \end{bmatrix} \begin{matrix} 1 \\ 2 \\ 3 \end{matrix}$$ ◄——— To eliminate the 5 in Row 1, multiply Row 1 by 7 and Row 2 by −5. Add these products. Replace Row 1 with the result.

The matrix is now in triangular form. This represents the following system, which can now be solved readily.

$$\begin{cases} 48x = -96 & \quad 1 \\ 24x + 7y = -6 & \quad 2 \\ 9x + 2y + 3z = 3 & \quad 3 \end{cases}$$

Since $48x = -96$, $x = -2$. Replace x in Equation 2 with −2 to find y; $y = 6$. Now replace x with −2 and y with 6 in Equation 3 to find z; $z = 3$.

Check: Replace x, y, and z in the original equations with this result.

Solution set: $\{(-2, 6, 3)\}$.

Try These

Write the matrix associated with each system.

1. $\begin{cases} 3x - 2y + z = 14 \\ 5x + 3y - 4z = -7 \\ 2x + 2y + 3z = 19 \end{cases}$ $\begin{bmatrix} 3 & -2 & 1 & 14 \\ 5 & 3 & -4 & -7 \\ 2 & 2 & 3 & 19 \end{bmatrix}$ **2.** $\begin{cases} 4x + 7y - 2z = 35 \\ 3x - 5y - 4z = 2 \\ -x + 9y + 6z = -7 \end{cases}$ $\begin{bmatrix} 4 & 7 & -2 & 35 \\ 3 & -5 & -4 & 2 \\ -1 & 9 & 6 & -7 \end{bmatrix}$

Exercises

Use the matrix method to solve each system.

a

1. $\begin{cases} 2x - y + 3z = 16 \\ 3x - 5y + 4z = -6 \\ 4x + 2y - 3z = 28 \end{cases}$ $\{(6,8,4)\}$

2. $\begin{cases} 3x - 2y + 7z = 80 \\ 5x + 3y - 4z = 2 \\ 2x + 5y + z = 42 \end{cases}$ $\{(6,4,10)\}$

3. $\begin{cases} 2x + y + z = 6 \\ 3x + 3y - 2z = -5 \\ -x + y - z = -5 \end{cases}$ $\{(1, 0, 4)\}$

4. $\begin{cases} 3x + 2y - z = 5 \\ 2x + y - 2z = -7 \\ 3x - 2y + 3z = 21 \end{cases}$ $\{(2, 3, 7)\}$

5. $\begin{cases} 6x + y - z = -2 \\ 2x + 5y - z = 2 \\ x + 2y + z = 5 \end{cases}$ $\{(0, 1, 3)\}$

6. $\begin{cases} 2x + 2y + z = 3 \\ 3x + 2y - 2z = -1 \\ 2x - 3y - z = 22 \end{cases}$ $\{(5, -5, 3)\}$

7. $\begin{cases} x + y + z = 6 \\ 2x + y - z = 2 \\ 3x - 2y + 2z = 10 \end{cases}$ $\{(2, 1, 3)\}$

8. $\begin{cases} 2x + 3y - 2z = 18 \\ 5x - 6y + z = 21 \\ 4y - 2z = 6 \end{cases}$ $\{(8, 4, 5)\}$

9. $\begin{cases} 3x + 2y = 12 \\ 4z + 3y = 25 \\ 5x + 2y = 16 \end{cases}$ $\{(2, 3, 4)\}$

10. $\begin{cases} 4x - 3y = 1 \\ 6x - 8z = 1 \\ 2y - 4z = 0 \end{cases}$ $\{(-\frac{1}{2}, -1, -\frac{1}{2})\}$

Represent each problem as a linear system. Solve by the matrix method.

b

11. Find the three angles of a triangle if the sum of the first angle and twice the second equals the third angle, and if four times the second angle is 15° more than the third. 45°, 30°, and 105°

12. On a 3-day grand opening sale, a store offered a special on cotton, orlon, and wool ski sweaters. On the first day, the store sold 5 cotton, 4 orlon, and 8 wool sweaters; on the second day, 4 cotton, 3 orlon, and 6 wool sweaters; and on the third day, 3 cotton, 5 orlon, and 4 wool sweaters. If the total sales for the three days were $210, $160 and $146, what was the sale price of each type sweater? cotton: $10; orlon: $12; wool: $14

PUZZLE

A block of cheese 4 centimeters by 5 centimeters by 6 centimeters is covered with wax. If the cheese is cut into cubes 1 centimeter by 1 centimeter by 1 centimeter, how many cubes will not have any wax on them? 2 × 3 × 4, or 24 cubes

7-10 Dependent and Inconsistent Systems

The objective for this section is on page 289.

Example

Solve the following system.

$$\begin{cases} x - 2y + 3z = 2 \\ x + 4y - 2z = 1 \\ -2x + 4y - 6z = -4 \end{cases}$$

1. Rewrite as a matrix.

$$\begin{bmatrix} 1 & -2 & 3 & 2 \\ 1 & 4 & -2 & 1 \\ -2 & 4 & -6 & -4 \end{bmatrix}$$

2. Multiply the first row by −1
and add this result to the second
row. Replace the second row
with the result. Add 2 times
the first row to the third.
Replace the third row with this result.

$$\begin{bmatrix} 1 & -2 & 3 & 2 \\ 0 & 6 & -5 & -1 \\ 0 & 0 & 0 & 0 \end{bmatrix}$$

Note that the last row consists only of zeros. This means that z can equal any number. Thus, there are infinitely many solutions, and the system is dependent. The goal is to find the general solution.

3. Multiply Row 2 by $\frac{1}{3}$. Add this to Row 1. Replace Row 1 with this result.

$$\begin{bmatrix} 1 & 0 & \frac{4}{3} & \frac{5}{3} \\ 0 & 6 & -5 & -1 \\ 0 & 0 & 0 & 0 \end{bmatrix} \begin{matrix} 1 \\ 2 \\ 3 \end{matrix}$$

4. Write this matrix as a system.

$$\begin{cases} x + \frac{4}{3}z = \frac{5}{3} \\ 6y - 5z = -1 \\ 0 \cdot z = 0 \end{cases} \text{ or } \begin{cases} x + \frac{4}{3}z = \frac{5}{3} \\ y - \frac{5}{6}z = -\frac{1}{6} \\ 0 \cdot z = 0 \end{cases}$$

This last system leads directly to the general solution.

$$x = \frac{5}{3} - \frac{4}{3}z; \ y = -\frac{1}{6} + \frac{5}{6}z; \ z \text{ is any complex number, or}$$

$$\{(\frac{5}{3} - \frac{4}{3}z, -\frac{1}{6} + \frac{5}{6}z, z) : z \in C\}.$$

If the last row of a matrix is of the form

$$0 \quad 0 \quad 0 \quad k$$

where $k \neq 0$, it implies that $0 \cdot z = k$. Since this is false for all z, you cannot find any ordered triple (x, y, z) that will satisfy the system. The solution set of such a system is <u>empty</u>, and the system is <u>inconsistent</u>.

Exercises

Use the matrix method to solve each system. The solution sets can have one element, infinitely many elements or no elements. Indicate the general solution for the systems with an infinite number of solutions.

1. $\begin{cases} x - 3y - 4z = 10 \\ -x + 3y - 5z = 2 \\ x + 3y + 8z = 10 \end{cases}$ $\{(\frac{38}{3}, \frac{8}{3}, -\frac{4}{3})\}$

2. $\begin{cases} x - y + 3z = 6 \\ 2x - 5y + z = 12 \\ x - y - 2z = -6 \end{cases}$ $\{(-\frac{26}{5}, -4, \frac{12}{5})\}$

3. $\begin{cases} x - 2y + 3z = 3 \\ 2x - 3y - z = 6 \\ -3x + 2y + z = 5 \end{cases}$ $\{(-\frac{50}{9}, -\frac{49}{9}, -\frac{7}{9})\}$

4. $\begin{cases} x + 3y - 4z = -8 \\ x + 9y + z = 2 \\ -3x - 9y + 12z = 24 \end{cases}$ See below.

5. $\begin{cases} x + 3y - 2z = 10 \\ 2x + 6y - 4z = -10 \\ 4y - 2z = 6 \end{cases}$ ϕ

6. $\begin{cases} -x + 2y + \frac{1}{2}z = -3 \\ 2x - 4y - z = 6 \\ 3x - 3y + 3z = 18 \end{cases}$ See below.

7. $\begin{cases} 2x + 4z = 20 \\ 2y - z = 2 \\ 5x - 3y = 12 \end{cases}$ $\{(\frac{90}{23}, \frac{58}{23}, \frac{70}{23})\}$

8. $\begin{cases} 2x + 3y = -2 \\ -4y + 2z = -10 \\ 3x + 5z = -1 \end{cases}$ $\{(-\frac{92}{11}, \frac{54}{11}, \frac{53}{11})\}$

4. $\{(-13 + \frac{13}{2}z, \frac{5}{3} - \frac{5}{6}z, z) : z \in c\}$ 6. $\{(9 - \frac{5}{2}z, 3 - \frac{3}{2}z, z) : z \in c\}$

The **determinant** of a 2 x 2 square matrix is defined as the following number.

$$\det \begin{bmatrix} a_{11} & a_{12} \\ a_{21} & a_{22} \end{bmatrix} = \begin{vmatrix} a_{11} & a_{12} \\ a_{21} & a_{22} \end{vmatrix} = a_{11}a_{22} - a_{21}a_{12}$$

Find the number represented by each of the following determinants.

9. $\begin{vmatrix} 5 & 2 \\ 6 & 3 \end{vmatrix}$ 3

10. $\begin{vmatrix} 3 & 7 \\ 4 & 1 \end{vmatrix}$ −25

11. $\begin{vmatrix} -4 & 8 \\ 2 & 3 \end{vmatrix}$ −28

12. $\begin{vmatrix} -1 & -2 \\ 6 & 7 \end{vmatrix}$ 5

13. $\begin{vmatrix} 2i & 3i \\ i & -i \end{vmatrix}$ 5

14. $\begin{vmatrix} i & i \\ -i & -i \end{vmatrix}$ 0

The solution of the general system of two equations in two variables

$$\begin{cases} a_1x + b_1y = c_1 \\ a_2x + b_2y = c_2 \end{cases}$$

can be expressed by these ratios of determinants.

$$x = \frac{\begin{vmatrix} c_1 & b_1 \\ c_2 & b_2 \end{vmatrix}}{\begin{vmatrix} a_1 & b_1 \\ a_2 & b_2 \end{vmatrix}} \quad \text{and} \quad y = \frac{\begin{vmatrix} a_1 & c_1 \\ a_2 & c_2 \end{vmatrix}}{\begin{vmatrix} a_1 & b_1 \\ a_2 & b_2 \end{vmatrix}}$$

Use the ratios of determinants above to solve these systems.

15. $\begin{cases} 2x + y = 6 \\ x - y = 4 \end{cases}$ $\left\{ \left(\frac{10}{3}, -\frac{2}{3} \right) \right\}$

16. $\begin{cases} 3x + 2y = 1 \\ 4x - y = 3 \end{cases}$ $\left\{ \left(\frac{7}{11}, -\frac{5}{11} \right) \right\}$

17. $\begin{cases} -3x + 6y = 4 \\ 2x - 3y = 5 \end{cases}$ $\left\{ \left(14, \frac{23}{3} \right) \right\}$

18. $\begin{cases} x + 2y - 2 = 2x \\ 3y - \frac{5}{6}x = \dfrac{4x + 1}{3} \end{cases}$ $\{(4, 3)\}$

The solution of the general system of three equations with three variables.

$$\begin{cases} a_1x + b_1y + c_1z = d_1 \\ a_2x + b_2y + c_2z = d_2 \\ a_3x + b_3y + c_3z = d_3 \end{cases}$$

can be determined from these ratios of determinants.

$$x = \frac{\begin{vmatrix} d_1 & b_1 & c_1 \\ d_2 & b_2 & c_2 \\ d_3 & b_3 & c_3 \end{vmatrix}}{\begin{vmatrix} a_1 & b_1 & c_1 \\ a_2 & b_2 & c_2 \\ a_3 & b_3 & c_3 \end{vmatrix}} \quad y = \frac{\begin{vmatrix} a_1 & d_1 & c_1 \\ a_2 & d_2 & c_2 \\ a_3 & d_3 & c_3 \end{vmatrix}}{\begin{vmatrix} a_1 & b_1 & c_1 \\ a_2 & b_2 & c_2 \\ a_3 & b_3 & c_3 \end{vmatrix}} \quad z = \frac{\begin{vmatrix} a_1 & b_1 & d_1 \\ a_2 & b_2 & d_2 \\ a_3 & b_3 & d_3 \end{vmatrix}}{\begin{vmatrix} a_1 & b_1 & c_1 \\ a_2 & b_2 & c_2 \\ a_3 & b_3 & c_3 \end{vmatrix}}$$

Use the above ratios of determinants to solve the following systems.

19. $\begin{cases} 0.4x + 0.3y + 0.6z = 17 \\ 0.6x + 0.5y + 0.8z = 24 \\ x + 0.2y + 0.3z = 13 \end{cases}$ $\{(5, 10, 20)\}$

20. $\begin{cases} 0.4x - 0.5y - 0.2z = 8 \\ 0.3x + 0.2y - 0.3z = 2.9 \\ 0.5x - 0.5y = 6.5 \end{cases}$
$\{(5, -8, -10)\}$

PUZZLE

From four positive integers, select three. Take the arithmetic mean of the three and add it to the fourth integer. Doing this in every possible way results in the numbers 17, 21, 23, and 29. Find the original integers. 3, 9, 12, 21

Proof by Contradiction

Every rational number can be expressed in exponential form.

$$2 = 4^{\frac{1}{2}} = 8^{\frac{1}{3}} = 16^{\frac{1}{4}} = \cdots$$

$$\frac{2}{3} = \left(\frac{4}{9}\right)^{\frac{1}{2}} = \left(\frac{8}{27}\right)^{\frac{1}{3}} = \left(\frac{16}{81}\right)^{\frac{1}{4}} = \cdots$$

$$\frac{a}{b} = \left(\frac{a^n}{b^n}\right)^{\frac{1}{n}}$$

Not every number that can be expressed in exponential form is a rational number, however. For example, you know that $2^{\frac{1}{2}}$, or $\sqrt{2}$, is not a rational number. It is an irrational number.

However, let's assume that $\sqrt{2}$ is rational. Then $\sqrt{2}$ can be expressed as the ratio of two integers p and q, where $q \neq 0$ and p and q have *no common factor;* that is, $\frac{p}{q}$ is in simplest form.

$$\sqrt{2} = \frac{p}{q}$$

$$2 = \frac{p^2}{q^2} \quad \longleftarrow \quad \text{Square both sides.}$$

$$2q^2 = p^2 \quad \longleftarrow \quad \text{Simplify.}$$

Notice that $2q^2$ is an even number, so p^2 is the same even number. In fact, p^2 is an even perfect square because it is the square of an integer. Since p^2 is an even perfect square, then p must also be even. (You can prove this on your own.) Since every even number can be expressed as $2k$, where k is an integer, let $2k = p$.

The expression $2k^2$ represents an even number. Hence, q^2 is even and q is even. Therefore, p and q are both multiples of 2. But this is a **contradiction** of the original assumption that p and q have no common factor. Thus, 2 cannot be expressed as the ratio $\frac{p}{q}$ in simplest form. This means that $\sqrt{2}$ is not a rational number. Then $\sqrt{2}$ must be an irrational number.

Chapter
Objectives
and
Review

Objective: To know the meanings of the important mathematical terms of this chapter.

1. Here are many of the mathematical terms used in this chapter. Be sure that you know their meanings and that you can use them correctly.

addition method (p. 261)
consistent system (p. 267)
dependent system (p. 268)
equivalent systems (p. 260)
inconsistent system (p. 267)
independent system (p. 268)

matrix (p. 281)
polygonal convex set (p. 275)
solution set of a system (p. 256)
substitution method (p. 265)
system of equations (p. 256)
triangular form (p. 281)

Objective: To solve a system of linear equations by graphing. (Section 7-1)

Find the solution set of each linear system by graphing.

2. $\begin{cases} 3x + 2y = 4 \\ -x + 3y = -5 \end{cases}$ $\{(2, -1)\}$

3. $\begin{cases} 4x - y = -5 \\ x + \frac{1}{2}y = 1 \end{cases}$ $\{(-\frac{1}{2}, 3)\}$

4. $\begin{cases} x - 3y = 6 \\ -2x + 6y = 2 \end{cases}$ $\emptyset$

Objective: To solve a system of linear equations by the addition method. (Section 7-2)

Use the addition method to solve each system.

5. $\begin{cases} -2x + y = 4 \\ x - 3y = 3 \end{cases}$ $\{(-3, -2)\}$

6. $\begin{cases} 3x + 2y = 3 \\ 6x - 2y = 5 \end{cases}$ $\{(\frac{8}{9}, \frac{1}{6})\}$

$\{(x,y): x - 3y = 2\}$
7. $\begin{cases} x - 3y = 2 \\ -2x + 6y = -4 \end{cases}$

Objective: To solve a system of linear equations by the substitution method. (Section 7-3)

Solve each system of linear equations by substitution. $\{(\frac{1}{3}, 1)\}$

8. $\begin{cases} 3x + 4y = 1 \\ x - 2y = 7 \end{cases}$ $\{(3, -2)\}$

9. $\begin{cases} \frac{1}{3}x - \frac{1}{2}y = 0 \\ x - 2y = -2 \end{cases}$ $\{(6, 4)\}$

10. $\begin{cases} 3x - 2y = -1 \\ -3x + 4y = 3 \end{cases}$

Objective: To classify a system of linear equations as <u>Consistent</u>, <u>Inconsistent</u>, <u>Dependent</u>, or <u>Independent</u>. (Section 7-4)

Solve each system. Classify each system as consistent or inconsistent. If the system is consistent, state whether it is dependent or independent.

11. $\begin{cases} x - y = 2 \\ x + y = 8 \end{cases}$ $\{(5, 3)\}$

Independent, consistent

12. $\begin{cases} x + y = 5 \\ x + y = 2 \end{cases}$ ϕ

Inconsistent

$\{(x, 3 - x)\}$ **13.** $\begin{cases} x + y = 3 \\ 2x + 2y = 6 \end{cases}$

Consistent, dependent

Objective: To use systems of linear equations to solve problems. (Section 7-5)

Write a system of equations to represent each problem. Solve the system.

14. The sum of two numbers is 17. The difference between the greater and twice the smaller is −1. What are the numbers? 11 and 6

15. John has 17 coins in dimes and quarters. If the value of the coins is $2.75, how many of each does he have? 10 dimes and 7 quarters

Objective: To solve systems of linear inequalities graphically. (Section 7-6)

Use a graph to find the solution set of each system. See key for Exercises 16-18.

16. $\begin{cases} 2x - y < 1 \\ -x + y < 1 \end{cases}$

17. $\begin{cases} x + y \le 5 \\ x + y \ge 3 \end{cases}$

18. $\begin{cases} -3x + 4y > 2 \\ x - y \le -1 \end{cases}$

Objective: To graph a polygonal convex set defined by a system of inequalities. (Section 7-7) Each solution set is a polygonal convex set bounded by a triangle with the given vertices.

Solve each system of inequalities by graphing.

19. $\begin{cases} 2x - y \le 1 \\ -x + y \le 1 \\ y \ge 0 \end{cases}$

$(-1, 0), (2, 3), \left(\frac{1}{2}, 0\right)$

20. $\begin{cases} x - 2y \le 10 \\ 3x - y \ge 9 \\ x + y \le 4 \end{cases}$

$\left(\frac{13}{4}, \frac{3}{4}\right), (6, -2), \left(\frac{8}{5}, -\frac{21}{5}\right)$

21. $\begin{cases} -3x + 4y \ge 2 \\ x - y \ge -1 \\ x \le 5 \end{cases}$

$(-2, -1), (5, 6), \left(5, \frac{17}{4}\right)$

Objective: To solve a system of linear equations in three variables (Section 7-8)

Solve the following systems.

22. $\begin{cases} 2x - 5y + 3z = 8 \\ x + y - z = 0 \\ 8y - 2z = 2 \end{cases}$ $\{(2, 1, 3)\}$

23. $\begin{cases} 3x - 2y + 5z = 1 \\ 2x + 3y + 4z = -2 \\ 4x - 5y - 3z = 40 \end{cases}$ $\{(7, 0, -4)\}$

Objective: To solve systems of linear equations by matrix methods. (Sections 7-9, 7-10)

Use the matrix method to solve each system in Exercises 22 and 23.

Chapter
Test

Complete each statement.

1. The solution set of an inconsistent system of equations is ___empty___.

2. A consistent system of linear equations with an infinite number of solutions is a(n) ___dependent___ system.

3. A rectangular array of numbers is a(n) ___matrix___.

For each system of equations, use the indicated method to find its solution set. If no method is indicated, use the method you prefer.

4. Graphing
$$\begin{cases} 2x - 3y = 33 \\ 4x + y = 11 \end{cases} \left\{ \left(\tfrac{33}{7}, -\tfrac{55}{7} \right) \right\}$$

5. Addition method
$$\begin{cases} 3x + 2y = -3 \\ 6x - 4y = -10 \end{cases} \left\{ \left(-\tfrac{4}{3}, \tfrac{1}{2} \right) \right\}$$

6. Substitution method
$$\begin{cases} 5x - 3y = -3 \\ 4x - y = -16 \end{cases} \left\{ \left(-\tfrac{45}{7}, -\tfrac{68}{7} \right) \right\}$$

7. Graphing See below.
$$\begin{cases} 2x + 3y \le 9 \\ x - 2y \le 8 \end{cases}$$

8. $\begin{cases} 2x - 3y = 8 \\ 4x = 10 + 6y \end{cases}$ ∅

9. $\begin{cases} 2x - y + 3z = 4 \\ x + y + 4z = -1 \\ -x + y - z = -3 \end{cases}$ $\{(1, -2, 0)\}$

10. Find two integers whose difference is 12 and whose sum is 2. 7, 5

7. The region below the line $2x + 3y = 9$ and above the line $x - 2y = 8$. This includes the point $(6, -1)$, the point of intersection of the lines, and all points on each line to the left of $x = 6$.

Answers to Remember

Page 259: **1.** $-\tfrac{2}{3}$ **2.** $-1\tfrac{2}{5}$ **3.** $\tfrac{3}{8}$ **4.** 2 **5.** $\tfrac{3}{2}$ **6.** $\tfrac{5}{7}$ **7.** $-\tfrac{8}{3}$ **8.** $-\tfrac{1}{2}$

Page 265: **1.** 0 **2.** $-\tfrac{6}{7}$ **3.** $\tfrac{14}{13}$

Cumulative Review

Write the letter of the response that best answers each question.

1. If the replacement set for x in the relation $y = 3 - x$ is the set of whole numbers, give the range of the relation.

    ⓐ $\{\cdots, -3, -2, -1, 0, 1, 2, 3\}$ **b.** $\{1, 2, 3, \cdots\}$
    c. Q **d.** $\{1, 2, 3\}$

2. Tell which relations are functions.

    ⓐ $y = -5$ **b.** $x = 3$ **c.** $y \geq x + 2$ **d.** $x = y^2 - 4$

3. If $g(x) = -2x^2 + x + 1$, find $g(a - 2)$.

    a. $-2a^2 + a - 1$ **b.** $-2a^2 + a + 1$ **ⓒ** $-(2a^2 - 9 + 9)$ **d.** $-a + 3$

4. If $f(x) = x^2 - 3$ and $g(x) = 2x + 5$, find $f[g(x)]$.

    a. $2x^2 + 2$ **ⓑ** $4x^2 + 20x + 22$ **c.** $2x^2 - 1$ **d.** $4x^2 + 22$

5. Name the inverse relation of $y = \frac{2}{3}x + 6$.

    ⓐ $y = \frac{3}{2}x - 9$ **b.** $x = \frac{3}{2}y - 9$ **c.** $y = \frac{3}{2}x - 18$ **d.** $x = 3y - 9$

6. Give the zeros of the function $f(x) = x^2 - 4x + 1$.

    a. $-2 + \sqrt{3}, -2 - \sqrt{3}$ **b.** $-2 + 2\sqrt{3}, 2 - 3\sqrt{3}$
    ⓒ $2 - \sqrt{3}, 2 + \sqrt{3}$ **d.** $4 - 2\sqrt{3}, 4 + 2\sqrt{3}$

7. If y varies directly as the square of x, and $y = 4$ when $x = 4$, find y when $x = 12$.

    a. 12 **b.** $\frac{4}{3}$ **ⓒ** 36 **d.** 576

8. Tell which statement is true for the parabola $y = 2x^2 - 12x + 28$.

    a. The parabola has two x intercepts.
    ⓑ The equation of its axis of symmetry is $x = 3$.
    c. The coordinates of its vertex are $(-3, 5)$.
    d. The maximum value of the function is 5.

9. For the equation $ax^2 + bx + c = 0$, $b^2 - 4ac > 0$. Tell which statements are true.

    a. The graph of $y = ax^2 + bx + c$ is tangent to the x axis.
    b. The graph of $y = ax^2 + bx + c$ does not intersect the x axis.
    ⓒ The equation has two unequal real roots.
    d. The equation has one real root.

10. Tell which statements are true for the given system of equations.

$$\begin{cases} 4x - y + 3 = 0 \\ 8x - 2y + 6 = 0 \end{cases}$$

a. The system is an inconsistent system.
(b.) The system is a consistent system.
c. The solution set is $\{(0, 0)\}$.
(d.) The system is a dependent system.

11. Tell which set of ordered pairs contains solutions of the given system of inequalities.

$$\begin{cases} y \le x + 3 \\ y > 3x - 2 \\ y > -1 \end{cases}$$

a. $\{(1, 3), (0, 3), (-4, -2)\}$
(b.) $\{(2, 5), (-3, -\frac{1}{2}), (0, 0)\}$
c. $\{(10, 10), (-5, 2), (0, \frac{1}{2})\}$
d. $\{(1, 4), (2, 4), (-2, -1)\}$

12. Solve: $(x - 2)(x + 3) = -4$

a. $\{2, -3\}$ b. $\{-2, 3\}$ (c.) $\{-2, 1\}$ d. $\{2, -1\}$

13. If $f(x) = 3x^2 + 2x - 5$ and $g(x) = x + 4$, tell which statements are true.

a. $g[f(x)] = f[g(x)]$
(b.) $f[g^{-1}(x)] = 3x^2 - 22x + 35$
c. $f[f^{-1}(x)] = 3x^2 + 20$
d. $g[g^{-1}(x)] = x + 4$

14. Find the value of k that will make the solutions of $x^2 - x + k = 0$ real and unequal.

(a.) $k < \frac{1}{4}$ b. $k = \frac{2}{3}$ c. $k > \frac{1}{2}$ d. $k = -3$

15. Tell which statement(s) are true for the set of complex numbers.

(a.) $(a, b) + (c, d) = (a + c, b + d)$
(b.) $(a, b) - (c, d) = (a - c, b - d)$
c. $(a, b) \cdot (c, d) = (ac + bd, ad + bc)$
d. $(a, b) \div (c, d) = \left(\dfrac{ac + bd}{c^2 + d^2}, \dfrac{ad + bc}{c^2 + d^2} \right)$

16. Tell which statements are true for the parabola $y = ax^2 + bx + c$.

a. The equation of its axis of symmetry is $x = \dfrac{b}{2a}$.
(b.) The vertex of the parabola always lies on its axis of symmetry.
(c.) If $a < 0$, the graph of the parabola opens downward.
(d.) If $a > 0$, the function $y = ax^2 + bx + c$ has a minimum value.

Chapter 8
Real Exponents

8-1 Negative Exponents

The objective for this section is on page 318.

An equation such as

$$y = a^x, \text{ where } a \neq 0$$

is called an **exponential equation**. For example, the graph of $y = 2^x$, where $x \in W$, is the graph of an exponential equation. To extend this graph to the left, $y = 2^x$ must be defined when x is a negative integer. To do this, you use the following properties of positive integral exponents and assume that they are true for negative integral exponents.

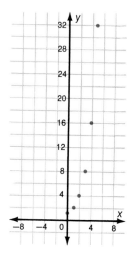

$$a^m \cdot a^n = a^{m+n}, \quad a \neq 0$$
$$a^0 = 1, \quad a \neq 0$$

Example 1

Use the above properties to simplify $2^7 \cdot 2^{-7}$ and $a^m \cdot a^{-m}$.

$$2^7 \cdot 2^{-7} = 2^{7+(-7)}$$
$$= 2^0$$
$$= 1$$
Thus, $2^7 \cdot 2^{-7} = 1$

Then $\quad 2^7 = \dfrac{1}{2^{-7}}$

or $\quad 2^{-7} = \dfrac{1}{2^7}$

$$a^m \cdot a^{-m} = a^{m+(-m)}$$
$$= a^0$$
$$= 1$$
Thus, $a^m \cdot a^{-m} = 1$

Then $\quad a^m = \dfrac{1}{a^{-m}}$

or $\quad a^{-m} = \dfrac{1}{a^m}$

Definition: A nonzero number raised to an integral exponent is equal to 1 divided by the same number raised to the additive inverse of the original exponent.

For all $a \neq 0$, $\quad a^{-m} = \dfrac{1}{a^m} \quad$ and $\quad a^m = \dfrac{1}{a^{-m}}$.

You know that $(a^m)^n = a^{mn}$ for nonnegative integral exponents. This property also holds for negative integral exponents.

Example 2

Write an equivalent expression with positive exponents and without parentheses for $(2^{-3})^4$.

Method I

$$(2^{-3})^4 = \left(\frac{1}{2^3}\right)^4$$

$$= \frac{1}{(2^3)^4}$$

$$= \frac{1}{2^{12}} = \frac{1}{4096}$$

Method II

$$(2^{-3})^4 = 2^{-3 \cdot 4}$$

$$= 2^{-12}$$

$$= \frac{1}{2^{12}} = \frac{1}{4096}$$

Example 3

Write an equivalent expression with positive exponents for each of the following. Remove all parentheses.

a. b^{-4} **b.** mn^{-2} **c.** $(ab)^{-5}$ **d.** $x^{-3}y^4$

a. $b^{-4} = \dfrac{1}{b^4}$ **b.** $mn^{-2} = \dfrac{m}{n^2}$ **c.** $(ab)^{-5} = \dfrac{1}{(ab)^5}$ **d.** $x^{-3}y^4 = \dfrac{y^4}{x^3}$

$$= \frac{1}{a^5 b^5}$$

Now $y = 2^x$ can be evaluated for negative integral values of x. For example, for $x = -1$, $y = \frac{1}{2}$; for $x = -2$, $y = \frac{1}{4}$; for $x = -3$, $y = \frac{1}{8}$. These points can be included in the graph of $y = 2^n$.

Try These

Evaluate each expression.

$5^8 = 390625$

1. 3^{-2} $\frac{1}{9}$ **2.** 2^{-4} $\frac{1}{16}$ **3.** 4^{-1} $\frac{1}{4}$ **4.** $\dfrac{1}{5^{-8}}$

5. $(2+3)^{-3}$ $\frac{1}{125}$ **6.** $2^{-3} + 4^{-2}$ $\frac{1}{8} + \frac{1}{16} = \frac{3}{16}$ **7.** $(2^{-3})^{-2}$ 64 **8.** $(3^{-1})^4$ $\frac{1}{81}$

Real Exponents   **295**

Exercises

Write each number without exponents. The replacement set for each variable is the set of complex numbers other than 0. (Remember that i is not a variable.)

1. 7^0 1

2. 2^{-2} $\frac{1}{4}$

3. 2^{-4} $\frac{1}{16}$

4. 3^{-2} $\frac{1}{9}$

5. 5^0 1

6. $(8a)^0$ 1

7. $8a^0$ 8

8. $(x+2y)^0$ $x \neq -2y$ 1

9. $x^0 + 2y^0$ 3

10. $(2+3)^{-2}$ $\frac{1}{25}$

11. $2^{-2} + 3^{-2}$ $\frac{13}{36}$

12. $(2 \cdot 3)^{-2}$ $\frac{1}{36}$

13. $2^{-2} \cdot 3^{-2}$ $\frac{1}{36}$

14. $4^{-2} - 1^{-2}$ $-\frac{15}{16}$

15. $3^{-3} + 2^{-3}$ $\frac{35}{216}$

16. $(2i)^0$ 1

17. $(3+4i)^0$ 1

18. $(5i)^{-2}$ $-\frac{1}{25}$

19. $(5i)^{-1}$ $\frac{1}{5i}$

20. $(2-i)^{-1}$ $\frac{1}{2-i}$

21. $(3+2i)^{-2}$ $\frac{1}{5+12i}$

22. $(\frac{1}{2})^{-1}$ 2

23. $(\frac{3}{4})^{-1}$ $\frac{4}{3}$

24. $(\frac{2}{3})^{-1}$ $\frac{3}{2}$

25. $(\frac{1}{2})^{-2}$ 4

26. $(\frac{3}{4})^{-2}$ $\frac{16}{9}$

27. $(\frac{3}{5})^{-1}$ $\frac{5}{3}$

28. $(\frac{2}{3})^{-3}$ $\frac{27}{8}$

Write an equivalent expression with positive exponents, and remove all parentheses. The replacement set for each variable is the set of complex numbers other than 0.

29. a^{-1} $\frac{1}{a}$

30. a^{-2} $\frac{1}{a^2}$

31. mn^{-1} $\frac{m}{n}$

32. $(mn)^{-1}$ $\frac{1}{mn}$

33. $2x^{-3}$ $\frac{2}{x^3}$

34. $(2x)^{-3}$ $\frac{1}{8x^3}$

35. a^2b^{-3} $\frac{a^2}{b^3}$

36. $x^{-3}y^5$ $\frac{y^5}{x^3}$

Find the value of the following when $a = 2$ and $b = 3$.

37. a^0 1

38. $2a^0b^{-2}$ $\frac{2}{9}$

39. $3a^2b^{-1}$ 4

40. $(ab)^{-2}$ $\frac{1}{36}$

41. $a^{-2}b^{-2}$ $\frac{1}{36}$

42. $(a+b)^0$ 1

43. $a^0 + b^0$ 2

44. $(\frac{2}{3} + 5b)^0$ 1

Write each number as the sum of multiples of powers of 10.

See key for Exercises 46-55.

Example: $62.37 = 6 \cdot 10^1 + 2 \cdot 10^0 + 3 \cdot 10^{-1} + 7 \cdot 10^{-2}$

45. $249.863 = 2 \cdot \underline{?}\ 10^2 + 4 \cdot \underline{?}\ 10^1 + 9 \cdot \underline{?}\ 10^0 + 8 \cdot \underline{?}\ 10^{-1} + 6 \cdot \underline{?}\ 10^{-2} + 3 \cdot \underline{?}\ 10^{-3}$

46. 7654

47. 8325.7

48. 500.03

49. 1234.567

50. 0.00009

51. 23000.07

52. 75,000

53. 75.004

54. On graph paper make a careful graph of $y = 2^x$, where the replacement set for x is $\{\pm5, \pm4, \pm3, \pm2, \pm1, 0\}$.

55. Graph $y = (-2)^x$ where the replacement set for x is $\{\pm5, \pm4, \pm3, \pm2, \pm1, 0\}$. How does this graph differ from the graph of $y = 2^x$?

8-2 Scientific Notation

The objective for this section is on page 318.

Definition: Scientific notation is a way of expressing a number as the indicated product of a number greater than or equal to 1 but less than 10 and an integral power of 10.

The mean distance from the earth to the sun is about 93,000,000 miles. Express this in scientific notation.

$93,000,000 = 9.3 \times \underline{}$ ⟵   The first factor must be between 1 and 10.

$= 9.3 \times 10,000,000$ ⟵   Divide to find the second factor.

$= 9.3 \times 10^7$ ⟵   Write 10,000,000 as a power of 10.

Compare the exponent in 10^7 with the number of places in 93,000,000 and the direction in which you moved the decimal point.

Example 2

The amount in grams of one cubic centimeter of air at 0° Celsius and 76 centimeters of mercury pressure is 0.00129. Express this in scientific notation.

$0.00129 = 1.29 \times \underline{}$ ⟵   The first factor must be between 1 and 10.

$= 1.29 \times 0.001$ ⟵   Divide to find the second factor.

$= 1.29 \times \frac{1}{1000}$ ⟵   Write the second factor as a fraction.

$= 1.29 \times \frac{1}{10^3}$ ⟵   Write the denominator as a power of 10.

$= 1.29 \times 10^{-3}$ ⟵   Write as a power of 10.

Compare the exponent in 10^{-3} with the number of places and the direction that you moved the decimal point in 0.00129.

Real Exponents   **297**

Example 3   The age of the earth is estimated by some scientists to be 2.5×10^9 years. Express this without using scientific notation.

$$2.5 \times 10^9 = 2.5 \times 1,000,000,000$$
$$= 2,500,000,000.$$

←   To multiply by 10^9, move the decimal point in 2.5 nine places to the right.

Exercises

Express the numbers in Exercises 1-8 in scientific notation.

1. Light travels 300,000,000 meters per second. 3×10^8

2. The radius of the earth is about 6371 kilometers. 6.371×10^3

3. The sun is one of about 100 billion stars making up the Milky Way. 1×10^{11}

4. The distance light travels in a year is about 9,460,000,000,000 kilometers. (This is called a light year.) 9.46×10^{12}

5. The half-life of uranium is $4\frac{1}{2}$ billion years. (Half-life is a convenient term used by scientists for the time required for half of the atoms originally present in a radioactive element to disintegrate.) 4.5×10^9

6. Electromagnetic waves whose lengths are between 0.000036 centimeter and 0.000077 centimeter cause the sensation of light. $3.6 \times 10^{-5}; 7.7 \times 10^{-5}$

7. Special balances for weighing small quantities can weigh a quantity as small as 0.00000001 gram. Such a quantity of matter would contain more than 10,000,000,000,000 atoms. $1 \times 10^{-8}; 1 \times 10^{13}$

8. A hydrogen atom weighs 0.000,000,000,000,000,000,000,001,67 gram.
1.67×10^{-24}

Express the numbers in Exercises 9-13 without using scientific notation.

9. The mass of the sun is 2×10^{30} kilograms. 2,000,000,000,000,000,000,000,000,000,000

10. The volume of the earth is about 1.08×10^{27} cubic centimeters.
1,080,000,000,000,000,000,000,000,000

11. The temperature of the sun is 6×10^3 degrees Celsius. 6000

12. One foot of copper wire expands 1.6×10^{-5} feet with an increase in temperature of 1° Celsius. 0.000016

13. A helium atom has a diameter of 2.2×10^{-8} centimeters. 0.000000022

Algebraic expressions involving integral exponents are usually much easier to handle if they are simplified first.

Example 1   Write $\dfrac{a^{-m}}{b^{-m}}$ as a fraction with positive exponents.

Method I $\dfrac{a^{-m}}{b^{-m}} = \dfrac{\frac{1}{a^m}}{\frac{1}{b^m}}$ ⟵ Rewrite with positive exponents.

$$= \frac{1}{a^m} \cdot \frac{b^m}{1} = \frac{b^m}{a^m}$$

Method II $\dfrac{a^{-m}}{b^{-m}} \cdot \dfrac{a^m b^m}{a^m b^m} = \dfrac{a^0 b^m}{b^0 a^m}$ ⟵ Multiply by $\frac{a^m b^m}{a^m b^m}$.

$$= \frac{b^m}{a^m}$$ ⟵ $\frac{a^0}{b^0} = 1$

Example 2   Use positive exponents to simplify the following algebraic expression.

$$3x^{-2}y - 2x^{-1}y^2 + 5 + \frac{7y^2}{x} - \frac{3y}{x^2}, \ x \neq 0$$

$$\frac{3y}{x^2} - \frac{2y^2}{x} + 5 + \frac{7y^2}{x} - \frac{3y}{x^2}$$ ⟵ Rewrite with positive exponents

$$5 + \frac{5y^2}{x}$$ ⟵ Combine like terms

Example 3 Use positive exponents to simplify.

$$\frac{1}{a^{-1}+b^{-1}}(a+b), \text{ where } a,\ b \neq 0.$$

$$\left(\frac{1}{a^{-1}+b^{-1}}\right)(a+b) = \frac{1}{\dfrac{1}{a}+\dfrac{1}{b}}(a+b) \quad \longleftarrow \quad \text{Rewrite with positive exponents.}$$

$$= \frac{1}{\dfrac{b+a}{ab}}(a+b)$$

$$= \frac{ab}{a+b}(a+b)$$

$$= ab$$

In the exercises that follow, assume that the replacement set has been restricted to exclude numbers that would lead to 0 in a denominator.

Try These Write each of the following using positive exponents.

1. $\dfrac{a^{-2}}{b^{-3}}$ $\frac{b^3}{a^2}$

2. $\dfrac{2ab^{-1}}{3c^{-3}d}$ $\frac{2ac^3}{3db}$

3. $\dfrac{(2x)^{-2}}{(3y)^{-2}}$ $\frac{(3y)^2}{(2x)^2}$

4. $\dfrac{2x^{-2}}{3y^{-2}}$ $\frac{2y^2}{3x^2}$

Use positive exponents to simplify the following.

5. $2x^{-1}y + \dfrac{y}{x}$ $\frac{3y}{x}$

6. $5x^{-2}y + x^{-1} - \dfrac{6y}{x^2} + \dfrac{3}{x}$ $\frac{-y}{x^2}+\frac{4}{x}$

7. $\dfrac{1}{a^{-1}}(a-b)$ $a^2 - ab$

8. $(a^{-1}+b^{-1})\left(\dfrac{a^2b}{a^2-b^2}\right)$ $\frac{a}{a-b}$

Exercises

Use positive exponents to simplify the following.

1. $\dfrac{x^{-1}y^{-1}}{z^{-3}}$ $\frac{z^3}{xy}$

2. $2^{-1}ab^{-3}$ $\frac{a}{2b^3}$

3. $a^{-2}+b^{-2}$ $\frac{a^2+b^2}{a^2b^2}$

4. $ab^{-3}+a^{-4}b^2$ $\frac{a^5+b^5}{a^4b^3}$

300   Chapter 8

5. $3^{-5}ab^{-4}c^{-2}$ $\frac{a}{3^5b^4c^2}$

6. $\dfrac{(a+b)^{-3}}{4^{-1}c^3b^{-1}}$ $\frac{4b}{c^3(a+b)^3}$

7. $\dfrac{x^{-2}y^3}{x^3y^{-2}}$ $\frac{y^5}{x^5}$

8. $\dfrac{a^5b^{-3}}{a^{-1}b^4}$ $\frac{a^6}{b^7}$

9. $\dfrac{2^{-1}a^{-1}}{3a^2b^{-1}}$ $\frac{b}{6a^3}$

10. $\dfrac{3^{-1}u^{-1}v^2}{2u^3v^{-4}}$ $\frac{v^6}{6u^4}$

11. $\dfrac{p^{-4}g^5r^{-6}}{p^{-2}g^{-2}r^{-7}}$ $\frac{g^7r}{p^2}$

12. $\left(\dfrac{s^{-4}m^{-4}}{s^{-2}m}\right)^0$ 1

13. $\dfrac{4a}{a^{-1}}+\dfrac{3}{a^{-2}}$ $7a^2$

14. $\dfrac{3m}{n^{-1}}+\dfrac{2n}{m^{-1}}$ $5mn$

15. $(r^{-1}s^2)^{-1}$ $\frac{r}{s^2}$

16. $(r^3s^{-4})^{-2}$ $\frac{s^8}{r^6}$

Simplify each of the following in such a way as to avoid the fraction form.

$2w^{-1}x^{-1}y^{-2}z^2 \leftarrow$

17. $\dfrac{1}{a^3}$ a^{-3}

18. $\dfrac{1}{x^2}+\dfrac{1}{y^2}$ $x^{-2}+y^{-2}$

19. $\dfrac{2xy^3}{z^2w}$ $2w^{-1}xy^3z^{-2}$

20. $\dfrac{2x^{-1}y^{-2}}{z^{-2}w}$

21. $\dfrac{x}{y^4}$ xy^{-4}

22. $\dfrac{1}{(x+y)^2}$ $(x+y)^{-2}$

23. $\dfrac{2}{b^2}+\dfrac{3}{c^{-3}}$ $2b^{-2}+3c^3$

24. $\dfrac{3}{b^{-2}}+\dfrac{4}{c^4}$

$3b^2+4c^{-4}$

Use positive exponents to simplify the following products.

25. $a^{-1}(b^{-1}a+c^{-2}a^2)$ $\frac{c^2+ab}{bc^2}$

26. $(a^{-1}+b^{-1})(a+b)$ $\frac{(a+b)^2}{ab}$

27. $(a+b)^{-2}(a^2-b^2)$ $\frac{a-b}{a+b}$

28. $(x+y)^{-2}(x^{-1}+y^{-1})$ $\frac{1}{(x+y)xy}$

Use positive exponents to simplify the following.

29. $(x^{-2}-y^{-2})(x^{-2}+y^{-2})(x+y)$ $\frac{(y^4-x^4)(x+y)}{x^4y^4}$

30. $\dfrac{x}{y^2}-2x^{-1}y^{-1}+\dfrac{6y^{-2}}{x}-3x^0$ $\frac{x^2-3xy^2-2y+6}{xy^2}$

31. $\left(\dfrac{1}{x}-\dfrac{1}{y}\right)(x-y)+\left(\dfrac{1}{x^{-1}-y^{-1}}\right)(x-y)$ $\frac{-(x-y)^2}{xy}-xy$

32. Show that $(x^{-1}+y^{-1})^{-1}=x+y$ is a false statement. See key.

33. Show that $(x+y)^{-1}=x^{-1}+y^{-1}$ is a false statement. See key.

Remember

Factor completely.

1. 72 $2^3\cdot3^2$

2. $-10x^2+29x-21$ $(2x-3)(-5x+7)$

3. x^3-8 $(x-2)(x^2+2x+4)$

4. x^3+x^2-6x $x(x+3)(x-2)$

The answers are on page 320.

PUZZLE

Complete the sequence: OTTFFSSE___? N; these are the first letters of names of the digits 1-9.

The objectives for this section are on page 319.

The graph of $y = 2^x$ for some integral values of x is shown at the right. Since there are "holes" in the graph, it seems reasonable to think that 2^x ought to be defined for nonintegral values of x also. To do this, you assume the following property of integral exponents holds also for rational exponents.

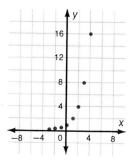

$$(a^m)^n = a^{mn}$$

Example 1   Use the above property to simplify $(2^{\frac{1}{7}})^7$ and $(a^{\frac{1}{n}})^n$.

$(2^{\frac{1}{7}})^7 = 2^{\frac{1}{7} \cdot 7}$

          $= 2^1$, or 2

Thus, $(2^{\frac{1}{7}})^7 = 2$

Also, $(\sqrt[7]{2})^7 = 2$

Then $2^{\frac{1}{7}} = \sqrt[7]{2}$

$(a^{\frac{1}{n}})^n = a^{\frac{1}{n} \cdot n}$

          $= a^{\frac{n}{n}}$, or a

Thus, $(a^{\frac{1}{n}})^n = a$

Also, $(\sqrt[n]{a})^n = a$

Then $a^{\frac{1}{n}} = \sqrt[n]{a}$

Definition: When a is a real number, $a \neq 0$ and $n \in N$,

$$a^{\frac{1}{n}} = \sqrt[n]{a}$$

Example 2   Evaluate: **a.** $4^{\frac{1}{2}}$ **b.** $125^{\frac{1}{3}}$

a. $4^{\frac{1}{2}} = \sqrt{4}$ **b.** $125^{\frac{1}{3}} = \sqrt[3]{125}$

       $= 2$ $= 5$

Notice that $4^{\frac{1}{2}}$ is not ± 2. According to the definition of *nth* root, $a^{\frac{1}{n}}$ is the **principal *nth* root** of a. That is, $a^{\frac{1}{n}}$ is the positive *nth* root when there is more than one real root, and the real root when there is exactly one real root.

Example 3   Evaluate: $4^{\frac{3}{2}}$

Method I $4^{\frac{3}{2}} = (4^{\frac{1}{2}})^3$

$= (\sqrt{4})^3$

$= (2)^3$

$= 8$

Method II $4^{\frac{3}{2}} = (4^3)^{\frac{1}{2}}$

$= (64)^{\frac{1}{2}}$

$= \sqrt{64}$

$= 8$

Example 3 illustrates two important ideas. First, in the fractional exponent $\frac{3}{2}$, the denominator, 2, tells you which root to take. The numerator, 3, tells how many factors you have. Secondly, you can raise the base to the exponent of the numerator before, or after, you take the root shown in the denominator.

Example 4   Evaluate: $8^{\frac{2}{3}}$

$8^{\frac{2}{3}} = (8^{\frac{1}{3}})^2$ ⟵ Take the root first.

$= (2)^2 = 4$

$8^{\frac{2}{3}} = (8^2)^{\frac{1}{3}}$ ⟵ Raise to the exponent first.

$= (64)^{\frac{1}{3}} = 4$

Theorem 8-1:   For all $a \in R$, $a \neq 0$, $m \in \mathcal{I}$ and $n \in N$,

$$a^{\frac{m}{n}} = (a^{\frac{1}{n}})^m = (\sqrt[n]{a})^m, \text{ or}$$

$$a^{\frac{m}{n}} = (a^m)^{\frac{1}{n}} = \sqrt[n]{a^m}$$

except when n is even and $a < 0$.

All of the properties of integral exponents that you have studied are also true for rational exponents.

Example 5   Evaluate: **a.** $(-64)^{-\frac{2}{3}}$ **b.** $-64^{-\frac{2}{3}}$

a. $(-64)^{-\frac{2}{3}} = \dfrac{1}{(-64)^{\frac{2}{3}}}$ **b.** $-64^{-\frac{2}{3}} = -\dfrac{1}{64^{\frac{2}{3}}}$

$\qquad = \dfrac{1}{(\sqrt[3]{-64})^2}$ $\qquad = -\dfrac{1}{(\sqrt[3]{64})^2}$

$\qquad = \dfrac{1}{(-4)^2} = \dfrac{1}{16}$ $\qquad = -\dfrac{1}{(4)^2} = -\dfrac{1}{16}$

Try These   *Evaluate each expression.*

1. $25^{\frac{1}{2}}$ 5
2. $9^{\frac{3}{2}}$ 27
3. $-64^{\frac{2}{3}}$ 16
4. $4^{-\frac{3}{2}}$ $\frac{1}{8}$

5. $-125^{-\frac{1}{3}}$ $-\frac{1}{5}$
6. $-8^{\frac{1}{3}}$ -2
7. $81^{-\frac{1}{2}}$ $\frac{1}{9}$
8. $-27^{-\frac{1}{3}}$ $-\frac{1}{3}$

Exercises

Evaluate each expression.

1. $9^{\frac{1}{2}}$ 3
2. $125^{\frac{1}{3}}$ 5
3. $16^{\frac{1}{4}}$ 2
4. $-27^{\frac{1}{3}}$ -3

5. $-36^{\frac{1}{2}}$ -6
6. $(-27)^{\frac{1}{3}}$ -3
7. $-(-27)^{\frac{1}{3}}$ 3
8. 8^0 1

9. $8^{\frac{2}{3}}$ 4
10. $8^{\frac{3}{3}}$ 8
11. $8^{\frac{5}{3}}$ 32
12. $81^{\frac{3}{4}}$ 27

13. $-27^{\frac{3}{3}}$ -27
14. $(-32)^{\frac{3}{5}}$ -8
15. $4^{\frac{5}{2}}$ 32
16. $25^{\frac{3}{2}}$ 125

17. $16^{\frac{1}{2}}$ 4
18. $64^{-\frac{1}{3}}$ $\frac{1}{4}$
19. $64^{-\frac{2}{3}}$ $\frac{1}{16}$
20. $16^{-\frac{3}{4}}$ $\frac{1}{8}$

21. $-25^{-\frac{1}{2}}$ $-\frac{1}{5}$
22. $27^{-\frac{4}{3}}$ $\frac{1}{81}$
23. $27^{-\frac{2}{3}}$ $\frac{1}{9}$
24. $27^{-\frac{1}{3}}$ $\frac{1}{3}$

25. $(-27)^{-\frac{4}{3}}$ $\frac{1}{81}$
26. $-(-27)^{-\frac{4}{3}}$ $-\frac{1}{81}$
27. $\left(\frac{4}{9}\right)^{-1}$ $\frac{9}{4}$
28. $\left(\frac{27}{8}\right)^{-\frac{2}{3}}$ $\frac{4}{9}$

Write with radical signs instead of with fractional exponents.

Example: $3x^{\frac{2}{3}}y = 3y\sqrt[3]{x^2}$ $\rightarrow \sqrt[4]{ab^3}$

29. $a^{\frac{1}{2}}$ $\sqrt{a}$
30. $b^{\frac{1}{3}}$ $\sqrt[3]{b}$
31. $x^{\frac{1}{4}}$ $\sqrt[4]{x}$
32. $n^{\frac{2}{3}}$ $\sqrt[3]{n^2}$

33. $a^{\frac{3}{4}}$ $\sqrt[4]{a^3}$
34. $2x^{\frac{3}{4}}$ $2\sqrt[4]{x^3}$
35. $3a^{\frac{1}{2}}$ $3\sqrt{a}$
36. $a^{\frac{1}{4}}b^{\frac{3}{4}}$

37. $2^{\frac{1}{2}}y^{\frac{1}{2}}$ $\sqrt{2y}$
38. $a^{\frac{1}{2}}+b^{\frac{1}{2}}$ $\sqrt{a}+\sqrt{b}$
39. $(x-y)^{\frac{1}{3}}$ $\sqrt[3]{x-y}$
40. $x^{\frac{1}{3}}-y^{\frac{1}{3}}$
$\qquad\qquad\qquad\qquad\qquad\quad \sqrt[3]{x}-\sqrt[3]{y}$

Write with fractional exponents instead of with radical signs.

$m^{\frac{1}{3}}n^{\frac{2}{3}}$

41. $\sqrt[3]{x^2}$ $x^{\frac{2}{3}}$ **42.** $\sqrt[4]{y^3}$ $y^{\frac{3}{4}}$ **43.** $\sqrt{mn}$ $(mn)^{\frac{1}{2}}$ **44.** $\sqrt[3]{mn^2}$

45. $\sqrt[4]{x^2y^3}$ $x^{\frac{1}{2}}y^{\frac{3}{4}}$ **46.** $2\sqrt[4]{a^3}$ $2a^{\frac{3}{4}}$ **47.** $a\sqrt[5]{b^2c^3}$ $ab^{\frac{2}{5}}c^{\frac{3}{5}}$ **48.** $2xy\sqrt{z}$

49. $\sqrt{a}\sqrt[3]{b^2}$ $a^{\frac{1}{2}}b^{\frac{2}{3}}$ **50.** $\sqrt{a+b}$ $(a+b)^{\frac{1}{2}}$ **51.** $\sqrt[4]{2x^5y^4}$ $2^{\frac{1}{4}}x^{\frac{5}{4}}y$ **52.** $\sqrt{4a-9b}$ $(4a-9b)^{\frac{1}{2}}$

$\longrightarrow 2xyz^{\frac{1}{2}}$

Complete the table.

	Radical Form	Exponential Form	Numerical Value	Radical Equation	Exponential Equation
53.	$\sqrt{16}$	$16^{\frac{1}{2}}$	4	$\sqrt{16}=4$	$16^{\frac{1}{2}}=4$
54.	$(\sqrt{4})^3$	$4^{\frac{3}{2}}$	8	$(\sqrt{4})^3=8$	$4^{\frac{3}{2}}=8$
55.	$\sqrt{25}$	$25^{\frac{1}{2}}$	5	$\sqrt{25}=5$	$25^{\frac{1}{2}}=5$
56.	$\sqrt[3]{64}$	$64^{\frac{1}{3}}$	4	$\sqrt[3]{64}=4$	$64^{\frac{1}{3}}=4$
57.	$(\sqrt[3]{8})^2$	$8^{\frac{2}{3}}$	4	$(\sqrt[3]{8})^2=4$	$8^{\frac{2}{3}}=4$
58.	$(\sqrt{9})^3$	$9^{\frac{3}{2}}$	27	$(\sqrt{9})^3=27$	$9^{\frac{3}{2}}=27$
59.	$(\sqrt[4]{16})^5$	$16^{\frac{5}{4}}$	32	$(\sqrt[4]{16})^5=32$	$16^{\frac{5}{4}}=32$
60.	$(\sqrt{16})^3$	$16^{\frac{3}{2}}$	64	$(\sqrt{16})^3=64$	$16^{\frac{3}{2}}=64$
61.	$\frac{1}{\sqrt{4}}$	$4^{-\frac{1}{2}}$	$\frac{1}{2}$	$\frac{1}{\sqrt{4}}=\frac{1}{2}$	$4^{-\frac{1}{2}}=\frac{1}{2}$
62.	$\frac{1}{(\sqrt[3]{8})}$	$8^{-\frac{1}{3}}$	$\frac{1}{2}$	$\frac{1}{(\sqrt[3]{8})}=\frac{1}{2}$	$8^{-\frac{1}{3}}=\frac{1}{2}$
63.	$\frac{1}{(\sqrt[3]{8})^2}$	$8^{-\frac{2}{3}}$	$\frac{1}{4}$	$\frac{1}{(\sqrt[3]{8})^2}=\frac{1}{4}$	$8^{-\frac{2}{3}}=\frac{1}{4}$

Evaluate when $a = 8$, $b = 1$, and $c = 4$.

64. $a^{\frac{2}{3}}b^{\frac{1}{2}}$ 4   **65.** $(a+b)^{\frac{3}{2}}$ 27   **66.** $a^{-\frac{1}{3}}c^{\frac{3}{2}}$ 4   **67.** $(a-c)^{-\frac{1}{2}}$ $\frac{1}{2}$

68. $\left(\dfrac{a+b}{c}\right)^{-\frac{3}{2}}$ $\frac{8}{27}$ **69.** $(3a+b)^{\frac{1}{2}}$ 5   **70.** $\left(\dfrac{a}{7c-b}\right)^{\frac{2}{3}}$ $\frac{4}{9}$ **71.** $(4a)^{-\frac{3}{5}}$ $\frac{1}{8}$

72. $(6c+b)^{\frac{3}{2}}$ 125   **73.** $c^{\frac{1}{2}}+b^{\frac{1}{2}}$ 3   **74.** $(c+b)^{\frac{1}{2}}$ $\sqrt{5}$ **75.** $(2ac)^{-\frac{1}{2}}$ $\frac{1}{8}$

Write the following using fractional and negative exponents.

76. $\sqrt{\dfrac{a}{b}}$ $a^{\frac{1}{2}}b^{-\frac{1}{2}}$ **77.** $\sqrt[3]{\dfrac{x^2}{y}}$ $x^{\frac{2}{3}}y^{-\frac{1}{3}}$ **78.** $\sqrt{\dfrac{x^3}{y}}$ $x^{\frac{3}{2}}y^{-\frac{1}{2}}$ **79.** $\dfrac{m}{\sqrt{n}}$ $mn^{-\frac{1}{2}}$

PUZZLE

Explain the following paradox.

$$(-4)^{\frac{2}{2}} = [(-4)^2]^{\frac{1}{2}} = 16^{\frac{1}{2}} = 4 \qquad\qquad (-4)^{\frac{2}{2}} = (\sqrt{-4})^2 = (2i)^2 = 4i^2 = -4$$

$a^{\frac{m}{n}} \neq (a^m)^{\frac{1}{n}}$ when n is even and $a < 0$. Thus, $(-4)^{\frac{2}{2}} = 4$ is false.

The objective for this section is on page 319.

The following properties of exponents are used to simplify radicals and to compute with radicals. In these properties, a and b are real numbers, and m and n are rational numbers.

a. $a^m \cdot a^n = a^{m+n}$ **b.** $(a^m)^n = a^{mn}$ **c.** $\dfrac{a^m}{a^n} = a^{m-n}$, $a \neq 0$

d. $(a^n)(b^n) = (a \cdot b)^n$ **e.** $\dfrac{a^n}{b^n} = \left(\dfrac{a}{b}\right)^n$, $b \neq 0$

Properties **a, b,** and **c** are familiar, but properties **d** and **e** are new to you. Property **d** says that $(2^3)(3^3)$ equals $(2 \cdot 3)^3$. Property **e** says that $\dfrac{4^3}{3^3} = \left(\dfrac{4}{3}\right)^3$.

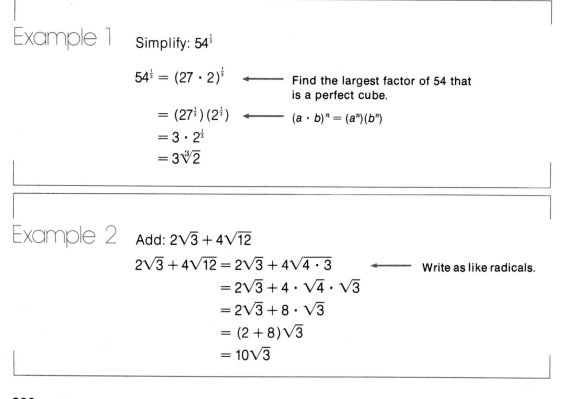

Example 1

Simplify: $54^{\frac{1}{3}}$

$54^{\frac{1}{3}} = (27 \cdot 2)^{\frac{1}{3}}$ ⟵ Find the largest factor of 54 that is a perfect cube.

$= (27^{\frac{1}{3}})(2^{\frac{1}{3}})$ ⟵ $(a \cdot b)^n = (a^n)(b^n)$

$= 3 \cdot 2^{\frac{1}{3}}$

$= 3\sqrt[3]{2}$

Example 2

Add: $2\sqrt{3} + 4\sqrt{12}$

$2\sqrt{3} + 4\sqrt{12} = 2\sqrt{3} + 4\sqrt{4 \cdot 3}$ ⟵ Write as like radicals.

$= 2\sqrt{3} + 4 \cdot \sqrt{4} \cdot \sqrt{3}$

$= 2\sqrt{3} + 8 \cdot \sqrt{3}$

$= (2 + 8)\sqrt{3}$

$= 10\sqrt{3}$

Example 3 Multiply: $\sqrt{2} \cdot \sqrt[3]{3}$

$\sqrt{2} \cdot \sqrt[3]{3} = 2^{\frac{1}{2}} \cdot 3^{\frac{1}{3}}$ ⟵ Rewrite the factors using fractional exponents.

$= 2^{\frac{3}{6}} \cdot 3^{\frac{2}{6}}$ ⟵ Write each exponent with a common denominator.

$= (2^3)^{\frac{1}{6}} \cdot (3^2)^{\frac{1}{6}}$ ⟵ Write the factors with equal exponents.

$= (8)^{\frac{1}{6}} \cdot (9)^{\frac{1}{6}}$

$= (8^{\frac{1}{6}}) \cdot (9^{\frac{1}{6}})$

$= (8 \cdot 9)^{\frac{1}{6}}$ ⟵ $(a^n)(b^n) = (a \cdot b)^n$

$= 72^{\frac{1}{6}}$

$= \sqrt[6]{72}$

To divide, follow the same procedure as in Example 3.

Example 4 Divide: $\sqrt[3]{2} \div \sqrt[4]{3}$

$$\frac{\sqrt[3]{2}}{\sqrt[4]{3}} = \frac{2^{\frac{1}{3}}}{3^{\frac{1}{4}}} = \frac{2^{\frac{4}{12}}}{3^{\frac{3}{12}}} = \frac{(2^4)^{\frac{1}{12}}}{(3^3)^{\frac{1}{12}}} = \left(\frac{16}{27}\right)^{\frac{1}{12}}$$

Example 5 Simplify $\sqrt[6]{27}$. Write your answer with a decimal exponent.

$$\sqrt[6]{27} = (27)^{\frac{1}{6}} = (3^3)^{\frac{1}{6}} = 3^{\frac{3}{6}} = 3^{\frac{1}{2}} = 3^{0.5}$$

Try These Simplify.

1. $16^{\frac{1}{3}}$ $2\sqrt[3]{2}$

2. $48^{\frac{1}{4}}$ $2\sqrt[4]{3}$

3. $\sqrt{48} - 5\sqrt{12}$ $-6\sqrt{3}$

4. $3\sqrt[3]{4} + 5\sqrt[3]{32}$ $13\sqrt[3]{4}$

5. $\dfrac{\sqrt{2}}{3} + \dfrac{\sqrt{3}}{2}$ $\frac{2\sqrt{2}\,+\,3\sqrt{3}}{6}$

6. $\sqrt[3]{3} \cdot \sqrt[4]{4}$ $\sqrt[3]{12}$

7. $\sqrt[3]{24} \div \sqrt[3]{3}$ 2

8. $\sqrt[3]{2} \cdot \sqrt{3}$ $\sqrt[6]{108}$

9. $\sqrt{2} \div \sqrt[3]{5}$ $\left(\frac{8}{25}\right)^{\frac{1}{6}}$

Exercises

Simplify. The replacement set for each variable is the set of real numbers.

a

1. $81^{\frac{1}{3}}$ $\;_{3\sqrt[3]{3}}$

2. $32^{\frac{1}{4}}$ $\;_{2\sqrt[4]{2}}$

3. $\sqrt[4]{64}$ $\;_{2\sqrt[4]{4}}$

4. $\sqrt[3]{128}$ $\;_{4\sqrt[3]{2}}$

5. $3\sqrt[3]{48}$ $\;_{6\sqrt[3]{3}}$

6. $2\sqrt[3]{250}$ $\;_{10\sqrt[3]{2}}$

7. $7\sqrt{18} - \sqrt{50}$ $\;_{16\sqrt{2}}$

8. $5\sqrt{12} + 3\sqrt{27}$ $\;_{19\sqrt{3}}$

9. $2\sqrt[3]{3} + \sqrt[3]{24}$ $\;_{4\sqrt[3]{3}}$

10. $4\sqrt[3]{16} + 3\sqrt[3]{54}$ $\;_{17\sqrt[3]{2}}$

11. $6\sqrt{20} - \sqrt{45} + 2\sqrt{5}$ $\;_{11\sqrt{5}}$

12. $2\sqrt[3]{27} - 3\sqrt[3]{16} - 5\sqrt[3]{54}$ $\;_{6 - 21\sqrt[3]{2}}$

13. $\dfrac{\sqrt{3}}{5} + \dfrac{\sqrt{5}}{3}$ $\;_{\frac{3\sqrt{3} + 5\sqrt{5}}{15}}$

14. $\dfrac{\sqrt[3]{1}}{2} - \dfrac{\sqrt[3]{1}}{16}$ $\;_{\frac{7}{16}}$

15. $2\sqrt[3]{32} - \sqrt[3]{108} - \dfrac{\sqrt[3]{1}}{2}$ $\;_{\sqrt[3]{4} - \frac{1}{2}}$

16. $5\sqrt[3]{24} - 2\sqrt[3]{81} - \dfrac{\sqrt[3]{1}}{9}$ $\;_{4\sqrt[3]{3} - \frac{1}{9}}$

17. $(\sqrt[3]{4})(\sqrt[3]{2})$ $\;_{2}$

18. $\sqrt[3]{2} \cdot \sqrt[3]{16}$ $\;_{2\sqrt[3]{4}}$

19. $(-4\sqrt{3})^2$ $\;_{48}$

20. $(3\sqrt{2})^3$ $\;_{54\sqrt{2}}$

21. $(6\sqrt[3]{9})\left(\dfrac{1}{2}\sqrt[3]{6}\right)$ $\;_{9\sqrt[3]{2}}$

22. $\sqrt{8x^2} \cdot \sqrt{9x^6y^2}$ $\;_{6x^4y\sqrt{2}}$

23. $18\sqrt{2} \div 3\sqrt{3}$ $\;_{2\sqrt{6}}$

24. $3\sqrt[3]{a^2} \cdot \sqrt[3]{ab}$ $\;_{3a\sqrt[3]{b}}$

25. $\dfrac{\sqrt[3]{21}}{\sqrt[3]{7}}$ $\;_{\sqrt[3]{3}}$

26. $\dfrac{\sqrt[4]{2}}{\sqrt[4]{32}}$ $\;_{\frac{1}{2}}$

27. $\dfrac{\sqrt[3]{6}}{\sqrt[3]{4}}$ $\;_{\left(\frac{3}{2}\right)^{\frac{1}{3}}}$

Example: $\quad 4 \div (2 + \sqrt{3}) = \dfrac{4}{2 + \sqrt{3}} = \dfrac{4}{2 + \sqrt{3}} \cdot \dfrac{(2 - \sqrt{3})}{(2 - \sqrt{3})}$

$$= \dfrac{8 - 4\sqrt{3}}{4 - 3}, \quad \text{or} \quad 8 - 4\sqrt{3}$$

28. $\dfrac{12}{\sqrt{5} - 2}$ $\;_{12\sqrt{5} + 24}$

29. $\dfrac{4}{\sqrt{5} + \sqrt{7}}$ $\;_{-2\sqrt{5} + 2\sqrt{7}}$

30. $\dfrac{\sqrt{3} + \sqrt{2}}{\sqrt{3} - \sqrt{2}}$ $\;_{5 + 2\sqrt{6}}$

Write each of the following without exponents.

b

31. $4^{0.5}$ $\;_{2}$

32. $16^{0.75}$ $\;_{8}$

33. $32^{1.2}$ $\;_{64}$

34. $9^{1.5}$ $\;_{27}$

35. $81^{1.25}$ $\;_{243}$

36. $256^{0.125}$ $\;_{2}$

c

37. Prove: $\sqrt[n]{a} \cdot \sqrt[n]{b} = \sqrt[n]{ab}$, if $a \geq 0$ and $b \geq 0$. (HINT: Show that $(\sqrt[n]{a} \cdot \sqrt[n]{b})^n = ab$) $\;_{\text{See key.}}$

Remember

Use the quadratic formula to solve each equation.

1. $x^2 - 3x + 1 = 0$ $\;_{\frac{3 \pm \sqrt{5}}{2}}$

2. $x^2 - 3x + 7 = 0$ $\;_{\frac{3 \pm i\sqrt{19}}{2}}$

3. $4x^2 + 5x - 7 = 0$ $\;_{\frac{-5 \pm \sqrt{137}}{8}}$

The answers are on page 320.

8-6 Equations with Radicals

The objective for this section is on page 319.

Equations like $\sqrt{x} = 7$ and $\sqrt{4x + 4} = 12$ are **radical equations.**

Example 1   Solve: $\sqrt{4x + 4} = 12$

$$\sqrt{4x + 4} = 12$$
$$(\sqrt{4x + 4})^2 = (12)^2 \longleftarrow \text{Square both sides to remove the } \sqrt{\,}.$$
$$4x + 4 = 144$$
$$4x = 140$$
$$x = 35$$

Check: $\sqrt{4(35) + 4} \stackrel{?}{=} 12 \longleftarrow$ Replace x in the original equation.
$$\sqrt{144} = 12 \qquad \textbf{Solution set: } \{35\}$$

Raising both sides of an equation to the same exponent does not always produce an equivalent equation. It can produce "wrong numbers" as solutions to the original equation. These "wrong numbers" are only **apparent solutions.**

Example 2   Solve: $\sqrt{x + 2} = 3$

$$\sqrt{x + 2} = 3$$
$$(\sqrt{x + 2})^2 = 3^2 \longleftarrow \text{Square both sides.}$$
$$x + 2 = 9$$
$$x = 7$$

Check: $\sqrt{7 + 2} \stackrel{?}{=} 3 \qquad \textbf{Solution set: } \{7\}$
$$\sqrt{9} = 3$$

Example 3   Solve: $\sqrt{2x-3} - \sqrt{5x-21} = 0$

$$(\sqrt{2x-3})^2 = (\sqrt{5x-21})^2$$
$$2x - 3 = 5x - 21$$
$$-3x = -18$$
$$x = 6$$

Check: $\sqrt{12-3} - \sqrt{30-21} \overset{?}{=} 0.$ **Solution set:** $\{6\}$
$$\sqrt{9} - \sqrt{9} = 0.$$

Example 4   Solve: $\sqrt{x} = -2$

$$(\sqrt{x})^2 = (-2)^2$$ **Check:** $\sqrt{4} \overset{?}{=} -2$ **Solution set:** $\emptyset$
$$x = 4$$ $$2 = -2$$

Thus, $\sqrt{x} = -2$ has no solution. The number 4 is an <u>apparent</u> solution.

Example 5   Solve: $x^{-\frac{2}{3}} = 4$

$$\frac{1}{(\sqrt[3]{x})^2} = 4$$ ⟵ Rewrite with positive exponents.

$$\left(\frac{1}{(\sqrt[3]{x})^2}\right)^{\frac{1}{2}} = 4^{\frac{1}{2}}$$ ⟵ Take the square root of both sides to remove the exponent 2 in $(\sqrt[3]{x})^2$.

$$\frac{1}{\sqrt[3]{x}} = \pm 2$$ ⟵ Take both the positive and negative square root to find all solutions.

$$\left(\frac{1}{\sqrt[3]{x}}\right)^3 = (\pm 2)^3$$ ⟵ Cube both sides.

$$\frac{1}{x} = \pm 8$$

$$x = \pm\frac{1}{8}$$ ⟵ Verify that $\left\{\frac{1}{8}, -\frac{1}{8}\right\}$ is the solution set.

1. $\sqrt{x} = 3$ ₉ 2. $\sqrt{x} = -3$ ∅ 3. $x^{\frac{1}{2}} = 2$ ₄ 4. $x^{\frac{1}{2}} = 3$ ₉

5. $x^{\frac{1}{3}} = 4$ ₆₄ 6. $\sqrt{y+3} = 7$ ₄₆ 7. $\sqrt{x-1} = 4$ ₁₇ 8. $\sqrt{2x} = 4$ ₈

Exercises

Solve. Be sure to check for any apparent solutions.

a 1. $\sqrt{x} = 6$ {36}

2. $\sqrt{5a} = 10$ {20}

3. $\sqrt{3y} + 4 = 5$ {$\frac{1}{3}$}

4. $5 - \sqrt{2m} = 3$ {2}

5. $x^{\frac{1}{2}} = 7$ {49}

6. $n^{\frac{1}{3}} = 2$ {8}

7. $x^{\frac{2}{3}} = 4$ {-8, 8}

8. $y^{\frac{3}{2}} = 8$ {4}

9. $15 = 3\sqrt{x}$ {25}

10. $2a^{\frac{1}{3}} = 8$ {64}

11. $\sqrt{x-1} = 4$ {17}

12. $\sqrt{2n-5} = 3$ {7}

13. $\sqrt[3]{y+4} = 3$ {23}

14. $\sqrt[3]{a+1} = 2$ {7}

15. $\sqrt{2x+5} - 7 = -4$ {2}

16. $-7 + \sqrt{2a-3} = -4$ {6}

17. $2\sqrt{3x-15} = 6$ {8}

18. $3\sqrt{2y+1} = -5$ ∅

19. $2a^{\frac{2}{3}} = \frac{1}{8}$ {$-\frac{1}{64}, \frac{1}{64}$}

20. $4x^{\frac{3}{2}} = -32$ ∅

21. $\sqrt[4]{x+1} = 2$ {15}

22. $\sqrt[4]{3y} + 8 = 11$ {27}

23. $2\sqrt{2n-3} + 4 = 1$ ∅

24. $\sqrt{x^2-9} = 4$ {-5, 5}

25. $\sqrt{1+x^2} = 5$ {$-2\sqrt{6}, 2\sqrt{6}$}

26. $2\sqrt{y} = 7\sqrt{2}$ {24.5}

27. $3 = \dfrac{6}{\sqrt{x}}$ {4}

28. $2 = \dfrac{8}{\sqrt{5a-4}}$ {4}

29. $5 + \sqrt[3]{a} = 1$ {-64}

30. $\sqrt{8+2x} = -6$ ∅

b 31. $x^{-\frac{1}{2}} = 2$ $\frac{1}{4}$

32. $y^{-\frac{1}{3}} = 4$ {$\frac{1}{64}$}

33. $a^{-\frac{2}{3}} = 25$ {$-\frac{1}{125}, \frac{1}{125}$}

34. $8n^{-\frac{3}{2}} = 1$ {4}

35. $\frac{1}{4}x^{-\frac{2}{3}} = 16$ {$-\frac{1}{512}, \frac{1}{512}$}

36. $\sqrt{y-2} = \dfrac{5}{\sqrt{y-2}}$ {7}

37. $\sqrt{x^2+3} = x+1$ {1}

38. $\sqrt{4y^2-1} = 2y+3$ {$-\frac{5}{6}$}

39. $\sqrt{4x-5} = \sqrt{6x-5}$ {0}

40. $\sqrt{2n-5} + \sqrt{2n+3} = 4$ {3}

8-7 Radical Equations Reducible to Quadratics

The objective for this section is on page 319.

Example 1

Solve: $\sqrt{4x+5} - \sqrt{2x-6} = 3$

$$\sqrt{4x+5} = 3 + \sqrt{2x-6}$$ ← Write with one radical on each side.

$$4x+5 = 9 + 6\sqrt{2x-6} + 2x-6$$ ← Square both sides.

$$2x+2 = 6\sqrt{2x-6}$$ ← Combine like terms.

$$x+1 = 3\sqrt{2x-6}$$ ← Divide both sides by 2.

$$x^2 + 2x + 1 = 9(2x-6)$$ ← Square both sides.

$$x^2 + 2x + 1 = 18x - 54$$

$$x^2 - 16x + 55 = 0$$ ← Combine like terms.

$$(x-5)(x-11) = 0$$ ← Factor.

$$x = 5 \quad \underline{or} \quad x = 11$$

Check: Verify that $\{5, 11\}$ is the solution set.

Example 2

Solve: $\sqrt{2x+7} - 2\sqrt{x} = -1$

$$\sqrt{2x+7} = 2\sqrt{x} - 1$$

$$2x+7 = 4x - 4\sqrt{x} + 1$$

$$4\sqrt{x} = 2x - 6$$

$$2\sqrt{x} = x - 3$$

$$4x = x^2 - 6x + 9$$

$$x^2 - 10x + 9 = 0$$

$$(x-9)(x-1) = 0$$

$$x = 1 \quad \underline{or} \quad x = 9$$

Check: $\sqrt{2+7} - 2\sqrt{1} \overset{?}{=} -1$ $\qquad$ $\sqrt{18+7} - 2\sqrt{9} \overset{?}{=} -1$

$\qquad\qquad\qquad 3 - 2 \neq -1$ $\qquad\qquad\qquad\qquad 5 - 6 = -1$

Solution set: $\{9\}$ $\quad$ The number 1 is an apparent solution.

Solve. Be sure to check for apparent solutions.

1. $\sqrt{x+2}=3$ 7

2. $\sqrt{3-x}=5$ −22

3. $\sqrt{4+2x}=-3$ ∅

4. $3x=5\sqrt{2}$ $\frac{5\sqrt{2}}{3}$

5. $2\sqrt{x}=5$ $\frac{25}{4}$

6. $5\sqrt{x}=\sqrt{3-2x}$ $\frac{1}{9}$

Exercises

Solve. Be sure to check for apparent solutions.

a

1. $\sqrt{x+2}+4=x$ {7}

2. $\sqrt{x+2}+x=4$ {2}

3. $x-3=\sqrt{4x+9}$ {10}

4. $\sqrt{x+4}+2x=13$ {5}

5. $\sqrt{x+4}-x=-8$ {12}

6. $2x-\sqrt{7x-3}=3$ {4}

7. $1-y=\sqrt{1-5y}$ {0, −3}

8. $\sqrt{x^2-8}+x=4$ {3}

9. $\sqrt{x+4}+\sqrt{x-3}=7$ {12}

10. $\sqrt{3x-5}-\sqrt{3x}=-1$ {3}

b

11. $4\sqrt{b-3}-\sqrt{b+2}=5$ {7}

12. $\sqrt{3x+1}-\sqrt{6x+1}=-2$ {8}

13. $a-\sqrt{a+3}=3$ {6}

14. $5x-\sqrt{2x+1}=4x+1$ {4}

15. $x+3=\sqrt{x-4}+7$ {4, 5}

16. $\sqrt{2n-1}=6+\sqrt{n+4}$ {221}

17. $\sqrt{x+1}+\sqrt{3x+1}=2$ {0}

18. $1+\sqrt{x-1}=\sqrt{2x-1}$ {5, 1}

19. $\dfrac{9}{\sqrt{2x-7}}=\sqrt{2x-7}$ {8}

20. $\sqrt{x}+\sqrt{1+x}=\dfrac{2}{\sqrt{1+x}}$ $\{\frac{1}{3}\}$

c

21. $\sqrt{x+7}+\sqrt{x-5}=\sqrt{3x-23}$ $\{-\frac{85}{3}\}$

22. $\sqrt{x+8}+\sqrt{3x-2}-\sqrt{8x+8}=0$ {17, 1}

23. $\sqrt{3x-11}+\sqrt{3x}=\sqrt{12x-23}$ {12}

Remember

1. Find the distance between $P(-1, 2)$ and $Q(4, -3)$. $5\sqrt{2}$

2. Find the midpoint of the segment with endpoints $P(-1, 2)$ and $Q(4, -3)$. $\left(\frac{3}{2}, -\frac{1}{2}\right)$

3. Find the distance between $A(3, 7)$ and $B(3, -5)$.   12

The answers are on page 320.

8-8 Exponential Equations

The objective for this section is on page 319.

The following property is needed to solve exponential equations.

If $a^m = a^n$, then $m = n$.　　If $m = n$, then $a^m = a^n$.

Example 1

Solve: $8 = 4^x$

$8 = 4^x$

$2^3 = (2^2)^x$ ⟵ —— Write with the same base.

$2^3 = (2)^{2x}$ ⟵ —— $(a^m)^n = a^{mn}$

$3 = 2x$ ⟵ —— If $a^m = a^n$, then $m = n$.

$\frac{3}{2} = x$

Check: $8 \overset{?}{=} 4^{\frac{3}{2}}$　　　**Solution set:** $\left\{\frac{3}{2}\right\}$

$8 \overset{?}{=} (\sqrt{4})^3$

$8 = 2^3$

Example 2

Solve: $125^{x-1} = 25$

$125^{x-1} = 25$　　　　　**Check:** $125^{x-1} = 25$

$(5^3)^{x-1} = 5^2$　　　　　　$125^{\frac{5}{3}-1} \overset{?}{=} 25$

$(5)^{3x-3} = 5^2$　　　　　　$125^{\frac{2}{3}} \overset{?}{=} 25$

$3x - 3 = 2$　　　　　　$(\sqrt[3]{125})^2 \overset{?}{=} 25$

$3x = 5$　　　　　　　$(5)^2 = 25$

$x = \frac{5}{3}$　　　　**Solution set:** $\left\{\frac{5}{3}\right\}$

Solve for x.

1. $2^x = 32$ {5}   **2.** $3^x = 81$ {4}   **3.** $9^x = 27$ $\{\frac{3}{2}\}$

4. $27^x = 81$ $\{\frac{4}{3}\}$ **5.** $2^x = \frac{1}{2}$ {-1}   **6.** $3^x = \frac{1}{9}$ {-2}

Exercises

Solve for x.

1. $2^x = 8$ {3}   **2.** $4^x = 2$ $\{\frac{1}{2}\}$ **3.** $2^x = 32$ {5}

4. $8^x = 2$ $\{\frac{1}{3}\}$ **5.** $8^x = 4$ $\{\frac{2}{3}\}$ **6.** $8^x = 0.5$ $\{-\frac{1}{3}\}$

7. $25^x = 5$ $\{\frac{1}{2}\}$ **8.** $25^x = 0.04$ {-1}   **9.** $16^x = 2$ $\{\frac{1}{4}\}$

10. $8^x = 32$ $\{\frac{5}{3}\}$ **11.** $25^x = 0.2$ $\{-\frac{1}{2}\}$ **12.** $4^x = 0.25$ {-1}

13. $4^x = 0.5$ $\{-\frac{1}{2}\}$ **14.** $27^x = 3$ $\{\frac{1}{3}\}$ **15.** $9^x = \frac{1}{27}$ $\{-\frac{3}{2}\}$

16. $8^x = \frac{1}{8}$ {-1}   **17.** $16^x = 0.5$ $\{-\frac{1}{4}\}$ **18.** $27^x = 9$ $\{\frac{2}{3}\}$

19. $9^{x-2} = 27$ $\{\frac{7}{2}\}$ **20.** $2^{-x} = 16$ {-4}   **21.** $2^{x+2} = 32$ {3}

More Challenging Problems   2. $(x^{-1} + y^{-1})^{-1} = \left(\frac{1}{x} + \frac{1}{y}\right)^{-1} = \frac{1}{\frac{1}{x} + \frac{1}{y}} = \frac{1}{\frac{y+x}{xy}} = \frac{xy}{x+y}$

1. Simplify and express without negative exponents. $\frac{1}{xy}$

$$(x+y)^{-1}(x^{-1} + y^{-1})$$

2. Show that $(x^{-1} + y^{-1})^{-1} = \frac{xy}{x+y}$. See above.   **3.** Simplify: $1 + \frac{1}{1-\sqrt{3}} - \frac{1}{1+\sqrt{3}}$

$1 - \sqrt{3}$

4. Simplify: $\left(\sqrt[6]{\sqrt[3]{a^9}}\right)^4 \left(\sqrt[6]{\sqrt{a^9}}\right)^4$ a^5 **5.** Given that $10^{2x} = 25$, find 10^{-x}. $\pm\frac{1}{5}$

PUZZLE

What is wrong with the following demonstration that $-1 = 1$?

$$\sqrt{a} \cdot \sqrt{b} = \sqrt{ab}$$

$$\sqrt{-1} \cdot \sqrt{-1} = \sqrt{(-1)(-1)}$$

$$\sqrt{(-1)^2} = \sqrt{1}$$

$$-1 = 1$$

$\sqrt{-1}$ is defined as i, and $i^2 = -1$. $\sqrt{a} \cdot \sqrt{b} = \sqrt{ab}$ when $a, b \geq 0$.

Mathematics and the Life Sciences

PERSONS seeking careers in the life sciences should obtain the broadest possible background of college-level courses in biology, physics, and mathematics. Courses in statistics, calculus, and computer programming are of increasing importance.

Some **microbiologists** study the relationship between bacteria and disease. Others specialize in studying the effects of microorganisms on soil. Still others study viruses or ways of developing methods for fighting infections.

Pathologists are concerned with the effects of diseases, parasites, and insects on human cells, tissues, and organs.

Pharmacologists conduct tests to determine the effects of drugs, gases, poisons, and dust on tissues and organs.

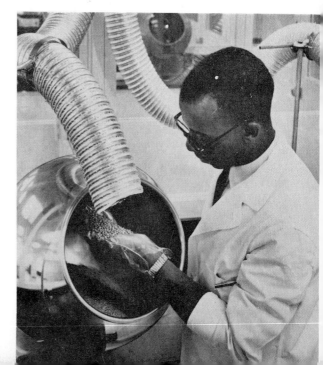

Ecologists study the effects of rainfall, temperature, altitude, and pollution on living things. For example, they extract microscopic plants from bodies of water to determine the effects of pollution.

These "before" and "after" photographs of Pittsburgh demonstrate how ecology can help solve pollution problems.

Chapter
Objectives
and
Review

Objective: To know the meanings of the important mathematical terms of this chapter.

1. Here are many of the mathematical terms used in this chapter. Be sure that you know their meanings and that you can use them correctly.

exponential equation (p. 294)   radical equation (p. 309)
principal root (p. 303)   scientific notation (p. 297)

Objective: To evaluate algebraic expressions with natural number exponents. (Section 8-1)

Simplify each expression.

2. $\left(\frac{4}{3}\right)^{-1}$ $\frac{3}{4}$

3. $(a^4)^3$ a^{12}

4. $a^4 \cdot a^3$ a^7

5. $5^7 \cdot 5^2$ 5^9

6. $7^4 \div 7^7$ 7^{-3}

7. $(2^3)^5$ 2^{15}

8. $(1735)^0$ 1

9. $(a^3 \cdot b^2)^2$ $a^6 b^4$

10. $(3^2)^4 \div 3^5$ 3^3

Objective: To express a number in scientific notation. (Section 8-2)

Write each number in scientific notation.

11. $6,800,000,000$ 6.8×10^9

12. 0.000000000587 5.87×10^{-10}

13. 5 5×10^0

Objective: To simplify algebraic expressions with integral exponents. (Section 8-3)

Use positive exponents to simplify the following.

14. $\left(\frac{2}{5}\right)^{-2}$ $\frac{25}{4}$

15. $\dfrac{a^{-1}b^{-2}}{b^{-2}a^1}$ $\frac{1}{a^2}$

16. $2^{-3} + 3^{-2}$ $\frac{17}{72}$

17. $(x + 2y)^{-1}$ $\frac{1}{x+2y}$

18. $(b^{-3})^{-2}$ b^6

19. $(c^{-7})^0$ 1

Simplify each of the following in such a way as to avoid the fraction form.

20. $\dfrac{1}{(5+2)^{-2}}$ 49

21. $\dfrac{2xy^2}{x^2zy}$ $2x^{-1}yz^{-1}$

22. $\dfrac{(a+b)^{-2}}{2(a+b)^{-1}}$

$[2(a+b)]^{-1}$

Objective: To evaluate expressions with rational exponents. (Section 8-4)

Evaluate each expression.

23. $8^{\frac{1}{3}}$ *2*

24. $81^{\frac{1}{4}}$ *3*

25. $25^{-\frac{1}{2}}$ *$\frac{1}{5}$*

26. -27^0 *−1*

Objective: To rewrite expressions involving radicals as expressions with rational number exponents. (Section 8-4)

Rewrite each expression using rational exponents.

27. $\sqrt[3]{x^2}$ *$x^{\frac{2}{3}}$*

28. $\sqrt[4]{x^5}$ *$x^{\frac{5}{4}}$*

29. $\sqrt{3x-1}$ *$(3x-1)^{\frac{1}{2}}$*

30. $\dfrac{1}{\sqrt[3]{b}}$ *$b^{-\frac{1}{3}}$*

Objective: To rewrite expressions with rational exponents as expressions with radicals. (Section 8-4)

31. $\dfrac{1}{\sqrt[4]{b^3}}$ *or* $\dfrac{1}{(\sqrt[4]{b})^3}$ *33.* $\sqrt[3]{8^5}$ *or* $(\sqrt[3]{8})^5$

Rewrite each expression using a radical.

31. $b^{-\frac{3}{4}}$ *see above*

32. $c^{\frac{1}{3}}$ *$\sqrt[3]{c}$*

33. $8^{\frac{5}{3}}$ *see above*

34. $2^{\frac{1}{2}}y^{\frac{3}{2}}$ *$\sqrt{2y^3}$*

Objective: To simplify, add, subtract, multiply, and divide radical expressions. (Section 8-5)

Simplify.

35. $108^{\frac{1}{3}}$ *$3\sqrt[3]{4}$*

36. $3\sqrt{8}+4\sqrt{18}$ *$18\sqrt{2}$*

37. $\sqrt{4}\cdot\sqrt[3]{5}$ *$2\sqrt[3]{5}$*

38. $\sqrt[3]{4}\div2^{\frac{1}{6}}$ *$8^{\frac{1}{6}}$*

39. $\sqrt{2}\cdot\sqrt[3]{2}$ *$\sqrt[6]{32}$*

40. $\sqrt[6]{36}$ *$6^{\frac{1}{3}}$*

Objective: To solve radical equations. (Sections 8-6, 8-7)

Solve. Remember to check for apparent solutions.

41. $\sqrt{x+1}=4$ *{15}*

42. $\sqrt{x}=-3$ *∅*

43. $2\sqrt{x}=7$ *$\left\{\frac{49}{4}\right\}$*

44. $\sqrt{x-2}+8=x$ *{11}*

45. $\sqrt{3x+3}-\sqrt{3x-2}=1$ *{2}*

Objective: To solve exponential equations. (Section 8-8)

Solve.

46. $4^x=32$ *$\left\{\frac{5}{2}\right\}$*

47. $9^x=27$ *$\left\{\frac{3}{2}\right\}$*

48. $4^x=\frac{1}{16}$ *{−2}*

Chapter Test

Simplify.

1. $(3^3)^2$ $3^6 = 729$

2. $(843)^0$ 1

3. $5^2 \div 5^5$ $5^{-3} = \frac{1}{125}$

4. $2^3 \cdot 2^5$ 2^8

5. Express 7,500,000,000 and 0.0000007892 in scientific notation. 7.5×10^9 7.892×10^{-7}

6. Simplify the following expression.

$$5x^{-3}y - 4x^{-1}y + \frac{3y^2}{x} - \frac{5y}{x^3} \qquad (x \neq 0) \quad \frac{y(3y-4)}{x}$$

Rewrite the following using fractional and negative exponents.

7. $\sqrt{\dfrac{x}{y}}$ $x^{\frac{1}{2}} y^{-\frac{1}{2}}$

8. $\sqrt[3]{\dfrac{a}{b^2}}$ $a^{\frac{1}{3}} b^{-\frac{2}{3}}$

9. $\dfrac{3xy}{\sqrt[4]{z^3}}$ $3xyz^{-\frac{3}{4}}$

10. $\dfrac{\sqrt[3]{m}}{\sqrt{n}}$ $m^{\frac{1}{3}} n^{-\frac{1}{2}}$

Evaluate each of the following expressions.

11. $\left(\dfrac{2}{3}\right)^{-3}$ $\frac{27}{8}$

12. $(x+y)^0$ 1

13. $36^{-\frac{1}{2}}$ $\frac{1}{6}$

14. $4^{-\frac{3}{2}}$ $\frac{1}{8}$

Solve and check.

15. $x^{\frac{1}{2}} = 2$ $\{4\}$

16. $\sqrt{2x-5} = 3$ $\{7\}$

17. $\sqrt{6x-8} + 2 = 0$ $\emptyset$

18. $\sqrt{x^2 - 5} + x = 5$ $\{3\}$

19. $8^x = 32$ $\left\{\frac{5}{3}\right\}$

20. $5^x = \dfrac{1}{125}$ $\{-3\}$

Answers to Remember

Page 301:   **1.** $2^3 \cdot 3^2$ **2.** $(2x-3)(-5x+7)$ **3.** $(x-2)(x^2+2x+4)$ **4.** $x(x+3)(x-2)$

Page 308:   **1.** $\dfrac{3 \pm \sqrt{5}}{2}$ **2.** $\dfrac{3 \pm i\sqrt{19}}{2}$ **3.** $\dfrac{-5 \pm \sqrt{137}}{8}$

Page 313:   **1.** $5\sqrt{2}$ **2.** $\left(\dfrac{3}{2}, -\dfrac{1}{2}\right)$ **3.** 12

Chapter 9
Logarithmic Functions

The objective for this section is on page 354.

By defining the replacement set for x in the exponential equation $y = 2^x$ as the set of real numbers, you can graph the equation without any "holes." The graph shows that $y = 2^x$ is a function.

Definition: An **exponential function** is defined by $f(x) = a^x$, where $a, x \in R$, $a \neq 1$, $a > 0$, and a is known as the base.

The exponential function $f(x) = 2^x$ has base 2. As x increases, the function increases; as x decreases, the function decreases. As x decreases the curve gets closer and closer to the x axis, but never touches it. The x axis is an asymptote of the graph.

From the graph, note that a change of one unit in the value of x does not always result in a change of one unit in the value of y. As x increases, a small change in x implies a large change in y. Thus, the curve becomes steeper as x increases. The steepness of the graph of the exponential function $f(x) = a^x$ depends on the value of the base a.

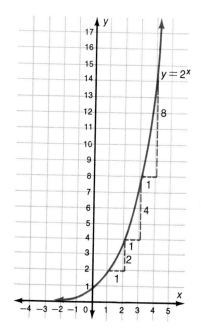

$y = 2^x$

Try These

Complete the following tables.

1. $y = 10^x$

x	−3	−2	−1	0	$\frac{1}{2}$	1	$1\frac{1}{2}$
y	0.001	0.01	0.1	1	3.162	10	31.62

(NOTE: To find $y = 10^{1\frac{1}{2}}$, write $10^{1\frac{1}{2}}$ as $10^1 \cdot 10^{\frac{1}{2}}$ and use the table of square roots on page 555.)

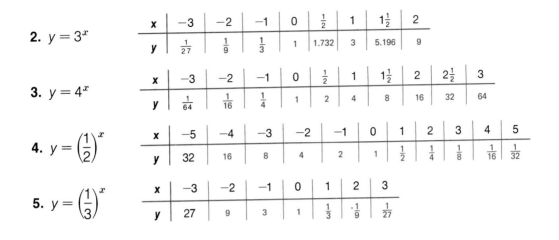

2. $y = 3^x$

x	-3	-2	-1	0	$\frac{1}{2}$	1	$1\frac{1}{2}$	2
y	$\frac{1}{27}$	$\frac{1}{9}$	$\frac{1}{3}$	1	1.732	3	5.196	9

3. $y = 4^x$

x	-3	-2	-1	0	$\frac{1}{2}$	1	$1\frac{1}{2}$	2	$2\frac{1}{2}$	3
y	$\frac{1}{64}$	$\frac{1}{16}$	$\frac{1}{4}$	1	2	4	8	16	32	64

4. $y = \left(\frac{1}{2}\right)^x$

x	-5	-4	-3	-2	-1	0	1	2	3	4	5
y	32	16	8	4	2	1	$\frac{1}{2}$	$\frac{1}{4}$	$\frac{1}{8}$	$\frac{1}{16}$	$\frac{1}{32}$

5. $y = \left(\frac{1}{3}\right)^x$

x	-3	-2	-1	0	1	2	3
y	27	9	3	1	$\frac{1}{3}$	$\frac{\cdot 1}{9}$	$\frac{1}{27}$

The graphs of the functions in Exercises 1-5 are smooth curves passing through the points given in the tables of Exercises 1-5, Try These.

Exercises

On the same set of axes, sketch the graph of the following functions. Use the tables of values that you completed in the Try These.

1. $y = 10^x$ **2.** $y = 3^x$ **3.** $y = 4^x$ **4.** $y = \left(\frac{1}{2}\right)^x$ **5.** $y = \left(\frac{1}{3}\right)^x$

Use the graphs in Exercises **1–5** to answer the questions.

6. Do the graphs have any common points? If so, specify them. <small>Yes. (0,1)</small>

7. Note the graphs of Exercises 1, 2, and 3 where a > 1. As a increases, what happens to the shape of the curves? <small>steeper</small>

8. Note the graphs of Exercises 4 and 5 where a < 1. As a increases, what happens to the shape of the curve? <small>less steep</small>

9. When a < 1, are the graphs asymptotic to the positive half of the x axis or to the negative half of the x axis? <small>Positive half.</small>

10. When a > 1, are the graphs asymptotic to the positive half of the x axis or to the negative half of the x axis? <small>Negative half.</small>

11. Will the curves ever intersect the x axis? Why? <small>No.; y will never equal 0 for any value of x.</small>

12. Is $y = a^x$ an exponential function when a = 1? Explain. <small>No; by definition of exponential function</small>

13. Sketch the graphs of $y = 2^x$ and $y = \left(\frac{1}{2}\right)^x$ on the same set of axes. Discuss the symmetry of the graphs. Do the graphs of $y = 3^x$ and $y = \left(\frac{1}{3}\right)^x$ have the same symmetry? Why or why not? <small>See key.</small>

Logarithmic Functions   **323**

14. An exponential function that is important in mathematical analysis is defined by $y = e^x$ where $e \approx 2.7182$. Sketch the graph of $y = e^x$ using the values given in the table below. It is an exponential curve.

x	−4	−3	−2	−1	0	1	2	3
y	0.02	0.05	0.14	0.37	1	2.72	7.39	20.1

*Use the graph in Exercise **14** to find approximations for the given powers of e.*

15. $e^{\frac{1}{2}}$ 1.6

16. $e^{-\frac{3}{2}}$ 0.2

17. $e^{\frac{5}{2}}$
12.2

18. Graph $y = 2^x$ and $x = 2^y$ on the same set of axes. Discuss the symmetry and asymptotic lines of the graphs. See key.

19. Prove that the graphs of $y = a^x$ and $y = \left(\frac{1}{a}\right)^x$ are symmetric with respect to the y axis. See key.

Remember

Simplify.

1. $\dfrac{3x}{4} - \dfrac{4x-5}{5}$ $\frac{20-x}{20}$

2. $\dfrac{2x+3}{x-1} - \dfrac{2x-3}{x+1}$ $\frac{10x}{x^2-1}$

3. $\dfrac{\dfrac{1}{a}+1}{\dfrac{2}{a}-1}$ $\frac{1+a}{2-a}$

4. If $\left|3a - \dfrac{1}{2}\right| = 7$, find a. $\left\{\frac{5}{2}, -\frac{13}{6}\right\}$

5. Find the sum and difference of the vectors $(4, 3)$ and $(2, -5)$.   Sum: (6, −2); Diff.: (2, 8)

6. Is $\{(2, 1), (3, 1), (4, 1)\}$ a relation? Is it a function?   Yes, Yes

The answers are on page 356.

PUZZLE

Two freight trains, 180 miles apart, start toward each other, each traveling at 40 miles per hour. A bee on the first train flies to the second at 60 miles per hour, then flies back to the first at the same rate. The bee flies back and forth in this way from one train to the other until the trains meet. How far does the bee fly?   135 miles

9-2 Using the Exponential Function

The objective for this section is on page 354.

The table below lists some integral powers of 2.

x	2^x		x	2^x		x	2^x
−8	$\frac{1}{256}$		0	1		8	256
−7	$\frac{1}{128}$		1	2		9	512
−6	$\frac{1}{64}$		2	4		10	1024
−5	$\frac{1}{32}$		3	8		11	2048
−4	$\frac{1}{16}$		4	16		12	4096
−3	$\frac{1}{8}$		5	32		13	8192
−2	$\frac{1}{4}$		6	64		14	16384
−1	$\frac{1}{2}$		7	128		15	32768

This table and the following properties of exponents can help to simplify computation.

Examples

$a^3 \cdot a^4 = a^{3+4}$

$(a^3)^4 = a^{12}$

$a^6 \div a^2 = a^4$

$\sqrt[3]{a^4} = a^{\frac{4}{3}}$

Properties

$a^m \cdot a^n = a^{m+n}$; $m, n, a \in R, a \neq 0$

$(a^m)^n = a^{mn}$; $m, n, a \in R, a \neq 0$

$\dfrac{a^m}{a^n} = a^{m-n}$; $m, n, a \in R, a \neq 0$

$\sqrt[n]{a^m} = a^{\frac{m}{n}}$; $m, a \in R, a \neq 0, n \in N$

Example 1   Evaluate: **a.** 64×512 **b.** $\sqrt[4]{4096}$

a. $64 \times 512 = 2^6 \times 2^9$ ⟵ Write as powers of 2.

$= 2^{15}$ ⟵ $a^m \cdot a^n = a^{m+n}$

$= 32{,}768$ ⟵ From the table.

b. $\sqrt[4]{4096} = (4096)^{\frac{1}{4}}$ ⟵ $\sqrt[n]{a^m} = a^{\frac{m}{n}}$

$= (2^{12})^{\frac{1}{4}}$

$= 2^3 = 8$

Example 2   Evaluate: $\sqrt{\dfrac{2048 \times 128}{256}}$

$$\sqrt{\frac{2048 \times 128}{256}} = \left(\frac{(2^{11})(2^{7})}{2^{8}} \right)^{\frac{1}{2}}$$

$$= \left(\frac{2^{18}}{2^{8}} \right)^{\frac{1}{2}}$$

$$= (2^{10})^{\frac{1}{2}}$$

$$= 2^{5}, \text{ or } 32$$

Example 3   Use the graph of $f(x) = 2^{x}$ to approximate $3^{1.3} \times 5^{0.3}$.

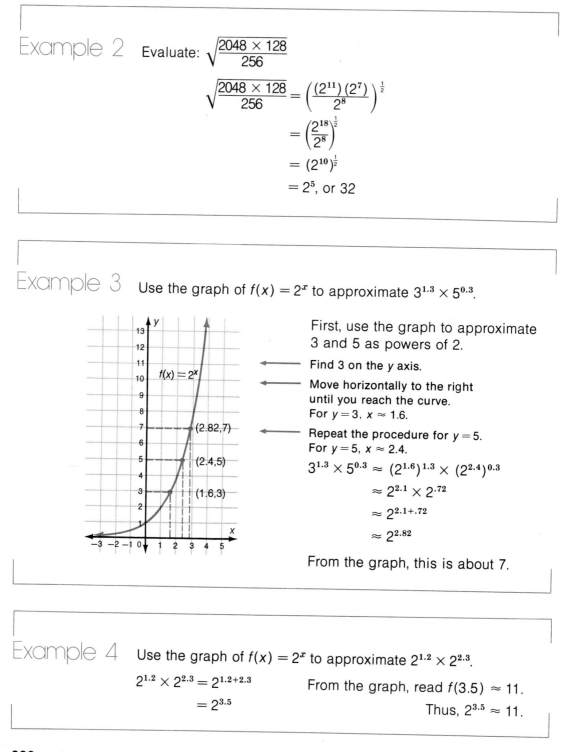

$f(x) = 2^{x}$

(2.82,7)

(2.4,5)

(1.6,3)

First, use the graph to approximate 3 and 5 as powers of 2.

Find 3 on the y axis.

Move horizontally to the right until you reach the curve. For $y = 3$, $x \approx 1.6$.

Repeat the procedure for $y = 5$. For $y = 5$, $x \approx 2.4$.

$$3^{1.3} \times 5^{0.3} \approx (2^{1.6})^{1.3} \times (2^{2.4})^{0.3}$$

$$\approx 2^{2.1} \times 2^{.72}$$

$$\approx 2^{2.1+.72}$$

$$\approx 2^{2.82}$$

From the graph, this is about 7.

Example 4   Use the graph of $f(x) = 2^{x}$ to approximate $2^{1.2} \times 2^{2.3}$.

$$2^{1.2} \times 2^{2.3} = 2^{1.2+2.3}$$

$$= 2^{3.5}$$

From the graph, read $f(3.5) \approx 11$.

Thus, $2^{3.5} \approx 11$.

Use the table of powers of 2 to evaluate each of the following.

1. $2^3 \cdot 2^5$ ₂₅₆   256

2. $2^6 \div 2^2$ 16

3. $\frac{1}{128} \times 4096$ 32

4. $32 \div \frac{1}{128}$ 4096

Use the graph of $f(x) = 2^x$ to approximate each of the following.

5. $2^{1.1} \cdot 2^{-1.5}$ 0.8

6. $3^{0.8} \div 5^{0.2}$ 1.7

Exercises

Use the table of powers of 2 to evaluate each of the following.

1. $2^{-2} \div 2^3$ $\frac{1}{32}$

2. $(2^3)^4$ 4096

3. $\sqrt[3]{2^{12}}$ 16

4. $\sqrt[4]{2^{-8}}$ $\frac{1}{4}$

5. $\frac{1}{16} \times \frac{1}{8}$ $\frac{1}{128}$

6. $32{,}768 \div 2048$ 16

7. 4^6 4096

8. 32^2 1024

9. $\left(\frac{1}{2}\right)^8$ $\frac{1}{256}$

10. $\sqrt[4]{4096}$ 8

11. $\sqrt[4]{\frac{1}{256}}$ $\frac{1}{4}$

12. $16^4 \div 4^4$ 256

Use the graph of $y = 2^x$ to approximate each of the following.

13. $2^{1.5} \times 2^{0.7}$ 4.6

14. $2^{-1.2} \times 2^{1.7}$ 1.4

15. $2^{3.1} \div 2^{1.7}$ 2.6

16. $2^{2.7} \div 2^{3.6}$ 0.5

17. $\sqrt[3]{2^{1.8}}$ 1.5

18. $\sqrt[4]{2^{-1.2}}$ 0.8

19. 7×1.6 11.2

20. 0.7×13

21. $7 \div 1.6$ 4.4

22. $0.7 \div 13$ 0.05

23. $\sqrt[4]{15}$ 2.0

24. $\sqrt[3]{5}$ 1.7
9.1 (actual answer)

Use the graph of $f(x) = 2^x$ to verify each of the following.
Simply carry out the calculations in Ex. 25-28.

25. $f(2) \times f(1.5) = f(2 + 1.5)$

26. $f(5) \div f(2) = f(5 - 2)$

27. $[f(\frac{1}{2})]^3 = f(\frac{1}{2} \times 3)$

28. $[f(4)]^{\frac{1}{3}} = f(4 \div 3)$

$f(x_1) \times f(x_2) = a^{x_1} \times a^{x_2} = a^{x_1 + x_2} = f(x_1 + x_2)$

If $(x) = a^x$, $a \neq 1$, $a > 0$, and x_1 and x_2 are fixed values of x, show that each of the following is true. $f(x_1) \div f(x_2) = a^{x_1} \div a^{x_2} = a^{x_1 - x_2} = f(x_1 - x_2)$

29. $f(x_1) \times f(x_2) = f(x_1 + x_2)$

30. $f(x_1) \div f(x_2) = f(x_1 - x_2)$

Remember

Solve each system.

1. $\begin{cases} 2x - 4y = 10 \\ x + y = 4 \end{cases}$ $\left(4\frac{1}{3}, -\frac{1}{3}\right)$

2. $\begin{cases} 3x + 6y = 3 \\ x - 4y = 4 \end{cases}$ $\left(2, -\frac{1}{2}\right)$

3. $\begin{cases} 4x + 7 = 5y \\ 8x - 10y = 5 \end{cases}$ ∅

The answers are on page 356.

The Logarithmic Function

The objective for this section is on page 354.

The inverse of the exponential function $y = 10^x$ is also a function. This inverse is called the **logarithmic function.**

$$y = \log_{10} x \quad \longleftarrow \quad \text{Read: "y is the logarithm of x to base 10."}$$

The table below gives corresponding coordinates for $y = 10^x$ and $y = \log_{10} x$. The numbers in the first column are exponents. These same numbers appear in the fourth column where they are logarithms. Thus, <u>a logarithm is an exponent.</u>

	$y = 10^x$		$y = \log_{10} x$	
x	10^x		**x**	$\log_{10} x$
−3	.001		.001	−3
−2	.01		.01	−2
−1	.1		.1	−1
0	1		1	0
1	10		10	1
2	100		100	2
3	1000		1000	3

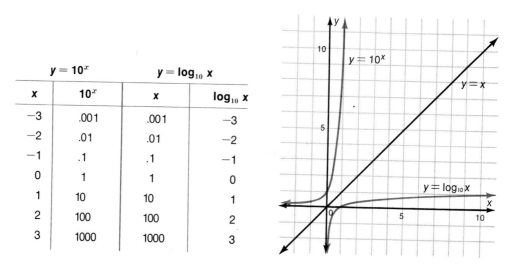

Compare the equivalent sentences in the following table.

Exponential Form	Logarithmic Form
$2^3 = 8$	$\log_2 8 = 3$
$10^3 = 1000$	$\log_{10} 1000 = 3$
$3^{-2} = \dfrac{1}{9}$	$\log_3 \dfrac{1}{9} = -2$
$3^5 = 243$	$\log_3 243 = 5$

This leads to the following definition.

328   Chapter 9

Definition: The **logarithmic function** $y = \log_a x$ is the inverse of the exponential function $y = a^x$, $a \neq 1$, $a > 0$. That is,

$$y = \log_a x \text{ if and only if } x = a^y.$$

A value of the logarithmic function is a **logarithm.**

Example 1   Find $\log_{10} 1000$.

$\log_{10} 1000 = y$ if and only if $10^y = 1000$.   ⟵   By definition

Thus, $y = 3$ and $\log_{10} 1000 = 3$.

Example 2   Find $\log_2 32$.

$\log_2 32 = y$ if and only if $2^y = 32$.   ⟵   By definition

Since $2^5 = 32$,

$\log_2 32 = 5$.

Example 3   Approximate $\log_{10} 65$ from the graph of $y = \log_{10} x$.

$y = \log_{10} 65$

$10^y = 65$ ⟵ $1 < y < 2$

$10^{1+d} = 65$ ⟵   Represent y as $1 + d$, where $0 < d < 1$.

$10^1 \cdot 10^d = 65$

$10^d = 6.5$

$\log_{10} 6.5 = d$

$0.8 = d$ ⟵   Approximate d from the graph.

$1.8 = d + 1$

$1.8 = \log_{10} 65$ ⟵   Since $y = d + 1$.

Try These

1. What is the domain of $y = \log_{10} x$?   Positive real numbers

2. What is the range of $y = \log_{10} x$?   Real numbers

3. Which axis is the asymptote for the graph of $y = \log_{10} x$?   y axis

Express in logarithmic form.

4. $2^3 = 8$ $\log_2 8 = 3$

5. $3^2 = 9$ $\log_3 9 = 2$

6. $10^{-2} = \frac{1}{100}$ $\log_{10} \frac{1}{100} = -2$

7. $6^3 = 216$ $\log_6 216 = 3$

8. $4^{0.5} = 2$ $\log_4 2 = 0.5$

9. $0.125^{\frac{1}{3}} = 0.5$ $\log_{0.125} 0.5 = \frac{1}{3}$

Express in exponential form.

10. $\log_2 16 = 4$ $2^4 = 16$

11. $\log_3 27 = 3$ $3^3 = 27$

12. $\log_8 64 = 2$ $8^2 = 64$

13. $\log_{0.5} 0.25 = 2$ $0.5^2 = 0.25$

14. $\log_2 \frac{1}{8} = -3$ $2^{-3} = \frac{1}{8}$

15. $\log_{10} 0.001 = -3$ $10^{-3} = 0.001$

Exercises

Evaluate.

1. $\log_{10} 10{,}000$ 4

2. $\log_2 8$ 3

3. $\log_2 16$ 4

4. $\log_2 64$ 6

5. $\log_{10} 0.01$ -2

6. $\log_{10} 0.0001$ -4

7. $\log_{10} 10$ 1

8. $\log_2 \frac{1}{4}$ -2

9. $\log_3 \frac{1}{27}$ -3

10. $\log_{10} 1$ 0

11. $\log_3 1$ 0

12. $\log_{10} \sqrt{10}$ $\frac{1}{2}$

13. $\log_{27} 81$ $\frac{4}{3}$

14. $\log_3 \frac{1}{9}$ -2

15. $\log_8 32$ $\frac{5}{3}$

16. $\log_{\frac{1}{2}} 8$ -3

17. $\log_{\frac{1}{3}} 27$ -3

18. $\log_{\sqrt{2}} 16$ 8

In Column A, insert two consecutive powers of 10 to make a true statement. Then use this information to insert two consecutive integers in the blanks in Column B to make a true statement.

A	B
$\underline{10^2} < 562 < \underline{10^3}$;	$\underline{2} < \log_{10} 562 < \underline{3}$
19. $\underline{?\ 10^1} < 50 < \underline{?}$; 10^2	$\underline{?\ 1} < \log_{10} 50 < \underline{?}$ 2
20. $\underline{?\ 10^1} < 30 < \underline{?}$; 10^2	$\underline{?\ 1} < \log_{10} 30 < \underline{?}$ 2
21. $\underline{?\ 10^1} < 15 < \underline{?}$; 10^2	$\underline{?\ 1} < \log_{10} 15 < \underline{?}$ 2

	A	B

22. $\underline{?\ 10^0} < 4 < \underline{\ ?\ }$; 10^1 $\underline{\ ?\ }0 < \log_{10} 4 < \underline{\ ?\ }1$

23. $\underline{?\ 10^2} < 697 < \underline{\ ?\ 10^3}$; $\underline{\ ?\ }2 < \log_{10} 697 < \underline{\ ?\ }3$

24. $\underline{?\ 10^3} < 1642 < \underline{\ ?\ }$; 10^4 $\underline{\ ?\ }3 < \log_{10} 1642 < \underline{\ ?\ }4$

Determine b, x, or y.

25. $\log_b 64 = 3$ $b = 4$

26. $\log_b 32 = 5$ 2

27. $\log_b 8 = \frac{3}{2}$ $b = 4$

28. $\log_3 x = 4$ $x = 81$

29. $\log_2 x = 7$ 128

30. $\log_{10} x = -3$ $x = 0.001$

31. $\log_{10} 1 = y$ $y = 0$

32. $\log_4 8 = y$ $y = \frac{3}{2}$

33. $\log_{\frac{1}{8}} \frac{1}{16} = y$ $y = \frac{4}{3}$

Use the graph of $y = 10^x$ to approximate each number.

34. $\log_{10} 3000$ 3.5

35. $\log_{10} 20{,}000$ 4.3

36. $\log_{10} 46$ 1.7

Use a large sheet of graph paper and graph the logarithmic functions in Exercises 37–39 on the same axes.

37. $y = \log_{10} x$ See page 328.

x	$\frac{1}{100}$	$\frac{1}{10}$	1	2	4	6	8	10	12	14	16	18	20
y	−2	−1	0	.30	.60	.78	.90	1	1.08	1.15	1.20	1.26	1.30

38.

x	$\frac{1}{16}$	$\frac{1}{8}$	$\frac{1}{4}$	$\frac{1}{2}$	1	2	4	8	16
y	−4	−3	−2	−1	0	1	2	3	4

38. $y = \log_2 x$, with $x = \frac{1}{16}, \frac{1}{8}, \frac{1}{4}, \frac{1}{2}, 1, 2, 4, 8, 16$ See above.

39. $y = \log_3 x$, with $x = \frac{1}{27}, \frac{1}{9}, \frac{1}{3}, 1, 3, 9, 27$

x	$\frac{1}{27}$	$\frac{1}{9}$	$\frac{1}{3}$	1	3	9	27
y	−3	−2	−1	0	1	2	3

Use the graphs of Exercises 37–39 to answer the following questions.

40. Do the graphs have a point in common? If so, which one(s)? Yes; (1, 0)

41. As the base for the logarithms increases, describe the shape of the curves. Curves rise less steeply to the right.

42. Is the logarithm of a negative number a real number? No

43. If $x > 1$, is the logarithm of x a positive number or a negative number? Positive

44. If $x = 1$, what is its logarithm with any base? 0

45. If $0 < x < 1$, is the logarithm of x a positive number or a negative number? Negative

Let M and N be any positive real numbers, and let $\log_{10} M = t$, $\log_{10} N = r$. Prove the following relationships.

46. $\log_{10} (M \times N) = \log_{10} M + \log_{10} N$ See key.

47. $\log_{10} \left(\frac{M}{N}\right) = \log_{10} M - \log_{10} N$. See key.

48. $\log_{10} M^s = s \log_{10} M$, where s is any real number. See key.

9-4 Common Logarithms

The objective for this section is on page 355.

Logarithms with base 10 are **common logarithms.** It is customary to write log 100 rather than $\log_{10} 100$. The table shows the logarithms for some powers of ten. The logarithms of numbers other than the integral powers of ten are irrational numbers. The irrational numbers are approximated by rational numbers, because *each positive real number can be expressed as ten raised to some exponent.*

Exponential Form	Logarithmic Form
$10{,}000 = 10^4$	$\log 10{,}000 = 4$
$1{,}000 = 10^3$	$\log 1000 = 3$
$100 = 10^2$	$\log 100 = 2$
$10 = 10^1$	$\log 10 = 1$
$1 = 10^0$	$\log 1 = 0$
$0.1 = 10^{-1}$	$\log 0.1 = -1$
$0.01 = 10^{-2}$	$\log 0.01 = -2$
$0.001 = 10^{-3}$	$\log 0.001 = -3$

The table on pages 548–549 is a four-place table that includes the logarithms of 900 numbers from 1.00 through 9.99. The logarithms range from 0 to .9996. Note that the decimal point for the logarithm is omitted in the table.

The column headed N contains numbers from 1.0 to 9.9. The entries in the column headed 0 are the logarithms of the corresponding numbers in the N column. Except for 1, the logarithms are approximations. For convenience, however, we use the symbol = when writing statements that involve logarithms. Use the following portion of the table for Examples 1 and 2.

N	0	1	2	3	4	5	6	7	8	9
5.8	7634	7642	7649	7657	7664	7672	7679	7686	7694	7701
5.9	7709	7716	7723	7731	7738	7745	7752	7760	7767	7774

Example 1

Find log 5.8 and log 5.80.

Find 5.8 in the N column.

$\log 5.80 = 0.7634$ ◄——— Read the entry to the right of 5.8 in the 0-column.

$\log 5.80 = 0.7634$ ◄——— Since 5.8 = 5.80

Example 2 Find log 5.84 and log 5.88.

Find 5.8 in the *N* column.

log 5.84 = 0.7664 ◄─────── Move horizontally to the right until you reach the column headed 4.

log 5.88 = 0.7694 ◄─────── Move horizontally to the right until you reach the column headed 8.

A table of logarithms can be used in two ways. Given a number *N*, you can find its logarithm. Also, given a logarithm (exponent), you can find the corresponding number *N*, called the <u>antilogarithm</u> (abbreviated antilog).

Definition: Antilogarithm

$$N = \text{antilog } L \text{ if and only if } L = \log_a N$$

Example 3 Find antilog 0.7767. That is, find *N* if log *N* = 0.7767.

Find 7767 in the body of the table. It is in the same row as 5.9 and under the column headed by 8. Thus, *N* = 5.98.

Example 4 Find antilog 0.8267. That is, find *N* when log *N* = 0.8267.

Locate 8267 in the same row as 6.7 and under the column headed by 1. Thus, antilog 0.8267 = 6.71 = *N*.

Example 5 Find *x* if $10^x = 3.26$.

log 3.26 = *x* ◄─────── Write in logarithmic form.

x = 0.5132 ◄─────── From the table.

Thus, log 3.26 = 0.5132 and $10^{0.5132} = 3.26$.

Use the table of logarithms to find the following numbers.

1. log 1.0 .0000   **2.** log 3.7 .5682   **3.** log 6.2 .7924

4. log 8.41 .9248   **5.** log 9.99 .9996   **6.** antilog .2553 1.8

7. antilog .7160 5.2   **8.** antilog .8451 7.0   **9.** antilog .8899 7.76

Exercises

Use the table to find these logarithms.

1. log 6.75 0.8293   **2.** log 4.32 0.6355   **3.** log 1.76 0.2455

4. log 7.84 0.8943   **5.** log 3.60 0.5563   **6.** log 7.03 0.8470

7. log 4.99 0.6981   **8.** log 4.00 0.6021   **9.** log 1.06 0.0253

10. log 8.63 0.9360   **11.** log 6.01 0.7789   **12.** log 9.65 0.9845

Use the table to find x.

13. $10^x = 4.85$ 0.6857   **14.** $10^x = 5.96$ 0.7752   **15.** $10^x = 4.09$ 0.6117

16. $10^x = 1.26$ 0.1004   **17.** $10^x = 9.86$ 0.9939   **18.** log x = .4624 2.90

19. log x = .6170 4.14   **20.** log x = .7316 5.39   **21.** log x = .8639 7.31

22. $10^{.9294} = x$ 8.50   **23.** $10^{.3464} = x$ 2.22   **24.** antilog .9886 = x 9.74

25. antilog .8615 = x 7.27   **26.** antilog .0253 = x 1.06   **27.** antilog .6096 = x 4.07

Remember

Determine the nature of the roots of each quadratic equation.

1. $x^2 - 4x + 4$ Rational, real, equal   **2.** $x^2 - 3x + 1 = 0$ Irrational, real, unequal   **3.** $x^2 + 2x + 10 = 0$ Complex, unequal

The answers are on page 356.

PUZZLE

What is the next number in this sequence?

11, 31, 71, 91, 32, 92, 13, 73, ___?___ 14; Each number is the reverse of the two digit primes in order of magnitude

9-5 Properties of Logarithms

The objectives for this section are on page 355.

You can multiply any two real numbers M and N by expressing them as powers of 10, adding the exponents, and locating the appropriate power in a table.

Theorem 9-1: Logarithm of a Product

The logarithm of the product of two real numbers M and N is the sum of the logarithms of the numbers. That is,

$$\log (M \cdot N) = \log M + \log N.$$

Proof: Let

$$\log M = a \quad \text{and} \quad \log N = b.$$

Then

$$10^a = M \quad \text{and} \quad 10^b = N.$$

Thus,

$$M \cdot N = 10^a \cdot 10^b$$
$$= 10^{a+b}$$

So,

$$\log (M \cdot N) = a + b$$

or,

$$\log (M \cdot N) = \log M + \log N.$$

Example 1   Use logarithms to compute 2.36×1.75.

$$\log (2.36 \times 1.75) = \log 2.36 + \log 1.75$$
$$= 0.3729 + 0.2430$$
$$= 0.6159$$

Now look in the table for the number closest to 6159 and determine its antilog. The closest number is 6160.

$$\text{antilog } 0.6160 = 4.13$$

Thus, 2.36×1.75 is about 4.13.

Theorem 9-2: Logarithm of a Quotient

The logarithm of a quotient of two real numbers M and N is the difference of the logarithms of the two numbers. That is,

$$\log (M \div N) = \log M - \log N.$$

Proof: Let

Let	$\log M = a$ and $\log N = b$.
Then	$10^a = M$ and $10^b = N$
Thus,	$M \div N = 10^a \div 10^b$
	$= 10^{a-b}$
So,	$\log (M \div N) = a - b$
or	$\log (M \div N) = \log M - \log N$

Theorem 9-3: The logarithm of a real number M raised to a power n is the product of the exponent and the logarithm of that number. That is,

$$\log N^a = a \log N.$$

Proof:

Let	$\log N = b.$
Then	$10^b = N$
and	$(10^b)^a = N^a$
or	$10^{ab} = N^a.$
Then	$\log N^a = ab.$
Since	$\log N = b,$
then	$\log N^a = a \log N.$

Example 2 Use logarithms to compute $9.99 \div 3.56$.

$\log 9.99 = 0.9996 \qquad \log 3.56 = 0.5514$

$\log (9.99 \div 3.56) = \log 9.99 - \log 3.56$ ◀——— Theorem 9-2

$= 0.9996 - 0.5514$

$= 0.4482$

antilog $0.4482 = 2.81$ ◀——— Thus, $9.99 \div 3.56$ is about 2.81.

Example 3   Use logarithms to compute $(4.73)^{\frac{1}{3}}$.

$$\log 4.73 = 0.6749$$

$$\tfrac{1}{3} \log 4.73 = 0.2250 \longleftarrow \text{Theorem 9-3}$$

$$\text{antilog } 0.2250 = 1.68$$

Thus, $(4.73)^{\frac{1}{3}}$ is about 1.68.

Try These

1. $\log M \cdot N = \underline{\ ?\ }$ **2.** $\log \dfrac{M}{N} = \underline{\ ?\ }$ **3.** $\log M^a = \underline{\ ?\ }$ **4.** $\log \sqrt[a]{M} = \underline{\ ?\ }$

$\log M + \log N$ $\log M - \log N$ $a \log M$ $\frac{1}{a} \log M$

Express as the logarithm of a single number.

5. $\log 4 + \log 9$ log 36

6. $\log 12 - \log 3$ log 4

7. $2 \log 5 + 3 \log 2$ log 200

8. $\frac{1}{2} \log 64 - 2 \log 4$ $\log \frac{1}{2}$

9. $\log 4 + \log 2 + \log 7$ log 56

10. $\log 8 - \log 2 + \log 6$ log 24

Exercises

Use logarithms to compute the following.

1. 4.91×1.05 5.16

2. $7.09 \div 3.62$ 1.96

3. $(2.76)^2$ 7.62

4. $\sqrt[4]{4.62}$ 1.47

5. 3.25×1.97 6.40

6. 2.34×2.43 5.69

7. $(1.11)^8$ 2.30

8. $\sqrt{4.62}$ 1.36

9. $\sqrt[4]{6.25}$ 1.58

10. 3.21×2.45 7.86

11. $(3.65)(1.83)$ 6.68

12. $8.91 \div 4.10$ 2.17

13. $(1.21)^4$ 2.14

14. $\sqrt[3]{9.99}$ 2.15

15. $(1.65)(3.83)$ 6.32

16. $(1.12)^3$ 1.40

17. $\sqrt[3]{7.06}$ 1.92

18. $9.81 \div 1.04$ 9.43

19. $\sqrt{6.93}$ 1.47

20. $8.42 \div 7.63$ 1.10

21. 3.26×1.25 4.08

22. $8.00 \div 3.76$ 2.13

23. $(1.51)^4$ 5.20

24. $\sqrt[4]{4.50}$ 1.46

Classify as True or False.

25. $\log \dfrac{10^5}{10^2} = \log 10^5 - \log 10^2$ True.

26. $\dfrac{\log 10^5}{\log 10^2} = \log 10^5 - \log 10^2$ False.

Classify as True or False.

27. $\log 10^n = \log n \cdot 10$ <small>False.</small>

28. $\log 10^n = n \log 10$ <small>True.</small>

29. $\log \dfrac{10^n}{10^m} = \log 10^n - \log 10^m$ <small>True.</small>

30. $\dfrac{\log 10^n}{\log 10^m} = \log 10^n - \log 10^m$ <small>False.</small>

31. $\log M^2 = 2 \log M$ <small>True.</small>

32. $\dfrac{\log M}{\log N} = \log M - \log N$ <small>False.</small>

33. $\log M^{\frac{1}{2}} = \dfrac{1}{2} \log M$ <small>True.</small>

34. $\log \dfrac{a}{b} = \dfrac{1}{b} \log a$ <small>False.</small>

35. $\log \sqrt{45} = \sqrt{\log 45}$ <small>False.</small>

36. $\log \sqrt[q]{m^p} = \dfrac{p}{q} \log m$ <small>True.</small>

37. $\log a^2 b = 2 \log a + \log b$ <small>True.</small>

38. $\log \sqrt{ab} = \frac{1}{2} \log a + \log b$ <small>False.</small>

39. If $5^4 = 625$, then $\log_4 625 = 5$. <small>False.</small>

40. $\log 1350 = \log 1.35 + \log 10^3$ <small>True.</small>

Given log 2 = .3010, log 3 = .4771 and log 5 = .6990, find:

41. $\log 30$ <small>1.4771</small>

42. $\log 24$ <small>1.3801</small>

43. $\log 45$ <small>1.6532</small>

44. $\log 7.5$ <small>0.8751</small>

45. $\log \sqrt{20}$ <small>0.6505</small>

46. $\log 360$ <small>2.5562</small>

Solve each equation.

47. $\log(x + 3) + \log 2 = 0$ <small>$x = -2\frac{1}{2}$</small>

48. $\log 8 - \log(n - 4) = 1$ <small>$n = 4.8$</small>

49. $3 \log_2 a = 6$ <small>$4 = a$</small>

50. $\log_3(2x + 3) = 4$ <small>$39 = x$</small>

Remember

Write each number in scientific notation.

1. 284750 <small>2.8475 × 10⁵</small>   **2.** 5 <small>5 × 10⁰</small>   **3.** −871 <small>−8.71 × 10²</small>   **4.** 0.00053 <small>5.3 × 10⁻⁴</small>   **5.** 0.10005 <small>1.0005 × 10⁻¹</small>   **6.** 0.02007 <small>2.007 × 10⁻²</small>

The answers are on page 356.

PUZZLE

Answer to Puzzle: No. Color alternate squares red and black. The two deleted squares are the same color. Each small strip covers one red and one black. This is impossible.

From a board that measures 8 centimeters by 8 centimeters, a 1–centimeter by 1–centimeter square is cut from diagonally opposite corners. Can the remainder of the board be covered by rectangular strips that measure 2 centimeters by 1 centimeter? (No overlapping is allowed). <small>See above.</small>

9-6 Characteristic and Mantissa

The objective for this section is on page 355.

Since any positive real number can be expressed in scientific notation, you can use the table of logarithms for any positive number.

Example 1   Find the logarithm of 13,600.

$$13{,}600 = 1.36 \times 10^4 \qquad \longleftarrow \text{Write in scientific notation.}$$
$$\log 13{,}600 = \log\ (1.36 \times 10^4)$$
$$\log 13{,}600 = \log 1.36 + \log 10^4 \quad \longleftarrow \text{Theorem 9-1}$$
$$\log 13{,}600 = 0.1335 + 4 = 4.1335$$

Every logarithm consists of two parts: the integral part, called the **characteristic,** and the part to the right of the decimal point, called the **mantissa.** In log $13{,}600 = 4.1335$, the characteristic is 4 and the mantissa is .1335.

Example 2   Find the logarithm of 275. Identify the characteristic and mantissa.

$$\log 275 = \log\ (2.75 \times 10^2) \quad \longleftarrow 275 = 2.75 \times 10^2$$
$$\log 2.75 + \log 10^2 = .4393 + 2 = 2.4393.$$

The characteristic is 2; the mantissa is .4393.

The mantissa of a logarithm is <u>always</u> kept nonnegative so that it may be found in the table. The characteristic may be positive, negative, or zero. Negative characteristics are associated with numbers between 0 and 1.

Logarithmic Functions   **339**

Example 3 Find the logarithm of 0.0342, and identify the characteristic and mantissa.

$$\log 0.0342 = \log 3.42 + \log 10^{-2} \longleftarrow \quad 0.0342 = (3.42 \times 10^{-2})$$
$$= .5340 + -2, \text{ or } -2 + .5340$$

The characteristic is -2; the mantissa is $+.5340$.

Note that in Example 3, the mantissa is positive and the characteristic is negative. Logarithms with negative characteristics are written in a standard form. You know that $-2 = 8 - 10 = 18 - 20$, etc. Therefore, write

$$-2 + .5340 \quad \text{as} \quad 8.5340 - 10.$$

Note that the characteristic is still -2, since $8 - 10 = -2$.

Example 4 Find the antilog of $9.3263 - 10$.

$2.12 \longleftarrow$ Look up 3263 in the table.
$-1 \longleftarrow$ Characteristic: $9 - 10$
$2.12 \times 10^{-1} \longleftarrow$ Meaning in scientific notation.

Thus, the number whose logarithm is $9.3263 - 10$ is 0.212.

Try These   State the characteristic of each logarithm.

1. log 42 1   2. log 325 2   3. log 7.86 0   4. log 0.842 −1

Find the logarithm of each number.

5. 97400 4.9886   6. 12.3 1.0899   7. 1.23 0.0899   8. 0.123
                                                                    9.0899 − 10

Find the antilogarithm of each number.

9. 2.7016 503   10. 1.9805 95.6   11. 9.8768 − 10   12. 7.3945 − 10
                                                0.753   0.00248

Exercises

Given log 3.62 = 0.5587, find the logarithm of each number.

1. 362 2.5587   **2.** 36.2 1.5587   **3.** 36,200 4.5587   **4.** 0.0362 8.5587− 10

Given log 0.7230 = 9.8591 − 10, find the logarithm of each number.

5. 0.07230 8.8591− 10   **6.** 7.230 0.8591   **7.** 7230 3.8591   **8.** 72.3 1.8591

Find the logarithm of each number. When the characteristic is negative, write the logarithm in standard form.

9. 42.7 1.6304

10. 5340 3.7275

11. 432 2.6355

12. .00623 7.7945− 10

13. .000752 6.8762− 10

14. 9.83 0.9926

15. 367,000 5.5647

16. .00000456 4.6590 − 10

17. 50 1.6990

18. .843 9.9258 − 10

19. 62,800 4.7980

20. .0106 8.0253 − 10

21. 720.00 2.8573

22. .000095 5.9777 − 10

23. 83.40 1.9212

24. .777 9.8904 − 10

25. .003 7.4771 − 10

26. 70,700 4.8494

27. 0.0055 7.7404 − 10

28. 9860 3.9939

29. .001 7.0000 − 10

Find the antilog to three digits of the following logarithms.

30. 2.8351 684

31. 1.9818 95.9

32. 3.2672 1850

33. 9.3118 − 10 0.205

34. 6.7372 − 10 0.000546

35. 8.9533 − 10 0.0898

36. 1.7143 51.8

37. 2.9085 810

38. 4.4713 29,600

39. 7.8461 − 10 0.00702

40. 8.4841 − 10 0.0305

41. 9.7298 − 10 0.537

42. 21.9647 9.22 × 10^{21}

43. 3.3096 2,040

44. 1.5539 35.8

45. 7.8007 − 10 0.00632

46. 4.9101 − 10 0.00000813

47. 5.3892 − 10 0.0000245

Remember

Perform the indicated operations. Write the answers in exponential form.

1. $3^5 \cdot 3^4$ 3^9

2. $5^{12} \div 5^8$ 5^4

3. $(3^5)^4$ 3^{20}

4. $\sqrt{15}$ $15^{\frac{1}{2}}$

5. $\sqrt{62}$ $62^{\frac{1}{2}}$

6. $\dfrac{5^7 \cdot 5^9}{5^4}$ 5^{12}

The answers are on page 356.

Logarithmic Functions   **341**

9-7 Computation with Logarithms

The objective for this section is on page 355.

Example 1

Use logarithms to multiply: 673×52.7

$$\log 673 = 2.\underline{\qquad}$$
$$\frac{\log 52.7 = 1.\underline{\qquad}}{\log(673 \times 52.7) =}$$

← Write the characteristic for each factor.

$$\log 673 = 2.8280$$
$$\frac{\log 52.7 = 1.7218}{\log(673 \times 52.7) = 4.5498}$$

← Write the mantissa for each logarithm.

$$\text{antilog } 4.5498 = 35,500$$

← Find the antilog.

You can estimate to check: $700 \times 50 = 35,000$.

In subtracting logarithms, it is sometimes necessary to add 10 (or some multiple of 10) to the number you are subtracting from, and then to subtract 10 (or the same multiple of 10).

$$0.9154 = 10.9154 - 10 = 20.9154 - 20$$

Add 10.   Subtract 10.   Add 20.   Subtract 20.

This is a necessary step to keep the mantissa positive.

Example 2

Use logarithms to divide: $8.23 \div 12.4$.

$$\log 8.23 = 0.9154$$
$$\log 12.4 = 1.0934$$

← Since $0.9154 < 1.0934$, the mantissa will <u>not</u> be positive when you subtract.

$$\log 8.23 = 0.9154 = 10.9154 - 10$$
$$\log 12.4 = 1.0934 = 1.0934$$

← Add 10 and subtract 10.

$$\log(8.23 \div 12.4) = 9.8220 - 10$$
$$\text{antilog}(9.8220 - 10) = 0.664$$

← Estimate to check: $8 \div 12 \approx 0.67$

Example 3

Use logarithms to evaluate: $\sqrt[3]{0.734}$

$\log \sqrt[3]{0.734} = \frac{1}{3}(\log 0.734)$ ◄——— Since $\sqrt[3]{0.734} = (0.734)^{\frac{1}{3}}$.

$\log 0.734 = 9.8657 - 10$ ◄——— The characteristic is −1,

$\frac{1}{3}(\log 0.734) = 3.2886 - 3\frac{1}{3}$ so write in standard form.

Since $\frac{1}{3}(-10) = -3\frac{1}{3}$, move the decimal point $\frac{1}{3}$ place to the left, which is impossible. Therefore, rewrite the logarithm of 0.734 in a form that will produce an integer when it is multiplied by $\frac{1}{3}$ (or divided by 3).

$\log 0.734 = 29.8657 - 30$ ◄——— Since $\frac{1}{3}(-30) = -10$

$\frac{1}{3}(\log 0.734) = 9.9552 - 10$

antilog $(9.9552 - 10) = 0.902$ ◄——— Estimate: $0.734 \approx 1$, $\sqrt[3]{1} = 1$.

Example 4

Use logarithms to evaluate: $\sqrt{\dfrac{130 \times 25.2}{0.78}}$

$\log \sqrt{\dfrac{130 \times 25.2}{0.78}} = \frac{1}{2}[(\log 130 + \log 25.2) - \log 0.78]$

$= \frac{1}{2}[(2.1139 + 1.4014) - (9.8921 - 10)]$

$= \frac{1}{2}[3.5153 - (9.8921 - 10)]$

$= \frac{1}{2}[13.5153 - 10 - (9.8921 - 10)]$

$= \frac{1}{2}(3.6232)$

$= 1.8116$

antilog $1.8116 = 64.8$ ◄——— The check is left for you.

Try These
Subtract the lower logarithm from the upper. Be sure to change the form of the upper so that the mantissa in the result is positive. State the characteristic of the result.

1. 2.3154
2. 4.2760
8.0394 − 10; −2

2. 0.2391
1.4562
8.7829 − 10; −2

3. 2.2345
9.6372 − 10
2.5973; 2

Perform the indicated operations. State the characteristic of the result.

4. 2.1389
    ×4   8.5556
      ‾‾‾‾‾

5. 9.3472 − 10
      ×2   18.6944 − 20; −2
      ‾‾‾‾‾‾‾

6. 25.7193 − 30; −5
    8.5731 − 10
           ×3
      ‾‾‾‾‾‾

7. 6.3857 ÷ 2   3.1929; 3

8. (7.4825 − 10) ÷ 3   9.1608 − 10; −1

9. (8.6134 − 10) ÷ 4
     4.6534 − 5; −1

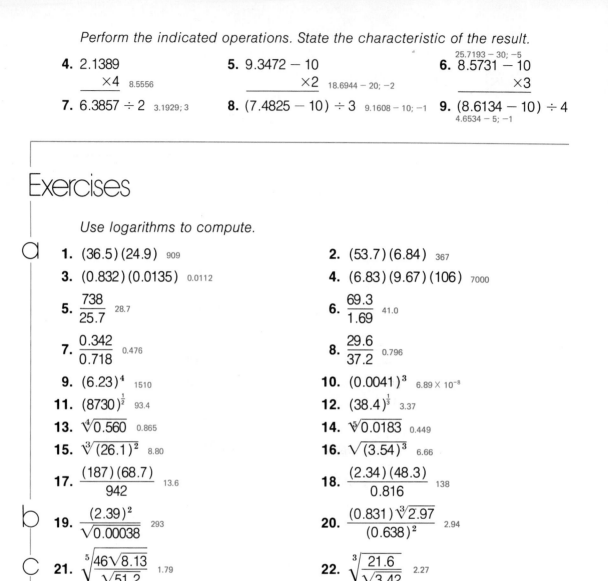

Exercises

Use logarithms to compute.

a

1. (36.5)(24.9)   909

2. (53.7)(6.84)   367

3. (0.832)(0.0135)   0.0112

4. (6.83)(9.67)(106)   7000

5. $\dfrac{738}{25.7}$ 28.7

6. $\dfrac{69.3}{1.69}$ 41.0

7. $\dfrac{0.342}{0.718}$ 0.476

8. $\dfrac{29.6}{37.2}$ 0.796

9. $(6.23)^4$ 1510

10. $(0.0041)^3$ 6.89 × 10⁻⁸

11. $(8730)^{\frac{1}{2}}$ 93.4

12. $(38.4)^{\frac{1}{3}}$ 3.37

13. $\sqrt[4]{0.560}$ 0.865

14. $\sqrt[4]{0.0183}$ 0.449

15. $\sqrt[3]{(26.1)^2}$ 8.80

16. $\sqrt{(3.54)^3}$ 6.66

17. $\dfrac{(187)(68.7)}{942}$ 13.6

18. $\dfrac{(2.34)(48.3)}{0.816}$ 138

b

19. $\dfrac{(2.39)^2}{\sqrt{0.00038}}$ 293

20. $\dfrac{(0.831)\sqrt[3]{2.97}}{(0.638)^2}$ 2.94

c

21. $\sqrt[5]{\dfrac{46\sqrt{8.13}}{\sqrt{51.2}}}$ 1.79

22. $\sqrt[3]{\dfrac{21.6}{\sqrt{3.42}}}$ 2.27

Remember

1. Find the slope of a line parallel to the line defined by $3x − 4y = 7$. $\frac{3}{4}$

2. Find the slope of a line perpendicular to the line defined by $7y + 3x = 5$. $\frac{7}{3}$

3. Find the equation of the line that contains (2, 5) and (−2, 3). $y = \frac{1}{2}x + 4$

The answers are on page 356.

9-8 Interpolation

The objective for this section is on page 355.

The table of logarithms in this book cannot be used directly when a number has more than three digits. But you can **interpolate** or "read between" the numbers. Interpolation is based on the properties of similar triangles.

Example 1   Find log 2.624.

The graph is an enlarged view of a small portion of the graph of $y = \log x$. To find log 2.624 is to find the y coordinate of point C.

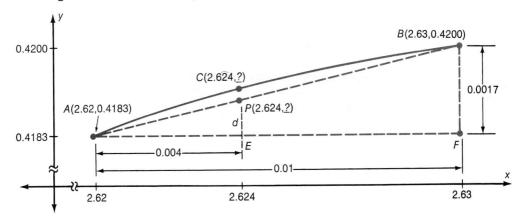

Since P is very close to C, the key to interpolation is assuming that arc AB is the same as segment AB. Thus, the y coordinate of P will provide a close approximation for the y coordinate of C. The y coordinate is $0.4183 + d$.

$$\triangle AEP \text{ is similar to } \triangle AFB.$$

Therefore, $$\frac{AE}{AF} = \frac{EP}{FB}, \text{ or } \frac{0.004}{0.01} = \frac{d}{0.0017}$$

Thus, $d \approx 0.0007$, and the y coordinate of P is $0.4183 + 0.0007 = 0.4190$. The y coordinate of C is also 0.4190.

Thus, $$\log 2.624 = 0.4190.$$

Example 2 shows the use of the table of logarithms.

Example 2 Find log 2.624.

$$0.01 \begin{cases} 0.004 \begin{cases} \begin{array}{cc} \textbf{Number} & \textbf{Log} \\ 2.620 & 0.4183 \\ 2.624 & \underline{\quad ? \quad} \\ 2.630 & 0.4200 \end{array} \end{cases} d \\ \end{cases} 0.0017$$

$$\frac{0.004}{0.01} = \frac{d}{0.0017} \quad \longleftarrow \quad \text{Set up the proportion.}$$

$$d = 0.0007 \quad \longleftarrow \quad \text{Solve for } d.$$

$$\log 2.624 = 0.4183 + 0.0007 = 0.4190$$

To find log 2624, the procedure is the same as in Example 2, but you would use 3 as the characteristic.

$$\log 2624 = 3.4190$$

Example 3 Find N, the antilog, to one decimal place: log $N = 2.2611$

$$1 \begin{cases} c \begin{cases} \begin{array}{cc} \textbf{Number} & \textbf{Log} \\ 182.0 & 2.2601 \\ N & 2.2611 \\ 183.0 & 2.2625 \end{array} \end{cases} 0.0010 \\ \end{cases} 0.0024$$

$$\frac{c}{1} = \frac{0.0010}{0.0024} \quad \longleftarrow \quad \text{Set up the proportion.}$$

$$c = 0.4 \quad \longleftarrow \quad \text{Solve for } c.$$

$$N = 182.0 + 0.4 = 182.4$$

You can find the value of the variable in an exponential function by first writing it in logarithmic form.

$$10^x = y \quad \longrightarrow \quad x = \log y$$

Example 4

Find x: $10^x = 1372$

$x = \log 1372 \longleftarrow$ Rewrite in logarithmic form.

$$10\left\{2\left\{\begin{array}{cc} \textbf{Number} & \textbf{Log} \\ 1370 & 3.1367 \\ 1372 & ? \\ 1380 & 3.1399 \end{array}\right\}d\right\}0.0032$$

$\dfrac{2}{10} = \dfrac{d}{0.0032} \longleftarrow$ Set up the proportion.

$d = 0.0006 \longleftarrow$ Solve for d.

$x = \log 1372 = 3.1367 + 0.0006 = 3.1373$

Try These

Interpolate to find the logarithm of each number.

1. 52.59 1.7209
2. 9.204 .9640
3. 772.3 2.8878
4. 0.1390 −.8570

Interpolate to find the antilogarithm of each number.

5. 1.2829 19.18
6. 0.2915 1.957
7. 3.8714 7437
8. 9.7375 − 10 .5464

Exercises

Interpolate to find the logarithms.

1. 56.25 1.7501
2. 7.832 0.8939
3. 432.4 2.6359
4. 0.6728 9.8279 − 10
5. 0.02137 8.3298 − 10
6. 32.41 1.5106
7. 1.233 0.0910
8. 8739 3.9415
9. 237.6 2.3758
10. 43.65 1.6400
11. 782.7 2.8936
12. .005294 7.7238 − 10

Interpolate to find the antilogarithms.

13. 2.7420 552.1
14. 3.8152 6,534
15. 1.5495 35.44
16. 0.1624 1.453
17. 1.1855 15.33
18. 9.5212 − 10 0.3321
19. 7.4015 − 10 0.002521
20. 8.9043 − 10 0.08022
21. 18.7478 − 20 0.05595

Compute by logarithms.

22. 25.43 × 8.265 210.2

23. 9.382 × 27.36 256.8

24. 533.7 × 0.1265 67.52

25. 78.12 × 6.537 510.8

26. 4.710 × 0.4931 2.322

27. 355.2 ÷ 74.25 4.783

28. 0.9328 ÷ 0.02130 43.79

29. 0.7239 ÷ 12.36 0.05856

30. 0.07215 ÷ 0.3272 0.2205

31. 8.763 ÷ 4.532 1.933

32. $(25.34)^3$ 16,270

33. $(4.361)^4$ 361.8

34. $(5.506)^3$ 167.0

35. $(6325)^2$ 40,010,000

36. $\sqrt{294.6}$ 17.16

37. $\sqrt[3]{92.83}$ 4.528

38. $\sqrt[3]{0.3468}$ 0.7024

39. $\sqrt[3]{0.02134}$ 0.2774

When you use logarithms to compute with negative numbers, as in Exercises 40–43, proceed as if the numbers were positive. Determine the sign of the result separately.

40. $(-6.321)(72.43) \div (36.45)$ −12.56

41. $\sqrt[3]{-53.62}$ −3.771

42. $(-2.344)^4$ 30.20

43. $(-18.72)(-4.836)$ 90.52

Compute by logarithms. Give your answers to the nearest tenth. When this is not possible, give them to the nearest hundredth.

44. $\sqrt[3]{983.4} \times \sqrt[4]{4.216}$ 14.3

45. $\sqrt[3]{8.926} \div \sqrt{1.635}$ 1.2

46. $\dfrac{97.6 \times \sqrt{47.3}}{(315)^2}$ 0.01

47. $\sqrt[3]{\dfrac{0.7621}{5.732}}$ 0.5

48. $\sqrt{\dfrac{17.2 \times 3.84}{2.96}}$ 4.7

49. $\sqrt[3]{\dfrac{53.2 \times 7.87}{5.00}}$ 4.4

9-9 Applications

The objective for this section is on page 355.

The following is the formula used in problems on <u>compound interest</u>.

If a sum of *p* dollars is invested at an interest rate *r*, compounded *k* times a year for *n* years, the total amount *A* (principal and interest) at the end of *n* years is given by the formula

$$A = p\left(1 + \frac{r}{k}\right)^{kn}$$

Find what $5000 will amount to in 10 years at 4% interest compounded semiannually.

$$A = 5000(1.02)^{20} \longleftarrow \quad p = 5000, \; r = 0.04, \; K = 2, \; n = 10$$

$$\log A = \log 5000 + 20 \log (1.02)$$

$$= 3.6990 + 20(0.0086)$$

$$= 3.6990 + (0.1720)$$

$$= 3.8710$$

$$A = 7430 \longleftarrow \quad \text{In ten years, the amount will be about } \$7430.$$

Exercises

Use logarithms to find the answers to each exercise. Give your answer to the nearest tenth.

1. How long is a side of a square whose area is 246.3 square centimeters?   15.7 centimeters

2. What is the volume of a bin 27.7 meters long, 9.2 meters wide, and 4.1 meters deep? 1044.7 cubic centimeters

3. The formula $PV = RT$ occurs frequently in chemical calculations. Find R when $P = 760.8$, $V = 22.40$, and $T = 288.7$. 59.0

4. The formula $t = \sqrt{\dfrac{\pi \ell}{g}}$ relates to the time for one swing of a pendulum. Find t when $\pi = 3.142$, $\ell = 50.62$, and $g = 980$. 0.4

5. The formula $A = \sqrt{s(s-a)(s-b)(s-c)}$ gives the area of a triangle. (a, b, and c are the lengths of the sides, and s is one half the perimeter.) How many acres are there in a triangular lot whose sides are 42.3 rods, 28.7 rods, and 37.0 rods? (1 acre = 160 square rods.) 3.3 acres

6. $\ell = ar^{n-1}$. Find ℓ when $a = 8$, $r = 2$, and $n = 12$. 16,400

7. $A = p(1 + r)^n$. Find A when $p = \$540$, $r = .03$, and $n = 6$. Find p when $A = \$1000$, $r = .04$, and $n = 5$. $645; $822

8. If $1500 is invested at 8% compounded annually, what will be its value after 8 years? $2780

Logarithmic Functions **349**

9. If you deposit $150 today at 6% interest compounded annually, how much will this sum become in 25 years? $644

10. Fifteen years ago, Mr. Hill invested $1000 at 5% interest compounded semiannually. How much has this $1000 investment earned for him during this time? $2100

11. Diego can buy a car for $850, or he can leave this sum in the bank at 6% interest compounded quarterly. What would it amount to in 5 years? $1150

12. Find the resulting amount of $2000 deposit compounded quarterly at 8% for 6 years. $3220

13. What principal will amount to $3000 if invested at 8% interest compounded semiannually for 10 years? (HINT: $A = 3000$; find p.) $1370

14. What principal will yield $3750 in 9 years at 6% compounded semiannually? $2210

15. Compute the depreciation on a $3000–automobile at 25% deducted annually for 4 years. (Follow the method of compound interest, but subtract the percentage instead of adding. The value of the automobile at the end of 4 years is $(.75)^4$ times the original value.) $2050

16. Find the cost of an automobile bought 5 years ago and now worth $750, if the depreciation is figured at 30% and deducted annually. $4460

17. Find the present sum that will amount to $10,000 in 18 years, interest being compounded at 6% semiannually. $3460

18. A rocket engine for a space craft has a noise level of 100 decibels. The noise level inside the space craft is 45 decibels. What is the ratio of the noise intensity outside to that inside the space craft? (HINT: The intensity level x is related to the decibel level b by the formula $b = 10 \log x$. Thus, if $b = 100$, then $100 = 10 \log x$.) $\frac{10^{10}}{10^{4.5}}$, or $\frac{10^{5.5}}{1}$

Remember

Solve each equation.

1. $2^x = 32$ {5}

2. $2^x = 128$ {7}

3. $3^x = 81$ {4}

4. $2^x = \frac{1}{2}$ {-1}

5. $3^x = \frac{1}{9}$ {-2}

6. $9^{x-2} = 81$ {4}

7. $9^x = 27$ $\{\frac{3}{2}\}$

8. $27^x = 81$ $\{\frac{4}{3}\}$

9. $2^{-x} = 16$ {-4}

The answers are on page 356.

Exponential Equations and Logarithms

The objective for this section is on page 356.

You learned a method of solving exponential equations in the previous chapter. Example 1 reviews this procedure.

Example 1

Solve: **a.** $2^x = 8$ **b.** $8^x = 32$

a. $2^x = 8$

$2^x = 2^3$

$x = 3$ **Solution set:** $\{3\}$

b. $8^x = 32$

$(2^3)^x = 2^5$

$2^{3x} = 2^5$

$3x = 5$

$x = \dfrac{5}{3}$ **Solution set:** $\left\{\dfrac{5}{3}\right\}$

Now that you can use logarithms, more difficult exponential equations can be solved. The procedure is based on the fact that if two numbers are equal, their logarithms are equal.

Example 2

Solve: $5.5^x = 2.345$

$\log 5.5^x = \log 2.345$ ⟵ Take the logarithm of both sides.

$x \log 5.5 = \log 2.345$

$x = \dfrac{\log 2.345}{\log 5.5}$

$= \dfrac{0.3701}{0.7404}$

$= 0.5$

Logarithmic Functions   **351**

Solve each equation for x.

1. $3^x = 733$ 6.005

2. $10^x = 41.63$ 1.6194

3. $5^x = 0.083$ −1.546

4. $(0.5)^x = 70$ −6.129

Exercises

Use logarithms to solve for x.

1. $2^x = 29$ 4.86

2. $25 = 3^x$ 2.93

3. $120 = 2^x$ 6.91

4. $275 = 4^x$ 4.05

5. $250 = 5^{2x}$ 1.72

6. $3.25 = 1.2^{3x}$ 2.15

7. $2^{x+1} = 37$ 4.21

8. $2^{3x+1} = 120$ 1.97

9. $5^{x+1} = 3^{x-2}$ −7.45

10. $7^{2x-1} = 8^{x-2}$ −1.22

11. $0.039^x = 15$ −0.835

12. $0.25^x = .75$ 0.207

Find the value of the following numbers by expressing them first in exponential form.

13. $\log_2 44$ 5.46

14. $\log_9 75$ 1.97

15. $\log_3 26$ 2.97

16. $\log_5 18$ 1.80

17. $\log_{100} 3$ 0.239

18. $\log_3 100$ 4.19

19. If you were to deposit money at 5% interest compounded annually, how soon would it be doubled? (HINT: Since each dollar is doubled, the equation is $(1.05)^n = 2$.)   14.2 years

20. If the interest is compounded annually, in how many years will a sum of money invested at 4% become three times as large?   28.1 years

21. A radioactive material decays at a rate expressed by $A = A_0 10^{-Kt}$ where A is in grams and t in years. If $A_0 = 500$ grams, find K if A is 450 grams when t is 1000 years.   0.0000458

22. Prove that if N, a, and b are positive real numbers, $a \neq 1$, $b \neq 1$, then

a. $\log_a N = \dfrac{\log_b N}{\log_b a}$

b. $\log_a b = \dfrac{1}{\log_b a}$ See key.

Use the results of Exercise 22 to determine each answer in Exercises 23–26.

23. $\log_2 7$ 2.81

24. $\log_3 2$ 0.631

25. $\log_4 9.6$ 1.63

26. $\log_3 10$ 2.10

Natural Logarithms

Logarithms to the base e (where $e \approx 2.72$), called **natural logarithms**, are often used in mathematics and science. To distinguish between common and natural logarithms, $\log_e x$ is often abbreviated as ln x.

The partial table below shows decimal approximations of natural logarithms to the nearest thousandth. Notice that the entries include the entire logarithm — both the characteristic and the mantissa.

N	0	1	2	3	4	5	6	7	8	9
4	1.386	1.411	1.435	1.459	1.482	1.504	1.526	1.548	1.569	1.589
5	1.609	1.629	1.649	1.668	1.686	1.705	1.723	1.740	1.758	1.775
6	1.792	1.808	1.825	1.841	1.856	1.872	1.887	1.902	1.917	1.932
7	1.946	1.960	1.974	1.988	2.001	2.015	2.028	2.041	2.054	2.067
8	2.079	2.092	2.104	2.116	2.128	2.140	2.152	2.163	2.175	2.186

How much does $4.70 amount to in 10 years at continuous compound interest of 6%?

$A = pe^{rn}$ ⟵ Interest formula for a principal, p, compounded continuously at r% for n years.

$A = 4.70e^{0.06(10)}$ ⟵ Replace p with 4.70, r with 0.06, and n with 10.

ln A = ln 4.70 + ln $e^{0.6}$

ln A = ln 4.70 + 0.6 ln e

ln A = 1.548 + 0.6 · 1, or 2.148 ⟵ From the table. Also, ln $e = \log_e e = 1$.

$A = 8.57$ ⟵ It will amount to about $8.57.

Use the partial table of natural logarithms to find how much $5.40 will amount to in 5 years at continuous compound interest of $7\frac{1}{2}$%.

Chapter
Objectives
and
Review

Objective: To know the meanings of the important mathematical terms of this chapter.

1. Here are many of the mathematical terms used in this chapter. Be sure that you know their meanings and that you can use them correctly.

antilogarithm (p. 333)
characteristic (p. 339)
common logarithm (p. 332)
exponential function (p. 322)

interpolation (p. 345)
logarithmic function (p. 329)
mantissa (p. 339)

Objective: To sketch the graph of an exponential function. (Section 9-1)

Sketch the graph of each function.

2. $y = 2^x$ See Ex. 13, Section 9.1

3. $y = (\frac{1}{2})^x$ See Ex. 4, Section 9.1

4. $y = 10^x$
See Ex. 1, Section 9.1

Objective: To use a graph of $y = 2^x$ to evaluate an expression. (Section 9-2)

Estimate the value of each expression, using a graph of $y = 2^x$.

5. $2^{1.1} \times 2^{2.1}$ 9.2

6. $3^{1.5}$ 5.3

7. $5^{0.5} \cdot 2^{1.5}$
6.5

Objective: To convert the logarithmic form of an expression to the exponential form. (Section 9-3)

Express in logarithmic form.

8. $64 = 4^3$ $\log_4 64 = 3$

9. $y = 5^2$ $\log_5 y = 2$

10. $y = a^x$
$\log_a y = x$

Objective: To convert the exponential form of an expression to the logarithmic form. (Section 9-3)

Express in exponential form.

11. $\log_3 81 = 4$ $3^4 = 81$

12. $y = \log_2 x$ $2^y = x$

13. $y = \log_b x$
$b^y = x$

Objective: To evaluate logarithms. (Section 9-3)

Evaluate.

14. $\log_5 125$ 3

15. $\log_3 \frac{1}{81}$ −4

16. $\log_{10} 0.001$ −3

Objective: To use tables to evaluate common logarithms and antilogarithms. (Sections 9-4 and 9-6)

Evaluate.

17. $\log 5.73$ 0.7582

18. $\log 584$ 2.7664

19. $\log 0.0135$ −2 + .1303 or 8.1303 − 10

20. antilog 0.9566 9.05

21. antilog 3.6085 4060

22. antilog $0.9671 - 3$ 0.00927

Objective: To use the properties of logarithms. (Section 9-5)

Complete each statement.

23. $\log(A \cdot B) = $ __?__   log A + log B

24. $\log C^n = $ __?__   n log C

25. $\log(x \div y) = $ __?__   log x − log y

26. $\frac{1}{2}\log c = $ __?__   log $c^{\frac{1}{2}}$

27. $\log A^{\frac{1}{3}} = $ __?__ $\frac{1}{3}$log A

28. $\log a^2 b = $ __?__   2 log a + log b

Objective: To use logarithms as a computational tool. (Sections 9-5, 9-6, 9-7)

Use logarithms to compute. Express answers correct to 3 places.

29. 843×763 643,000

30. $1.71 \div 8.74$ 0.196

31. 384^2 147,000

Objective: To interpolate to find the logarithm and the antilogarithm of a number. (Section 9-8)

Interpolate to find each of the following.

32. $\log 3.4593$ 0.5390

33. $\log 0.009146$ 7.9612 − 10

34. $\log 427.8$ 2.6312

35. antilog $7.4017 - 10$ 0.002522

36. antilog 1.5483 35.34

37. antilog 0.1656 1.464

Objective: To use logarithms to solve problems that involve formulas. (Section 9-9)

Use logarithms to solve these problems.

38. Find the side of a square whose area is 71 square centimeters.   8.43 centimeters

39. If $2000 is invested at 5% compounded annually, what will be its value after 10 years? $3260

40. If you deposited some money at 8% interest compounded annually, how long would it take to double the deposit?   9.0 years

Objective: To use logarithms to solve exponential equations. (Section 9-10)

Solve each equation.

41. $12^x = 18$ 1.16   **42.** $3^{2x} = 105$ 2.12   **43.** $2^{x+1} = 47$ 4.56

Chapter Test

Use logarithms to do these computations. Round answers to the nearest tenth.

1. 674×35.7 24,100   **2.** $75.6 \div 2.94$ 25.7

3. $\sqrt[5]{47.2}$ 2.16   **4.** $\dfrac{(43.2)^2 \times 124}{\sqrt{742}}$ 8,500

5. If $2500 is invested at 4% interest for 10 years, compounded semiannually, what will be the amount at the end of the 10 year period? $3,710

Solve each equation.

6. $4^x = \dfrac{1}{16}$ {-2}   **7.** $7^{2x} = 39$ {0.941}   **8.** $\log 10^4 = x$
                                                                            {4}

Complete each sentence.

9. $\log x^5 y = \underline{\quad ? \quad}$ 5 log x + log y   **10.** If $\log_x 64 = 6$, then $x = \underline{\quad ? \quad}$ 2

11. The statement, $5^4 = 625$, written in logarithmic form would be $\underline{\quad ? \quad}$. $\log_5 625 = 4$

12. Sketch the graphs of $y = 10^x$ and $y = \log_{10} x$ on the same set of coordinate axes. Label each graph. See page 328.

Answers to Remember

Page 324:   **1.** $\dfrac{20 - x}{20}$ **2.** $\dfrac{10x}{x^2 - 1}$ **3.** $\dfrac{1 + a}{2 - a}$ **4.** $\left\{\dfrac{5}{2}, -\dfrac{13}{6}\right\}$ **5.** Sum: $(6, -2)$; Difference: $(2, 8)$ **6.** Yes, Yes

Page 327:   **1.** $\left(4\dfrac{1}{3}, -\dfrac{1}{3}\right)$ **2.** $\left(2, -\dfrac{1}{2}\right)$ **3.** $\emptyset$

Page 334:   **1.** Rational, real, equal   **2.** Irrational, real, unequal   **3.** Complex, unequal

Page 338:   **1.** 2.8475×10^5 **2.** 5×10^0 **3.** -8.71×10^2 **4.** 5.3×10^{-4} **5.** 1.0005×10^{-1} **6.** 2.007×10^{-2}

Page 341:   **1.** 3^9 **2.** 5^4 **3.** 3^{20} **4.** $15^{\frac{1}{2}}$ **5.** $62^{\frac{1}{2}}$ **6.** 5^{12}

Page 344:   **1.** $\dfrac{3}{4}$ **2.** $\dfrac{7}{3}$ **3.** $y = \dfrac{1}{2}x + 4$

Page 350:   **1.** $\{5\}$ **2.** $\{7\}$ **3.** $\{4\}$ **4.** $\{-1\}$ **5.** $\{-2\}$ **6.** $\{4\}$ **7.** $\left\{\dfrac{3}{2}\right\}$ **8.** $\left\{\dfrac{4}{3}\right\}$ **9.** $\{-4\}$

Chapter 10
Conic Sections

The Circle

The objectives for this section are on page 387.

Conic sections are formed by the intersection of a plane and a right circular cone. A **circle** is the conic section formed by the intersection of a right circular cone and a plane perpendicular to the axis of the cone.

A circle can also be defined as a set of points, or **locus**.

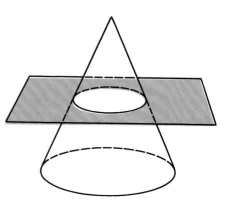

Definitions: A **circle** is the locus of points in a plane at a given distance from a fixed point. The distance is the **radius,** r. The fixed point is the **center,** C.

Using the conditions that define a circle, you can write an equation (algebraic model) of the locus.

Example 1

Write an equation for a circle with $r = 3$ and center, C, at $(0, 0)$. Let $P(x, y)$ be any point on the circle.

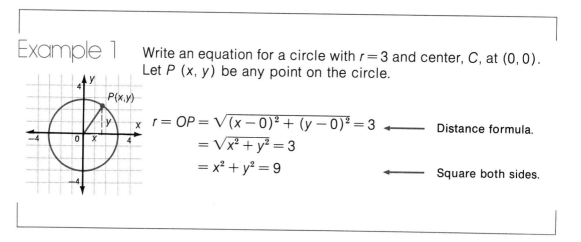

$$r = OP = \sqrt{(x-0)^2 + (y-0)^2} = 3 \quad \longleftarrow \text{Distance formula.}$$
$$= \sqrt{x^2 + y^2} = 3$$
$$= x^2 + y^2 = 9 \quad \longleftarrow \text{Square both sides.}$$

Example 1 suggests the following theorem.

Theorem 10-1: The equation of a circle with center at $(0, 0)$ and radius r, where $x, y, r \in R$, $r \geq 0$, is

$$x^2 + y^2 = r^2.$$

The graph of every equation of the form $x^2 + y^2 = r^2$, where $x, y, r \in R$, $r \geq 0$, is a circle with radius r and center at the origin.

You can use the procedure of Example 1 to find the equation of a circle whose center is <u>not</u> the origin.

Example 2  Write an equation for a circle with $r = 5$ and center at $(3, 6)$. Let $P(x, y)$ be any point on the circle.

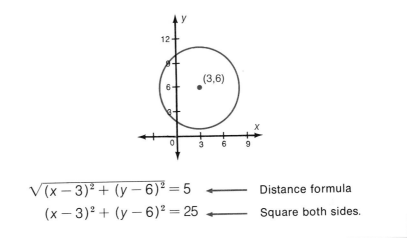

$\sqrt{(x-3)^2 + (y-6)^2} = 5$ ⟵ Distance formula

$(x-3)^2 + (y-6)^2 = 25$ ⟵ Square both sides.

Example 2 suggests the following theorem.

Theorem 10-2: The equation of a circle with center at (h, k) and radius r, where $h, k, r \in R$, $r \geq 0$, is

$$(x - h)^2 + (y - k)^2 = r^2.$$

Throughout the remainder of this chapter, the replacement set for all variables will be the set of real numbers.

Example 3 Find the center and radius of the circle defined by the following equation.

$$(x + 5)^2 + (y - 6)^2 = 25$$

$$h = -5, \ k = 6, \ r = 5 \qquad \longleftarrow \quad \text{Compare with } (x - h)^2 + (y - k)^2 = r^2$$

$$C(-5, 6) \qquad \qquad \longleftarrow \quad C(h, k)$$

Try These For each equation of a circle, write the length of the radius and the coordinates of its center.

1. $x^2 + y^2 = 4$ ⁣ $r = 2, \ (0, 0)$

2. $x^2 + y^2 = 25$ ⁣ $r = 5, \ (0, 0)$

3. $3x^2 + 3y^2 = 9$ ⁣ $r = \sqrt{3}, \ (0, 0)$

4. $(x - 2)^2 + (y - 3)^2 = 16$ ⁣ $r = 4, \ (2, 3)$

5. $(x + 4)^2 + (y - 5)^2 = 49$ ⁣ $r = 7, \ (-4, 5)$

6. $(x - 1)^2 + (y + 3)^2 = 36$ ⁣ $r = 6, \ (1, -3)$

Write the equation of each circle with the given center and radius.

7. $C(0, 0); \ r = 8$ ⁣ $x^2 + y^2 = 64$

8. $C(2, -3); \ r = 2$ ⁣ $(x - 2)^2 + (y + 3)^2 = 4$

Exercises

For each circle, the radius and the coordinates of the center are given. Write an equation for each circle. Then sketch its graph.

1. $r = 4; \ C(0, 0)$ ⁣ $x^2 + y^2 = 16$

2. $r = 2; \ C(0, 0)$ ⁣ $x^2 + y^2 = 4$

3. $r = 1; \ C(3, 4)$ ⁣ $(x - 3)^2 + (y - 4)^2 = 1$

4. $r = 3; \ C(2, -3)$ ⁣ $(x - 2)^2 + (y + 3)^2 = 9$

5. $r = 5; \ C(-3, 2)$ ⁣ $(x + 3)^2 + (y - 2)^2 = 25$

6. $r = 1\frac{1}{2}; \ C(-5, -2)$ ⁣ $(x + 5)^2 + (y + 2)^2 = \frac{9}{4}$

7. $r = \sqrt{3}; \ C(0, 6)$ ⁣ $x^2 + (y - 6)^2 = 3$

8. $r = 6; \ C(\frac{1}{2}, -\frac{5}{2})$ ⁣ $\left(x - \frac{1}{2}\right)^2 + \left(y + \frac{5}{2}\right)^2 = 36$

9. $r = \frac{5}{2}; \ C(-7, 0)$ ⁣ $(x + 7)^2 + y^2 = \frac{25}{4}$

10. $r = \sqrt{2}; \ C(-8, -4)$ ⁣ $(x + 8)^2 + (y + 4)^2 = 2$

Write the coordinates of the center, and the radius, of each circle.

11. $x^2 + y^2 = 36$ ⁣ $c(0, 0); \ 6$

12. $x^2 + y^2 = 7$ ⁣ $c(0, 0); \ r = \sqrt{7}$

13. $(x - 7)^2 + (y - 3)^2 = 4$ ⁣ $c(7, 3); \ 2$

14. $(x - 4)^2 + (y + 5)^2 = 3$ ⁣ $c(4, -5); \ r = \sqrt{3}$

15. $(x + \frac{1}{2})^2 + (y - \frac{1}{4})^2 = 9$ ⁣ $c\left(-\frac{1}{2}, \frac{1}{4}\right); \ r = 3$

16. $(x + \frac{3}{2})^2 + (y + \frac{5}{2})^2 = 10$

$$c\left(-\frac{3}{2}, -\frac{5}{2}\right); \ r = \sqrt{10}$$

Find the center and radius of the circle defined by each equation.

Example: $x^2 + y^2 + 6x + 8y = 15$

$(x^2 + 6x) + (y^2 + 8y) = 15$ ⟵ Group the x-terms and y-terms.

$(x^2 + 6x + 9) + (y^2 + 8y + 16) = 15 + 9 + 16$ ⟵ Complete the square twice.

$(x + 3)^2 + (y + 4)^2 = 40$

The center is at $(-3, -4)$ and the radius is $\sqrt{40}$.

17. $x^2 + 8x + y^2 - 4y = 16$ $\ (-4, 2); 6$ **18.** $x^2 + 4x + y^2 - 10y + 13 = 0$ $\ (-2, 5); 4$

19. $x^2 + y^2 - 6x + 8y = 24$ $\ (3, -4); 7$ **20.** $4x^2 + 4y^2 + 16x - 8y = 24$ $\ (-2, 1); \sqrt{11}$

21. $x^2 + y^2 + 4y - 6 = 0$ $\ (0, -2); \sqrt{10}$ **22.** $x^2 + y^2 + \frac{5}{2}x + 2y = 0$ $\ \left(-\frac{5}{4}, -1\right); \frac{\sqrt{41}}{4}$

23. A circle has its center at the origin and passes through the point $(3, 4)$. Write its equation. $\ x^2 + y^2 = 25$

24. A circle with center at $C(2, 5)$ contains the point $P(8, -3)$. Write the equation of the circle. $\ (x - 2)^2 + (y - 5)^2 = 100$

25. Write the equation of the circle whose diameter has endpoints at $(2, 3)$ and $(-6, 7)$. $\ (x + 2)^2 + (y - 5)^2 = 20$

26. For the second degree equation in two variables,

$$Ax^2 + Bxy + Cy^2 + Dx + Ey + F = 0,$$

suppose $A = C \neq 0$, and $B = 0$. Show that the graph of this equation is a circle, a point, or that it does not exist in the real number plane. (HINT: Complete the square in x and y.) See key.

Remember

Use the quadratic formula to solve for x.

1. $x^2 + 3x + 7 = 0$ $\quad \frac{-3 \pm i\sqrt{19}}{2}$

2. $x^2 + 3ax + 4a = 0$ $\quad x = \frac{-3a \pm \sqrt{9a^2 - 16a}}{2}$

Solve for x, where $x \in R$.

3. $x = \sqrt{2x - 1}$ $\ \{1\}$

4. $2x = \sqrt{7x - 3}$ $\ \{1\}$

5. $\sqrt{x} - 2 = \sqrt{x - 4}$ $\ \{4\}$

6. $\sqrt{x + 4} + \sqrt{x - 3} = 7$ $\ \{12\}$

The answers are on page 386.

The Ellipse

The objectives for this section are on pages 387-388.

An **ellipse** is the conic section formed by the intersection of a right circular cone and a plane. If the plane that intersects the cone to form a circle is tilted (as shown in the figure), the closed curve formed by this intersection is an ellipse.

An ellipse can also be defined as a locus.

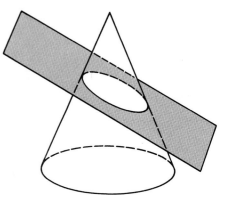

Definitions: An **ellipse** is the locus of all points in a plane such that the sum of the distances from two fixed points to a point of the locus is constant. Each of the fixed points is a **focus** (plural : foci).

Example 1

Write an equation for an ellipse where $F(-4, 0)$ and $F'(4, 0)$ are the foci and $FP + F'P = 10$.

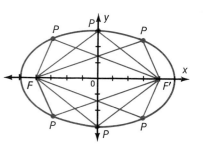

Let $P(x, y)$ be any point on the ellipse. The figure shows six different locations of P. In each case, $FP + F'P = 10$.

$FP = \sqrt{(x+4)^2 + (y-0)^2}$ $\qquad F'P = \sqrt{(x-4)^2 + (y-0)^2}$ ⟵ Distance formula

$\sqrt{(x+4)^2 + y^2} + \sqrt{(x-4)^2 + y^2} = 10$, or   ⟵ $FP + F'P = 10$

$\qquad \sqrt{(x-4)^2 + y^2} = 10 - \sqrt{(x+4)^2 + y^2}$

$\quad (x-4)^2 + y^2 = 100 - 20\sqrt{(x+4)^2 + y^2} + (x+4)^2 + y^2$ ⟵ Square both sides.

$x^2 - 8x + 16 + y^2 = 100 - 20\sqrt{(x+4)^2 + y^2} + x^2 + 8x + 16 + y^2$

$$16x + 100 = 20\sqrt{(x+4)^2 + y^2}$$

$$4x + 25 = 5\sqrt{(x+4)^2 + y^2} \qquad\qquad \longleftarrow \text{Divide by 4.}$$

$$16x^2 + 200x + 625 = 25x^2 + 200x + 400 + 25y^2 \qquad \longleftarrow \text{Square both sides.}$$

$$9x^2 + 25y^2 = 225$$

Example 2   Draw the graph of $9x^2 + 16y^2 = 144$.

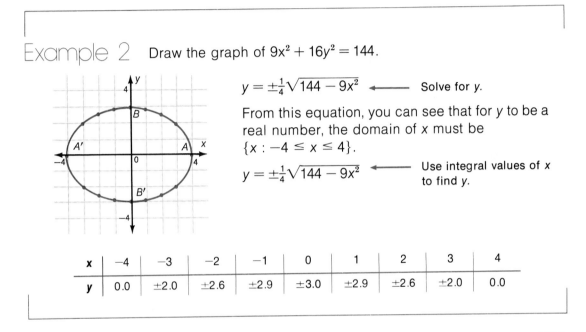

$$y = \pm\tfrac{1}{4}\sqrt{144 - 9x^2} \qquad \longleftarrow \text{Solve for } y.$$

From this equation, you can see that for y to be a real number, the domain of x must be $\{x : -4 \le x \le 4\}$.

$$y = \pm\tfrac{1}{4}\sqrt{144 - 9x^2} \qquad \longleftarrow \begin{array}{l}\text{Use integral values of } x \\ \text{to find } y.\end{array}$$

x	−4	−3	−2	−1	0	1	2	3	4
y	0.0	±2.0	±2.6	±2.9	±3.0	±2.9	±2.6	±2.0	0.0

In Example 2, $\overline{AA'}$ is the **major axis,** since it is longer than $\overline{BB'}$, the **minor axis.** The standard form for the equation of an ellipse with center at $(0, 0)$, semimajor axis of length a, and semiminor axis of length b, is

$$\frac{x^2}{a^2} + \frac{y^2}{b^2} = 1.$$

The coordinates of the four points in which the ellipse intersects the x and y axes are $(\pm a, 0)$ and $(0, \pm b)$.

If the major axis is the y axis rather than the x axis, then the standard form for the equation of an ellipse with center at $(0, 0)$, semimajor axis of length a and semiminor axis of length b is

$$\frac{x^2}{b^2} + \frac{y^2}{a^2} = 1.$$

Example 3 Find the coordinates of the x and y intercepts for the following equations. Tell whether the major axis is horizontal or vertical, and find its length.

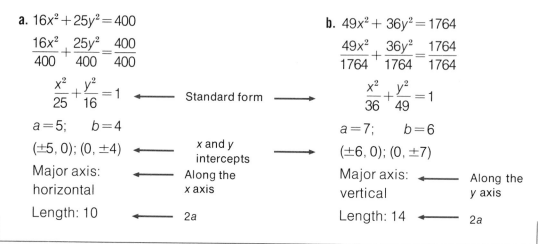

a. $16x^2 + 25y^2 = 400$

$$\frac{16x^2}{400} + \frac{25y^2}{400} = \frac{400}{400}$$

$$\frac{x^2}{25} + \frac{y^2}{16} = 1$$ ◄──── Standard form ──────►

$a = 5; \quad b = 4$

$(\pm 5, 0); (0, \pm 4)$ ◄──── x and y intercepts ──────►

Major axis: horizontal ◄──── Along the x axis

Length: 10 ◄──── 2a

b. $49x^2 + 36y^2 = 1764$

$$\frac{49x^2}{1764} + \frac{36y^2}{1764} = \frac{1764}{1764}$$

$$\frac{x^2}{36} + \frac{y^2}{49} = 1$$

$a = 7; \quad b = 6$

$(\pm 6, 0); (0, \pm 7)$

Major axis: vertical ◄──── Along the y axis

Length: 14 ◄──── 2a

It can be shown that

$$c^2 = a^2 - b^2$$

where the coordinates of the foci are

$$(\pm c, 0)$$

if the major axis is horizontal, and

$$(0, \pm c)$$

if the major axis is vertical.

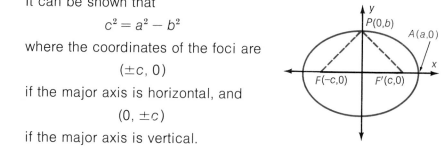

Example 4 Find the foci for the two equations in Example 3.

a. $\dfrac{x^2}{25} + \dfrac{y^2}{16} = 1$

$c^2 = a^2 - b^2$

$c^2 = 25 - 16 = 9$

$c = \pm 3$

Foci: $(\pm 3, 0)$

b. $\dfrac{x^2}{36} + \dfrac{y^2}{49} = 1$

$c^2 = a^2 - b^2$

$c^2 = 49 - 36 = 13$

$c = \pm\sqrt{13}$

Foci: $(0, \pm\sqrt{13})$

Try These *Classify each equation as defining an ellipse or a circle.*

1. $x^2 + 4y^2 = 100$ Ellipse   **2.** $36x^2 + 4y^2 = 144$ Ellipse   **3.** $x^2 + y^2 = 49$ Circle

4. $y^2 = 4 - x^2$ Circle   **5.** $3x^2 + 3y^2 = 22$ Circle   **6.** $x^2 + 9y^2 = 144$
                                                                                                  Ellipse

Give the lengths of the major and minor axes of each ellipse.

7. $x^2 + 4y^2 = 4$ 4, 2   **8.** $9x^2 + y^2 = 36$ 12, 4   **9.** $36x^2 + 4y^2 = 144$
                                                                                                                       12, 4

Exercises
The center for each of Exercises 1-9 is (0, 0).
The x and y intercepts are given.

Sketch the graph of each equation.

a

(3, 0), (−3, 0), (0, 2), (0, −2)

1. $\dfrac{x^2}{9} + \dfrac{y^2}{4} = 1$

(6, 0), (−6, 0), (0, 4), (0, −4)

2. $\dfrac{x^2}{36} + \dfrac{y^2}{16} = 1$

(2, 0), (−2, 0), (0, 4), (0, −4)

3. $\dfrac{x^2}{4} + \dfrac{y^2}{16} = 1$

4. $\dfrac{x^2}{49} + \dfrac{y^2}{25} = 1$ (7, 0), (−7, 0), (0, 5), (0, −5)

5. $x^2 + 4y^2 = 100$ (10, 0), (−10, 0), (0, 5), (0, −5)

6. $9x^2 + y^2 = 81$ (3, 0), (−3, 0), (0, 9), (0, −9)

7. $4x^2 + 9y^2 = 36$

(3, 0), (−3, 0), (0, 2), (0, −2)

8. $25x^2 + 9y^2 = 225$

(3, 0), (−3, 0), (0, 5), (0, −5)

9. $4x^2 + 36y^2 = 144$

(6, 0), (−6, 0), (0, 2), (0, −2)

For each ellipse, write the coordinates of the x intercepts, the y intercepts, and the foci.

foci: $(0, \sqrt{17})$, $(0, -\sqrt{17})$; (8, 0), (−8, 0), (0, 9), 0, −9)

10. $\dfrac{x^2}{36} + \dfrac{y^2}{25} = 1$

11. $\dfrac{x^2}{64} + \dfrac{y^2}{81} = 1$

12. $16x^2 + 9y^2 = 144$
foci: $(0, \sqrt{7})$, $(0, -\sqrt{7})$; (3, 0), (−3, 0), (0, 4), (0, −4)

foci: $(\sqrt{11}, 0)$, $(-\sqrt{11}, 0)$; (6, 0), (−6, 0), (0, 5), (0, −5)

Write the equation of each ellipse given the following information.

b

13. x intercepts at (5, 0) and (−5, 0), y intercepts at (0, 3) and (0, −3). $\frac{x^2}{25} + \frac{y^2}{9} = 1$

14. x intercepts at (2, 0) and (−2, 0), y intercepts at (0, 4) and (0, −4). $\frac{x^2}{4} + \frac{y^2}{16} = 1$

15. Foci at (4, 0) and (−4, 0), y intercepts at (0, 3) and (0, −3). $\frac{x^2}{25} + \frac{y^2}{9} = 1$

16. Foci at (0, 6) and (0, −6), x intercepts at (8, 0) and (−8, 0). $\frac{x^2}{64} + \frac{y^2}{100} = 1$

17. Major axis is horizontal and its length is 8; length of minor axis is 6; major and minor axes intersect at (0, 0). $\frac{x^2}{16} + \frac{y^2}{9} = 1$

18. Major axis is vertical and its length is 12; length of minor axis is 4; major and minor axis intersect at (0, 0). $\frac{x^2}{4} + \frac{y^2}{36} = 1$

19. Foci: (3, 0) and (−3, 0); one end point of major axis at (6, 0). $\frac{x^2}{36} + \frac{y^2}{27} = 1$

20. End points of major axis: (0, 7) and (0, −7); a focal point at (0, 5). $\frac{x^2}{24} + \frac{y^2}{49} = 1$

*The equations of an ellipse with center at (h, k) and with a and b the measures of the **semimajor** and **semiminor** axes (either half of a major or minor axis) are* $\dfrac{(x-h)^2}{a^2} + \dfrac{(y-k)^2}{b^2} = 1$ *and* $\dfrac{(x-h)^2}{b^2} + \dfrac{(y-k)^2}{a^2} = 1.$

Find the equation of the ellipse with the given center and given values for and b.

21. (3, 6); $a = 4$, $b = 3$; major axis is horizontal. $\dfrac{(x-3)^2}{16} + \dfrac{(y-6)^2}{9} = 1$

22. (−5, −6); $a = 9$, $b = 7$; major axis is vertical. $\dfrac{(x+5)^2}{49} + \dfrac{(y+6)^2}{81} = 1$

23. (−4, 4); $a = 5$, $b = \sqrt{7}$; major axis is horizontal. $\dfrac{(x+4)^2}{25} + \dfrac{(y-4)^2}{7} = 1$

C **24.** Use the figure to help you prove that

$$c^2 = a^2 - b^2,$$

where the foci are (±c, 0). See key.

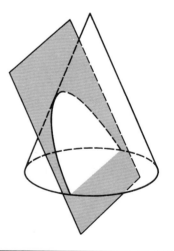

10-3 The Parabola

The objectives for this section are on page 388.

A **parabola** is the conic section formed by the intersection of a right circular cone and a plane. If the plane that intersects the cone to form an ellipse is tilted (as shown in the figure), the open curve formed is a parabola.

A parabola can also be defined as a locus.

Definitions: A **parabola** is the locus of points in the plane that are the same distance from a given line and a fixed point. The given line is the **directrix.** The fixed point is the **focus** of the parabola.

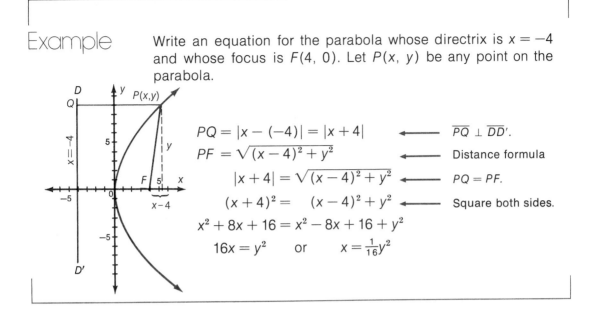

Example   Write an equation for the parabola whose directrix is $x = -4$ and whose focus is $F(4, 0)$. Let $P(x, y)$ be any point on the parabola.

$$PQ = |x - (-4)| = |x + 4| \quad \longleftarrow \quad \overline{PQ} \perp \overline{DD'}.$$

$$PF = \sqrt{(x-4)^2 + y^2} \quad \longleftarrow \quad \text{Distance formula}$$

$$|x + 4| = \sqrt{(x-4)^2 + y^2} \quad \longleftarrow \quad PQ = PF.$$

$$(x+4)^2 = (x-4)^2 + y^2 \quad \longleftarrow \quad \text{Square both sides.}$$

$$x^2 + 8x + 16 = x^2 - 8x + 16 + y^2$$

$$16x = y^2 \quad \text{or} \quad x = \tfrac{1}{16}y^2$$

The distance between the focus, $(4, 0)$, and the directrix in the example is 8. Also, the coefficient of $16x$ in $y^2 = 16x$ is 2×8. This illustrates a general relationship for a parabola whose **vertex** (turning point) is $(0, 0)$. When the distance between the focus and directrix is $2p$, the coefficient in the equation of the parabola is $4p$.

Parabola Facts

Equation	Axis of Symmetry	Opens
$y^2 = 4px$ or $x = \dfrac{1}{4p}y^2$	horizontal	to the right
$y^2 = -4px$ or $x = \dfrac{1}{-4p}y^2$	horizontal	to the left
$x^2 = 4py$ or $y = \dfrac{1}{4p}x^2$	vertical	up
$x^2 = -4py$ or $y = \dfrac{1}{-4p}x^2$	vertical	down

Try These   *Identify each equation as a circle, an ellipse, or a parabola.*

1. $x^2 + y^2 = 100$ Circle

2. $y = x^2 + 3$ Parabola

3. $3x^2 + 4y^2 = 5$ Ellipse

4. $x^2 = -y$ Parabola

5. $x^2 = 4 - y^2$ Circle

6. $y^2 = 2x + 3$ Parabola

Conic Sections   **367**

In Exercises 1-8, the graphs are parabolas with vertex at (0, 0). The axis of symmetry is horizontal in Exercises 1, 2, 5, and 7 and vertical in Exercises 3, 4, and 8.

Exercises

	1	2	3	4	5	6	7	8
Opens	right	right	up	down	left	up	left	up
Focus	(1, 0)	(2, 0)	(0, 4)	(0, −9)	$\left(-\frac{1}{2}, 0\right)$	(0, 3)	(−2, 0)	(0, 6)
Directrix	$x = -1$	$x = -2$	$y = -4$	$y = 9$	$x = \frac{1}{2}$	$y = -3$	$x = 2$	$y = -6$

Sketch the graph of each equation. Label the focus, vertex and directrix.

See key for Exercises 1-8.

1. $x = \frac{1}{4} y^2$ 2. $x = \frac{1}{8} y^2$ 3. $y = \frac{1}{16} x^2$ 4. $y = -\frac{1}{36} x^2$

5. $x = -\frac{1}{2} y^2$ 6. $x^2 = 12y$ 7. $y^2 = -8x$ 8. $x^2 = 24y$

Write the equation of each parabola given the following information.

9. Focus: (2, 0); directrix: $x = -2$ $\;y^2 = 8x$ 10. Focus: (−3, 0); directrix: $x = 3$ $\;y^2 = -12x$

11. Focus: (0, −4); directrix: $y = 4$ $\;x^2 = -16y$ 12. Focus: (0, 6); directrix: $y = -6$ $\;x^2 = 24y$

13. Focus: (5, 0), directrix: $x = -6$ $\;x = \frac{y^2}{22} - \frac{1}{2}$ 14. Focus: (−7, 0), directrix: $x = 2$ $\;x = -\frac{y^2}{18} - \frac{5}{2}$

15. Focus: (3, 0), directrix: $y = 5$ $\;x = \frac{1}{16}(y - 3)^2 - 7$ 16. Vertex: (5, 4), directrix: $x = -6$ $\;x = \frac{1}{44}(y - 4)^2 + 5$

17. Vertex: (−7, 3), focus: (−3, 3) $\;y = -\frac{1}{10}(x - 3)^2 + \frac{5}{2}$ 18. Vertex: (−4, −6), focus: (−4, −3) $\;y = \frac{1}{12}(x + 4)^2 - 6$

The general forms of the equation of a parabola with vertex at (h, k) are:

$$y - k = \pm\frac{1}{4p}(x - h)^2;\ \text{Focus: } (h, k + p) \text{ or } (h, k - p);\ \text{Directrix: } y = k - p \text{ for}$$

the positive sign or $y = k + p$ for the negative sign.

$$x - h = \pm\frac{1}{4p}(y - k)^2;\ \text{Focus: } (h + p, k) \text{ or } (h - p, k);\ \text{Directrix: } x = h - p \text{ for}$$

the positive sign or $x = h + p$ for the negative sign.

Use the general forms to sketch the graph of each equation. (HINT: *Write the equation in standard form by completing the square on x or y.*)

See key for Exercises 19-22.

19. $x^2 - 4x + 4y + 12 = 0$ 20. $y^2 + 4y - 2x + 2 = 0$

21. $2x^2 + 8x + y - 4 = 0$ 22. $3y^2 + 6y + 2x - 5 = 0$

PUZZLE

Simplify each fraction. Then generalize and explain. Each fraction is $\frac{1}{3}$.

$$\frac{1 + 3}{5 + 7} \qquad \frac{1 + 3 + 5}{7 + 9 + 11} \qquad \frac{1 + 3 + 5 + 7 + 9 + 11}{13 + 15 + 17 + 19 + 21 + 23}$$

$$\frac{1 + 3 + 5 + \cdots + 95 + 97 + 99}{101 + 103 + 105 + \cdots + 195 + 197 + 199} \qquad \frac{\frac{n}{2}[1 + (2n - 1)]}{\frac{n}{2}[(2n + 1) + (4n - 1)]} = \frac{1}{3}$$

The Hyperbola

The objectives for this section are on page 388.

A **hyperbola** is the conic section formed by the intersection of a right circular cone and a plane. If the plane that intersects the cone to form a parabola is tilted so that it is parallel to the axis of the cone, the open curve formed is a branch of a hyperbola.

A hyperbola can also be defined as a locus.

Definition: A **hyperbola** is the locus of all points in the plane such that the difference of the distances from two fixed points to a point of the locus is a constant. The fixed points are called foci.

Example 1 Write the equation of a hyperbola with foci at $F(0, 5)$ and $F'(0, -5)$ for which the constant difference is 8. Let $P(x, y)$ be any point on the hyperbola.

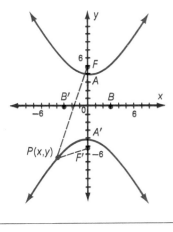

$FP - F'P = 8$ ◄——— By definition

$\sqrt{x^2 + (y - 5)^2} - \sqrt{x^2 + (y + 5)^2} = 8$, or

$\sqrt{x^2 + (y - 5)^2} = 8 + \sqrt{x^2 + (y + 5)^2}$

Now square both sides of the equation and simplify.

$x^2 + (y - 5)^2 = 8^2 + 16\sqrt{x^2 + (y + 5)^2} + x^2 + (y + 5)^2$

$-5y - 16 = 4\sqrt{x^2 + (y + 5)^2}$

Square both sides of the equation.

$25y^2 + 160y + 256 = 16(x^2 + y^2 + 10y + 25)$

$9y^2 - 16x^2 = 144$

In Example 1, the **major axis**, $\overline{AA'}$, is 8 units long. The **minor axis**, $\overline{BB'}$, is 6 units long. The center of the hyperbola is $(0, 0)$. The distance c from each focus to the center is $\sqrt{4^2 + 3^2} = 5$.

The standard form for the equation of a hyperbola with center at $(0, 0)$ is

Opens vertically. $\rightarrow$ $\dfrac{y^2}{a^2} - \dfrac{x^2}{b^2} = 1$ or $\dfrac{x^2}{a^2} - \dfrac{y^2}{b^2} = 1.$ $\leftarrow$ Opens horizontally.

Hyperbola Facts

For either $\dfrac{y^2}{a^2} - \dfrac{x^2}{b^2} = 1$ or $\dfrac{x^2}{a^2} - \dfrac{y^2}{b^2} = 1,$

a is one–half the length of the major axis;
b is one–half the length of the minor axis; and
$c = \sqrt{a^2 + b^2}$, the distance from each focus to the center.

Example 2   Sketch $\dfrac{x^2}{36} - \dfrac{y^2}{4} = 1$. Here $a = 6$ and $b = 2$.

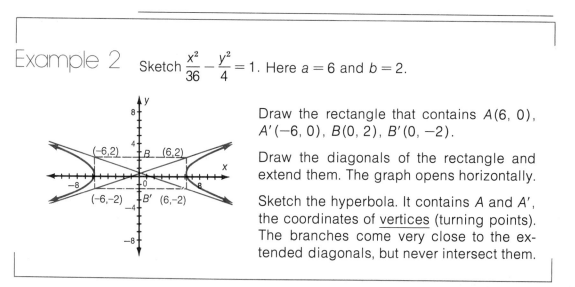

Draw the rectangle that contains $A(6, 0)$, $A'(-6, 0)$, $B(0, 2)$, $B'(0, -2)$.

Draw the diagonals of the rectangle and extend them. The graph opens horizontally.

Sketch the hyperbola. It contains A and A', the coordinates of <u>vertices</u> (turning points). The branches come very close to the extended diagonals, but never intersect them.

The extended diagonals are the <u>asymptotes</u> of the hyperbola. A hyperbola is asymptotic to (comes very close to, but never intersects) these two lines. The <u>equations of the asymptotes</u> are

$$y = \frac{b}{a}x \text{ and } y = -\frac{b}{a}x \text{ for } \frac{x^2}{a^2} - \frac{y^2}{b^2} = 1, \text{ or}$$

$$y = \frac{a}{b}x \text{ and } y = -\frac{a}{b}x \text{ for } \frac{y^2}{a^2} - \frac{x^2}{b^2} = 1.$$

Since $a = 6$ and $b = 2$ in Example 2, the asymptote equations are

$$y = \tfrac{2}{6}x, \text{ or } y = \tfrac{1}{3}x \quad \text{and} \quad y = -\tfrac{2}{6}x, \text{ or } y = -\tfrac{1}{3}x.$$

Try These

Tell which hyperbolas open horizontally and which open vertically. Give the coordinates of the vertices.

Vertically; (0,5), (0,−5)

1. $\dfrac{x^2}{9} - \dfrac{y^2}{16} = 1$ Horizontally; (3,0), (−3,0)   **2.** $\dfrac{x^2}{4} - \dfrac{y^2}{4} = 1$ Horizontally; (2,0), (−2,0)   **3.** $\dfrac{y^2}{25} - \dfrac{x^2}{16} = 1$

4. $4y^2 - 25x^2 = 100$ **5.** $4x^2 - y^2 = 16$ **6.** $2y^2 - 3x^2 = 6$

Vertically; (0,5), (0,−5)   Horizontally; (2,0), (−2,0)   Vertically; (0,√3), (0,−√3)

Exercises

Sketch the graph of each equation. Write the equations of the asymptotes.

See key for Exercises 1-9.

1. $\dfrac{x^2}{16} - \dfrac{y^2}{4} = 1$ **2.** $\dfrac{x^2}{25} - \dfrac{y^2}{9} = 1$ **3.** $\dfrac{y^2}{49} - \dfrac{x^2}{36} = 1$

4. $\dfrac{y^2}{64} - \dfrac{x^2}{25} = 1$ **5.** $9y^2 - x^2 = 81$ **6.** $x^2 - 4y^2 = 36$

7. $25x^2 - 4y^2 = 100$ **8.** $4y^2 - 9x^2 = 36$ **9.** $x^2 - y^2 = 9$

Write the equation of each hyperbola given the following information.

10. Center: (0, 0); opens horizontally; $a = 2$, $b = 5$. $\frac{x^2}{4} - \frac{y^2}{25} = 1$

11. Center: (0, 0); opens vertically; $a = 4$, $b = 4$. $\frac{y^2}{16} - \frac{x^2}{16} = 1$

12. Foci: (10, 0), (−10, 0); vertices: (6, 0), (−6, 0). $\frac{x^2}{36} - \frac{y^2}{64} = 1$

13. Foci: (0, 5), (0, −5); vertices: (0, 4), (0, −4). $\frac{y^2}{16} - \frac{x^2}{9} = 1$

14. Vertices: (3, 0), (−3, 0); asymptotes: $x - 3y = 0$, $x + 3y = 0$. $\frac{x^2}{9} - \frac{y^2}{1} = 1$

15. Find the coordinates of the foci for each hyperbola in Exercises **4-9.**

The general forms of the equation of a hyperbola with center at (h, k) are:

See key.

$$\frac{(x - h)^2}{a^2} - \frac{(y - k)^2}{b^2} = 1, \text{ if it opens horizontally.}$$

$$\frac{(y - k)^2}{a^2} - \frac{(x - h)^2}{b^2} = 1, \text{ if it opens vertically.}$$

Use the general form to sketch the graph of each equation.   See key for Exercises 16-18.

16. $\dfrac{(x - 3)^2}{16} - \dfrac{(y - 2)^2}{9} = 1$ **17.** $\dfrac{(y - 3)^2}{49} - \dfrac{x^2}{25} = 1$ **18.** $\dfrac{(x - 1)^2}{9} - \dfrac{y^2}{4} = 1$

10-5 Rectangular Hyperbolas

The objective for this section is on page 388.

The hyperbola whose asymptotes are the x and y axes is defined by

$$xy = k.$$

If $k > 0$, the branches of the hyperbola lie in Quadrants I and III. If $k < 0$, the branches lie in Quadrants II and IV. These special hyperbolas are called **rectangular hyperbolas.**

Example

Draw the graph of $xy = 12$.

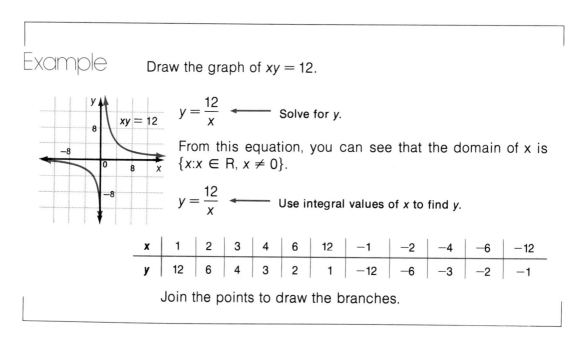

$$y = \frac{12}{x} \quad \longleftarrow \quad \text{Solve for } y.$$

From this equation, you can see that the domain of x is $\{x : x \in R, x \neq 0\}$.

$$y = \frac{12}{x} \quad \longleftarrow \quad \text{Use integral values of } x \text{ to find } y.$$

x	1	2	3	4	6	12	−1	−2	−4	−6	−12
y	12	6	4	3	2	1	−12	−6	−3	−2	−1

Join the points to draw the branches.

The graph of $xy = -12$ is symmetric to that of $xy = 12$ with respect to either the x axis or the y axis.

Note that the foci and vertices of a rectangular hyperbola, $xy = k$, lie on the line $y = x$ when $k > 0$ and on the line $y = -x$ when $k < 0$.

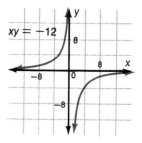

Exercises

Identify each equation as that of a line, a circle, an ellipse, a parabola, a hyperbola, or a rectangular hyperbola.

a

1. $x^2 + y^2 = 25$ Circle

2. $xy = 8$ Rectangular hyperbola

3. $x + y = 7$ Line

4. $x - y = 1$ Line

5. $y = x^2 + 1$ Parabola

6. $x^2 + 3y = 15$ Parabola

7. $3x - y^2 = 5$ Parabola

8. $4x^2 - 2y = 17$ Parabola

9. $4x + 2y = 17$ Line

10. $3x^2 = 27 - 7y$ Parabola

11. $x^2 + 2y^2 = 2$ Ellipse

12. $x^2 + y^2 = 17$ Circle

13. $2x^2 + y^2 = 17$ Ellipse

14. $2y^2 + 3x^2 = 11$ Ellipse

15. $x^2 - y^2 = 4$ Hyperbola

16. $4x^2 + 9y^2 = 36$ Ellipse

Plot a few points and sketch the graph of each equation.

See key for Exercises 17-20.

17. $xy = 18$

18. $xy = -18$

19. $xy - 9 = 0$

20. $xy + 9 = 0$

b

21. Use the locus definition of a hyperbola to find the equation of the hyperbola with foci at $(2, 0)$ and $(-2, 0)$ when the constant difference between any point of the hyperbola and the foci is $2\sqrt{2}$. $\frac{x^2}{2} - \frac{y^2}{2} = 1$

10-6 Applications: Variation

The objective for this section is on page 389.

The graph of the rectangular hyperbola is used as a geometric model of the relationship between the pressure, P, and volume, V, of a gas at constant temperature, k.

$$PV = k$$

As the value of P increases, the value of V decreases; as the value of V increases, the value of P decreases. This is an example of **inverse variation.**

    An inverse variation is often written as a proportion in problem solving situations.

Example 1

Write $xy = k$ as a proportion, where (x_1, y_2) and (x_2, y_2) satisfy the equation.

$$x_1y_1 = k \qquad \longleftarrow \qquad \text{Replace } x \text{ and } y.$$
$$x_2y_2 = k \qquad \longleftarrow \qquad \text{Replace } x \text{ and } y.$$

Therefore, $x_1y_1 = x_2y_2$

$$\frac{x_1}{x_2} = \frac{y_2}{y_1} \qquad \longleftarrow \qquad \text{Divide both sides by } x_2y_1.$$

The ratio of two values for x is the same as the reciprocal of the corresponding values for y.

Example 2

If x varies inversely as y and $y = 9$ when $x = 5$, find y when $x = 25$.

$$\frac{x_1}{x_2} = \frac{y_2}{y_1}$$

$$\frac{5}{25} = \frac{y_2}{9} \qquad \longleftarrow \qquad x_1 = 5,\ y_1 = 9,\ x_2 = 25$$

$$45 = 25y_2$$

$$y_2 = \frac{45}{25} = \frac{9}{5} = 1\tfrac{4}{5}$$

If $y = \dfrac{k}{x^2}$, or $x^2y = k$, then y is said to **vary inversely as the square** of x.

It is written below as a proportion.

$$\frac{y_1}{y_2} = \frac{x_2^{\,2}}{x_1^{\,2}}$$

Example 3

If y varies inversely as the square of x and $y = 12$ when $x = 7$, find y when $x = 6$.

$$\frac{y_1}{y_2} = \frac{x_2{}^2}{x_1{}^2}$$

$$\frac{12}{y_2} = \frac{(6)^2}{(7)^2} \longleftarrow x_1 = 7,\ y_1 = 12,\ x_2 = 6$$

$$588 = 36y_2$$

$$y_2 = \frac{588}{36} = 16\tfrac{1}{3}$$

Joint variation is expressed by the equation $x = kyz$, where x, y, and z are variables and k is a constant. This equation means that x varies jointly as y and z.

Example 4   If y varies jointly as x and z, write an equation that expresses this. Then write a proportion for (x_1, y_1, z_1) and (x_2, y_2, z_2).

$$y = kxz \qquad \text{or} \qquad \frac{y}{xz} = k \longleftarrow \text{Equation}$$

$$\frac{y_1}{x_1 z_1} = k \qquad \text{and} \qquad \frac{y_2}{x_2 z_2} = k$$

Therefore, $\dfrac{y_1}{x_1 z_1} = \dfrac{y_2}{x_2 z_2}$, or $\dfrac{y_1}{y_2} = \dfrac{x_1 z_1}{x_2 z_2}$

Try These   *In Exercises **1-10,** supply the missing words in the sentences that can be completed, using such phrases as: increases; decreases; is unchanged; is multiplied by, or is divided by, 2, 4, etc. If a sentence cannot be completed, say "One cannot tell." The replacement set for each variable is the set of positive real numbers.*

Use the formula $A = s^2$ in Exercises **1** and **2.**

1. As the value of s increases, the value of A __?__. increases.
2. If the value of s is multiplied by 3, the value of A __?__. is multiplied by 9.

Use P = 3a, the formula for the perimeter of an equilateral triangle, in
*Exercises **3-6.***

is multiplied by 4.

3. If some value of *a* is multiplied by 4, the corresponding value of *P*__?__.

4. If some value of *a* is divided by 2, the corresponding value of *P*__?__.

is divided by 2.

5. If *a* is decreased, the perimeter __?__. decreases.

6. If *a* is increased, the perimeter __?__. increases.

Use V = ℓwh, the formula for the volume of a rectangular solid, in
*Exercises **7-10.***

7. If ℓ is increased and *w* and *h* remain the same, *V*__?__. increases.

8. If *h* is decreased and ℓ and *w* remain the same, *V*__?__. decreases.

9. If ℓ is increased, *w* is decreased, and *h* remains the same, *V*__?__.

one cannot tell.

10. If ℓ is multiplied by 2, *w* by 2, and *h* by 3, *V*__?__.

is multiplied by 12.

Exercises

The formula for the area of a rectangular region with dimensions ℓ and
*w is A = ℓw. Use this formula to answer Exercises **1-4.***

Yes. If A is constant, values of ℓ must increase if w decreases, and ℓ must decrease if w increases.

1. Is *A = ℓw* an example of inverse variation? Explain.

2. Let *A* = 100. Then *ℓw* = 100. When ℓ = 5, *w* = __?__ (20); when ℓ = 10, *w* = __?__ (10).
If you choose a value of ℓ and double it, the corresponding value of *w* is __?__.

halved

3. Using *ℓw* = 100, if you choose a value for ℓ and triple it, the corresponding
value for *w* is __?__. divided by 3.

4. Using *ℓw* = 100, if you choose a value for ℓ and multiply it by *a*, the
corresponding value for *w* is __?__. divided by a.

*In Exercises **5-9,** use k for the constant of variation and write an equation*
that expresses the variation described in each statement.

5. *y* varies jointly as *x* and *z*. $y = kxz$

6. *y* varies jointly as *x* and *z* and inversely as the square of *m*. $y = \frac{kxz}{m^2}$

7. *A* varies jointly as *m*, *n*, and *p*. $A = kmnp$

8. *y* varies jointly as *x* and inversely as the square root of *z*. $y = \frac{kx}{\sqrt{z}}$

9. *y* varies jointly as *x* and *z* and inversely as *m* and *n*. $y = \frac{kxz}{mn}$

10. The Kelleys took a 300-kilometer trip. Write an equation showing the relation between average velocity, v, and time traveled, t. Is this an example of inverse variation? Express this relation as (v_1, t_1) and (v_2, t_2). Make a table showing at least six pairs of numbers that satisfy the equation.

$vt = 300$; yes; $v_1 t_1 = v_2 t_2$ or $\frac{v_1}{v_2} = \frac{t_2}{t_1}$;

v	60	50	30	15	10	5
t	5	6	10	20	30	60

The law of the lever states that wd = WD, where w and W represent weights and d and D represent distances from the fulcrum.

11. Express the relation as a proportion. Is this an example of direct or of inverse variation? If $w = 10$, $d = 5$, and $D = 20$, find W. $\frac{w}{W} = \frac{D}{d}$; Inverse; $\frac{5}{2}$

12. A 70-kilogram boy sits 2.5 meters from the fulcrum on a seesaw. Where must a 90-kilogram boy sit to balance the seesaw? About 1.9 meters

13. The weight of a body, w, varies inversely as the square of the distance, d, from the center of the earth. Express this relation with an equation, using k as the constant of variation. Express this relation as a proportion. If a body weighs 100 pounds on the surface of the earth (4000 miles from the center), how much would it weigh if it is raised 200 miles above the earth? See below.

14. If x varies inversely as y and $y = 10$ when $x = 4$, what is y when x is 8? 5

$\left(\text{HINT: Use } xy = k \text{ and find } k, \text{ or use } \dfrac{x_1}{x_2} = \dfrac{y_2}{y_1}.\right)$

15. If y varies inversely as x and $x = 4$ when $y = 12$, what is x when $y = 6$? 8

16. If y varies inversely as the square of x and $y = 2$ when $x = 4$, find y when $x = 16$. $\frac{1}{8}$

17. If x varies inversely as the square of y and $y = 5$ when $x = 4$, what is y when $x = 6$? $\pm\frac{5}{3}\sqrt{6}$

18. If y varies jointly as x and z, and $y = 12$ when $x = 1$ and $z = 4$, find y when $x = 4$ and $z = 2$. 24

19. If y varies jointly as z and the square of x, and $y = 15$ when $z = 5$ and $x = 1$, find y when $z = 1$ and $x = 2$. 12

20. A bicycle wheel with a 26-inch diameter takes 10 revolutions to go a certain distance. How many revolutions will a 20-inch diameter wheel make in covering the same distance? 13 revolutions

21. A pulley connects a 30-centimeter wheel with a 6-centimeter wheel. How many revolutions will the small wheel make for each revolution of the large wheel? How will the speed of the two wheels compare? 5 revolutions; the speed of the smaller wheel is 5 times the speed of the large wheel.

22. Knowing that intensity, I, varies inversely as the square of the distance, d, how far should a book be placed from a light to receive four times as intense illumination as it received when it was 2 meters from the light?
1 meter

13. $w = \frac{k}{d^2}$; $\frac{w_1}{w_2} = \frac{d_2^2}{d_1^2}$; about 90.7 pounds

The figures in the example show some ways in which the graphs of linear and second-degree equations can intersect.

Every point of intersection accounts for one pair of real numbers in the solution set. A point of tangency means one distinct pair of real numbers. When the graphs do not intersect, the solution set contains pairs of imaginary numbers.

Example

Name the number of distinct pairs of real numbers in the solution set of each pair of equations graphed below.

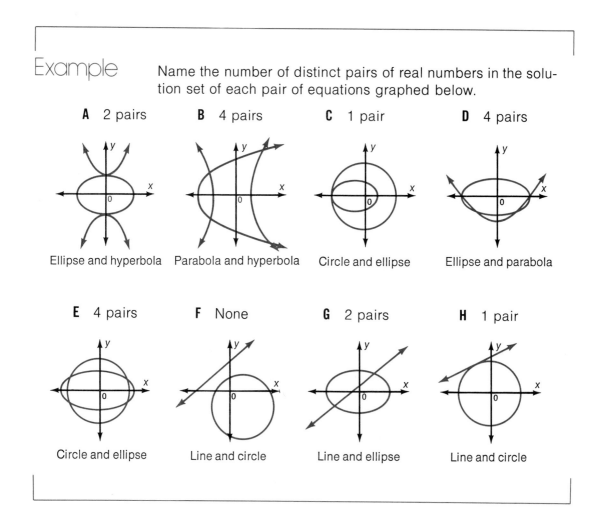

A 2 pairs

Ellipse and hyperbola

B 4 pairs

Parabola and hyperbola

C 1 pair

Circle and ellipse

D 4 pairs

Ellipse and parabola

E 4 pairs

Circle and ellipse

F None

Line and circle

G 2 pairs

Line and ellipse

H 1 pair

Line and circle

Exercises

Match each pair of equations in Exercises 1–9 with its corresponding graph below.

a.

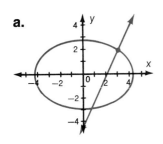

b.

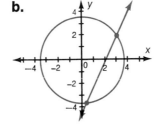

c.

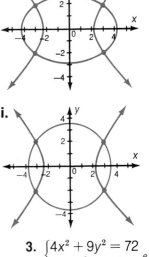

d.

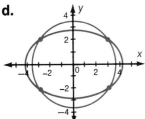

e.

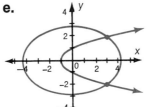

f.

g.

h.

i.

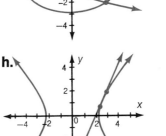

1. $\begin{cases} x^2 + y^2 = 13 \\ 2x - y = 4 \end{cases}$ *b*

2. $\begin{cases} 4x^2 + 9y^2 = 72 \\ 2x - y = 4 \end{cases}$ *a*

3. $\begin{cases} 4x^2 + 9y^2 = 72 \\ x - y^2 = -1 \end{cases}$ *e*

4. $\begin{cases} x = y^2 - 1 \\ 2x - y = 4 \end{cases}$ *c*

5. $\begin{cases} 4x^2 + 9y^2 = 72 \\ x^2 - y^2 = 5 \end{cases}$ *f*

6. $\begin{cases} x^2 + y^2 = 13 \\ 4x^2 + 9y^2 = 72 \end{cases}$ *d*

7. $\begin{cases} x^2 - y^2 = 5 \\ 2x - y = 4 \end{cases}$ *h*

8. $\begin{cases} x^2 + y^2 = 13 \\ x^2 - y^2 = 5 \end{cases}$ *i*

9. $\begin{cases} x - y^2 = -1 \\ x^2 + y^2 = 13 \end{cases}$ *g*

Solve each system by graphing. Estimate solutions to the nearest integer.

10. $\begin{cases} y = x^2 \\ y = x \end{cases}$ $\{(0, 0), (1, 1)\}$

11. $\begin{cases} x^2 + y^2 = 9 \\ y = x + 3 \end{cases}$ $\{(0, 3), (-3, 0)\}$

12. $\begin{cases} x^2 - y^2 = 16 \\ x - y = 2 \end{cases}$ $\{(5, 3)\}$

13. $\begin{cases} x^2 + 4y^2 = 36 \\ 2y = x - 6 \end{cases}$ $\{(6, 0), (0, -3)\}$

14. $\begin{cases} xy = 8 \\ x - y = 6 \end{cases}$ Approximate solution set: $\{(7, 1), (-1, -7)\}$

15. $\begin{cases} 4x^2 + 9y^2 = 36 \\ y - x = 3 \end{cases}$ Approximate solution set: $\{(-3, 0), (-1, 2)\}$

10-8 First-and Second-Degree Equations

The objective for this section is on page 389.

A system of equations consisting of one linear or first-degree equation and one second-degree equation may have two, one, or no pairs of real numbers in the solution set.

 If the graphs of the equations of the system have no points in common, the solution set contains no real solutions. A system involving a second-degree equation and a linear equation may have two elements in its solution set. One or both solutions may be complex numbers.

Example

Solve the following system.

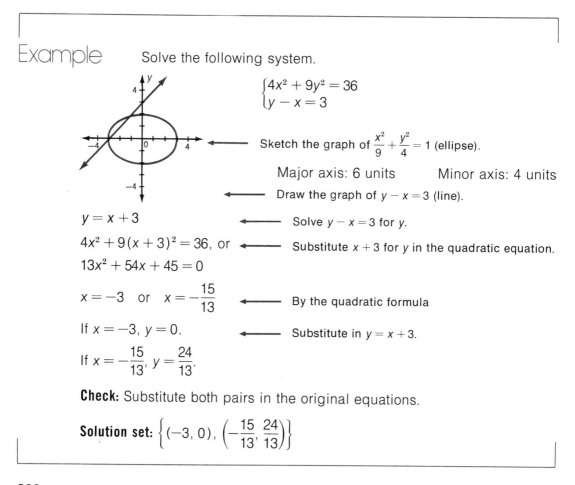

$$\begin{cases} 4x^2 + 9y^2 = 36 \\ y - x = 3 \end{cases}$$

⟵ Sketch the graph of $\dfrac{x^2}{9} + \dfrac{y^2}{4} = 1$ (ellipse).

Major axis: 6 units   Minor axis: 4 units

⟵ Draw the graph of $y - x = 3$ (line).

$y = x + 3$ ⟵ Solve $y - x = 3$ for y.

$4x^2 + 9(x + 3)^2 = 36$, or ⟵ Substitute $x + 3$ for y in the quadratic equation.
$13x^2 + 54x + 45 = 0$

$x = -3$ or $x = -\dfrac{15}{13}$ ⟵ By the quadratic formula

If $x = -3$, $y = 0$. ⟵ Substitute in $y = x + 3$.

If $x = -\dfrac{15}{13}$, $y = \dfrac{24}{13}$.

Check: Substitute both pairs in the original equations.

Solution set: $\left\{ (-3, 0), \left(-\dfrac{15}{13}, \dfrac{24}{13} \right) \right\}$

Steps for Solving a Linear/Second-Degree System

1. Sketch the graphs defined by equations of the system.
2. Solve the linear equation for one of the variables.
3. Substitute the result in the second-degree equation.
4. Solve this second-degree equation in one variable.
5. Find the other solution by substituting both numbers found in Step 4 in the linear equation.
6. Check by substituting each number pair in both equations.

Exercises

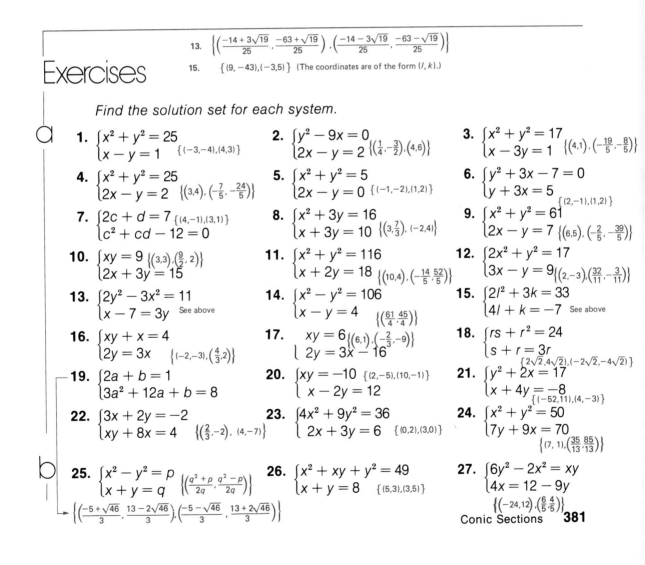

13. $\left\{\left(\dfrac{-14 + 3\sqrt{19}}{25}, \dfrac{-63 + \sqrt{19}}{25}\right), \left(\dfrac{-14 - 3\sqrt{19}}{25}, \dfrac{-63 - \sqrt{19}}{25}\right)\right\}$

15. $\{(9, -43),(-3,5)\}$ (The coordinates are of the form (l, k).)

Find the solution set for each system.

1. $\begin{cases} x^2 + y^2 = 25 \\ x - y = 1 \end{cases}$ $\{(-3,-4),(4,3)\}$

2. $\begin{cases} y^2 - 9x = 0 \\ 2x - y = 2 \end{cases}$ $\{(\frac{1}{4}, -\frac{3}{2}),(4,6)\}$

3. $\begin{cases} x^2 + y^2 = 17 \\ x - 3y = 1 \end{cases}$ $\{(4,1),(-\frac{19}{5}, -\frac{8}{5})\}$

4. $\begin{cases} x^2 + y^2 = 25 \\ 2x - y = 2 \end{cases}$ $\{(3,4),(-\frac{7}{5}, -\frac{24}{5})\}$

5. $\begin{cases} x^2 + y^2 = 5 \\ 2x - y = 0 \end{cases}$ $\{(-1,-2),(1,2)\}$

6. $\begin{cases} y^2 + 3x - 7 = 0 \\ y + 3x = 5 \end{cases}$ $\{(2,-1),(1,2)\}$

7. $\begin{cases} 2c + d = 7 \\ c^2 + cd - 12 = 0 \end{cases}$ $\{(4,-1),(3,1)\}$

8. $\begin{cases} x^2 + 3y = 16 \\ x + 3y = 10 \end{cases}$ $\{(3,\frac{7}{3}), (-2,4)\}$

9. $\begin{cases} x^2 + y^2 = 61 \\ 2x - y = 7 \end{cases}$ $\{(6,5), (-\frac{2}{5}, -\frac{39}{5})\}$

10. $\begin{cases} xy = 9 \\ 2x + 3y = 15 \end{cases}$ $\{(3,3),(\frac{9}{2}, 2)\}$

11. $\begin{cases} x^2 + y^2 = 116 \\ x + 2y = 18 \end{cases}$ $\{(10,4), (-\frac{14}{5}, \frac{52}{5})\}$

12. $\begin{cases} 2x^2 + y^2 = 17 \\ 3x - y = 9 \end{cases}$ $\{(2,-3),(\frac{32}{11}, -\frac{3}{11})\}$

13. $\begin{cases} 2y^2 - 3x^2 = 11 \\ x - 7 = 3y \end{cases}$ See above

14. $\begin{cases} x^2 - y^2 = 106 \\ x - y = 4 \end{cases}$ $\{(\frac{61}{4}, \frac{45}{4})\}$

15. $\begin{cases} 2l^2 + 3k = 33 \\ 4l + k = -7 \end{cases}$ See above

16. $\begin{cases} xy + x = 4 \\ 2y = 3x \end{cases}$ $\{(-2,-3),(\frac{4}{3},2)\}$

17. $\begin{cases} xy = 6 \\ 2y = 3x - 16 \end{cases}$ $\{(6,1),(-\frac{2}{3},-9)\}$

18. $\begin{cases} rs + r^2 = 24 \\ s + r = 3r \end{cases}$ $\{2\sqrt{2},4\sqrt{2}),(-2\sqrt{2},-4\sqrt{2})\}$

19. $\begin{cases} 2a + b = 1 \\ 3a^2 + 12a + b = 8 \end{cases}$

20. $\begin{cases} xy = -10 \\ x - 2y = 12 \end{cases}$ $\{(2,-5),(10,-1)\}$

21. $\begin{cases} y^2 + 2x = 17 \\ x + 4y = -8 \end{cases}$ $\{(-52,11),(4,-3)\}$

22. $\begin{cases} 3x + 2y = -2 \\ xy + 8x = 4 \end{cases}$ $\{(\frac{2}{3},-2), (4,-7)\}$

23. $\begin{cases} 4x^2 + 9y^2 = 36 \\ 2x + 3y = 6 \end{cases}$ $\{(0,2),(3,0)\}$

24. $\begin{cases} x^2 + y^2 = 50 \\ 7y + 9x = 70 \end{cases}$ $\{(7, 1),(\frac{35}{13}, \frac{85}{13})\}$

25. $\begin{cases} x^2 - y^2 = p \\ x + y = q \end{cases}$ $\{(\frac{q^2 + p}{2q}, \frac{q^2 - p}{2q})\}$

26. $\begin{cases} x^2 + xy + y^2 = 49 \\ x + y = 8 \end{cases}$ $\{(5,3),(3,5)\}$

27. $\begin{cases} 6y^2 - 2x^2 = xy \\ 4x = 12 - 9y \end{cases}$ $\{(-24,12),(\frac{6}{5}, \frac{4}{5})\}$

19. $\left\{\left(\dfrac{-5+\sqrt{46}}{3}, \dfrac{13 - 2\sqrt{46}}{3}\right), \left(\dfrac{-5-\sqrt{46}}{3}, \dfrac{13 + 2\sqrt{46}}{3}\right)\right\}$

Conic Sections **381**

Systems of Two Second-Degree Equations

The objective for this section is on page 390.

Systems of two second-degree equations can be solved by the substitution method or by the addition method.

Example

Solve the following system.

$$\begin{cases} x^2 + y^2 = 4 & \text{1} \\ 4x^2 + 9y^2 = 36 & \text{2} \end{cases}$$

$x^2 = 4 - y^2$ ⟵ Solve Equation **1** for x^2.

$4(4 - y^2) + 9y^2 = 36$ ⟵ Substitute for x^2 in Equation **2**.

$16 - 4y^2 + 9y^2 = 36$ ⟵ Solve for y.

$5y^2 = 20$

$y = \pm 2$

If $y = 2$, $x = 0$. ⟵ Replace y with 2 in Equation **1**.

If $y = -2$, $x = 0$. ⟵ Replace y with -2 in Equation **1**.

Solution set: $\{(0, 2), (0, -2)\}$ ⟵ The check is left for you.

Exercises

9. $\left\{\left(\pm\sqrt{\frac{a+b}{a^2+b^2}}, \sqrt{\frac{b-a}{a^2+b^2}}\right), \left(\pm\sqrt{\frac{a+b}{a^2+b^2}}, -\sqrt{\frac{b-a}{a^2+b^2}}\right)\right\}$

Solve each system. Check.

a

1. $\begin{cases} x^2 + y^2 = 9 \\ 2x^2 + 3y^2 = 18 \end{cases}$ $\{(3,0),(-3,0)\}$

2. $\begin{cases} 2x^2 - y^2 = -1 \\ x^2 + 2y^2 = 22 \end{cases}$

3. $\begin{cases} 4x^2 + y^2 = 17 \\ 3x^2 - 5y^2 = 7 \end{cases}$ $\{(2,1),(2,-1),(-2,1),(-2,-1)\}$

4. $\begin{cases} a^2 - 3b^2 = 13 \\ 2a^2 - 8b^2 = 18 \end{cases}$

5. $\begin{cases} y = x^2 \\ y = -x^2 + 2 \end{cases}$ $\{(1,1),(-1,1)\}$ $\{(2,3),(2,-3),(-2,3),(-2,-3)\}$

6. $\begin{cases} y = x^2 \\ x^2 + y^2 = 2 \end{cases}$ $\{(1,1),(-1,1)\}$

b

7. $\begin{cases} x^2 + y^2 = 2 \\ xy = 1 \end{cases}$ $\{(-1,-1),(1,1)\}$ $\{(5,2),(5,-2),(-5,2),(-5,-2)\}$

8. $\begin{cases} x^2 + y^2 = 25 \\ x + y^2 = 5 \end{cases}$ $\{(5,0),(-4,3),(-4,-3)\}$

9. $\begin{cases} ax^2 + by^2 = 1 \\ bx^2 - ay^2 = 1 \end{cases}$ see above.

382 Chapter 10

Inequalities of the Second Degree

The objective for this section is on page 390.

To graph the solution set of an inequality of the second degree, you first graph its corresponding equation. Then you determine the set of points that satisfy the inequality.

Example   Graph: $x^2 + y^2 < 25$

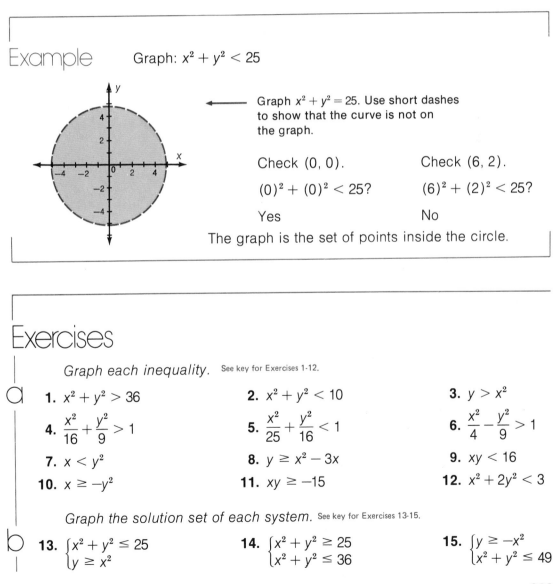

Graph $x^2 + y^2 = 25$. Use short dashes to show that the curve is not on the graph.

Check $(0, 0)$.

$(0)^2 + (0)^2 < 25$?

Yes

Check $(6, 2)$.

$(6)^2 + (2)^2 < 25$?

No

The graph is the set of points inside the circle.

Exercises

Graph each inequality.   See key for Exercises 1-12.

a   **1.** $x^2 + y^2 > 36$

2. $x^2 + y^2 < 10$

3. $y > x^2$

4. $\dfrac{x^2}{16} + \dfrac{y^2}{9} > 1$

5. $\dfrac{x^2}{25} + \dfrac{y^2}{16} < 1$

6. $\dfrac{x^2}{4} - \dfrac{y^2}{9} > 1$

7. $x < y^2$

8. $y \geq x^2 - 3x$

9. $xy < 16$

10. $x \geq -y^2$

11. $xy \geq -15$

12. $x^2 + 2y^2 < 3$

Graph the solution set of each system.   See key for Exercises 13-15.

b   **13.** $\begin{cases} x^2 + y^2 \leq 25 \\ y \geq x^2 \end{cases}$

14. $\begin{cases} x^2 + y^2 \geq 25 \\ x^2 + y^2 \leq 36 \end{cases}$

15. $\begin{cases} y \geq -x^2 \\ x^2 + y^2 \leq 49 \end{cases}$

Conic Sections   **383**

Mathematics and the
Environmental Sciences

Many **geologists** are involved with locating natural resources, such as minerals and oil, and working in laboratories, where they examine the various properties of rocks, minerals, and fossils. Much of this effort requires taking measurements and recording data. A bachelor's degree is the minimal requirement for entry into this field. About one-third of a college program consists of courses in mathematics, physics, chemistry, and engineering. Statistics and computer courses are especially recommended.

Geophysicists are concerned with the study of the earth's electric, magnetic, and gravitational fields. Highly technical measuring devices are used in their work. The use of satellites for conducting tests in outer space and of computers for collecting and analyzing data are growing in importance. Although the minimal requirement for this career is a bachelor's degree in geophysics, a degree in engineering or in a related science can suffice provided the person has taken mathematics and physical science courses.

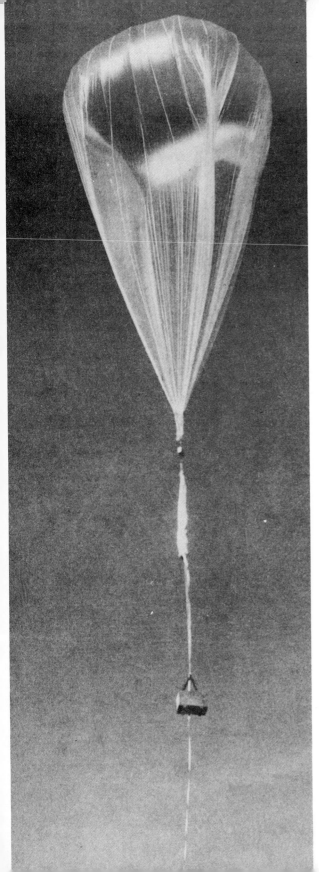

Most **meteorologists** specialize in weather forecasting. Some do research related to the effect of the atmosphere on the transmission of light, sound, and radio waves. As with other careers in the environmental sciences, taking measurements, collecting and recording data, and evaluation of data play an important role. In general, a bachelor's degree in meteorology is required for this field, but entry is possible with a degree in a related science of engineering. A person's background in mathematics and physics are the essential qualifications.

More Challenging Problems

1. Given $x^2(y^2 + y - 6) = x^4 + x^3 - 4x^2 + x + 1$, find y as a function of x. (There should be no radical in your answer.)

$$y = \frac{x^2 + 1}{x} \text{ or } y = \frac{-x^2 - x - 1}{x}$$

2. If $3a \neq b$, $a > 0$, and $b > 0$, show that $\dfrac{b}{3a} + \dfrac{3a}{b} > 2$. See key.

3. Show that $a^2 + \dfrac{16}{a^2} \geq 8$, if $a \neq 0$. See key.

4. Solve the following system. $\left\{ (4,-2),(-2,4) \right\}, \left(\frac{-5 + 3\sqrt{5}}{4}, \frac{-5 - 3\sqrt{5}}{4} \right), \left(\frac{-5 - 3\sqrt{5}}{4}, \frac{-5 + 3\sqrt{5}}{4} \right) \right\}$

$$\begin{cases} x^2 + y^2 + xy - x - y - 10 = 0 \\ 2xy + 3x + 3y + 10 = 0 \end{cases}$$

(HINT: For x substitute $u + v$ and for y substitute $u - v$, thus eliminating the xy terms. Solve for $u + v$.)

5. Under what conditions will a substitution as in Exercise 4 eliminate the xy term of a second-degree equation? If the coefficients of the x^2 and y^2 terms are equal.

6. Solve the following system. $\left\{ (12,9), (-9,-12) \right\}$

$$\begin{cases} x^3 - y^3 = 999 \\ x - y = 3 \end{cases}$$

7. Solve the following system. $\left\{ (9,4), (4,9) \right\}$

$$\begin{cases} x^2 + xy + y^2 = 133 \\ x - \sqrt{xy} + y = 7 \end{cases}$$

8. Find the equation of the circle that has the same center as $x^2 + y^2 - 5x + 3y = 0$ and is tangent to the line $x - y + 1 = 0$. $\left(x - \frac{5}{2} \right)^2 + \left(y + \frac{3}{2} \right)^2 = \frac{25}{2}$

9. Find the equation of the circle inscribed in the triangle with its sides formed by $x - y = 8$, $x + y = 8$, and $x = 0$. $(-8 + 8\sqrt{2})^2 = (x + 8 - 8\sqrt{2})^2 + y^2$

10. Solve the following system. $\left\{ \left(\frac{1}{2}, 1 \right) \right\}$

$$\begin{cases} \dfrac{1}{x^2} + \dfrac{4}{xy} - \dfrac{3}{y^2} = 9 \\ \dfrac{1}{x} + \dfrac{1}{y} = 3 \end{cases}$$

Answers to Remember

Page 361: 1. $x = \dfrac{-3 \pm \sqrt{19}i}{2}$ 2. $x = \dfrac{-3a \pm \sqrt{9a^2 - 16a}}{2}$ 3. {1}   4. {1}   5. {4}   6. 12

386   Chapter 10

Objective: To know the meanings of the important mathematical terms of this chapter.

1. Here are many of the mathematical terms used in this chapter. Be sure that you know their meanings and that you can use them correctly.

circle (p. 358)
center (p. 358)
directrix (p. 366)
ellipse (p. 362)
focus (p. 362)
hyperbola (p. 369)
inverse variation (p. 373)

joint variation (p. 375)
major axis (p. 363)
minor axis (p. 363)
parabola (p. 366)
radius (p. 358)
rectangular hyperbola (p. 372)
vertex (p. 367)

Objectives: To write the equation of a circle and to graph it given the center and the radius. (Section 10-1)

Write the equation of each circle with the given center and radius. Then sketch its graph.

2. $r = 2$; $(-1, 4)$
$(x + 1)^2 + (y - 4)^2 = 4$

3. $r = 5$; $(3, 0)$
$(x - 3)^2 + y^2 = 25$

4. $r = 3$; $(-2, -3)$
$(x + 2)^2 + (y + 3)^2 = 9$

Objectives: To write the length of the radius and the coordinates of the center of of a circle given its equation. (Section 10-1)

For each equation of a circle, write the length of the radius and the coordinates of its center.

5. $x^2 + y^2 = 16$ $r = 4; (0, 0)$

6. $(x + 2)^2 + (y - 3)^2 = 36$ $r = 6; (-2, 3)$

Objectives: To sketch the graph of an ellipse and to write the coordinates of the x intercepts, y intercepts, and foci from its equation. (Section 10-2)

Sketch the graph of each equation. Write the coordinates of the x intercepts, the y intercepts, and the foci. See key.

7. $36x^2 + 9y^2 = 324$

8. $64x^2 + 4y^2 = 256$

9. $25x^2 + 16y^2 = 400$

Conic Sections   **387**

Objectives: To write the equation of an ellipse given the x and y intercepts. (Section 10-2)

Write the equation of each ellipse given the following information.

10. x intercepts at $(3, 0)$ and $(-3, 0)$; y intercepts at $(0, 6)$ and $(0, -6)$. $\frac{x^2}{9} + \frac{y^2}{36} = 1$

11. x intercepts at $(5, 0)$ and $(-5, 0)$; y intercepts at $(0, 4)$ and $(0, -4)$. $\frac{x^2}{25} + \frac{y^2}{16} = 1$

Objectives: To sketch the graph of a parabola given its equation. (Section 10-3)

Sketch the graph of each equation. Label the focus, vertex, and directrix. See key.

12. $x = \frac{1}{36}y^2$ **13.** $y = -\frac{1}{64}x^2$ **14.** $y^2 = -4x$

Objectives: To write the equation of a parabola given the focus and the directrix. (Section 10-3)

Write the equation of each parabola given the following information.

15. Focus: $(-2, 0)$; directrix: $x = 2$ $y^2 = -8x$

16. Focus: $(0, 5)$; directrix: $y = -5$ $x^2 = 20y$

Objective: To sketch the graph of a hyperbola given its equation. (Section 10-4)

Sketch the graph of each equation. See key.

17. $\dfrac{x^2}{36} - \dfrac{y^2}{4} = 1$ **18.** $\dfrac{y^2}{64} - \dfrac{x^2}{16} = 1$ **19.** $25x^2 - 9y^2 = 225$

Objective: To write the equation of a hyperbola. (Section 10-4)

Write the equation of each hyperbola given the following information.

20. Center: $(0, 0)$; opens vertically; $a = 2$, $b = 3$ $\frac{y^2}{4} - \frac{x^2}{9} = 1$

21. Foci: $(0, 4)$, $(0, -4)$; Vertices: $(0, 3)$, $(0, -3)$ $\frac{y^2}{9} - \frac{x^2}{7} = 1$

22. Vertices: $(2, 0)$, $(-2, 0)$; asymptotes: $x - 4y = 0$, $x + 4y = 0$ $\frac{x^2}{4} - 4y^2 = 1$

Objective: To identify a given equation as that of a circle, ellipse, hyperbola, or rectangular hyperbola. (Section 10-5)

Identify each equation as that of a circle, an ellipse, a parabola, a hyperbola, or a rectangular hyperbola.

23. $xy = 15$ Rectangular hyperbola   **24.** $\dfrac{x^2}{100} + \dfrac{y^2}{36} = 1$ Ellipse   **25.** $x = y^2 - 6y + 5$ Parabola

26. $4x^2 + 9y^2 = 25$ Ellipse   **27.** $(x + 2)^2 + (y - 5)^2 = 10$ Circle   **28.** $y = -x^2 + 5x + 6$ Parabola

Objective: To solve variation problems. (Section 10-6)

For Exercises 29–31, use k as the constant of variation to write the equation that expresses each relation.

29. y varies inversely as x. $xy = k \text{ or } y = \frac{k}{x}$ **30.** y varies jointly as a and b. $y = kab$

31. y varies inversely as the square of x. $y = \frac{k}{x^2}$

32. If y varies directly as x, and $x = 10$ when $y = 3$, find y when $x = 7$. $\frac{21}{10}$

33. If y varies jointly as x and z, and $y = 20$ when $x = 4$ and $z = 2$, find y when $x = 3$ and $z = 1$. $\frac{15}{2}$

34. If y varies inversely as the square of x, and $y = 5$ when $x = 3$, find y when $x = 4$. $\frac{45}{16}$

Objective: To associate the equation of a conic section with its graph. (Section 10-7)

Match each graph below with its equation.

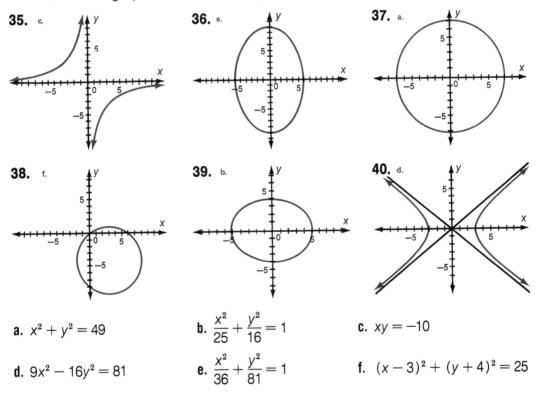

35. c.   **36.** e.   **37.** a.

38. f.   **39.** b.   **40.** d.

a. $x^2 + y^2 = 49$

b. $\dfrac{x^2}{25} + \dfrac{y^2}{16} = 1$

c. $xy = -10$

d. $9x^2 - 16y^2 = 81$

e. $\dfrac{x^2}{36} + \dfrac{y^2}{81} = 1$

f. $(x - 3)^2 + (y + 4)^2 = 25$

Objective: To solve a system of a first and second degree equation algebraically. (Section 10-8)

Solve each system algebraically. 43. $\{(\frac{4}{5}\sqrt{5},\frac{2}{5}\sqrt{5}),(-\frac{4}{5}\sqrt{5},-\frac{2}{5}\sqrt{5})\}$

41. $\begin{cases} 3x^2 + xy = 5 \\ 2x + y = 2 \end{cases}$ $\quad$ **42.** $\begin{cases} x^2 - y = 3 \\ x - y = -3 \end{cases}$ $\{(3,6),(-2,1)\}$ $\quad$ **43.** $\begin{cases} x^2 + y^2 = 4 \\ x - 2y = 0 \end{cases}$

$\{(-1+\sqrt{6}, 4-2\sqrt{6}),(-1-\sqrt{6}, 4+2\sqrt{6})\}$ $\qquad\qquad\qquad\qquad\qquad\qquad\qquad\qquad$ See above

Objective: To solve a system of two second-degree equations. (Section 10-9)

Sove each system. 45. $\{(\sqrt{6},\sqrt{6}),(-\sqrt{6},-\sqrt{6}),(2\sqrt{3},\sqrt{3}),(-2\sqrt{3},-\sqrt{3})\}$

44. $\begin{cases} x^2 + y^2 = 25 \\ 3x^2 - 2y^2 = 30 \end{cases}$ $\{(4,3),(4,-3),(-4,3),(-4,-3)\}$ $\quad$ **45.** $\begin{cases} x^2 + 2y^2 = 18 \\ xy = 6 \end{cases}$ see above

Objective: To graph the solution set of an inequality of the second degree. (Section 10-10)

Graph each inequality.

46. $x^2 + y^2 < 16$ The graph is the set of points inside the circle with center at (0,0) and radius 4. $\quad$ **47.** $4x^2 + 9y^2 \geq 36$ The graph is the set of points on and outside the ellipse with center (0,0) and intercepts (3,0),(−3,0), (0,2) and (0, −2).

Chapter
Test

Name and graph the conic section defined by the given equations.

1. $x^2 + y^2 = 36$ Circle; center (0,0); $r = 6$ $\quad$ **2.** $xy = -5$ Rectangular hyperbola; vertices: $(\sqrt{5}, -\sqrt{5}),(-\sqrt{5},\sqrt{5})$

3. $\dfrac{x^2}{16} + \dfrac{y^2}{25} = 1$ Ellipse; center (0,0); intercepts: (±4,0),(0,±5) **4.** $\dfrac{x^2}{25} - \dfrac{y^2}{49} = 1$ Hyperbola; center (0,0); vertices: (5,0),(−5,0)

5. $4x^2 - 16y^2 = 24$ Hyperbola; center (0,0); vertices: $(\sqrt{6}, 0),(-\sqrt{6},0)$ $\quad$ **6.** $(x - 2)^2 + (y + 4)^2 = 16$ Circle: Center (2,−4); $r = 4$

Find the solution set of each system.

7. $\begin{cases} 3x^2 - 2y^2 = 15 \\ x - y = 1 \end{cases}$ $\{(-2+\sqrt{21}, -3+\sqrt{21},)(-2-\sqrt{21},-3-\sqrt{21})\}$ $\quad$ **8.** $\begin{cases} 2x^2 + xy = 10 \\ x + 2y = 2 \end{cases}$ $\left\{\left(\dfrac{-1-\sqrt{61}}{3}, \dfrac{7+\sqrt{61}}{6}\right),\left(\dfrac{-1+\sqrt{61}}{3}, \dfrac{7-\sqrt{61}}{6}\right)\right\}$

For Exercises 9–11, use k as the constant of variation and write an equation that expresses the given relationship.

9. *a* varies inversely as *b*. $a = \frac{k}{b}$

10. *x* varies directly as *y*. $x = ky$

11. *r* varies jointly as *x* and *t* and inversely as the square of *w*. $r = \frac{kx \cdot t}{w^2}$

12. If *a* varies jointly as *b* and *c*, and *a* = 16 when *b* = 10 and *c* = 5, find *a* when *b* = 9 and *c* = 4. $a = \frac{288}{25}$

Chapter 11
Sequences and Series

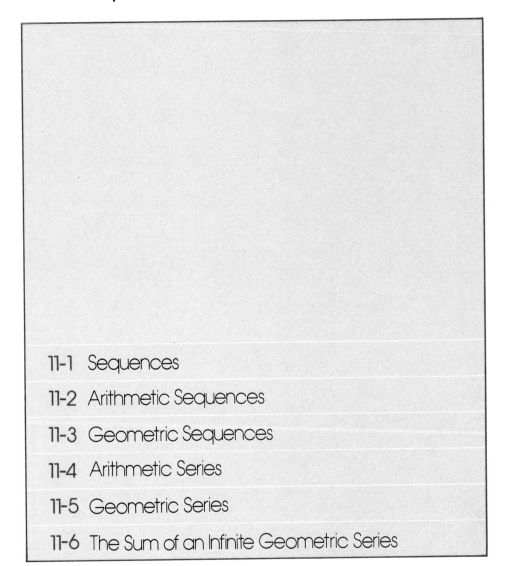

The objective for this section is on page 412.

Each of the following has a pattern.

a. 1, 7, 13, 19, 25, · · ·
b. 2, 4, 8, 16, 32, · · ·
c. 1, 4, 9, 16, 25, · · ·

To find the <u>rule</u> that describes the pattern, pair each number of the pattern with a positive integer.

Example

Write the rule for pattern **a.** Use the rule to find the next three numbers.

To find the rule means to find the nth number in pattern **a,** which is written a_n (read: "a sub n").

$$\begin{array}{cccccc} 1 & 2 & 3 & 4 & 5 & \cdots & n \\ \updownarrow & \updownarrow & \updownarrow & \updownarrow & \updownarrow & & \updownarrow \\ 1 & 7 & 13 & 19 & 25 & \cdots & a_n \end{array}$$

←——— Positive integers

←——— Pattern **a**

<u>Rule:</u> Each number in pattern **a** is equal to 5 less than 6 times the positive integer with which it is paired. In symbols,

$$a_n = 6n - 5$$

To find the next three numbers means to find the sixth, seventh, and eighth numbers in **a,** which are a_6, a_7, and a_8.

$a_6 = 6(6) - 5 = 31$ ←——— Replace n with 6.
$a_7 = 6(7) - 5 = 37$ ←——— Replace n with 7.
$a_8 = 6(8) - 5 = 43$ ←——— Replace n with 8.

The pairings can be written as a set of ordered pairs.

$\{(1, 1), (2, 7), (3, 13), (4, 19), (5, 25), \cdots, (n, 6n - 5) \cdots\}$

This set describes a function called a <u>sequence</u>.

Definitions: A **sequence** is a function whose domain is the set of positive integers. The numbers contained in the range of the function are the **terms of the sequence.**

$$\{(1, a_1), (2, a_2), (3, a_3), (4, a_4), \cdots, (n, a_n), \cdots\}$$

Patterns **a-c** are **infinite sequences,** because there is no last term. A sequence that has a last term is a **finite sequence.**

Try These　*Verify that each rule gives the first three terms of the given sequence. Use the rule to find the next three terms.*

1. $a_n = 3n$; 3, 6, 9, $\cdots$　12, 15, 18

2. $a_n = 2n - 3$; -1, 1, 3, $\cdots$　5, 7, 9

3. $a_n = n^2$; 1, 4, 9, $\cdots$　16, 25, 36

4. $a_n = 2^n$; 2, 4, 8, $\cdots$　16, 32, 64

Exercises

Use the rule to find the first three terms of a sequence.

1. $a_n = n^3$　1, 8, 27

2. $a_n = n^2 + 1$　2, 5, 10

3. $a_n = n + \dfrac{1}{n}$　2, $2\frac{1}{2}$, $3\frac{1}{3}$

Write the rule for each sequence. Use the rule to find the next three terms.

4. $a_n = 2n$; 2, 4, 6, 8, $\cdots$　10, 12, 14

5. $a_n = 3n + 1$; 4, 7, 10, 13, $\cdots$　16, 19, 22

6. $a_n = n$; 1, 2, 3, 4, $\cdots$　5, 6, 7

7. 0, -1, -2, -3, $\cdots$　$-4, -5, -6$

8. $a_n = 3n - 1$; 2, 5, 8, 11, $\cdots$　14, 17, 20

9. 3, 6, 12, 24, $\cdots$　48, 96, 192

10. $a_n = -n + 1$; -2, -1, 0, 1, $\cdots$　2, 3, 4

11. -4, -2, 0, 2, $\cdots$　4, 6, 8

12. $a_n = \dfrac{3 \cdot 2^{n-1}}{1}$; 1, $\dfrac{1}{2}$, $\dfrac{1}{3}$, $\dfrac{1}{4}$, $\cdots$　$\frac{1}{5}, \frac{1}{6}, \frac{1}{7}$

13. $a_n = \dfrac{1}{3} - 3$; 1, $\dfrac{1}{3}$, $\dfrac{1}{9}$, $\dfrac{1}{27}$, $\cdots$　$\frac{1}{81}, \frac{1}{243}, \frac{1}{729}$

14. $a_n = 2n - 6$; 2, 1, $\dfrac{1}{2}$, $\dfrac{1}{4}$, $\cdots$　$\frac{1}{8}, \frac{1}{16}, \frac{1}{32}$

15. $a_n = n^{-1}$; 2.5, 3, 3.5, 4, $\cdots$　4.5, 5, 5.5

Use the rule to write the first four terms of a sequence.

16. $a_n = n^2(n - 1)$　0, 4, 18, 48

17. $a_n = (-1)^{n+1}$　1, -1, 1, -1

18. $a_n = \dfrac{n}{2}(n + 1)$　1, 3, 6, 10

19. $a_n = 3^{1-n}$　1, $\frac{1}{3}, \frac{1}{9}, \frac{1}{27}$

20. $a_n = a + (n - 1)d$　$a, a + d, a + 2d, a + 3d$

21. $a_n = ar^{n-1}$　a, ar, ar^2, ar^3

11-2 Arithmetic Sequences

The objectives for this section are on pages 412-413.

If each term of a sequence is obtained by adding some fixed number to the preceding term, the sequence is called an <u>arithmetic sequence</u> or an <u>arithmetic progression</u>.

Definitions: An **arithmetic sequence** is a sequence in which the difference obtained by subtracting any term from the following term is a constant called the **common difference.**

Example 1

If a_1 is the first term of an arithmetic sequence, find the next four terms.

$$a_2 - a_1 = d \quad \text{or} \quad a_2 = a_1 + d \quad \longleftarrow \quad \text{By definition.}$$

Similarly: $a_3 = a_2 + d$ $\qquad a_4 = a_3 + d$ $\qquad a_5 = a_4 + d$

$\qquad\qquad a_3 = (a_1 + d) + d$ $\qquad a_4 = (a_1 + 2d) + d$ $\qquad a_5 = (a_1 + 3d) + d$

$\qquad\qquad a_3 = a_1 + 2d$ $\qquad\qquad a_4 = a_1 + 3d$ $\qquad\qquad a_5 = a_1 + 4d$

Generalizing Example 1, you have the following.

$$a_n = a_{n-1} + d$$
$$a_n = a_1 + (n-1)d$$

Example 2

The first term of an arithmetic sequence is 3 and the common difference between successive terms is 2. Find the twentieth term.

$$a_{20} = a_1 + (n-1)d$$
$$= 3 + (20 - 1)2 \quad \longleftarrow \quad a_1 = 3, \ d = 2, \ n = 20$$
$$= 41$$

Example 3 The sixth term of an arithmetic sequence is -2 and the twelfth term is -14. Find the first term and the common difference.

$$\begin{cases} -2 = a_1 + 5d \\ -14 = a_1 + 11d \end{cases} \longleftarrow \quad \begin{aligned} a_6 &= a_1 + (6-1)d \\ a_{12} &= a_1 + (12-1)d \end{aligned}$$

$$\begin{cases} a_1 + 5d = -2 \\ a_1 + 11d = -14 \end{cases} \longleftarrow \quad \text{Solve this system to find } a_1 \text{ and } d.$$

$$a_1 = 8; \; d = -2$$

The terms between any two given terms of an arithmetic sequence are called **arithmetic means.** For example, in the sequence 2, 8, 14, 20, 26, $\cdots$ the terms 8, 14, and 20 are the three arithmetic means between 2 and 26.

Example 4 Find three arithmetic means between 6 and 12.

Consider 6 and 12 as the first and fifth terms.

$$a_n = a_1 + (n-1)d$$
$$12 = 6 + (5-1)d \longleftarrow \quad a_1 = 6, \; n = 5$$
$$12 = 6 + 4d$$
$$\tfrac{3}{2} = d$$

$$a_2 = a_1 + \tfrac{3}{2} \qquad\qquad a_3 = a_2 + \tfrac{3}{2} \qquad\qquad a_4 = a_3 + \tfrac{3}{2}$$
$$a_2 = 6 + \tfrac{3}{2} = 7\tfrac{1}{2} \qquad a_3 = 7\tfrac{1}{2} + \tfrac{3}{2} = 9 \qquad a_4 = 9 + \tfrac{3}{2} = 10\tfrac{1}{2}$$

Try These *Classify each sequence as arithmetic or non-arithmetic. Find the difference between successive terms for each arithmetic sequence.*

1. $-6, -2, 2, 6, 10, \cdots$ Arithmetic, d = 4

2. $\tfrac{1}{3}, \tfrac{1}{9}, \tfrac{1}{27}, \tfrac{1}{81}, \tfrac{1}{243}, \cdots$ Non-Arithmetic

3. $6, 3, 0, -3, -6, \cdots$ Arithmetic, d = -3

4. $1, \tfrac{3}{2}, 2, \tfrac{5}{2}, 3, \cdots$ Arithmetic, $d = \tfrac{1}{2}$

5. $2x, x, 0, -x, -2x, \cdots$ Arithmetic, d = -x

6. $x + 1, 2x, 3x - 1, 4x - 2, \cdots$ Arithmetic, d = x - 1

Sequences and Series **395**

Exercises

Write the first five terms of each arithmetic sequence.

1. $a_1 = 1$, $d = 5$ 1,6,11,16,21

2. $a_1 = -5$, $d = 6$ -5,1,7,13,19

3. $a_1 = -30$, $d = -2$ -30,-32,-34,-36,-38

4. $a_1 = 25b$, $d = -5b$

                                                 25b, 20b, 15b,10b,5b

5. $a_1 = c$, $d = x - c$

    $c, x, 2x - c, 3x - 2c, 4x - 3c$

6. $a_1 = x$, $d = x + m$

    $x, 2x + m, 3x + 2m, 4x + 3m, 5x + 4m$

In each of the following sequences, find the required term.

7. The 10th term of 4, 5, 6, $\cdots$ 13

8. The 20th term of 5, 7, 9, $\cdots$ 43

9. The 18th term of 18, 14, 10, $\cdots$ -50

10. The 24th term of -3, 0, 3, $\cdots$ 66

11. The 9th term of a, $a + 2$, $a + 4$, $\cdots$ $a + 16$

12. The 11th term of $2\sqrt{3}$, $\sqrt{3}$, 0, $\cdots$ $-8\sqrt{3}$

13. The 15th term of $\frac{1}{2}$, 2, $\frac{7}{2}$, $\cdots$ $\frac{43}{2}$

14. The 25th term of 5, $4\frac{1}{3}$, $3\frac{2}{3}$, $\cdots$ -11

Find the indicated number of arithmetic means.

15. Find two arithmetic means between 3 and 15.   7 and 11

16. Find two arithmetic means between 4 and 80. $29\frac{1}{3}$ and $54\frac{2}{3}$

17. Find three arithmetic means between 6 and 11. $7\frac{1}{4}$, $8\frac{1}{2}$, and $9\frac{3}{4}$

18. Find four arithmetic means between 4 and 179.   39, 74, 109, and 144

19. Find the arithmetic mean between x and y. $\frac{x+y}{2}$ (See Ex. 35)

20. Find five arithmetic means between 2 and 11. $3\frac{1}{2}$, 5, $6\frac{1}{2}$, 8, and $9\frac{1}{2}$

21. The third term of an arithmetic sequence is 5 and the eighth term is 20. Find the first term, the common difference, and the first three terms of the sequence. $d = 3$; $a_1 = -1$; The first three terms are -1, 2, and 5.

22. The seventh term of an arithmetic sequence is 6 and the thirteenth term is -18. Find the first five terms of the sequence.   30, 26, 22, 18 and 14

23. If the fourth term of an arithmetic sequence is 9 and the seventh term is 10, find the twentieth term. $14\frac{1}{3}$

24. Find the common difference in an arithmetic sequence if there are 75 terms, where the first term is 38 and the last term is 1. $-\frac{1}{2}$

25. How many terms are there in an arithmetic sequence if the first term is 100, the last term is -14, and the common difference is -2?   58

26. Which term in the sequence 5, 2, -1, $-4 \cdots$ is -85?   31

27. How many even integers are there between 12 and 238? (HINT: $a_1 = 14$, $a_n = 236$, and $d = 2$.)   112

28. How many odd integers are there between 133 and 351?   108

29. How many integers divisible by 3 are there between 1 and 100?   33

30. Find the value of x so that $x + 1$, $3x - 2$, and $4x + 5$ form an arithmetic sequence.   10

31. The top row of a pile of logs contains 6 logs, the row below the top one contains 7 logs, the third row from the top contains 8 logs, and so on. If there are 45 rows, how many logs are there in the bottom row?   50

32. It costs $1650 to attend a state university. If the cost increases $75 each year, how much will it cost to attend this university in 13 years? $2625

33. The rise in the cost of living has increased the Oliver family's grocery bill $84 each year for 6 consecutive years. If the Oliver's grocery expenditure one year ago was $1056, what was their grocery expenditure 6 years ago? Approximately how many years will it take for last year's expenditure to double, if the rate of increase stays the same? $636; 11.6 years

34. A consumer buys a foreign car for $1800. Rising import taxes increase the price of the car $125 each year. When will the consumer pay $2300 for the car?   4 years

35. Prove that finding one arithmetic mean between two numbers is the same as finding the "average" of the numbers.   See key.

36. Prove that adding corresponding terms of two arithmetic sequences forms another arithmetic sequence. Illustrate with an example.   See key.

37. Show that multiplying corresponding terms of two arithmetic sequences does not, in general, form another arithmetic sequence.   See key.

38. Prove that if each term of an arithmetic sequence is multiplied by a constant, the resulting sequence is an arithmetic sequence.   See key.

11-3 Geometric Sequences

The objectives for this section are on page 413.

In arithmetic sequences, there is a constant difference, d, between successive terms. A sequence in which the ratio of each term to its preceding term is the same constant, r, (called a **common ratio**) is a geometric sequence or a geometric progression.

Definition: A **geometric sequence** is one in which the ratio r of any term to its predecessor is always the same number.

$$\frac{a_{n+1}}{a_n} = r$$

Example 1

If a_1 is the first term of a geometric sequence, find the next four terms.

$$\frac{a_2}{a_1} = r \quad \text{or} \quad a_2 = a_1 r \quad \longleftarrow \quad \text{By definition}$$

Similarly:

$a_3 = a_2 r$	$a_4 = a_3 r$	$a_5 = a_4 r$
$a_3 = (a_1 r) r$	$a_4 = (a_1 r^2) r$	$a_5 = (a_1 r^3) r$
$a_3 = a_1 r^2$	$a_4 = a_1 r^3$	$a_5 = a_1 r^4$

Generalizing Example 1, you have the following.

$$\begin{cases} a_n = a_{n-1} r \\ a_n = a_1 r^{n-1} \end{cases}$$

The symbolism for the first term is often given without the subscript. That is, $a_1 = a$. You then have

$$a_n = a r^{n-1}.$$

Example 2
Find the eighth term of 4, 8, 16, 32, $\cdots$.

$a_n = a_1 \cdot r^{n-1}$

$a_8 = 4 \cdot (2^{8-1})$ $\longleftarrow$ $a_1 = 4, r = 2, n = 8$

$a_8 = 4 \cdot (2^7)$

$a_8 = 4(128) = 512$

The terms between any two given terms of a geometric sequence are called the **geometric means** between these terms.

Example 3
Insert three geometric means between 3 and $\dfrac{3}{16}$.

$a_n = ar^{n-1}$

$\dfrac{3}{16} = 3r^4$ $\longleftarrow$ $a_n = \dfrac{3}{16}, a = 3, n = 5$

$r = \pm \dfrac{1}{\sqrt[4]{16}} = \pm \dfrac{1}{2}$

$a_2 = 3\left(\dfrac{1}{2}\right) = \dfrac{3}{2}$ or $a_2 = 3\left(-\dfrac{1}{2}\right) = -\dfrac{3}{2}$ $\longleftarrow$ $a_2 = ar$

$a_3 = 3\left(\dfrac{1}{2}\right)^2 = \dfrac{3}{4}$ or $a_3 = 3\left(-\dfrac{1}{2}\right)^2 = \dfrac{3}{4}$ $\longleftarrow$ $a_3 = ar^2$

$a_4 = 3\left(\dfrac{1}{2}\right)^3 = \dfrac{3}{8}$ or $a_4 = 3\left(-\dfrac{1}{2}\right)^3 = -\dfrac{3}{8}$ $\longleftarrow$ $a_4 = ar^3$

Thus, either $\dfrac{3}{2}, \dfrac{3}{4}, \dfrac{3}{8}$ or $-\dfrac{3}{2}, \dfrac{3}{4}, -\dfrac{3}{8}$ may be inserted between 3 and $\dfrac{3}{16}$ to form a geometric sequence.

Try These
Find the common ratio for each geometric sequence.

1. 3, 9, 27, $\cdots$ 3

2. 8, 2, $\dfrac{1}{2}, \dfrac{1}{8}, \cdots$ $\dfrac{1}{4}$

3. $ar, ar^2, ar^3, \cdots$ r

Find the missing term in each geometric sequence.

4. 2, 8, 32, $\underline{\quad?\quad}$ $\cdots$ 128

5. $\underline{\quad?\quad}$, 3, 1, $\dfrac{1}{3} \cdots$ 9

6. $\sqrt{3}$, $\underline{\quad?\quad}$, $3\sqrt{3}$, 9 $\cdots$ 3

Sequences and Series **399**

Exercises

Write the first four terms of each geometric sequence.

1. $a = 2$, $r = 3$ 2, 6, 18, 54

2. $a = 2$, $r = -2$ 2, −4, 8, −16

3. $a = \frac{1}{2}$, $r = 4$ $\frac{1}{2}$, 2, 8, 32

4. $a = -\frac{1}{2}$, $r = -2$ $-\frac{1}{2}$, 1, −2, 4

5. $a = \frac{1}{4}$, $r = 2$ $\frac{1}{4}$, $\frac{1}{2}$, 1, 2

6. $a_1 = -27$, $r = \frac{2}{3}$ See above

7. $a_1 = 0.7$, $r = -4$ See above

8. $a_1 = \sqrt{2}$, $r = \sqrt{2}$ $\sqrt{2}$, 2, 2$\sqrt{2}$, 4

9. $a_1 = i$, $r = i$ i, −1, −i, 1

10. The second term is $4x^8$ and $r = -2x^2$. $-2x^6$, $4x^8$, $-8x^{10}$, $16x^{12}$

11. The fourth term is −18 and $r = -\frac{3}{2}$. $\frac{16}{3}$, −8, 12, −18

12. The third term is y^{12} and $r = y^3$. y^6, y^9, y^{12}, y^{15}

13. The fifth term is $(1.03)^4$ and $r = 1.03$. 1, 1.03, 1.03^2, 1.03^3

Find the specified term for each of the following geometric sequences.

14. 8th term: 1, 2, 4, · · · 128

15. 8th term: −1, −2, −4, · · · −128

16. 6th term: −6, −3, −$\frac{3}{2}$, · · · $-\frac{3}{16}$

17. 14th term: x, −x, x, · · · −x

18. 10th term: $\sqrt{2}$, 2, 2$\sqrt{2}$, · · · 32

19. 6th term: 96, 24, 6, · · · $\frac{3}{32}$

20. 9th term: 0.3, 0.03, 0.003, · · · 0.000000003

21. 12th term: i, −1, −i, · · · 1

Find the indicated geometric means. (A single geometric mean between two numbers is called the geometric mean, or mean proportional, of the two numbers.)

22. One positive geometric mean between 3 and 48. 12

23. One negative geometric mean between −3 and −27. −9

24. Three geometric means between 3 and 48. 6, 12 and 24 or −6, 12, and −24

25. Five geometric means between −2 and −128. −4, −8, −16, −32, and −64 or 4, −8, 16, −32, 64

26. Four geometric means between $\sqrt{2}$ and 8. 2, 2$\sqrt{2}$, 4, 4$\sqrt{2}$

27. Find the mean proportional between $\sqrt{6}$ and $\sqrt{24}$. $\sqrt{12}$ or −$\sqrt{12}$

28. The geometric mean between two numbers is 15. If one number is 9, find the other. 25

29. Which term of the geometric sequence 5, −10, 20, · · · is 320? seventh

30. Which term of the geometric sequence $\frac{1}{4}$, $\frac{1}{2}$, 1, · · · is 128? tenth

31. Find the value of x so that $x + 1$, $x - 1$ and $x - 2$ form a geometric sequence. 3

32. The third term of a geometric sequence is 9 and the seventh term is 81. Find the fifth term. ₂₇ 27

33. The population in a town of 3125 increased 20 per cent each year. When will the population reach 7776? 5 years

34. A car which originally cost $3200 depreciates each year $\frac{1}{4}$ of its value the preceding year. What is the value of the car at the end of 5 years? $759.38

35. The figure at the right contains a large square with a side of length 12 and a succession of smaller squares formed by connecting midpoints of consecutive sides. The areas of the squares form a geometric sequence. Find the common ratio and the area of the red square. $\frac{1}{2}$; 9 square units

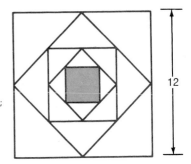

C **36.** There are 3 amoebas in a jar. They double every minute. If the jar is completely filled in 20 minutes, when is the jar half full? 19 minutes

37. Prove that if a_1, a_2, a_3 form a geometric sequence, then a_1^2, a_2^2, a_3^2, form a geometric sequence. See key.

11-4 Arithmetic Series

The objectives for this section are on page 413.

The following are examples of arithmetic series.

$$1 + 2 + 3 + \cdots + n$$
$$2 + 4 + 6 + \cdots + 2n$$
$$1 + 4 + 7 + \cdots + (3n - 2)$$

A **series** is an indicated sum of the terms of a sequence. The terms of a series are the same as the terms of the sequence.

Definition: An **arithmetic series** is the indicated sum of the terms of an arithmetic sequence.

The **sum of a series** is the standard name for the indicated sum.

Example 1   Find the sum of the series $4 + 8 + 12 + 16 + 20 + 24$.

$$\begin{array}{ll} S_6 = 4 + 8 + 12 + 16 + 20 + 24 & \\ \underline{S_6 = 24 + 20 + 16 + 12 + 8 + 4} & \longleftarrow \text{Reverse the order.} \\ 2S_6 = 28 + 28 + 28 + 28 + 28 + 28 & \longleftarrow \text{Add.} \\ 2S_6 = 6 \cdot 28 & \\ S_6 = \frac{6}{2} \cdot 28 & \longleftarrow \text{Note: The 6 in } \frac{6}{2} \text{ is the number of} \\ S_6 = 3 \cdot 28, \text{ or } 84 & \text{terms, and 28 is the sum of the first} \\ & \text{and last terms.} \end{array}$$

The general case is done similarly.

$$\begin{array}{l} S_n = a_1 + (a_1 + d) + (a_1 + 2d) + \cdots + [a_1 + (n-1)d] \\ \underline{S_n = [a_1 + (n-1)d] + [a_1 + (n-2)d] + [a_1 + (n-3)d] + \cdots + a_1} \\ 2S_n = [2a_1 + (n-1)d] + [2a_1 + (n-1)d] + [2a_1 + (n-1)d] + \cdots + [2a_1 + (n-1)d] \\ 2S_n = n[2a_1 + (n-1)d] \quad \longleftarrow \text{There are } n \text{ terms.} \\ S_n = \frac{n}{2}[2a_1 + (n-1)d] \end{array}$$

This result is summarized in Theorem 11-1.

Theorem 11-1: Sum of an Arithmetic Series

If S_n represents the sum of the arithmetic series
$a_1 + (a_1 + d) + (a_1 + 2d) + \cdots + a_1 + (n-1)d$, then

$$S_n = \frac{n}{2}[2a_1 + (n-1)d].$$

The formula

$$S_n = \frac{n}{2}(a_1 + a_n),$$

where a is the first term and a_n is the last term, can be derived from the formula in Theorem 11-1.

Example 2   Find the sum of the first fifteen terms of $2 + 5 + 8 + \cdots$.

Method I

$$S_n = \frac{n}{2}[2a_1 + (n-1)d]$$

$$S_{15} = \frac{15}{2}[2(2) + 14(3)]$$

$$S_{15} = \frac{15(4 + 42)}{2}$$

$$S_{15} = \frac{15(46)}{2} = 345$$

Method II

$$a_n = a_1 + (n-1)d$$

$$a_{15} = 2 + 14(3) \quad \longleftarrow \text{ Find } a_{15}.$$

$$a_{15} = 44$$

$$S_n = \frac{n}{2}(a_1 + a_n)$$

$$S_{15} = \frac{15}{2}(2 + 44) = 345$$

Try These   *Write the required term in each arithmetic series.*

1. The seventh term of $2 + 6 + 10 + \cdots$ 26
2. The sixty-fourth term of $1 + 3 + 5 + \cdots$ 127
3. The tenth term of $5 + 8 + 11 + \cdots$ 32

Find the sum of the terms as indicated.

4. $3 + 5 + 7 + \cdots$ to eight terms.   80
5. $17 + 15 + 13 + \cdots$ to thirty terms.   −360

Exercises

Write the required term in each arithmetic series.

a **1.** The eighth term of $14 + 10 + 6 + \cdots$ −14
2. The twentieth term of $5 + 4\frac{1}{2} + 4 + \cdots$ $-\frac{9}{2}$
3. The seventh term of $-7 - 9 - 11 - \cdots$ −19

4. The eighth term of $2\sqrt{2} + \sqrt{2} + 0 + \cdots$ $-5\sqrt{2}$

5. The sixth term of $-6 - 4 - 2 - \cdots$ 4

6. The twelfth term of $-6 - 2 + 2 + \cdots$ 38

7. The twentieth term of $\frac{1}{2} + 2 + 3\frac{1}{2} + \cdots$ 29

8. The fifteenth term of $2x + 5x + 8x + \cdots$ $44x$

9. The ninth term of $(a + 7) + (a + 4) + (a + 1) + \cdots$ $a - 17$

10. The tenth term of $(a + b) + (a + 2b) + (a + 3b) + \cdots$ $a + 10b$

11. Write the first five terms of an arithmetic series where the second term is x and the third term is y. $(2x - y) + (x) + (y) + (2y - x) + (3y - 2x)$

$24 + 60 + 96 + 132 + 168 + 204 + 240$

Write the arithmetic series that results from each procedure.

$6 + 12 + 18 + 24 + 30 + 36 + 42 + 48 + 54 + 60$

12. Eight arithmetic means are inserted between 6 and 60.

13. Five arithmetic means are inserted between 24 and 240.

14. One arithmetic mean is inserted between $\frac{1}{8}$ and $\frac{1}{16}$. $\frac{1}{8} + \frac{3}{32} + \frac{1}{16}$

15. Four arithmetic means are inserted between x and y.

$x + \frac{4x + y}{5} + \frac{3x + 2y}{5} + \frac{2x + 3y}{5} + \frac{x + 4y}{5} + y$

Find the sum of the terms as indicated.

16. $-7 - 5 - 3 - \cdots$ to sixteen terms 128

17. $7 + 12 + 17 + \cdots$ to ten terms 295

18. $-13 - 11 - 9 - \cdots$ to twenty terms 120

19. $-10 - 5 - 0 + \cdots$ to ten terms 125

20. $7 + 11 + 15 + \cdots$ to fifteen terms 525

21. $2b + 5b + 8b + \cdots$ to twelve terms $222b$

22. $x + 0 - x - \cdots$ to eighteen terms $-135x$

23. $\frac{1}{4} + \frac{1}{2} + \frac{3}{4} + \cdots$ to ten terms $\frac{55}{4}$

24. $3 + \frac{7}{2} + 4 + \cdots$ to fifteen terms $\frac{195}{2}$

25. $(2x - 5y) + (3x - 4y) + (4x - 3y) + \cdots$ to ten terms $65x - 5y$

Find the missing data for each arithmetic series.

	a_1	a_n	n	d	S_n
26.	2	31	$\underline{?}$ 10	$\underline{?}\frac{29}{9}$	165
27.	-1	$\underline{?}$ 64	14	$\underline{?}$ 5	441
28.	5	-33	20	$\underline{?}-\frac{38}{19}$	$\underline{?}$ -280
29.	-3	$\underline{?}$ 65	18	$\underline{?}$ 4	558

	a_1	a_n	n	d	S_n
30.	? 6	? $25\frac{1}{2}$	40	$\frac{1}{2}$	630
31.	? 7	-113	25	? -5	-1325

32. The sequence 16, 48, 80, $\cdots$ represents the distance in feet an object will fall during the first second, the second second, the third second, and so on. How far will an object fall in the tenth second? How far will it fall in the first ten seconds?   304 feet; 1,600 feet

33. The sequence 2, 5, 8, $\cdots$ shows how fast a certain object rolls down an inclined plane. That is, it rolls 2 meters the first second, 5 the next second, and so on. How far will it roll in the twelfth second? in twelve seconds?
35 meters; 222 meters

34. Find the sum of the integers between 1 and 100 that are not divisible by 3.
3266

35. If $a_1 + a_2 + a_3 + a_4 + a_5 + \cdots$ is an arithmetic series, prove that the terms $a_1 + a_3 + a_5 + \cdots$ also form an arithmetic series. See key.

Remember

Perform the indicated operations.

1. $4(2)^5 - 4$ 124

2. $\frac{1}{8}(2)^{16} - \frac{1}{8}$ $8191\frac{7}{8}$

3. $\dfrac{2(-2)^6 - 2}{-3}$ -42

The answers are on page 414.

11-5 Geometric Series

The objectives for this section are on page 413.

A geometric series is related to a geometric sequence in the same way that an arithmetic series is related to an arithmetic sequence.

Definition: A **geometric series** is the indicated sum of the terms of a geometric sequence.

The general term of a geometric series is the same as the general term of the corresponding geometric sequence.

$$a_n = a_1 \cdot r^{n-1}$$

A formula for the sum of a geometric series can be found.

$$S_n = a_1 + a_1r + a_1r^2 + \cdots + a_1r^{n-1}$$ ⟵ Sum of n terms

$$rS_n = \qquad a_1r + a_1r^2 + a_1r^3 + \cdots + a_1r^n$$ ⟵ Multiply by r.

$$rS_n = \qquad a_1r + a_1r^2 + a_1r^3 + \cdots + a_1r^n$$ ⟵ Find $rS_n - S_n$.

$$-S_n = -a_1 - a_1r - a_1r^2 - \cdots - a_1r^{n-2} - a_1r^{n-1}$$

$$rS_n - S_n = a_1r^n - a_1$$

$$S_n(r-1) = a_1r^n - a_1$$

$$S_n = \frac{a_1(r^n - 1)}{r - 1}$$ ⟵ $r \neq 1$

Theorem 11-2: Sum of a Geometric Series
If S_n represents the sum of the geometric series, then

$$S_n = a_1 + a_1r + a_1r^2 + \cdots + a_1r^{n-1}.$$

$$S_n = \frac{a_1r^n - a_1}{r - 1}, \; r \neq 1$$

Or, $$S_n = \frac{a_1(r^n - 1)}{r - 1}, \; r \neq 1$$

Example

Find the sum of the series $2 + 6 + 18 + 54 + 162$.

$$S_n = \frac{a_1(r^n - 1)}{r - 1}$$

$$S_5 = \frac{2(3^5 - 1)}{3 - 1}$$ ⟵ $n = 5, a = 2, r = 3$

$$S_5 = \frac{2(242)}{2} = 242$$

Try These

In finding the nth term of a geometric series, you will need to find products involving powers. Find each product. (The use of prime factors is helpful.)

1. $3(2)^6$ 192

2. $1(-4)^7$ −16,384

3. $6(\frac{1}{2})^5$ $\frac{3}{16}$

4. $5(\frac{1}{2})^8$ $\frac{5}{256}$

5. $128(\frac{1}{2})^{11}$ $\frac{1}{16}$

6. $27(\frac{1}{3})^7$ $\frac{1}{81}$

7. $2(\frac{1}{4})^8$ $\frac{1}{32,768}$

8. $5(\frac{3}{5})^5$ $\frac{243}{625}$

Exercises

Find the specified term for each geometric series.

1. 6th term: $-6 + -3 + -\frac{3}{2} + \cdots$ $-\frac{3}{16}$

2. 5th term: $48 + 12 + 3 + \cdots$ $\frac{3}{16}$

Find the sum to the required number of terms for each geometric series.

3. $4 + 8 + 16 + \cdots$ to five terms   124

4. $2 - 8 + 32 - \cdots$ to five terms   410

5. $12 - 6 + 3 - \cdots$ to eight terms $\frac{255}{32}$

6. $3 + \frac{9}{2} + \frac{27}{4} + \cdots$ to six terms $\frac{1995}{32}$

7. $2 - 10a + 50a^2 - \cdots$ to five terms $\frac{2(3125a^5 + 1)}{5a + 1}$

8. $\frac{1}{2} - \frac{1}{4} + \frac{1}{8} + \cdots$ to six terms $\frac{21}{64}$

Find the number of terms in each series.

9. $6 + 12 + 24 + \cdots + 384$ 7

10. $64 + 96 + 144 + \cdots + 729$ 7

Use logarithms to compute the desired term of each of the following series.

11. 20th term when $a = 1$ and $r = 1.03$ About 1.75

12. 30th term when $a = 600$ and $r = 1.02$ About 1070

Find the sum of the first six terms of each series.

13. $25 + 45 + 81 + \cdots$ 1031.632

14. $6.4 + 9.6 + 14.4 + \cdots$ 133

15. How much would you have saved at the end of seven days if you had set aside 64¢ on the first day, 96¢ on the second day, $1.44 on the third day, and so on through the period? $20.59

16. A ball is dropped to the ground from a height of 30 meters. If it rebounds to a height of 10 meters on the first bounce, $3\frac{1}{3}$ meters on the second bounce, and so on, what is the total distance traveled by the ball at the time it hits the ground the sixth time?   59.9 meters

17. If the population of a city of 100,000 increases 10% for each of ten years, what will the population be after ten years?   260,000

18. During each year, the value of a computer decreases 20%. If the computer cost $20,000, what is its value after four years? $8,192

Remember

Express each repeating decimal as a fraction.

Example: $0.\overline{15}$

$N = 0.151515 \cdots$ ⟵ $0.\overline{15}$

$100N = 15.151515 \cdots$ ⟵ Multiply by 100 because it repeats after hundredths.

$\underline{-N = -0.151515 \cdots}$ ⟵ Subtract.

$99N = 15$, and $N = \frac{15}{99}$

1. $0.\overline{8}$ $\frac{8}{9}$ **2.** $0.\overline{4}$ $\frac{4}{9}$ **3.** $0.\overline{5}$ $\frac{5}{9}$ **4.** $0.\overline{12}$ $\frac{12}{99}$, or $\frac{4}{33}$ **5.** $0.\overline{03}$ $\frac{3}{99}$, or $\frac{1}{33}$ **6.** $0.\overline{06}$ $\frac{6}{99}$, or $\frac{2}{33}$

The answers are on page 414.

11-6 The Sum of an Infinite Geometric Series

The objective for this section is on page 414.

The formulas for the sum of a finite geometric series,

$$S_n = \frac{a_1(r^n - 1)}{r - 1}, \ r \neq 1 \quad \text{or} \quad S_n = \frac{a_1(1 - r^n)}{1 - r}, \ r \neq 1,$$

can be used to find the partial sums of an infinite geometric series.

Example 1

Find the partial sums S_4 and S_5 for $\frac{1}{2} + \frac{1}{4} + \frac{1}{8} + \frac{1}{16} + \cdots$

$$S_n = \frac{a_1(1 - r^n)}{1 - r} \quad \longleftarrow \quad |r| < 1$$

$$S_4 = \frac{\frac{1}{2}(1 - (\frac{1}{2})^4)}{1 - \frac{1}{2}} \qquad\qquad S_5 = \frac{\frac{1}{2}(1 - (\frac{1}{2})^5)}{1 - \frac{1}{2}} \quad \longleftarrow \quad a = \frac{1}{2}, r = \frac{1}{2}$$

$$= \frac{\frac{1}{2}(1 - \frac{1}{16})}{\frac{1}{2}} \qquad\qquad\qquad = \frac{\frac{1}{2}(1 - \frac{1}{32})}{\frac{1}{2}}$$

$$= \frac{\frac{1}{2}(\frac{15}{16})}{\frac{1}{2}} = \frac{15}{16} \qquad\qquad = \frac{\frac{1}{2}(\frac{31}{32})}{\frac{1}{2}} = \frac{31}{32}$$

in Example 1, r^n becomes smaller as you use larger and larger values of n. (Note: This will not occur unless $|r| < 1$.) In fact, r^n approaches zero as n increases in value. Therefore, the value of $(1 - r^n)$ approaches 1 as r^n approaches zero.

Therefore, it seems reasonable to use the formula

$$S = \frac{a_1}{1 - r}$$

to find the sum of an infinite geometric series when $|r| < 1$. Thus, you only need to know a_1 and r to find S.

The sum of the infinite geometric series in Example 1 is 1.

$$S = \frac{\frac{1}{2}}{1 - \frac{1}{2}} = \frac{\frac{1}{2}}{\frac{1}{2}} = 1$$

This sum, 1, is called the limit of the infinite geometric series, $\frac{1}{2} + \frac{1}{4} + \frac{1}{8} + \frac{1}{16} + \cdots$. You can think of the limit of a series as a certain number that the sum of the series will approach as you add more and more terms.

Example 2   Find the sum of $5 - \frac{5}{3} + \frac{5}{9} - \frac{5}{27} + \cdots$.

$$S = \frac{5}{1 + \frac{1}{3}} \quad \longleftarrow \quad a_1 = 5, \ r = -\frac{1}{3}$$

$$= \frac{5}{\frac{4}{3}} = \frac{15}{4} = 3\frac{3}{4}$$

Exercises

Find the sum of each infinite geometric series.

1. $4 + 2 + 1 + \cdots$ 8
2. $12 + 4 + \frac{4}{3} + \cdots$ 18
3. $5 + \frac{5}{3} + \frac{5}{9} + \cdots$ $\frac{15}{2}$
4. $6 + 4 + \frac{8}{3} + \cdots$ 18
5. $100 + 60 + 36 + \cdots$ 250
6. $1 - \frac{1}{3} + \frac{1}{9} - \cdots$ $\frac{3}{4}$
7. $0.3 + 0.03 + 0.003 + \cdots$ $(a = 0.3, \ r = 0.1)$ $\frac{1}{3}$
8. $0.6 + 0.06 + 0.006 + \cdots$ $(a = 0.6, \ r = 0.1)$ $\frac{2}{3}$

9. Find the value of the repeating decimal 0.151515 ⋯ . (HINT: This is the same as finding the sum of $0.15 + 0.0015 + 0.000015 + \cdots$. Any repeating decimal can be expressed as a fraction by this method.) $\frac{5}{33}$

Express each repeating decimal as a fraction.

10. $0.\overline{8}$ $\frac{8}{9}$

11. $0.\overline{4}$ $\frac{4}{9}$

$\frac{5}{9}$ 12. $0.\overline{5}$

13. $0.\overline{12}$ $\frac{4}{33}$

14. $0.\overline{03}$ $\frac{1}{33}$

$\frac{2}{33}$ 15. $0.\overline{06}$

16. A ball is thrown vertically upward a distance of 54 meters. After hitting the ground, it rebounds $\frac{2}{3}$ the distance fallen and continues to rebound in the same manner. What distance does the ball cover before coming to rest?
324 meters

17. The midpoints of the sides of a 12 centimeter equilateral triangle are connected to form a second inscribed triangle, whose sides are in turn connected to form a third equilateral triangle, and so on. If this process is continued indefinitely, find the sum of the perimeters of the triangles.
72 centimeters

18. A pendulum swings through an arc of 20 centimeters on the first swing, $\frac{7}{8}$ this distance on the second swing, and continues to swing $\frac{7}{8}$ of the previous distance in each succeeding swing. If this process continues until the pendulum comes to rest, what distance is covered by the pendulum?
160 centimeters

19. An abstract piece of art depicts an infinite series of concentric circles. The largest of these circles has a circumference of 20 decimeters and each successive circle has a circumference of $\frac{1}{2}$ the circumference of each preceding circle. Find the sum of the circumferences of the infinite series.
40 decimeters

PUZZLE

Can you find x?

$$x = 1 + \cfrac{x}{1 + \cfrac{x}{1 + \cfrac{x}{1 + \cfrac{x}{\cdot}}}}$$

2

$$x = 1 + \cfrac{1}{1 + \cfrac{1}{1 + \cfrac{1}{1 + \cdot}}}$$

$\frac{1 \pm \sqrt{5}}{2}$

Finite Fields

The set of real numbers satisfies the eleven postulates listed on page 560 with respect to the operations of addition and multiplication. Any set that has these properties with respect to two operations is a **field**.

The finite set T = {0, 1, 2} under the operations + and × as defined in these tables is a field.

+	0	1	2
0	0	1	2
1	1	2	0
2	2	0	1

×	0	1	2
0	2	0	1
1	0	1	2
2	1	2	0

The finite set S = {3, O} under the operations + and × as defined in these tables is a field.

+	E	O
E	E	O
O	O	E

×	E	O
E	E	E
O	E	O

The finite set M = {i, j, k, n} is <u>not</u> a field. It has an additive identity, but does <u>not</u> have a multiplicative identity.

+	i	j	k	n
i	k	n	i	j
j	n	k	j	i
k	i	j	k	n
n	j	i	n	k

×	i	j	k	n
i	i	j	k	n
j	k	k	k	k
k	k	k	k	k
n	i	j	k	n

Can You Solve These?

1. For the set T above, name the additive identity and the multiplicative identity.
2. For the set S, name the additive identity and the multiplicative identity.
3. For the set M, name the additive identity.
4. Name two field postulates (other than multiplicative identity) that the set M does not satisfy.

Chapter
Objectives
and
Review

Objective: To know the meanings of the important mathematical terms of this chapter.

1. Here are many of the mathematical terms used in this chapter. Be sure that you know their meanings and that you can use them correctly.

arithmetic means (p. 395)
arithmetic series (p. 401)
arithmetic sequence (p. 394)
common difference (p. 394)
common ratio (p. 398)
finite sequence (p. 393)
geometric means (p. 399)

geometric series (p. 405)
geometric sequence (p. 398)
infinite sequence (p. 393)
series (p. 401)
sequence (p. 393)
sum of a series (p. 402)
terms of a sequence (p. 393)

Objective: To write the rule for a given sequence and to use the rule to find other terms. (Section 11-1).

Write the rule for each of the following. Use the rule to find the next three terms.

$a_n = 2n$

2. 2, 4, 6, 8, · · ·   10, 12, 14

$a_n = \dfrac{1}{n^2}$

3. $1, \dfrac{1}{4}, \dfrac{1}{9}, \dfrac{1}{16},$ · · · $\dfrac{1}{25}, \dfrac{1}{36}, \dfrac{1}{49}$

4. −8, −3, 2, 7, · · ·   12, 17, 22

$a_n = 5n - 13$

5. 1, 4, 13, 40, · · ·   121, 364, 1093

$a_n = 3a_{n-1} + 1$

Objective: To write the first n terms of an arithmetic sequence. (Section 11-2).

Write the first five terms of each arithmetic sequence.

6. $a = 6; d = 3$ 6, 9, 12, 15, and 18

7. $a = 12; d = -2$ 12, 10, 8, 6, and 4

8. $a = -7; d = 10$ −7, 3, 13, 23, and 33

9. $a = 1; d = -4$ 1, −3, −7, −11, and −15

Objective: To find n, a_n, a, or d for an arithmetic sequence. (Section 11-2).

Find the unknown.

10. $a_1 = 3, d = 4, n = 18, a_n = $ ___?___ 71

11. $a_1 = $ ___?___, $d = 3, n = 15, a_n = 54$ 12

12. Find the tenth term of 44, 57, 70, 83, · · ·   161

412   Chapter 11

Objective: To find n arithmetic means between two terms. (Section 11-2)

13. Find one arithmetic mean between -5 and 17. ⁶ 6

14. Find three arithmetic means between -5 and 19. 1, 7, and 13

Objective: To write the first n terms of a geometeic sequence. (Section 11-3)

Write the first four terms of each geometric sequence.

15. $a = 2$; $r = \frac{1}{2}$ $\quad$ 2, 1, $\frac{1}{2}$, and $\frac{1}{4}$

16. $a = -16$; $r = \frac{1}{2}$ $\quad$ $-16, -8, -4,$ and -2

17. $a = 25$; $r = 2$ $\quad$ 25, 50, 100, and 200

18. $a = -3$; $r = 2$ $\quad$ $-3, -6, -12,$ and -24

Objective: To write n, a_n, a, or r for a geometric sequence. (Section 11-3)

19. $a_1 = 3$, $r = 4$, $n = 6$, $a_n = $ __?__ 3072

20. $a_1 = $ __?__, $r = \frac{1}{2}$, $n = 5$, $a_5 = \frac{9}{8}$ $\quad$ 18

21. Find the ninth term of $64, 32, 16, 8, \cdots$ $\quad$ $\frac{1}{4}$

Objective: To find n geometric means between two terms. (Section 11-3)

22. Find one geometric mean between 3 and 12. $\quad$ ± 6

23. Find three geometric means between 3 and $\frac{3}{81}$. $\quad$ 1, $\frac{1}{3}, \frac{1}{9}$ or $-1, \frac{1}{3}, -\frac{1}{9}$

Objective: To write a specified term of an arithmetic series. (Section 11-4)

24. Find the eighth term of $-6 + (-9) + (-12) + \cdots$. $\quad$ -27

25. Find the tenth term of $1 + 4 + 7 + \cdots$. $\quad$ 28

Objective: To find the sum of an arithmetic series. (Section 11-4)

26. Find S_{10} for $-6 + (-9) + (-12) + \cdots$. $\quad$ -195

27. Find S_8 for $1 + 7 + 13 + \cdots$. $\quad$ $S_8 = 176$

Objective: To write a specified term of a geometric series. (Section 11-5)

28. Find the seventh term of $1 + 4 + 16 + \cdots$. $\quad$ 4096

29. Find the ninth term of $1 + \frac{1}{3} + \frac{1}{9} + \cdots$. $\quad$ $\frac{1}{6561}$

Objective: To find the sum of a geometric series. (Section 11-5)

30. Find S_{10} for $1 + 4 + 16 + \cdots$. $\quad$ 349, 525

31. Find S_5 for $1 + \frac{1}{3} + \frac{1}{9} + \cdots$. $\quad$ $\frac{121}{81}$

Objective: To find the sum of an infinite geometric series. (Section 11-6)

32. Find the sum of $\frac{1}{3} + \frac{1}{9} + \frac{1}{27} + \cdots$. $\frac{1}{2}$

33. Find the sum of $0.1 + 0.01 + 0.001 + \cdots$. $\frac{1}{9}$

Chapter
Test

Identify each sequence as <u>*Arithmetic*</u>, <u>*Geometric*</u>, *or* <u>*Neither*</u>. *Then list the next three terms for each arithmetic and geometric sequence.*

1. $\frac{1}{5}, -\frac{1}{10}, \frac{1}{20}, -\frac{1}{40}, \cdots$ Geometric $\frac{1}{80}, -\frac{1}{160}, \frac{1}{320}$

2. $\frac{1}{3}, 1, \frac{5}{3}, \frac{7}{3}, \cdots$ Arithmetic $3, \frac{11}{3}, \frac{13}{3}$

3. $\frac{1}{2}, \frac{3}{4}, \frac{7}{8}, \frac{15}{16}, \cdots$ Neither

4. $-\frac{1}{2}, \frac{1}{4}, -\frac{1}{8}, \frac{1}{16}, \cdots$ $-\frac{1}{32}, \frac{1}{64}, -\frac{1}{128}$ Geometric

5. Find the 20th term in the sequence $-3, -1, 1, 3, 5, \cdots$ 35

6. Find the 10th term in the sequence $-2, 4, -8, 16, \cdots$ 1024

7. Find the sum of the odd integers between 30 and 70.   1000

8. Insert three arithmetic means between 4 and 12.   6, 8, 10

9. Insert two geometric means between 10 and $-\frac{2}{25}$. $-2, \frac{2}{5}$

10. Find the first five terms in the sequence of partial sums of the following series. That is, find S_1, S_2, S_3, S_4, S_5.

$\frac{1}{2}, \frac{7}{6}, \frac{23}{12}, \frac{163}{60}, \frac{213}{60}$

$$\frac{1}{2} + \frac{2}{3} + \frac{3}{4} + \frac{4}{5} + \cdots + \frac{n}{n+1} + \cdots$$

11. Find the sum of the infinite geometric series $-25 - 5 - 1 - \frac{1}{5} \cdots$. $-31\frac{1}{4}$

Cumulative Review

Write the letter of the response that best answers each question.

1. Use positive exponents to simplify $(x^{-1} + y^{-1})\left(\dfrac{x^2 y}{x^2 - y^2}\right)$.

    a. $\dfrac{y}{x^2 - y^2}$
    b. $\dfrac{x}{x - y}$
    c. $\dfrac{xy}{x - y}$
    d. $\dfrac{xy}{x + y}$

2. Write $\dfrac{10^3 \cdot 10^{\frac{1}{2}} \cdot 10^{2x}}{10^4 \cdot 10^{-3x} \cdot 10^{x-5}}$ in simplest exponential form.

    a. $10^{\frac{1}{2}}$
    b. $10^{\frac{3}{2}}$
    c. $10^{4x + \frac{9}{2}}$
    d. $10^{4x + \frac{11}{2}}$

3. Tell which expression is equivalent to $(a + b)^{\frac{3}{2}}$.

    a. $\sqrt[3]{a^2 + 2ab + b^2}$
    b. $\sqrt[3]{a^3 + b^3}$
    c. $\sqrt[3]{a^2 + b^2}$
    d. $\sqrt{(a + b)^3}$

4. Find the solution set of $\sqrt{x + 13} - \sqrt{7 - x} = 2$.

    a. $\{3\}$
    b. $\{-1\}$
    c. $\{-6\}$
    d. $\{3, -9\}$

5. Solve: $(x - 4)^{\frac{1}{2}} = \left(\dfrac{1}{8}\right)^{\frac{1}{3}}$

    a. $\{\frac{25}{4}\}$
    b. $\{\frac{5}{4}\}$
    c. $\{\frac{9}{2}\}$
    d. $\{\frac{17}{4}\}$

6. Tell which statement is <u>false</u>.

    a. For every ordered pair (x, y) in a function f, there is an ordered pair (y, x) in f^{-1}.

    b. If $x = \log_b y$, then $b^x = y$.

    c. $\log 4 + \log 9 = \log 13$

    d. $\log \dfrac{10^7}{10^3} = 4 \log 10$

7. Write the equation of the circle with center at $(-2, -5)$ and radius 4.

    a. $(x + 2)^2 + (y - 5)^2 = 16$
    b. $(x - 2)^2 + (y + 5)^2 = 4$

    c. $(x + 2)^2 + (y - 5)^2 = 4$
    d. $(x + 2)^2 + (y + 5)^2 = 16$

8. Write the equation of the ellipse with center at $(0, 0)$, x intercepts at $(-3, 0)$ and $(3, 0)$, and y intercepts at $(0, -6)$ and $(0, 6)$.

    a. $\dfrac{x^2}{9} + \dfrac{y^2}{36} = 1$
    b. $\dfrac{x^2}{6} + \dfrac{y^2}{12} = 1$

    c. $\dfrac{x^2}{9} - \dfrac{y^2}{36} = 1$
    d. $9x^2 + 36y^2 = 1$

9. Choose the word or words that best describe the graph of $xy = -16$.

    a. circle   **b.** ellipse   **c.** parabola   (**d**) rectangular hyperbola

10. If x varies inversely as y and $y = \frac{8}{3}$ when $x = \frac{9}{2}$, find x when $y = 144$.

    (**a**) $\frac{1}{12}$ **b.** $\frac{9}{64}$ **c.** 12   **d.** $\frac{64}{9}$

11. If A varies jointly as m, n, and p, describe the change in A when m is doubled, n is tripled, and p remains the same.

    a. The value of A is multiplied by $\frac{1}{6}$.
    (**b**) The value of A is multiplied by 6.
    c. The value of A is multiplied by 5.
    d. The value of A is unchanged.

12. Tell which statements are true for the hyperbola defined by the equation $4y^2 - 25x^2 = 100$.

    (**a**) Its center is at the origin and it opens vertically.
    (**b**) The length of the major axis is 10.
    c. The equations of the asymptotes are $y = \pm\frac{2}{5}x$.
    d. The coordinates of the foci are $(0, \pm\sqrt{21})$.

13. Tell which of the following is an arithmetic sequence.

    a. 7, 14, 28, 56, 112 $\cdots$ **b.** 1, 3, 6, 10, 15 $\cdots$
    (**c**) 5, 8, 11, 14, 17 $\cdots$ **d.** 2, 3, 5, 7, 11 $\cdots$

14. Tell which of the following is a geometric series.

    a. 7, 14, 28, 56, 112 $\cdots$ **b.** 2, 4, 6, 8, 10 $\cdots$
    c. $2 + 4 + 6 + 8 + 10 + \cdots$ (**d**) $2 + 4 + 8 + 16 + 32 + \cdots$

15. Find the sum of the series $a + an + an^2 + an^3 + an^4 + an^5$.

    a. $\dfrac{6(a + an^5)}{2}$ (**b**) $\dfrac{a(1 - n^6)}{1 - n}$ **c.** $a(1 + n)^5$ **d.** $6a(1 + n + n^2 + n^3 + n^4 + n^5)$

16. Find the 14th term of $\frac{1}{3}$, 4, $7\frac{2}{3}$, $11\frac{1}{3}$, $\cdots$

    (**a**) 48   **b.** $47\frac{2}{3}$ **c.** 46   **d.** $\dfrac{4^{13}}{3^{14}}$

17. For the parabola $x^2 = 64y$, tell which statements are true.

    (**a**) The axis of symmetry is vertical and the graph of the parabola opens upward.
    b. The axis of symmetry is vertical and the graph of the parabola opens to the left.
    (**c**) The coordinates of the focus are $(0, 16)$.
    (**d**) The equation of the directrix is $y = -16$.

Chapter 12
Probability

12-1 Permutations

The objective for this section is on page 436.

You can arrange the four letters **a, b, c,** and **d** in the following ways.

abcd,	abdc,	acbd,	acdb,	adbc,	adcb,
bacd,	badc,	bdac,	bdca,	bcad,	bcda,
cabd,	cadb,	cbad,	cbda,	cdab,	cdba,
dabc,	dacb,	dbac,	dbca,	dcab,	dcba

Each is an ordered arrangement. That is, **abcd** is not the same as **acbd** or **abdc** or **adbc**. An ordered arrangement is a <u>permutation</u>.

Definition: A **permutation** of a set of elements is an arrangement of a specified number of those elements in a definite order.

In ordering the four letters, there are four choices for the first position. For each choice for the first position, there are three choices for the second position. For each choice for the second position, there are two choices for the third position. For each choice for the third position, there is one choice for the fourth position. Thus, there are $4 \cdot 3 \cdot 2 \cdot 1$ or 24 permutations for the 4 letters **a, b, c,** and **d.**

Position	1	2	3	4
Choices	4	3	2	1

$\longrightarrow 4 \cdot 3 \cdot 2 \cdot 1 = 24$

The number of permutations for the five letters **a, b, c, d,** and **e,** is $5 \cdot 4 \cdot 3 \cdot 2 \cdot 1 = 120$. The number of permutations for n distinct objects is

$$n(n-1)(n-2)(n-3)(n-4) \cdot \cdots \cdot (3)(2)(1).$$

Symbolically, the number of permutations of n elements taken n at a time (this means you have n elements and n positions) is $_nP_n$. Thus,

$$_nP_n = n(n-1)(n-2)(n-3)(n-4) \cdot \cdots \cdot (3)(2)(1).$$

Note that $_nP_n$ is the product of the integer n and all positive integers less than n. The symbol $n!$ (read n factorial) represents this product.

$$_nP_n = n!$$

Now consider n elements and r positions, where $r < n$.

Example 1 In how many ways can 5 of 8 people be seated in a row of 5 vacant chairs?

Position	1	2	3	4	5
Choices	8	7	6	5	4

In all, there are $8 \cdot 7 \cdot 6 \cdot 5 \cdot 4$ permutations when 8 elements are taken 5 at a time. The symbol $_8P_5$ represents this.

$$_8P_5 = 8 \cdot 7 \cdot 6 \cdot 5 \cdot 4 = 6720$$

Symbolically, the number of permutations of n elements taken r at a time is $_nP_r$. To generalize, match each position with the number of choices for that position.

Position	1	2	3	4	$\cdots$	r
Choices	n	$n-1$	$n-2$	$n-3$	$\cdots$	$n-(r-1)$

There are $n - (r-1)$ or $n - r + 1$ choices for the rth position.

$$_nP_r = n(n-1)(n-2) \cdots (n-r+1)$$

This formula can be simplified by multiplying by $\dfrac{(n-r)!}{(n-r)!}$, which, of course, is 1.

$$_nP_r = \frac{n(n-1)(n-2) \cdots (n-r+1)(n-r)!}{(n-r)!}$$

$$_nP_r = \frac{n(n-1)(n-2) \cdots (n-r+1)(n-r)(n-r-1) \cdots (3)(2)(1)}{(n-r)!}$$

$$_nP_r = \frac{n!}{(n-r)!}$$

Example 2   If you have 10 different books to choose from, how many permutations can be formed on a shelf that holds 6 books?

$$_{10}P_6 = \frac{10!}{(10-6)!} \quad\longleftarrow\quad n = 10, r = 6$$

$$= \frac{10 \cdot 9 \cdot 8 \cdot 7 \cdot 6 \cdot 5 \cdot 4 \cdot 3 \cdot 2 \cdot 1}{4 \cdot 3 \cdot 2 \cdot 1}$$

$$= 10 \cdot 9 \cdot 8 \cdot 7 \cdot 6 \cdot 5 = 151, 200$$

If n is replaced by r in $_nP_r$, you have the following.

$$_nP_r = \frac{n!}{(n-r)!}$$

$$_rP_r = \frac{r!}{(r-r)!} = \frac{r!}{0!}$$

Since $_rP_r = r!$, then $\frac{r!}{0!} = r!$

Thus, 0! must equal 1 for this to be true.

Definition: The number **0! is equal to 1.**

Try These   *Evaluate the following.*

1. 2! ₂   **2.** 6! ₇₂₀   **3.** $\frac{5!}{3!}$ ₂₀   **4.** $\frac{n!}{(n-1)!}$ ₙ   **5.** $_3P_3$ ₆   **6.** $_4P_2$ ¹²

Exercises

Find the number designated by each expression.

α   **1.** 3! 0! ₆   **2.** 5! 4! ₂₈₈₀   **3.** 8! −4! ₄₀,₉₂₆   **4.** $\frac{_6P_2}{_3P_2}$ ₅   **5.** $\frac{_5P_5}{_5P_2}$ ₆   **6.** $\frac{_6P_6}{_3P_3}$ ¹²⁰

7. Write the 12 permutations of 2 letters each, using the letters of the set
{**a, b, c, d**}. {(a, b), (a, c), (a, d), (b, a), (b, c), (b, d), (c, a), (c, b), (c, d), (d, a), (d, b), (d, c)}

8. How many permutations of the letters in the word **FACTOR** can be formed by using all of the letters? 720

9. How many permutations of 4 letters each can be formed from the letters of the word **NUMBERS?** 840

10. How many four-digit positive integers can be formed from the digits 1, 2, 3, and 4, if no digit is repeated in a numeral? 24

11. How many different positive integers greater than 2000 can be formed by using 1, 2, 3, and 4, if each is used just once in every numeral? 18

12. How many positive four-digit integers can be formed by using the digits 1, 2, 3, 4, 5, 6, 7 if no digit is repeated in any numeral? How many are possible if repetitions are allowed? 840; 2401

13. In how many ways can 6 different books be arranged on a shelf? 720

14. How many positive five-digit even integers can be formed with the digits 2, 3, 5, 7, 9 if no repetitions are allowed? 24

15. In how many ways can 6 out of 8 people be seated in 6 empty seats? 20,160

16. In how many ways can 6 girls occupy a row of 6 seats? 720

17. In how many ways can a family of a mother, father, and three children stand in a row to be photographed if the mother and father stand at the ends of the row? 12

18. In how many ways can a baseball team be arranged if one player always plays first base and one player always is the catcher? 5040

19. In how many ways can three cars park in 10 parking spaces? 720

20. Each of 10 basketball players can play any of the 5 positions on the team. How many ways may the coach arrange a team? 30,240

21. How many license plate numbers consisting of two letters followed by four digits are possible if repetition of numbers and letters is allowed? How many are possible if repetition of numbers and letters is not allowed? 6,760,000; 3,276,000

22. Show that $_5P_3 = 5(_4P_2)$. $_5P_3 = 60; 5(_4P_2) = 60$

23. Show that $_nP_r = n(_{n-1}P_{r-1})$. ·See key.

24. If $_nP_4 = 4(_nP_3)$, find n. 7   25. If $_nP_5 = 6(_{n-1}P_4)$, find n. 6

If the three **E**'s in the word **EERIE** are distinguished from one another as **E₁**, **E₂**, and **E₃**, then the number of permutations of the 5 letters is $_5P_5 = 5!$, or 120. However, **E₁**, **E₂**, and **E₃** cannot really be distinguished. That is,

$$E_1E_2E_3RI, \quad E_2E_1E_3RI, \quad E_2E_3E_1RI, \text{ and so on,}$$

are the same.

There are $5 \cdot 4$, or 20, different arrangements if you just consider **R** and **I** in the 5 positions.

R I _ _ _	I R _ _ _	_ R I _ _	_ I R _ _
R _ I _ _	I _ R _ _	_ R _ I _	_ I _ R _
R _ _ I _	I _ _ R _	_ R _ _ I	_ I _ _ R
R _ _ _ I	I _ _ _ R		
_ _ R I _	_ _ I R _	_ _ _ R I	_ _ _ I R
_ _ R _ I	_ _ I _ R		

For <u>each</u> one of these distinct arrangements, you can rearrange the three **E**'s in 3! ways. Thus, if T represents the number of distinct arrangements of the 5 letters, then

$$3!T = {}_5P_5$$

$$T = \frac{{}_5P_5}{3!} = \frac{5!}{3!} = \frac{120}{6} = 20$$

In general, the number of distinct permutations of n things where p of these are alike is

$$T = \frac{n!}{p!}$$

Further, if there is more than one set of like elements, say p things alike, q things alike, r things alike, and so on, then

$$T = \frac{n!}{p!q!r! \cdots}$$

Example

How many different permutations can you make with the letters in **CONNECTICUT?**

$$T = \frac{11!}{3!2!2!} \longleftarrow \begin{array}{l} n = 11 \text{ letters} \\ p = 3 \text{ C's, } q = 2 \text{ N's, } r = 2 \text{ T's} \end{array}$$

$$= \frac{11 \cdot 10 \cdot 9 \cdot 8 \cdot 7 \cdot 6 \cdot 5 \cdot 4 \cdot 3 \cdot 2 \cdot 1}{3 \cdot 2 \cdot 1 \cdot 2 \cdot 1 \cdot 2 \cdot 1}$$

$$= 11 \cdot 10 \cdot 9 \cdot 8 \cdot 7 \cdot 6 \cdot 5$$

$$= 1,663,200$$

Try These

Use the numeral 1213 to answer these exercises.

1. How many permutations can be made from these digits? 12

2. How many permutations can be made if the first digit must be 2? 3

3. How many permutations can be made if the numeral must be greater than 2000? 6

Exercises

1. How many permutations can be made from the letters of the word **COLORADO?** 6720

2. How many permutations can be made from the letters of the word **MICHIGAN?** 20,160

3. How many permutations can be made from the letters of the word **SATELLITE?** 45,360

4. How many permutations can be made from the digits in the numeral 121221? 20

5. How many distinct ways can 10 balloons be arranged in a row if 3 are red, 2 are blue, 2 are green, and the rest are yellow? 25,200

6. At a safety program, a traffic instructor wishes to display 9 traffic signs. In how many different ways can she display the signs in a row if there are four identical stop signs, two identical direction signs, and three identical speed limit signs? 1260

7. Each of 7 cheerleaders stands in a line holding a Pom Pom. If 3 of the Pom Poms are white, 2 are blue, and the rest are yellow, in how many distinguishable ways can the Pom Poms be arranged? 210

8. A father loses a bet to his 6 children and agrees to distribute the coins in his pockets among them. If he has 3 dimes, 2 quarters, and one half dollar, in how many ways can he distribute the coins equally? 60

9. In how many different ways can 12 books be arranged on a shelf if 5 of them are identical books with blue covers, 4 are identical books with green covers, and 3 are identical books with black covers? In how many different ways can they be arranged if books of the same color must be grouped? 27,720; 6

10. How many different line-ups, each consisting of 2 forwards, 2 guards and one center, can be made from a basketball squad of 5 forwards, 4 guards, and 2 centers? 120

An arrangement of elements in a circle is called a <u>circular permutation</u>. *If n elements are arranged in a circle, any one of the* <u>n elements may be</u> *selected as the first position. Then the other n − 1 elements can be arranged in the remaining positions. Hence, the total number of distinguishable circular permutations is*

$$_nP_n = \frac{n!}{n}$$

$$= \frac{n(n-1)!}{n} = (n-1)!$$

11. Find the number of ways 6 people can be seated at a round table. 120

12. In how many ways can a family of 4 be seated at a round table? 6

13. Ten members of a football team huddle in a circle around the quarterback to hear the next play. In how many ways can they arrange themselves? 362,880

14. In how many ways can 5 different keys be arranged on a key ring? (HINT: Objects such as keys can be flipped over to produce arrangements identical to those originally counted by $(n-1)!$. For such objects, there are only half the usual number of circular permutations, $\frac{(n-1)!}{2}$.) 12

15. In how many ways can 6 objects be fastened to a circular piece of wire? 60

16. In how many ways can 4 boys and 4 girls be seated alternately in a circle? 72

17. In how many ways could King Arthur and six of his court sit at the Round Table if one of the chairs was the throne chair for King Arthur, and there were six other chairs? 720

18. How many ways are there to seat ten persons at a round table if two people must sit next to each other? 80,640

The objective for this section is on page 436.

The number of permutations of the letters **a**, **b**, and **c** is 6.

| abc | acb | bac | bca | cab | cba |

However, the permutations listed above consist of only one combination. That is, **abc, acb, bac,** and so on are the same combination.

Definition: A **combination** is an arrangement of the elements of a set without consideration of the order of the elements.

For the 3 letters **a**, **b**, and **c**, there is one combination but 3! permutations. For 4 different letters there is one combination but 4! permutations. In general, there are $r!$ permutations for each combination of r objects.

You can generalize this for n things taken r at a time by dividing $_nP_r$ by $r!$, and by using $_nC_r$ or $\binom{n}{r}$ to represent the number of combinations of n things taken r at a time.

$$_nC_r = \binom{n}{r} = \frac{_nP_r}{r!} = \frac{n!}{r!(n-r)!}$$

Example

In how many ways can a committee of 3 be chosen from a class of 30 students?

$$_{30}C_3 = \frac{30!}{3!(30-3)!} \quad \longleftarrow \quad n = 30, \ r = 3$$

$$= \frac{30 \cdot 29 \cdot 28 \cdot \cdots \cdot 2 \cdot 1}{3 \cdot 2 \cdot 1 \cdot 27 \cdot 26 \cdot \cdots \cdot 1}$$

$$= \frac{30 \cdot 29 \cdot 28}{3 \cdot 2 \cdot 1} = 4060$$

Exercises

Determine the number of ways that each selection can be made.

1. Five boys for a basketball team from a physical education class of 30 boys. 142,506

2. Two student officers from a group of 100. 4950

3. A group of 4 from a group of 7. 35

4. A group of 4 or more from a group of 7. 64

5. A committee of 5 girls and 7 boys from a group of 10 girls and 11 boys. (HINT: Find the number of combinations for girls, then for boys, and then find this product.) 83,160

6. Prove that $_nC_n = 1$ and that $_nC_1 = n$. See key.

7. Prove that $_nC_r = {_nC_{n-r}}$. See key.

8. How many lines are determined by 10 points, no 3 of which are on the same line? 45

9. How many diagonals can be drawn in a hexagon? 9

10. You may choose 5 classmates out of a group of 15 to accompany you on a camping trip. In how many ways could you choose the group to go with you? 3003

11. How many committees of 4 can be chosen from 12 students? How many of these will include a given student? How many will exclude a given student? 495; 165; 330

12. In how many ways can you draw 56 marbles from a bag that contains 59 marbles? 32,509

13. A sample of 10 light bulbs is to be chosen from a set of 100 light bulbs. In how many ways can the sample be selected? 1.731×10^{13}

14. From a group of 12 Republicans and 10 Democrats, how many different committees of 6 can be formed if:
    a. at least 4 are Democrats? 17,094
    b. no more than 4 are Democrats? 71,379
    c. at least 3 are Republicans? 57,519
    d. no more than 3 are Republicans? 43,494

15. In how many ways can a person invite one or more of four friends to dinner? 15

16. From a group of 6 persons, how many committees of 3 can be formed if two of the 6 people cannot be on the same committee? 10

426   Chapter 12

Combinations and the Binomial Theorem

The objective for this section is on page 437.

The Binomial Theorem tells you how to expand $(a + b)^n$. Now you can use combinations to write the coefficients in a binomial expansion.

Example

Expand $(a + b)^5$.

$$(a+b)^5 = \binom{5}{0}a^5 + \binom{5}{1}a^4b + \binom{5}{2}a^3b^2 + \binom{5}{3}a^2b^3 + \binom{5}{4}ab^4 + \binom{5}{5}b^5$$

$$= 1a^5 + \frac{5}{1}a^4b + \frac{5 \cdot 4}{1 \cdot 2}a^3b^2 + \frac{5 \cdot 4 \cdot 3}{1 \cdot 2 \cdot 3}a^2b^3 + \frac{5 \cdot 4 \cdot 3 \cdot 2}{1 \cdot 2 \cdot 3 \cdot 4}ab^4 + \frac{5 \cdot 4 \cdot 3 \cdot 2 \cdot 1}{1 \cdot 2 \cdot 3 \cdot 4 \cdot 5}b^5$$

Similarly,

$$(a+b)^n = \binom{n}{0}a^n + \binom{n}{1}a^{n-1}b + \binom{n}{2}a^{n-2}b^2 + \binom{n}{3}a^{n-3}b^3 + \cdots + \binom{n}{n}b^n.$$

You can write the rth term of $(a + b)^n$ as $\binom{n}{r-1}a^{n-r+1}b^{r-1}$. For example, the sixth term of $(a + b)^{10}$ is $\binom{10}{5}a^5b^5$.

Exercises

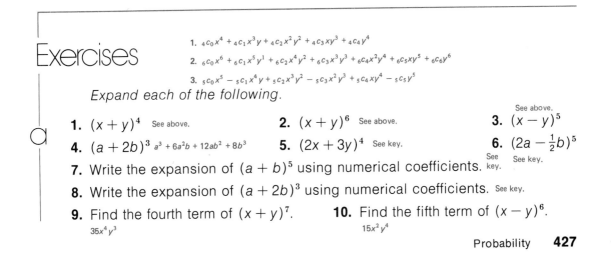

1. $_4C_0 x^4 + {}_4C_1 x^3 y + {}_4C_2 x^2 y^2 + {}_4C_3 xy^3 + {}_4C_4 y^4$

2. $_6C_0 x^6 + {}_6C_1 x^5 y^1 + {}_6C_2 x^4 y^2 + {}_6C_3 x^3 y^3 + {}_6C_4 x^2 y^4 + {}_6C_5 xy^5 + {}_6C_6 y^6$

3. $_5C_0 x^5 - {}_5C_1 x^4 y + {}_5C_2 x^3 y^2 - {}_5C_3 x^2 y^3 + {}_5C_4 xy^4 - {}_5C_5 y^5$

Expand each of the following.

1. $(x + y)^4$ See above.

2. $(x + y)^6$ See above.

3. $(x - y)^5$ See above.

4. $(a + 2b)^3$ $a^3 + 6a^2b + 12ab^2 + 8b^3$

5. $(2x + 3y)^4$ See key.

6. $(2a - \frac{1}{2}b)^5$ See key.

7. Write the expansion of $(a + b)^5$ using numerical coefficients.   See key.

8. Write the expansion of $(a + 2b)^3$ using numerical coefficients.   See key.

9. Find the fourth term of $(x + y)^7$.
$35x^4 y^3$

10. Find the fifth term of $(x - y)^6$.
$15x^2 y^4$

Probability   **427**

12-5 Probability

The objective for this section is on page 437.

If you toss a coin, there are 2 possible <u>outcomes</u>: Heads or Tails. The chances of tossing a head are one out of two, or $\frac{1}{2}$. Similarly, the chances of tossing a tail are one out of two, or $\frac{1}{2}$.

The ratio of the number of successful outcomes to the number of possible outcomes is the **probability** that an outcome will occur.

The probability that you will get <u>neither</u> a head nor a tail when you toss a coin is zero. The probability that you will get <u>either</u> a head <u>or</u> a tail is one. A probability is a number p, where $0 \leq p \leq 1$.

Postulate 12-1
The probability of an outcome that cannot occur is 0.

Postulate 12-2
The probability of an outcome that must occur is 1.

Example 1

In rolling a die, what is the probability of getting a 5?

1, 2, 3, 4, 5, 6 ←——— Possible outcomes

5 ←——— Successful outcomes

$p = \dfrac{1}{6}$ ←——— $\dfrac{\text{Number of successful outcomes}}{\text{Number of possible outcomes}}$

In probability, the set of possible outcomes is called a **sample space.** Each outcome or element in a sample space is a **sample point.**

Example 2 In rolling a die, what is the probability of getting an even number?

1, 2, 3, 4, 5, 6 ⟵ Possible outcomes

2, 4, 6 ⟵ Successful outcomes

$p = \dfrac{3}{6} = \dfrac{1}{2}$ ⟵ $\dfrac{\text{Number of successful outcomes}}{\text{Number of possible outcomes}}$

In Example 2, each of the successful outcomes, 2, 4, or 6, is equally likely, and they cannot occur together. Because of this, you can find the probability of _each_ successful outcome and then add these 3 probabilities to find the probability of rolling either a 2, a 4, or a 6.

Probability of Rolling a 2 4 6	Probability of Rolling a 2, 4, or 6.
$\dfrac{1}{6}$ $\dfrac{1}{6}$ $\dfrac{1}{6}$	$\dfrac{1}{6} + \dfrac{1}{6} + \dfrac{1}{6} = \dfrac{3}{6} = \dfrac{1}{2}$

Postulate 12-3: If two or more outcomes cannot occur simultaneously, the probability of either of the outcomes occurring is the sum of the probabilities that each will occur.

In Examples 1 and 2, the set of successful outcomes is a subset of the sample space. This subset is called an **event**. In Example 1, the event {5} is a **simple event** because there is only one element in the sample space. In Example 2, the event {2, 4, 6} is the union of three simple events, {2}, {4}, and {6}.

Try These   *Exercises* **1-4** *refer to a single toss of a die.*

1. What is the probability of getting a 1 or a 6? $\frac{1}{3}$
2. What is the probability of getting a number less than 5? $\frac{2}{3}$
3. What is the probability of getting a prime number? a composite number? $\frac{1}{2}; \frac{1}{3}$
4. What is the probability of getting 1, 2, 3, 4, 5, or 6? 1

Exercises

a

1. A bridge deck consists of two black suits (spades and clubs) and two red suits (hearts and diamonds). Each suit contains an ace, a king, a queen, a jack and one each of cards numbered 2, 3, 4, 5, 6, 7, 8, 9, 10. What is the probability of drawing an ace in a single draw from a bridge deck of cards? $\frac{1}{13}$

2. In a single draw from a bridge deck, what is the probability of drawing a spade? a black card? $\frac{1}{4}; \frac{1}{2}$

3. In a single draw from a bridge deck, what is the probability of drawing a red 7? $\frac{1}{26}$

4. In a single draw from a bridge deck, what is the probability of drawing a 2 or a 3? $\frac{2}{13}$

5. Ten slips of paper numbered from 6 to 15 are placed in a hat. What is the probability that the number of the slip drawn is a prime? $\frac{3}{10}$

6. A bag contains 4 red cubes and 5 black cubes. What is the probability that a cube drawn at random is blue? that it is red or black? $0; 1$

7. If C and D are distinct points on $\overline{AB}$ and C is the midpoint of $\overline{AB}$, what is the probability that D is the midpoint of $\overline{AB}$? 0

8. If P is a point on the bisector of angle ABC, what is the probability that P is equidistant from the sides of the angle? 1

9. If a bag contains 2 red tokens, 3 white tokens, and 4 black tokens, what is the probability of choosing a red token? a white token? a black token? What is the sum of these probabilities? $\frac{2}{9}; \frac{3}{9}; \frac{4}{9}; 1$

10. If a bag contains 3 red cubes and 6 white cubes, what is the probability of choosing a red cube? a white cube? neither a white cube nor a red cube? either a white cube or a red cube? a cube that is not white? a cube that is not red? $\frac{1}{3}; \frac{2}{3}; 0; 1; \frac{1}{3}; \frac{2}{3}$

*Five books labeled {**a, b, c, d, e**} are placed on a shelf at random.*

11. What is the probability that they will be placed in the order {**b, d, e, c, a**}? $\frac{1}{120}$

Exercises 12–14 refer to a single toss of a pair of dice.

12. What is the total number of possible outcomes in the sample space? 36

13. What is the probability of getting a 6? $\frac{5}{36}$

14. What is the probability of getting a 2 or a 6? $\frac{1}{6}$

Mutually Exclusive Events

The objective for this section is on page 437.

Example 1   Six discs of the same size are labeled as shown in the figure and placed in a box. What is the probability that the disc you draw at random is labeled **A**?

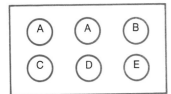

{**A, B, C, D, E**}   ⟵ Sample space

Since 2 discs are labeled **A,** consider them as being labeled A_1 and A_2. The sample space will now have 6 sample points.

{$A_1, A_2,$ **B, C, D, E**}   ⟵ Sample space

{A_1, A_2}   ⟵ Successful outcomes

$$p = \frac{2}{6} = \frac{1}{3}$$ ⟵ $\dfrac{\text{Number of successful outcomes}}{\text{Number of sample points}}$

Example 2   Five red tokens labeled **1, 2, 3, 4, 5** and five white tokens labeled **3, 4, 5, 6,** and **7** are placed in a box. What is the probability of drawing an odd-numbered red token or an even-numbered white token?

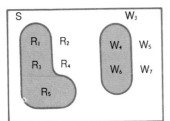

The events,

E_1 ⟵ Drawing an odd-numbered token

and E_2 ⟵ Drawing an even-numbered token

are disjoint sets. That is, they do not have any elements in common. Such events are **mutually exclusive events.** Thus, the union of E_1 and E_2 is the set of successful outcomes.

{$R_1, R_2, R_3, R_4, R_5, W_3, W_4, W_5, W_6, W_7$}   ⟵ Sample space

$E_1 \cup E_2 = \{R_1, R_3, R_5, W_4, W_6\}$ ⟵ Successful outcomes

$$p(E_1 \cup E_2) = \frac{5}{10} = \frac{1}{2}$$ ⟵ $\dfrac{\text{Number of successful outcomes}}{\text{Number of sample points}}$

Probability   **431**

Example 3   Using the same sample space as in Example 2, what is the probability of drawing a red token or an even-numbered token?

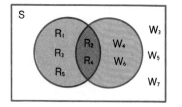

The events,

E_1 ◄——— Drawing a red token

and E_2 ◄——— Drawing an even-numbered token

are not mutually exclusive events as shown in the figure.

$$E_1 \cup E_2 = \{R_1, R_2, R_3, R_4, R_5, W_4, W_6\}$$

The elements that are common to E_1 and E_2 are not listed twice in $E_1 \cup E_2$.

To find the probability of $E_1 \cup E_2$, which is symbolized as $p(E_1 \cup E_2)$, refer to the figure and count the number of successful outcomes in $E_1 \cup E_2$.

$$p(E_1 \cup E_2) = \frac{7}{10} \quad \text{◄———} \quad \frac{\text{Number of successful outcomes}}{\text{Number of sample points}}$$

This suggests the following theorem.

Theorem 12-1:   For any two events E_1 and E_2 for a given sample space,

$$p(E_1 \cup E_2) = p(E_1) + p(E_2) - p(E_1 \cap E_2).$$

Example 4   What is the probability that one card drawn from a bridge deck of 52 cards will be a club or queen?

The events,

E_1 ◄——— Drawing a club

and E_2 ◄——— Drawing a queen

are not mutually exclusive. (Note: There are 13 clubs and 4 queens, one of which is a club.)

$$p(E_1 \cup E_2) = p(E_1) + p(E_2) - p(E_1 \cap E_2)$$

$$p(E_1 \cup E_2) = \frac{13}{52} + \frac{4}{52} - \frac{1}{52} = \frac{16}{52} = \frac{4}{13} \quad \text{◄——— Probability}$$

Exercises

If one card is drawn from a bridge deck of 52 cards, identify each of the following pairs of events as mutually exclusive or not.

1. E_1: a spade; E_2: a diamond   Mutually exclusive.   **2.** E_1: a queen; E_2: a heart   Not mutually exclusive.

3. E_1: a face card; E_2: a card numbered at least 2   Mutually exclusive.

*Six slips of red paper are numbered **2, 3, 4, 5, 8, 9** and four slips of blue paper are numbered **3, 6, 8, 10** and placed in a hat. The slips are shuffled and one slip is drawn at random. Identify each of the following pairs of events as mutually exclusive or not.*

4. E_1: a blue slip; E_2: a red slip   Mutually exclusive.

5. E_1: a red slip; E_2: a slip numbered **8** or **10**   Not mutually exclusive.

6. E_1: a blue slip; E_2: a slip number is a prime number   Not mutually exclusive.

7. Indicate sample spaces for Exercises 1–6.   See key.

8. Determine $P(E_1 \cup E_2)$ for Exercises 1–6. $\frac{1}{2}; \frac{4}{13}; \frac{12}{13}; 1\frac{4}{5}; \frac{7}{10}$

9. What is the probability of getting an even number with one spin of a spinner (shown at the right)? of getting a multiple of 3? of getting an even number or a multiple of 3? $\frac{1}{2}; \frac{1}{3}; \frac{2}{3}$

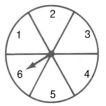

10. On two spins of the spinner, what is the probability of getting two successive 5's? of getting a sum of 10? of getting two successive 5's or a sum of 10? $\frac{1}{36}; \frac{1}{12}; \frac{1}{12}$

11. A collection of books contains 5 French books, 6 physics books, 4 mathematics books, and 7 English books. In one draw, what is the probability of drawing either a French or a mathematics book? either a physics, a mathematics, or an English book? $\frac{9}{22}; \frac{17}{22}$

12. If a single die is thrown, what is the probability of getting an even number or a number less than 4? $\frac{5}{6}$

13. One license plate is randomly selected from fifty license plates numbered from 1 to 50. Find the probabilities.
   a. The number begins with a 2 or a 3. $\frac{11}{25}$
   b. The number is divisible by 3 or 6. $\frac{8}{25}$
   c. The number ends in a 2 or a 3. $\frac{1}{5}$

14. A pair of dice is thrown and the outcomes are recorded. Determine the probability of throwing a double or getting a sum of 7. $\frac{1}{3}$

Mathematical Induction

It is impossible to test <u>all</u> natural numbers to prove the following theorem.

Theorem: For any natural number, n,

$$1 + 2 + 3 + \cdots + n = \frac{n(n+1)}{2}.$$

You can verify the theorem by a method called **mathematical induction**.

Theorem: Mathematical Induction

If a statement involving natural numbers is
i. true for $n = 1$, and
ii. whenever this statement is true for $n = k$ it is true for $n = k + 1$, then it is true for all natural numbers.

Assume that you are in line at a theater waiting to buy a ticket, and an unspecified number of persons are in line ahead of you. You can prove that you will get a ticket if you can establish these two statements.

i. The first person in line gets a ticket, $n = 1$.
ii. If any person in line gets a ticket, $n = k$, the next person in line will get a ticket, $n = k + 1$.

It is this kind of process that is used in applying the <u>Theorem of Mathematical Induction</u>.

i. Verify that $n = 1$ is true.

$$\frac{1(1+1)}{2} = 1 \quad \longleftarrow \quad \text{Replace } n \text{ with 1 in } 1 + 2 + 3 \cdots + n = \frac{n(n+1)}{2}.$$

ii. Assume that the theorem is true for $n = k$.

$$1 + 2 + 3 + \cdots + k = \frac{k(k+1)}{2}$$

To prove that the theorem is true for $n = k + 1$, add $k + 1$ to both sides of the equation.

$$1 + 2 + 3 + \cdots + k + (k + 1) = \frac{k(k + 1)}{2} + (k + 1)$$

$$= \frac{k(k + 1) + 2(k + 1)}{2}$$

$$= \frac{(k + 1)(k + 2)}{2}$$

$$1 + 2 + 3 + \cdots + k + (k + 1) = \frac{(k + 1)(k + 1 + 1)}{2}$$

This last statement shows that the theorem is true for $n = k + 1$. Thus, $n = k + 1$ follows from $n = k$. By mathematical induction, the theorem is true for all natural numbers.

Prove that for any natural number, n, $n^3 + 2n$ is divisible by 3.

i. Verify that $n = 1$ is true.

$1^3 + 2(1)$ is divisible by 3. ⟵ $1^3 + 2(1) = 3$ and 3 is divisible by 3.

ii. Assume the statement is true for $n = k$: $k^3 + 2k$ is divisible by 3.

To prove that the statement $n = k + 1$ is true, replace k with $k + 1$.

$$(k + 1)^3 + 2(k + 1) = k^3 + 3k^2 + 3k + 1 + 2k + 2$$

$$= (k^3 + 2k) + 3k^2 + 3k + 3$$

$$= (k^3 + 2k) + 3(k^2 + k + 1)$$

You know that $(k^3 + 2k)$ is divisible by 3 by the assumption in ii. Since $3(k^2 + k + 1)$ is also clearly divisible by 3, then $(k + 1)^3 + 2(k + 1)$ is divisible by 3. Thus, by mathematical induction, $n^3 + 2n$ is divisible by 3 for any natural number, n.

Can You Solve These?

Use mathematical induction to prove each of the following.

1. $1 + 3 + 5 + \cdots + (2n - 1) = n^2$

2. For any natural number n, $n^2 + n$ is divisible by 2.

Chapter Objectives and Review

Objective: To know the meanings of the important mathematical terms in this chapter.

1. Here are many of the mathematical terms used in this chapter. Be sure that you know their meanings and that you can use them correctly.

combination (p. 425)   probability (p. 428)
event (p. 429)   sample point (p. 428)
factorial (p. 419)   sample space (p. 428)
mutually exclusive events (p. 431)   simple event (p. 429)
permutation (p. 418)

Objective: To calculate the number of permutations of a set of elements. (Sections 12-1 and 12-2)

(a,b,c), (a,c,b), (b,c,a), (b,a,c), (c,a,b), (c,b,a)
2. Write the permutations of 3 elements each of {**a, b, c**}.

3. How many four-digit integers can be formed from the digits 0, 1, 2, 3, 4, 5, 6, if no digit is repeated in a number? How many are possible if repetitions are allowed? 720; 2058

4. In how many ways can 7 different books be arranged on a shelf? 5040

5. How many permutations can be made from the letters of the word **STATISTICS**? 50,400

6. In how many ways can 3 identical mathematics books, 4 identical physics books, and 7 identical English books be placed on a shelf? 120,120

Objective: To calculate the number of combinations of a set of elements. (Section 12-3)

7. Write the combinations of 2 elements each taken from {**a, b, c, d**}. 6

8. In how many ways can you choose a committee of 3 boys and 5 girls from a group of 7 boys and 6 girls? 210

9. Five boys are to be chosen from a group of 12 to make one basketball team. In how many ways can the team be chosen? How many of these will include Phil, a member of the group? 792; 330

10. Prove that $_nC_r = {}_nC_{n-r}$. See key.

Objective: To use combinations to expand a binomial. (Section 12-4)

Write each expression, using binomial coefficients.
See key for Exercises 11-13.

11. $(x-y)^4$ **12.** $(x+y)^7$ **13.** $(2a-3b)^5$

14. Find the fourth term of $(x+y)^9$. $84x^6y^3$

Objective: To compute the probability that an event will occur. (Section 12-5)

Compute the probability of each event. The sample space is
$\{1, 2, 3, 4, 5, 6, 7, 8\}$.

15. What is the probability of drawing a 3 in one random selection? $\frac{1}{8}$

16. What is the probability of drawing an even number in one random selection? $\frac{1}{2}$

17. What is the probability of drawing one of 1, 2, 3, 4, 5, 6, 7, 8, in one random selection? 1

18. What is the probability of drawing 0 in one random selection? 0

Objective: To compute the probability of mutually exclusive events. (Section 12-6)

19. If a single card is drawn from a deck of 52 cards, what is the probability that it will be an ace or a face card? $\frac{4}{13}$

20. If a pair of dice is thrown, what is the probability of getting a 3 or a 4? $\frac{5}{36}$

21. If a pair of dice is thrown, what is the probability of getting a double or a 9? $\frac{5}{18}$

22. If a single die is thrown, what is the probability of getting a 3 or a 4? $\frac{1}{3}$

Chapter
Test

Evaluate.

1. $_5C_3$ 10

2. $_8P_4$ 1680

3. $\dfrac{(n-1)!}{n!}$ $\frac{1}{n}$

4. 0! 1

5. A sample space for tossing three coins consists of 8 points representing the possible outcomes. List them. What is the probability of each point? See below.

6. How many 5-digit numbers can be formed from the integers 1, 2, 3, 5, 7, 9 if no integer can be used more than once? 720

7. In how many ways can you arrange five people in a straight line? 120

8. How many committees of three people each can you form from a set of eight people? 56

9. How many permutations can be made of the letters of the word **HAWAII**? 180

10. From a bag containing 9 red cubes and 6 green cubes, 2 cubes are drawn in succession. What is the probability of drawing a red cube or a green cube? 1

Two dice are thrown.

11. Find the probability that the numbers on the two dice are the same. $\frac{1}{6}$

12. Find the probability that the number is less than 3 or greater than 3. $\frac{34}{36}$

13. Find the probability that the number is greater than or equal to 4 or that the number is 12. $\frac{33}{36}$

14. Find the probability that the sum of the numbers on the two dice is greater than 8. $\frac{10}{36}$

15. Write the expansion of $(2a + b)^5$. Express the coefficients in combination notation. $\binom{5}{0}(2a)^5 + \binom{5}{1}(2a)^4 b + \binom{5}{2}(2a)^3 b^2 + \binom{5}{3}(2a)^2 b^3 + \binom{5}{4}(2a)b^4 + \binom{5}{5}b^5$

16. Find the fifth term of $(x - y)^8$. $70x^4y^4$

17. The numbers from 1 through 15 are printed on 15 tokens, one number per token. If one token is drawn at random, what is the probability that the number on it is divisible by 5? that the number is even? that the number is odd? that the number is a perfect square? $\frac{3}{15}; \frac{7}{15}; \frac{8}{15}; \frac{3}{15}$

5. {(H,H,H),(T,H,H),(H,H,T),(H,T,H),(T,T,H), (T,H,T),(H,T,T),(T,T,T)}; $\frac{1}{8}$

Chapter 13
Trigonometric Functions

The objective for this section is on page 472.

An angle can be formed by rotating a ray about its endpoint, or <u>vertex</u>, in a fixed plane. The initial position of the ray is the **initial side,** ray *OA*. The terminal position of the ray is the **terminal side,** ray *OB*.

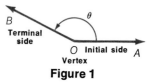

Figure 1

The amount and direction of rotation is the measure of the angle represented by θ (theta) in Figure 1. Angles with measures of 45°, −45°, 390°, and −390° are shown below.

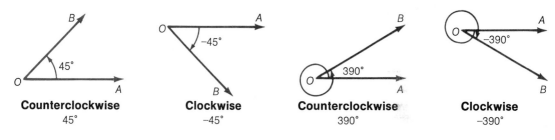

| **Counterclockwise** 45° | **Clockwise** −45° | **Counterclockwise** 390° | **Clockwise** −390° |

An angle of 360° is one full counterclockwise rotation. The terminal and initial sides coincide.

An angle of 180° is one–half a counterclockwise rotation. An angle of −180° is one–half a clockwise rotation.

An angle is in <u>standard position</u> when the vertex is at the origin and the initial side is on the positive *x* axis. Angle *AOB* is a <u>first-quadrant angle</u> because its terminal side is in that quadrant. An angle is a **quadrantal angle** if the terminal side is on an axis, such as ∠ *AOC* at the right.

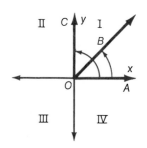

Exercises

Sketch each angle in standard position. Use a curved arrow to show the amount and direction of rotation. See key for Exercises 1-6.

1. 90° **2.** −90° **3.** 135°

4. −180° **5.** 315° **6.** 450°

*In Exercises **9-12**, the rotation of an angle is given. Sketch the angle in a coordinate plane, and find its measure.*

Same as Ex. 1; 90° Same as Ex. 4; −180°

7. $\frac{1}{4}$ rotation counterclockwise **8.** $\frac{1}{2}$ rotation clockwise
Similar to Ex. 3; but 120° See text page 440.

9. $\frac{1}{3}$ rotation counterclockwise **10.** 1 rotation counterclockwise

11. $2\frac{1}{4}$ rotations counterclockwise 810° **12.** $1\frac{1}{3}$ rotations clockwise −480°

In which quadrant will the terminal side of each angle lie?

13. 37° First **14.** 98° Second **15.** 156° Third

16. 287° Fourth **17.** 350° Fourth **18.** 375° First

19. 400° First **20.** 735° First **21.** −60° Fourth

22. −135° Third **23.** −240° Second **24.** −315° First

Find the coordinates of a point P on the terminal side of each angle if the distance of P from the origin is r.

25. 30°, $r = 2$ $(\sqrt{3}, 1)$ **26.** 45°, $r = 1$ $\left(\frac{\sqrt{2}}{2}, \frac{\sqrt{2}}{2}\right)$ **27.** 150°, $r = 4$ $(-2\sqrt{3}, 2)$

28. −135°, $r = 3$ $\left(-\frac{3}{2}\sqrt{2}, -\frac{3}{2}\sqrt{2}\right)$ **29.** 60°, $r = 6$ $(3, 3\sqrt{2})$ **30.** −240°, $r = 2$ $(-1, \sqrt{3})$

31. Draw an angle in standard position with the terminal side passing through a point in Quadrant III that has $r = 5$. If $y = -3$, find x, $\frac{y}{r}$, $\frac{x}{r}$ and $\frac{y}{x}$.
$x = -4$; $\frac{y}{r} = \frac{-3}{5}$, $\frac{x}{r} = \frac{-4}{5}$, $\frac{y}{x} = \frac{-3}{-4}$ or $\frac{3}{4}$

32. Through how many meters does a wheel of radius 6 centimeters roll in 3 revolutions? (HINT: Find the circumference. Use $\pi = 3.14$) 1.1304 meters

33. How many revolutions does a wheel 8 meters in diameter make in going 1 kilometer? 39.8 revolutions

34. A merry-go-round 20 meters in diameter makes 3 revolutions in 1 minute. What is the speed in meters per second of a boy standing at the edge?
3.14 m/sec.

Remember

Use the figure at the right for the following exercises.

1. Use the distance formula to find the measure of $\overline{OA}$, $\overline{OB}$, $\overline{OC}$, and $\overline{OD}$. $OA = 5, OB = 10, OC = 15, OD = 20$

2. If r represents the distance from O to each of the points A, B, C, D, find $\frac{y}{r}$, $\frac{x}{r}$, and $\frac{y}{x}$.

    For each of the points, $\frac{y}{r} = \frac{4}{5}, \frac{x}{r} = \frac{3}{5}$, and $\frac{y}{x} = \frac{4}{3}$.

3. For any point (x, y) on ray OA, what is the value of $\frac{y}{r}$? $\frac{x}{r}$? $\frac{y}{x}$? $\frac{y}{r} = \frac{4}{5}, \frac{x}{r} = \frac{3}{5}, \frac{y}{x} = \frac{4}{3}$

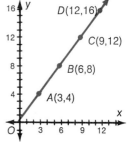

The answers are on page 475.

13-2 Trigonometric Functions Defined

The objective for this section is on page 472.

Think of point $P(x, y)$ on the terminal side of an angle with measure θ. Let P be r units from the origin. The ratios $\frac{y}{r}$, $\frac{x}{r}$, and $\frac{y}{x}$ are the three basic relationships of trigonometry.

The distance r is the measure of the <u>radius vector</u> of the point P. The triangle formed by drawing a perpendicular from point P on the radius vector to the x axis is the **reference triangle.**

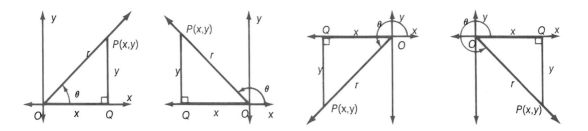

The ratios $\frac{y}{r}$, $\frac{x}{r}$, and $\frac{y}{x}$ have special names.

Definitions

$$\text{sine } \theta \text{ (abbreviated sin } \theta) = \frac{\text{ordinate of } P}{r} = \frac{y}{r}$$

$$\text{cosine } \theta \text{ (abbreviated cos } \theta) = \frac{\text{abscissa of } P}{r} = \frac{x}{r}$$

$$\text{tangent } \theta \text{ (abbreviated tan } \theta) = \frac{\text{ordinate of } P}{\text{abscissa of } P} = \frac{y}{x}, \ x \neq 0$$

Theorem 13-1: Each of the ratios $\frac{y}{r}$, $\frac{x}{r}$, and $\frac{y}{x}$ $(x \neq 0)$ is the same for every point P on the terminal side of an angle with measure θ.

Proof: Triangles OP_1Q_1 and OP_2Q_2 are similar.

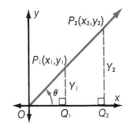

Therefore, $\frac{y_1}{r_1} = \frac{y_2}{r_2}$.

Also, $\frac{x_1}{r_1} = \frac{x_2}{r_2}$,

and, for $x_1 \neq 0$, $x_2 \neq 0$, $\frac{y_1}{x_1} = \frac{y_2}{x_2}$.

By Theorem 13-1, the sine, cosine, and tangent ratios depend only on the measure of the angle. Further, for each given θ, each ordered pair $(\theta, \sin \theta)$, $(\theta, \cos \theta)$, and $(\theta, \tan \theta)$ is unique. Thus, $\sin \theta$, $\cos \theta$ and $\tan \theta$ are functions.

The table below shows how these functions increase or decrease for values of θ where $0° \leq \theta \leq 360°$.

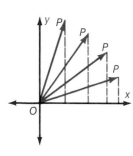

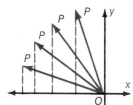

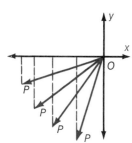

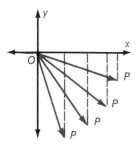

Angle Measure	Function	Changes in the Function
$0° \leq \theta < 90°$	sine	Increasing from 0 to nearly 1
	cosine	Decreasing from 1 to nearly 0
	tangent	Increasing from 0 to very large values
$\theta = 90°$	sine	$\sin 90° = 1$
	cosine	$\cos 90° = 0$
	tangent	tan 90° is not defined.
$90° < \theta \leq 180°$	sine	Decreasing from nearly 1 to 0
	cosine	Decreasing from nearly 0 to -1
	tangent	Increasing
$180° < \theta < 270°$	sine	Decreasing from 0 to nearly -1
	cosine	Increasing from -1 to nearly 0
	tangent	Increasing from 0 to very large values
$270°$	sine	$\sin 270° = -1$
	cosine	$\cos 270° = 0$
	tangent	tan 270° is not defined.
$270° < \theta \leq 360°$	sine	Increasing from -1 to 0
	cosine	Increasing from 0 to 1
	tangent	Increasing

The domain of the sine and cosine functions is the set of real numbers. However, certain real numbers are excluded from the domain of the tangent function.

Example 1   Evaluate $\sin\theta$, $\cos\theta$, and $\tan\theta$ for angle QOP.

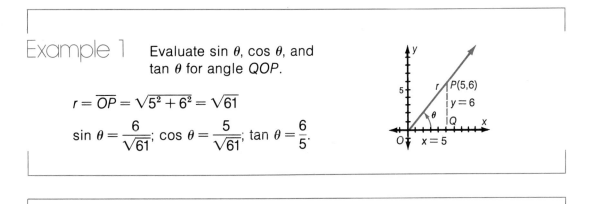

$r = \overline{OP} = \sqrt{5^2 + 6^2} = \sqrt{61}$

$\sin\theta = \dfrac{6}{\sqrt{61}}$; $\cos\theta = \dfrac{5}{\sqrt{61}}$; $\tan\theta = \dfrac{6}{5}$.

Example 2   Sketch the angle whose terminal side contains $P(-5, 12)$. Find the quadrant of the angle and use the reference triangle to find $\sin\theta$, $\cos\theta$, and $\tan\theta$.

The angle is in Quadrant II.

$r = \sqrt{(-5)^2 + 12^2} = 13$

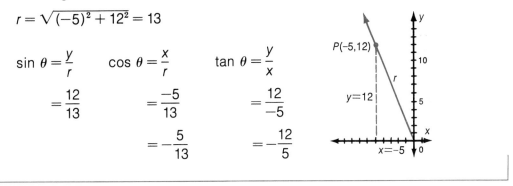

$\sin\theta = \dfrac{y}{r}$ $\cos\theta = \dfrac{x}{r}$ $\tan\theta = \dfrac{y}{x}$

$\quad = \dfrac{12}{13}$ $\quad = \dfrac{-5}{13}$ $\quad = \dfrac{12}{-5}$

$\qquad\qquad\qquad = -\dfrac{5}{13}$ $\quad = -\dfrac{12}{5}$

Try These   *Evaluate $\sin\theta$, $\cos\theta$, and $\tan\theta$ when θ is an angle in standard position whose terminal side contains the given point.*

1. $(3, 4)$ $\frac{4}{5}, \frac{3}{5}, \frac{4}{3}$ **2.** $(5, 12)$ $\frac{12}{13}, \frac{5}{13}, \frac{12}{5}$ **3.** $(-5, -12)$ $-\frac{12}{13}, -\frac{5}{13}, \frac{12}{5}$ **4.** $(5, -12)$

$-\frac{12}{13}, \frac{5}{13}, -\frac{12}{5}$

Exercises

9. $\dfrac{10}{5\sqrt{5}}$ or $\dfrac{2\sqrt{5}}{5}$; $\dfrac{5}{5\sqrt{5}}$ or $\dfrac{\sqrt{5}}{5}$; $\dfrac{10}{5}$ or 2

10. $\dfrac{4}{2\sqrt{13}}$ or $\dfrac{2\sqrt{13}}{13}$; $\dfrac{-6}{2\sqrt{13}}$ or $-\dfrac{3\sqrt{13}}{13}$; $-\dfrac{4}{6}$ or $-\dfrac{2}{3}$

11. $-\dfrac{5\sqrt{61}}{61}$; $-\dfrac{6\sqrt{61}}{61}$; $\dfrac{5}{6}$

Evaluate sin θ, cos θ, and tan θ where θ is the measure of an angle in standard position whose terminal side contains the given point. Leave answers in simplified radical form. Note that the values of some of the functions are negative and the values of some are positive.

1. $(-3, 4)$ $\frac{4}{5}; -\frac{3}{5}; -\frac{4}{3}$ **2.** $(10, -24)$ $-\frac{12}{13}; \frac{5}{13}; -\frac{12}{5}$ **3.** $(-6, 8)$ $\frac{4}{5}; -\frac{3}{5}; -\frac{4}{3}$ **4.** $(-6, -8)$ $-\frac{4}{5}; -\frac{3}{5}; \frac{4}{3}$

5. $(6, -8)$ $-\frac{4}{5}; \frac{3}{5}; -\frac{4}{3}$ **6.** $(8, -6)$ $-\frac{3}{5}; \frac{4}{5}; -\frac{3}{4}$ **7.** $(12, -5)$ $-\frac{5}{13}; \frac{12}{13}; -\frac{5}{12}$ **8.** $(-12, -5)$ $-\frac{5}{13}; -\frac{12}{13}; \frac{5}{12}$

9. $(5, 10)$ See above   **10.** $(-6, 4)$ See above   **11.** $(-12, -10)$ See above   **12.** $(3, 0)$ $0; 1; 0$

13. $(-1, -1)$ $-\frac{1}{\sqrt{2}}$ or $-\frac{\sqrt{2}}{2}$; $-\frac{1}{\sqrt{2}}$ or $\frac{-\sqrt{2}}{2}$; $\frac{-1}{-1}$ or $+1$ **14.** $(12, 0)$ $0; 1; 0$ **15.** $(0, -4)$ $-1; 0;$ Undefined   **16.** $(0, 7)$ $1; 0;$ Undefined

Evaluate sin θ and cos θ when θ is in the first quadrant, and when

17. $\tan \theta = \frac{2}{3}$ $\sin\theta = \frac{2}{\sqrt{13}}$ or $\frac{2\sqrt{13}}{13}$; $\cos\theta = \frac{3}{\sqrt{13}}$ or $\frac{3\sqrt{13}}{13}$ **18.** $\tan \theta = \frac{5}{12}$ $\sin\theta = \frac{5}{13}$; $\cos\theta = \frac{12}{13}$

Replace each __?__ with + or − to indicate whether the values of the given functions are positive or negative in the quadrants named.

	I	II	III	IV
19. sin θ	__?__ +	__?__ +	__?__ −	__?__ −
20. cos θ	__?__ +	__?__ −	__?__ −	__?__ +
21. tan θ	__?__ +	__?__ −	__?__ +	__?__ −

State the quadrants in which θ lies under the given conditions.

22. $\sin \theta > 0$ First and second quadrants.

23. $\cos \theta < 0$ Second and third quadrants

24. $\sin \theta > 0$ and $\cos \theta < 0$ Second quadrant

25. $\tan \theta > 0$ First or third quadrant

26. $\tan \theta > 0$ and $\cos \theta < 0$ Third quadrant

27. $\sin \theta < 0$ and $\tan \theta > 0$ Third quadrant

Find the value of the missing function.

Example: $\sin \theta = \frac{1}{2}$; $\cos \theta < 0$ **Solution:** $\cos \theta = \dfrac{x}{r} = \dfrac{-\sqrt{3}}{2} = -\dfrac{\sqrt{3}}{2}$

$$\tan \theta = \dfrac{y}{x} = \dfrac{1}{-\sqrt{3}} = -\dfrac{\sqrt{3}}{3}$$

28. $\sin \theta = -\frac{1}{2}$; $\cos \theta < 0$ $\cos\theta = -\frac{\sqrt{3}}{2}$; $\tan\theta = \frac{-1}{-\sqrt{3}}$ or $\frac{\sqrt{3}}{3}$

29. $\sin \theta = -\frac{1}{2}$; $\cos \theta > 0$ $\cos\theta = \frac{\sqrt{3}}{2}$; $\tan\theta = -\frac{1}{\sqrt{3}}$ or $-\frac{\sqrt{3}}{3}$

30. $\tan \theta = 1$; $\cos \theta < 0$ $\cos\theta = -\frac{1}{\sqrt{2}}$ or $-\frac{\sqrt{2}}{2}$; $\sin\theta = -\frac{1}{\sqrt{2}}$ or $\frac{-\sqrt{2}}{2}$

31. $\cos \theta = \frac{3}{5}$; $\tan \theta < 0$ $\sin\theta = -\frac{4}{5}$; $\tan\theta = -\frac{4}{3}$

Sketch a positive angle θ in each of Quadrants I-IV so that each angle has the same reference triangle. Choose a point P(x, y) on the terminal sides of the angles so that each angle has the same radius vector, r. Express the values of the sine, cosine and tangent of each angle in terms of x, y and r.

Which of the following is <u>not</u> true about the domain and range of the sine, cosine and tangent functions?

32. As θ increases from 0° to 90°, tan θ increases from 1 without bound. True

33. As θ varies from 0° to 360°, sin θ takes all values from −1 to 1. True

34. As θ varies from 0° to 360°, the range of cos θ is the set of all numbers from 0 to −1. Not true

35. As θ decreases from 180° to 90°, sin θ decreases from 1 to 0. Not true

36. As θ increases from 180° to 270°, tan θ decreases from 0 without bound. Not true

37. As θ decreases from 90° to 0°, cos θ decreases from 1 to 0. Not true

13-3 Functions of Special Angles

The objective for this section is on page 472.

Recall that 30-60-90 and 45-45-90 right triangles have sides whose lengths are related as shown in Figure 1, where s is any real number.

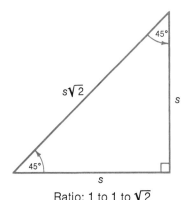

Ratio: 1 to 1 to $\sqrt{2}$

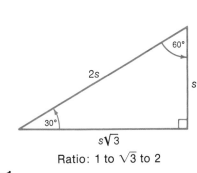

Ratio: 1 to $\sqrt{3}$ to 2

Figure 1

Finding unknown sides or angles in a triangle is called <u>solving the triangle.</u>

Example 1

Solve the 30-60-90 triangle whose hypotenuse is 10 centimeters.

From Figure 1 on page 447, the leg opposite the 30° angle is one–half the hypotenuse.

$\frac{1}{2}(10) = 5$ ⟵ The length is 5 centimeters.

$\sqrt{10^2 - 5^2} = \sqrt{75}$ ⟵ Pythagorean Theorem

$= 5\sqrt{3}$ ⟵ The other leg is $5\sqrt{3}$ centimeters.

Example 2

Solve the 45-45-90 triangle whose hypotenuse is 16 meters.

METHOD I Let x be the length of each leg.

$x^2 + x^2 = 16^2$ ⟵ Pythagorean Theorem.

$2x^2 = 256$

$x^2 = 128$

$x = 8\sqrt{2}$ ⟵ The length is $8\sqrt{2}$ meters.

METHOD II From Figure 1, s is the length of a leg and

$\sqrt{2}s = 16$.

Thus, $s = \dfrac{16}{\sqrt{2}}$

$= 8\sqrt{2}$

The relationships of the lengths of the sides of 30-60-90 and 45-45-90 triangles are used to find the trigonometric functions of angles whose reference triangles have a 30°, a 60°, or a 45° angle. It is helpful to sketch the angle and the reference triangle.

Example 3   Find sin 135°, cos 135°, and tan 135°.

The reference triangle is 45-45-90.
By Figure 1, the sides of the reference triangle have the same measures, s, and $r = s\sqrt{2}$.
    Thus, the coordinates of P are
$(-s, s)$, because P is in Quadrant
II.

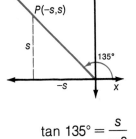

$$\sin 135° = \frac{s}{s\sqrt{2}} = \frac{1}{\sqrt{2}} \qquad \cos 135° = \frac{-s}{s\sqrt{2}} \qquad \tan 135° = \frac{s}{-s}$$

$$= \frac{\sqrt{2}}{2} \qquad\qquad\qquad = -\frac{\sqrt{2}}{2} \qquad\qquad = -1$$

Example 4   Find sin 330°, cos 330°, and tan 330°.

As the figure shows, the reference
triangle is a 30-60-90 triangle. By
Figure 1, the lengths of its sides
are proportional to 1, 2, and $\sqrt{3}$.
This means that the length of the
radius vector of some point P on
the terminal side of the 330° angle
is 2. Thus, the coordinates of P
are $(\sqrt{3}, -1)$, So,

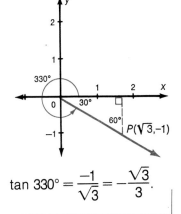

$$\sin 330° = \frac{-1}{2} = -\frac{1}{2} \qquad \cos 330° = \frac{\sqrt{3}}{2} \qquad \tan 330° = \frac{-1}{\sqrt{3}} = -\frac{\sqrt{3}}{3}.$$

Try These

1. If a point P lies on the terminal side of a 30° angle in standard position and
   the radius vector of P measures 2 units, find the coordinates of P. $P(\sqrt{3}, 1)$

2. Use the results of Exercise 1 to find sin 30° cos 30°, and tan 30°. Leave
   your answers in radical form, but rationalize any irrational denominators.
   $\sin 30° = \frac{1}{2}$; $\cos 30° = \frac{\sqrt{3}}{2}$; $\tan 30° = \frac{\sqrt{3}}{3}$

Exercises

2. $\sin 60° = \dfrac{\sqrt{3}}{2}$; $\cos 60° = \dfrac{1}{2}$; $\tan 60° = \dfrac{\sqrt{3}}{1}$ or $\sqrt{3}$

a

1. If a point P lies on the terminal side of a 60° angle that is in standard position and the radius vector of P measures 2 units, find the coordinates of P. $(1,\sqrt{3})$

2. Use the results of Exercise 1 to find sin 60°, cos 60°, and tan 60°. See above.

3. If a point P lies on the terminal side of a 45° angle that is in standard position and the abcissa of point P is 1, find the ordinate and the length of the radius vector of P. $y=1, r=\sqrt{2}$

4. Use the results of Exercise 3 to find sin 45°, cos 45°, and tan 45°. $\dfrac{\sqrt{2}}{2}$; $\dfrac{\sqrt{2}}{2}$; 1

5. If a point P lies on the terminal side of a 315° angle that is in standard position and the abcissa of point P is 1, find the ordinate and the length of the radius vector of P. Use your results to find sin 315°, cos 315°, and tan 315°. $y=-1; r=\sqrt{2}$; $\sin 315° = \dfrac{-\sqrt{2}}{2}$; $\cos 315° = \dfrac{\sqrt{2}}{2}$; $\tan 315° = -1$

6. If a point P lies on the terminal side of a 225° angle in standard position and the ordinate of P is −1, find the abcissa and radius vector of P. Use your results to find sin 225°, cos 225°, and tan 225°. $x=-1; r=\sqrt{2}$; $-\dfrac{\sqrt{2}}{2}$; $-\dfrac{\sqrt{2}}{2}$; 1

7. If the point P lies on the terminal side of a 120° angle in standard position and the radius vector of P is 2 units, find the coordinates of P. Use your results to find sin 120°, cos 120°, and tan 120°. $(-1,\sqrt{3})$; $\dfrac{\sqrt{3}}{2}$; $-\dfrac{1}{2}$; $-\sqrt{3}$

Repeat Exercise 7 for angles with the following measures.

8. 150° **9.** 210° **10.** 240° **11.** 300°

$(-\sqrt{3}, 1); \dfrac{1}{2}; -\dfrac{\sqrt{3}}{2}; -\dfrac{\sqrt{3}}{3}$ $-\dfrac{1}{2}; -\dfrac{\sqrt{3}}{2}; \dfrac{\sqrt{3}}{3}$ $-\dfrac{\sqrt{3}}{2}; -\dfrac{1}{2}; \sqrt{3}$ $-\dfrac{\sqrt{3}}{2}; \dfrac{1}{2}; -\sqrt{3}$

Use a reference triangle to find each function value.

b

12. cos 405° $\dfrac{\sqrt{2}}{2}$ **13.** sin 570° $-\dfrac{1}{2}$ **14.** tan 420° $\sqrt{3}$ **15.** sin 330° $-\dfrac{1}{2}$

16. cos 660° $\dfrac{1}{2}$ **17.** tan 585° 1 **18.** tan 870° $-\dfrac{\sqrt{3}}{3}$ **19.** cos 495°

20. Show that $\sin^{2}3\theta + \cos^{2}3\theta = 1$. (HINT: $\sin^{2}3\theta$ means $(\sin 3\theta)^{2}$.) $-\dfrac{\sqrt{2}}{2}$

See key.

21. Show that $\tan 60° = \dfrac{\sin 60°}{\cos 60°}$ See key.

22. Prove that the following two statements are identities. That is, for all angles θ for which no denominator is zero, See key.

$$\sin^{2}\theta + \cos^{2}\theta = 1 \qquad \text{and} \qquad \tan\theta = \dfrac{\sin\theta}{\cos\theta}.$$

Using Trigonometric Functions in Triangles

The objective for this section is on page 473.

The reference triangle of every angle in the coordinate plane that is not a quadrantal angle is a right triangle. The length of the hypotenuse is r, and the lengths of the sides opposite, and adjacent to, the acute angle with measure θ are $|y|$ and $|x|$, where x and y are the coordinates of P. By substituting for x, y and r in the coordinate system definitions, the right-triangle definitions can be stated as follows.

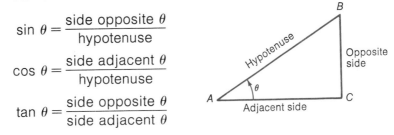

$$\sin \theta = \frac{\text{side opposite } \theta}{\text{hypotenuse}}$$

$$\cos \theta = \frac{\text{side adjacent } \theta}{\text{hypotenuse}}$$

$$\tan \theta = \frac{\text{side opposite } \theta}{\text{side adjacent } \theta}$$

The table on pages 543–547 gives the sine, cosine, and tangent function values for angles of 0° to 90° to the nearest ten-thousandth. Angles that measure 45° or less are read in the left column using the headings at the top of the table. Angles of 45° or greater are read in the right column using the headings at the bottom.

Although the values in the table are approximations, we shall use the symbol "=" when writing statements involving these values because it is more convenient.

Example

If c, the length of the hypotenuse, is 220 meters and A (the measure of $\angle A$) is 28° 40′ (40′ is read "forty minutes") in right triangle ABC, find b, the leg opposite $\angle B$.

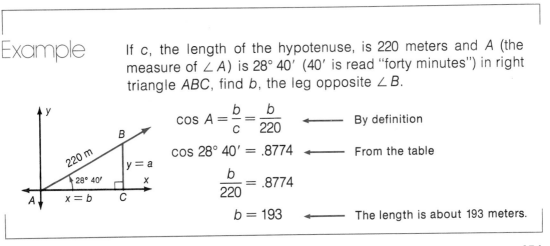

$$\cos A = \frac{b}{c} = \frac{b}{220} \quad \longleftarrow \quad \text{By definition}$$

$$\cos 28° \, 40′ = .8774 \quad \longleftarrow \quad \text{From the table}$$

$$\frac{b}{220} = .8774$$

$$b = 193 \quad \longleftarrow \quad \text{The length is about 193 meters.}$$

Trigonometric Functions **451**

In Figure 1, angle *BEP* is the **angle of elevation** of *E* from *P*. To measure ∠*BEP*, a surveyor places his transit at *E* and first points the telescope horizontally toward the flagpole. Then the telescope is pointed to the top of the pole, *P*.

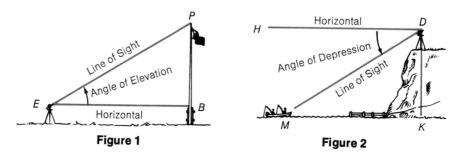

Figure 1   **Figure 2**

Figure 2 shows an **angle of depression**. When the telescope is turned from the horizontal position to *DM* (looking at the persons in the boat), it turns through the angle of depression, *HDM*.

Try These   *Use the table on pages 543–547 to find the values of the following functions.*

1. sin 14° 50' .2560

2. tan 27° 20' .5169

3. cos 67° 30'
.3827

Use the table on pages 543–547 to find θ, the measure of an acute angle, when

4. sin θ = 0.4014 23° 40'

5. tan θ = 1.5798 57° 40'

6. cos θ = 0.6539
49° 10'

Exercises

Use the drawing of △ABC to answer Exercises 1-4.

1. If you know the measure of ∠*B* and the value of *b*, which trigonometric function would you use to find *a*? to find *c*? tan B; sin B

2. If you know the measure of ∠*A* and the value of *b*, which trigonometric function would you use to find *c*? to find *a*? cos A; tan A

3. If you know the measure of ∠*B* and the value of *a*, which trigonometric function would you use to find *c*? to find *b*? cos B; tan B

4. If you know the values of *a* and *b*, which trigonometric function would you use to find *B*, the measure of ∠*B*?   tan *B*

Find the values of the sine, cosine, and tangent of each acute angle in the triangles of Exercises 5-8.   See key for Exercises 5-8.

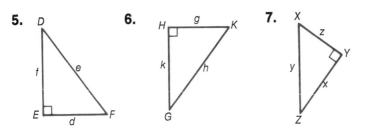

5. D   **6.**   **7.**   **8.**

9. Name the angle of elevation if you are looking from *B* to *A*; from *C* to *D*.   α; φ

10. Name the angle of depression if you are looking from *D* to *C*; from *A* to *B*.   θ; β

11. If α = 40°, then β = __?__   40°
If θ = 50°, then φ = __?__   50°

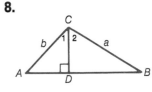

12. The railroad that runs to the summit of Pikes Peak makes, at the steepest place, a 27° angle with the horizontal. How many meters would you rise in going 400 meters up this track?   About 182 meters

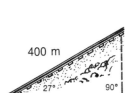

13. The distance *AB* shown in the picture can be found by placing stakes at *A, B,* and *C* in such a way as to make ∠*A* a right angle, and by measuring *AC* and ∠*C*. If *AC* is 532 meters and *C* is 42° 10′, how long is *AB*?   About 482 meters

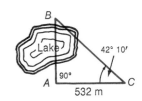

14. A line to the sun and a line directly under it on the ground make an angle of 33°. At the same time, a pole casts a shadow 124 feet long on level ground. How high is the pole?   About 80.5 feet

15. The angle of depression from the top of a cliff 800 meters high to the base of a log cabin is 37° 20′. How far is the cabin from the foot of the cliff?   About 1049 meters

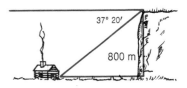

16. Two boats are observed from a tower 75 meters above a lake. The angles of depression seen are 12° 30′ and 7° 10′. How far apart are the boats? About 259 meters

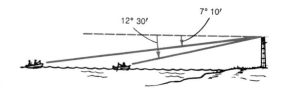

13-5 Interpolation

The objectives for this section are on page 473.

Interpolation for trigonometric functions involves the same principle as interpolation for logarithms.

The graphs of trigonometric functions are not straight lines. For small portions of the graphs, however, a straight line approximates the graphs quite well.

Example 1   Evaluate tan 76° 33′.

Use the table of tangents to interpolate.

$$10\left[\ 3\left[\begin{matrix} 76°\ 30' \\ 76°\ 33' \end{matrix}\right.\right.\quad \text{From the table} \longrightarrow \left.\left.\begin{matrix} 4.1653 \\ ? \end{matrix}\right]d\right]0.0540$$
$$76°\ 40' \qquad \text{From the table} \longrightarrow 4.2193$$

$$\frac{3}{10} = \frac{d}{0.054} \qquad \longleftarrow \quad \text{Write the ratios.}$$

$$d = \frac{3 \times 0.0540}{10}, \text{ or } d = 0.0162$$

$$\tan 76° 33' = 4.1653 + 0.0162$$
$$= 4.1815$$

Example 2   Evaluate cos 32° 17'

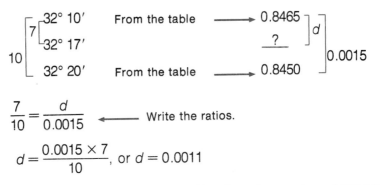

$$\frac{7}{10} = \frac{d}{0.0015}$$ ← Write the ratios.

$$d = \frac{0.0015 \times 7}{10}, \text{ or } d = 0.0011$$

The cosine of 32° 17' is smaller than the cosine of 32° 10' because the cosine function for angles in the first quadrant decreases as the measure of the angle increases.

cos 32° 17' = 0.8465 − 0.0011
= 0.8454

Example 3   Find B to the nearest minute if tan B = 1.3456.

$$10 \begin{bmatrix} d \begin{bmatrix} 53° \ 20' \\ B \end{bmatrix} \begin{matrix} 1.3432 \\ 1.3456 \end{matrix} \end{bmatrix} 0.0024 \\ 53° \ 30' \quad 1.3514 \end{bmatrix} 0.0082$$

$$\frac{d}{10} = \frac{0.0024}{0.0082}$$ ← Write the ratios.

$$d = \frac{0.0024 \times 10}{0.0082}$$

d = 2.92, or d is about 3'.

B = 53° 20' + 3'
= 53° 23'

Exercises

Evaluate.

1. tan 34° 23′ 0.6843   **2.** tan 51° 36′ 1.2617   **3.** tan 75° 29′ 3.8621   **4.** sin 42° 18′ 0.6730

5. sin 64° 23′ 0.9017   **6.** cos 22° 12′ 0.9259   **7.** cos 40° 36′   **8.** cos 64° 45′ 0.4266

Find θ to the nearest minute.

9. If tan θ = .7325 36° 13′   **10.** If tan θ = 1.9371 62° 42′   **11.** If sin θ = .8537 58° 37′

12. If sin θ = .8670 60° 7′   **13.** If cos θ = .7561 40° 53′   **14.** If cos θ = .3890 67° 7′

15. If, in the figure, B = 48° 13′ and c = 735 centimeters find a. Find b. a = 490 cm; b = 548 cm

16. If, in the same figure, A = 52° 28′ and a = 452 centimeters what is b? What is c? b = 347 cm; c = 570 cm

17. Lighthouse C is due west from a ship A. Lighthouse B, which is due north of C, is so situated that angle CAB measures 25° 37′. If the distance from C to B is 13.12 kilometers, how far is the ship from C? 27.36 km

18. In the triangle below, sides AC and BC are each 462 centimeters long and side AB is 302 centimeters. What are the measures of A and B to the nearest minute? 70° 56′

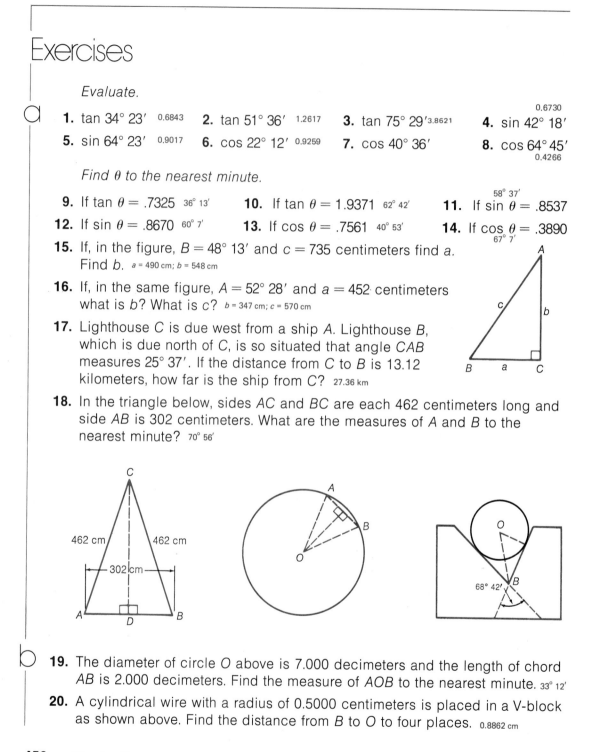

19. The diameter of circle O above is 7.000 decimeters and the length of chord AB is 2.000 decimeters. Find the measure of AOB to the nearest minute. 33° 12′

20. A cylindrical wire with a radius of 0.5000 centimeters is placed in a V-block as shown above. Find the distance from B to O to four places. 0.8862 cm

13-6 Logarithms of Trigonometric Functions

The objectives for this section are on page 473.

The multiplication and division necessary to solve triangles can be done by logarithms. The logarithms of the trigonometric functions are given in the table on pages 550–554 for every 10′ of angle. Interpolate for other values.

Many trigonometric functions have values smaller than one. Thus, their logarithms have negative characteristics. To simplify matters, the negative characteristic is not included in the table. However, each value in the table is assumed to have −10 added to it. Thus,

$$\log \sin 17° \ 20' = 9.4741 - 10 \ (\text{not } 9.4741),$$

and

$$\log \tan 87° \ 30' = 11.3599 - 10 \ (\text{not } 11.3599).$$

Example

Find the value of 26.5 cos 11° 30′.

$$\log 26.5 = \ \ 1.4232 \quad \longleftarrow \quad \text{From the table}$$
$$\log \cos 11° \ 30' = \ \ 9.9912 - 10$$
$$\log (26.5 \cos 11° \ 30') = 11.4144 - 10$$
$$= 1.4144$$

$$26.5 \cos 11° \ 30' = 26.0 \quad \longleftarrow \quad \text{From the table}$$

Try These

Find the values of the following.

1. log sin 43° 9.8338 − 10

2. log sin 22°, 30′ 9.5828 − 10

3. log sin 75° 10′ 9.9853 − 10

4. log cos 34° 9.9186 − 10

5. log cos 72° 20′ 9.4821 − 10

6. log cos 43° 15′ 9.8624 − 10

7. log tan 32° 9.7958 − 10

8. log tan 53° 30′ 0.1308

Exercises

Given the following values, find θ to the nearest 10'.

1. log sin θ = 9.7642 − 10   <small>35° 30'</small>

2. log cos θ = 9.6666 − 10   <small>62° 20'</small>

3. log tan θ = 0.3529   <small>66°</small>

4. log tan θ = 9.3456 − 10   <small>12° 30'</small>

Interpolate to approximate the following values.

5. log sin 22° 12'   <small>9.5773 −10</small>

6. log cos 48° 16'   <small>9.8233 − 10</small>

7. log tan 58° 48'   <small>0.2178</small>

Use logarithms to evaluate.

8. 3.43 sin 40° 30'   <small>2.23</small>

9. 67.2 cos 62° 30'   <small>31.0</small>

10. 453 tan 72° 30'   <small>1,440</small>

11. $\dfrac{62.3}{\cos 45° 30'}$ <small>88.9</small>

12. $\dfrac{754}{\tan 54° 00'}$ <small>548</small>

13. $\dfrac{982}{\sin 35° 30'}$ <small>1,690</small>

14. 4500 tan 32° 00'   <small>2,810</small>

15. 745 sin 51° 30'   <small>583</small>

16. 4.62 cos 36° 30'   <small>3.71</small>

*Use triangle ABC for Exercises **17–22**.*

17. If A = 64° 30' and b = 3.8 meters, a = __?__.   <small>7.97</small>

18. If B = 47° 30' and a = 194 meters, b = __?__.   <small>212 meters</small>

19. If A = 36° 00' and a = 254 meters, c = __?__.   <small>432 meters</small>

20. If B = 73° 00' and c = 63.5 meters, a = __?__.   <small>18.6 meters</small>

21. If a = 25.3 meters and b = 60.0 meters, find ∠A to the nearest 30'.   <small>23° 00'</small>

22. If c = 90.8 meters and b = 25.5 meters, find ∠B to the nearest 30'.   <small>16° 30'</small>

23. An aviator observes the measure of the angle of depression of a marker to be 36° 00'. She is 2000 meters above the ground. How far from the marker is the point on the ground directly under the plane?   <small>2750 meters</small>

24. A camp director wishes to buy a new rope for the flagpole at his camp. At a point 4 meters from the foot of the pole, he measured the angle of elevation of the top of the pole and found it to be 82° 30'. What length of rope should he buy if he wishes it to be double the distance from the top of the pole to the spot from which he measured the angle?   <small>61.4 meters</small>

Angles with Negative Measures

The objective for this section is on page 474.

Example 1

Evaluate sin (−45°), cos (−45°), tan (−45°), sin (−210°), cos (−210°), and tan (−210°).

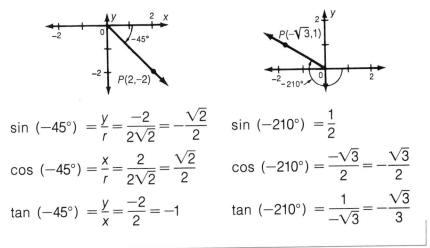

$$\sin(-45°) = \frac{y}{r} = \frac{-2}{2\sqrt{2}} = -\frac{\sqrt{2}}{2} \qquad \sin(-210°) = \frac{1}{2}$$

$$\cos(-45°) = \frac{x}{r} = \frac{2}{2\sqrt{2}} = \frac{\sqrt{2}}{2} \qquad \cos(-210°) = \frac{-\sqrt{3}}{2} = -\frac{\sqrt{3}}{2}$$

$$\tan(-45°) = \frac{y}{x} = \frac{-2}{2} = -1 \qquad \tan(-210°) = \frac{1}{-\sqrt{3}} = -\frac{\sqrt{3}}{3}$$

For any angle QOP whose measure is θ, there is one and only one angle whose measure is $-\theta$. If P' is chosen so that $\overline{OP'}$ is congruent to $\overline{OP}$, the reference triangles for angles QOP and QOP' are congruent. In each of four possible cases shown, $x' = x$, $y' = -y$, and $r' = r$.

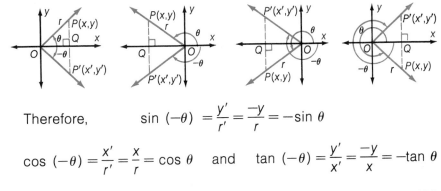

Therefore,
$$\sin(-\theta) = \frac{y'}{r'} = \frac{-y}{r} = -\sin\theta$$

$$\cos(-\theta) = \frac{x'}{r'} = \frac{x}{r} = \cos\theta \qquad \text{and} \qquad \tan(-\theta) = \frac{y'}{x'} = \frac{-y}{x} = -\tan\theta$$

Trigonometric Functions **459**

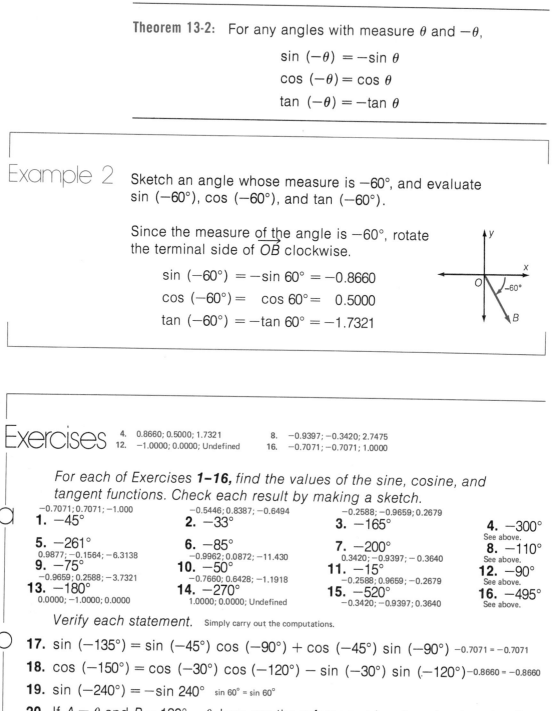

Theorem 13-2: For any angles with measure θ and $-\theta$,

$$\sin(-\theta) = -\sin\theta$$
$$\cos(-\theta) = \cos\theta$$
$$\tan(-\theta) = -\tan\theta$$

Example 2　Sketch an angle whose measure is −60°, and evaluate
sin (−60°), cos (−60°), and tan (−60°).

Since the measure of the angle is −60°, rotate
the terminal side of $\overrightarrow{OB}$ clockwise.

$$\sin(-60°) = -\sin 60° = -0.8660$$
$$\cos(-60°) = \cos 60° = 0.5000$$
$$\tan(-60°) = -\tan 60° = -1.7321$$

Exercises

4.　0.8660; 0.5000; 1.7321　　　8.　−0.9397; −0.3420; 2.7475
12.　−1.0000; 0.0000; Undefined　16.　−0.7071; −0.7071; 1.0000

For each of Exercises **1–16,** find the values of the sine, cosine, and
tangent functions. Check each result by making a sketch.

1. −45° −0.7071; 0.7071; −1.000

2. −33° −0.5446; 0.8387; −0.6494

3. −165° −0.2588; −0.9659; 0.2679

4. −300° See above.

5. −261° 0.9877; −0.1564; −6.3138

6. −85° −0.9962; 0.0872; −11.430

7. −200° 0.3420; −0.9397; −0.3640

8. −110° See above.

9. −75°

10. −50° −0.7660; 0.6428; −1.1918

11. −15° −0.2588; 0.9659; −0.2679

12. −90° See above.

13. −180° 0.0000; −1.0000; 0.0000

14. −270° 1.0000; 0.0000; Undefined

15. −520° −0.3420; −0.9397; 0.3640

16. −495° See above.

9. −0.9659; 0.2588; −3.7321

Verify each statement. Simply carry out the computations.

17. sin (−135°) = sin (−45°) cos (−90°) + cos (−45°) sin (−90°) −0.7071 = −0.7071

18. cos (−150°) = cos (−30°) cos (−120°) − sin (−30°) sin (−120°)−0.8660 = −0.8660

19. sin (−240°) = −sin 240° sin 60° = sin 60°

20. If $A = \theta$ and $B = 180° - \theta$, how are the reference triangles of $\angle A$ and $\angle B$
related if $\theta < 180°$? if $\theta > 180°$? See key.

13-8 Reduction Formulas

The objective for this section is on page 474.

In Figure 1, if $A = \theta$ and $B = 180° - \theta$, then the reference triangles of angles A and B are similar for any points P and P' chosen on the terminal sides of $\angle A$ and $\angle B$, respectively.

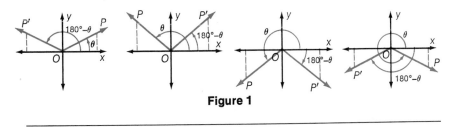

Figure 1

Theorem 13-3	$\sin (180° - \theta) = \sin \theta$
	$\cos (180° - \theta) = -\cos \theta$
	$\tan (180° - \theta) = -\tan \theta$

Suppose $A = \theta$ and $B = 180° + \theta$.

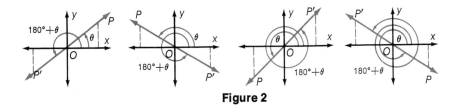

Figure 2

The reference triangles for the angles A and B are similar regardless of how points P and P' are chosen.

Theorem 13-4	$\sin (180° + \theta) = -\sin \theta$
	$\cos (180° + \theta) = -\cos \theta$
	$\tan (180° + \theta) = \tan \theta$

A similar relationship exists between any angles with measures θ and $360° - \theta$. Verify the following theorem for several values of θ.

Trigonometric Functions **461**

Theorem 13-5

$$\sin (360° - \theta) = -\sin \theta$$
$$\cos (360° - \theta) = \cos \theta$$
$$\tan (360° - \theta) = -\tan \theta$$

A different relationship exists between the values of the sine, cosine, and tangent functions for the angles whose measures are θ and $(90° - \theta)$.

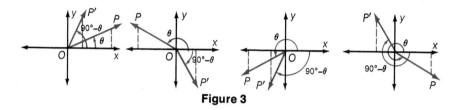

Figure 3

If points P and P' are chosen on the terminal sides of the angles so that $OP' = OP$, the reference triangles are congruent right triangles with $r' = r$, $x' = y$, and $y' = x$.

If P and P' are chosen so that $OP' \neq OP$, the reference triangles of the angles with measures θ and $(90° - \theta)$ are similar, and the same relationships hold for the coordinates and radius vectors of P and P'.

Theorem 13-6

$$\sin (90° - \theta) = \cos \theta$$
$$\cos (90° - \theta) = \sin \theta$$
$$\tan (90° - \theta) = \frac{1}{\tan \theta}$$

Consider the angles whose measures are θ and $(90° + \theta)$.

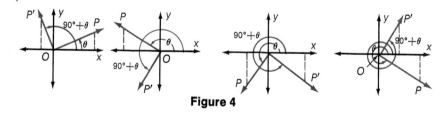

Figure 4

If P and P' are chosen so that $r' = r$, and if the coordinates of P are (x, y), the coordinates of P' are $(-y, x)$.

Theorem 13-7	$\sin(90° + \theta) = \cos\theta$
	$\cos(90° + \theta) = -\sin\theta$
	$\tan(90° + \theta) = -\dfrac{1}{\tan\theta}$

Example   Evaluate: cos 159° 30'

$$\cos 159° 30' = \cos(180° - 20° 30')$$
$$\cos 159° 30' = -\cos 20° 30' \quad\longleftarrow\quad \cos(180° - \theta) = -\cos\theta$$
$$= -0.9367$$

Exercises

Express in the form (180° − θ).

1. 125° 30'   **2.** 145° 48'   **3.** 116° 32'   **4.** 134° 26'   **5.** 99° 58'   **6.** 156° 45'
(180° − 54° 30')   (180° − 34° 12')   (180° − 63° 28')   (180° − 45° 34')   (180° − 80° 2')   (180° − 23° 15')

Express in the form (180° + θ).

7. 217°   **8.** 200°   **9.** 225° 20'   **10.** 237° 40'   **11.** 250° 17'   **12.** 267° 54'
(180° + 37°)   (180° + 20°)   (180° + 45° 20')   (180° + 57° 40')   (180° + 70° 17')   (180° + 87° 54')

Express in the form (360° − θ).

13. 275°   **14.** 283°   **15.** 302° 10'   **16.** 326° 40'   **17.** 345° 36'   **18.** 357° 24'
(360° − 85°)   (360° − 77°)   (360° − 57° 50')   (360° − 33° 20')   (360° − 14° 24')   (360° − 2° 36')

Express in the form (90° + θ).

19. 123° 14' (90° + 33° 14')   **20.** 162° 36' (90° + 72° 36')   **21.** 149° 57' (90° + 59° 57')

Find sin θ, cos θ, and tan θ for the following values of θ.

0.4592; −0.8884; −0.5169   −0.5592; −0.8290; 0.6745   −0.9063; 0.4226; −2.1445
22. 152° 40'   **23.** 143° 30'   **24.** 214°   **25.** 227° 10'   **26.** 295°   **27.** 304° 14'
        0.5948; −0.8039; −0.7400   −0.7333; −0.6799; 1.0786   −0.8268; 0.5626; −1.4696

Other Trigonometric Functions

The objective for this section is on page 474.

The reciprocals of the sine, cosine, and tangent ratios define the following functions.

Definitions: cotangent θ (cot θ) $= \dfrac{1}{\tan \theta} = \dfrac{1}{\frac{y}{x}} = \dfrac{x}{y}$, $\tan \theta \neq 0$

secant θ (sec θ) $= \dfrac{1}{\cos \theta} = \dfrac{1}{\frac{x}{r}} = \dfrac{r}{x}$, $\cos \theta \neq 0$

cosecant θ (csc θ) $= \dfrac{1}{\sin \theta} = \dfrac{1}{\frac{y}{r}} = \dfrac{r}{y}$, $\sin \theta \neq 0$

Example 1   Find the cotangent, secant, and cosecant of 30°.

$$\cot 30° = \frac{1}{\tan 30°} = \frac{1}{\frac{1}{\sqrt{3}}} = \sqrt{3} \qquad \sec 30° = \frac{1}{\cos 30°} = \frac{1}{\frac{\sqrt{3}}{2}} = \frac{2}{\sqrt{3}} = \frac{2\sqrt{3}}{3}$$

$$\csc 30° = \frac{1}{\sin 30°} = \frac{1}{\frac{1}{2}} = 2$$

Example 2   Evaluate: sec 57°

$$\sec 57° = \frac{1}{\cos 57°} = \frac{1}{0.5446} \quad \longleftarrow \quad \text{From the table}$$

$$= 1.8362$$

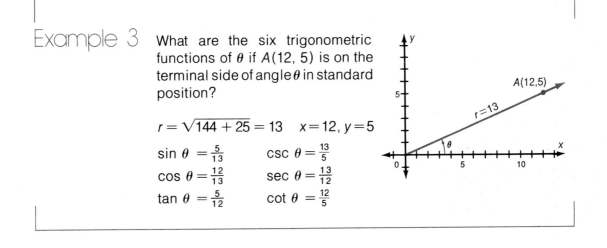

Example 3   What are the six trigonometric functions of θ if $A(12, 5)$ is on the terminal side of angle θ in standard position?

$r = \sqrt{144 + 25} = 13$ $x = 12, y = 5$

$\sin \theta = \frac{5}{13}$ $\csc \theta = \frac{13}{5}$

$\cos \theta = \frac{12}{13}$ $\sec \theta = \frac{13}{12}$

$\tan \theta = \frac{5}{12}$ $\cot \theta = \frac{12}{5}$

Try These   *Find the secant, cosecant, and cotangent (when defined) of each angle.*

6.3924, 1.0125, 0.1584

1. $45°$ $\sqrt{2}, \sqrt{2}, 1$ **2.** $60°$ $2, \frac{2\sqrt{3}}{3}, \frac{\sqrt{3}}{3}$ **3.** $30°$ $\frac{2\sqrt{3}}{3}, 2, \sqrt{3}$ **4.** $90°$ Undefined, 1,0   **5.** $37°$ 1.2521, 1.6616, 1.3270   **6.** $81°$

Exercises

See key for Exercises 1-4.

Find the values of the six trigonometric functions of the angle θ in standard position, if its terminal side contains the given point.

a   **1.** $(-24, 7)$ **2.** $(4, -5)$ **3.** $(-5, -12)$ **4.** $(4, 0)$

Find each value.

8.403

5. $\cot 110°$ −0.3640   **6.** $\sec 245°$ −2.366   **7.** $\csc 340°$ −2.924   **8.** $\sec 83° \, 10'$

9. $\csc 210° \, 20'$ −1.980   **10.** $\cot 326° \, 14'$ −1.496   **11.** $\cot 240° \, 18'$ 0.5704   **12.** $\sec 108° \, 09'$ −3.210

Find the acute angle θ, given the following information.

13. $\sec \theta = 1.236$ 36°   **14.** $\cot \theta = 1.8165$ 28° 50'

15. $\csc \theta = 5.575$ 10° 20'   **16.** $\sec \theta = 1.187$ 32° 35'

In which quadrant must θ lie under the given conditions?

b   **17.** $\sec \theta < 0$ and $\cot \theta > 0$ III   **18.** $\csc \theta > 0$ and $\cot \theta < 0$ II

19. $\sec \theta > 0$ and $\csc \theta > 0$ I   **20.** $\sec \theta > 0$ and $\csc \theta < 0$ IV

13-10 The Law of Sines

The objective for this section is on page 475.

The Law of Sines is useful in solving triangles.

Theorem 13-8: Law of Sines

In any triangle, the measures of the sides are proportional to the sines of the measure of the angles opposite the sides.

In $\triangle ABC$, $\qquad \dfrac{a}{\sin A} = \dfrac{b}{\sin B} = \dfrac{c}{\sin C}$.

Proof: CASE I: Angles A, B, and C are acute.

Construct $\overline{CD}$ perpendicular to side AB.

In $\triangle ADC$, $\sin A = \dfrac{h}{b}$, or $h = b \sin A$.

In $\triangle DBC$, $\sin B = \dfrac{h}{a}$, or $h = a \sin B$.

Thus, $a \sin B = b \sin A$.

$$\dfrac{a}{\sin A} = \dfrac{b}{\sin B} \qquad \longleftarrow \text{Divide by } \sin A \sin B.$$

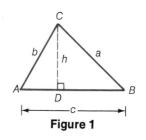

Figure 1

Similarly, by constructing a perpendicular to $\overline{BC}$, you can show that $\dfrac{c}{\sin C} = \dfrac{b}{\sin B}$.

So, $\dfrac{a}{\sin A} = \dfrac{b}{\sin B} = \dfrac{c}{\sin C}$.

CASE II: Angle A is obtuse.

In Figure 2, $\sin B = \dfrac{h}{a}$, or $h = a \sin B$

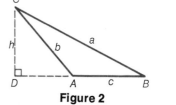

Figure 2

$\sin (180° - A) = \sin A = \dfrac{h}{b}$, or $h = b \sin A$

Now you can complete the proof.

466   Chapter 13

Example

In $\triangle ABC$, $A = 35°$, $C = 115°$, $b = 250$ units. How long are sides AB and BC?

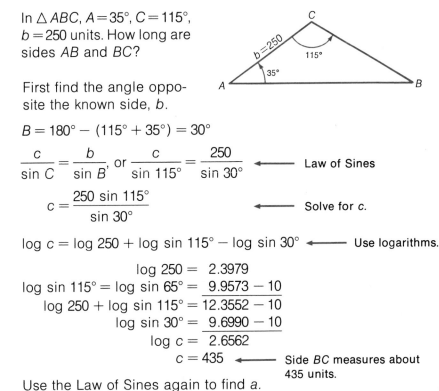

First find the angle opposite the known side, b.

$B = 180° - (115° + 35°) = 30°$

$$\frac{c}{\sin C} = \frac{b}{\sin B}, \text{ or } \frac{c}{\sin 115°} = \frac{250}{\sin 30°} \quad \longleftarrow \text{ Law of Sines}$$

$$c = \frac{250 \sin 115°}{\sin 30°} \quad \longleftarrow \text{ Solve for } c.$$

$\log c = \log 250 + \log \sin 115° - \log \sin 30° \quad \longleftarrow$ Use logarithms.

$$
\begin{array}{rl}
\log 250 = & 2.3979 \\
\log \sin 115° = \log \sin 65° = & 9.9573 - 10 \\
\log 250 + \log \sin 115° = & \overline{12.3552 - 10} \\
\log \sin 30° = & 9.6990 - 10 \\
\log c = & \overline{2.6562} \\
c = & 435 \quad \longleftarrow \text{ Side } BC \text{ measures about} \\
& \qquad\qquad\qquad 435 \text{ units.}
\end{array}
$$

Use the Law of Sines again to find a.

Exercises

Solve each triangle.

1. $c = 16.5$, $A = 38°$, $C = 54°$
$a = 12.6; B = 88°; b = 20.4$

2. $b = 224$, $A = 21° 10'$, $B = 84° 40'$
$C = 74° 10'; a = 81.2; c = 216$

3. $a = 1.50$, $B = 32° 30'$, $C = 54° 50'$
$A = 92° 40'; b = 0.807; c = 1.23$

4. $c = 916$, $A = 15° 40'$, $B = 60° 30'$
$C = 103° 50'; a = 255; b = 821$

5. $a = 75.36$, $A = 18° 25'$, $C = 32° 5'$
$B = 129° 30'; b = 184.1; c = 126.7$

6. A ship at sea is sighted at two observation posts, A and B, on shore. Points A and B are 24 kilometers apart. The measure of the angle at A between $\overline{AB}$ and the ship is 41° 40'. The angle at B is 36° 10'. Find the distance, to the nearest tenth of a kilometer, from A to the ship. 14.5 kilometers

7. To find the distance from a point A to a point B across a river, some boys established a base line $\overline{AC}$ that measured 495 meters. They found $\angle BAC$ and $\angle BCA$ to measure 89° and 55°, respectively. Find the distance AB. 690 meters

8. To find the height of a tree standing at point C across a river from point A, a base line $\overline{AB}$ 80 meters long is established on one side of the river. The measure of $\angle BAC$ was found to be 54° 20′ and that of $\angle CBA$ was 74° 10′. The angle of elevation of the top of the tree from A measures 10° 20′. What is the height of the tree? 17.9 meters

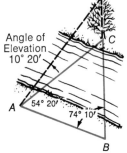

Angle of Elevation 10° 20′

A   54° 20′   74° 10′   B   C

9. If each diagonal of a regular pentagon is 57.2 feet, how long is the radius of the inscribed circle? 24.3 feet

10. From the top and bottom of a tower 28 meters high, the angles of depression of a ship are 18° 40′ and 14° 20′, respectively. What is the distance of the ship from the foot of the tower? (HINT: The distance is not measured along a horizontal segment in this case.) 351 meters

13-11 Law of Cosines

The objective for this section is on page 475.

When the measures of three sides of a triangle, or the measures of two sides and the angle included by those sides are known, the Law of Cosines can be used to solve the triangle.

Theorem 13-9: Law of Cosines
In any triangle, the square of a side is equal to the sum of the squares of the other two sides minus twice their product times the cosine of the measure of their included angle.

In $\triangle ABC$,
$$a^2 = b^2 + c^2 - 2bc \cos A$$
$$b^2 = a^2 + c^2 - 2ac \cos B$$
$$c^2 = a^2 + b^2 - 2ab \cos C$$

Proof: CASE I   Suppose △ ABC is acute and $\overline{CD} \perp \overline{AB}$.

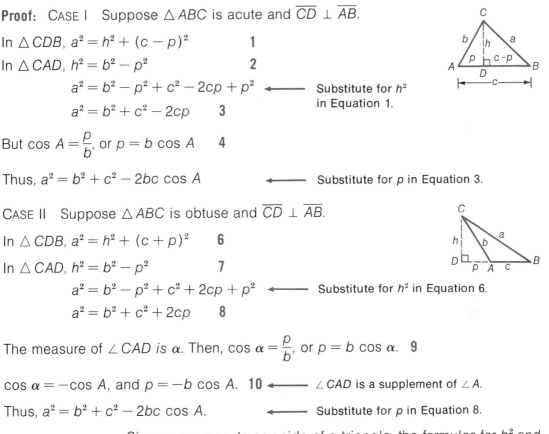

In △ CDB, $a^2 = h^2 + (c - p)^2$ **1**

In △ CAD, $h^2 = b^2 - p^2$ **2**

$a^2 = b^2 - p^2 + c^2 - 2cp + p^2$ ⟵ Substitute for h^2 in Equation 1.

$a^2 = b^2 + c^2 - 2cp$ **3**

But $\cos A = \dfrac{p}{b}$, or $p = b \cos A$ **4**

Thus, $a^2 = b^2 + c^2 - 2bc \cos A$ ⟵ Substitute for p in Equation 3.

CASE II   Suppose △ ABC is obtuse and $\overline{CD} \perp \overline{AB}$.

In △ CDB, $a^2 = h^2 + (c + p)^2$ **6**

In △ CAD, $h^2 = b^2 - p^2$ **7**

$a^2 = b^2 - p^2 + c^2 + 2cp + p^2$ ⟵ Substitute for h^2 in Equation 6.

$a^2 = b^2 + c^2 + 2cp$ **8**

The measure of ∠ CAD is α. Then, $\cos \alpha = \dfrac{p}{b}$, or $p = b \cos \alpha$.   **9**

$\cos \alpha = -\cos A$, and $p = -b \cos A$.   **10** ⟵ ∠ CAD is a supplement of ∠ A.

Thus, $a^2 = b^2 + c^2 - 2bc \cos A$. ⟵ Substitute for p in Equation 8.

Since a represents any side of a triangle, the formulas for b^2 and c^2 may be derived by interchanging the letters.

Example
     The distance at the ground between the sides of the roof on an A–frame cabin is 20 meters. If the length of each side is 12 meters, what is the measure of the angle between them?

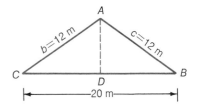

$$\cos A = \frac{b^2 + c^2 - a^2}{2bc}$$

$$= \frac{(12)^2 + (12)^2 - (20)^2}{2(12)(12)} = -0.3889$$

For $\cos A < 0$, ∠ A is either in Quadrant II or Quadrant III. From the conditions of the problem, ∠ A is in Quadrant II. Thus, ∠ A is about 112° 50′.

Exercises

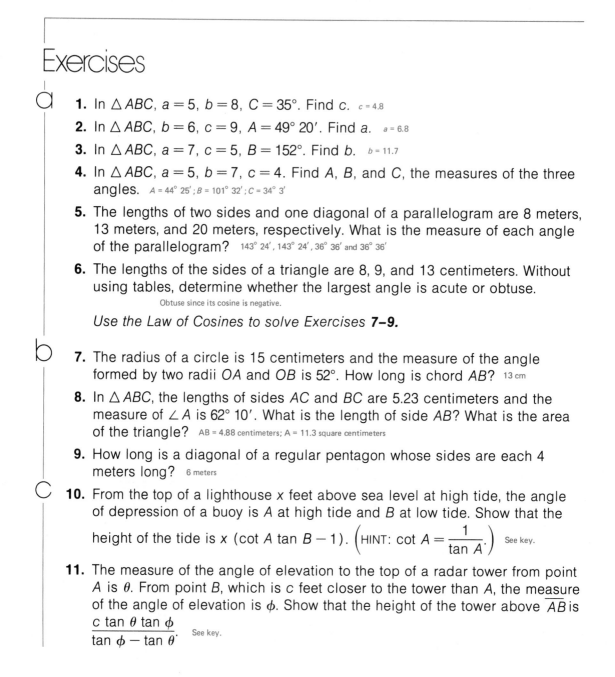

a

1. In $\triangle ABC$, $a = 5$, $b = 8$, $C = 35°$. Find c. $c = 4.8$

2. In $\triangle ABC$, $b = 6$, $c = 9$, $A = 49° \, 20'$. Find a. $a = 6.8$

3. In $\triangle ABC$, $a = 7$, $c = 5$, $B = 152°$. Find b. $b = 11.7$

4. In $\triangle ABC$, $a = 5$, $b = 7$, $c = 4$. Find A, B, and C, the measures of the three angles. $A = 44° \, 25'$; $B = 101° \, 32'$; $C = 34° \, 3'$

5. The lengths of two sides and one diagonal of a parallelogram are 8 meters, 13 meters, and 20 meters, respectively. What is the measure of each angle of the parallelogram? $143° \, 24'$, $143° \, 24'$, $36° \, 36'$ and $36° \, 36'$

6. The lengths of the sides of a triangle are 8, 9, and 13 centimeters. Without using tables, determine whether the largest angle is acute or obtuse.
Obtuse since its cosine is negative.

Use the Law of Cosines to solve Exercises 7–9.

b

7. The radius of a circle is 15 centimeters and the measure of the angle formed by two radii OA and OB is 52°. How long is chord AB? 13 cm

8. In $\triangle ABC$, the lengths of sides AC and BC are 5.23 centimeters and the measure of $\angle A$ is $62° \, 10'$. What is the length of side AB? What is the area of the triangle? AB = 4.88 centimeters; A = 11.3 square centimeters

9. How long is a diagonal of a regular pentagon whose sides are each 4 meters long? 6 meters

c

10. From the top of a lighthouse x feet above sea level at high tide, the angle of depression of a buoy is A at high tide and B at low tide. Show that the height of the tide is $x \, (\cot A \tan B - 1)$. $\left(\text{HINT: } \cot A = \dfrac{1}{\tan A}. \right)$ See key.

11. The measure of the angle of elevation to the top of a radar tower from point A is θ. From point B, which is c feet closer to the tower than A, the measure of the angle of elevation is ϕ. Show that the height of the tower above $\overline{AB}$ is $\dfrac{c \tan \theta \tan \phi}{\tan \phi - \tan \theta}$. See key.

Mathematics and
Electronics

There are various types of technicians that provide assistance to engineers. **Electronics technicians** inspect, assemble, and repair equipment; **draftsmen** prepare drawings based on the engineers specifications; **engineering aids** test equipment; and **mathematical assistants** follow outlined procedures to solve problems. Technicians require specialized training that can involve two years of college. Others receive apprenticeship training over a three or four year period. High school courses in mathematics and science are essential in both instances.

Electrical and **electronic engineers** solve problems in the areas of research, development, production, and quality control of products that range from extremely small components such as transistors and micro circuits to radio and television broadcasting equipment, computers, and microwave ovens. Although a college degree in engineering is the minimum requirement, engineers must keep up with new developments by continued formal study and the reading of technical publications.

Chapter
Objectives
and
Review

Objective: To know the meanings of the important mathematical terms of this chapter.

1. Here are many of the mathematical terms used in this chapter. Be sure that you know their meanings and that you can use them correctly.

angle of depression (p. 452)
angle of elevation (p. 452)
cosecant ratio (p. 464)
cosine ratio (p. 443)
cotangent ratio (p. 464)
initial side of an angle (p. 440)

quadrantal angle (p. 440)
reference triangle (p. 442)
secant ratio (p. 464)
sine ratio (p. 443)
tangent ratio (p. 443)
terminal side of an angle (p. 440)

Objective: To draw an angle in standard position. (Section 13-1)

Draw each angle in standard position. The quadrant for each is given.

2. 30° I

3. −120° III

4. −270° Positive y axis.

5. 405° I

Objective: To evaluate sin θ, cos θ, and tan θ, given a point on the terminal side of an angle. (Section 13-2)

Evaluate sin θ, cos θ, and tan θ. The given point is on the terminal side of the angle.

6. (0, 1) 1; 0; tan θ is undefined.

7. (−3, 2) $\frac{2\sqrt{13}}{13}, \frac{-3\sqrt{13}}{13}, -\frac{2}{3}$

8. (−2, −5) $-\frac{5\sqrt{29}}{29}, -\frac{2\sqrt{29}}{29}, \frac{5}{2}$

9. (4, −3) $-\frac{3}{5}, \frac{4}{5}, -\frac{3}{4}$

Objective: To use the ratio properties of 30-60-90 and 45-45-90 triangles to evaluate the sine, cosine, and tangent of certain angles. (Section 13-3)

Evaluate.

10. sin 30° $\frac{1}{2}$

11. cos 30° $\frac{\sqrt{3}}{2}$

12. tan 30° $\frac{\sqrt{3}}{3}$

13. sin 45° $\frac{\sqrt{2}}{2}$

14. cos 45° $\frac{\sqrt{2}}{2}$

15. tan 45° 1

16. sin 120° $\frac{\sqrt{3}}{2}$

17. tan 315° −1

Objective: To use tables and interpolation to evaluate sin θ, cos θ, and tan θ.
(Section 13-5)

Evaluate.

18. sin 115° 0.9063   **19.** tan 317° −0.9325   **20.** cos 137° −0.7314 **21.** sin 315° −0.7071

22. cos 212° 30′ −0.8434 **23.** cos 196° 10′ −0.9605 **24.** sin 63° 13′ 0.8927 **25.** tan 37° 46′ 0.7748

Find θ to the nearest minute.

26. sin θ = .4132 24° 24′   **27.** cos θ = .4261   64° 47′

28. tan θ = .4050 22° 3′   **29.** tan θ = 2.4240   67° 35′

Objective: To use the table of logarithms of trigonometric functions to compute with trigonometric functions. (Section 13-6)

Use logarithms to evaluate.

30. 3.25 cos 58° 10′ 1.71

31. $\dfrac{28.12}{\sin 27° 18′}$ 61.3

Objective: To use the trigonometric functions to solve problems.
(Sections 13-4, 13-5, 13-6)

32. To find the distance CA across the river, as shown at the right, a length CB of 50 meters was measured on one bank. The measure of $\angle B$ was found to be 34° 10′. If $\angle C$ is a right angle, how long is $\overline{CA}$?   34 meters

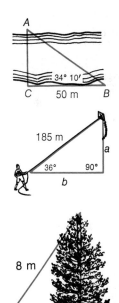

33. A kite string is 185 meters long and makes an angle of 36° with the horizontal, as shown at the right. How high is the kite above the ground? (Assume that the string is straight and that it is held 1 meter above the ground.)   110 meters

34. A 8-meter pole is leaning against a tree. What angle does it make with the tree (to the nearest 10 minutes) if the foot of the pole is 5 meters from the foot of the tree?   38° 40′

35. A canopy 10 meters long extends from the wall of a hotel. It makes an angle of 30° with the horizontal and is supported by a chain that makes an angle of 45° with the wall of the building.

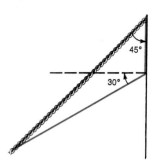

  a. How far from the wall is the end of the canopy? 8.7 meters

  b. How far above the point where the canopy is fastened to the wall is the chain fastened? 3.7 meters

  c. What is the full length of the chain? 12 meters

Objective: To evaluate sin θ, cos θ, and tan θ for angles with negative measures. (Section 13-7)

  Evaluate.

36. sin (−231°)   **37.** tan (−17°)   **38.** cos (−125°)   **39.** tan (−125°)
  −0.7771   −0.3057   0.5736   1.4281

Objective: To apply the reduction formulas. (Section 13-8)

  Express in terms of the functions of θ.

40. sin (180° − θ) = __?__ sin θ **41.** cos (180° − θ) = __?__ − cos θ

42. sin (180° + θ) = __?__ − sin θ **43.** cos (180° + θ) = __?__ − cos θ

44. sin (360° − θ) = __?__ − sin θ **45.** cos (360° − θ) = __?__ cos θ

Objective: To evaluate cot θ, sec θ, and csc θ and to find measures of angles. (Section 13-9)

  Evaluate.

46. cot 318° 16′ −1.121   **47.** sec 220° −1.305

48. csc 118° 06′ 1.134   **49.** cot 265° 0.0875

  Find θ to the nearest minute.

50. sec θ = 1.064 20° 00′   **51.** csc θ = 6.277 9° 10′

52. cot θ = 6.4350 8° 50′   **53.** cot θ = 1.6340 31° 28′

Objective: To use the Law of Sines to solve triangles. (Section 13-10)

Solve each triangle.

54. In △ABC, $A = 40°$, $C = 53°$, $c = 20$ $B = 87°; a = 16; b = 25$

55. In △ABC, $a = 9$, $B = 30° \ 10'$, $C = 54° \ 40'$ $A = 95° \ 10'; b = 4.5; c = 7.4$

Objective: To use the Law of Cosines to solve triangles. (Section 13-11)

Solve each triangle.

56. In △ABC, $a = 6$, $b = 11$, $C = 40°$. Find c. 7.5

57. In △ABC, $a = 7$, $b = 9$, $c = 6$. Find A, B, and C, the measures of the three angles. $A = 50° \ 59'; B = 87° \ 16'; C = 41° \ 45'$

Chapter
Test

8. $\frac{\sqrt{3}}{2}, -\frac{1}{2}, -\sqrt{3}, \frac{2\sqrt{3}}{3}, -2, \frac{-\sqrt{3}}{3}$

Without using tables, find the values of the six trigonometric functions for angles with the following measures.

4. $\frac{\sqrt{3}}{2}, \frac{1}{2}, \sqrt{3}, \frac{2\sqrt{3}}{3}, 2, \frac{\sqrt{3}}{3}$

0, 1, 0, undefined, 1 undefined

1. 0°

2. 30° $\frac{1}{2}, \frac{\sqrt{3}}{2}, \frac{\sqrt{3}}{3}, 2, \frac{2\sqrt{3}}{3}, \sqrt{3}$ **3.** 45° $\frac{\sqrt{2}}{2}, \frac{\sqrt{2}}{2}, 1, \sqrt{2}, \sqrt{2}, 1$ **4.** 60°

5. 135°

6. 240°

7. 330°

8. 120°

$\frac{\sqrt{2}}{2}, -\frac{\sqrt{2}}{2}, -1, \sqrt{2}, -\sqrt{2}, -1$ $-\frac{\sqrt{2}}{2}, \frac{1}{2}, \sqrt{3}, -\frac{2\sqrt{3}}{\sqrt{3}}, -2, \frac{\sqrt{3}}{3}$ $-\frac{1}{2}, \frac{\sqrt{3}}{2}, -\frac{\sqrt{3}}{3}, -2, \frac{2\sqrt{3}}{3}, -\sqrt{3}$

Use trigonometric tables to evaluate the following.

9. cos 275° .0872   **10.** tan 46° 1.0355   **11.** sin 203° −.3907   **12.** cos 195° −.9659

13. sin 163° 40′ .2812   **14.** cos(−321°) .7771   **15.** sin(−175°) −.0872   **16.** cos(−245°) .4226

17. Interpolate to find tan 72° 12′. 3.1147

18. The tread on the stairway in a school is 30 centimeters wide. Each step rises 20 centimeters above the next lower step. Find, to the nearest minute, the angle at which the staircase rises. 33° 41′

19. In Figure 1, $AC = BC = 15$ meters; $\angle A = 63°$ and $\angle B = 63°$. Find the length of $\overline{AB}$. (Use either one of the right triangles.) 13.6 meters

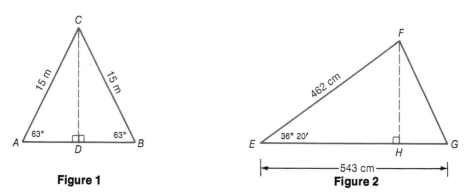

Figure 1   **Figure 2**

20. In Figure 2, $EF = 462$ centimeters, $EG = 543$ centimeters, and $E = 36° 20′$. Find the area of $\triangle EFG$. 74,300 square centimeters

Use the Law of Sines or the Law of Cosines for Exercises 21–22.

21. In triangle ABC, $AB = 81$ meters, $A = 61°$, and $C = 73°$. Find the length of $\overline{AC}$ to the nearest meter. 61 meters

22. In triangle ABC, $a = 5$, $b = 8$, and $c = 5$. Find the measure of angle C. 37°

Chapter 14
More Topics
in Trigonometry

14-1 Radian Measure

The objective for this section is on page 506.

In mathematics, it is often convenient to use a unit of angular measure called a <u>radian</u>. In the figure at the right, if the measure of arc *AB* intercepted by angle *AOB* is equal to radius *r*, then the measure of the central angle *AOB* is one radian.

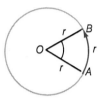

Example 1

If *r* is 3 units and the measure of $\widehat{AB}$ is 6 units, find the number of radians in the central angle *subtended* by $\widehat{AB}$. (If $\angle AOB$ intercepts $\widehat{AB}$, then $\widehat{AB}$ subtends $\angle X$.)

Since the radius of the circle is 3 units, the measure of $\angle AOB$ will be 1 radian when arc *AB* measures 3 units. Since the arc length of $\widehat{AB}$ is 6 units, the measure of $\angle AOB$ is 2 radians.

Definition: A **radian** is the measure of an angle that, with its vertex placed at the center of a circle, intercepts an arc equal in length to the radius of the circle.

Example 2

Find the number of radians in a circle with radius *r*.

You must find the number of times *r* can be laid off on the circle.

Since $C = 2\pi r$, the number of *r*'s in the circumference is 2π. Therefore, there are 2π radians in a circle, or

$$2\pi \text{ radians} = 360°.$$

Example 3

Express 1° in terms of radian measure, and express 1 radian in terms of degree measure.

$$360° = 2\pi \text{ radians} \qquad 2\pi \text{ radians} = 360°$$

$$1° = \frac{2\pi}{360} \text{ radians} \qquad 1 \text{ radian} = \frac{360°}{2\pi}$$

$$1° = \frac{\pi}{180} \text{ radians} \qquad 1 \text{ radian} = \frac{180°}{\pi}$$

Therefore, **1° is about 0.0174533 radian** and **1 radian is about 57°17′44.8″.**

When no unit of measure is indicated in giving the measure of an angle, it is understood to be a radian.

Exercises

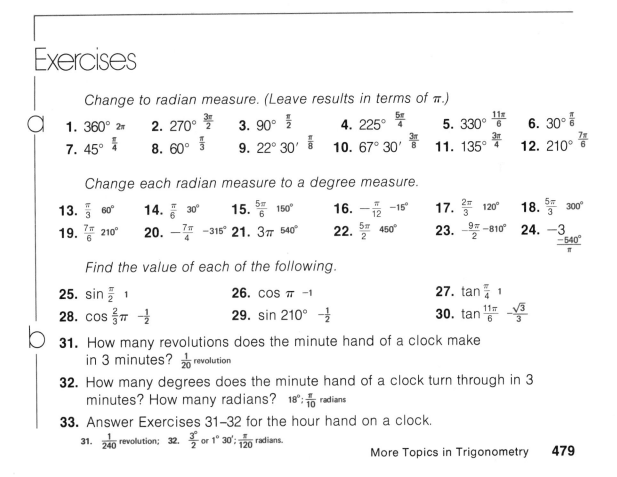

Change to radian measure. (Leave results in terms of π.)

a

1. 360° 2π **2.** 270° $\frac{3\pi}{2}$ **3.** 90° $\frac{\pi}{2}$ **4.** 225° $\frac{5\pi}{4}$ **5.** 330° $\frac{11\pi}{6}$ **6.** 30° $\frac{\pi}{6}$

7. 45° $\frac{\pi}{4}$ **8.** 60° $\frac{\pi}{3}$ **9.** 22° 30′ $\frac{\pi}{8}$ **10.** 67° 30′ $\frac{3\pi}{8}$ **11.** 135° $\frac{3\pi}{4}$ **12.** 210° $\frac{7\pi}{6}$

Change each radian measure to a degree measure.

13. $\frac{\pi}{3}$ 60°   **14.** $\frac{\pi}{6}$ 30°   **15.** $\frac{5\pi}{6}$ 150°   **16.** $-\frac{\pi}{12}$ −15°   **17.** $\frac{2\pi}{3}$ 120°   **18.** $\frac{5\pi}{3}$ 300°

19. $\frac{7\pi}{6}$ 210°   **20.** $-\frac{7\pi}{4}$ −315°   **21.** 3π 540°   **22.** $\frac{5\pi}{2}$ 450°   **23.** $-\frac{9\pi}{2}$ −810°   **24.** −3 $\frac{-540°}{\pi}$

Find the value of each of the following.

25. $\sin \frac{\pi}{2}$ 1   **26.** $\cos \pi$ −1   **27.** $\tan \frac{\pi}{4}$ 1

28. $\cos \frac{2}{3}\pi$ $-\frac{1}{2}$ **29.** $\sin 210°$ $-\frac{1}{2}$ **30.** $\tan \frac{11\pi}{6}$ $-\frac{\sqrt{3}}{3}$

b

31. How many revolutions does the minute hand of a clock make in 3 minutes? $\frac{1}{20}$ revolution

32. How many degrees does the minute hand of a clock turn through in 3 minutes? How many radians?   18°; $\frac{\pi}{10}$ radians

33. Answer Exercises 31–32 for the hour hand on a clock.

31. $\frac{1}{240}$ revolution;   **32.** $\frac{3°}{2}$ or 1° 30′; $\frac{\pi}{120}$ radians.

Given a circle of radius r, the length S of the arc intercepted by a central angle θ, expressed in radians, is found by $S = r\theta$.

Example: Find the length of the arc intercepted by a central angle of 30° in a circle with a 12-centimeter radius.

$$\theta = 30 \left(\tfrac{\pi}{180}\right) = \tfrac{\pi}{6} \text{ radians}$$
$$S = r\theta = 12\left(\tfrac{\pi}{6}\right) = 2\pi, \text{ or } S \approx 2(3.14) = 6.28 \text{ cm}$$

34. Find the length of the arc intercepted by a central angle of 120° in a wheel of radius 10 centimeters. 20.93 centimeters

35. A central angle of 45° intercepts an arc of 5.5 decimeters. Find the radius.
7.0 decimeters

14-2 Radian Measure and Trigonometric Functions

The objective for this section is on page 506.

The measure of angle AOB, 50°, can also be expressed as 0.8727 radian. Also, for every angle of measure θ, there is one and only one value for sin θ, cos θ, and tan θ. Thus, you can write the following with respect to $\angle AOB$.

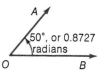

$$\sin 0.8727 = \sin 50° = 0.7660$$
$$\cos 0.8727 = \cos 50° = 0.6428 \quad \longleftarrow \quad \text{From the table}$$
$$\tan 0.8727 = \tan 50° = 1.1918$$

Example 1   Verify that tan 1.2 = tan 68° 47′ = 2.5759.

$$1 \text{ radian} = \frac{180°}{\pi}; \; 1.2 \text{ radians} = (1.2)\frac{180°}{\pi} = \frac{216°}{\pi}$$

$$\frac{216°}{\pi} = 68.79°, \text{ or } 68° 47′ \quad \longleftarrow \quad \text{Use } \pi = 3.14.$$

$$\tan 68° 47′ = 2.5759 \quad \longleftarrow \quad \text{From the table}$$

Tan 1.2 can also be found in the tables on pages 543–547. The second column of these tables gives the radian measure equivalent of degree measures between 0° and 90° inclusive. That is, the tables give radian measures between 0 and 1.5708 inclusive.

Example 2 Evaluate: $\cos \dfrac{3\pi}{2}$

$\cos \dfrac{3\pi}{2}$ means $\cos \left(\dfrac{3\pi}{2}\ \text{radians}\right)$ and $\dfrac{3\pi}{2}$ radians $= 270°$.

$\cos \dfrac{3\pi}{2} = \cos 270° = 0$

Exercises

Without using the table, find the value of each trigonometric function.

1. $\sin \frac{\pi}{6}$ $\frac{1}{2}=0.5000$
2. $\cos \frac{\pi}{3}$ $\frac{1}{2}=0.5000$
3. $\tan \frac{\pi}{4}$ 1
4. $\cos \pi$ −1

5. $\sin \frac{\pi}{2}$ 1
6. $\cot \frac{3}{4}\pi$ −1
7. $\csc \frac{7}{6}\pi$ −2
8. $\sec \frac{2}{3}\pi$ −2

9. $\tan (-\pi)$ 0
10. $\sin \left(-\frac{\pi}{3}\right)$ $-\frac{\sqrt{3}}{2} \approx -0.8660$
11. $\csc \frac{8}{3}\pi$ $\frac{2\sqrt{3}}{3} \approx 1.1547$
12. $\sec \left(-\frac{11}{6}\pi\right)$ $\frac{2\sqrt{3}}{3} \approx 1.1547$

Use tables to find the six trigonometric functions of the given angle θ.

See key for Exercises 13-18.

13. 0.7156 radians
14. 1.3963 radians

15. 1.4923 radians
16. 0.3054 radians

17. 0.8116 radians
18. 0.1949 radians

Find all radian measures ($0 \le \theta \le 2\pi$) that make each equation true.

19. $\sin \theta = 0$ $0, \pi, 2\pi$
20. $\cos \theta = \frac{1}{2}$ $\frac{\pi}{3}$ or $\frac{5\pi}{3}$

21. $\cos \theta = -\frac{\sqrt{2}}{2}$ $\frac{3\pi}{4}$ or $\frac{5\pi}{4}$
22. $\sin \theta = \frac{\sqrt{3}}{2}$ $\frac{\pi}{3}$ or $\frac{2\pi}{3}$

23. $\tan \theta = -1$ $\frac{3\pi}{4}$ or $\frac{7\pi}{4}$
24. $\cot \theta = -\sqrt{3}$ $\frac{5\pi}{6}$ or $\frac{11\pi}{6}$

25. $\sec \theta = 2$ $\frac{\pi}{3}$ or $\frac{5\pi}{3}$
26. $\csc \theta = \frac{2}{3}\sqrt{3}$ $\frac{\pi}{3}$ or $\frac{2\pi}{3}$

27. Find the value of $\dfrac{2 \sin \frac{\pi}{6} + \cot \frac{\pi}{4}}{\tan \frac{\pi}{4} - 3 \cos \frac{\pi}{3}}$ −4

28. Show that $\sin \frac{\pi}{2} = 2 \sin \frac{\pi}{4} \cos \frac{\pi}{4}$ Each side equals 1.

More Topics in Trigonometry   481

The objective for this section is on page 506.

Example 1 Sketch the graph of $y = \sin x$, where $0 \le x \le 2\pi$.

x	y = sin x	x	y = sin x
0	0	$\frac{7\pi}{6}$	−.5000
$\frac{\pi}{6}$	.5000	$\frac{5\pi}{4}$	−.7071
$\frac{\pi}{4}$	.7071	4	−.7568
1	.8415	$\frac{4\pi}{3}$	−.8660
$\frac{\pi}{3}$	.8660	$\frac{3\pi}{2}$	−1
$\frac{\pi}{2}$	1	5	−.9589
2	.9093	$\frac{5\pi}{3}$	−.8660
$\frac{2\pi}{3}$	.8660	$\frac{7\pi}{4}$	−.7071
$\frac{3\pi}{4}$	.7071	$\frac{11\pi}{6}$	−.5000
$\frac{5\pi}{6}$	.5000	6	−.2794
3	.1411	2π	0
π	0		

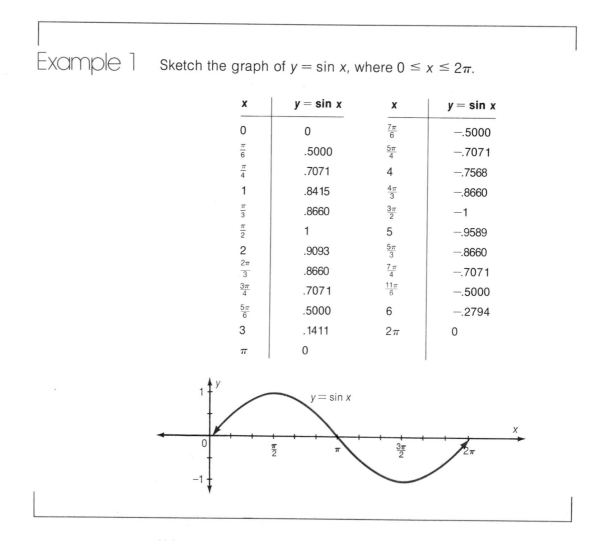

Although the domain of x in Example 1 is $0 \le x \le 2\pi$, the graph can be extended for $x < 0$ and $x > 2\pi$. Thus, the domain of $y = \sin x$ is the set of real numbers. However, the range is $\{y: -1 \le y \le 1\}$.

Example 2 Sketch the graph of $y = \cos x$, where $0 \le x \le 2\pi$.

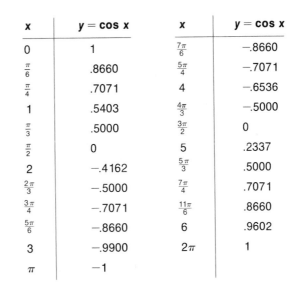

x	y = cos x	x	y = cos x
0	1	$\frac{7\pi}{6}$	−.8660
$\frac{\pi}{6}$	.8660	$\frac{5\pi}{4}$	−.7071
$\frac{\pi}{4}$	.7071	4	−.6536
1	.5403	$\frac{4\pi}{3}$	−.5000
$\frac{\pi}{3}$	.5000	$\frac{3\pi}{2}$	0
$\frac{\pi}{2}$	0	5	.2337
2	−.4162	$\frac{5\pi}{3}$	.5000
$\frac{2\pi}{3}$	−.5000	$\frac{7\pi}{4}$	.7071
$\frac{3\pi}{4}$	−.7071	$\frac{11\pi}{6}$	.8660
$\frac{5\pi}{6}$	−.8660	6	.9602
3	−.9900	2π	1
π	−1		

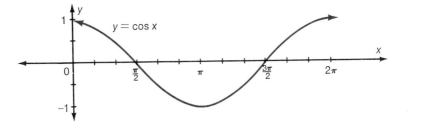

As with $y = \sin x$, the graph can be extended for $x < 0$ and $x > 2\pi$. Thus, the domain of $y = \cos x$ is the set of real numbers. However, the range is $\{y: -1 \le y \le 1\}$.

Example 3 Sketch the graph of $y = 2 \sin x$, where $0 \le x \le 2\pi$.

For each x between 0 and 2π, the corresponding value of y is twice the value of y in $y = \sin x$. All you need to do, then, is multiply each y value in the table of Example 1 by 2, and plot the resulting pairs.

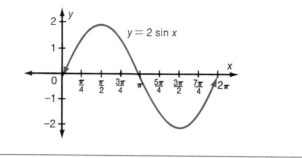

To graph $y = A \sin x$ or $y = A \cos x$, the y values are A times those in $y = \sin x$ or $y = \cos x$. The number $|A|$ is the **amplitude**.

Knowing the amplitude and the general shape of the sine and cosine curves, you can sketch the graph readily.

Example 4

Sketch the graph of $y = 2 \cos x$ for $-2\pi \le x \le 2\pi$.

Amplitude: 2   General shape: $y = \cos x$

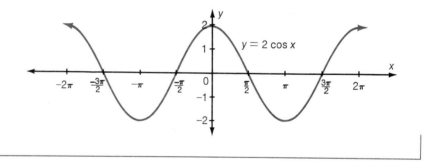

In Example 4, the graph of $y = 2 \cos x$ in the interval $-2\pi \le x \le 0$ is the same as the graph in the interval $0 \le x \le 2\pi$. After each interval of 2π, the graphs of the sine and cosine functions repeat. The distance you need to travel along the x axis before the graph repeats itself for the first time is the period of the function. Thus, 2π is the period of the sine and cosine functions. A function that repeats in this way is called a **periodic function**.

Definition: The smallest positive number p for which $f(p + x) = f(x)$ is always true is the **period** of the function f.

Write the amplitude and period of each function.

1. $y = 3 \sin x$ 3, 2π

2. $y = \frac{1}{2} \cos x$ ½, 2π

3. $y = 7 \cos x$ 7, 2π

4. $y = \frac{1}{8} \sin x$ ⅛, 2π

5. $y = -2 \sin x$ 2, 2π

6. $y = \frac{1}{4} \cos x$ ¼, 2π

7. $y = -1000 \sin x$ 1000, 2π

8. $y = -\cos x$ 1, 2π

9. $y = \pi \sin x$ π, 2π

Exercises

1. General shape of graph is that of $y = \cos x$; amplitude is 4 and period is 2π.

2. General shape of graph is that of $y = \sin x$; amplitude is $\frac{1}{2}$ and period is 2π.

3. General shape of graph is that of $y = \cos x$; however, the amplitude is 6; the period is 2π.

4. General shape of graph is that of $y = \cos x$; amplitude is $\frac{1}{3}$; period is 2π.

5. General shape of graph is that of $y = \sin x$; amplitude is $\frac{2}{3}$; period is 2π.

For each function in Exercises 1-6 make a table of the pairs of real numbers (x, y), where $0 \le x \le 2\pi$. Plot these points on a rectangular coordinate system, and connect the points with a smooth curve.

a

1. $y = 4 \cos x$ See above.

2. $y = \frac{1}{2} \sin x$ See above.

3. $y = 6 \cos x$ See above.

4. $y = \frac{1}{3} \cos x$ See above.

5. $y = \frac{2}{3} \sin x$ See above.

6. $y = 3 \sin x$ See below.

6. General shape is that of $y = \sin x$. The amplitude is 3; the period is 2π.

Sketch the graphs on the same coordinate system for $0 \le x \le 2\pi$.

7. This graph has the general shape of $y = -\cos x$; amplitude is 4; period is 2π.

7. $y = -4 \cos x$ See above

8. $y = -2 \cos x$ See below

9. $y = -\frac{1}{2} \cos x$ See below

8. General shape of graph is that of $y = -\cos x$; amplitude is 2; period is 2π.

9. General shape of graph is that of $y = -\cos x$; amplitude is $\frac{1}{2}$; period is 2π.

Sketch the graphs on the same coordinate system for $0 \le x \le 2\pi$.

10. This has the general shape of $y = \sin x$; amplitude is 2; period is 2π.

10. $y = 2 \sin x$ See above

11. $y = -2 \sin x$ See below

11. This has the general shape of $y = -\sin x$; amplitude is 2; period is 2π.

12. Make a table of values and draw the graph of $y = \sin 2x$. Note that $y = \sin 2x$ is not the same as $y = 2 \sin x$.   See key.

13. How does the amplitude of $y = \sin 2x$ compare with that of $y = \sin x$?

The amplitude of both $y = \sin 2x$ and $y = \sin x$ equals 1.

14. How does the period of $y = \sin 2x$ compare with that of $y = \sin x$?

The period of $y = \sin 2x$ is π; the period of $y = \sin x$ is 2π.

15. Make a table of values and draw the graph of $y = \cos 2x$.   See key.

16. How does the amplitude of $y = \cos 2x$ compare with that of $y = \cos x$?

The amplitude of both $y = \cos 2x$ and $y = \cos x$ equals 1.

17. How do the periods of $y = \cos 2x$ and $y = \cos x$ compare?

The period of $y = \cos 2x$ is π; the period of $y = \cos x$ is 2π.

The period of $y = \sin (bx)$ or $y = \cos (bx)$ is $\left|\frac{1}{b}\right|$ times the period of $y = \sin x$ or $y = \cos x$. Find the period of each of the following.

b

18. $y = \cos 3x$ $\frac{2\pi}{3}$

19. $y = \sin 5x$ $\frac{2\pi}{5}$

20. $y = \sin \frac{1}{2} x$ 4π

21. $y = \cos \frac{1}{4} x$ 8π

22. $y = \cos (-2x)$ π

23. $y = \sin \left(-\frac{1}{3} x\right)$ 6π

The Graph of the Tangent Function

The objective for this section is on page 506.

You can proceed as before to graph $y = \tan x$.

Example   Graph $y = \tan x$, where $0 \leq x \leq 2\pi$.

x	y
0	0
$\frac{\pi}{6}$	.5774
$\frac{\pi}{4}$	1.000
1	1.557
$\frac{\pi}{3}$	1.732
$\frac{\pi}{2}$	undefined
2	−2.185
$\frac{2\pi}{3}$	−1.732
$\frac{5\pi}{6}$	−.5774
3	−.1425
π	0

x	y
$\frac{7\pi}{6}$	.5774
$\frac{5\pi}{4}$	1.000
4	1.158
$\frac{4\pi}{3}$	1.732
$\frac{3\pi}{2}$	undefined
5	−3.381
$\frac{5\pi}{3}$	−1.732
$\frac{7\pi}{4}$	−1.000
6	−.2910
2π	0

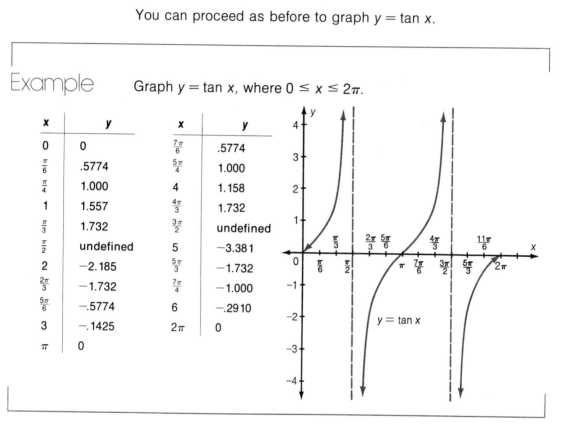

Recall that for angles in standard position, $\tan \theta = \frac{y}{x}$. Thus the tangent function is <u>not</u> defined when $x = 0$. Since $x = 0$ when $\theta = \frac{\pi}{2}$ and $\frac{3\pi}{2}$, $\tan \theta$ is undefined there. To show this, dashed lines are drawn on the graph of $y = \tan x$ at $x = \frac{\pi}{2}$ and $x = \frac{3\pi}{2}$. These lines are asymptotes for the graph of $y = \tan x$.

The domain of the tangent function is the set of real numbers except for the numbers $\frac{\pi}{2}, \frac{3\pi}{2}, \frac{5\pi}{2}$, etc. Its range is the set of real numbers. The period for $y = \tan x$ is π, because it repeats at intervals of π units.

486   Chapter 14

The tangent function, unlike the sine and cosine functions, has "breaks" in its graph at multiples of $x = \frac{\pi}{2}$. Thus, the function is not a continuous function. A continuous function is a curve with no "breaks" or jumps in it. The sine and cosine functions are continuous.

Try These

1. For what values of x, where $-\frac{\pi}{2} \le x \le \frac{5}{2}\pi$, is $y = \tan x$ undefined? $-\frac{\pi}{2}, \frac{\pi}{2}, \frac{3\pi}{2}, \frac{5\pi}{2}$

2. What are the equations of the asymptotes for $y = \tan x$, where $-\frac{\pi}{2} \le x \le \frac{5}{2}\pi$?
   $x = -\frac{\pi}{2}, x = \frac{\pi}{2}, x = \frac{3\pi}{2}, x = \frac{5\pi}{2}$

3. Describe the domain, range, and period of the tangent function. Domain: the set of real numbers, except for $\frac{\pi}{2}, \frac{3\pi}{2}, \frac{5\pi}{2}$, etc.; Range: the set of real numbers; period: π radians.

Exercises

2. The general shape is the same as the graph in Exercise 1, but each ordinate is one-half times the corresponding ordinate.

3. The general shape is the same as the graph in Exercise 1, but each ordinate is two times the corresponding ordinate.

Sketch the graph of each function over the interval $-\frac{\pi}{2} \le x \le \frac{5}{2}\pi$.

a

1. $y = \tan x$ See key.

2. $y = \frac{1}{2} \tan x$ See above.

3. $y = 2 \tan x$ See above.

b

4. Make a table of values for $y = \tan\left(\frac{1}{4}x\right)$ and graph the function. See key.

5. What is the period of $y = \tan\left(\frac{1}{4}x\right)$? 4π

6. How does the period of $y = \tan\left(\frac{1}{4}x\right)$ compare with the period of $y = \tan x$? The period of $y = \tan\left(\frac{1}{4}x\right)$ is 4π and the period of $y = \tan x$ is π.

7. Write a general rule for the period of $y = \tan(bx)$. Period of $y = \tan(bx)$ is $\frac{\pi}{|b|}$

Find the period of each function and sketch the graph over the interval indicated.

8. $y = \tan 3x$; $x = -\pi$ to $x = \pi$ See key.

9. $y = \tan \frac{1}{3}x$; $x = -2\pi$ to $x = 2\pi$ See key.

10. $y = \frac{1}{2} \tan 3x$; $x = -\frac{\pi}{2}$ to $x = \frac{\pi}{2}$ See key.

11. $y = 2 \tan \frac{1}{3}x$; $x = -\frac{3}{2}\pi$ to $x = \frac{3}{2}\pi$ See key.

12. Use the relationship $\cot x = \dfrac{1}{\tan x}$ to determine the period of $y = \cot x$. π

More Topics in Trigonometry **487**

The objective for this section is on page 506.

Recall that a conditional equation may be true for no, one, or several replacements of the variable and that an identity is true for all replacements of the variable for which the statement is defined. The symbol ≡ (read "is identical to") is sometimes used to distinguish an identity from a conditional equation. However, we shall use = for both the identity and the conditional equation.

Theorem 14-1: Reciprocal Identities

$$1. \ \csc \theta = \frac{1}{\sin \theta}, \ \sin \theta \neq 0$$

$$2. \ \sec \theta = \frac{1}{\cos \theta}, \ \cos \theta \neq 0$$

$$3. \ \cot \theta = \frac{1}{\tan \theta}, \ \tan \theta \neq 0$$

Proof: Only the proof of 1 is given.

$$\csc \theta = \frac{r}{y} \longleftarrow \text{By definition}$$

$$= \frac{1}{\frac{y}{r}} = \frac{1}{\sin \theta}$$

Two additional identities are the ratio identities.

Theorem 14-2: Ratio Identities

$$4. \ \tan \theta = \frac{\sin \theta}{\cos \theta}, \ \cos \theta \neq 0$$

$$5. \ \cot \theta = \frac{\cos \theta}{\sin \theta}, \ \sin \theta \neq 0$$

Proof: 4. $\tan \theta = \dfrac{y}{x} = \dfrac{\frac{y}{r}}{\frac{x}{r}} = \dfrac{\sin \theta}{\cos \theta}$.

5. $\cot \theta = \dfrac{1}{\tan \theta} = \dfrac{1}{\frac{\sin \theta}{\cos \theta}} = \dfrac{\cos \theta}{\sin \theta}$.

Three identities are called <u>Pythagorean identities.</u>

Theorem 14-3: Pythagorean Identities
For all replacements of θ for which the functions are defined,

$$6.\ \sin^2 \theta + \cos^2 \theta = 1.$$
$$7.\ 1 + \cot^2 \theta = \csc^2 \theta.$$
$$8.\ \tan^2 \theta + 1 = \sec^2 \theta.$$

The symbol "$\sin^2 \theta$" means $(\sin \theta)^2$. For example, if $\sin \theta = \frac{1}{2}$, then $\sin^2 \theta = (\frac{1}{2})^2$, or $\frac{1}{4}$.

The Pythagorean Identities are proved as follows.

Proof: **6.** $y^2 + x^2 = r^2$ ◄——— True for any point $P(x, y)$ on radius vector.

$\dfrac{y^2}{r^2} + \dfrac{x^2}{r^2} = \dfrac{r^2}{r^2}$ ◄——— Divide by r^2, $r^2 \neq 0$.

$\left(\dfrac{y}{r}\right)^2 + \left(\dfrac{x}{r}\right)^2 = 1$

$\sin^2 \theta + \cos^2 \theta = 1$ ◄——— Since $\sin \theta = \dfrac{y}{r}$ and $\cos \theta = \dfrac{x}{r}$.

Identities **7** and **8** may be proven similarly or by using **6, 5** and **1**.

Proof: **7.** $\sin^2 \theta + \cos^2 \theta = 1$ ◄——— Identity **6.**

$\dfrac{\sin^2 \theta}{\sin^2 \theta} + \dfrac{\cos^2 \theta}{\sin^2 \theta} = \dfrac{1}{\sin^2 \theta}$ ◄——— Multiply by $\dfrac{1}{\sin^2 \theta}$, $\sin^2 \theta \neq 0$.

$1 + \cot^2 \theta = \csc^2 \theta$ ◄——— By **5** and **1.**

Try These *Write an equivalent expression for each of the following.*

1. $\csc \theta$ $\frac{1}{\sin \theta}$

2. $\sec \theta$ $\frac{1}{\cos \theta}$

3. $\cot \theta$ $\frac{1}{\tan \theta}$

4. $\dfrac{1}{\cos \theta}$ sec θ

5. $\dfrac{\cos \theta}{\sin \theta}$ cot θ

6. $\dfrac{\sin \theta}{\cos \theta}$ tan θ

7. $1 - \sin^2 \theta$ cos² θ

8. $1 + \tan^2 \theta$ sec² θ

9. $1 + \cot^2 \theta$ csc² θ

10. $1 - \cos^2 \theta$ sin² θ

11. $\sec^2 \theta - 1$ tan² θ

12. $\csc^2 \theta - 1$ cot² θ

Exercises

Write an equivalent expression for each of the following. Simplify as much as possible.

1. cot x · sin x cos x

2. tan x · cot x 1

3. $\dfrac{\sin^2 x}{\cos^2 x}$ tan²x

4. $\dfrac{\sin^2 x - 1}{\cos^2 x}$ −1

5. $\sin^4 x - \sin^2 x$ −sin²x cos²x

6. csc θ · cos θ cot θ

7. cos θ tan θ sin θ

8. $\dfrac{\tan \theta}{\sec \theta}$ sin θ

9. $\dfrac{\cos \theta}{\cot \theta}$ sin θ

10. $\dfrac{\cos^2 \theta}{1 - \sin^2 \theta}$ 1

11. $\dfrac{1 + \tan^2 x}{1 + \cot^2 x}$ cot² θ

12. csc x − cos x cot x sin x

Express in terms of sin θ, cos θ, or both. Simplify.

13. $\dfrac{\cot \theta}{\csc \theta}$ cos θ

14. cot θ + tan θ $\frac{1}{\sin \theta \cos \theta}$

15. sec θ − tan θ $\frac{1 - \sin \theta}{\cos \theta}$

16. $\dfrac{\sec^2 \theta}{\tan \theta \csc \theta}$ $\frac{1}{\cos \theta}$

17. $\dfrac{1 + \tan \theta}{\sec \theta}$ cos θ + sin θ

18. $\dfrac{\sec \theta}{\cot \theta + \tan \theta}$ sin θ

Use the definitions of the trigonometric functions to prove that each statement is true for all values of θ for which the statement is defined. For each statement, indicate the replacement set for which it is an identity.

See key for Exercises 19-27.

19. $\csc \theta = \dfrac{1}{\sin \theta}$

20. cos θ · sec θ = 1

21. tan θ · cot θ = 1

22. $\tan \theta = \dfrac{\sin \theta}{\cos \theta}$

23. $\cot \theta = \dfrac{\cos \theta}{\sin \theta}$

24. $\tan \theta = \dfrac{\sec \theta}{\csc \theta}$

25. cot θ = cos θ · csc θ

26. $\cos^2 \theta = 1 - \sin^2 \theta$

27. $\tan^2 \theta + 1 = \sec^2 \theta$

Sum and Difference Identities

The objective for this section is on page 507.

The <u>sum and difference identities</u> are very useful.

Theorem 14-4: For any α and β,

$$\sin (\alpha + \beta) = \sin \alpha \cos \beta + \cos \alpha \sin \beta.$$

Before proving this identity, check to see that it makes sense.
Let $\alpha = \dfrac{\pi}{6}$ and $\beta = \dfrac{\pi}{3}$.

$$\sin \left(\frac{\pi}{6} + \frac{\pi}{3}\right) = \sin \frac{\pi}{6} \cos \frac{\pi}{3} + \cos \frac{\pi}{6} \sin \frac{\pi}{3}$$

$$\sin \frac{\pi}{2} = \frac{1}{2} \cdot \frac{1}{2} + \frac{\sqrt{3}}{2} \cdot \frac{\sqrt{3}}{2}$$

$$1 = \frac{1}{4} + \frac{3}{4}$$

Proof: Assume the angles with measures α, β, and $(\alpha + \beta)$ are positive acute angles as shown.
From A, draw $\overline{AD} \perp \overline{OD}$, and $\overline{AB} \perp \overline{OC}$. Draw $\overline{DC} \perp \overline{OC}$ and $\overline{DE} \perp \overline{AB}$.
Notice that $\angle BOD$ and $\angle BAD$ have their sides perpendicular in pairs. Thus,

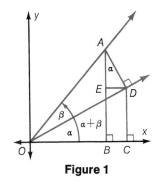

Figure 1

$$\angle BAD \cong \angle BOD \text{ and } m\angle BAD = \alpha.$$

$$\sin (\alpha + \beta) = \frac{AB}{OA} = \frac{EB + EA}{OA} = \frac{DC + EA}{OA} = \frac{DC}{OA} + \frac{EA}{OA} \quad \textbf{1.}$$

In $\triangle OCD$, $\quad \sin \alpha = \dfrac{DC}{OD}$, or $OD \cdot \sin \alpha = DC \quad \textbf{2.}$

In $\triangle AED$, $\quad \cos \alpha = \dfrac{AE}{AD}$, or $AD \cdot \cos \alpha = AE \quad \textbf{3.}$

Substitute Equations **2** and **3** in Equation **1**.

$$\sin (\alpha + \beta) = \frac{OD \sin \alpha}{OA} + \frac{AD \cos \alpha}{OA}$$

$$= \sin \alpha \cos \beta + \cos \alpha \sin \beta$$

You can also use Figure 1 to demonstrate Theorem 14-5.

Theorem 14-5: For any α and β,

$$\cos (\alpha + \beta) = \cos \alpha \cos \beta - \sin \alpha \sin \beta$$

Proof:

$$\cos (\alpha + \beta) = \frac{OB}{OA} = \frac{OC - BC}{OA} = \frac{OC}{OA} - \frac{BC}{OA}$$

In $\triangle OCD$,

$$\cos \alpha = \frac{OC}{OD}; \text{ or } OD \cos \alpha = OC$$

In $\triangle AED$,

$$\sin \alpha = \frac{ED}{AD} = \frac{BC}{AD}; \text{ or } AD \sin \alpha = BC$$

$$\cos (\alpha + \beta) = \frac{OD}{OA} \cos \alpha - \frac{AD}{OA} \sin \alpha$$

$$= \cos \alpha \cos \beta - \sin \alpha \sin \beta$$

Theorem 14-6: For any α and β,

    a. $\sin (\alpha - \beta) = \sin \alpha \cos \beta - \cos \alpha \sin \beta$
    b. $\cos (\alpha - \beta) = \cos \alpha \cos \beta + \sin \alpha \sin \beta$

Only the proof of **a** is given.

Proof: $\sin (\alpha - \beta) = \sin (\alpha + [-\beta])$

$= \sin \alpha \cos (-\beta) + \cos \alpha \sin (-\beta)$ ⟵ By Theorem 14-4

$= \sin \alpha \cos \beta - \cos \alpha \sin \beta$ ⟵ $\cos (-\beta) = \cos \beta$
                                             $\sin (-\beta) = -\sin \beta$

The sine and cosine of 30°, 45°, 60°, 90°, 180°, and 270° can be used to evaluate certain other angles.

Example 1   Evaluate cos 210° by using Theorem 14-5.

$$\cos 210° = \cos (180° + 30°)$$
$$= \cos 180° \cos 30° - \sin 180° \sin 30°$$
$$= -1 \cdot \frac{\sqrt{3}}{2} - 0 \cdot \frac{1}{2}, \text{ or } -\frac{\sqrt{3}}{2}$$

Example 2   Evaluate sin 15° by using Theorem 14-6.

$$\sin 15° = \sin (45° - 30°)$$
$$= \sin 45° \cos 30° - \cos 45° \sin 30°$$
$$= \frac{\sqrt{2}}{2} \cdot \frac{\sqrt{3}}{2} - \frac{\sqrt{2}}{2} \cdot \frac{1}{2}$$
$$= \frac{\sqrt{2}}{4} (\sqrt{3} - 1)$$

Try These   *Write each angle measure as the sum or difference of the measures of angles whose sines and cosines are known.* Answers will vary.

1. 105°   **2.** 75°   **3.** 15°   **4.** 60°   **5.** 135°   **6.** 120°
60° + 45°   45° + 30°   60° − 45°   90° − 30°   90° + 45°   180° − 60°

Exercises

Use the tables to evaluate sin $(\alpha + \beta)$ and cos $(\alpha + \beta)$.

a   **1.** $\alpha = 63°$, $\beta = 50°$ **2.** $\alpha = 30°$, $\beta = 30°$ **3.** $\alpha = 90°$, $\beta = 20°$
0.9205; −0.3907   0.8660; 0.5000   0.9397; −0.3420

Use the tables to evaluate sin $(\alpha - \beta)$ and cos $(\alpha - \beta)$.

4. $\alpha = 60°$, $\beta = 45°$ **5.** $\alpha = 45°$, $\beta = 30°$ **6.** $\alpha = 73°$, $\beta = 43°$
0.2588; 0.9659   0.2588; 0.9659   0.5000; 0.8660

Use the addition and difference formulas to evaluate the sine and cosine of each measure.

7. 120° $\frac{\sqrt{3}}{2}; -\frac{1}{2}$ **8.** 135° $\frac{\sqrt{2}}{2}; -\frac{\sqrt{2}}{2}$ **9.** 150° $\frac{1}{2}; -\frac{\sqrt{3}}{2}$ **10.** 225° $-\frac{\sqrt{2}}{2}; -\frac{\sqrt{2}}{2}$ **11.** 330° $-\frac{1}{2}; \frac{\sqrt{3}}{2}$ **12.** 240° $-\frac{\sqrt{3}}{2}; -\frac{1}{2}$

13. Find the sine and cosine of $45° + \theta$ in terms of θ. See key.

14. Find the sine and cosine of $45° - \theta$ in terms of θ. See key.

15. Find the sine and cosine of $270° + \theta$ in terms of θ. See key.

16. Find the sine and cosine of $270° - \theta$ in terms of θ. See key.

Use $\sin (\alpha + \alpha) = \sin (2\alpha) = 2 \sin \alpha \cos \alpha$ to find $\sin (2\alpha)$ for each α.

17. $\alpha = 45°$ 1   **18.** $\alpha = 30°$ $\frac{\sqrt{3}}{2}$ **19.** $\alpha = 60°$ $\frac{\sqrt{3}}{2}$ **20.** $\alpha = 120°$

21. Derive a formula for $\cos (2\alpha)$ and use the formula to find $\cos (2\alpha)$ for the $\frac{-\sqrt{3}}{2}$ values of α given in Exercises **17-20.**

$\cos (2\alpha) = \cos (\alpha + \alpha) = \cos \alpha \cos \alpha - \sin \alpha \sin \alpha = \cos^2 \alpha - \sin^2 \alpha$

17. 0; 18. $\frac{1}{2}$; 19. $-\frac{1}{2}$; 20. $-\frac{1}{2}$

14-7 Proving Trigonometric Identities

The objective for this section is on page 506.

The general procedure for proving trigonometric identities is to rewrite the expression on the right side or the expression on the left side of the = sign.

Example 1   Prove: $\cos \theta = \sin \theta \cot \theta$

$\cos \theta = \sin \theta \cot \theta$

$= \sin \theta \cdot \dfrac{\cos \theta}{\sin \theta}$ ⟵ Using $\cot \theta = \dfrac{\cos \theta}{\sin \theta}$

$= \dfrac{\sin \theta \cdot \cos \theta}{\sin \theta}$

$= \dfrac{\sin \theta}{\sin \theta} \cdot \cos \theta$

$= 1 \cdot \cos \theta$

$\cos \theta = \cos \theta$

Example 2 Prove: $(\cos\theta - \sec\theta)^2 = \tan^2\theta - \sin^2\theta$

$$(\cos\theta - \sec\theta)^2 = \tan^2\theta - \sin^2\theta$$

$$\cos^2\theta - 2\cos\theta\sec\theta + \sec^2\theta = \quad \longleftarrow \quad \text{Square the left side.}$$

$$\cos^2\theta - 2\cos\theta\left(\frac{1}{\cos\theta}\right) + \sec^2\theta = \quad \longleftarrow \quad \text{Reciprocal identity}$$

$$\cos^2\theta - 2 + \sec^2\theta =$$

$$\cos^2\theta - 1 - 1 + \sec^2\theta =$$

$$(\cos^2\theta - 1) + (-1 + \sec^2\theta) =$$

$$-\sin^2\theta + \tan^2\theta = \quad \longleftarrow \quad \text{Pythagorean identity}$$

$$\tan^2\theta - \sin^2\theta = \tan^2\theta - \sin^2\theta$$

The two methods used in Example 3 show that you can rewrite either the expression on the left side or the expression on the right side.

Example 3 Prove: $1 - 2\sin^2\theta = 2\cos^2\theta - 1$

Method I

$$1 - 2\sin^2\theta = 2\cos^2\theta - 1$$
$$1 - 2(1 - \cos^2\theta) =$$
$$1 - 2 + 2\cos^2\theta =$$
$$2\cos^2\theta - 1 = 2\cos^2\theta - 1$$

Method II

$$1 - 2\sin^2\theta = 2\cos^2\theta - 1$$
$$= 2(1 - \sin^2\theta) - 1$$
$$= 2 - 2\sin^2\theta - 1$$
$$1 - 2\sin^2\theta = 1 - 2\sin^2\theta$$

A third method, shown below, illustrates that you can rewrite both sides of an identity. This method, however, is not recommended.

$$1 - 2\sin^2\theta = 2\cos^2\theta - 1$$
$$(1 - \sin^2\theta) - \sin^2\theta = \cos^2\theta + (\cos^2\theta - 1)$$
$$\cos^2\theta - \sin^2\theta = \cos^2\theta - \sin^2\theta$$

Example 4   **Prove:** $\sin^4 \theta - \cos^4 \theta = \sin^2 \theta - \cos^2 \theta$

$$\sin^4 \theta - \cos^4 \theta = \sin^2 \theta - \cos^2 \theta$$
$$(\sin^2 \theta - \cos^2 \theta)(\sin^2 \theta + \cos^2 \theta) =$$
$$(\sin^2 \theta - \cos^2 \theta) \cdot 1 =$$
$$\sin^2 \theta - \cos^2 \theta = \sin^2 \theta - \cos^2 \theta$$

Exercises

*In Exercises **1-6,** prove that the first expression is equal to the second for all values of θ for which the first expression is defined.* See key for Ex. 1-25.

1. $(1 - \tan \theta)^2$, $\sec^2 \theta - 2 \tan \theta$

2. $(1 - \sin^2 \theta)(1 + \tan^2 \theta)$, 1

3. $\dfrac{\cos^2 \theta}{\sin \theta} + \sin \theta$, $\csc \theta$

4. $\tan \theta + \cot \theta$, $\sec \theta \csc \theta$

5. $\dfrac{\tan \theta}{1 - \cos^2 \theta}$, $\dfrac{\sec \theta}{\sin \theta}$

6. $\dfrac{\cot \theta}{\cos \theta} + \dfrac{\sec \theta}{\cot \theta}$, $\sec^2 \theta \csc \theta$

*In Exercises **7–16,** prove that each statement is an identity.*

7. $\dfrac{\cos x - \sin x}{\cos x} = 1 - \tan x$

8. $\dfrac{\cot \theta + 1}{\cot \theta} = 1 + \tan \theta$

9. $\tan x \,(\tan x + \cot x) = \sec^2 x$

10. $(\sec \theta - \tan \theta)(\sec \theta + \tan \theta) = 1$

11. $\sec^4 x - \tan^4 x = \sec^2 x + \tan^2 x$

12. $\sin^4 x + 2 \sin^2 x \cos^2 x + \cos^4 x = 1$

13. $\dfrac{\sin^4 \theta - \cos^4 \theta}{1 - \cot^4 \theta} = \sin^4 \theta$

14. $\dfrac{1 - 2 \sin x - 3 \sin^2 x}{\cos^2 x} = \dfrac{1 - 3 \sin x}{1 - \sin x}$

15. $\csc \theta + \dfrac{\tan \theta}{\sin \theta} - \sec \theta = \dfrac{\cot \theta}{\cos \theta}$

16. $\dfrac{\sin^3 x + \cos^3 x}{1 - 2 \cos^2 x} = \dfrac{\sec x - \sin x}{\tan x - 1}$

Use the addition formulas for sine and cosine functions along with the eight fundamental identities to prove that each statement is an identity.

Example: $\sin 2x = 2 \sin x \cos x$
   Let $\alpha = \beta = x$ in $\sin (\alpha + \beta) = \sin \alpha \cos \beta + \cos \alpha \sin \beta$.

Then, $\sin 2x = \sin (x + x)$

$$= \sin x \cos x + \cos x \sin x$$

$$= 2 \sin x \cos x$$

17. $\tan (\alpha + \beta) = \dfrac{\tan \alpha + \tan \beta}{1 - \tan \alpha \tan \beta}$ $\left(\text{HINT: Use } \tan \alpha = \dfrac{\sin \alpha}{\cos \alpha} \text{ and } \tan \beta = \dfrac{\sin \beta}{\cos \beta}.\right)$

18. $\tan (\alpha - \beta) = \dfrac{\tan \alpha - \tan \beta}{1 + \tan \alpha \tan \beta}$ (HINT: Use $\tan [\alpha - \beta] = \tan [\alpha + (-\beta)]$ and Exercise 17.)

The formulas in Exercises **19-22** are called **double-angle formulas.** Prove that each is an identity.

19. $\cos 2x = \cos^2 x - \sin^2 x$ **20.** $\cos 2x = 2 \cos^2 x - 1$

21. $\cos 2x = 1 - 2 \sin^2 x$ **22.** $\tan 2x = \dfrac{2 \tan x}{1 - \tan^2 x}$

The formulas in Exercises **23-25** and in the following example are called **half-angle formulas.** Prove that each is an identity.

Example: Prove that $\sin \dfrac{\theta}{2} = \pm \sqrt{\dfrac{1 - \cos \theta}{2}}$.

Apply the addition formula for cosines and let $\alpha = \beta = \dfrac{\theta}{2}$.

$$\cos \left(\dfrac{\theta}{2} + \dfrac{\theta}{2}\right) = \cos^2 \dfrac{\theta}{2} - \sin^2 \dfrac{\theta}{2}$$

$$\cos \theta = 1 - 2 \sin^2 \dfrac{\theta}{2} \qquad\qquad \text{Why?}$$

$$\sin^2 \dfrac{\theta}{2} = \dfrac{1 - \cos \theta}{2} \qquad\qquad \begin{aligned} &\cos^2 \tfrac{\theta}{2} + \sin^2 \tfrac{\theta}{2} = 1 \\ &\cos^2 \tfrac{\theta}{2} = 1 - \sin^2 \tfrac{\theta}{2} \end{aligned}$$

$$\sin \dfrac{\theta}{2} = \pm \sqrt{\dfrac{1 - \cos \theta}{2}}$$

23. $\cos \dfrac{\theta}{2} = \pm \sqrt{\dfrac{1 + \cos \theta}{2}}$ $\left(\text{HINT: Use Exercise 20 with } x = \dfrac{\theta}{2}.\right)$

24. $\tan \dfrac{\theta}{2} = \pm \sqrt{\dfrac{1 - \cos \theta}{1 + \cos \theta}}$ (HINT: Use the above example and Exercise 23.)

25. $\tan \dfrac{\theta}{2} = \pm \sqrt{\dfrac{1 - \cos^2 \theta}{(1 + \cos \theta)^2}} = \pm \dfrac{\sin \theta}{1 + \cos \theta}$

14-8 Inverse Trigonometric Functions

The objective for this section is on page 507.

The graph of the inverse of a relation can be obtained by drawing the graph of $y = x$ and finding the "mirror image" of the original curve with respect to the graph of $y = x$. In Figure 1 this is done for the function $y = \sin x$. The resulting mirror image is the inverse of $y = \sin x$ and is denoted by $y = \text{arc } \sin x$. Check several points such as A, B, and C of $y = \sin x$ to see that they have image points A', B', and C', respectively, in the curve $y = \text{arc } \sin x$.

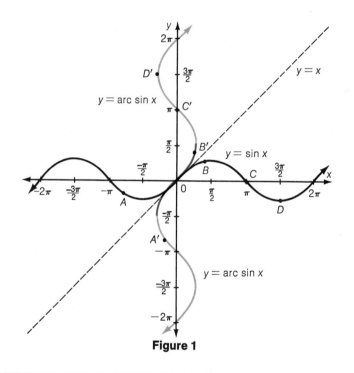

Figure 1

Definition: $y = \text{arc } \sin x$ if and only if $x = \sin y$.

A good way to think about the inverse of the sine function is that $y = \text{arc } \sin x$ means "y is the measure of the angle whose sine is x."

Example 1   What is arc sin $\frac{1}{2}$?

What is the measure of an angle whose sine is $\frac{1}{2}$?

$$\frac{1}{2} = \sin y \qquad \longleftarrow \quad \text{Write as an equation.}$$

$$y = \frac{\pi}{6}, \, y = \frac{5\pi}{6}, \, y = \frac{-7\pi}{6}, \, y = \frac{-11\pi}{6}, \text{ and so on.} \qquad \longleftarrow \quad \text{Solve for } y.$$

Since solving $\sin y = \frac{1}{2}$ gives an infinite number of solutions, $y = $ arc sin x is not a function. To get an inverse that is a function you use the **principal values** of the inverse of the sine function. When the word "arc" in $y = $ Arc sin x is written with a capital A, the principal value is desired. The graph of $y = $ Arc sin x is shown as the heavy portion of the curve $y = $ arc sin x in Figure 1.

$$y = \text{Arc sin } x \qquad \left(-1 \leq x \leq 1 \text{ and } -\frac{\pi}{2} \leq y \leq \frac{\pi}{2} \right)$$

Example 2   What is Arc sin $\frac{1}{2}$?

$$\text{Arc sin } \frac{1}{2} = \frac{\pi}{6} \qquad \longleftarrow \quad \text{The principal value of } y = \text{arc sin } \frac{1}{2}.$$

The functions $y = \cos x$ and $y = \tan x$ also have inverses.

Definitions

$y = $ arc cos x if and only if $x = \cos y$.

$y = $ arc cos x for $-1 \leq x \leq 1$ and $0 \leq y \leq \pi$ is the **principal value of the inverse cosine relation** and is written $y = $ Arc cos x.

$y = $ arc tan x if and only if $x = \tan y$.

$y = $ arc tan x for $-\infty \leq x \leq \infty$ and $-\frac{\pi}{2} \leq y \leq \frac{\pi}{2}$ is the **principal value of the inverse tangent relation**, written $y = $ Arc tan x.

Example 3   Evaluate: sin (Arc tan 8)

Let $\alpha = $ Arc tan 8.

Then $\tan \alpha = \frac{8}{1}$

and $y = 8$ $x = 1$ ⟵———— $\tan \alpha = \frac{y}{x}$

Thus, $r = \sqrt{8^2 + 1} = \sqrt{65}$ ⟵———— Pythagorean Theorem

$$\sin \alpha = \frac{y}{r} = \frac{8}{\sqrt{65}} \quad \text{and} \quad \sin (\text{Arc tan } 8) = \frac{8}{\sqrt{65}}$$

Try These   *Evaluate.*

1. Arc sin $\left(-\frac{\sqrt{2}}{2}\right)$ $-\frac{\pi}{4}$ **2.** Arc tan (-1) $-\frac{\pi}{4}$ **3.** Arc cos (-1) π

4. Arc sin 0 $_0$ **5.** Arc cos 0 $\frac{\pi}{2}$ **6.** Arc tan 1.3764
                                                                      54° or 0.9425 radians

Exercises

Evaluate.

a

1. Arc cos 0.4848   **2.** Arc sin 0.6691   **3.** Arc sin $\left(-\frac{\sqrt{3}}{2}\right)$
   61° or 1.0647 radians   42° or .7330 radians $-60°$ or $-\frac{\pi}{3}$

4. Arc cos 0.9272   **5.** sin (Arc cos $\frac{1}{3}$) $\frac{2\sqrt{2}}{3}$ **6.** cos (Arc tan 3) $\frac{\sqrt{10}}{10}$
   22° or .3840 radians

7. tan [Arc sin $\left(-\frac{1}{6}\right)$] $-\frac{\sqrt{35}}{35}$ **8.** cos (Arc sin $\frac{2}{3}$) $\frac{\sqrt{5}}{3}$ **9.** tan (Arc tan 5) $_5$

10. sin (Arc sin $\frac{4}{5}$) $\frac{4}{5}$ **11.** sin [Arc tan (-2)] $-\frac{2\sqrt{5}}{5}$ **12.** tan [Arc cos $\left(-\frac{12}{13}\right)$] $-\frac{5}{12}$

13. sec (Arc sin $\frac{1}{2}$) $\frac{2\sqrt{3}}{3}$ **14.** cot (Arc cos $\frac{3}{5}$) $\frac{3}{4}$ **15.** csc [Arc tan (-4)] $-\frac{\sqrt{17}}{4}$

16. csc (Arc sin $\frac{3}{7}$) $\frac{7}{3}$ **17.** cot (Arc tan $\frac{2}{5}$) $\frac{5}{2}$ **18.** sec (Arc cos $\frac{1}{7}$) $_7$

19. cot (Arc sin $\frac{2}{3}$) $\frac{\sqrt{5}}{2}$ **20.** sec [Arc tan (-7)] $_{5\sqrt{2}}$ **21.** csc [Arc cos $\left(-\frac{3}{4}\right)$]
   22. $0 \le y \le \pi$ **23.** $-\frac{\pi}{2} < y < \frac{\pi}{2}$ $\frac{4\sqrt{7}}{7}$

Sketch the graph of each inverse over the interval stated. Indicate the portion of each curve that represents the principal values.

See above.

22. $y = $ arc cos x; $y = -\pi$ to $y = 2\pi$ **23.** $y = $ arc tan x; $y = -2\pi$ to $y = 2\pi$

b **24.** $y = $ arc sin $\frac{1}{2}x$; $y = -\pi$ to $y = \pi$ **25.** $y = $ arc sin 2x; $y = -\pi$ to $y = \pi$

   $-\pi \le y \le \pi$ $-\frac{\pi}{4} \le y \le \frac{\pi}{4}$

500   Chapter 14

14-9 Trigonometric Equations

The objective for this section is on page 507.

To solve a trigonometric equation such as $\sin x = \frac{1}{2}$ where $0 \le x \le 2\pi$, you find all the real values of x such that $\sin x = \frac{1}{2}$ is true for the given domain.

Example 1

Solve: $\sin x = \frac{1}{2}$, $0 \le x \le 2\pi$

$\sin x = \frac{1}{2}$

$x = \dfrac{\pi}{6}$ and $\dfrac{5\pi}{6}$ ◄—— Since $\sin \dfrac{\pi}{6} = \dfrac{1}{2}$ and $\sin \dfrac{5\pi}{6} = \dfrac{1}{2}$.

Solution set: $\left\{ \dfrac{\pi}{6}, \dfrac{5\pi}{6} \right\}$

If x is any real number, $\sin x$ is periodic and has a period of 2π. Therefore, any integral multiple of 2π added to $\dfrac{\pi}{6}$ or $\dfrac{5\pi}{6}$ will give additional solutions. The solution set for $\sin x = \dfrac{1}{2}$ where x is a real number is $\left\{ 2k\pi + \dfrac{\pi}{6},\ 2k\pi + \dfrac{5\pi}{6} \right\}$, when k is any integer. The graphic solution below shows that there are two solutions for each period.

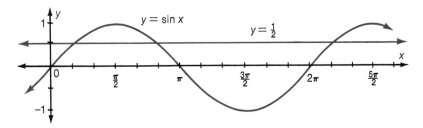

Trigonometric identities can be useful in solving trigonometric equations.

More Topics in Trigonometry **501**

Example 2   Solve: $2 \sin^2 x - \cos^2 x - 1 = 0$, where $0 \le x \le 2\pi$.

Since the equation has a squared term, it may be possible to factor it. To factor, however, it is necessary for the equation to be in terms of the sine or cosine only.

$$2 \sin^2 x - \cos x - 1 = 0$$
$$2(1 - \cos^2 x) - \cos x - 1 = 0 \quad \longleftarrow \quad \sin^2 x = 1 - \cos^2 x$$
$$2 - 2 \cos^2 x - \cos x - 1 = 0$$
$$-2 \cos^2 x - \cos x + 1 = 0$$
$$2 \cos^2 x + \cos x - 1 = 0 \quad \longleftarrow \quad \text{Multiply by } -1.$$
$$(2 \cos x - 1)(\cos x + 1) = 0 \quad \longleftarrow \quad \text{Factor.}$$
$$2 \cos x - 1 = 0 \text{ or } \cos x + 1 = 0$$
$$\cos x = \tfrac{1}{2} \text{ or } \cos x = -1$$

The solution set for $\cos x = \frac{1}{2}$ is $\left\{ \dfrac{\pi}{3}, \dfrac{5\pi}{3} \right\}$. The solution set for $\cos x = -1$ is $\{\pi\}$.

Thus, the solution set is $\left\{ \dfrac{\pi}{3}, \dfrac{5\pi}{3}, \pi \right\}$.

Exercises

Solve each equation, where $0 \le x \le 2\pi$.

1. $\cos x = \frac{\sqrt{2}}{2}$ $\left\{ \frac{\pi}{4}, \frac{7\pi}{4} \right\}$

2. $\tan x = \sqrt{3}$ $\left\{ \frac{\pi}{3}, \frac{4\pi}{3} \right\}$

3. $\cot x = 0$ $\left\{ \frac{\pi}{2}, \frac{3\pi}{2} \right\}$

4. $\sec x = 2$ $\left\{ \frac{\pi}{3}, \frac{5\pi}{3} \right\}$

5. $2 \cos^2 x - \cos x = 0$ $\left\{ \frac{\pi}{3}, \frac{\pi}{2}, \frac{3\pi}{2}, \frac{5\pi}{3} \right\}$

6. $2 \sin^2 x - \sin x - 1 = 0$ $\left\{ \frac{\pi}{2}, \frac{7\pi}{6}, \frac{11\pi}{6} \right\}$

7. $\sin^2 x = \frac{1}{2}$ $\left\{ \frac{\pi}{4}, \frac{3\pi}{4}, \frac{5\pi}{4}, \frac{7\pi}{4} \right\}$

8. $\tan^2 x = 1$ $\left\{ \frac{\pi}{4}, \frac{3\pi}{4}, \frac{5\pi}{4}, \frac{7\pi}{4} \right\}$

9. $3 \sin^2 x - \cos^2 x = 0$ $\left\{ \frac{\pi}{6}, \frac{5\pi}{6}, \frac{7\pi}{6}, \frac{11\pi}{6} \right\}$

10. $2 \tan^2 x - 3 \sec x + 3 = 0$
$\{0, 2\pi\}$

Solve each equation, where θ is any real number.

11. $\cos \theta = 0$ $\left\{ k\pi + \frac{\pi}{2} \right\}$, where k is any integer.

12. $3 \cot \theta + \sqrt{3} = 0$ $\left\{ k\pi + \frac{2\pi}{3} \right\}$, where k is any integer.

13. $(\sin \theta - 1)(2 \sin \theta + 1) = 0$ _{See key.} **14.** $(2 \cos \theta + 1)(\cos \theta - 1) = 0$
_{See key.}

15. $3 \tan^2 \theta - \sqrt{3} \tan \theta = 0$ $\{k\pi, k\pi + \frac{\pi}{6}\}$ **16.** $\sec^2 \theta + 2 \sec \theta = 0$ $\{2k\pi + \frac{2\pi}{3}, 2k\pi + \frac{4\pi}{3}\}$

Use the tables on pages 543-547 to find all solutions of each equation to the nearest minute, where $0 \le \theta \le 2\pi$.

17. $4 \sin \theta - 2 = 1$ _{48° 35' or 131° 25'} **18.** $\tan \theta = -2.1290$ _{115° 10' or 295° 10'}

19. $\cos \theta = 0.1263$ _{82° 45' or 277° 15'} **20.** $2 \sec \theta = -3$ _{131° 48' or 228° 12'}

More Challenging Problems

_{See key for Exercises 1-11.}

1. Graph $y = \sin (2x + \frac{\pi}{2})$ and $y = \sin 2x$ on the same coordinate system. How is the graph of $y = \sin (2x + \frac{\pi}{2})$ related to the graph of $y = \sin 2x$?

2. Graph $y = \sin (3x + \frac{\pi}{2})$ and $y = \sin 3x$ on the same coordinate system. How are the two graphs related?

Use the reciprocal definitions for sec θ, csc θ, and cot θ to show that the statements in Exercises 3 and 4 are true.

3. $\tan \theta \cdot \cos \theta \cdot \csc \theta = 1$ **4.** $\cos^2 \theta \cdot \sec \theta = \sin \theta \cdot \cot \theta$

5. Prove: $\cos 3\theta = 4 \cos^3\theta - 3 \cos \theta$ **6.** Prove: $1 + \tan^2 \theta = \sec^2 \theta$

7. Prove: $1 + 2 \cot^2 \theta + \cot^4 \theta = \csc^4 \theta$

Prove the identities in Exercises **8–11.**

8. $\sin \alpha \cos \beta = \frac{1}{2}[\sin (\alpha + \beta) + \sin (\alpha - \beta)]$

9. $\cos \alpha \sin \beta = \frac{1}{2}[\sin (\alpha + \beta) - \sin (\alpha - \beta)]$

10. $\cos \alpha \cos \beta = \frac{1}{2}[\cos (\alpha + \beta) + \cos (\alpha - \beta)]$

11. $\sin \alpha \sin \beta = \frac{1}{2}[\cos (\alpha - \beta) - \cos (\alpha + \beta)]$

12. Solve the conditional equation $\dfrac{\csc x}{\cot x} = \tan x$. _ϕ

13. Evaluate $\cos (\text{Arc} \tan 2 + \text{Arc} \sec 3)$. _{$\frac{\sqrt{5} - 4\sqrt{10}}{15}$}

14. Prove Arc $\cos \frac{3}{5}$ + Arc $\sin \frac{5}{13}$ = Arc $\tan \frac{63}{16}$. _{See key.}

15. Prove Arc $\tan x$ + Arc $\cot x = \dfrac{\pi}{2}$. _{See key.}

16. Let $K = \frac{1}{2}bc \sin A$ be the area of a triangle. Use the Law of Cosines to show that $K = \sqrt{s(s - a)(s - b)(s - c)}$, where a, b, and c are the measures of the sides of a triangle and $s = \frac{1}{2}(a + b + c)$. _{See key.}

Complex Numbers in Polar Form

A complex number, $a + bi$, can be expressed in terms of r, where $r = \sqrt{a^2 + b^2}$, and the sine and cosine of an angle, θ, in standard position, where $P(a, b)$ is a point on the terminal side of θ.

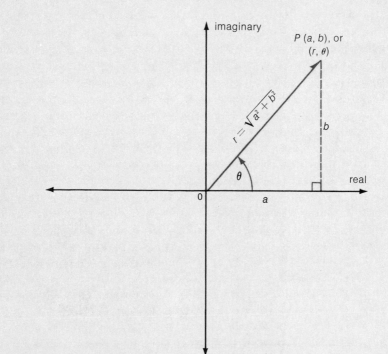

From the graph, note that

$$\cos \theta = \frac{a}{r} \qquad \text{and} \qquad \sin \theta = \frac{b}{r}$$

then,
$$a = r \cos \theta \qquad \text{and} \qquad b = r \sin \theta$$

Thus,
$$a + bi = r \cos \theta + ir \sin \theta.$$
$$a + bi = r(\cos \theta + i \sin \theta)$$

This is the **polar form** of the complex number, $a + bi$. The numbers r and θ, written (r, θ) are the **polar coordinates** of point P.

The **polar-coordinate plane** is used to graph complex numbers in polar form.

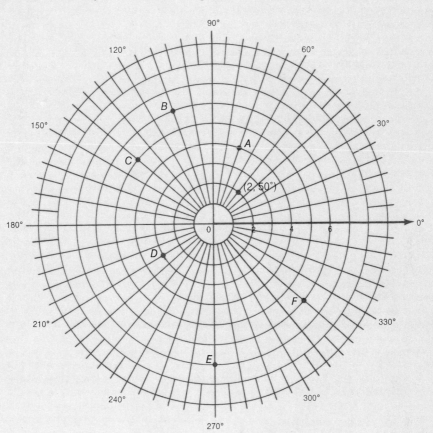

To graph $2(\cos 50° + i \sin 50°)$, you graph the coordinates $(2, 50°)$. First, move 2 units along the zero or polar axis. Then, move along the circle to the ray for 50°.

Can You Solve These?

Use the graph of the polar coordinate plane to match each complex number with its graph.

1. $6(\cos 110° + i \sin 110°)$ **2.** $7(\cos 270° + i \sin 270°)$

3. $3(\cos 210° + i \sin 210°)$ **4.** $4 \cos 70° + 4i \sin 70°$

5. $5 \cos(-210°) + 5i \sin(-210°)$ **6.** $6 \cos(-40°) + 6i \sin(-40°)$

Chapter Objectives and Review

Objective: To know the meanings of the important mathematical terms of this chapter.

1. Here are many of the mathematical terms used in this chapter. Be sure that you know their meanings and that you can use them correctly.

amplitude (p. 484)
period (p. 484)

periodic function (p. 484)
principal value (p. 499)
radian (p. 478)

Objective: To change radian measure to degree measure and degree measure to radian measure. (Section 14-1)

Change each radian measure to degrees.

2. $\frac{7\pi}{6}$ 210°

3. 2 $\frac{360°}{\pi}$

4. $\frac{11\pi}{15}$ 132°

5. $\frac{15\pi}{9}$ 300°

Change each degree measure to radians.

6. 360° 2π

7. 135° $\frac{3\pi}{4}$

8. 70° $\frac{7\pi}{18}$

9. 228° $\frac{19\pi}{15}$

Objective: To evaluate trigonometric functions with the measure of the angle expressed in radians. (Section 14-2)

Evaluate.

10. $\sin \frac{7\pi}{18}$ .9397

11. $\tan \frac{11\pi}{15}$ −1.1106

12. $\cos 0.7$ .7648

13. $\cot \frac{37\pi}{45}$
−1.6003

Objective: To graph trigonometric functions. (Sections 14-3 and 14-4)

Sketch the graph of each function where $-2\pi \le x \le 2\pi$.
State the domain, range, amplitude and period of each.

14. $y = 2 \sin 3x$
See key.

15. $y = \frac{1}{4} \cos \frac{1}{2} x$
See key.

16. $y = \tan 2x$
See key.

Objective: To prove trigonometric identities. (Sections 14-5 and 14-7)

Prove each identity. See key for Exercises 17-20.

17. $(1 - \sin^2 x)(1 + \tan^2 x) = 1$

18. $\sec x \csc x - \dfrac{\sin x}{\cos x} = \cot x$

19. $\sin^4 x - 2 \sin^2 x + 1 = \cos^4 x$

20. $\dfrac{1 + \sin x}{\cot^2 x} = \dfrac{\sin x}{\csc x - 1}$

Objective: To use the sum and difference identities to evaluate trigonometric functions. (Section 14-6)

Use the sum and difference identities to evaluate each function. $\frac{\sqrt{2} - \sqrt{6}}{4}$

21. $\sin 15°$ $\frac{\sqrt{6} - \sqrt{2}}{4}$ **22.** $\cos 75°$ $\frac{\sqrt{6} - \sqrt{2}}{4}$ **23.** $\sin 105°$ $\frac{\sqrt{6} + \sqrt{2}}{4}$ **24.** $\cos 255°$

Objective: To evaluate expressions that involve inverse trigonometric functions. (Section 14-8)

Evaluate.

25. $\tan (\text{Arc} \cos \frac{\sqrt{3}}{2})$ $\frac{\sqrt{3}}{3}$ **26.** $\cos (\text{Arc} \sin \frac{\sqrt{3}}{2})$ $\frac{1}{2}$

Objective: To solve trigonometric equations. (Section 14-9)

Solve each equation where $0 \le x \le 2\pi$.

27. $2 \sin x - 1 = 0$ $\{\frac{\pi}{6}, \frac{5\pi}{6}\}$ **28.** $3 + 2(\cos^2 x - 1) = \cos x + 1$
$\{\frac{\pi}{3}, \frac{\pi}{2}, \frac{3\pi}{2}, \frac{5\pi}{3}\}$

Chapter
Test

Change the following radian measures to degrees.

1. $\frac{2}{3}\pi$ 120°   **2.** $\frac{17}{12}\pi$ 255°   **3.** $\frac{10}{6}\pi$ 300°

Evaluate.

4. $\sin \frac{3}{4}\pi$ $\frac{\sqrt{2}}{2}$ **5.** $\cos \frac{7}{6}\pi$ $-\frac{\sqrt{3}}{2}$ **6.** $\tan \frac{5}{3}\pi$ $-\sqrt{3}$

Sketch the graph of each function for $0 \le x \le 2\pi$. State the domain, range, amplitude, and period of each.

D: the set of real numbers   D: the set of real numbers   D: the set of real numbers except

7. $y = \sin x$ R: $\{y: -1 \le y \le 1\}$ **8.** $y = \cos x$ R: $\{y: -1 \le 1\}$ **9.** $y = \tan x$ $\frac{\pi}{2}, \frac{3\pi}{2}$, etc.
Amp.: 1; Period: 2π Amp.: 1; Period: 2π R: the set of real numbers
                                                                              Amp.: undefined; Period: π

Complete each of the following statements by giving the simplest trigonometric expression that makes the sentence an identity.

10. $\sin^2 \theta + \underline{\quad?\quad} = 1$ $\cos^2\theta$ **11.** $1 + \tan^2 \theta = \underline{\quad?\quad}$ $\sec^2\theta$ **12.** $1 + \underline{\quad?\quad} = \csc^2 \theta$ $\cot^2\theta$

13. $\frac{\sin \theta}{\cos \theta} = \underline{\quad?\quad}$ $\tan\theta$ **14.** $\frac{1}{\cos \theta} = \underline{\quad?\quad}$ $\sec\theta$ **15.** $\cot \theta = \frac{1}{?}$ $\tan\theta$

Prove each identity.

16. $\tan x = \sin x \cdot \sec x$ $= \sin x \frac{1}{\cos x} = \tan x$ **17.** $\frac{\cos x - \sin x}{\cos x} = 1 - \tan x$

18. $\sin^4 x - \cos^4 x = \sin^2 x - \cos^2 x$
$\sin^4 x - \cos^4 x = (\sin^2 x + \cos^2 x)(\sin^2 x - \cos^2 x) = 1(\sin^2 x - \cos^2 x)$

$\frac{\cos x - \sin x}{\cos x} = 1 - \frac{\sin x}{\cos x} = 1 - \tan x$

More Topics in Trigonometry   **507**

Cumulative Review

Write the letter of the response that best answers each question.

1. Choose the set that contains $\sqrt{-5}$.

    a. Ir   **ⓑ** C   **c.** Q   **d.** R

2. Tell which statement is <u>not</u> true for the given vectors.

    ⓐ The additive inverse of $(-3, 4)$ is $(-3, -4)$.
    b. The length of $(3, -4)$ is 5 units.
    c. $(6, 2)$ has the same direction as $(3, 1)$.
    d. The vector $(7, 11)$ is equivalent to $-(-7, -11)$.

3. Solve for x: $4x - 4c = ax - ac$

    a. $\{4\}$ **b.** $\{2\}$ **ⓒ** $\{c\}$ **d.** $\{-c\}$

4. Use the Remainder theorem to find the remainder when $x^5 + x^4 - x^3 - x^2 - 2x - 2$ is divided by $x - 1$.

    a. 4   **ⓑ** -4 **c.** 0   **d.** -2

5. Divide and simplify: $\dfrac{x^4 - 16}{x^6 - 27} \div \dfrac{x^2 - 4}{(x^4 - 9)(x^4 + 3x^2 + 9)}$

    a. $\dfrac{(x^2 + 4)(x^2 + 3)(x^4 + 3x^2 + 9)}{x^3 + 9}$ **b.** $(x + 2)^2(x^2 + 3)$

    c. $(x + 2)^2(x + 3)^2$ **ⓓ** $(x^2 + 4)(x^2 + 3)$

6. Given the line containing the points $(5, -3)$ and $(x, 9)$ and with slope $-\frac{3}{2}$, find x.

    a. $2\frac{3}{8}$ **b.** -6 **c.** 3   **ⓓ** -3

7. Find the equations that have irrational solutions.

    a. $x^2 + 2x + 2 = 0$ **b.** $x^2 = 3x - 2$
    c. $21x - 10x^2 + 10 = 0$ **ⓓ** $4x^2 = 12x - 7$

8. Tell which statement is true.

    a. $\sqrt{-10} \div \sqrt{-2}$ is a pure imaginary number.
    b. $\sqrt{6} \cdot \sqrt{6}$ is an irrational number.
    ⓒ $\sqrt{-8} - \sqrt{-7}$ is an imaginary number.
    d. $\sqrt{-5} \cdot \sqrt{-2}$ is an imaginary number.

9. If the domain of $f(x) = |x| + 2$ is $\{-1, 1, 3, 5, 7\}$, state its range.

    a. $\{0, 2, 4, 6, 8\}$ **b.** $\{-1, 1, 3, 5, 7\}$ **ⓒ** $\{3, 5, 7, 9\}$ **d.** $\{2, 4, 6, 8, 10\}$

10. Tell which statement about the fifth term of $(3x - y)^8$ is <u>false</u>.

   (**a.**) The coefficient is 70.
            b. The exponent of x is 4.
   c. The exponent of y is 4.
            d. The fifth term is $5670x^4y^4$.

11. Find the number of permutations of 5 things taken 3 at a time.

   a. 10   (**b.**) 60   **c.** 30   **d.** 120

12. Tell which statement is <u>true</u>.

   a. $_nP_r = n!$ **b.** $0! = 0$ (**c.**) $\dfrac{n!}{(n-1)!} = n$ **d.** $_nC_r = \dfrac{n!}{r!}$

13. Find the number of ways that a committee of 5 can be chosen from a class of 25 students.

   a. $\dfrac{25!}{5!}$ (**b.**) $\dfrac{25!}{20!\,5!}$ **c.** $\dfrac{25!}{20!}$ **d.** $\dfrac{25!}{24!}$

14. If a single die is thrown, find the probability of getting an even number or an odd number.

   a. 0   **b.** $\dfrac{1}{2}$ **c.** $\dfrac{2}{3}$ (**d.**) 1

15. If a single die is thrown, find the probability of getting a number less than 3.

   a. 0   (**b.**) $\dfrac{1}{3}$ **c.** $\dfrac{2}{3}$ **d.** 1

16. For a given angle whose measure is θ, $\sin \theta = .45$ and $\cos \theta = .90$. Find $\tan \theta$.

   (**a.**) $\dfrac{1}{2}$ or 0.500   **b.** 2   **c.** 1.3500   **d.** .0405

17. A ray makes an angle measuring 25° with the negative x axis. Choose the measure(s) of the angles that it could also make with the positive x axis.

   (**a.**) 205°   **b.** −165°   **c.** −155°   **d.** 155°

18. Tell which statement is <u>false</u>.

   a. $\cos \theta = \cos (-\theta)$ **b.** $\cos \theta = \dfrac{1}{\sec \theta}$

   (**c.**) $\cos \theta = \sin (90° + \theta)$ **d.** $\cos \theta = \sin \theta \cot \theta$

19. Tell which of the following is not a statement of the Law of Cosines?

   (**a.**) $a^2 = b^2 + c^2 - 2ab \cos C$ **b.** $c^2 = a^2 + b^2 - 2ab \cos C$

   c. $b^2 = a^2 + c^2 - 2ac \cos B$ **d.** $\cos A = \dfrac{b^2 + c^2 - a^2}{2bc}$

20. Triangle *ABC* is a right triangle with *C* at the vertex of the right angle. Tell which of the following is not a side of $\triangle ABC$.

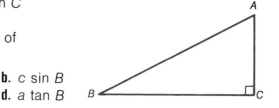

  a. $c \cos B$
  c. $a \cos B$ ⟵ circled

  b. $c \sin B$
  d. $a \tan B$

21. Tell which statements are <u>true</u>.

  a. The period of the function $y = \tan x$ is 2π.

  b. The amplitude of the function $y = \frac{1}{2} \cos 2x$ is $\frac{1}{2}$. ⟵ circled

  c. The period of the function $y = \frac{1}{2} \cos 2x$ is π. ⟵ circled

  d. The range of the function $y = \sin x$ is the set of real numbers.

22. Tell which statement(s) are <u>false</u>.

  a. Arc $\sin \frac{1}{2} = \frac{\pi}{6}$

  b. Arc $\tan (-1) = -\frac{\pi}{4}$

  c. Arc $\cos (-1) = \pi$

  d. Arc $\sin 0 = \frac{\pi}{2}$ ⟵ circled

23. Tell which statements are <u>true</u> for all replacements for θ for which the functions are defined.

  a. $\cos^2 \theta = 1 - \sin^2 \theta$ ⟵ circled
  c. $1 + \cos^2 \theta = \cot^2 \theta$

  b. $\sin^2 \theta - \cos^2 \theta = 1$
  d. $\sin^2 \theta - 1 = \tan^2 \theta$

24. Choose the statement that is <u>not</u> true.

  a. $\sin 75° = \sin 45° \cos 30° + \cos 45° \sin 30°$
  b. $\cos 120° = \cos 60° \cos 60° - \sin 60° \sin 60° = \cos^2 60° - \sin^2 60°$
  c. $\sin 15° = \sin 45° \cos 30° + \cos 45° \sin 30°$ ⟵ circled
  d. $\cos 30° = \cos 90° \cos 60° + \sin 90° \sin 60°$

25. Solve for *x* where $0 \le x \le 2\pi$: $2 \cos^2 x + \cos x - 1 = 0$

  a. $\left\{ \frac{\pi}{3} \right\}$ **b.** $\left\{ \frac{\pi}{6}, \pi \right\}$ **c.** $\left\{ \frac{\pi}{3}, \pi, \frac{5\pi}{3} \right\}$ ⟵ circled   **d.** $\left\{ \frac{\pi}{3}, \pi, \frac{5\pi}{3}, \frac{9\pi}{3} \right\}$

26. Tell which statement is <u>true</u> for the graphs of $y = 2$ and $y = 2 \sin x$ as *x* varies from 0 to π radians.

  a. They intersect in one point. ⟵ circled
  b. They intersect in two points.
  c. They intersect in three points.
  d. They do not intersect.

Chapter 15
Computer Programming

15-1 Introduction

A **program** is a sequence of commands to carry out a step-by-step procedure. In this book, programs are written in the BASIC language. A BASIC program that computes the perimeter of a rectangle is shown.

Statement 1Ø is an **input** command. It tells the machine to accept from the DATA listed in line 5Ø a value for the variable L (length) and a value for W (width). These values are stored in **memory locations** in the machine. Each memory cell is like a box that can hold one number at a time. When Program 1 is executed, the box called "L" will first contain 7 and box "W" will hold 5.

PROGRAM 1

```
1Ø READ L,W

2Ø LET P = 2 * L + 2 * W

3Ø PRINT "PERIMETER = ";P

4Ø GO TO 1Ø

5Ø DATA 7, 5, 9.2, 4.7

6Ø END
```

The computer moves in order to statement 2Ø. The word LET indicates a computation step. In this case, the values of L and W are used to calculate a value for P. Since L = 7 and W = 5, P = 24 when execution of statement 2Ø ends. Statement 3Ø causes **output** of the message PERIMETER = 24 on a keyboard terminal attached to the computer by cable or by a telephone line. Note that in line 3Ø, the letter P is outside the quotation marks. In this way the machine will put the current value of P at the end of the message, PERIMETER = .

Statement 4Ø tells the machine to "loop" back to statement 1Ø until there is no more DATA in line 5Ø. In this situation the machine automatically jumps to line 6Ø and ends execution of the program.

The complete listing of Program 1 as it appeared on a terminal follows, along with the output from a "run" (execution) of the program. Comments explain the printout.

```
NEW PERIM                           ←————  Tells the machine to expect a new
                                           program to be named "PERIM".
READY

1Ø READ L,W                         ←————  The user types the statements
2Ø LET P = 2 * L + 2 * W                   of the program.
3Ø PRINT "PERIMETER = ";P
4Ø GO TO 1Ø
5Ø DATA 7, 5, 9.2, 4.7
6Ø END
RUN                                 ←————  The user types RUN to tell the
                                           machine to execute the program.
PERIM  Ø8:Ø8 AM Ø7-JUN-76  ←————           The computer types this output.
PERIMETER = 24
PERIMETER = 27.8
OUT OF DATA AT LINE 1Ø

READY                               ←————  Indicates the computer is
                                           ready for a new command or another
                                           program.
```

It is customary to number statements in multiples of ten. This makes it easy to add a statement later. For example, to insert a statement between lines 1Ø and 2Ø, simply number the statement 15 and the computer will put the new line in sequence properly. The following symbols are used for operations in BASIC.

+ addition   / division
− subtraction   ↑ raising to a power
* multiplication

Examples showing the use of these symbols are given below. The usual order of operations is followed in BASIC. Unlike algebra, however, the * for multiplication is always written.

Algebraic Equation	BASIC Statement
$y = 2x^2$	2Ø LET Y = 2 * X ↑ 2
$y = (2x)^2$	2Ø LET Y = (2 * X) ↑ 2
$z = 5(x + y) - 6$	2Ø LET Z = 5 * (X + Y) - 6
$z = (a + 7)(b - 3)$	2Ø LET Z = (A + 7) * (B - 3)
$r = \dfrac{6xy}{z - 1}$	2Ø LET R = 6*X*Y/(Z - 1)

Exercises

See key for Exercises 9-18.

Write each equation as a BASIC LET statement. Then write a program for each exercise.

1. $y = (x - 8)^2$ 2 0 LET Y = (X − 8) ↑ 2

2. $r = \dfrac{2t^2}{u}$ 2 0 LET R = 2 * T ↑ 2/U

3. $a = \dfrac{c + d}{2}$ 2 0 LET A = (C + D)/2

4. $y = 2x^2 - 3x + 6$ 2 0 LET Y = 2 * X ↑ 2 − 3 * X + 6

5. $p = 2(\ell + w)$ 2 0 LET P = 2 * (L + W)

6. $k = \dfrac{mn}{c + 2}$ 2 0 LET K = M * N/(C + 2)

7. $s = \dfrac{x - a^3}{3y}$ 2 0 LET S = (X − A ↑ 3)/(3 * Y)

8. $\ell = -7 + \dfrac{b}{c - d}$
   2 0 LET L = −7 + B/(C − D)

9. Read the length and width of a rectangle. Compute and print the area.

10. Given the number of wins and losses, compute a team's winning percentage. Assume that there are no ties.

Given the length of a side of a square, print each of the following.

11. The perimeter of the square

12. The area of the square

Compute the average of each of the following.

13. Two given real numbers

14. Three real numbers

15. Given the length of the base and the height of a triangle, calculate the area.

16. Calculate a man's gross weekly pay, given his rate per hour, overtime rate per hour, number of regular hours, and number of overtime hours worked that week.

Read the radius of a circle. Then compute and print each of the following. (Note: There is no key for π on a terminal. Use 3.14159 for π.)

17. The circumference of the circle

18. The area of the circle

BASIC programs usually involve decisions. In BASIC, an IF . . . THEN statement is used to make a decision.

Example

Read a real number. Print its principal square root.

PROGRAM 2

```
1Ø PRINT "NUMBER", "SQUARE ROOT"
2Ø PRINT
3Ø READ X
4Ø IF X < Ø THEN 7Ø
5Ø PRINT X,SQR(X)
6Ø GO TO 3Ø
7Ø PRINT X,SQR(-X);"I"
8Ø GO TO 3Ø
9Ø DATA 7,Ø,-16,37,-59
1ØØ END
```

When run, Program 2 produces this output.

```
NUMBER              SQUARE ROOT
  7                 2.64575
  Ø                 Ø
-16                 4 I
 37                 6.Ø8276
-59                 7.68115 I
OUT OF DATA AT LINE 3Ø
```

Statement 1Ø prints the headings for the two columns of output. Line 2Ø skips a line between these headings and the first line of output data. Statement 4Ø requires a decision for each value of X. If X is negative, the computer jumps to statement 7Ø. If X is not negative, the machine continues in sequence to line 5∅. "SQR" refers to a built-in BASIC function that takes the principal square root of the positive real number in parentheses behind SQR.

In statements 1∅, 5∅, and 7∅, commas are used to separate the quantities to be printed. The output page is separated into five print "zones" of equal width. The comma causes the computer to skip to the next zone to print the next item. In this way the headings can be fixed over the columns of output. The semicolon in line 7∅, on the other hand, causes the "I" to be printed close behind the previous item.

In an IF . . . THEN statement, the relation in the IF clause may be complicated. Here are some examples.

```
3∅ IF X + Y = A - B THEN 9∅
2∅ IF B↑2 - 4*A*C >= ∅ THEN 1∅∅
4∅ IF X <= 7*Y THEN 1∅
6∅ IF R/(.5*Y) <> K + 6 THEN 8∅
```

Relation	BASIC Equivalent
=	=
<	<
>	>
≤	<=
≥	>=
≠	<>

While the sample programs in these computer units are in BASIC, all problems assigned for programming can be done in FORTRAN as well. A difficulty with FORTRAN, however, is that it is not as standardized as BASIC.

Exercises See key.

Write a program for each problem. Be sure that the DATA chosen produces each possible outcome at least once.

1. Given the length of a side of a square, compute the length of a diagonal.

2. Given the length of a side of an equilateral triangle, print the area of the triangle.

3. Read real numbers X and Y. Decide whether X = Y, X > Y, or X < Y.

4. Read three positive numbers A, B, and C. Decide whether these numbers could be the sides of a right triangle. Do not assume that C is the largest number.

5. Read a real number X. Print X and its absolute value.

6. For an equation of the form $Ax + B = Cx + D$, read A, B, C, and D and an additional number N. Decide whether N is a solution of the equation.

7. Given an inequality of the form $Ax + B < Cx + D$, decide whether a given number is in the solution set of the inequality.

15-3 Coordinate Geometry

Thus far we have used only one type of BASIC variable, namely, a single letter. For coordinate geometry it is often convenient to use another type: one letter followed by one digit. Examples are AØ, A1, A2, ..., A9, ..., Z8, Z9.

Example 1

Given the coordinates of two points, compute the slope of the line containing the points.

PROGRAM 3

```
1Ø READ X1,Y1,X2,Y2
2Ø IF X2 - X1 = Ø THEN 5Ø
3Ø PRINT "SLOPE = ";(Y2 - Y1)/(X2 - X1)
4Ø GO TO 1Ø
5Ø PRINT "SLOPE UNDEFINED"
6Ø GO TO 1Ø
7Ø DATA 6,-2,8,1Ø,4,Ø,4,-2,-6,7,-3,7
8Ø END

READY

RUN
SLOPE     1Ø:1Ø AM            Ø1-JUN-76
SLOPE =   6
SLOPE UNDEFINED
SLOPE =   Ø
OUT OF DATA AT LINE 1Ø
```

In statement 3Ø, the formula for slope is entered directly into the PRINT line. This saves a LET statement.

BASIC cannot handle complex numbers as such. To the computer, "I" is just another real variable. Likewise, a statement such as, 3Ø LET I = SQR(-1), is meaningless since SQR handles only positive values. Instead operations are performed with the real numbers A and B from the complex number $A + Bi$.

Example 2   Write a program to add the complex numbers $A + Bi$ and $C + Di$.

PROGRAM 4

```
1Ø  READ A,B,C,D
2Ø  LET R = A + C
3Ø  LET S = B + D
4Ø  IF S < Ø THEN 7Ø
5Ø  PRINT R;" + ";S;"I"
6Ø  GO TO 1Ø
7Ø  PRINT R;S;"I"
8Ø  GO TO 1Ø
9Ø  DATA 4, 6,-3,7,5,2,-5,-4,-6,1,8,-1,4
95  DATA  -9,-2,5
1ØØ END

READY

RUN
CPLXNO   1Ø:16 AM        Ø1-JUN-76
  1  + 13 I
  Ø  -2 I
  2  +  Ø I
  2  -4 I
OUT OF DATA AT LINE 1Ø

READY
```

The decision in statement 4Ø is used to print the sums as neatly as possible. When S is negative, line 7Ø prints the result without the + sign.

Exercises

1. Revise Program 3 so that it prints a complete message that includes the coordinates of the points. Here is a sample:

```
SLOPE OF THE LINE THROUGH ( 6 ,-2 ) AND ( 8 , 1Ø )
IS 6
SLOPE OF THE LINE THROUGH ( 4 , Ø ) AND ( 4 ,-2 )
IS UNDEFINED
SLOPE OF THE LINE THROUGH (-6 , 7 ) AND (-3 ,   7 )
IS Ø
```

2. Change Program 4 so that it prints the numbers being added as well as their sum.

   Write programs for Exercises 3-12. Make sure the DATA illustrates all possible outcomes.

   Given the coordinates of two points in the Cartesian plane.

3. Compute the distance between them.

4. Print the coordinates of the midpoint of the segment joining them.

5. Read the x and y coordinates of points A, B, C, and D. Decide whether ABCD is a parallelogram.

   Print the equation of a line in standard form, $Ax + By = C$, given the following information.

6. The coordinates of a point on the line and the slope of the line

7. The slope of the line and its y-intercept

8. The coordinates of two points on the line

   Given a complex number $A + Bi$, print each of the following.

9. Its absolute value

10. Its conjugate in standard form

11. Its reciprocal (if it has one) in standard form

12. Read the coordinates of a point in the coordinate plane. Print the number of the quadrant in which the point lies, or whether it lies on the x axis, on the y axis, or on both.

15-4 Quadratic Functions

A computer is useful in analyzing quadratic functions. A simple application prints a table of XY-pairs from which a graph can be drawn. The program is made easier by a new pair of BASIC statements: the FOR and NEXT statements.

PROGRAM 5

```
10  PRINT " X"," Y"
20  PRINT
30  READ A,B,C
40  FOR X = -5 TO 5
50  LET Y = A*X↑2 + B*X + C
60  PRINT X,Y
70  NEXT X
80  DATA 2,-3,7
90  END
```

READY

RUN
QUADRA   10:19 AM   01-JUN-76
  X   Y

X	Y
-5	72
-4	51
-3	34
-2	21
-1	12
0	7
1	6
2	9
3	16
4	27
5	42

READY

The FOR and NEXT statements set up a loop, statements 4Ø through 7Ø, that the computer executes over and over. X is first set to −5, Y is computed (line 5Ø), and the X−Y pair printed (6Ø). The statement, NEXT X, signals the machine to add one to X and to change its value to −4. The loop is now executed again. The program continues for X equal to −3, −2, −1, 0, 1, 2, 3, 4, 5. When X = 5, the loop is finished.

To obtain more XY−pairs from Program 5, change line 4Ø to 4Ø FOR X = −5 TO 5 STEP .5. "STEP.5" means that instead of adding one to obtain each value of X, the computer adds .5. Thus X will then take on the values −5, −4.5, −4, −3.5, ... 4, 4.5, 5.

Exercises See key.

For the parabola defined by $y = Ax^2 + Bx + C$, $A \neq 0$, *read* A, B, *and* C.

1. Print the coordinates of the vertex.

2. Give the equation of the axis of symmetry.

3. Decide whether the vertex is a maximum or a minimum point.

For the quadratic equation $Ax^2 + Bx + C = 0$, *read* A, B, *and* C.

4. Evaluate the discriminant.

5. Determine the nature of the roots.

6. Without solving, print the sum and the product of the roots.

7. Read the complex number $D + Ei$ and decide whether it is a root.

8. Given a quadratic inequality and the coordinates of a point, decide whether the point lies in the solution set of the inequality.

9. Given the two real roots of a quadratic equation, print the equation.

Systems of Sentences

Many computer applications involve matrix operations. Hence BASIC provides a set of "MAT" commands for handling matrices.

In BASIC, as in algebra, a matrix is named by a capital letter. To refer to a particular element of the matrix, two subscripts are used. In BASIC, since terminal keyboards cannot print lowered characters, the subscripts are placed in parentheses. Thus $A_{i,j}$ becomes A(I,J) in BASIC. Likewise $M_{3,4}$ is M(3,4).

Example

Write a program to read a 2 × 2 matrix and print its determinant.

PROGRAM 6

```
1Ø DIM A(2,2)
2Ø MAT READ A
3Ø LET D = A(1,1)*A(2,2)-A(1,2)*A(2,1)
4Ø PRINT "FOR THE MATRIX"
5Ø MAT PRINT A,
7Ø PRINT "THE DETERMINANT IS";D
8Ø PRINT
9Ø GO TO 2Ø
1ØØ DATA 1,2,-1,4,2,-2,4,-4
11Ø END

READY

RUN
DETERM  1Ø:38 AM       Ø1-JUN-76
FOR THE MATRIX
   1                2

  -1                4

 THE DETERMINANT IS 6
```

```
FOR THE MATRIX
  2              -2

  4              -4

THE DETERMINANT IS Ø

OUT OF DATA AT LINE 2Ø
```

In executing the MAT READ and MAT PRINT operations, BASIC passes across the rows of matrix A, as is customary in algebra. 10 DIM A(2,2) is a <u>dimension</u> statement that tells the computer how big a matrix A is. Without this statement, BASIC would not know how many elements to input for A in line 2Ø. The dimensions of every matrix used in a program must be listed in a DIM statement.

Here are some MAT commands available on most systems.

Command	Explanation
1. MAT READ A,B,C, · · ·	Read the matrices A,B,C, · · ·, where all elements of A are read from DATA first, in row–wise sequence, then all elements of B, then C, · · · .
2. MAT PRINT A,B;C · · ·	Print the matrices A,B,C, · · · with A and C in regular format (one entry per zone per line) but matrix B closely packed (because of the semicolon).
3. MAT C = A + B	Add the matrices A and B and store the result as matrix C. A and B must have the same dimensions.
4. MAT C = A * B	Multiply the matrix A times the matrix B and store the result as matrix C. A and B must be conformable.
5. MAT C = INV(A)	Form the multiplicative inverse of the square matrix A (if the inverse exists) and store it as C.

Exercises <small>See key.</small>

Write a program for Exercises 1-5. Use a variety of DATA sets.

1. For the system $\begin{cases} Ax + By = C \\ Dx + Ey = F \end{cases}$, read the coefficients A,B,C,D,E, and F. Determine whether the system is consistent or inconsistent.

2. Determine whether the system in Exercise 1 is dependent or independent.

3. For the system given in Exercise 1, read the coefficients. Solve the system or print NO UNIQUE SOLUTION.

4. Given two linear inequalities and the coordinates of a point, decide whether the point lies in the common solution set of the inequalities.

5. Read the elements of a 3 × 3 matrix M. Print M and its determinant.

15-6 Sequences and Series

Computer work with sequences and series uses the FOR-NEXT loop introduced in Program 5.

Example

Given the first term of an arithmetic sequence and the common difference, print the first N terms, where N is read from DATA.

PROGRAM 7

```
1Ø  READ A,D,N
2Ø  PRINT A;
3Ø  FOR I = 2 TO N
4Ø  LET A = A + D
5Ø  PRINT A;
6Ø  NEXT I
7Ø  PRINT
8Ø  GO TO 1Ø
9Ø  DATA 5,3,1Ø,6,-.5,8,-12,3.5,15
1ØØ  END
```

```
READY

RUN
AP       Ø8:12 AM           Ø7-JUN-76
  5   8   11   14   17   2Ø   23   26   29   32
  6  5.5   5  4.5   4  3.5   3  2.5
-12 -8.5 -5 -1.5 2 5.5 9 12.5 16 19.5 23 26.5 3Ø 33.5 37
OUT OF DATA AT LINE 1Ø

READY
```

Program 7 uses several new features. Lines 2Ø and 5Ø use a semicolon after PRINT A to keep the terminal on the same line. This approach avoids wasting space by printing the terms one-per-line. Statement 7Ø is used to move the terminal off the line before the next DATA is read.

Statement 4Ø, LET A = A + D, would be contradictory if it were an algebraic equation, but it is not. The computer executes the command as follows:

1. Begin with the right side of the =. The current values of A and D are taken from memory and added.
2. This sum is stored back in location A since A appears on the left side of the =.

Think of the = in a LET statement as a left-pointing arrow. Thus, LET A = A + D has the effect A ← A + D. This statement causes location A to take on, in order, the successive values of the terms of the sequence.

The variable I in Program 7 functions as a <u>counter</u>. It counts the number of terms printed.

Exercises See key.

1. Change Program 7 so that only the Nth term is printed.

   Write programs for Exercises 2-10. Given the first term, A, and the common difference, D, of an arithmetic sequence:
2. Print the sum of the first N terms, where N is read from DATA.
3. Print the first N partial sums. Use the statement LET S = S + A to accumulate the sum in location S.

Read the first term A *and the ratio* R *(R ≠ 1) of a geometric sequence. Also, read a positive integer* N.

4. Print the first N terms.

5. Print only the Nth term.

6. Print the first N partial sums.

7. Print only the Nth partial sum.

8. Given the first term A and the ratio R of a geometric series, print the infinite sum of the geometric series if such a sum exists.

9. Accept two real numbers A and B and a positive integer N. Print the N arithmetic means between A and B.

10. Read two positive real numbers A and B and a positive integer N. Print the N geometric means between A and B.

15-7 Permutations and Combinations

Example 1   Write a program to compute N! where N (a nonnegative integer) is read from DATA.

PROGRAM 8

```
1Ø  READ N
2Ø  LET F = 1
3Ø  FOR I = 2 TO N
4Ø  LET F = F * I
5Ø  NEXT I
6Ø  PRINT N;" FACTORIAL =";F
7Ø  GO TO 1Ø
8Ø  DATA 5,Ø,1,8
9Ø  END
```

READY

```
RUN
FACTRL   11:Ø6 AM      Ø1-JUN-76
  5 FACTORIAL = 12Ø
  Ø FACTORIAL = 1
  1 FACTORIAL = 1
  8 FACTORIAL = 4Ø32Ø
OUT OF DATA AT LINE 1Ø

READY
```

The computer can simulate chance events if the RND (random) function of BASIC is used. RND produces a "random" number between Ø and 1. As an example of how the RND function can be used, consider the next program.

Example 2

Simulate tossing a coin one thousand times. Count the number of heads and the number of tails.

PROGRAM 9

```
1Ø RANDOMIZE
2Ø LET H = Ø
3Ø FOR I = 1 TO 1ØØØ
4Ø IF RND(I) > .5 THEN 6Ø
5Ø LET H = H + 1
6Ø NEXT I
7Ø PRINT H;"HEADS AND";1ØØØ-H;"TAILS"
8Ø END

READY

RUN
COIN   11:16 AM      Ø1-JUN-76
 5Ø2 HEADS AND 498 TAILS

READY

RUN
COIN   11:16 AM      Ø1-JUN-76
 512 HEADS AND 488 TAILS
```

Note that Program 9 needs no READ or DATA statements, since the RND function generates its own data. Secondly, the RANDOMIZE statement is used to start the "random number generator," a preprogrammed routine BASIC uses to produce random numbers. Thirdly, the "coin" comes up "heads" when the random number generated is less than .5. ("Heads" could just as easily have been numbers greater than .5.) Since the random number is just as likely to be less than .5 as greater than .5, this breakdown corresponds to the probabilities for the physical coin-tossing. Statement 5Ø is used to count the number of heads. The number of tails is obtained in line 7Ø by subtracting H from 1ØØØ.

Exercises   See key.

Write programs for the following.

a 1. Modify Program 8 to print N! for N = Ø,1,2,3, ···, 1Ø. The output should be a table with two columns, N and N FACTORIAL.

b 2. Compute the number of permutations of N things taken R at a time.

3. Repeat Exercise 2, but assume that P of the things are alike.

4. Calculate the number of combinations of N things taken R at a time.

15-8 Trigonometry

BASIC includes several "built-in" trigonometric functions.

Function	Meaning
SIN(X)	Gives the sine of x, where x is a radian measure.
COS(X)	Gives the cosine of x, where x is a radian measure.
TAN(X)	Gives the tangent of x, where x is a radian measure.
ATN(X)	Gives, in radians, the principal angle whose tangent is x.

In each case 'X' may be any valid arithmetic expression.

A good computer application is the solution of triangles.

Example

Given the lengths of two sides of a triangle and the degree measure of the included angle, find the remaining parts of the triangle.

The figure on the right was used as a reference in writing this program. A, B, and C represent the lengths of the sides; A1, B1, and C1 are the measures of the angles.

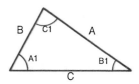

PROGRAM 10

```
1Ø READ B,C,A1
2Ø LET R1 = A1*3.14159/18Ø
3Ø LET A = SQR(B↑2+C↑2-2*B*C*COS(R1))
4Ø IF C < B THEN 12Ø
5Ø LET S = B*SIN(R1)/A
6Ø LET D = SQR(1 - S↑2)
7Ø LET R2 = ATN(S/D)
8Ø LET B1 = R2*18Ø/3.14159
9Ø LET C1 = 18Ø - (A1 + B1)
1ØØ PRINT "SIDES ARE:";A;B;C
1Ø5 PRINT "ANGLES ARE:";A1;B1;C1
1Ø7 PRINT
11Ø GO TO 1Ø
12Ø LET S = C*SIN(R1)/A
13Ø LET D = SQR(1 - S↑2)
14Ø LET R2 = ATN(S/D)
15Ø LET C1 = R2*18Ø/3.14159
16Ø LET B1 = 18Ø - (A1 + C1)
17Ø GO TO 1ØØ
18Ø DATA 5,8,35,6,9,49.33,7,5,152
19Ø END
```

Here is the output from Program 10.

```
SIDES ARE: 4.84436   5   8
ANGLES ARE: 35   36.2994   1Ø8.7Ø1
```

```
SIDES ARE: 6.82761   6   9
ANGLES ARE: 49.33   41.8004   88.8696

SIDES ARE: 11.6536   7   5
ANGLES ARE: 152   16.3795   11.6205

OUT OF DATA AT LINE 10
```

Exercises See key.

a
1. Given the coordinates of a point P, print the values of the six trigonometric functions of the angle with P on its terminal side. Note: It is illegal to write: LET SIN(X) = A/C. A function may not appear on the left side of the = in a LET statement. Instead use S for SIN(X), C for COS(X), T for TAN(X), etc.

2. Read two parts of a right triangle. (Assume that the right angle is an additional known part.) Solve the triangle. Four cases are possible: HA, LA, HL, LL.

3. Given A and sin A, B and sin B, and C where A < C < B. Use interpolation to find sin C.

4. Given the measure X of an angle in standard position, where −360° < X < 360°, print the number of the quadrant in which the terminal side of X lies or the axis on which the terminal side lies.

b
5. Write programs similar to Program 10 to solve the other cases: SSS, ASA, SAA, SSA.

6. Given the lengths of three sides of a triangle use Hero's Formula to compute the area of the triangle. Hero's Formula is

$$\text{Area} = \sqrt{s(s-a)(s-b)(s-c)}$$

where a, b, and c are the lengths of the sides and s is the "semiperimeter" (half the perimeter).

Answers to Review of Algebra One

Diagnostic Test 1 **1.** e **2. a.** False **b.** True **c.** True **d.** True **3.** 1-c; 2-d; 3-b; 4-e; 5-a **4.** Commutative postulate **5.** Associative postulate **6.** Distributive postulate **7. b;** the correct answer is the distributive postulate.

Review Unit 1 **R-2: a.** True **b.** True **c.** True **R-3: A:** $-\dfrac{25}{6}$ **B:** $-\dfrac{3}{1}$ **C:** $-\dfrac{9}{4}$ **D:** $\dfrac{0}{1}$ **E:** $\dfrac{3}{1}$

R-4: a. Rational **b.** Rational **c.** Rational **d.** Irrational **R-5: a.** Yes **b.** No **c.** Yes **d.** Yes **e.** Yes **R-6: a.** True **b.** True **c.** False **d.** True **R-7: a.** True **b.** False **c.** True **d.** False **R-8: a.** True **b.** False; $\dfrac{1}{3} = 0.333\cdots$ **c.** False **d.** True **e.** True

R-9: a. Associative postulate for multiplication **b.** Commutative postulate for multiplication **c.** Associative postulate for addition **d.** Commutative postulate for addition **e.** Closure postulate for addition **R-10: a.** True **b.** True **c.** True **d.** True **e.** True **R-11: a.** Distributive postulate **b.** Additive inverse postulate **c.** Multiplicative identity postulate **d.** Additive identity postulate **e.** Multiplicative inverse postulate **f.** Additive inverse postulate **R-12: a.** Additive inverse postulate **b.** Distributive postulate **c.** Commutative postulate for multiplication **d.** Associative postulate for multiplication **e.** Multiplicative inverse postulate **f.** Multiplicative identity postulate

Mastery Test 1 **1.** d **2.** e **3.** a **4.** c **5.** f **6.** b **13.** Commutative postulate for addition **14.** Commutative postulate for multiplication **15.** Additive identity postulate **16.** Multiplicative identity postulate **17.** Associative postulate for addition **18.** Associative postulate for multiplication **19.** Multiplicative inverse postulate **20.** Distributive postulate **21.** Additive inverse postulate **22.** Closure postulate for multiplication

Diagnostic Test 2 **1.** b **2.** d **3.** c **4.** d **5.** b **6.** c **7.** a, c **8.** c **9.** c **10.** d **11.** d

Review Unit 2 **R-1: a.** −10 **b.** 5 **c.** −6.5 **d.** 0 **R-2: a.** 11 **b.** $-\dfrac{4}{8}$, or $-\dfrac{1}{2}$ **c.** 33 **d.** −15.2

R-3: a. 7 **b.** −5 **c.** $\dfrac{2}{8}$, or $\dfrac{1}{4}$ **d.** −72.8 **R-4: a.** −5 **b.** 11.2 **c.** −8 **d.** 1

R-5: a. −10 **b.** $\dfrac{5}{7}$ **c.** 5.1 **d.** 7 **R-6: a.** −10 **b.** $-\dfrac{1}{2}$ **c.** 7 **d.** 1.17 **R-7: a.** 16

b. $-\dfrac{3}{16}$ **c.** 40 **d.** −25.50 **R-8: a.** > **b.** < **c.** < **d.** > **e.** = **R-9: a.** −7 **b.** −5

c. 0.9   d. 3   **R-10: a.** 4; 0; -6 **b.** 2; -4; -13 **c.** 4; 0; 9   **d.** 0; 0; 15   **R-11: a.** $x \neq 0$
b. $x \neq 2$ **c.** $x \neq -4$ **d.** $x \neq 3$, $x \neq -3$ **R-12: a.** Equivalent   **b.** Not equivalent
c. Equivalent   **d.** Equivalent   **R-13: a.** Addition postulate   **b.** Multiplication
postulate   **c.** Addition postulate   **d.** Multiplication postulate   **e.** Multiplication
postulate   **R-14: a.** {4}   **b.** {-13}   **c.** {4}   **d.** {-33}   **R-15: a.** {10}   **b.** {2}   **c.** {12}
d. {3.9}   **R-16: a.** {5}   **b.** $\left\{\dfrac{28}{5}\right\}$ **c.** {-4}   **d.** {3}   **R-17: a.** {18}   **b.** {64}   **c.** {4.8}
d. {85}   **R-18: a.** {7}   **b.** $\left\{-\dfrac{33}{4}\right\}$ **c.** {36}   **d.** {-40}   **R-19: a.** $\{b + a\}$ **b.** $\left\{\dfrac{A}{b}\right\}$ **c.** $\{ab\}$
d. $\left\{\dfrac{p - 2\ell}{2}\right\}$ **R-20: a.** $n > -1$ **b.** $x < -3$ **c.** $n < -4$ **d.** $x < -6$
R-21: a. $\{n: n > -2\}$ **b.** $\{n: n > 2\}$ **c.** $\{x: x < -3\}$ **d.** $\{a: a < 1\}$

Mastery
Test 2
1. 9   **2.** 6   **3.** 0   **4.** -1 **5.** 2   **6.** -16 **7.** 2.1   **8.** -9 **9.** 20   **10.** -7 **11.** 11   **12.** 8
13. -2 **14.** 3   **15.** 0.62   **16.** -2.84 **17.** $-7\frac{1}{2}$ **18.** 0.32   **19.** -32 **20.** 15   **21.** -14
22. $\dfrac{3}{8}$ **23.** 0   **24.** 12   **25.** 5   **26.** -8 **27.** -6 **28.** 1   **29.** 0   **30.** -4 **31.** 45   **32.** $-\dfrac{2}{9}$
33. 1.2   **34.** $-7, -5, -1, 3, 9$ **35.** $x \neq \dfrac{9}{2}$ **36. a.** Add -2.   **b.** Add 5.   **c.** Multiply by 2.
d. Multiply by $\dfrac{1}{6}$.   **37.** {24}   **38.** {-21}   **39.** {3}   **40.** {-8}   **41.** {2}   **42.** $\left\{-\dfrac{75}{2}\right\}$
43. $\{c^2 - b^2\}$ **44.** $\left\{\dfrac{p - 2w}{2}\right\}$ **45.** $\{x: x > 9\}$ **46.** $\{n: n < -17\}$ **47.** $\{a: a < -5\}$
48. $\{y: y < 3\}$ **49.** c   **50.** a   **51.** d   **52.** b

Diagnostic
Test 3
1. d   **2.** a   **3.** d   **4.** b   **5.** c   **6.** b   **7.** a   **8.** c   **9.** d   **10.** b

Review
Unit 3
R-1: 2; 1; x squared; x cubed or x to the third power   **R-2: a.** x^8 **b.** x^5 **c.** $\dfrac{1}{x^5}$ **d.** $27x^6$
R-3: a. 3^{10} **b.** 5^4 **c.** 2^{15} **d.** 1   **R-4: a.** coefficient 5, degree 4   **b.** coefficient -3,
degree 6   **c.** coefficient 1, degree 2   **d.** coefficient 8, degree 0   **R-5: a.** binomial
b. trinomial   **c.** monomial   **d.** monomial   **R-6: a.** $9m^3$ **b.** $8b^3 + 5a^2$ **c.** $3x^2y - 2xy^2$
d. $-11x + 8y$ **R-7: a.** $4x^2 - 4x + 5$ **b.** $x^2 - 9x + 11$ **c.** $-4b^3 - 6b^2 + 7b - 4$
d. $11x^3 - 2x^2 + 2x - 2$ **R-8: a.** $14x^4$ **b.** $-6a^3b^3$ **c.** $12b^3$ **d.** $-2y^4$ **R-9: a.** $18x^2 - 9x$
b. $2x^2y - 3xy^2$ **c.** $-28a^3 + 12a^2 - 20a$ **d.** $-2a^3x + 14a^2x^2 - 6ax^3$ **R-10: a.** $x^2 + 7x + 10$
b. $x^2 + 4x + 3$ **c.** $m^2 - 9$ **d.** $2c^2 + 5c + 3$ **R-11: a.** $a^2 + 4a + 4$ **b.** $b^2 - 6b + 9$
c. $25 - 10x + x^2$ **d.** $9y^2 - 6y + 1$ **R-12: a.** y^3 **b.** $6x^4$ **c.** $\dfrac{1}{n^5}$ **d.** $-\dfrac{8m^4}{n^3}$ **R-13: a.** $x + 5$
b. $ab^2 - b$ **c.** $3x^3 - 4x^2 + x$ **d.** $4m^2 - 2mn - 3$ **R-14: a.** $x + 4$ **b.** $3a + 2$, $R - 10$
c. $x + 2$ **d.** $2y + 1$, R 12

Mastery
Test 3
1. x^9 **2.** a^7 **3.** n^3 **4.** $\dfrac{1}{y^4}$ **5.** x^{10} **6.** x^{15} **7.** $4x^6$ **8.** $-27a^6$ **9.** $16x^8y^4$ **10.** 4
11. 2^3, or 8   **12.** 3^{12} **13.** $\dfrac{1}{4^6}$ **14.** 1   **15.** $17y$ **16.** $6x + 6y$ **17.** coefficient 3, degree 4
18. coefficient -1, degree 5   **19.** trinomial   **20.** monomial   **21.** monomial
22. binomial   **23.** $7x + 9$ **24.** $5a - 8$ **25.** $-x^2 + 3x + 7$ **26.** $3y^2 - 7y - 3$ **27.** $-10x^7$

28. $72y^5$ **29.** $-8x^4y^4$ **30.** $3x^2 - 15x$ **31.** $4y^5 - 12y^3 + 16y^2$ **32.** $x^2 + 5x + 6$
33. $n^2 + 5n - 14$ **34.** $y^2 - 64$ **35.** $2a^2 + 11a + 12$ **36.** $3x^2 - x - 10$ **37.** $n^2 + 8n + 16$
38. $y^2 - 4y + 4$ **39.** $4m^2 + 4m + 1$ **40.** $9a^2 - 12a + 4$ **41.** $4x^6$ **42.** $-\dfrac{8}{n^6}$ **43.** $\dfrac{a^3b}{3}$
44. $-\dfrac{5x^5}{y}$ **45.** $x - 7$ **46.** $m^2 - 2m + 3$ **47.** $x + 5$ **48.** $2y + 1$, R 2

1. b   **2.** d   **3.** c   **4.** c   **5.** c   **6.** b   **7.** a   **8.** d   **9.** b   **10.** a

R-1: a. $2(x + 5y)$ **b.** $5(c - 6)$ **c.** $a(b + c)$ **d.** $3(x^2 - 3x + 5)$ **R-2:** c
R-3: a. $(a + b)(2 - x)$ **b.** $(4 - b)(a + c)$ **c.** $(x + y)(m - n)$ **d.** $(3a - 2b)(x + y)$
R-4: a. $(c + d)(w + a)$ **b.** $(b + c)(a + 2)$ **c.** $(x - 5)(5 + a)$ **d.** $(a^2 + 1)(a - 1)$
R-5: a. $(x + 4)(x - 4)$ **b.** $(m + n)(m - n)$ **c.** $(2a + b)(2a - b)$ **d.** prime
R-6: a. $5(x + y)(x - y)$ **b.** $4(x + 2)(x - 2)$ **c.** Prime   **d.** $3(2c + 3)(2c - 3)$
R-7: a. $(x + 4)(x + 3)$ **b.** $2(c + 3)(c + 2)$ **c.** $(x - 7)(x - 3)$ **d.** $3(n - 2)(n - 1)$
R-8: a. $(2x + 1)(x + 4)$ **b.** $(3x - 2)(2x - 3)$ **c.** $(4n + 5)(n - 4)$ **d.** $(6a - 1)(a - 3)$
R-9: a, b, d   **R-10: a.** $(x + 2)^2$ **b.** $(x - 2)^2$ **c.** $(a - 7)^2$ **d.** $(b + 5)^2$

1. A; 5; monomial   **2.** B   **3.** D   **4.** A; $-3a$; monomial   **5.** A; $c + 2$; binomial   **6.** C
7. $2(4n - 1)$ **8.** $3x(x + 5)$ **9.** $(a + b)(6 - x)$ **10.** $(m - n)(x - y)$
11. $(y - 2)(5 + x)$ **12.** $(b + f)(a + c)$ **13.** $(3m + 1)(3m - 1)$ **14.** $(y + 3)(y - 3)$
15. $(2x + 1)(2x - 1)$ **16.** $3(n + 2)(n - 2)$ **17.** $(a + 3)(a + 2)$ **18.** $(y - 8)(y + 3)$
19. $(2n + 1)(n + 6)$ **20.** $(3x + 4)(x - 2)$

Answers to Try These and Chapter Tests

Chapter 1

Page 4 **1.** T **2.** F **3.** F **4.** F **5.** T **6.** F **7.** F **8.** T

Page 8 **1.** 11 **2.** $6|x|$ **3.** $10|x|$ **4.** $5|x^5|$

Page 11 **1.** $\sqrt{15}$ **2.** $30\sqrt{6}$ **3.** $\dfrac{\sqrt{6}}{4}$ **4.** $\frac{1}{6}\sqrt{210}$ **5.** $\dfrac{\sqrt{3}}{4}$

Page 14 **1.** $7\sqrt{7}$ **2.** $16\sqrt{3}$ **3.** $6\sqrt{2}$ **4.** $2\sqrt{7}$ **5.** $8\sqrt{3}$ **6.** $\dfrac{3\sqrt{2}}{2}$

Page 18 **1.** $5i$ **2.** $i\sqrt{3}$ **3.** $2i\sqrt{2}$ **4.** $8i$ **5.** $-i$ **6.** -6 **7.** $\sqrt{2}$ **8.** $\dfrac{\sqrt{6}}{2}$

Page 21 **1.** $2+\sqrt{3}i$ **2.** $0+4i$ **3.** $-1+0i$ **4.** $1+(-1)i$ **5.** $0+(-1)i$ **6.** $-1+(-1)i$ **7.** $\sqrt{5}+\sqrt{5}i$ **8.** $1+1i$

Page 24 **1.** $7+8i$ **2.** $-4+7i$ **3.** $-13+2i$ **4.** $-21+5i$ **5.** $2-6i$ **6.** $2+8i$

Page 27 **1.** $-7+22i$ **2.** $82-39i$ **3.** $26-87i$ **4.** $4+9i$ **5.** $2\frac{2}{5}-\frac{1}{5}i$ **6.** $(-28+3\sqrt{2})+(4\sqrt{3}+7\sqrt{6})i$

Page 31 **1.** $\frac{2}{5}-\frac{1}{5}i$ **2.** $0-\frac{5}{3}i$ **3.** $0-1i$

Chapter Test **1.** R **2.** The set of complex numbers **3.** $2+6i$ **4.** $\frac{3}{13}-\frac{2}{13}i$ **5.** -7 **6.** T **7.** T **8.** F
Page 36 **9.** T **10.** T **11.** $6|y|$ **12.** $4\sqrt{3}$ **13.** $3\sqrt{30}$ **14.** $-\sqrt{3}$ **15.** $8\sqrt{2}-3\sqrt{3}$ **16.** 1 **17.** $-3+3i$ **18.** $1+3i$ **19.** $-5-14i$ **20.** $-\frac{1}{2}+\frac{5}{2}i$

Chapter 2

Page 39 **1.** Polynomial over the integers **2.** Not a polynomial **3.** Not a polynomial **4.** Polynomial over the complex numbers **5.** Polynomial over the real numbers **6.** Polynomial over the integers

Page 42 **1.** $-2x+7$ **2.** $4\sqrt{3}y^3-2\sqrt{7}y^2+5y$ **3.** $-2x+20$ **4.** $(5i-6)z^2$ **5.** $3c^3-8c^2+10c+4$ **6.** $4x^3-5x^2+8x$

Page 47 **1.** $-6x^3y^4$ **2.** $63c-42cd$ **3.** $6x^2-x-2$ **4.** x^2+ix+6

Page 51 **1.** T **2.** T **3.** T **4.** T **5.** F **6.** F

Page 55   **1.** $(x+3)(x+5)$ **2.** $(2n-1)(n+4)$ **3.** $(a+2)(3a+1)$ **4.** $(3y-1)(4y-1)$ **5.** $(2c-3)(5c+4)$ **6.** $(w-6)(3w+2)$

Page 57   **1.** Prime   **2.** $5(z^2+1)$ **3.** $(3y+\sqrt{10})(3y-\sqrt{10})$ **4.** $(x+3i)(x-3i)$ **5.** $6(x+2i)(x-2i)$ **6.** $5(a+i)(a-i)$

Page 61   **1.** x^3 **2.** $-a^3$ **3.** $\dfrac{1}{m^5}$ **4.** $-3a^4$ **5.** $x+3$ **6.** $a-b$

Page 67   **1.** Yes   **2.** No   **3.** Yes   **4.** No   **5.** No   **6.** Yes

Page 73   **1.** $\{-7, 9\}$ **2.** $\{-3, 3\}$ **3.** $\{-3i, 3i\}$ **4.** $\{-\frac{1}{4}, \frac{1}{4}\}$ **5.** $\{-\frac{1}{4}i, \frac{1}{4}i\}$ **6.** $\{-\frac{1}{2}, \frac{5}{3}\}$

1. Since $a+b$ is not a factor of $z+2(a+b)$, the expression cannot be simplified.
2. Since factors of x^2+y^2 do not include $x+y$, the expression cannot be simplified.
3. Since $a+b$ is not a factor of $a+b+c$, the expression cannot be simplified.
4. The answer should be $\dfrac{1}{x+y}$.   **5.** Since $a+b$ is not a factor of $2a+b$, the expression cannot be simplified.   **6.** Since a^2 is added to x^2 and z^2 (not multiplied by them) the expression cannot be simplified.   **7.** The answer should be 1.   **8.** Since x is not a factor of $x+y$, the expression cannot be simplified.   **9.** The answer should be -1.
10. The answer should be $\dfrac{-1}{a+b}$.

Page 76   **1.** $\dfrac{25}{4}$ **2.** $\dfrac{x-3}{6}$ **3.** $\dfrac{3}{b^2}$ **4.** $\dfrac{9x-15}{2}$ **5.** $\dfrac{9b^2}{8}$ **6.** $(y-3)(y-4)=y^2-7y+12$

Page 79   **1.** $\dfrac{4}{3}$ **2.** $\dfrac{14}{27c^2}$ **3.** $\dfrac{5}{2(x+3)}$ **4.** $\dfrac{y+1}{y^2}$

Page 82   **1.** $\dfrac{4x}{2}$, or $2x$ **2.** $\dfrac{-22}{2}$, or -11 **3.** $\dfrac{2x-3y}{x+y}$

Page 86   **1.** $\dfrac{10a}{15a^2}, \dfrac{9}{15a^2}$ **2.** $\dfrac{4a(a+b)}{12a^4b^2}, \dfrac{15b}{12a^4b^2}$ **3.** $\dfrac{5(x+2)}{20}, \dfrac{4(x-5)}{20}$ **4.** $\dfrac{3(x-2)}{3(x+2)^2}, \dfrac{5(x+2)}{3(x+2)^2}$ **5.** $\dfrac{(2x-3)(2x+5)}{(2x-5)(2x+5)}, \dfrac{25x^2}{(2x-5)(2x+5)}$ **6.** $\dfrac{-2(x+1)}{(x-1)(x+1)}, \dfrac{2x}{(x-1)(x+1)}$

Page 93   **1.** $20x^3y^3$ **2.** $-20x^3y^3$ **3.** $160x^3y^3$ **4.** $-\frac{5}{2}x^3y^3$

Chapter Test
Page 100
1. $-3x^2-3x-7$ **2.** $m^4-2m^3+3m^2-2m+6$ **3.** $(3x-12)(3x+12)=9(x-4)(x+4)$ **4.** $(5m+2)(3m+7)$ **5.** $2(a+3)(a^2-3a+9)$ **6.** $(6s+5t)^2$ **7.** $2(y-5)^2$ **8.** $(n-5)(n^2+5n+25)$ **9.** $(2x-\sqrt{5})(2x+\sqrt{5})$ **10.** $(a-b)(a+b)(a+bi)(a-bi)$ **11.** 37   **12.** Yes   **13.** $2xy^2+4y-6$ **14.** $2y^2-5y-3$ **15.** $\dfrac{x+2}{x-2}$ **16.** $\dfrac{5a^2}{a+b}$ **17.** $\dfrac{-2n+5m}{n(m-n)}$ **18.** $\dfrac{c+d}{cd}$ **19.** $a^4-8a^3b+24a^2b^2-32ab^3+16b^4$ **20.** $21 \cdot 32 \cdot m^5n^4$, or $672m^5n^4$

Chapter 3

Page 103   **1.** $\{4\}$ **2.** $\{-7\}$ **3.** $\{-6\}$ **4.** $\{-4\}$ **5.** $\{-3\}$ **6.** $\{10\}$

Page 106   **1.** 6   **2.** 12   **3.** $7a$ **4.** $9m$ **5.** $3y$ **6.** $4c$

1. $x = \dfrac{2ab}{a+b}$, $a \neq -b$ **2.** $x = \dfrac{a^3 - 2a^2 - 48}{a - 8}$, $a \neq 8$ **3.** $x = \dfrac{-2}{a+b-c}$, $a+b-c \neq 0$

4. $x = \dfrac{ab}{c}$, $c \neq 0$

Page 113 **1.** $x = 2$ or $x = -2$ **2.** $3y = 9$ or $3y = -9$ **3.** $n + 7 = 3$ or $n + 7 = -3$
4. $n - 4 = 2$ or $n - 4 = -2$ **5.** $\{3, -2\}$ **6.** $\{14, -18\}$

Page 117 **1.** Same **2.** Same **3.** Reverse **4.** Reverse

Page 121 **1.** $\frac{1}{6}t = A$ **2.** $\frac{1}{5}t = A$ **3.** $\frac{1}{5}t + \frac{1}{4}t = A$ **4.** $\frac{1}{4}t + \frac{1}{5}t + \frac{1}{6}t = A$ **5.** $\frac{1}{4}t + \frac{1}{5}t + \frac{1}{6}t = 2$

Page 128 **1.** $\{x: x > -4\} \cap \{x: x < 4\}$ **2.** $\{y: y < -2\} \cup \{y: y > 2\}$
3. $\{c: c \geq 2\} \cap \{c: c \leq 8\}$ **4.** $\{n: n \leq -2\} \cup \{n: n \geq 14\}$

Chapter Test **1.** -7 **2.** -1 **3.** $\dfrac{1}{2}$ **4.** $\dfrac{5}{2}$ **5.** 8 **6.** 5 **7.** 3 **8.** 4 **9.** -5 **10.** 15 **11.** $\{3, -10\}$

Page 132 **12.** $\{3, \dfrac{3}{4}\}$ **13.** $r = s + \dfrac{t}{a}$ **14.** $a = \dfrac{S(r-1)}{r^n - 1}$ **15.** $x > -2$ **16.** $y \leq 5$ **17.** $w = 3$, $\ell = 5$

18. 7 hours

Chapter 4

Pages 134-135 **1.** I, III, IV, II **2.** 4, 6 **3.** I, III, IV, II **4.** y axis, x axis, x axis, y axis **5.** (0, 0)

Page 138 **1.** 5 **2.** 10 **3.** $10\sqrt{2}$ **4.** $\sqrt{(a-3)^2 + (b-3)^2}$

Page 151 **1.** Parallel, $-\dfrac{1}{6}$; perpendicular, 6 **2.** Parallel, $-\dfrac{5}{3}$; perpendicular, $\dfrac{3}{5}$

3. Parallel, $\dfrac{4}{5}$; perpendicular, $-\dfrac{5}{4}$ **4.** Parallel, $\dfrac{b}{a}$; perpendicular, $-\dfrac{a}{b}$

Page 156 **1.** $y = -3x + 5$ **2.** $y = -\frac{3}{5}x$ **3.** $y = 3x - 4$ **4.** $y = 3x - 5$; $m = 3$; y intercept: (0, -5)
5. $y = x$; $m = 1$; y intercept: (0, 0) **6.** $y = -\frac{1}{2}x + \frac{5}{2}$; $m = -\frac{1}{2}$; y intercept: (0, $\frac{5}{2}$)

Page 160 **1.** $x = -2$ **2.** $y = 3$ **3.** $y \geq 3$ **4.** $x < 0$ and $y > 0$ **5.** $x < 0$ and $y < 0$
6. The set of all points in the coordinate plane that are at a distance of 3 units or more below the x axis. **7.** The set of all points in the coordinate plane that are 3 units or more to the right of the y axis. **8.** The set of all points in the coordinate plane that are 3 units or more below the x axis and 3 units or more to the right of the y axis.

Page 164 **1.** $A(1, 1)$, $B(0, 6)$, $C(-6, 2)$, $D(-1, -2)$, $E(7, -3)$ **2.** $x = 3$ **3.** $y = 5$
4. $x = 6$, $y = -2$ **5.** $x = -2$, $y = -3$ **6.** $x = 0$, $y = 0$ **7.** $x = 3$, $y = -4$ **8.** $y = 6$
9. $x = -1$

Page 168 **1.** D **2.** L **3.** L **4.** L, D, E **5.** D **6.** L

1. 2 **2.** 3 **3.** (0, 1) **4.** Complex **5.** Real; imaginary **6.** $4\sqrt{5}$ **7.** (1, 4) **8.** -1
9. 2 **10.** $\dfrac{2}{3}$ **11.** $y = 2x + 2$ **12.** $y = 2x - 9$ **13.** $y = -3x + 5$ **14.** $\overline{AB} = 1 + 3i$,
$\overline{OC} = -3 + i$, $\overline{DE} = -1 - 5i$ **15.** A line that contains (0, 0) and (1, 2) **16.** The
half-plane above the line defined by $y = 2x - 6$. The line is not included.

Chapter 5

1. D: {1, 2, 5, 8}; R: {4, 3, 6, 13} **2.** D: {4, 6, 2, -2}; R: {3, -1, -3} **3.** D: {-1, 2};
R: {1, 4, 7, 9} **4.** D: {-2, 0, 5}: R: {0, 1, 3, 6}

1. Function **2.** Not a function; the ordered pairs (2, 1) and (2, 7) have the same
first number paired with different second members. **3.** Function **4.** Not a function;
the ordered pairs (-1, 2) and (-1, 3) have the same first members paired with different
second members. **5.** 6; 30; -26 **6.** 8; -4; -19

1. {3, 5, 7, 9, 11} **2.** {0, 1, 2, 3} **3.** {0, 1, 4, 9} **4.** {-3, -2, -1, 0, 1, 2, 3}
5. $\left\{-3, -2, -\dfrac{1}{3}, \dfrac{1}{5}, 1\right\}$

1. $\dfrac{3}{2}$ **2.** $-\dfrac{1}{5}$ **3.** 2, 3 **4.** 0, -2, 2

1. $f = \{(1, 3), (2, 5), (3, 7)\}$; $g = \{(3, 7), (5, 5), (7, 3)\}$; $g(f) = \{(1, 7), (2, 5), (3, 3)\}$
2. $f = \{(1, 4), (2, 5), (3, 4)\}$; $g = \{(4, 6), (5, 7)\}$; $g(f) = \{(1, 6), (2, 7), (3, 6)\}$

1. {(1, 1), (3, 2), (4, 3), (5, 4)}; function **2.** {(2, 0), (2, 2), (4, 3), (5, 1)};
not a function

1. A set of ordered pairs **2.** Identity **3.** f^{-1} **4.** {2, 3} **5.** Linear **6.** {7, 6, 5, 4, 3}
7. $f(-2) = -2$; $f(1) = -\dfrac{1}{2}$ **8.** Answers will vary. **9.** The graph consists of the set of
points, {(-2, -5), (-1, -4), (0, -3), (2, -1), (4, 1)}. **10.** $-\dfrac{2}{3}$ **11.** $\dfrac{2}{5}$ **12.** 0, $\dfrac{1}{2}$
13. $g(h) = 6x + 1$ **14.** $h^{-1}(x) = \frac{1}{3}x + \frac{2}{3}$

Chapter 6

1. 48 **2.** -20 **3.** 75 **4.** 98

1. L **2.** Q **3.** L **4.** Q **5.** Q **6.** Q

1. U **2.** U **3.** D **4.** D **5.** U **6.** D

1. f_1, f_4, f_5; f_2, f_6; **2.** f_1, f_3, f_5, and f_6 open upward; f_2 and f_4 open downward
3. f_1: (0, 0); f_2: (0, 1); f_3: (0, 0); f_4: (0, -1); f_5: (0, 6); f_6: (0, 4)

1. $x = 0$ **2.** $x = \dfrac{7}{2}$ **3.** $x = 2$ **4.** (0, 1): minimum **5.** (0, 4): maximum
6. $\left(\dfrac{1}{4}, -\dfrac{23}{8}\right)$: maximum

1. Minimum of $-\frac{1}{4}$ **2.** Maximum of $2\frac{1}{4}$ **3.** Maximum of $6\frac{1}{4}$ **4.** $(x+4)x = 221$, or $x^2 + 4x = 221$ **5.** $\pi r^2 = 440$

232 **1.** Two **2.** None **3.** One **4.** $\{1\}$; $-(1)^2 + 2(1) - 1 = 0$

ge 235 **1.** $\{5, -5\}$ **2.** $\{4, -4\}$ **3.** $\{i\sqrt{2}, -i\sqrt{2}\}$ **4.** $\{\sqrt{10}, -\sqrt{10}\}$ **5.** $\{0\}$ **6.** $\{5, 1\}$

'age 240 **1.** $x^2 + 14x + 49$; $(x+7)^2$ **2.** $a^2 - 16a + 64$; $(a-8)^2$ **3.** $x^2 + 12x + 36$; $(x+6)^2$
4. $x^2 + 5x + \dfrac{25}{4}$; $\left(x + \dfrac{5}{2}\right)^2$

Page 242 **1.** $a = 2$, $b = 5$, $c = -6$ **2.** $a = 1$, $b = 2$, $c = 3$ **3.** $a = 5$, $b = 3$, $c = -4$
4. $a = 2$, $b = -5$, $c = -12$ **5.** $a = -1$, $b = 3$, $c = -5$ **6.** $a = 1$, $b = -5$, $c = -14$

Page 247 **1.** 25 **2.** 0 **3.** 40 **4.** Two unequal real roots; one real root; two unequal real roots

Chapter
Test **1.** $x = -\dfrac{b}{2a}$ **2.** $x = \dfrac{-b \pm \sqrt{b^2 - 4ac}}{2a}$ **3.** Downward **4.** Imaginary **5.** $y = 8$

Page 254 **6.** $\{-1 \pm i\sqrt{2}\}$ **7.** $\left\{\dfrac{1}{2}, -3\right\}$ **8.** $\{-3 \pm \sqrt{3}\}$ **9.** $x = 1$ **10.** $(0, 1)$ **11.** $V(1, -1)$

12. 5 and 5 **13.** $k > \dfrac{4}{5}$ or $k < -\dfrac{4}{5}$; $-\dfrac{4}{5} < k < \dfrac{4}{5}$

Chapter 7

Page 257 **1.** No **2.** Yes **3.** No **4.** $\begin{cases} x + y = 14 \\ x - y = 4 \end{cases}$ **5.** $\begin{cases} xy = 6 \\ 2y - x = 1 \end{cases}$

Page 263 (In each exercise, the order of the numbers is the same as the order of the equations.)
1. 2, 1 **2.** 5, 4 **3.** 1, -7 or -1, 7 **4.** 1, -2 or -1, 2 **5.** -2, 3 or 2, -3 **6.** 1, 2

Page 266 **1.** $y = 6 - x$ **2.** $y = -4 - 2x$ **3.** $x = 8 + y$ **4.** $x = 3 - \frac{1}{2}y$

Page 271 **1.** $2x - y = 25$ **2.** $3x + 24 = 2y + 18$ **3.** $5x + 10y$ **4.** $5x + 10y = 750$ **5.** $10t + u$
6. $10u + t$ **7.** $0.3x + 0.04y$ **8.** $0.06x + 0.08y = 370$ and $x + y = 5000$

Page 282 **1.** $\begin{bmatrix} 3 & -2 & 1 & 14 \\ 5 & 3 & -4 & -7 \\ 2 & 2 & 3 & 19 \end{bmatrix}$ **2.** $\begin{bmatrix} 4 & 7 & -2 & 35 \\ 3 & -5 & -4 & 2 \\ -1 & 9 & 6 & -7 \end{bmatrix}$

Chapter
Test **1.** Empty **2.** Dependent **3.** Matrix **4.** $\left\{\left(\dfrac{33}{7}, \dfrac{-55}{7}\right)\right\}$ **5.** $\left\{\left(-\dfrac{4}{3}, \dfrac{1}{2}\right)\right\}$

Page 290 **6.** $\left\{\left(\dfrac{-45}{7}, \dfrac{-68}{7}\right)\right\}$ **7.** The region below the line $2x + 3y = 9$ and above the line
$x - 2y = 8$. This includes the point $(6, -1)$, the point of intersection of the lines, and all
points on each line to the left of $x = 6$. **8.** $\emptyset$ **9.** $\{(1, -2, 0)\}$ **10.** 7; 5

Chapter 8

Page 295 **1.** $\dfrac{1}{9}$ **2.** $\dfrac{1}{16}$ **3.** $\dfrac{1}{4}$ **4.** $5^8 = 390625$ **5.** $\dfrac{1}{125}$ **6.** $\dfrac{1}{2^3} + \dfrac{1}{4^2} = \dfrac{1}{8} + \dfrac{1}{16} = \dfrac{3}{16}$ **7.** $2^6 = 64$

8. $3^{-4} = \dfrac{1}{3^4} = \dfrac{1}{81}$

Page 300 1. $\dfrac{b^3}{a^2}$ 2. $\dfrac{2ac^3}{3bd}$ 3. $\dfrac{(3y)^2}{(2x)^2}$ 4. $\dfrac{2y^2}{3x^2}$ 5. $\dfrac{3y}{x}$ 6. $\dfrac{-y}{x^2}+\dfrac{4}{x}$ 7. a^2-ab 8. $\dfrac{a}{a-b}$

Page 304 1. 5 2. 27 3. -16 4. $\dfrac{1}{8}$ 5. $-\dfrac{1}{5}$ 6. -2 7. $\dfrac{1}{9}$ 8. $-\dfrac{1}{3}$

Page 307 1. $2\sqrt[3]{2}$ 2. $2\sqrt[4]{3}$ 3. $-6\sqrt{3}$ 4. $13\sqrt[3]{4}$ 5. $\dfrac{2\sqrt{2}+3\sqrt{3}}{6}$ 6. $\sqrt[3]{12}$ 7. 2 8. $\sqrt[6]{108}$

9. $\left(\dfrac{8}{25}\right)^{\frac{1}{6}}$

Page 311 1. 9 2. $\emptyset$ 3. 4 4. 9 5. 64 6. 46 7. 17 8. 8

Page 313 1. 7 2. -22 3. $\emptyset$ 4. $\dfrac{5\sqrt{2}}{3}$ 5. $\dfrac{25}{4}$ 6. $\dfrac{1}{9}$

Page 315 1. {5} 2. {4} 3. $\left\{\dfrac{3}{2}\right\}$ 4. $\left\{\dfrac{4}{3}\right\}$ 5. $\{-1\}$ 6. $\{-2\}$

Chapter Test 1. 729 2. 1 3. $\dfrac{1}{5^3}=\dfrac{1}{125}$ 4. 2^8 5. 7.5×10^9; 7.892×10^{-7} 6. $\dfrac{y(3y-4)}{x}$ 7. $x^{\frac{1}{2}}y^{-\frac{1}{2}}$
Page 320 8. $a^{\frac{1}{3}}b^{-\frac{2}{3}}$ 9. $3xyz^{-\frac{3}{4}}$ 10. $m^{\frac{1}{3}}n^{-\frac{1}{2}}$ 11. $\dfrac{27}{8}$ 12. 1 13. $\dfrac{1}{6}$ 14. $\dfrac{1}{8}$ 15. 4 16. {7}

17. $\emptyset$ 18. {3} 19. $\left\{\dfrac{5}{3}\right\}$ 20. $\{-3\}$

Chapter 9

Pages 1. 0.01, 0.1, 1, 3.162, 10, 31.62 2. $\dfrac{1}{9}$, $\dfrac{1}{3}$, 1, 1.732, 3, 5.196, 9 3. $\dfrac{1}{16}$, $\dfrac{1}{4}$, 1, 2, 4, 8, 16,
322-323
32, 64 4. 16, 8, 4, 2, 1, $\dfrac{1}{2}$, $\dfrac{1}{4}$, $\dfrac{1}{8}$, $\dfrac{1}{16}$, $\dfrac{1}{32}$ 5. 9, 3, 1, $\dfrac{1}{3}$, $\dfrac{1}{9}$, $\dfrac{1}{27}$

Page 327 1. 256 2. 16 3. 32 4. 4096 5. 0.8 6. 1.7

Page 330 1. Positive real numbers 2. Real numbers 3. y axis 4. $\log_2 8=3$ 5. $\log_3 9=2$
6. $\log_{10}\dfrac{1}{100}=-2$ 7. $\log_6 216=3$ 8. $\log_4 2=0.5$ 9. $\log_{0.125}0.5=\dfrac{1}{3}$ 10. $2^4=16$

11. $3^3=27$ 12. $8^2=64$ 13. $0.5^2=0.25$ 14. $2^{-3}=\dfrac{1}{8}$ 15. $10^{-3}=0.001$

Page 334 1. .0000 2. .5682 3. .7924 4. .9248 5. .9996 6. 1.8 7. 5.2 8. 7.0 9. 7.76

Page 337 1. $\log M+\log N$ 2. $\log M-\log N$ 3. $a\log M$ 4. $\dfrac{1}{a}\log M$ 5. $\log 36$ 6. $\log 4$

7. $\log 5^2+\log 2^3=\log 200$ 8. $\log\dfrac{1}{2}$ 9. $\log 56$ 10. $\log 24$

Page 340 1. 1 2. 2 3. 0 4. -1 5. 4.9886 6. 1.0899 7. 0.0899 8. $9.0899-10$ 9. 503
10. 95.6 11. 0.753 12. 0.00248

1. $8.0394 - 10; -2$ **2.** $8.7829 - 10; -2$ **3.** $2.5973; 2$ **4.** $8.5556; 8$ **5.** $18.6944 - 20; -2$
6. $25.7193 - 30; -5$ **7.** $3.1929; 3$ **8.** $9.1608 - 10; -1$ **9.** $4.6534 - 5; -1$

47 **1.** 1.7209 **2.** 0.9640 **3.** 2.8878 **4.** -0.8570 **5.** 19.18 **6.** 1.957 **7.** 7437 **8.** .5464

352 **1.** 6.005 **2.** 1.6194 **3.** -1.546 **4.** -6.129

Chapter
Test
Page 356 **1.** 24,100 **2.** 25.7 **3.** 2.16 **4.** 8,500 **5.** $3,710 **6.** $\{-2\}$ **7.** $\{0.941\}$ **8.** $\{4\}$
9. $5 \log x + \log y$ **10.** 2 **11.** $\log_5 625 = 4$ **12.** See page 328.

Chapter 10

Page 360 **1.** $r = 2$; $(0, 0)$ **2.** $r = 5$; $(0, 0)$ **3.** $r = \sqrt{3}$; $(0, 0)$ **4.** $r = 4$; $(2, 3)$ **5.** $r = 7$;
$(-4, 5)$ **6.** $r = 6$; $(1, -3)$ **7.** $x^2 + y^2 = 64$ **8.** $(x-2)^2 + (y \pm 3)^2 = 4$

Page 365 **1.** Ellipse **2.** Ellipse **3.** Circle **4.** Circle **5.** Circle **6.** Ellipse **7.** 4, 2
8. 12, 4 **9.** 12, 4

Page 367 **1.** Circle **2.** Parabola **3.** Ellipse **4.** Parabola **5.** Circle **6.** Parabola

Page 371 **1.** Horizontally; $(3, 0)$, $(-3, 0)$. **2.** Horizontally; $(2, 0)$, $(-2, 0)$. **3.** Vertically;
$(0, 5)$, $(0. -5)$. **4.** Vertically; $(0, 5)$, $(0 -5)$. **5.** Horizontally; $(2, 0)$, $(-2, 0)$.
6. Vertically; $(0, \sqrt{3})$, $(0, -\sqrt{3})$.

Pages
375–376 **1.** Increases. **2.** Is multiplied by 9. **3.** Is multiplied by 4. **4.** Is divided by 2.
5. Decreases. **6.** Increases. **7.** Increases. **8.** Decreases. **9.** One cannot tell.
10. Is multiplied by 12.

Chapter
Test
Page 390 **1.** Circle: center $(0, 0)$, radius: 6 **2.** Rectangular hyperbola; vertices $(\sqrt{5}, -\sqrt{5})$
and $(-\sqrt{5}, \sqrt{5})$. **3.** Ellipse: center $(0, 0)$; intercepts $(4, 0)$, $(-4, 0)$, $(0, 5)$, and
$(0, -5)$. **4.** Hyperbola: center $(0, 0)$; vertices $(5, 0)$ and $(-5, 0)$. **5.** Hyperbola:
center $(0, 0)$; vertices $(\sqrt{6}, 0)$ and $(-\sqrt{6}, 0)$. **6.** Circle: center $(2. -4)$; radius 4.
7. $\{(-2 + \sqrt{21}, -3 + \sqrt{21}), (-2 - \sqrt{21}, -3 - \sqrt{21})\}$ **8.** $\left\{\left(\dfrac{-1 - \sqrt{61}}{3}, \dfrac{7 + \sqrt{61}}{6}\right),\right.$
$\left.\left(\dfrac{-1 + \sqrt{61}}{3}, \dfrac{7 - \sqrt{61}}{6}\right)\right\}$ **9.** $a = \dfrac{k}{b}$ **10.** $x = ky$ **11.** $r = \dfrac{kx \cdot t}{w^2}$ **12.** $a = \dfrac{288}{25}$

Chapter 11

Page 393 **1.** 12, 15, 18 **2.** 5, 7, 9 **3.** 16, 25, 36 **4.** 16, 32, 64

Page 395 **1.** Arithmetic, $d = 4$ **2.** Non–arithmetic **3.** Arithmetic, $d = -3$ **4.** Arithmetic, $d = \dfrac{1}{2}$
5. Arithmetic, $d = -x$ **6.** Arithmetic, $d = x - 1$.

Page 399 **1.** 3 **2.** $\dfrac{1}{4}$ **3.** r **4.** 128 **5.** 9 **6.** 3

Page 403 **1.** 26 **2.** 127 **3.** 32 **4.** 80 **5.** -360

Page 406 **1.** 192 **2.** $-16,384$ **3.** $\dfrac{3}{16}$ **4.** $\dfrac{5}{256}$ **5.** $\dfrac{1}{16}$ **6.** $\dfrac{1}{81}$ **7.** $\dfrac{1}{32,768}$ **8.** $\dfrac{243}{625}$

1. Geometric; $\frac{1}{80}$, $-\frac{1}{160}$, $\frac{1}{320}$ **2.** Arithmetic; 3, $\frac{11}{3}$, $\frac{13}{3}$ **3.** Neither **4.** Geometric;

$-\frac{1}{32}$, $\frac{1}{64}$, $-\frac{1}{128}$ **5.** 35 **6.** 1024 **7.** 1000 **8.** 6, 8, 10 **9.** $-2, \frac{2}{5}$ **10.** $\frac{1}{2}$, $\frac{7}{6}$, $\frac{23}{12}$, $\frac{163}{60}$, $\frac{213}{60}$

11. $-31\frac{1}{4}$

Chapter 12

1. 2 **2.** 720 **3.** 20 **4.** n **5.** 6 **6.** 12

1. 12 **2.** 3 **3.** 6

1. $\frac{1}{3}$ **2.** $\frac{2}{3}$ **3.** $\frac{1}{2}$; $\frac{1}{3}$ **4.** 1

1. 10 **2.** 1680 **3.** $\frac{1}{n}$ **4.** 1 **5.** {(H, H, H), (T, H, H), (H, H, T), (H, T, H), (T, T, H),

(T, H, T), (H, T, T), (T, T, T)}; $\frac{1}{8}$ **6.** 720 **7.** 120 **8.** 56 **9.** 180 **10.** 1 **11.** $\frac{1}{6}$ **12.** $\frac{34}{36}$

13. $\frac{33}{36}$ **14.** $\frac{10}{36}$ **15.** $\binom{5}{0}(2a)^5 + \binom{5}{1}(2a)^4b + \binom{5}{2}(2a)^3b^2 + \binom{5}{3}(2a)^2b^3 + \binom{5}{4}(2a)b^4 + \binom{5}{5}b^5$

17. $\frac{3}{15}$; $\frac{7}{15}$; $\frac{8}{15}$; $\frac{3}{15}$

Chapter 13

1. $\frac{4}{5}$; $\frac{3}{5}$; $\frac{4}{3}$ **2.** $\frac{12}{13}$; $\frac{5}{13}$; $\frac{12}{5}$ **3.** $-\frac{12}{13}$; $-\frac{5}{13}$; $\frac{12}{5}$ **4.** $-\frac{12}{13}$; $\frac{5}{13}$; $-\frac{12}{5}$

1. $P(\sqrt{3}, 1)$ **2.** $\sin 30° = \frac{1}{2}$; $\cos 30° = \frac{\sqrt{3}}{2}$; $\tan 30° = \frac{\sqrt{3}}{3}$

1. .2560 **2.** .5169 **3.** .3827 **4.** 23°40′ **5.** 57°40′ **6.** 49°10′

1. $9.8338 - 10$ **2.** $9.5828 - 10$ **3.** $9.9853 - 10$ **4.** $9.9186 - 10$ **5.** $9.4821 - 10$
6. $9.8624 - 10$ **7.** $9.7958 - 10$ **8.** 0.1308

1. $\sqrt{2}$; $\sqrt{2}$; 1 **2.** 2, $\frac{2\sqrt{3}}{3}$; $\frac{\sqrt{3}}{3}$ **3.** $\frac{2\sqrt{3}}{3}$, 2, $\sqrt{3}$ **4.** Undefined; 1; 0 **5.** 1.2521; 1.6616;
1.3270 **6.** 6.3924; 1.0125; .1584

θ	$\sin \theta$	$\cos \theta$	$\tan \theta$	$\csc \theta$	$\sec \theta$	$\cot \theta$
1. 0°	0	1	0	Undefined	1	Undefined
2. 30°	$\frac{1}{2}$	$\frac{\sqrt{3}}{2}$	$\frac{\sqrt{3}}{3}$	2	$\frac{2\sqrt{3}}{3}$	$\sqrt{3}$
3. 45°	$\frac{\sqrt{2}}{2}$	$\frac{\sqrt{2}}{2}$	1	$\sqrt{2}$	$\sqrt{2}$	1
4. 60°	$\frac{\sqrt{3}}{2}$	$\frac{1}{2}$	$\sqrt{3}$	$\frac{2\sqrt{3}}{3}$	2	$\frac{\sqrt{3}}{3}$

θ	$\sin \theta$	$\cos \theta$	$\tan \theta$	$\csc \theta$	$\sec \theta$	$\cot \theta$
5. 135°	$\dfrac{\sqrt{2}}{2}$	$-\dfrac{\sqrt{2}}{2}$	-1	$\sqrt{2}$	$-\sqrt{2}$	-1
6. 240°	$-\dfrac{\sqrt{3}}{2}$	$-\dfrac{1}{2}$	$\sqrt{3}$	$-\dfrac{2\sqrt{3}}{3}$	-2	$\dfrac{\sqrt{3}}{3}$
7. 330°	$-\dfrac{1}{2}$	$\dfrac{\sqrt{3}}{2}$	$-\dfrac{\sqrt{3}}{3}$	-2	$\dfrac{2\sqrt{3}}{3}$	$-\sqrt{3}$
8. 120°	$\dfrac{\sqrt{3}}{2}$	$-\dfrac{1}{2}$	$-\sqrt{3}$	$\dfrac{2\sqrt{3}}{3}$	-2	$-\dfrac{\sqrt{3}}{3}$

9. .0872 **10.** 1.0355 **11.** −.3907 **12.** −.9659 **13.** .2812 **14.** .7771 **15.** −.0872
16. .4226 **17.** 3.1147 **18.** 33°41′ **19.** 13.6 meters **20.** 74,300 square centimeters
21. 61 meters **22.** 37°

Chapter 14

Page 485 **1.** 3; 2π **2.** $\dfrac{1}{2}$; 2π **3.** 7; 2π **4.** $\dfrac{1}{8}$; 2π **5.** 2; 2π **6.** $\dfrac{1}{4}$; 2π **7.** 1000; 2π **8.** 1; 2π
9. π; 2π

Page 487 **1.** $-\dfrac{\pi}{2}, \dfrac{\pi}{2}, \dfrac{3\pi}{2}, \dfrac{5\pi}{2}$ **2.** $x = -\dfrac{\pi}{2}, x = \dfrac{\pi}{2}, x = \dfrac{3\pi}{2}, x = \dfrac{5\pi}{2}$ **3.** Domain: the set of real
numbers, except for $\dfrac{\pi}{2}, \dfrac{3\pi}{2}, \dfrac{5\pi}{2}$, etc.; Range: the set of real numbers; period: π radians

Pages 489–490 **1.** $\dfrac{1}{\sin \theta}$ **2.** $\dfrac{1}{\cos \theta}$ **3.** $\dfrac{1}{\tan \theta}$ **4.** $\sec \theta$ **5.** $\cot \theta$ **6.** $\tan \theta$ **7.** $\cos^2 \theta$ **8.** $\sec^2 \theta$
9. $\csc^2 \theta$ **10.** $\sin^2 \theta$ **11.** $\tan^2 \theta$ **12.** $\cot^2 \theta$

Page 493 Answers will vary. **1.** 60° + 45° **2.** 45° + 30° **3.** 60° − 45° or 45° − 30° **4.** 90° − 30°
or 150° − 90° **5.** 90° + 45° **6.** 180° − 60°

Page 500 **1.** $-\dfrac{\pi}{4}$ **2.** $-\dfrac{\pi}{4}$ **3.** π **4.** 0 **5.** $\dfrac{\pi}{2}$ **6.** 54° or 0.9425 radians

Chapter Test Page 507 **1.** 120° **2.** 255° **3.** 300° **4.** $\dfrac{\sqrt{2}}{2}$ **5.** $-\dfrac{\sqrt{3}}{2}$ **6.** $-\sqrt{3}$ **7.** Domain: the set of real
numbers; Range: {y: −1 ≤ y ≤ 1}; Amplitude: 1; Period: 2π **8.** Domain: the set of
real numbers; Range: {y: −1 ≤ y ≤ 1}; Amplitude: 1; Period: 2π **9.** Domain: the set
of real numbers except for $\dfrac{\pi}{2}, \dfrac{3\pi}{2}, \dfrac{5\pi}{2}$ etc.; Range: the set of real numbers; Amplitude:
undefined; Period: π **10.** $\cos^2 \theta$ **11.** $\sec^2 \theta$ **12.** $\cot^2 \theta$ **13.** $\tan \theta$ **14.** $\sec \theta$
15. $\tan \theta$ **16.** $\tan x = \sin x \cdot \sec x = \sin x \cdot \dfrac{1}{\cos x} = \dfrac{\sin x}{\cos x} = \tan x$ **17.** $\sin^4 x - \cos^4 x$
$= (\sin^2 x + \cos^2 x)(\sin^2 x - \cos^2 x) = 1(\sin^2 x - \cos^2 x) = \sin^2 x - \cos^2 x$
18. $\dfrac{\cos x - \sin x}{\cos x} = \dfrac{\cos x}{\cos x} - \dfrac{\sin x}{\cos x} = 1 - \tan x$

Table of Values of the Trigonometric Functions

θ Deg.	θ Rad.	Sin θ	Cos θ	Tan θ	Cot θ	Sec θ	Csc θ		
0° 00′	.0000	.0000	1.0000	.0000		1.000		1.5708	90° 00′
10′	.0029	.0029	1.0000	.0029	343.77	1.000	343.8	1.5679	50′
20′	.0058	.0058	1.0000	.0058	171.89	1.000	171.9	1.5650	40′
30′	.0087	.0087	1.0000	.0087	114.59	1.000	114.6	1.5621	30′
40′	.0116	.0116	.9999	.0116	85.940	1.000	85.95	1.5592	20′
50′	.0145	.0145	.9999	.0145	68.750	1.000	68.76	1.5563	10′
1° 00′	.0175	.0175	.9998	.0175	57.290	1.000	57.30	1.5533	89° 00′
10′	.0204	.0204	.9998	.0204	49.104	1.000	49.11	1.5504	50′
20′	.0233	.0233	.9997	.0233	42.964	1.000	42.98	1.5475	40′
30′	.0262	.0262	.9997	.0262	38.188	1.000	38.20	1.5446	30′
40′	.0291	.0291	.9996	.0291	34.368	1.000	34.38	1.5417	20′
50′	.0320	.0320	.9995	.0320	31.242	1.001	31.26	1.5388	10′
2° 00′	.0349	.0349	.9994	.0349	28.636	1.001	28.65	1.5359	88° 00′
10′	.0378	.0378	.9993	.0378	26.432	1.001	26.45	1.5330	50′
20′	.0407	.0407	.9992	.0407	24.542	1.001	24.56	1.5301	40′
30′	.0436	.0436	.9990	.0437	22.904	1.001	22.93	1.5272	30′
40′	.0465	.0465	.9989	.0466	21.470	1.001	21.49	1.5243	20′
50′	.0495	.0494	.9988	.0495	20.206	1.001	20.23	1.5213	10′
3° 00′	.0524	.0523	.9986	.0524	19.081	1.001	19.11	1.5184	87° 00′
10′	.0553	.0552	.9985	.0553	18.075	1.002	18.10	1.5155	50′
20′	.0582	.0581	.9983	.0582	17.169	1.002	17.20	1.5126	40′
30′	.0611	.0610	.9981	.0612	16.350	1.002	16.38	1.5097	30′
40′	.0640	.0640	.9980	.0641	15.605	1.002	15.64	1.5068	20′
50′	.0669	.0669	.9978	.0670	14.924	1.002	14.96	1.5039	10′
4° 00′	.0698	.0698	.9976	.0699	14.301	1.002	14.34	1.5010	86° 00′
10′	.0727	.0727	.9974	.0729	13.727	1.003	13.76	1.4981	50′
20′	.0756	.0756	.9971	.0758	13.197	1.003	13.23	1.4952	40′
30′	.0785	.0785	.9969	.0787	12.706	1.003	12.75	1.4923	30′
40′	.0814	.0814	.9967	.0816	12.251	1.003	12.29	1.4893	20′
50′	.0844	.0843	.9964	.0846	11.826	1.004	11.87	1.4864	10′
5° 00′	.0873	.0872	.9962	.0875	11.430	1.004	11.47	1.4835	85° 00′
10′	.0902	.0901	.9959	.0904	11.059	1.004	11.10	1.4806	50′
20′	.0931	.0929	.9957	.0934	10.712	1.004	10.76	1.4777	40′
30′	.0960	.0958	.9954	.0963	10.385	1.005	10.43	1.4748	30′
40′	.0989	.0987	.9951	.0992	10.078	1.005	10.13	1.4719	20′
50′	.1018	.1016	.9948	.1022	9.7882	1.005	9.839	1.4690	10′
6° 00′	.1047	.1045	.9945	.1051	9.5144	1.006	9.567	1.4661	84° 00′
10′	.1076	.1074	.9942	.1080	9.2553	1.006	9.309	1.4632	50′
20′	.1105	.1103	.9939	.1110	9.0098	1.006	9.065	1.4603	40′
30′	.1134	.1132	.9936	.1139	8.7769	1.006	8.834	1.4573	30′
40′	.1164	.1161	.9932	.1169	8.5555	1.007	8.614	1.4544	20′
50′	.1193	.1190	.9929	.1198	8.3450	1.007	8.405	1.4515	10′
7° 00′	.1222	.1219	.9925	.1228	8.1443	1.008	8.206	1.4486	83° 00′
10′	.1251	.1248	.9922	.1257	7.9530	1.008	8.016	1.4457	50′
20′	.1280	.1276	.9918	.1287	7.7704	1.008	7.834	1.4428	40′
30′	.1309	.1305	.9914	.1317	7.5958	1.009	7.661	1.4399	30′
40′	.1338	.1334	.9911	.1346	7.4287	1.009	7.496	1.4370	20′
50′	.1367	.1363	.9907	.1376	7.2687	1.009	7.337	1.4341	10′
8° 00′	.1396	.1392	.9903	.1405	7.1154	1.010	7.185	1.4312	82° 00′
10′	.1425	.1421	.9899	.1435	6.9682	1.010	7.040	1.4283	50′
20′	.1454	.1449	.9894	.1465	6.8269	1.011	6.900	1.4254	40′
30′	.1484	.1478	.9890	.1495	6.6912	1.011	6.765	1.4224	30′
40′	.1513	.1507	.9886	.1524	6.5606	1.012	6.636	1.4195	20′
50′	.1542	.1536	.9881	.1554	6.4348	1.012	6.512	1.4166	10′
9° 00′	.1571	.1564	.9877	.1584	6.3138	1.012	6.392	1.4137	81° 00′
		Cos θ	Sin θ	Cot θ	Tan θ	Csc θ	Sec θ	θ Rad.	θ Deg.

Table of Values of the Trigonometric Functions

θ Rad.	Sin θ	Cos θ	Tan θ	Cot θ	Sec θ	Csc θ		
.1571	.1564	.9877	.1584	6.3138	1.012	6.392	1.4137	81° 00′
.1600	.1593	.9872	.1614	6.1970	1.013	6.277	1.4108	50′
.1629	.1622	.9868	.1644	6.0844	1.013	6.166	1.4079	40′
.1658	.1650	.9863	.1673	5.9758	1.014	6.059	1.4050	30′
.1687	.1679	.9858	.1703	5.8708	1.014	5.955	1.4021	20′
.1716	.1708	.9853	.1733	5.7694	1.015	5.855	1.3992	10′
.1745	.1736	.9848	.1763	5.6713	1.015	5.759	1.3963	80° 00′
.1774	.1765	.9843	.1793	5.5764	1.016	5.665	1.3934	50′
.1804	.1794	.9838	.1823	5.4845	1.016	5.575	1.3904	40′
.1833	.1822	.9833	.1853	5.3955	1.017	5.487	1.3875	30′
.1862	.1851	.9827	.1883	5.3093	1.018	5.403	1.3846	20′
.1891	.1880	.9822	.1914	5.2257	1.018	5.320	1.3817	10′
11° 00′ .1920	.1908	.9816	.1944	5.1446	1.019	5.241	1.3788	79° 00′
10′ .1949	.1937	.9811	.1974	5.0658	1.019	5.164	1.3759	50′
20′ .1978	.1965	.9805	.2004	4.9894	1.020	5.089	1.3730	40′
30′ .2007	.1994	.9799	.2035	4.9152	1.020	5.016	1.3701	30′
40′ .2036	.2022	.9793	.2065	4.8430	1.021	4.945	1.3672	20′
50′ .2065	.2051	.9787	.2095	4.7729	1.022	4.876	1.3643	10′
12° 00′ .2094	.2079	.9781	.2126	4.7046	1.022	4.810	1.3614	78° 00′
10′ .2123	.2108	.9775	.2156	4.6382	1.023	4.745	1.3584	50′
20′ .2153	.2136	.9769	.2186	4.5736	1.024	4.682	1.3555	40′
30′ .2182	.2164	.9763	.2217	4.5107	1.024	4.620	1.3526	30′
40′ .2211	.2193	.9757	.2247	4.4494	1.025	4.560	1.3497	20′
50′ .2240	.2221	.9750	.2278	4.3897	1.026	4.502	1.3468	10′
13° 00′ .2269	.2250	.9744	.2309	4.3315	1.026	4.445	1.3439	77° 00′
10′ .2298	.2278	.9737	.2339	4.2747	1.027	4.390	1.3410	50′
20′ .2327	.2306	.9730	.2370	4.2193	1.028	4.336	1.3381	40′
30′ .2356	.2334	.9724	.2401	4.1653	1.028	4.284	1.3352	30′
40′ .2385	.2363	.9717	.2432	4.1126	1.029	4.232	1.3323	20′
50′ .2414	.2391	.9710	.2462	4.0611	1.030	4.182	1.3294	10′
14° 00′ .2443	.2419	.9703	.2493	4.0108	1.031	4.134	1.3265	76° 00′
10′ .2473	.2447	.9696	.2524	3.9617	1.031	4.086	1.3235	50′
20′ .2502	.2476	.9689	.2555	3.9136	1.032	4.039	1.3206	40′
30′ .2531	.2504	.9681	.2586	3.8667	1.033	3.994	1.3177	30′
40′ .2560	.2532	.9674	.2617	3.8208	1.034	3.950	1.3148	20′
50′ .2589	.2560	.9667	.2648	3.7760	1.034	3.906	1.3119	10′
15° 00′ .2618	.2588	.9659	.2679	3.7321	1.035	3.864	1.3090	75° 00′
10′ .2647	.2616	.9652	.2711	3.6891	1.036	3.822	1.3061	50′
20′ .2676	.2644	.9644	.2742	3.6470	1.037	3.782	1.3032	40′
30′ .2705	.2672	.9636	.2773	3.6059	1.038	3.742	1.3003	30′
40′ .2734	.2700	.9628	.2805	3.5656	1.039	3.703	1.2974	20′
50′ .2763	.2728	.9621	.2836	3.5261	1.039	3.665	1.2945	10′
16° 00′ .2793	.2756	.9613	.2867	3.4874	1.040	3.628	1.2915	74° 00′
10′ .2822	.2784	.9605	.2899	3.4495	1.041	3.592	1.2886	50′
20′ .2851	.2812	.9596	.2931	3.4124	1.042	3.556	1.2857	40′
30′ .2880	.2840	.9588	.2962	3.3759	1.043	3.521	1.2828	30′
40′ .2909	.2868	.9580	.2994	3.3402	1.044	3.487	1.2799	20′
50′ .2938	.2896	.9572	.3026	3.3052	1.045	3.453	1.2770	10′
17° 00′ .2967	.2924	.9563	.3057	3.2709	1.046	3.420	1.2741	73° 00′
10′ .2996	.2952	.9555	.3089	3.2371	1.047	3.388	1.2712	50′
20′ .3025	.2979	.9546	.3121	3.2041	1.048	3.356	1.2683	40′
30′ .3054	.3007	.9537	.3153	3.1716	1.049	3.326	1.2654	30′
40′ .3083	.3035	.9528	.3185	3.1397	1.049	3.295	1.2625	20′
50′ .3113	.3062	.9520	.3217	3.1084	1.050	3.265	1.2595	10′
18° 00′ .3142	.3090	.9511	.3249	3.0777	1.051	3.236	1.2566	72° 00′
	Cos θ	Sin θ	Cot θ	Tan θ	Csc θ	Sec θ	θ Rad.	θ Deg.

Table of Values of the Trigonometric Functions

θ Deg.	θ Rad.	Sin θ	Cos θ	Tan θ	Cot θ	Sec θ	Csc θ		
18° 00'	.3142	.3090	.9511	.3249	3.0777	1.051	3.236	1.2566	72° 00'
10'	.3171	.3118	.9502	.3281	3.0475	1.052	3.207	1.2537	50'
20'	.3200	.3145	.9492	.3314	3.0178	1.053	3.179	1.2508	40'
30'	.3229	.3173	.9483	.3346	2.9887	1.054	3.152	1.2479	30'
40'	.3258	.3201	.9474	.3378	2.9600	1.056	3.124	1.2450	20'
50'	.3287	.3228	.9465	.3411	2.9319	1.057	3.098	1.2421	10'
19° 00'	.3316	.3256	.9455	.3443	2.9042	1.058	3.072	1.2392	71° 00'
10'	.3345	.3283	.9446	.3476	2.8770	1.059	3.046	1.2363	50'
20'	.3374	.3311	.9436	.3508	2.8502	1.060	3.021	1.2334	40'
30'	.3403	.3338	.9426	.3541	2.8239	1.061	2.996	1.2305	30'
40'	.3432	.3365	.9417	.3574	2.7980	1.062	2.971	1.2275	20'
50'	.3462	.3393	.9407	.3607	2.7725	1.063	2.947	1.2246	10'
20° 00'	.3491	.3420	.9397	.3640	2.7475	1.064	2.924	1.2217	70° 00'
10'	.3520	.3448	.9387	.3673	2.7228	1.065	2.901	1.2188	50'
20'	.3549	.3475	.9377	.3706	2.6985	1.066	2.878	1.2159	40'
30'	.3578	.3502	.9367	.3739	2.6746	1.068	2.855	1.2130	30'
40'	.3607	.3529	.9356	.3772	2.6511	1.069	2.833	1.2101	20'
50'	.3636	.3557	.9346	.3805	2.6279	1.070	2.812	1.2072	10'
21° 00'	.3665	.3584	.9336	.3839	2.6051	1.071	2.790	1.2043	69° 00'
10'	.3694	.3611	.9325	.3872	2.5826	1.072	2.769	1.2014	50'
20'	.3723	.3638	.9315	.3906	2.5605	1.074	2.749	1.1985	40'
30'	.3752	.3665	.9304	.3939	2.5386	1.075	2.729	1.1956	30'
40'	.3782	.3692	.9293	.3973	2.5172	1.076	2.709	1.1926	20'
50'	.3811	.3719	.9283	.4006	2.4960	1.077	2.689	1.1897	10'
22° 00'	.3840	.3746	.9272	.4040	2.4751	1.079	2.669	1.1868	68° 00'
10'	.3869	.3773	.9261	.4074	2.4545	1.080	2.650	1.1839	50'
20'	.3898	.3800	.9250	.4108	2.4342	1.081	2.632	1.1810	40'
30'	.3927	.3827	.9239	.4142	2.4142	1.082	2.613	1.1781	30'
40'	.3956	.3854	.9228	.4176	2.3945	1.084	2.595	1.1752	20'
50'	.3985	.3881	.9216	.4210	2.3750	1.085	2.577	1.1723	10'
23° 00'	.4014	.3907	.9205	.4245	2.3559	1.086	2.559	1.1694	67° 00'
10'	.4043	.3934	.9194	.4279	2.3369	1.088	2.542	1.1665	50'
20'	.4072	.3961	.9182	.4314	2.3183	1.089	2.525	1.1636	40'
30'	.4102	.3987	.9171	.4348	2.2998	1.090	2.508	1.1606	30'
40'	.4131	.4014	.9159	.4383	2.2817	1.092	2.491	1.1577	20'
50'	.4160	.4041	.9147	.4417	2.2637	1.093	2.475	1.1548	10'
24° 00'	.4189	.4067	.9135	.4452	2.2460	1.095	2.459	1.1519	66° 00'
10'	.4218	.4094	.9124	.4487	2.2286	1.096	2.443	1.1490	50'
20'	.4247	.4120	.9112	.4522	2.2113	1.097	2.427	1.1461	40'
30'	.4276	.4147	.9100	.4557	2.1943	1.099	2.411	1.1432	30'
40'	.4305	.4173	.9088	.4592	2.1775	1.100	2.396	1.1403	20'
50'	.4334	.4200	.9075	.4628	2.1609	1.102	2.381	1.1374	10'
25° 00'	.4363	.4226	.9063	.4663	2.1445	1.103	2.366	1.1345	65° 00'
10'	.4392	.4253	.9051	.4699	2.1283	1.105	2.352	1.1316	50'
20'	.4422	.4279	.9038	.4734	2.1123	1.106	2.337	1.1286	40'
30'	.4451	.4305	.9026	.4770	2.0965	1.108	2.323	1.1257	30'
40'	.4480	.4331	.9013	.4806	2.0809	1.109	2.309	1.1228	20'
50'	.4509	.4358	.9001	.4841	2.0655	1.111	2.295	1.1199	10'
26° 00'	.4538	.4384	.8988	.4877	2.0503	1.113	2.281	1.1170	64° 00'
10'	.4567	.4410	.8975	.4913	2.0353	1.114	2.268	1.1141	50'
20'	.4596	.4436	.8962	.4950	2.0204	1.116	2.254	1.1112	40'
30'	.4625	.4462	.8949	.4986	2.0057	1.117	2.241	1.1083	30'
40'	.4654	.4488	.8936	.5022	1.9912	1.119	2.228	1.1054	20'
50'	.4683	.4514	.8923	.5059	1.9768	1.121	2.215	1.1025	10'
27° 00'	.4712	.4540	.8910	.5095	1.9626	1.122	2.203	1.0996	63° 00'
		Cos θ	Sin θ	Cot θ	Tan θ	Csc θ	Sec θ	θ Rad.	θ Deg.

Table of Values of the Trigonometric Functions

θ Deg.	θ Rad.	Sin θ	Cos θ	Tan θ	Cot θ	Sec θ	Csc θ		
27° 00'	.4712	.4540	.8910	.5095	1.9626	1.122	2.203	1.0996	**63° 00'**
10'	.4741	.4566	.8897	.5132	1.9486	1.124	2.190	1.0966	50'
20'	.4771	.4592	.8884	.5169	1.9347	1.126	2.178	1.0937	40'
30'	.4800	.4617	.8870	.5206	1.9210	1.127	2.166	1.0908	30'
40'	.4829	.4643	.8857	.5243	1.9074	1.129	2.154	1.0879	20'
50'	.4858	.4669	.8843	.5280	1.8940	1.131	2.142	1.0850	10'
28° 00'	.4887	.4695	.8829	.5317	1.8807	1.133	2.130	1.0821	**62° 00'**
10'	.4916	.4720	.8816	.5354	1.8676	1.134	2.118	1.0792	50'
20'	.4945	.4746	.8802	.5392	1.8546	1.136	2.107	1.0763	40'
30'	.4974	.4772	.8788	.5430	1.8418	1.138	2.096	1.0734	30'
40'	.5003	.4797	.8774	.5467	1.8291	1.140	2.085	1.0705	20'
50'	.5032	.4823	.8760	.5505	1.8165	1.142	2.074	1.0676	10'
29° 00'	.5061	.4848	.8746	.5543	1.8040	1.143	2.063	1.0647	**61° 00'**
10'	.5091	.4874	.8732	.5581	1.7917	1.145	2.052	1.0617	50'
20'	.5120	.4899	.8718	.5619	1.7796	1.147	2.041	1.0588	40'
30'	.5149	.4924	.8704	.5658	1.7675	1.149	2.031	1.0559	30'
40'	.5178	.4950	.8689	.5696	1.7556	1.151	2.020	1.0530	20'
50'	.5207	.4975	.8675	.5735	1.7437	1.153	2.010	1.0501	10'
30° 00'	.5236	.5000	.8660	.5774	1.7321	1.155	2.000	1.0472	**60° 00'**
10'	.5265	.5025	.8646	.5812	1.7205	1.157	1.990	1.0443	50'
20'	.5294	.5050	.8631	.5851	1.7090	1.159	1.980	1.0414	40'
30'	.5323	.5075	.8616	.5890	1.6977	1.161	1.970	1.0385	30'
40'	.5352	.5100	.8601	.5930	1.6864	1.163	1.961	1.0356	20'
50'	.5381	.5125	.8587	.5969	1.6753	1.165	1.951	1.0327	10'
31° 00'	.5411	.5150	.8572	.6009	1.6643	1.167	1.942	1.0297	**59° 00'**
10'	.5440	.5175	.8557	.6048	1.6534	1.169	1.932	1.0268	50'
20'	.5469	.5200	.8542	.6088	1.6426	1.171	1.923	1.0239	40'
30'	.5498	.5225	.8526	.6128	1.6319	1.173	1.914	1.0210	30'
40'	.5527	.5250	.8511	.6168	1.6212	1.175	1.905	1.0181	20'
50'	.5556	.5275	.8496	.6208	1.6107	1.177	1.896	1.0152	10'
32° 00'	.5585	.5299	.8480	.6249	1.6003	1.179	1.887	1.0123	**58° 00'**
10'	.5614	.5324	.8465	.6289	1.5900	1.181	1.878	1.0094	50'
20'	.5643	.5348	.8450	.6330	1.5798	1.184	1.870	1.0065	40'
30'	.5672	.5373	.8434	.6371	1.5697	1.186	1.861	1.0036	30'
40'	.5701	.5398	.8418	.6412	1.5597	1.188	1.853	1.0007	20'
50'	.5730	.5422	.8403	.6453	1.5497	1.190	1.844	.9977	10'
33° 00'	.5760	.5446	.8387	.6494	1.5399	1.192	1.836	.9948	**57° 00'**
10'	.5789	.5471	.8371	.6536	1.5301	1.195	1.828	.9919	50'
20'	.5818	.5495	.8355	.6577	1.5204	1.197	1.820	.9890	40'
30'	.5847	.5519	.8339	.6619	1.5108	1.199	1.812	.9861	30'
40'	.5876	.5544	.8323	.6661	1.5013	1.202	1.804	.9832	20'
50'	.5905	.5568	.8307	.6703	1.4919	1.204	1.796	.9803	10'
34° 00'	.5934	.5592	.8290	.6745	1.4826	1.206	1.788	.9774	**56° 00'**
10'	.5963	.5616	.8274	.6787	1.4733	1.209	1.781	.9745	50'
20'	.5992	.5640	.8258	.6830	1.4641	1.211	1.773	.9716	40'
30'	.6021	.5664	.8241	.6873	1.4550	1.213	1.766	.9687	30'
40'	.6050	.5688	.8225	.6916	1.4460	1.216	1.758	.9657	20'
50'	.6080	.5712	.8208	.6959	1.4370	1.218	1.751	.9628	10'
35° 00'	.6109	.5736	.8192	.7002	1.4281	1.221	1.743	.9599	**55° 00'**
10'	.6138	.5760	.8175	.7046	1.4193	1.223	1.736	.9570	50'
20'	.6167	.5783	.8158	.7089	1.4106	1.226	1.729	.9541	40'
30'	.6196	.5807	.8141	.7133	1.4019	1.228	1.722	.9512	30'
40'	.6225	.5831	.8124	.7177	1.3934	1.231	1.715	.9483	20'
50'	.6254	.5854	.8107	.7221	1.3848	1.233	1.708	.9454	10'
36° 00'	.6283	.5878	.8090	.7265	1.3764	1.236	1.701	.9425	**54° 00'**
		Cos θ	Sin θ	Cot θ	Tan θ	Csc θ	Sec θ	θ Rad.	θ Deg.

Table of Values of the Trigonometric Functions

θ Deg.	θ Rad.	Sin θ	Cos θ	Tan θ	Cot θ	Sec θ	Csc θ		
36° 00′	.6283	.5878	.8090	.7265	1.3764	1.236	1.701	.9425	54° 00′
10′	.6312	.5901	.8073	.7310	1.3680	1.239	1.695	.9396	50′
20′	.6341	.5925	.8056	.7355	1.3597	1.241	1.688	.9367	40′
30′	.6370	.5948	.8039	.7400	1.3514	1.244	1.681	.9338	30′
40′	.6400	.5972	.8021	.7445	1.3432	1.247	1.675	.9308	20′
50′	.6429	.5995	.8004	.7490	1.3351	1.249	1.668	.9279	10′
37° 00′	.6458	.6018	.7986	.7536	1.3270	1.252	1.662	.9250	53° 00′
10′	.6487	.6041	.7969	.7581	1.3190	1.255	1.655	.9221	50′
20′	.6516	.6065	.7951	.7627	1.3111	1.258	1.649	.9192	40′
30′	.6545	.6088	.7934	.7673	1.3032	1.260	1.643	.9163	30′
40′	.6574	.6111	.7916	.7720	1.2954	1.263	1.636	.9134	20′
50′	.6603	.6134	.7898	.7766	1.2876	1.266	1.630	.9105	10′
38° 00′	.6632	.6157	.7880	.7813	1.2799	1.269	1.624	.9076	52° 00′
10′	.6661	.6180	.7862	.7860	1.2723	1.272	1.618	.9047	50′
20′	.6690	.6202	.7844	.7907	1.2647	1.275	1.612	.9018	40′
30′	.6720	.6225	.7826	.7954	1.2572	1.278	1.606	.8988	30′
40′	.6749	.6248	.7808	.8002	1.2497	1.281	1.601	.8959	20′
50′	.6778	.6271	.7790	.8050	1.2423	1.284	1.595	.8930	10′
39° 00′	.6807	.6293	.7771	.8098	1.2349	1.287	1.589	.8901	51° 00′
10′	.6836	.6316	.7753	.8146	1.2276	1.290	1.583	.8872	50′
20′	.6865	.6338	.7735	.8195	1.2203	1.293	1.578	.8843	40′
30′	.6894	.6361	.7716	.8243	1.2131	1.296	1.572	.8814	30′
40′	.6923	.6383	.7698	.8292	1.2059	1.299	1.567	.8785	20′
50′	.6952	.6406	.7679	.8342	1.1988	1.302	1.561	.8756	10′
40° 00′	.6981	.6428	.7660	.8391	1.1918	1.305	1.556	.8727	50° 00′
10′	.7010	.6450	.7642	.8441	1.1847	1.309	1.550	.8698	50′
20′	.7039	.6472	.7623	.8491	1.1778	1.312	1.545	.8668	40′
30′	.7069	.6494	.7604	.8541	1.1708	1.315	1.540	.8639	30′
40′	.7098	.6517	.7585	.8591	1.1640	1.318	1.535	.8610	20′
50′	.7127	.6539	.7566	.8642	1.1571	1.322	1.529	.8581	10′
41° 00′	.7156	.6561	.7547	.8693	1.1504	1.325	1.524	.8552	49° 00′
10′	.7185	.6583	.7528	.8744	1.1436	1.328	1.519	.8523	50′
20′	.7214	.6604	.7509	.8796	1.1369	1.332	1.514	.8494	40′
30′	.7243	.6626	.7490	.8847	1.1303	1.335	1.509	.8465	30′
40′	.7272	.6648	.7470	.8899	1.1237	1.339	1.504	.8436	20′
50′	.7301	.6670	.7451	.8952	1.1171	1.342	1.499	.8407	10′
42° 00′	.7330	.6691	.7431	.9004	1.1106	1.346	1.494	.8378	48° 00′
10′	.7359	.6713	.7412	.9057	1.1041	1.349	1.490	.8348	50′
20′	.7389	.6734	.7392	.9110	1.0977	1.353	1.485	.8319	40′
30′	.7418	.6756	.7373	.9163	1.0913	1.356	1.480	.8290	30′
40′	.7447	.6777	.7353	.9217	1.0850	1.360	1.476	.8261	20′
50′	.7476	.6799	.7333	.9271	1.0786	1.364	1.471	.8232	10′
43° 00′	.7505	.6820	.7314	.9325	1.0724	1.367	1.466	.8203	47° 00′
10′	.7534	.6841	.7294	.9380	1.0661	1.371	1.462	.8174	50′
20′	.7563	.6862	.7274	.9435	1.0599	1.375	1.457	.8145	40′
30′	.7592	.6884	.7254	.9490	1.0538	1.379	1.453	.8116	30′
40′	.7621	.6905	.7234	.9545	1.0477	1.382	1.448	.8087	20′
50′	.7650	.6926	.7214	.9601	1.0416	1.386	1.444	.8058	10′
44° 00′	.7679	.6947	.7193	.9657	1.0355	1.390	1.440	.8029	46° 00′
10′	.7709	.6967	.7173	.9713	1.0295	1.394	1.435	.7999	50′
20′	.7738	.6988	.7153	.9770	1.0235	1.398	1.431	.7970	40′
30′	.7767	.7009	.7133	.9827	1.0176	1.402	1.427	.7941	30′
40′	.7796	.7030	.7112	.9884	1.0117	1.406	1.423	.7912	20′
50′	.7825	.7050	.7092	.9942	1.0058	1.410	1.418	.7883	10′
45° 00′	.7854	.7071	.7071	1.0000	1.0000	1.414	1.414	.7854	45° 00′
		Cos θ	Sin θ	Cot θ	Tan θ	Csc θ	Sec θ	θ Rad.	θ Deg.

Table of Common Logarithms

N	0	1	2	3	4	5	6	7	8	9
1.0	0000	0043	0086	0128	0170	0212	0253	0294	0334	0374
1.1	0414	0453	0492	0531	0569	0607	0645	0682	0719	0755
1.2	0792	0828	0864	0899	0934	0969	1004	1038	1072	1106
1.3	1139	1173	1206	1239	1271	1303	1335	1367	1399	1430
1.4	1461	1492	1523	1553	1584	1614	1644	1673	1703	1732
1.5	1761	1790	1818	1847	1875	1903	1931	1959	1987	2014
1.6	2041	2068	2095	2122	2148	2175	2201	2227	2253	2279
1.7	2304	2330	2355	2380	2405	2430	2455	2480	2504	2529
1.8	2553	2577	2601	2625	2648	2672	2695	2718	2742	2765
1.9	2788	2810	2833	2856	2878	2900	2923	2945	2967	2989
2.0	3010	3032	3054	3075	3096	3118	3139	3160	3181	3201
2.1	3222	3243	3263	3284	3304	3324	3345	3365	3385	3404
2.2	3424	3444	3464	3483	3502	3522	3541	3560	3579	3598
2.3	3617	3636	3655	3674	3692	3711	3729	3747	3766	3784
2.4	3802	3820	3838	3856	3874	3892	3909	3927	3945	3962
2.5	3979	3997	4014	4031	4048	4065	4082	4099	4116	4133
2.6	4150	4166	4183	4200	4216	4232	4249	4265	4281	4298
2.7	4314	4330	4346	4362	4378	4393	4409	4425	4440	4456
2.8	4472	4487	4502	4518	4533	4548	4564	4579	4594	4609
2.9	4624	4639	4654	4669	4683	4698	4713	4728	4742	4757
3.0	4771	4786	4800	4814	4829	4843	4857	4871	4886	4900
3.1	4914	4928	4942	4955	4969	4983	4997	5011	5024	5038
3.2	5051	5065	5079	5092	5105	5119	5132	5145	5159	5172
3.3	5185	5198	5211	5224	5237	5250	5263	5276	5289	5302
3.4	5315	5328	5340	5353	5366	5378	5391	5403	5416	5428
3.5	5441	5453	5465	5478	5490	5502	5514	5527	5539	5551
3.6	5563	5575	5587	5599	5611	5623	5635	5647	5658	5670
3.7	5682	5694	5705	5717	5729	5740	5752	5763	5775	5786
3.8	5798	5809	5821	5832	5843	5855	5866	5877	5888	5899
3.9	5911	5922	5933	5944	5955	5966	5977	5988	5999	6010
4.0	6021	6031	6042	6053	6064	6075	6085	6096	6107	6117
4.1	6128	6138	6149	6160	6170	6180	6191	6201	6212	6222
4.2	6232	6243	6253	6263	6274	6284	6294	6304	6314	6325
4.3	6335	6345	6355	6365	6375	6385	6395	6405	6415	6425
4.4	6435	6444	6454	6464	6474	6484	6493	6503	6513	6522
4.5	6532	6542	6551	6561	6571	6580	6590	6599	6609	6618
4.6	6628	6637	6646	6656	6665	6675	6684	6693	6702	6712
4.7	6721	6730	6739	6749	6758	6767	6776	6785	6794	6803
4.8	6812	6821	6830	6839	6848	6857	6866	6875	6884	6893
4.9	6902	6911	6920	6928	6937	6946	6955	6964	6972	6981
5.0	6990	6998	7007	7016	7024	7033	7042	7050	7059	7067
5.1	7076	7084	7093	7101	7110	7118	7126	7135	7143	7152
5.2	7160	7168	7177	7185	7193	7202	7210	7218	7226	7235
5.3	7243	7251	7259	7267	7275	7284	7292	7300	7308	7316
5.4	7324	7332	7340	7348	7356	7364	7372	7380	7388	7396

Table of Common Logarithms

N	0	1	2	3	4	5	6	7	8	9
5.5	7404	7412	7419	7427	7435	7443	7451	7459	7466	7474
5.6	7482	7490	7497	7505	7513	7520	7528	7536	7543	7551
5.7	7559	7566	7574	7582	7589	7597	7604	7612	7619	7627
5.8	7634	7642	7649	7657	7664	7672	7679	7686	7694	7701
5.9	7709	7716	7723	7731	7738	7745	7752	7760	7767	7774
6.0	7782	7789	7796	7803	7810	7818	7825	7832	7839	7846
6.1	7853	7860	7868	7875	7882	7889	7896	7903	7910	7917
6.2	7924	7931	7938	7945	7952	7959	7966	7973	7980	7987
6.3	7993	8000	8007	8014	8021	8028	8035	8041	8048	8055
6.4	8062	8069	8075	8082	8089	8096	8102	8109	8116	8122
6.5	8129	8136	8142	8149	8156	8162	8169	8176	8182	8189
6.6	8195	8202	8209	8215	8222	8228	8235	8241	8248	8254
6.7	8261	8267	8274	8280	8287	8293	8299	8306	8312	8319
6.8	8325	8331	8338	8344	8351	8357	8363	8370	8376	8382
6.9	8388	8395	8401	8407	8414	8420	8426	8432	8439	8445
7.0	8451	8457	8463	8470	8476	8482	8488	8494	8500	8506
7.1	8513	8519	8525	8531	8537	8543	8549	8555	8561	8567
7.2	8573	8579	8585	8591	8597	8603	8609	8615	8621	8627
7.3	8633	8639	8645	8651	8657	8663	8669	8675	8681	8686
7.4	8692	8698	8704	8710	8716	8722	8727	8733	8739	8745
7.5	8751	8756	8762	8768	8774	8779	8785	8791	8797	8802
7.6	8808	8814	8820	8825	8831	8837	8842	8848	8854	8859
7.7	8865	8871	8876	8882	8887	8893	8899	8904	8910	8915
7.8	8921	8927	8932	8938	8943	8949	8954	8960	8965	8971
7.9	8976	8982	8987	8993	8998	9004	9009	9015	9020	9025
8.0	9031	9036	9042	9047	9053	9058	9063	9069	9074	9079
8.1	9085	9090	9096	9101	9106	9112	9117	9122	9128	9133
8.2	9138	9143	9149	9154	9159	9165	9170	9175	9180	9186
8.3	9191	9196	9201	9206	9212	9217	9222	9227	9232	9238
8.4	9243	9248	9253	9258	9263	9269	9274	9279	9284	9289
8.5	9294	9299	9304	9309	9315	9320	9325	9330	9335	9340
8.6	9345	9350	9355	9360	9365	9370	9375	9380	9385	9390
8.7	9395	9400	9405	9410	9415	9420	9425	9430	9435	9440
8.8	9445	9450	9455	9460	9465	9469	9474	9479	9484	9489
8.9	9494	9499	9504	9509	9513	9518	9523	9528	9533	9538
9.0	9542	9547	9552	9557	9562	9566	9571	9576	9581	9586
9.1	9590	9595	9600	9605	9609	9614	9619	9624	9628	9633
9.2	9638	9643	9647	9652	9657	9661	9666	9671	9675	9680
9.3	9685	9689	9694	9699	9703	9708	9713	9717	9722	9727
9.4	9731	9736	9741	9745	9750	9754	9759	9763	9768	9773
9.5	9777	9782	9786	9791	9795	9800	9805	9809	9814	9818
9.6	9823	9827	9832	9836	9841	9845	9850	9854	9859	9863
9.7	9868	9872	9877	9881	9886	9890	9894	9899	9903	9908
9.8	9912	9917	9921	9926	9930	9934	9939	9943	9948	9952
9.9	9956	9961	9965	9969	9974	9978	9983	9987	9991	9996

Table of Values of the Logarithms of Trigonometric Functions

θ Deg.	θ Rad.	Log Sin θ	Log Cos θ	Log Tan θ	Log Cot θ		
0°00'	.0000	—	10.0000	—	—	1.5708	90°00'
10'	.0029	7.4637	10.0000	7.4637	12.5363	1.5679	50'
20'	.0058	7.7648	10.0000	7.7648	12.2352	1.5650	40'
30'	.0087	7.9408	10.0000	7.9409	12.0591	1.5621	30'
40'	.0116	8.0658	10.0000	8.0658	11.9342	1.5592	20'
50'	.0145	8.1627	10.0000	8.1627	11.8373	1.5563	10'
1°00'	.0175	8.2419	9.9999	8.2419	11.7581	1.5533	89°00'
10'	.0204	8.3088	9.9999	8.3089	11.6911	1.5504	50'
20'	.0233	8.3668	9.9999	8.3669	11.6331	1.5475	40'
30'	.0262	8.4179	9.9999	8.4181	11.5819	1.5446	30'
40'	.0291	8.4637	9.9998	8.4638	11.5362	1.5417	20'
50'	.0320	8.5050	9.9998	8.5053	11.4947	1.5388	10'
2°00'	.0349	8.5428	9.9997	8.5431	11.4569	1.5359	88°00'
10'	.0378	8.5776	9.9997	8.5779	11.4221	1.5330	50'
20'	.0407	8.6097	9.9996	8.6101	11.3899	1.5301	40'
30'	.0436	8.6397	9.9996	8.6401	11.3599	1.5272	30'
40'	.0465	8.6677	9.9995	8.6682	11.3318	1.5243	20'
50'	.0495	8.6940	9.9995	8.6945	11.3055	1.5213	10'
3°00'	.0524	8.7188	9.9994	8.7194	11.2806	1.5184	87°00'
10'	.0553	8.7423	9.9993	8.7429	11.2571	1.5155	50'
20'	.0582	8.7645	9.9993	8.7652	11.2348	1.5126	40'
30'	.0611	8.7857	9.9992	8.7865	11.2135	1.5097	30'
40'	.0640	8.8059	9.9991	8.8067	11.1933	1.5068	20'
50'	.0669	8.8251	9.9990	8.8261	11.1739	1.5039	10'
4°00'	.0698	8.8436	9.9989	8.8446	11.1554	1.5010	86°00'
10'	.0727	8.8613	9.9989	8.8624	11.1376	1.4981	50'
20'	.0756	8.8783	9.9988	8.8795	11.1205	1.4952	40'
30'	.0785	8.8946	9.9987	8.8960	11.1040	1.4923	30'
40'	.0814	8.9104	9.9986	8.9118	11.0882	1.4893	20'
50'	.0844	8.9256	9.9985	8.9272	11.0728	1.4864	10'
5°00'	.0873	8.9403	9.9983	8.9420	11.0580	1.4835	85°00'
10'	.0902	8.9545	9.9982	8.9563	11.0437	1.4806	50'
20'	.0931	8.9682	9.9981	8.9701	11.0299	1.4777	40'
30'	.0960	8.9816	9.9980	8.9836	11.0164	1.4748	30'
40'	.0989	8.9945	9.9979	8.9966	11.0034	1.4719	20'
50'	.1018	9.0070	9.9977	9.0093	10.9907	1.4690	10'
6°00'	.1047	9.0192	9.9976	9.0216	10.9784	1.4661	84°00'
10'	.1076	9.0311	9.9975	9.0336	10.9664	1.4632	50'
20'	.1105	9.0426	9.9973	9.0453	10.9547	1.4603	40'
30'	.1134	9.0539	9.9972	9.0567	10.9433	1.4573	30'
40'	.1164	9.0648	9.9971	9.0678	10.9322	1.4544	20'
50'	.1193	9.0755	9.9969	9.0786	10.9214	1.4515	10'
7°00'	.1222	9.0859	9.9968	9.0891	10.9109	1.4486	83°00'
10'	.1251	9.0961	9.9966	9.0995	10.9005	1.4457	50'
20'	.1280	9.1060	9.9964	9.1096	10.8904	1.4428	40'
30'	.1309	9.1157	9.9963	9.1194	10.8806	1.4399	30'
40'	.1338	9.1252	9.9961	9.1291	10.8709	1.4370	20'
50'	.1367	9.1345	9.9959	9.1385	10.8615	1.4341	10'
8°00'	.1396	9.1436	9.9958	9.1478	10.8522	1.4312	82°00'
10'	.1425	9.1525	9.9956	9.1569	10.8431	1.4283	50'
20'	.1454	9.1612	9.9954	9.1658	10.8342	1.4254	40'
30'	.1484	9.1697	9.9952	9.1745	10.8255	1.4224	30'
40'	.1513	9.1781	9.9950	9.1831	10.8169	1.4195	20'
50'	.1542	9.1863	9.9948	9.1915	10.8085	1.4166	10'
9°00'	.1571	9.1943	9.9946	9.1997	10.8003	1.4137	81°00'
		Log Cos θ	Log Sin θ	Log Cot θ	Log Tan θ	θ Rad.	θ Deg.

The tables give the logarithms increased by 10. In each case, 10 should be subtracted.

Table of Values of the Logarithms of Trigonometric Functions

θ Deg.	θ Rad.	Log Sin θ	Log Cos θ	Log Tan θ	Log Cot θ		
9° 00′	.1571	9.1943	9.9946	9.1997	10.8003	1.4137	81° 00′
10′	.1600	9.2022	9.9944	9.2078	10.7922	1.4108	50′
20′	.1629	9.2100	9.9942	9.2158	10.7842	1.4079	40′
30′	.1658	9.2176	9.9940	9.2236	10.7764	1.4050	30′
40′	.1687	9.2251	9.9938	9.2313	10.7687	1.4021	20′
50′	.1716	9.2324	9.9936	9.2389	10.7611	1.3992	10′
10° 00′	.1745	9.2397	9.9934	9.2463	10.7537	1.3963	80° 00′
10′	.1774	9.2468	9.9931	9.2536	10.7464	1.3934	50′
20′	.1804	9.2538	9.9929	9.2609	10.7391	1.3904	40′
30′	.1833	9.2606	9.9927	9.2680	10.7320	1.3875	30′
40′	.1862	9.2674	9.9924	9.2750	10.7250	1.3846	20′
50′	.1891	9.2740	9.9922	9.2819	10.7181	1.3817	10′
11° 00′	.1920	9.2806	9.9919	9.2887	10.7113	1.3788	79° 00′
10′	.1949	9.2870	9.9917	9.2953	10.7047	1.3759	50′
20′	.1978	9.2934	9.9914	9.3020	10.6980	1.3730	40′
30′	.2007	9.2997	9.9912	9.3085	10.6915	1.3701	30′
40′	.2036	9.3058	9.9909	9.3149	10.6851	1.3672	20′
50′	.2065	9.3119	9.9907	9.3212	10.6788	1.3643	10′
12° 00′	.2094	9.3179	9.9904	9.3275	10.6725	1.3614	78° 00′
10′	.2123	9.3238	9.9901	9.3336	10.6664	1.3584	50′
20′	.2153	9.3296	9.9899	9.3397	10.6603	1.3555	40′
30′	.2182	9.3353	9.9896	9.3458	10.6542	1.3526	30′
40′	.2211	9.3410	9.9893	9.3517	10.6483	1.3497	20′
50′	.2240	9.3466	9.9890	9.3576	10.6424	1.3468	10′
13° 00′	.2269	9.3521	9.9887	9.3634	10.6366	1.3439	77° 00′
10′	.2298	9.3575	9.9884	9.3691	10.6309	1.3410	50′
20′	.2327	9.3629	9.9881	9.3748	10.6252	1.3381	40′
30′	.2356	9.3682	9.9878	9.3804	10.6196	1.3352	30′
40′	.2385	9.3734	9.9875	9.3859	10.6141	1.3323	20′
50′	.2414	9.3786	9.9872	9.3914	10.6086	1.3294	10′
14° 00′	.2443	9.3837	9.9869	9.3968	10.6032	1.3265	76° 00′
10′	.2473	9.3887	9.9866	9.4021	10.5979	1.3235	50′
20′	.2502	9.3937	9.9863	9.4074	10.5926	1.3206	40′
30′	.2531	9.3986	9.9859	9.4127	10.5873	1.3177	30′
40′	.2560	9.4035	9.9856	9.4178	10.5822	1.3148	20′
50′	.2589	9.4083	9.9853	9.4230	10.5770	1.3119	10′
15° 00′	.2618	9.4160	9.9849	9.4281	10.5719	1.3090	75° 00′
10′	.2647	9.4177	9.9846	9.4331	10.5669	1.3061	50′
20′	.2676	9.4223	9.9843	9.4381	10.5619	1.3032	40′
30′	.2705	9.4269	9.9839	9.4430	10.5570	1.3003	30′
40′	.2734	9.4314	9.9836	9.4479	10.5521	1.2974	20′
50′	.2763	9.4359	9.9832	9.4527	10.5473	1.2945	10′
16° 00′	.2793	9.4403	9.9828	9.4575	10.5425	1.2915	74° 00′
10′	.2822	9.4447	9.9825	9.4622	10.5378	1.2886	50′
20′	.2851	9.4491	9.9821	9.4669	10.5331	1.2857	40′
30′	.2880	9.4533	9.9817	9.4716	10.5284	1.2828	30′
40′	.2909	9.4576	9.9814	9.4762	10.5238	1.2799	20′
50′	.2938	9.4618	9.9810	9.4808	10.5192	1.2770	10′
17° 00′	.2967	9.4659	9.9806	9.4853	10.5147	1.2741	73° 00′
10′	.2996	9.4700	9.9802	9.4898	10.5102	1.2712	50′
20′	.3025	9.4741	9.9798	9.4943	10.5057	1.2683	40′
30′	.3054	9.4781	9.9794	9.4987	10.5013	1.2654	30′
40′	.3083	9.4821	9.9790	9.5031	10.4969	1.2625	20′
50′	.3113	9.4861	9.9786	9.5075	10.4925	1.2595	10′
18° 00′	.3142	9.4900	9.9782	9.5118	10.4882	1.2566	72° 00′
		Log Cos θ	Log Sin θ	Log Cot θ	Log Tan θ	θ Rad.	θ Deg.

Table of Values of the Logarithms of Trigonometric Functions

θ Deg.	θ Rad.	Log Sin θ	Log Cos θ	Log Tan θ	Log Cot θ		
18°00′	.3142	9.4900	9.9782	9.5118	10.4882	1.2566	72°00′
10′	.3171	9.4939	9.9778	9.5161	10.4839	1.2537	50′
20′	.3200	9.4977	9.9774	9.5203	10.4797	1.2508	40′
30′	.3229	9.5015	9.9770	9.5245	10.4755	1.2479	30′
40′	.3258	9.5052	9.9765	9.5287	10.4713	1.2450	20′
50′	.3287	9.5090	9.9761	9.5329	10.4671	1.2421	10′
19°00′	.3316	9.5126	9.9757	9.5370	10.4630	1.2392	71°00′
10′	.3345	9.5163	9.9752	9.5411	10.4589	1.2363	50′
20′	.3374	9.5199	9.9748	9.5451	10.4549	1.2334	40′
30′	.3403	9.5235	9.9743	9.5491	10.4509	1.2305	30′
40′	.3432	9.5270	9.9739	9.5531	10.4469	1.2275	20′
50′	.3462	9.5306	9.9734	9.5571	10.4429	1.2246	10′
20°00′	.3491	9.5341	9.9730	9.5611	10.4389	1.2217	70°00′
10′	.3520	9.5375	9.9725	9.5650	10.4350	1.2188	50′
20′	.3549	9.5409	9.9721	9.5689	10.4311	1.2159	40′
30′	.3578	9.5443	9.9716	9.5727	10.4273	1.2130	30′
40′	.3607	9.5477	9.9711	9.5766	10.4234	1.2101	20′
50′	.3636	9.5510	9.9706	9.5804	10.4196	1.2072	10′
21°00′	.3665	9.5543	9.9702	9.5842	10.4158	1.2043	69°00′
10′	.3694	9.5576	9.9697	9.5879	10.4121	1.2014	50′
20′	.3723	9.5609	9.9692	9.5917	10.4083	1.1985	40′
30′	.3752	9.5641	9.9687	9.5954	10.4046	1.1956	30′
40′	.3782	9.5673	9.9682	9.5991	10.4009	1.1926	20′
50′	.3811	9.5704	9.9677	9.6028	10.3972	1.1897	10′
22°00′	.3840	9.5736	9.9672	9.6064	10.3936	1.1868	68°00′
10′	.3869	9.5767	9.9667	9.6100	10.3900	1.1839	50′
20′	.3898	9.5798	9.9661	9.6136	10.3864	1.1810	40′
30′	.3927	9.5828	9.9656	9.6172	10.3828	1.1781	30′
40′	.3956	9.5859	9.9651	9.6208	10.3792	1.1752	20′
50′	.3985	9.5889	9.9646	9.6243	10.3757	1.1723	10′
23°00′	.4014	9.5919	9.9640	9.6279	10.3721	1.1694	67°00′
10′	.4043	9.5948	9.9635	9.6314	10.3686	1.1665	50′
20′	.4072	9.5978	9.9629	9.6348	10.3652	1.1636	40′
30′	.4102	9.6007	9.9624	9.6383	10.3617	1.1606	30′
40′	.4131	9.6036	9.9618	9.6417	10.3583	1.1577	20′
50′	.4160	9.6065	9.9613	9.6452	10.3548	1.1548	10′
24°00′	.4189	9.6093	9.9607	9.6486	10.3514	1.1519	66°00′
10′	.4218	9.6121	9.9602	9.6520	10.3480	1.1490	50′
20′	.4247	9.6149	9.9596	9.6553	10.3447	1.1461	40′
30′	.4276	9.6177	9.9590	9.6587	10.3413	1.1432	30′
40′	.4305	9.6205	9.9584	9.6620	10.3380	1.1403	20′
50′	.4334	9.6232	9.9579	9.6654	10.3346	1.1374	10′
25°00′	.4363	9.6259	9.9573	9.6687	10.3313	1.1345	65°00′
10′	.4392	9.6286	9.9567	9.6720	10.3280	1.1316	50′
20′	.4422	9.6313	9.9561	9.6752	10.3248	1.1286	40′
30′	.4451	9.6340	9.9555	9.6785	10.3215	1.1257	30′
40′	.4480	9.6366	9.9549	9.6817	10.3183	1.1228	20′
50′	.4509	9.6392	9.9543	9.6850	10.3150	1.1199	10′
26°00′	.4538	9.6418	9.9537	9.6882	10.3118	1.1170	64°00′
10′	.4567	9.6444	9.9530	9.6914	10.3086	1.1141	50′
20′	.4596	9.6470	9.9524	9.6946	10.3054	1.1112	40′
30′	.4625	9.6495	9.9518	9.6977	10.3023	1.1083	30′
40′	.4654	9.6521	9.9512	9.7009	10.2991	1.1054	20′
50′	.4683	9.6546	9.9505	9.7040	10.2960	1.1025	10′
27°00′	.4712	9.6570	9.9499	9.7072	10.2928	1.0996	63°00′
		Log Cos θ	Log Sin θ	Log Cot θ	Log Tan θ	θ Rad.	θ Deg.

552   Tables

Table of Values of the Logarithms of Trigonometric Functions

θ Deg.	θ Rad.	Log Sin θ	Log Cos θ	Log Tan θ	Log Cot θ		
27° 00′	.4712	9.6570	9.9499	9.7072	10.2928	1.0996	63° 00′
10′	.4741	9.6595	9.9492	9.7103	10.2897	1.0966	50′
20′	.4771	9.6620	9.9486	9.7134	10.2866	1.0937	40′
30′	.4800	9.6644	9.9479	9.7165	10.2835	1.0908	30′
40′	.4829	9.6668	9.9473	9.7196	10.2804	1.0879	20′
50′	.4858	9.6692	9.9466	9.7226	10.2774	1.0850	10′
28° 00′	.4887	9.6716	9.9459	9.7257	10.2743	1.0821	62° 00′
10′	.4916	9.6740	9.9453	9.7287	10.2713	1.0792	50′
20′	.4945	9.6763	9.9446	9.7317	10.2683	1.0763	40′
30′	.4974	9.6787	9.9439	9.7348	10.2652	1.0734	30′
40′	.5003	9.6810	9.9432	9.7378	10.2622	1.0705	20′
50′	.5032	9.6833	9.9425	9.7408	10.2592	1.0676	10′
29° 00′	.5061	9.6856	9.9418	9.7438	10.2562	1.0647	61° 00′
10′	.5091	9.6878	9.9411	9.7467	10.2533	1.0617	50′
20′	.5120	9.6901	9.9404	9.7497	10.2503	1.0588	40′
30′	.5149	9.6923	9.9397	9.7526	10.2474	1.0559	30′
40′	.5178	9.6946	9.9390	9.7556	10.2444	1.0530	20′
50′	.5207	9.6968	9.9383	9.7585	10.2415	1.0501	10′
30° 00′	.5236	9.6990	9.9375	9.7614	10.2386	1.0472	60° 00′
10′	.5265	9.7012	9.9368	9.7644	10.2356	1.0443	50′
20′	.5294	9.7033	9.9361	9.7673	10.2327	1.0414	40′
30′	.5323	9.7055	9.9353	9.7701	10.2299	1.0385	30′
40′	.5352	9.7076	9.9346	9.7730	10.2270	1.0356	20′
50′	.5381	9.7097	9.9338	9.7759	10.2241	1.0327	10′
31° 00′	.5411	9.7118	9.9331	9.7788	10.2212	1.0297	59° 00′
10′	.5440	9.7139	9.9323	9.7816	10.2184	1.0268	50′
20′	.5469	9.7160	9.9315	9.7845	10.2155	1.0239	40′
30′	.5498	9.7181	9.9308	9.7873	10.2127	1.0210	30′
40′	.5527	9.7201	9.9300	9.7902	10.2098	1.0181	20′
50′	.5556	9.7222	9.9292	9.7930	10.2070	1.0152	10′
32° 00′	.5585	9.7242	9.9284	9.7958	10.2042	1.0123	58° 00′
10′	.5614	9.7262	9.9276	9.7986	10.2014	1.0094	50′
20′	.5643	9.7282	9.9268	9.8014	10.1986	1.0065	40′
30′	.5672	9.7302	9.9260	9.8042	10.1958	1.0036	30′
40′	.5701	9.7322	9.9252	9.8070	10.1930	1.0007	20′
50′	.5730	9.7342	9.9244	9.8097	10.1903	.9977	10′
33° 00′	.5760	9.7361	9.9236	9.8125	10.1875	.9948	57° 00′
10′	.5789	9.7380	9.9228	9.8153	10.1847	.9919	50′
20′	.5818	9.7400	9.9219	9.8180	10.1820	.9890	40′
30′	.5847	9.7419	9.9211	9.8208	10.1792	.9861	30′
40′	.5876	9.7438	9.9203	9.8235	10.1765	.9832	20′
50′	.5905	9.7457	9.9194	9.8263	10.1737	.9803	10′
34° 00′	.5934	9.7476	9.9186	9.8290	10.1710	.9774	56° 00′
10′	.5963	9.7494	9.9177	9.8317	10.1683	.9745	50′
20′	.5992	9.7513	9.9169	9.8344	10.1656	.9716	40′
30′	.6021	9.7531	9.9160	9.8371	10.1629	.9687	30′
40′	.6050	9.7550	9.9151	9.8398	10.1602	.9657	20′
50′	.6080	9.7568	9.9142	9.8425	10.1575	.9628	10′
35° 00′	.6109	9.7586	9.9134	9.8452	10.1548	.9599	55° 00′
10′	.6138	9.7604	9.9125	9.8479	10.1521	.9570	50′
20′	.6167	9.7622	9.9116	9.8506	10.1494	.9541	40′
30′	.6196	9.7640	9.9107	9.8533	10.1467	.9512	30′
40′	.6225	9.7657	9.9098	9.8559	10.1441	.9483	20′
50′	.6254	9.7675	9.9089	9.8586	10.1414	.9454	10′
36° 00′	.6283	9.7692	9.9080	9.8613	10.1387	.9425	54° 00′
		Log Cos θ	Log Sin θ	Log Cot θ	Log Tan θ	θ Rad.	θ Deg.

Table of Values of the Logarithms of Trigonometric Functions

θ Deg.	θ Rad.	Log Sin θ	Log Cos θ	Log Tan θ	Log Cot θ		
36° 00'	.6283	9.7692	9.9080	9.8613	10.1387	.9425	54° 00'
10'	.6312	9.7710	9.9070	9.8639	10.1361	.9396	50'
20'	.6341	9.7727	9.9061	9.8666	10.1334	.9367	40'
30'	.6370	9.7744	9.9052	9.8692	10.1308	.9338	30'
40'	.6400	9.7761	9.9042	9.8718	10.1282	.9308	20'
50'	.6429	9.7778	9.9033	9.8745	10.1255	.9279	10'
37° 00'	.6458	9.7795	9.9023	9.8771	10.1229	.9250	53° 00'
10'	.6487	9.7811	9.9014	9.8797	10.1203	.9221	50'
20'	.6516	9.7828	9.9004	9.8824	10.1176	.9192	40'
30'	.6545	9.7844	9.8995	9.8850	10.1150	.9163	30'
40'	.6574	9.7861	9.8985	9.8876	10.1124	.9134	20'
50'	.6603	9.7877	9.8975	9.8902	10.1098	.9105	10'
38° 00'	.6632	9.7893	9.8965	9.8928	10.1072	.9076	52° 00'
10'	.6661	9.7910	9.8955	9.8954	10.1046	.9047	50'
20'	.6690	9.7926	9.8945	9.8980	10.1020	.9018	40'
30'	.6720	9.7941	9.8935	9.9006	10.0994	.8988	30'
40'	.6749	9.7957	9.8925	9.9032	10.0968	.8959	20'
50'	.6778	9.7973	9.8915	9.9058	10.0942	.8930	10'
39° 00'	.6807	9.7989	9.8905	9.9084	10.0916	.8901	51 °00'
10'	.6836	9.8004	9.8895	9.9110	10.0890	.8872	50'
20'	.6865	9.8020	9.8884	9.9135	10.0865	.8843	40'
30'	.6894	9.8035	9.8874	9.9161	10.0839	.8814	30'
40'	.6923	9.8050	9.8864	9.9187	10.0813	.8785	20'
50'	.6952	9.8066	9.8853	9.9212	10.0788	.8756	10'
40' 00'	.6981	9.8081	9.8843	9.9238	10.0762	.8727	50° 00'
10'	.7010	9.8096	9.8832	9.9264	10.0736	.8698	50'
20'	.7039	9.8111	9.8821	9.9289	10.0711	.8668	40'
30'	.7069	9.8125	9.8810	9.9315	10.0685	.8639	30'
40'	.7098	9.8140	9.8800	9.9341	10.0659	.8610	20'
50'	.7127	9.8155	9.8789	9.9366	10.0634	.8581	10'
41° 00'	.7156	9.8169	9.8778	9.9392	10.0608	.8552	49° 00'
10'	.7185	9.8184	9.8767	9.9417	10.0583	.8523	50'
20'	.7214	9.8198	9.8756	9.9443	10.0557	.8494	40'
30'	.7243	9.8213	9.8745	9.9468	10.0532	.8465	30'
40'	.7272	9.8227	9.8733	9.9494	10.0506	.8436	20'
50'	.7301	9.8241	9.8722	9.9519	10.0481	.8407	10'
42° 00'	.7330	9.8255	9.8711	9.9544	10.0456	.8378	48° 00'
10'	.7359	9.8269	9.8699	9.9570	10.0430	.8348	50'
20'	.7389	9.8283	9.8688	9.9595	10.0405	.8319	40'
30'	.7418	9.8297	9.8676	9.9621	10.0379	.8290	30'
40'	.7447	9.8311	9.8665	9.9646	10.0354	.8261	20'
50'	.7476	9.8324	9.8653	9.9671	10.0329	.8232	10'
43° 00'	.7505	9.8338	9.8641	9.9697	10.0303	.8203	47° 00'
10'	.7534	9.8351	9.8629	9.9722	10.0278	.8174	50'
20'	.7563	9.8365	9.8618	9.9747	10.0253	.8145	40'
30'	.7592	9.8378	9.8606	9.9772	10.0228	.8116	30'
40'	.7621	9.8391	9.8594	9.9798	10.0202	.8087	20'
50'	.7650	9.8405	9.8582	9.9823	10.0177	.8058	10'
44° 00'	.7679	9.8418	9.8569	9.9848	10.0152	.8029	46° 00'
10'	.7709	9.8431	9.8557	9.9874	10.0126	.7999	50'
20'	.7738	9.8444	9.8545	9.9899	10.0101	.7970	40'
30'	.7767	9.8457	9.8532	9.9924	10.0076	.7941	30'
40'	.7796	9.8469	9.8520	9.9949	10.0051	.7912	20'
50'	.7825	9.8482	9.8507	9.9975	10.0025	.7883	10'
45° 00'	.7854	9.8495	9.8495	10.0000	10.0000	.7854	45° 00'
		Log Cos θ	Log Sin θ	Log Cot θ	Log Tan θ	θ Rad.	θ Deg.

Table of Squares, Cubes, Square and Cube Roots

No.	Squares	Cubes	Square Roots	Cube Roots	No.	Squares	Cubes	Square Roots	Cube Roots
1	1	1	1.000	1.000	51	2,601	132,651	7.141	3.708
2	4	8	1.414	1.260	52	2,704	140,608	7.211	3.733
3	9	27	1.732	1.442	53	2,809	148,877	7.280	3.756
4	16	64	2.000	1.587	54	2,916	157,464	7.348	3.780
5	25	125	2.236	1.710	55	3,025	166,375	7.416	3.803
6	36	216	2.449	1.817	56	3,136	175,616	7.483	3.826
7	49	343	2.646	1.913	57	3,249	185,193	7.550	3.849
8	64	512	2.828	2.000	58	3,364	195,112	7.616	3.871
9	81	729	3.000	2.080	59	3,481	205,379	7.681	3.893
10	100	1,000	3.162	2.154	60	3,600	216,000	7.746	3.915
11	121	1,331	3.317	2.224	61	3,721	226,981	7.810	3.936
12	144	1,728	3.464	2.289	62	3,844	238,328	7.874	3.958
13	169	2,197	3.606	2.351	63	3,969	250,047	7.937	3.979
14	196	2,744	3.742	2.410	64	4,096	262,144	8.000	4.000
15	225	3,375	3.873	2.466	65	4,225	274,625	8.062	4.021
16	256	4,096	4.000	2.520	66	4,356	287,496	8.124	4.041
17	289	4,913	4.123	2.571	67	4,489	300,763	8.185	4.062
18	324	5,832	4.243	2.621	68	4,624	314,432	8.246	4.082
19	361	6,859	4.359	2.668	69	4,761	328,509	8.307	4.102
20	400	8,000	4.472	2.714	70	4,900	343,000	8.367	4.121
21	441	9,261	4.583	2.759	71	5,041	357,911	8.426	4.141
22	484	10,648	4.690	2.802	72	5,184	373,248	8.485	4.160
23	529	12,167	4.796	2.844	73	5,329	389,017	8.544	4.179
24	576	13,824	4.899	2.884	74	5,476	405,224	8.602	4.198
25	625	15,625	5.000	2.924	75	5,625	421,875	8.660	4.217
26	676	17,576	5.099	2.962	76	5,776	438,976	8.718	4.236
27	729	19,683	5.196	3.000	77	5,929	456,533	8.775	4.254
28	784	21,952	5.292	3.037	78	6,084	474,552	8.832	4.273
29	841	24,389	5.385	3.072	79	6,241	493,039	8.888	4.291
30	900	27,000	5.477	3.107	80	6,400	512,000	8.944	4.309
31	961	29,791	5.568	3.141	81	6,561	531,441	9.000	4.327
32	1,024	32,768	5.657	3.175	82	6,724	551,368	9.055	4.344
33	1,089	35,937	5.745	3.208	83	6,889	571,787	9.110	4.362
34	1,156	39,304	5.831	3.240	84	7,056	592,704	9.165	4.380
35	1,225	42,875	5.916	3.271	85	7,225	614,125	9.220	4.397
36	1,296	46,656	6.000	3.302	86	7,396	636,056	9.274	4.414
37	1,369	50,653	6.083	3.332	87	7,569	658,503	9.327	4.431
38	1,444	54,872	6.164	3.362	88	7,744	681,472	9.381	4.448
39	1,521	59,319	6.245	3.391	89	7,921	704,969	9.434	4.465
40	1,600	64,000	6.325	3.420	90	8,100	729,000	9.487	4.481
41	1,681	68,921	6.403	3.448	91	8,281	753,571	9.539	4.498
42	1,764	74,088	6.481	3.476	92	8,464	778,688	9.592	4.514
43	1,849	79,507	6.557	3.503	93	8,649	804,357	9.644	4.531
44	1,936	85,184	6.633	3.530	94	8,836	830,584	9.695	4.547
45	2,025	91,125	6.708	3.557	95	9,025	857,375	9.747	4.563
46	2,116	97,336	6.782	3.583	96	9,216	884,736	9.798	4.579
47	2,209	103,823	6.856	3.609	97	9,409	912,673	9.849	4.595
48	2,304	110,592	6.928	3.634	98	9,604	941,192	9.899	4.610
49	2,401	117,649	7.000	3.659	99	9,801	970,299	9.950	4.626
50	2,500	125,000	7.071	3.684	100	10,000	1,000,000	10.000	4.642

Glossary

The following definitions and statements reflect the usage of terms in this textbook.

Abscissa The first number, *x*, in an ordered pair, (*x*, *y*) is the *abscissa*. (Page 134)

Absolute value The *absolute value* of *x*, written |*x*|, is *x* if *x* is nonnegative and −*x* if *x* is negative. (Page 7)

Absolute value of a complex number The *absolute value of the complex number a + bi* is $\sqrt{a^2 + b^2}$. It represents the length of the vector (*a*,*b*). (Page 168)

Antilogarithm If $L = \log_a N$, then *N* is the *antilogarithm* of *L*. (Page 333)

Arithmetic means The terms between any two given terms of an arithmetic sequence are *arithmetic means*. (Page 395)

Arithmetic sequence A sequence in which each term is obtained by adding some fixed number to the preceding term is an *arithmetic sequence*. (Page 394)

Arithmetic series An *arithmetic series* is the indicated sum of the terms of an arithmetic sequence. (Page 401)

Characteristic In a logarithm, the number to the left of the decimal point is the *characteristic*. (Page 339)

Circle A *circle* is the locus of points in a plane at a given distance from a fixed point. (Page 358)

Combination A *combination* is an arrangement of the elements of a set without consideration of the order of the elements. (Page 425)

Common difference The difference obtained by subtracting any term in an arithmetic sequence from the following term is a constant called the *common difference*. (Page 394)

Complex conjugate Two complex numbers of the form *a* + *bi* and *a* − *bi* are complex conjugates. (Page 29)

Complex number A *complex number* is a number of the form *a* + *bi*, where *a* and *b* are real numbers and $i = \sqrt{-1}$. (Page 20)

Composite function If *f* is the function {(*x*, *y*): *y* = *f*(*x*)} and *g* is the function {(*x*, *y*): *y* = *g*(*x*)}, and the range of *f* includes the domain of *g*, then {(*x*, *y*): *y* = *g*[*f*(*x*)]} is called the composition of *g* with *f*, or the *composite function g*(*f*). (Page 198)

Consistent system A system of equations or inequalities whose solution set has one or more elements is a *consistent system*. (Page 267)

Coordinate(s) The *coordinate* of a point on a line is the number associated with the point. The *coordinates* of a point in a plane are the numbers in the ordered pair associated with the point. (Page 134)

Cosecant ratio The *cosecant ratio* is the reciprocal of the sine ratio. (Page 464)

Cosine ratio Let a point *P*(*x*, *y*) be on the terminal side of an angle *θ* and let *P* be *r* units from the origin. Then

$$\text{cosine } \theta \ (\cos \theta) = \frac{x}{r}.$$

(Page 443)

Cotangent ratio The *cotangent ratio* is the reciprocal of the tangent ratio. (Page 464)

Degree of a polynomial The *degree of a polynomial* is the greatest degree of the terms of the polynomial. (Page 38)

Degree of a term The *degree of a term* of a polynomial is the sum of the exponents of its variables. (Page 38)

Dependent system A consistent system of linear equations whose solution set is infinite is called a *dependent system*. (Page 268)

Direct variation The equation $y = kx$, where k is a constant, expresses *direct variation* between x and y. (Page 191)

Discriminant The *discriminant* of the quadratic equation $ax^2 + bx + c = 0$ is the number $b^2 - 4ac$. (Page 245)

Domain For a relation, the set of first elements of its ordered pairs is the *domain* of the relation. (Page 180)

Ellipse An *ellipse* is the locus of points in a plane such that the sum of the distances from two fixed points to a point of the locus is constant. (Page 362)

Equivalent equations Equations that have the same solution set are *equivalent equations*. (Page 102)

Equivalent systems Systems of equations that have the same solution set are *equivalent systems*. (Page 260)

Equivalent vectors Vectors that represent the same number are *equivalent vectors*. (Page 166)

Event The subset of a sample space that represents the set of successful outcomes is an *event*. (Page 429)

Exponential function A function defined by $f(x) = a^x$, where a and x are real numbers and $a \neq 1$, $a > 0$, is an *exponential function*. (Page 322)

Factorial The symbol $n!$ is read *n factorial*.
$$n! = {}_nP_n = n(n-1)(n-2) \cdots 3 \cdot 2 \cdot 1$$
(Page 419)

Function A *function* is a relation such that for every element in the domain of the relation, there is one and only one element of the range. (Page 183)

Geometric means The terms between any two given terms of a geometric sequence are the *geometric means* between these terms. (Page 399)

Geometric sequence A *geometric sequence* is one in which the ratio r of any term to its predecessor is always the same number. (Page 398)

Geometric series A *geometric series* is the indi-cated sum of a geometric sequence. (Page 405)

Greatest common factor The *greatest common factor* of two expressions is the greatest expression that is a factor of both expressions. (Page 83)

Hyperbola A *hyperbola* is the locus of points in the plane such that the difference of the distances from two fixed points to a point of the locus is a constant. (Page 369)

Imaginary number Any complex number for which $b \neq 0$ is an *imaginary number*. (Page 20)

Inconsistent system A system of equations or inequalities whose solution set is the empty set is an *inconsistent system*. (Page 267)

Independent system A consistent system of linear equations whose solution set has exactly one element is an *independent system*. (Page 268)

Integers The set of *integers*, $\mathscr{I}$ is the set consisting of the natural numbers, the opposites of the natural numbers, and zero. (Page 2)

Inverse relation Relations Q and S are *inverse relations* if and only if for every ordered pair (x, y) in Q, there is an ordered pair (y, x) is S. (Page 202)

Inverse variation If the product of two variables is a nonzero constant, the variables are in *inverse variation*. The equation for the inverse variation may be written as $xy = k$ or $y = \dfrac{k}{x}$, where k is the constant of variation. (Page 373)

Irrational number A number that cannot be written as the ratio of an integer and a natural number is an *irrational number*. Irrational numbers cannot be represented as terminating, or as nonterminating, repeating decimals. (Page 3)

Joint variation *Joint variation* is expressed by the equation $x = kyz$ where x, y, and z are variables and k is a constant. This equation means that x varies jointly as y and z. (Page 375)

Least common denominator The *least common denominator, LCD,* of two or more rational expressions is the least common multiple of their denominators. (Page 84)

Least common multiple   The *least common multiple, LCM,* of m and n is the least polynomial that has both m and n as factors. (Page 83)

Linear function   A function that can be expressed as $f(x) = mx + b$ is a *linear function.* (Page 191)

Logarithmic function   The inverse of the exponential function $y = a^x$, $a \neq 1$, $a > 0$, is called the *logarithmic function.* It is written, $y = \log_a x$. (Page 329)

Mantissa   The part of a logarithm to the right of the decimal point is called the *mantissa.* (Page 339)

Mapping   A *mapping* is a correspondence that associates the elements of two sets. (Page 187)

Matrix   A *matrix* is a rectangular array of numbers. (Page 281)

Monomial   A *monomial* is a term that consists only of the product of complex numbers and variables with exponents that are whole numbers. (Page 38)

Mutually exclusive events   Events that do not have any elements in common are *mutually exclusive events.* (Page 431)

Natural number   The set of *natural numbers, N,* is the set of numbers whose members are 1 and every number found by adding 1 to a member of the set. (Page 2)

Open sentence   Sentences with variables are *open sentences.* They may be true for all, some, or no replacements of the variables. (Page 6)

Ordinate   The second number, y, in an ordered pair (x, y) is the *ordinate.* (Page 134)

Parabola   A *parabola* is the locus of points in the plane that are the same distance from a given line and a fixed point. (Page 366)

Perfect square   A *perfect square* is the square of an integer. (Page 6)

Period   The smallest positive number p for which $f(p + x) = f(x)$ is always true is the *period* of the function f. (Page 484)

Periodic function   A function for which $f(p + x) = f(x)$ for some positive p and for all x is a *periodic function.* (Page 484)

Permutation   A *permutation* of a set of elements is an arrangement of a specified number of those elements in a definite order. (Page 418)

Polygonal convex set   A *polygonal convex set* is the nonempty intersection of a finite number of closed half-planes. (Page 275)

Polynomial   A *polynomial* is a monomial or the sum of monomials. (Page 38)

Prime polynomial   A polynomial that has no polynomial factors other than itself, its opposite, and 1, is a *prime polynomial.* (Page 50)

Principal root   For $a \in \mathrm{R}$, $a \neq 0$, and $n \in \mathrm{N}$, $a^{\frac{1}{n}}$ is the principal nth root of a. It is the positive nth root when there is more than one real root and the real root when there is exactly one real root. (Page 303)

Probability   The ratio of the number of successful outcomes to the number of possible outcomes is the *probability* that an outcome will occur. (Page 428)

Proper subset   For two sets A and B, if there is at least an element in B that is not in A, then A is a *proper subset* of B. This is written, $A \subset B$. (Page 3)

Pure imaginary number   A *pure imaginary number* is a square root of a negative real number. (Page 16)

Quadratic equation   An equation that can be written in the form $ax^2 + bx + c = 0$, where a, b, and c are complex numbers and $a \neq 0$, is a *quadratic equation.* (Page 231)

Quadratic formula   For any quadratic equation $ax^2 + bx + c = 0$, the solutions are
$$x = \frac{-b \pm \sqrt{b^2 - 4ac}}{2a}.$$
This is called the *quadratic formula.* (Page 242)

Quadratic function   A *quadratic function* is a function defined by $y = ax^2 + bx + c$, where a, b, and c are complex number constants, and $a \neq 0$. (Page 215)

Radian If the vertex of an angle is placed at the center of a circle, and the angle intercepts an arc equal in length to the radius of the circle, then the angle is said to have a measure of *1 radian*. (Page 478)

Radical The expression $\sqrt{25}$ is called a *radical*. (Page 6)

Radicand In the expression $\sqrt{25}$, 25 is the *radicand*. (Page 6)

Range The set of second elements of the relation is the *range*. (Page 180)

Rational expression A *rational expression* is an expression of the form $\frac{P}{Q}$ where P and Q are polynomials and $Q \neq 0$. (Page 71)

Rational numbers The set of *rational numbers, Q*, is the set of numbers that can be expressed in the form $\frac{a}{b}$, where a is an integer and b is a natural number. (Page 2)

Real numbers The union of the set of rational numbers with the set of irrational numbers is the set of *real numbers, R*. (Page 3)

Relation A *relation* is a set of ordered pairs. (Page 180)

Replacement set The given set of elements that a variable may represent is the replacement set. (Page 6)

Sample space In probability, a set of possible outcomes is a *sample space*. (Page 428)

Scientific notation When a number is represented as a power of 10 multiplied by a number greater than or equal to 1 and less than 10, it is expressed in *scientific notation*. (Page 297)

Secant ratio The reciprocal of the cosine ratio is the *secant ratio*. (Page 464)

Sequence A *sequence* is a function whose domain is the set of positive integers. (Page 393)

Series A *series* is an indicated sum of the terms of a sequence. (Page 401)

Sine ratio Let a point $P(x, y)$ be on the terminal side of an angle θ and let P be r units from the origin. Then
$$\text{sine } \theta \ (\sin \theta) = \frac{y}{r}. \quad \text{(Page 443)}$$

Slope The *slope m* of a line that contains the points $P_1(x_1, y_1)$ and $P_2(x_2, y_2)$ is
$$m = \frac{y_2 - y_1}{x_2 - x_1} = \frac{y_1 - y_2}{x_1 - x_2}, \ (x_1 \neq x_2). \text{ (Page 145)}$$

Solution set The *solution set* of an open sentence is the set of numbers that makes the sentence true. (Page 70)

Solution set of a system The *solution set of a system* of two equations in two variables is the set of ordered pairs that make the equations true. (Page 256)

Standard form of the linear equation Any line in the xy plane defined by an equation of the form $Ax + By + C = 0$, where $A, B, C, \in$ R and A and B are not both zero is said to be written in standard form. (Page 156)

Symmetry of two points Two points A and B are said to be symmetric with respect to a line q if and only if q is the perpendicular bisector of line segment AB. (Page 202)

System of equations A set of two or more equations is called a *system of equations*. (Page 256)

Tangent ratio Let $P(x, y)$ be a point on the terminal side of an angle θ and let P be r units from the origin. Then
$$\text{tangent } \theta \ (\tan \theta) = \frac{y}{x}. \quad \text{(Page 443)}$$

Variable A *variable* is a symbol that represents any element of a specified replacement set. (Page 6)

Vector A *vector* is a directed line segment. (Page 166)

Whole numbers The set of *whole numbers, W*, is the set that is the union of the set of natural numbers and zero. (Page 2)

Zero of a function A *zero of a function* f is any number a for which $f(a) = 0$. (Page 194)

Postulates for Real Numbers

For all real numbers a, b, and c,

$a + b$ is one and only one real number.	Closure postulate for addition
$a \cdot b$ is one and only one real number.	Closure postulate for multiplication
$a + b = b + a$	Commutative postulate for addition
$a \cdot b = b \cdot a$	Commutative postulate for multiplication
$a + (b + c) = (a + b) + c$	Associative postulate for addition
$a \cdot (b \cdot c) = (a \cdot b) \cdot c$	Associative postulate for multiplication
$a(b + c) = ab + ac$	Distributive postulate for multiplication over addition
$a + 0 = a$	Additive identity postulate
$a \cdot 1 = a$	Multiplicative identity postulate
$a + (-a) = 0$	Additive inverse postulate
$a \cdot \dfrac{1}{a} = 1$, $a \neq 0$	Multiplicative inverse postulate

Index

Boldfaced numerals indicate the pages that contain formal or informal definitions.

Point (continued)
  of tangency, 378
Point-slope form of the linear
  equation, **153**–54
Polygonal convex set, **275**–76
Polynomial(s), **38**–39
  addition of, **40**–41
  classification of, 38–39
  coefficients of, **39**
  degree, **38**
  depressed, **71**
  division of, **59**–61
  equation, 69–70
  Factor theorem, **65**–66
  factoring, **49**–51, 53–55, 57
  multiplication of, **45**–47
  prime, **50**–51, 57
  in rational expressions, 71
  subtraction of, **41**
Postulates
  addition of equations, **102**–
    03
  addition of inequalities, **115**
  addition of real numbers, **4**
  multiplication of equations,
    102
  multiplication of inequalities,
    115–16
  multiplication of real
    numbers, **4**
Prime polynomials(s), **50**–51
  over the integers, **50**, 57
  over the real numbers, 57
Principal nth root, **302**–03
PRINT statements, **512**,
  516–18, 525
Probability, **428**–29
  postulates, **428**–29
Problems
  compound interest, **348**–49
  math models for, 119–20,
    123–24
  maximum and minimum,
    228–29
  rate, **119–20**
  solved using systems, 270
Product(s)
  renaming a polynomial as,
    49
  rewriting as a sum, 88

of the solution of quadratic
  equations, **248**–49
of the sum and difference of
  two numbers, 49–51, 57
of trigonometric functions,
  503
Program(s), **512**
  to add complex numbers,
    518
  to compute the determinant
    of a matrix, 522–23
  to compute N!, 526–27
  to compute the perimeter of
    a rectangle, 512–13
  to compute slopes of lines,
    517
  to compute square roots,
    515
  to evaluate a quadratic
    function and print a table
    of X, Y pairs, 520
  to generate terms of an
    arithmetic sequence,
    524–25
  to simulate a chance event,
    527–28
  to solve a triangle, 529–30
Proof(s)
  by contradiction, 287
  double-angle formula for
    sine, 497
  fundamental identities of
    trigonometry, **488–89**
  half-angle formula for
    cosine, 497
  law of cosines, 469
  law of sines, 466
  properties of logarithms,
    335–36
  quadratic formula, 241
  sum of an arithmetic series,
    402
  sum and difference identi-
    ties, 491–92
  sum of a geometric series,
    406
  sum of an infinite geometric
    series, 408–09
  trigonometric identities,
    494–96

Proportions, 212
Pythagorean identities, **489**

Quadrant(s), 134, 440, 445
Quadratic equations, **231**–32,
    234–35
  discriminants of, **245**–46
  incomplete, **234**
  nature of solutions of, **245**–
    46
  roots, **231**
  solving by completing the
    square, **237**–39
  solving graphically, 231–32
  solving by quadratic
    formula, **242**
  sum and product of solu-
    tions, **248**–49
Quadratic formula, **242**
Quadratic function(s), **215**–16,
    218–19, 221–22, 224–26
  graphs of, 215, 218–19,
    221–22, 225–26
  zeros of, **196**

Radian, 478--79
Radical(s), **6**
  addition and subtraction of,
    13–14, 306
  division of, **10,** 307
  equations, 309–12
  multiplication of, **9,** 307, 308
  rationalizing the
    denominator of, **11**
  simplifying, 9–11, 302,
    306–07
Radicand, **6**
Radius vector, **442**
Range, **180**
Ratio(s)
  of determinants of matrices,
    286
  trigonometric, **443, 464**
Rational expressions, **71**
  addition of, **81,** 83–85, 88
  division of, **78**–79
  equations with, 105–06
  multiplication of, **75**–76
  simplification of, 71–72
  subtraction of, **81,** 83–85

Picture Credits

567

B
C
D
E 7
F 8
G 9
H 0
I 1
J 2